# THEATRE STUDIES

*Series of Occasional Publications*

Edited by
ALAN WOODS AND
NENA COUCH

*Sidney Kingsley at work, 1930s. Courtesy of Sidney Kingsley.*

# SIDNEY KINGSLEY:
# FIVE
# PRIZEWINNING
# PLAYS

•

*With introductions by Sidney Kingsley*

Edited by Nena Couch

Published for *Theatre Studies* by
Ohio State University Press

OHIO STATE UNIVERSITY PRESS

COLUMBUS

All of the plays in this volume are the sole property of the playwright (with the estate of Arthur Koestler for *Darkness at Noon*) and are fully protected under the copyright laws of the United States of America, the British Commonwealth, including Canada, and all other countries of the Copyright Union. All rights, including professional and amateur performances, motion pictures, recitation, lecturing, public reading, radio or television broadcasting as well as cable, videocassettes, or any recording whatsoever, and the rights of translation into foreign languages are strictly reserved. In their present form, these plays are dedicated to the reading public only.

Amateur rights to *Men in White,* amateur and stock rights to *Darkness at Noon,* and stock rights to *Detective Story* and *The Patriots* are controlled by Samuel French, Inc., 45 West 25th Street, New York, NY 10010. Stock rights to *Men in White* are controlled by Robert A. Freedman Dramatic Agency, Inc., 1501 Broadway, Suite 2310, New York, NY 10036. Amateur rights to *Dead End, The Patriots,* and *Detective Story* are controlled by Dramatists Play Service, Inc., 440 Park Avenue North, New York, NY 10016. Permissions for all other rights whatsoever must be obtained in writing from the playwright, Sidney Kingsley, c/o The Dramatists Guild, Inc., 234 West 44th Street, New York, NY 10036.

Library of Congress Cataloging-in-Publication Data
Kingsley, Sidney, 1906–1995.
    Sidney Kingsley : five prizewinning plays, with introductions by
Sidney Kingsley / edited by Nena Couch.
        p.   cm.—(Theatre studies series of occasional publications)
    "Published for Theatre studies by Ohio State University Press."
    Includes bibliographical references.
    ISBN 0-8142-0665-4 (alk. paper)
    I. Couch, Nena.   II. Theatre studies.   III. Series.
PS3521.I55A6   1995
812'.52—dc20                                                                         95-10843
                                                                                             CIP

Text and jacket design by Bruce Gore.
Type set in Sabon by Graphic Composition, Inc., Athens, Georgia.
Printed by Bookcrafters, Inc. Chelsea, Michigan.

9 8 7 6 5 4 3 2 1

*In Memoriam*

# SIDNEY KINGSLEY

22 October 1906–20 March 1995

Sidney Kingsley's respect for life is reflected in his work—but this extended far beyond human life. He possessed a great reverence for all life—on the land, in the air, and in the sea. There are many instances, such as the time he rescued a little fawn that was floating down the Ramapo River on a chunk of ice. He waded out into the frigid water and carried the little animal to the warmth and safety of his furnace room.

Sidney and Madge had many dogs—they were their family. For his final resting place with Madge, Sidney chose a beautiful area at the foot of a waterfall near the bank of the Ramapo River, on the property he so dearly loved, with the ashes of their dogs scattered in a circle around them.

—DORIS DAVIS

*The following reminiscences of Mr. Kingsley were shared by friends and colleagues at a gathering in his memory held at the Players Club, New York City, 19 May 1995.*

Sidney was part of that extraordinary group of playwrights who came into being in the 30s and 40s, which heralded the arrival of the new American theatre and the new American drama. . . . Sidney was not only an influence through his plays, he was also kind and generous in helping young playwrights. . . . He applauded enthusiastically the success of each and every young playwright. And as president of the Dramatists Guild, Sidney guided us through the most difficult period of reorganization at the end of which we emerged as a separate and most effective guild. . . .

Sidney was a greatly gifted man, a witty man, a kind man, a good man. His plays excited us to become playwrights, his presence at our meetings encouraged us, and his leadership as president of the Dramatists Guild strengthened us. He was an important part of all our lives.

—ROBERT ANDERSON

My first meeting with Sidney was at the Dakota. Eli [Wallach] and I had gone to a Martha Graham concert and were invited to an after-theatre party being given for her and her company of modern dancers. I knew of Sidney Kingsley, successful Pulitzer Prize–winning author of Hollywood fame and Broadway's plays *Dead End* and *Detective Story*. I didn't know that he was on the board of the Martha Graham Dance Company, and that he was hosting the party. I was very impressed with that cultural side of him. As the years went by, I came to discover many more intriguing and different sides to him—his interests in architecture, painting, and sculpture—but his support of Martha and her modern dance company was the most surprising and endearing to me.

—ANNE JACKSON

I was Sidney's stage manager for *Lunatics and Lovers*. . . . It was a great experience for me. Sidney Kingsley was a hero to me. After working with him while he was writing the play, we began rehearsals. . . . Sidney started to direct—he was very fast, knew exactly what he wanted—but as he directed, I was second-guessing him. . . . I said, "That's not the way to do it, that's not the thing to say to the actor, why should he do that?" And as I'm saying this underneath my breath, my assistant hands me a piece of paper. On it is something in code which says, "1 PP, 2 DCCA, 5007H, SMYOFB." So I said, "What the hell is that?" He said, "One Pulitzer Prize, two Drama Critics Circle Awards, five out of seven hits, so mind your own f******g business!"

—SAMUEL (BIFF) LIFF

Sidney Kingsley was a landmark playwright, and every playwright who followed is indebted to him, for he created the technique of "going behind the scenes" not only of hospitals and detective squad rooms but of our national and personal lives.

—JEROME LAWRENCE

After Madge [Evans] died, Sidney was occupied day and night with the work on the estate, and I had suggested to him that some accountants or lawyers could find a way [to] save some taxes and save part of the estate, and I said I would be willing to help in any way that I could. But Sidney looked at me and said, "But Jack, you don't understand, I believe in the system."

Later, I thought about that little incident, and it seemed to me a reflection of Sidney's life and his work. . . . He was a revolutionary writer and it was Thomas Paine, Jefferson, and Madison that inspired him in his ideas and in his work. . . . His real contribution, which we will turn to over and over again, is his belief that up to this point the best system, or the best potential, for the realization of the dreams of man lie in the origins of this country.

—JACK GARFEIN

# CONTENTS

# ACKNOWLEDGMENTS

THE PERSON who is owed the greatest thanks for making this publication possible is, of course, Sidney Kingsley, for his outstanding plays. I would also like to thank him for his generosity in inviting me into his home to work with his collection of materials documenting his remarkable career in the American theatre. His longtime secretary, Maureen Lake, who worked with Mr. Kingsley on his autobiography, has been an invaluable resource to me. In particular I thank Doris Davis, Mr. Kingsley's friend of many years who brought me into this project, for her ongoing help and support in all phases of the work. Her interest, energy, and commitment were vital to this publication—it would not have happened without her. I am grateful for the personal support and encouragement I have received from Peter and Alexander Coccia, for advice from colleagues Alan Woods and Phil Thompson, and for administrative and institutional support from the Department of Theatre and the Libraries of The Ohio State University.

My introduction to this volume is just the opening statement on Mr. Kingsley's contributions to the theatre. It is hoped that this collection of his plays will encourage others to examine his works both as they are situated in the history of American theatre and as a part of the fabric of twentieth-century American life.

# AN INTRODUCTION

SIDNEY KINGSLEY is a playwright, but through his writing he has had many more careers—as a social and political activist, a health-care reformer, an advocate for children, a patriot, a visionary. This collection of Kingsley's award-winning plays fills a void in American dramatic publishing: while critical statements on Kingsley's work appear in the significant studies of American theatre and his plays continue to be produced, there has never been a standard edition of his major works. Of his nine professionally produced plays, *Men in White* (1933) received the Pulitzer Prize and the Theatre Club Award; *Dead End* (1935), the Theatre Club Award; *The Patriots* (1943), the New York Drama Critics Circle Award, Newspaper Guild Front Page Award, and Theatre Club Award; *Detective Story* (1949), the Edgar Allen Poe Award; and *Darkness at Noon* (1951), the New York Drama Critics Circle Award and the Donaldson Award. This collection provides the definitive edition of these plays, each with an introduction by Sidney Kingsley.

As a playwright who has found life "infinitely rich, poetic and dramatic,"[1] Sidney Kingsley has used his naturalistic writing style to present major American social problems on the stage. His pioneering work for the stage led the way for new genres and character types in film and television: hospital and doctor dramas such as *General Hospital, Dr. Kildare, Ben Casey,* and *ER;* numerous clever bad boys, starting with the Dead End Kids; and the detectives and criminals populating shows such as *NYPD Blue.*

Born Sidney Kirshner on 22 October 1906, Sidney Kingsley grew up in New York City, the locale for most of his plays. He attended Cornell University, where he had the good fortune to encounter one of those rare teachers who sometimes change one's life—Alec Drummond. Drummond "was possessed by a vision, beautiful beyond words, by a dream called Theatre,"[2] a

*Scene from* Wonder-Dark Epilogue *produced by the Cornell Dramatic Club,*
*1928. Courtesy of Sidney Kingsley.*

dream that became Kingsley's dream and life as well. Facing the constant
lack of theatre resources at Cornell with which Drummond struggled,
Kingsley wrote, acted, directed, and designed—experiences that would
stand him well in the professional theatre world. He was a member of the
dramatic club and of the freshman and varsity debate teams. He received the
94 Memorial Stage, a Cornell University prize in debate. Kingsley's first
published play, *Wonder-Dark Epilogue,*[3] about artist Eugene Travers and
death, was a one-act produced at Cornell by the Cornell Dramatic Club in
May 1928. In this play, Kingsley tried out some of the techniques and ideas
he would later put to good use in *Darkness at Noon:* the flashback, the
character reviewing his life as he approaches his death, and a setting that
provides a variety of areas and levels for acting. In 1981 Kingsley returned
to the topics of artists and death in *Falling Man,* produced by the Florida
State University School of Theatre.

     After graduating from Cornell, he acted briefly in a stock company and
then appeared in *Broadway Express* on Broadway. But Kingsley really
wanted to write for the stage and directed his efforts toward that end, beginning quite successfully with *Men in White,* closely followed by *Dead End.*

     *Ten Million Ghosts* (1936), Kingsley's third Broadway play, was a techni-
cally complex production about conspiracy and the hypocrisy of French and
German branches of a family of munitions magnates during World War I.

The playwright/director himself felt that he had rushed the play into production. While the play was a box-office failure, the multimedia aspect of *Ten Million Ghosts*, with projections and sound design, foreshadowed by many years the technical virtuosity that has become a hallmark of many recent Broadway productions.

In 1939 Kingsley produced and directed *The World We Make*. Based on the novel *The Outward Room* by Millen Brand, *The World We Make* is the story of a mentally ill young woman who tries to reclaim a normal life. The play was a moderate box-office success, and was praised by groups interested in mental health and treatment of mental illness.[4] It was considered by Burns Mantle to be "one of his [Kingsley's] minor successes."[5] The research papers that remain to document the development of this play reveal Kingsley's meticulous attention to detail that was a hallmark of his work. They include extensive interviews he had commissioned with laundry workers on wages and hours, working conditions, the union, living conditions, employer-employee relations, family life, education, recreation, health, insurance, reasons for coming to the United States, politics, and hopes for the future.

Toward the end of his service in the United States Army (1939–43), Kingsley returned to the Broadway stage with *The Patriots*. In 1949 and 1951, in rather quick succession, he was back on Broadway with *Detective Story* and *Darkness at Noon,* respectively. Then, in a total departure from his past plays dealing with issues of social and political import, Kingsley wrote *Lunatics and Lovers* (1954), bringing his careful writing and staging to the fore for this farce in which con men and women, a judge, a dentist and his wife, a house detective, and a policeman create chaos in a hotel. In 1962 Kingsley returned to naturalism in *Night Life,* a study of the denizens of a New York key club. The play failed, probably for a variety of reasons. Morgan Y. Himelstein felt that "sensational realism" was "passé" by 1962 because of "the advent of television as medium for documentary reporting and with the growing cynicism of the audience."[6] But *Night Life* may have suffered from strikes against New York newspapers in November and December 1962 that affected newspaper coverage and advertisement, so it is difficult to judge what the box-office popularity of the play might have been. John Wharton felt that the play could have been successful had the Playwrights Company been able to produce it.[7]

It is interesting that, while Kingsley had successes produced by both the Group Theatre and the Playwrights Producing Company, he never officially affiliated himself with either organization. Nevertheless, he credited the Group Theatre with drawing his attention to the social problems of the 1930s.[8] In his history of the Playwrights Producing Company, John Wharton speculated on why Kingsley had not been made a member of the company, or, if the suggestion had been made to him, why he did not accept. In all obvious aspects, Kingsley seemed a good fit.[9] Perhaps his strong independence as a theatre professional was necessary for him to write on the variety of topics he chose.

While Kingsley wrote a number of playscripts, screenplays and treatments, and notes that were not produced, one must regret in particular that *Napoleon the First,* adapted from Theodor Tagger's play written under the pseudonym Ferdinand Bruckner, was not performed. This play, which Kingsley also would have directed, was to have starred Peter Lorre.

In 1939 Kingsley married the actress Madge Evans. The couple lived both in New York and in Kingsley's pre–Revolutionary War home in Oakland, New Jersey, where he continued to live following his wife's death in 1981. In this house one still finds books, amid thousands of others on the shelves, that were used in his research: medical dictionaries, psychology texts, Thomas Jefferson's letters, Washington's diaries. These books and other research materials easily support Kingsley's assertion that each play has entailed immersion in a different segment of American culture and history: "Each has been a new view of life, and I've led many lives."[10] His current project is an autobiography of those many lives.

Kingsley did occasional Hollywood work, such as the original story for MGM's *Homecoming* (1948), a tragic love story starring Lana Turner and Clark Gable, but his greatest efforts were for the stage. Nevertheless, he always had a keen interest in film and in later years was active on the New Jersey Motion Picture and Television Development Commission, serving as chair from 1976–80, appointed by Governor Brendan Byrne.

Kingsley's plays have received numerous professional, community, and university productions worldwide over the decades and continue to be produced today. For example, revivals of *Detective Story* include the Richard Barr–Charles Woodward production for their Theatre 1973 and a production by the Royal Exchange Theatre of Manchester, England, in 1982. Charlton Heston starred in a 1984 production of *Detective Story* at the Ahmanson in Los Angeles. *Detective Story* was produced by the State Theatre in Istanbul, Turkey, in 1988, and by the Tokyo Gendaigeki Centre Manatsuza in 1989. Samuel French records show a production of *Men in White* in 1983 and six productions of *Darkness at Noon* from 1984 to 1992, including productions by the State Theatre in Istanbul in 1988, by Vigszinhaz in Budapest in 1989, and Teatr Ateneum in Warsaw in 1989.

Because of their popularity abroad, his plays have been translated into many languages, including Spanish, German, Russian, and Hungarian for *Men in White;* German, Spanish, Korean, Chinese, Arabic, and several languages of the Indian subcontinent for *The Patriots;* Italian, German, and

*Sidney Kingsley and his wife, actress Madge Evans, working on a script at the pool of their New Jersey home. Courtesy of Sidney Kingsley.*

Japanese for *Detective Story;* and Arabic, German, and three different Spanish translations for *Darkness at Noon.* Only *Dead End* seems not to have been translated, perhaps because of the difficulty in rendering New York street slang, as well as the frequent phonetic spellings in the play, into another language.

In addition to winning awards for specific plays, Sidney Kingsley has been the recipient of numerous awards recognizing his body of work. In 1951 he was given the Academy of Arts and Letters Medal of Merit. He was inducted into the Theater Hall of Fame in 1983. In 1986, also from the Academy of Arts and Letters, Kingsley received the Gold Medal for Drama, which is given, not annually, but as it is appropriate, for a body of work that demonstrates outstanding accomplishment in the field. And in 1988 he received the William Inge Award for Distinguished Achievement in the American Theatre, an honor whose recent recipients include Edward Albee, Peter Shaffer, Wendy Wasserstein, and Terrence McNally.

## Men in White

Kingsley's first widely successful work was *Men in White*, produced by the Group Theatre in 1933. This play about hospital life dealt with one young intern's struggle to fulfill his commitment to society and medicine while being tempted by the easy medical practice and social advantages offered by his wealthy fiancée. His brief affair with a sympathetic nurse ends disastrously when she obtains an illegal, unsafe abortion.

Although it was acted by such theatre greats as Luther Adler, Morris Carnovsky, Sanford Meisner, Elia Kazan, and Clifford Odets, Group Theatre codirector Harold Clurman wrote that "Kingsley's *Men in White* was a well-constructed play with an interesting background, but the lofty quality given it by the Group Theatre company was not due to the excellence of its individual members but to the direction of Lee Strasberg."[11] In fact, Clurman was pleased with the play and production on several levels: it was a critical and popular success, and its box office provided the funds for him to make a theatre trip to Russia in 1934;[12] it proved to be what Clurman called, in a defense of Method acting, "a 'classic' Method production."[13]

Kingsley's meticulous approach to research and writing is apparent in *Men in White,* establishing the way he continued to work on all his projects. Optioned four times before finally being produced by the Group Theatre, *Men in White* was a critical, as well as popular, success. More than one critic rejoiced that the theatre was not dead after all, despite the Great Depression and its resulting effects, and Kingsley's play was the proof.[14] In fact, in retrospect on the theatre in New York during 1933–34, Burns Mantle felt that the season signaled a return of the theatre to a state of health, and that *Men in White* was one of the early heralds of that return.[15] Robert Garland's "Poll of Twelve Critics Reveals Their Favorite Plays and Players" found that ten of twelve critics[16] considered *Men in White* one of the best plays of the year, the dissenters being Gilbert W. Gabriel and John Mason Brown.

Brooks Atkinson found *Men in White* to be "a good, brave play," one that, while not perfect, "has force in the theatre . . . , warm with life and high in aspiration." Nevertheless, he questioned Kingsley's adherence to medical terminology as overly strict and the seduction scene as "hackneyed." In contrast to Atkinson, Eugene Burr of *Billboard* felt that in the seduction scene *Men in White* "reache[d] its finest psychological heights."[17]

John Mason Brown was the major naysayer among the critics of *Men in White*, and he continued to be for most of Kingsley's productions, lauding the Group's production but disliking the play. In fact, most critics acknowledged Kingsley's inexperience in the professional theatre but found both play and production worthy of praise. Arthur Pollock wrote that *Men in White* "shines continuously with a steady intelligence, is made notable by a crisp simplicity and austere skill, in spite of the fact that the author, Sidney Kingsley, has not heretofore been known to be a dramatist." Joseph Wood Krutch, admitting to not being predisposed to enthusiasm for *Men in White*, instead found it, "on the contrary, so immediately interesting, so completely absorbing, that one forgets to ask whether or not it is 'significant' or 'important.' And that, I submit, is one of the signs by which a genuine work of art may be recognized."[18]

Nor was *Men in White*'s popularity limited to New York. The touring company also received an enthusiastic response from such writers as Claudia Cassidy in Chicago: "*Men in White* is one of those rare plays that pleases actors, audiences and producers—it is written with a shrewd blend of zeal for a cause and zest for the stage."[19] Following immediately upon its U.S. success, the play was produced in London, in Vienna, and in Budapest, where Kingsley found the production to be outstanding.[20] *Men in White* opened in London at the Lyric Theatre in June 1934 (with Merton Hodge's adaptation to accommodate British medical practice), where it received good reviews from theatre as well as medical critics, although Kingsley himself felt that the anglicization was not "entirely successful," and the Lord Chamberlain had required some changes, such as the elimination of the scalpel and the placement of a screen around the surgical table, that inevitably affected the realistic presentation.[21] At almost the same time, the film of *Men in White*, with Clark Gable, Myrna Loy, and Jean Hersholt, opened in London to good reviews. While the play and film were running in London, the censor in Germany banned the play because "it shows doctors in a light contrary to the spirit of Nazi Germany."[22]

In *Men in White* Kingsley did what was clearly characteristic of him and what has marked his long career—to present on the stage a major human concern boldly and without apology or disguise—in this first instance, the issue of legalized abortion and the consequences of unregulated illegal abortion. It was not until forty years after the premiere of *Men in White* that the famous U.S. Supreme Court decision in *Roe* v. *Wade* legalized abortion in the United States, and the incendiary issue of abortion continues to be debated. Nevertheless, it must be acknowledged that Kingsley showed great strength of purpose and bravery in raising the question long before the public was prepared to confront it. And while it is to the credit of the critics of the time that the abortion did not alter their assessments of the play, it must also be noted that they were not as eager as Kingsley to discuss it. With Brooks Atkinson as a notable exception,[23] most avoided even the use of the word "abortion," either refraining from mentioning Nurse Dennin's illegal abortion and its disastrous outcome or referring to the situation euphemistically or circuitously.

As was also true of Kingsley's other works, *Men in White* attracted a critical audience bound by a common thread, in this case, their work in the field of health care. While these doctors and nurses surely attended other theatrical productions as individuals, *Men in White* brought them to the theatre for shared reasons—for self-examination, pride in the best representatives of their professions, and gratitude for Kingsley's understanding of the difficulties of their professional and personal lives. While two scenes in the play (one in which Ferguson stops a doctor from administering insulin to a patient and instead gives glucose; the other, the surgical scene of Nurse Dennin's hysterectomy) caused discussion among some health-care professionals with respect to the appropriateness of treatment or the reality of the situation,[24] other doctors and nurses gave the play their wholehearted approval.[25]

Kingsley became a highly desirable speaker for doctors' groups[26] and was asked to participate in a radio broadcast to raise funds for the United Hospital Fund of New York.[27] Both the stage and film versions of *Men in White* were favorably reviewed in medical journals and bulletins. The *Medical Record* found it to be "of especial value to wives and fiancées of physicians and those who depend or expect to depend on a physician's income for present or future comforts. . . . The play should be recommended by every medical man, for it gives to the public a clearer idea of the ideals and the problems of our profession, than could years of close contact between the physician and his patients."[28] The *Weekly Bulletin of the St. Louis Medical Society* declared that Kingsley "has caught the spirit of medicine and has portrayed as has never been done before on any stage the emotions, the heartbreaks, the struggles, the ambitions, the inhibitions, of the profession of today in the big city . . . with a pitying exactitude and truthfulness that we have never seen before."[29]

Reviews of the script of *Men in White* as published by Covici-Friede were slightly more mixed than those for the play, but nonetheless were generally favorable. Charles A. Wagner wrote that there was an "almost complete lack of memorable lines," but "technically and structurally, the play is a perfect whole, riding dramatically, even melodramatically, to logical wave on wave of a tidal force in professional duty and ambition pitted against the homing instinct." Almost diametrically opposed to Wagner's viewpoint was John Chamberlain's: "If one can forget the cardboard structure of *Men in White,* however, the individual lines are often amazingly effective."[30]

This disagreement among the critics carried over into a somewhat different arena than the daily newspaper—that of the Pulitzer Prize. The jury, made up of Clayton Hamilton, Walter Prichard Eaton, and Austin Strong, recommended Maxwell Anderson's *Mary of Scotland* for the prize; however, the Pulitzer advisory committee declined to accept the jury's recommendation and instead chose *Men in White.* While not an unprecedented move in Pulitzer history, this situation precipitated a good deal of discussion by the theatre critics. Brooks Atkinson voted with the jury for *Mary of Scotland,* although in reviewing *Dead End* two years later he wrote, "When the Pulitzer judges gave Mr. Kingsley a prize for *Men in White,* they picked a first-rate man." Perhaps more inclined to look at audience preference, Burns Mantle found it "significant . . . that while the specialists of the jury selected *Mary of Scotland* the playgoers of the larger Pulitzer committee reversed their decision and substituted *Men in White,*" for as playgoers, not experts, the advisory committee judged *Men in White* to be "the original American play, performed in New York, which shall best represent the educational value and power of the stage."[31]

It is quite likely that the dispute over *Men in White* was the impetus for some 1934 changes in the Pulitzer process. According to William Lyon Phelps, the addition to the prize of the phrase "preferably one dealing with American life" aided the committee when they might have to choose "between (let us say) two plays that might be of about equal artistic merit." In other words, a play such as *Men in White,* set in America, would have an advantage over a play such as Anderson's *Mary of Scotland.* In addition, a procedural change was instituted regarding the manner in which the jury's work was communicated. Rather than select a single play, the jurists were thenceforth to submit a short list in priority order, a method that had "always been desirable"[32] but had not been in practice.

## Dead End

Kingsley's second major production was *Dead End,* which frankly and shockingly put both profanity in the mouths of children and the hope-

lessness of poverty and slum life on the stage. With the major success of
*Dead End,* Kingsley proved to the critics that he was an American playwright of significance. According to Whitney Bolton: "There can no longer
be the slightest doubt (and there had been plenty) that Sidney Kingsley was
man and dramatist enough to follow up his first and Pulitzer prize-winning
play, *Men in White,* with a drama of equal brilliance. His new play is *Dead
End,* a thing of beautiful strength, of ferocity, contempt and possessed of a
rolling, cumulative force." Joseph Wood Krutch praised Kingsley as a "first-
rate theatrical craftsman," stating, "It is hard to see how [the corrupting
influence of poverty] could be made to serve as the basis for a more rapidly
moving or more exciting melodrama than the one which Mr. Kingsley has
written."[33]

With this second solid success as a playwright, recognition also came to
Mr. Kingsley as a fine director: "of an expertness seldom equaled"; "free of
false moves"; "[Kingsley's] directing keeps its vitality, clings hard to a claim
of the finest pieces of directing we've seen in recent seasons." Even John
Mason Brown, Kingsley's harshest critic, praised the direction, although he
credited that activity erroneously to Norman Bel Geddes.[34]

As did Stark Young and Eugene Burr, Brown also lauded both Bel Geddes's production and set: "it can safely be said that no native playwright of
our day has owed more to, or been more fortunate in, the productions his
dramas have received than Mr. Kingsley has been"; and "Mr. Geddes's waterfront scene is a triumph of realistic designing. . . . It is breath-taking, alive
with atmosphere, brilliantly contrived, fortunate in the angle from which it
is seen, and full of both acting opportunities and illusion." Percy Hammond,
on the other hand, felt that the stunning set was "the play's most artificial
component, half real and half palpable counterfeit," but consolingly went
on to say, "Any setting of any school of scene-making would probably seem
false in contrast to writing, acting and directing of the integrity that makes
*Dead End* important and successful."[35]

The 1935–36 season was an impressive one. It included Robert Emmet
Sherwood's Pulitzer Prize-winning *Idiot's Delight,* as well as Maxwell Anderson's *Winterset,* given the first award of the prize established by the New
York theatre critics in response to their earlier disagreement with the Pulitzer
committee. Nevertheless, *Dead End* showed well in the usual rankings as
number two in Robert Garland's best plays list[36] and appearing in *The Best
Plays, 1935–1936.*

Kingsley brought the experiences of his own childhood to bear in writing
*Dead End,* particularly in the language used. Years after the play, while
Kingsley was serving in the U.S. Army, some of his fellow soldiers decided
to use some spicy language to needle the quiet writer. To their great surprise,

he came back with a mouthful worthy of a Dead End Kid and, to their even greater surprise, informed them that he had written the book.[37]

While a number of critics noted the profane and graphic language in *Dead End,* either simply mentioning it or questioning the need for its use, most accepted and respected Mr. Kingsley's commitment to realism. Nevertheless, that language put the play on another theatre list in 1936—that of the Catholic Theatre Movement, which found *Dead End,* along with *Boy Meets Girl, The Children's Hour, Mulatto, One Good Year, A Room in Red and White,* and *Tobacco Road* to be "wholly objectionable."[38]

And yet, *Dead End* was wholly truthful. Kingsley again performed his characteristically exhaustive research. In looking at the hopelessness depicted in the photographs Kingsley acquired during his work, one understands what fueled the passion with which he wrote. Photographs of homeless children, street kids creating games with whatever was available— fire hydrants and piers—families receiving handouts, and shoe-shine boys are filed alongside photographs of juvenile delinquents, the bodies of John Dillinger, the Barkers, "Baby Face" Nelson, "Pretty Boy" Floyd, and Bonnie Parker, interiors of reformatories and prisons, and the electric chair at Sing Sing. Kingsley described his commitment and conviction in his writing in a radio interview: ". . . the root of every private life has its basis in social conditions, so that any play about human beings, living today, must of necessity consider, either to a lesser or greater degree, contemporary social conditions."[39]

*Dead End* was compared by the critics to Elmer Rice's *Street Scene* as well as, inevitably, to Anderson's *Winterset.* Comments ranged from nonjudgmental noting of their similarities and the differences within those similarities to strong partisan stands for one play or the other. Burns Mantle called *Dead End* "another dramatic exposure as was Elmer Rice's *Street Scene* . . . with the brooding gloom of Maxwell Anderson's *Winterset* without the Anderson verse to give it glamour," while Gilbert Gabriel found in *Dead End* and *Winterset* a "picturesqueness common to both . . . , common vitality, too, a kindred savagery of themes."[40]

The primary criticism made by several critics was their perception of a weak and conventional romantic subplot involving Gimpty and Kay. Nevertheless, the dramatic strength of *Dead End*'s message and social statement was compelling. Brooks Atkinson predicted that "*Dead End* is a play that will be missed only by the feeble-minded among those who pretend to be interested in the theater or in the poor or in intelligence or in the way this ruthless world wags—and need not wag at all."[41]

In fact, the stunning realism of *Dead End* confirmed Kingsley's commitment to writing plays that dug below the surface, not only to reveal social problems that many would rather have ignored, but to force society and government to address those problems. He did not pander to a well-to-do theatre audience: as Burns Mantle said, *Dead End* "provides another prod to the self-sufficient who look upon their tax receipts as complete vindication that they are giving their all for the betterment of the country and the protection of its future citizens."[42] Nor did Kingsley rely on the audience's powers of perception—he made his message unmistakably clear.

In finding and communicating that realism, Kingsley was supported to a significant extent by his actors, the seasoned professionals as well as the child actors. John Anderson found that "the kids are all incredibly right and persuasive in their performances." For Gilbert W. Gabriel, there was "not a single one from the ages of (let's say) 16 to 60 who is not absolutely, unalterably right."[43]

The Samuel Goldwyn film of *Dead End* included the boys from the original cast, and the "Dead End Kids" completed the transition some of them had begun on stage from being street toughs to playing street toughs. They made over 80 films in several film series, including "Dead End Kids and Little Tough Guys," "East Side Kids," and the "Bowery Boys."

Again, as with *Men in White,* Kingsley found a nontheatrical constituency seeking an articulate voice. That the voice was that of a playwright, rather than that of a legislator or journalist, mattered not—the public heard the message, either firsthand in the theatre or from numerous other sources. Even Eleanor Roosevelt cited *Dead End* in discussing the housing problem.[44] In newspaper articles on juvenile delinquency, poverty, low-cost housing, slums, youth clubs, child welfare, and workers' strikes, in publications from the *New York Times* to the *Daily Worker, Dead End* was praised, cited as true testimony, and appropriated to numerous causes. One of the more interesting appearances of the play in the nontheatrical press was in coverage of a strike threatened by some New York City housewives that there would be "no more babies until better housing were provided." *Dead End* was credited with influencing this idea.[45]

Humorous or not, the problem was real, and out of the awareness raised of the inadequacy of housing and the spotlight cast on the related health, safety, and social issues, the Wagner Housing Bill (S. 4424) was passed by the United States Congress "to provide financial assistance to the States and political subdivisions thereof for the elimination of unsafe and insanitary housing conditions, for the development of decent, safe, and sanitary dwellings for families of low income, and for the reduction of unemployment and the stimulation of business activity, to create a United States Housing Authority, and for other purposes."[46] And perhaps the passage of that bill and other legislation that followed would be the most satisfying review a playwright like Sidney Kingsley could want.

## The Patriots

*The Patriots*, which won the New York Drama Critics Circle award for 1942–43, was a four-year project for Kingsley, finished during his service in the army during World War II. The playwright was deeply concerned about the dissension he saw globally and in so many areas of society: "dissension is being whipped up between us and our Allies; party hates are being aggravated. North and South, farmer and labor and capital are being pitted one against the other, religious and racial antagonisms are being sharpened to a dangerous degree."[47] Rather than write a contemporary war play to air his concerns, he chose the period following the American Revolution when the difficult work of building a democracy that could survive was under way, a time of political and social instability. Jefferson, as secretary of state and friend of the people, and Hamilton, as secretary of the Treasury and royalist, held opposing views on how to accomplish the task and were frequently at odds. Kingsley dramatized their differences of opinion regarding the nature of the new nation as well as methods to stabilize it. The play ends with Hamilton supporting Jefferson, his longtime rival, against Aaron Burr for the presidency. *The Patriots* points out that national unity is established by contributions from different people with varying methods of reaching the common goal in a form of government. In Jefferson's "We are all republicans—we are all federalists,"[48] echoed by a statement in the prospectus of the *New York Evening Post* (established by Hamilton) "that honest and virtuous men are to be found in each party,"[49] Kingsley found the perfect sentiment and setting through which to express his concerns.

Kingsley's choice to set *The Patriots* in an earlier period was a wise one because American audiences in the first years of the U.S. involvement in the war did not want to see war plays. Burns Mantle's assessment of theatre audiences over the 1941–42 and 1942–43 seasons was that "[t]hey did not care for, nor would they support, plays written on war themes and plays reproducing, however impressively, an active wartime realism."[50]

Unlike *Men in White* and *Dead End*, very realistic productions of their own present times, *The Patriots* is set in the historical past, built on a partially documented and partially imagined relationship between two of the founding fathers of the United States—Thomas Jefferson and Alexander Hamilton—with George Washington as their sometime mediator. Kingsley wrote of Washington as having "been deified out of the human race,"[51] and the same sort of immutable character was assigned to Jefferson and Hamilton, although both were vilified as well as deified. Kingsley again brought his exhaustive research techniques to the task of first cutting through the mythology that had arisen around each man in the ensuing years, then determining as carefully as possible their relationship from contemporary documentation, and finally extrapolating the missing pieces of the relationship from the existing evidence. In the end, he felt that he had fairly treated the men and their impact on the new democracy.

In 1974 John Wharton, member of The Playwrights Producing Company and its legal counsel, remembered that Maxwell Anderson had brought Kingsley and an early draft of *The Patriots* to the company. Wharton did not specifically mention Elmer Rice's opposition to the play, which Kingsley describes in his introduction, but he did note that "there was still some hesitation on the part of some of the playwright-members" and that he and the manager were concerned about the cost of the production.[52] While the order of the players is somewhat obscure (Burns Mantle states that Rowland Stebbins wanted to produce *The Patriots* and sought out the Playwrights Company as coproducer;[53] Wharton says that Stebbins entered the picture after the company had already begun consideration of the script),[54] Rowland Stebbins and the Playwrights Company did collaborate on the successful production of *The Patriots*. Because of his commitment to the U.S. armed services, Kingsley was unable to direct the play, a job taken on by Shepard Traube; nevertheless, Kingsley was able to put in appearances from time to time at rehearsals to work through problems.

In general, the critics were very supportive of *The Patriots,* awarding it the New York Drama Critics Circle Award. In the inaugural volume of George Jean Nathan's *The Theatre Book of the Year, The Patriots* received honors as the best full-length American play, as did Cecil Humphreys's depiction of George Washington as the best male performance.[55] While some noted problems in the structure or writing of the play, those same critics praised Kingsley's selection of material and the striking parallels of that material with the war years: "In writing of the past, Mr. Kingsley has written most excellently of the immediate present";[56] "though Mr. Kingsley, beset with all the difficulties of a dramatist turned historian, has hardly caught the countenance of history, he has found its pulse and at times its voice, and written a play that is steadily interesting and occasionally eloquent and dramatic";[57] "the violence and importance of the conflict, the vivid personalities and the issues involved gave it an absorbing interest. . . . Altogether these elements go to make up an evening in the theatre which owes more to history than to drama, but which is, in any case, thoughtful, provocative and pertinent";[58] "Sidney Kingsley has written a stirring, eloquent and timely stage biography."[59] Samuel Grafton, political columnist for the *New York Post,* gleefully praised Kingsley's putting Thomas Jefferson, rather than a contemporary figure, onstage because it "gives [the politicians] the worrisome feeling that he is talking about social security, and a decent peace, even though his dialogue never steps out of chronological bounds in these haunting and thrilling scenes."[60]

As with *Dead End* and *Men in White,* Kingsley sparked audience interest in nontheatrical circles. *The Patriots* and Kingsley were invited to play a major role in the birthday celebration of Thomas Jefferson in Washington, D.C., and the dedication of the Jefferson statue by sculptor Rudolph Evans. The play was given in the Coolidge Auditorium of the Library of Congress, where "a distinguished audience thrilled to the presentation."[61]

In addition to the strongly positive feelings that many audience members had for *The Patriots,* Kingsley also managed to attract attention from a very unified opposition—the Hamilton Club. In a pamphlet circulated by the club in response to *The Patriots*'s playing the Library of Congress, Kingsley was decried as a "non-commissioned upstart, who so brazenly incriminates an intrepid Major-General of the Army of the Revolution." In fact, others were also taken to task: "But it is unmitigated shame, when a playwright, an aping coterie of critics, the Librarian of Congress [Archibald MacLeish] and a Justice of the Supreme Court [Felix Frankfurter] make this laceration of a Founding Father a Roman holiday!"[62]

In casting the play, Kingsley chose several radio actors, an action that John Wharton, at least, regretted. Although these actors gave excellent auditions due to their practice in making something out of a script quickly, Wharton felt that some of them never developed their roles past that first quick characterization.[63] The reviews for Raymond Edward Johnson, the radio actor playing Jefferson, tended to be good, noting a physical resemblance to Jefferson and particularly complimenting his voice and reading, such as his delivery of Jefferson's inaugural address. Nevertheless, Ward Morehouse gave him a mixed review: "a curiously uneven performance. In some scenes he was awkward but in many others he was genuinely moving";[64] and other critics concurred. Cecil Humphreys was widely praised as George Washington—"a minor masterpiece of stage characterization at its best,"[65] according to Burns Mantle. House Jameson as Hamilton received generally good notices, and Juano Hernandez, who had played the title role of *John Henry* on the radio, was praised as Jupiter. Kingsley's wife, Madge Evans, was complimented for her performance as Patsy. The reviews were mixed for many of the smaller roles.

While Warner Brothers, closely following the original stage production, announced a forthcoming film production of *The Patriots,* it was never made. Nevertheless, twenty years later, the script, adapted by Robert Hartung, did make it to the television screen as a Hallmark Hall of Fame production. According to Richard F. Shepard, the production "effected a rare and fine combination of television's much-vaunted but seldom-linked functions of entertaining and informing." Charlton Heston, playing Jefferson, "captured the statesmanship" but not "the warmth and weariness of the man."[66]

*The Patriots* toured North America very successfully, receiving good reviews in Boston, Providence, Hartford, Toronto, Buffalo, Philadelphia, Rochester, Baltimore, St. Louis, Washington, Richmond, Wilmington, Cincinnati, Pittsburgh, Indianapolis, Cleveland, Madison, Columbus, Milwaukee, Chicago, and Detroit. Some critics who had seen the New York production as well as the touring production preferred the latter. E. B. Radcliffe of the *Cincinnati Enquirer* liked the restaged prologue, but missed the fire generated during the Declaration of Independence scene "when voices of aroused debaters came from all parts of the house, thus making the audience a direct party to the Jeffersonian fight for an ideal."[67]

The tour ran with an almost entirely new cast: of the major roles, only Cecil Humphreys remained as Washington. When it came back to New York City for an appearance at City Center, the play was well received even by Burton Rascoe, who had been extremely negative about the Broadway production. Rascoe stated that the script had been revised for the better.[68] An examination of multiple copies of script drafts, including very early and middle versions, the production script, and the published version of the play, does not support Rascoe's statement that those substantial revisions, especially in act II, scene 1, were, in fact, made. The script did undergo some minor revisions, as well as a major revision from the earliest drafts, then entitled *Thomas Jefferson,* which included the character of Maria Cosway, a romantic interest for Jefferson. That subplot was eliminated in the production and published versions; however, the scene to which Rascoe referred remained constant. Perhaps in viewing *The Patriots* after an absence of eleven months and with entirely new casting for Jefferson and Hamilton, Rascoe simply saw a new set of actors making characters their own and distinctly different from the first cast, while speaking the original words.

## Detective Story

*Detective Story,* produced by Howard Lindsay and Russel Crouse, was directed by Kingsley himself. Set in a detective squad room of a police precinct populated by the amazing variety of people Kingsley found in real life, the play deals with issues of theft, paranoia, illegal abortion, and personal obsession. Foreshadowing *Darkness at Noon, Detective Story* warns against the abuse of power, whether by the individual or the state. In preparation for this play, Kingsley again immersed himself in on-site research, attaching himself to a New York police precinct for study.

The play takes place in that milieu, pulling many small stories together in support of the main story—Detective McLeod's unrelenting pursuit of an illegal abortionist who, unbeknownst to McLeod, had aborted his wife Mary's illegitimate child before they met and married. Finally, caught between his love for Mary and his inability to accept her past, McLeod is forced to recognize the truths she hurls at him: "You think you're on the side of the angels? You're not! You haven't even a drop of ordinary human forgiveness in your whole nature. . . . You're everything you've always said you hated in your own father."[69] Having lost Mary and his chance at humanity, McLeod loses his life during an escape attempt by the burglar Charley.

That Kingsley again succeeded in creating a real-life situation, intriguing because of that reality, is clear from the enthusiastic critical response. Interestingly, a few of the critics, as former police-beat reporters, were well qualified to review the play as an accurate representation of a police station squad room as well as a successful theatre work. Having been on the police beat, John Chapman and Robert Coleman vouched for the play's authenticity; Chapman called Kingsley's invented 21st Precinct station "typical of them all," acknowledging at the same time that the play had "a deceptive naturalness which conceals the know-how of an experienced and intelligent dramatist." Coleman praised the playwright/director, producers, and cast for a play with "heart, thrills and humanity." In agreement, George Jean Nathan, having had "the honor of knowing more or less intimately all kinds of detectives," felt that Kingsley's squad room was full of "the genuine article caught from the flesh: the hard, direct, and inexorable type; the tough-fibred but genial; the plodding but restless and impatient; the calmly dutiful." In fact, the play was so realistic that Chapman was impelled to inform readers that the playwright was not a detective, as Burns Mantle in 1933 had been obliged to let them know that Kingsley was not a doctor.[70]

Of the critics who had never had (or did not own up to having had) police-beat experience, the response was also enthusiastic. Richard Watts found that Kingsley's "pungent and fascinating detail, . . . interesting, dramatic and thoughtful narrative, . . . and racy and colorful characters" made up "one of the season's most triumphant combinations of a good show and a good play." In a season that included *Death of a Salesman, Anne of the Thousand Days, Summer and Smoke, Life with Mother, Kiss Me, Kate,* and *South Pacific,* this was indeed no small praise. Robert Garland found Kingsley's police detectives "as blood-filled and believable as were his bad guys in

*Dead End* and his good guys in *Men in White*," men who "in turn, deal believably with us all-too-human human beings."[71]

Among the few less-than-enthusiastic reviews, Brooks Atkinson compared Kingsley with Tennessee Williams and Arthur Miller, concluding that Kingsley was unable to "express ideas so deeply and forcefully [as Williams and Miller] because he is imprisoned by his method [naturalism]." However, he did admit that, "beginning with Ibsen, it is nevertheless a method that has resulted in some trenchant pieces of work, and *Detective Story* is one of the best." Several critics, including Ward Morehouse (the *Sun*), John Chapman (this time for the *Daily News*), and Wolcott Gibbs (the *New Yorker*) noted a kinship to Hecht and MacArthur's *The Front Page*: a similarity in "uproar and raucousness," "clatter, clutter and impudence," and "much the same place spiritually."[72]

A study of theatre criticism by writers/reporters for the popular media is interesting both theatrically and socially because it provides us directly with their views of the play and its production elements, but also indirectly with the barometer of issues that may be acceptably addressed in a widely distributed print forum. In contrast to the reviewers of 1933's *Men in White*, by 1949 virtually all the writers used the words "abortion" and "abortionist" in their coverage of *Detective Story*, without apology or circumlocution.

Ironically, Paramount, as with the rest of the film industry under its censorship code, had to change the abortion issue in *Detective Story*. Instead of being an abortionist, in the film Schneider becomes a doctor who delivers illegitimate or unwanted babies. While this alteration does not hold up on a contemporary viewing of the film, it seems to have been perfectly acceptable and comprehensible to film reviewers in 1951.[73] Presumably, the moviegoing public also understood the euphemism for abortion. Certainly, lines from the film such as McLeod's comments on Schneider's "baby farm grist mill," his biting statement that Schneider would "take care of both mother and child for a fee," and Tami Giacoppetti's "the baby was born dead"[74] suggest strongly a situation more sinister than the provision of obstetrical care for unwed mothers. In any event, the film followed the play's popularity and was selected as one of the top ten films of the year by the New York Film Critics.[75]

As usual by this time for Kingsley, *Detective Story*'s audiences and supporters again included a population who were probably not regular theatregoers—large numbers of police, the same ones who had been the trainers for Kingsley during his research period and later for Ralph Bellamy in his research for the role of McLeod. For the tryout in Philadelphia, the police of that city provided authentic supplies, such as fingerprint paper, for the production. The chief of police went so far as to check, after the play had transferred to New York, to see if they needed anything.[76]

For a play with a large cast, almost all the actors received remarkable notices, a number of the critics apologizing for not being able to single out every outstanding performance.[77] Ralph Bellamy as McLeod was praised widely by the critics, more than one identifying this role as his best to date, calling it a performance with "stature and dignity, evoking pity as well as terror, . . . a personal triumph";[78] "magnificently played";[79] an "unswerving portrayal [that] never fails the script."[80] In fact, the role of McLeod was a significant one for Bellamy and a major change from his usual lightweight parts in romantic comedy films. Bellamy seemed to recognize the importance of this role to his career because he viewed Jim McLeod as a multifaceted character whose successful portrayal would challenge him more than his other roles,[81] especially his film roles in which he played many "amiable, dull, slightly ridiculous gentlemen who were invariably fated to lose Irene Dunne to Cary Grant."[82] Wearing his director's hat, Kingsley found working with Bellamy a very satisfying experience, both professionally and personally.[83]

The role of Mary McLeod was one of the few areas of disagreement among the critics, some of whom found the script to be the problem,[84] and others simply recognizing that the role was intended to be a secondary one.[85] Intended or not, the part is underwritten in comparison to the other major roles in the play. The audience sees only one side of Mary McLeod: the wife who has tried to make herself into the woman she thinks her husband wants. From Schneider and Giacoppetti, it hears of another, younger, perhaps carefree and careless Mary. But Mary is seen only in relation to others—the playwright does not develop her character through dialogue, and, unlike other characters in the play, she is not onstage enough to show the audience through action who she is.

Of all the actors in *Detective Story*, Meg Mundy as Mary McLeod fared the least well, receiving mixed reviews—one kinder critic citing her for "exciting moments," others contenting themselves with objective descriptions of her role rather than qualitative comments on her performance, and still others, with Ward Morehouse, finding her "never too convincing." George Jean Nathan tried to explain why this actress who, from all accounts, had been excellent in *The Respectful Prostitute,* had failed in a company whose performances were uniformly good. Basing his opinion on information received from an anonymous, reliable source, he wrote that Mundy had pretended during rehearsals to follow Kingsley's direction, but when performances began she "elected to forget it and to go it on her own," which "was not good enough."[86]

Lee Grant as the Shoplifter, Horace McMahon as Lieutenant Monoghan, Joseph Wiseman as the First Burglar (Charles Gennini), Michael Strong as the Second Burglar (Lewis Abbott), and James Maloney as Mr. Pritchett all received outstanding notices for these roles, which they later re-created successfully in the film.

Regardless of their views on the play, the critics uniformly credited Kingsley with an excellent job of directing *Detective Story*. With a cast of thirty-four actors, many of whom were onstage at the same time, and a script with multiple dovetailing stories, the play had a potential for disaster if the stage movement and timing were less than precise. Richard Watts praised Kingsley as "one of the stage's most brilliant directors," specifically, as having "done a superb job in keeping his narrative moving with smoothness and dispatch." While criticizing Kingsley's writing style as "dated," Brooks Atkinson joined his fellow critics in finding much to praise in his directing: "[H]e has directed an honest performance that is always interesting and becomes exciting and shattering in the last act," and "Kingsley has organized a pungent and meticulous performance."[87]

While following Kingsley's established patterns of extensive research and realistic staging, *Detective Story* differs from the playwright's earlier works. His underlying message about the dangers of a police state, while not entirely lost on the critics and audiences, was not so clearly and emphatically presented as were the statements in *Men in White, Dead End,* and *The Patriots* on abortion, the evils of slum life, and the nature of democracy, respectively. And critical and popular response to *Detective Story* was overwhelmingly to the exciting, action-packed stage, rather than to the message the action was intended to convey. Again, unlike the earlier plays whose messages either found specific audiences (health care professionals) or had a broad audience appeal (to all citizens regarding the problems of slum housing and juvenile delinquency; to all U.S. patriots during a war effort), *Detective Story* did not have that same kind of built-in constituency. Indeed, it is an irony that the police—the professional group responding to *Detective Story*—were, in fact, those who could have been most offended had the police state message been explicit.

## Darkness at Noon

*Darkness at Noon,* while not Kingsley's first produced adaptation, preceded in 1939 by *The World We Make,* was certainly his most successful. Almost a dozen years had passed before Kingsley produced this second adaptation, which is based on the Arthur Koestler novel. Lester Markel, Sunday editor of the *New York Times,* suggested that the playwright read the novel, and Kingsley found that the work "crystallized [his] feeling of the Soviet experiment."[88] Markel also assisted Kingsley in establishing a correspondence with Koestler through which the right to adapt the novel into a play was obtained.[89] Kingsley himself considered *Darkness at Noon* a companion piece to *The Patriots:* "I began examining the other side of the medal—the Soviet way, and I came upon *Darkness at Noon*. I really picked up where I left off with *The Patriots*."[90] In this stage adaptation, Kingsley creates a prison setting in which scenes from the imprisoned Rubashov's Bolshevik past come back to him and in which he realizes that his torturer is the product of the cruel ideology of Rubashov's own generation.

In a flamboyant gesture before the opening of the play, Koestler donated his earnings from the stage version of *Darkness at Noon* to the Fund for Intellectual Freedom, established by Graham Greene, John Dos Passos, James Farrell, Aldous Huxley, and Koestler.[91] It seems likely that the novelist regretted this hasty display of generosity, since the play became a huge success. Koestler later attempted to obtain control over all foreign productions of the play. In an arbitration proceeding on Kingsley's claim that Koestler had breached their contract by these and other demands, the arbitrator found in favor of Kingsley and disallowed Koestler's claims.[92]

Nevertheless, the collaboration was of importance to Koestler in his bid for permanent residency in the United States. Because of his previous communist activities, he was not eligible by law for such status. The major success of *Darkness at Noon* as a play, which made a definite anti-communist statement by Kingsley in contrast to the vagueness of the novel, at the time Koestler was applying for residency certainly had an effect. In spite of objections by the U.S. Justice Department, both the Senate and the House of Representatives passed a bill allowing Koestler to stay in the United States.[93] Even though President Truman did not sign the bill, neither did he veto it; it therefore became law without his signature.[94]

Coproduced by the Playwrights Company and May Kirshner, Kingsley's sister, *Darkness at Noon* came at a critical time for the Playwrights Company, which was in a decline due, in part, to Kurt Weill's death and to problems of the individual playwright members. John Wharton viewed this play as "an accompanying tiny gleam" in the company's currently dark situation.[95]

Opening in Philadelphia at the Forrest Theatre, *Darkness at Noon* received reviews that would set the tone for its run there, in New York, and on tour. Henry T. Murdock called it "a timely play, a useful play, a thoughtful play and, since these things are not always enough in the theater—it is a profoundly gripping play." The majority of the critics in New York agreed and gave raves; disagreement came from a small minority. Richard Watts described the play: "Brilliantly staged by Mr. Kingsley, with Claude Rains giving the portrayal of his career in an enormously exacting role, and fine supporting cast playing with unfailing skill, *Darkness at Noon* emerges as a drama of great emotional and intellectual impact that never falls into the easy primrose path of conventional anti-Kremlin hysteria." John Chapman called the play "the only contemporary and contemporarily important drama we have on the stage."[96] These writers were joined in their praise-singing by Howard Barnes, William Hawkins, John McClain, Robert Coleman, Whitney Bolton, Ward Morehouse, and others.

Indeed, the play was regarded widely as so fine that it might be a Pulitzer Prize contender, and there was much speculation regarding its chances. Ironically, it is likely that the Pulitzer Prize revision regarding an American topic, instituted in 1934 following the public discussion and criticism regarding the committee's award to Kingsley's *Men in White* over Maxwell Anderson's *Mary of Scotland*, put *Darkness at Noon* out of the running. In any event, no Pulitzer play award was given in 1951.

Brooks Atkinson gave the play a somewhat negative review, comparing it unfavorably with the novel: "Somewhere between the novel and the theatre the intellectual distinction has gone out of the work." In contrast, William Hawkins wrote that Kingsley had "done an amazing job . . . of dramatizing what must at first have seemed the undramatizable." John Chapman (who admitted that he had been unable to get through the novel) felt that Kingsley had "taken an involved novel filled with the literary tricks of the fictioneer and [had] made it into a grim and frightening work for the stage." Elliot Norton gave Kingsley high marks for his adaptation of Koestler's ideas to the stage, since "philosophical notions are not truly dramatic." Max Lerner gave a good review, with some reservations: "His [Kingsley's] forte has always been that he is a kind of seismograph to register the convulsions of his era. He has set down here with a deep seriousness the consciousness and conscience of an anti-Communist generation." But even in his recognition of Kingsley's presentation of a broadly based public sentiment through his writing, Lerner felt that the playwright had focused on the political issues and, in doing so, had "almost by-passed the darkness of the human heart." One of the very few truly negative theatre reviews was by Hobe Morrison of *Variety*, who predicted "slight boxoffice prospects," a prediction quickly disproved by both critical and popular viewers.[97]

The most negative, vitriolic, and extended commentary, however, was the *New York Daily Worker*'s review by Bob Lauter, who had also found *Detective Story*'s statement on the police state to be a little too close to home. Furious with both Koestler for writing *Darkness at Noon* and Kingsley for adapting it to the stage, Lauter loosed a scathing diatribe on the two men and their work, the "corruption and decadence of the Broadway stage," and the Hearst publication empire. The review is so remarkable that excerpts can hardly demonstrate its outrageousness:

The Alvin Theatre is now offering a spectacle, a rather dull and pompous spectacle, but a dangerous one: the spectacle of two minds [Koestler's and Kingsley's] completely stripped of all integrity. . . . Its [the play's] current purposes are clear. They are first, to contribute to the lowest level of anti-Soviet hysteria—the Hearst level. Second, to equate fascism and Communism. Third, to present the theory that the Soviet Union invents non-existent spies and saboteurs. . . . Fourth, and perhaps most important, *Darkness at Noon* is an attempt to justify the sniveling cowardice, the colossal duplicity, and the utter moral bankruptcy of Koestler's heroes: the Trotzkyite criminals. . . .[98]

Kingsley, Koestler, and Broadway made no reply, but Hearst had both the means and the will to respond. Howard Rushmore, writing for the *New York Journal American,* retaliated by citing the *Daily Worker's* review as the "best proof that the play is a damaging and effective indictment of communism." Lauter replied by criticizing Rushmore "of the Hearst press—a press which is notorious throughout the world for its gutter journalism and cheap sensationalism," for his championing of the play. Indeed, in the salvos fired by two diametrically opposed ideologies, Kingsley and the play almost became lost as the discussion veered into an arena not usually frequented by theatre issues.[99]

Speculation began as early as the spring of 1950 that film star Claude Rains would play the lead role in *Darkness at Noon,* which was indeed the case. While it was a most successful role for him, it was also a difficult transition from film to the stage, according to Kingsley.[100] And perhaps there was more behind Rains's attitude than nervousness in returning to the stage: Kingsley felt at the time that communists had "even worked on Claude Rains in California, trying to frighten him, and telling him if he appeared in it it would ruin his career."[101] Yet it was certainly a successful undertaking. Many critics joined Richard Watts in praising Rains's portrayal of the Communist Rubashov. John Chapman called his performance "remarkable physically . . . [and] even more notable intellectually."[102]

Alexander Scourby received excellent notices in his role as Rubashov's comrade and sometime friend Ivanoff, while newcomer Walter J. Palance (Jack Palance of later film and television fame) was praised for his "chillingly wonderful performance as Gletkin."[103] Kim Hunter as Luba received generally good reviews. Although several critics were not overly enthusiastic,[104] others found her work pleasing, including Robert Coleman who felt that she had "add[ed] another fine page to her biography with a forthright and tender portrayal."[105] Kingsley and Frederick Fox also were praised in their capacities as director and designer.

In February 1951 Jack Gould wrote a *New York Times* article on a current necessity "in broadcasting [that] is the program which deals effectively and maturely with the evils of communism." Using Kingsley's *Darkness at Noon* and Robert E. Sherwood's *There Shall Be No Night* as examples, Gould pointed out that "the fate of a single individual or family can be a far more eloquent editorial than even the most impassioned preachment on the Soviet menace."[106] A week later, Walter Winchell announced that *Darkness at Noon* was to become a Voice of America broadcast.[107] In addition, it would have the distinction of having all regular programs canceled for its broadcast, something previously done only for major speeches by the president of the United States. The anticipated audience for this broadcast was estimated at 100,000,000 listeners in Eastern Europe and the Soviet Union, Latin America, and the Far East.[108]

In an effort to reach an even broader audience in the United States "because of the topical immediacy of the anti-Communist theme,"[109] Kingsley and the Playwrights Company decided to release *Darkness at Noon* to colleges simultaneously with the Broadway production. This new idea in play production foreshadowed by more than a decade the American Playwrights Theatre, founded in 1963, whose purpose was to provide first-run plays by established playwrights to college, university, regional, and community theatres.

*Darkness at Noon* followed the pattern established by Kingsley's earlier works and took its place in the broader context of discussion on politics, communism, human rights, and betrayal of one's country. The *New York Socialist Call*, in decrying the dismal working conditions in Russian mines as described by recent refugees, felt that Kingsley had allowed his "stagecraft to obscure rather thoroughly the intellectual content of the novel."[110] *Darkness at Noon*, both play and novel, were cited as providing needed answers in a consideration of Alger Hiss's guilt and motivation for his actions.[111] The play was discussed as revealing "the Soviet mentality" in an article on the support of unions for the U.S. administration's foreign policy, in particular, that for Russia.[112] The unions also provided the unusual theatre audience that Kingsley's plays tended to draw with "a dozen New York unions [buying] more than 10,000 seats."[113] An American businessman, after seventeen months in a Budapest prison on espionage charges, compared his life there to prison life in *Darkness at Noon*: "I didn't have much else to do but listen to the sound of footsteps."[114] Even entertainment columnist Earl Wilson compared the torture endured by a Hungarian political prisoner to that of Rubashov.[115]

## Conclusion

In examining the negative criticism of Kingsley's plays, one finds some common threads: criticism of his treatment of personal relationships and of weak or inadequately developed romantic subplots; criticism of underdeveloped female roles; criticism of his dated method, whether called naturalism, realism, or journalistic style; criticism of his dialogue for not reaching the heights of poetry. And yet even stronger threads weave these plays inextricably into the fabric of twentieth-century American theatre—their meticulous, depressing, frightening, gut-wrenching, and inspiring realism; roles of great breadth for actors; masterfully constructed scripts that in combination with outstanding design and direction provided first-rate theatrical presentations; and, perhaps most importantly, an unswerving attention to grave human issues.

Even though the responses of society to particular concerns have differed from decade to decade, those human issues are in many ways unchanging. A *Western Hospital Review* article cited deficiencies in health care, an issue weighing heavily on Americans in the 1990s: "many persons either cannot and do not receive the care they need, or are heavily burdened by the costs, . . . the poorer the family, the less medical care it received."[116] That article was published in 1934 and included a very positive review of *Men in White*.

The inadequacies of housing and schools for inner-city children, those children's association with gangs, their use of weapons for protection or power, and the frequently tragic outcomes for them are a part of current American society. While neither contributing factors nor solutions to these problems are the same as those for 1935, *Dead End* continues to speak to the hopelessness of such situations for individuals and society alike.

With the balance of political power changing on an almost daily basis throughout the world, a reconsideration of the nature of a democracy such as *The Patriots*'s is again appropriate. Kingsley would approve because he believes, as he learned from Thomas Jefferson, that "a democracy must always be working out its destiny."[117]

The abuse of power by the individual is an issue as old as humankind, and certainly the abuse of power by police is an ongoing problem as well. A most prominent recent example would be the internationally followed Rodney King case, but certainly corollaries could be drawn to such governments as that of pre-Mandela South Africa. To the extent that audiences perceive Kingsley's message regarding the police state, *Detective Story* remains timely.

Given the recent changes in formerly communist countries, *Darkness at Noon* would seem to be the most dated of Kingsley's work, in the same way that free-world-versus-communist spy thrillers are no longer current. U.S. anticommunist sentiment has waned since the play and novel were written. Nevertheless, attempts to control thought and expression are not unique to communism, but are possible in many forms of government.

In all of his plays, Kingsley's style of writing for the theatre dates his work more than do the issues he confronts in that writing. But while realism or a journalistic style may not now be in vogue in the theatre, it is still in use not only by numerous fiction writers, many of whom deal with the same topics introduced to the stage by Kingsley, but also on television in news coverage, documentaries, pseudodocumentaries, soap operas, and dramatic series.

We live in a time in which the specter of illegal abortion has again been raised and the inadequacy of the health-care system is a daily topic, in which children facing hopelessness and poverty stare at us on the evening news, in which police brutality cases are before the courts, and in which issues of individual patriotism and the position of the United States as a democracy in a rapidly changing world arise. And in this time in which some form of all the human rights issues and social problems dealt with in these plays are still, or again, with us, Sidney Kingsley has proven to be a playwright whose work is timely as well as timeless.

## NOTES

1. Sean Mitchell, "Sidney Kingsley Still Has Something to Say to the World," *Los Angeles Herald Examiner,* 10 February 1984.

2. Sidney Kingsley, "The Professor and the Critic" (Address delivered at Cornell University for the Fiftieth Anniversary of the Cornell Dramatic Club, 7 March 1959), 2.

3. Sidney S. Kirshner, *Wonder-Dark Epilogue,* in *Cornell University Plays,* ed. A. M. Drummond (New York and Los Angeles: Samuel French, 1932), 213–32.

4. Martin Abramson, "Large as Life," *Esquire,* February 1952, 52–53, 108–9.

5. Burns Mantle, *The Best Plays of 1942–43* (New York: Dodd, Mead, 1943), 411.

6. Morgan Y. Himelstein, "Sidney Kingsley," in *Contemporary Dramatists,* 2d ed. (London: St. James Press; New York: St. Martin's Press, 1977), 448.

7. John F. Wharton, *Life among the Playwrights: Being Mostly the Story of The Playwrights Producing Company* (New York: Quadrangle/New York Times Book Company, 1974), 120.

8. "Conversations with . . . Sidney Kingsley," interview by John Guare and Ruth Goetz, *Dramatists Guild Quarterly* (Autumn 1984): 8, 21–31.

9. Wharton, *Life among the Playwrights,* 120–21.

10. Alan Jenkins, "Playwright Kingsley 'Dead End's' Success," *Austin American Statesman,* 2 August 1981.

11. Harold Clurman, *The Divine Pastime: Theatre Essays* (New York: Macmillan, 1974), 72–73.

12. Harold Clurman, *All People Are Famous* (New York: Harcourt Brace Jovanovich, 1974), 81.

13. Clurman, *The Divine Pastime,* 79.

14. See Arthur Pollock, "*Men in White*," *Brooklyn Daily Eagle* (New York), 27 September 1933; Arthur Ruhl, "Second Nights: A Prelude to Drama," *New York Herald Tribune*, 22 October 1933.

15. Burns Mantle, *The Best Plays of 1933–34* (New York: Dodd, Mead, 1934), 3, 6, 15.

16. The critics included Kelcey Allan of *Women's Wear Daily*, John Anderson of the *New York Evening Journal*, Brooks Atkinson of the *New York Times*, Whitney Bolton of the *Morning Telegraph*, John Mason Brown of the *New York Evening Post*, Julius Cohen of the *Journal of Commerce*, Gilbert W. Gabriel of the *New York American*, Robert Garland of the *New York World-Telegram*, Percy Hammond of the *New York Herald Tribune*, Richard Lockridge of the *Sun*, Burns Mantle of the *New York Daily News*, and Walter Winchell of the *New York Daily Mirror*.

17. Brooks Atkinson, "Men of Medicine in a Group Theatre . . .," *New York Times*, 27 September 1933; Brooks Atkinson, "Medicine Men: Realities of Professional Life in a Hospital Play That Restores the Group Theatre to Its High Estate," *New York Times*, 1 October 1933; Eugene Burr, "The New Plays on Broadway: *Men in White*," *Billboard*, 7 October 1933.

18. John Mason Brown, "Hospitals and the Stage: Further Remarks on the Group Theatre's Production of *Men in White*," *New York Evening Post*, 7 October 1933; Arthur Pollock, "*Men in White*, a Play about the Integrity of Doctors, Is Presented Brilliantly at the Broadhurst Theater," *Brooklyn Daily Eagle*, 27 September 1933; Joseph Wood Krutch, "Drama: An Event," *The Nation*, 11 October 1933.

19. Claudia Cassidy, "*Men in White* Is Rare Play—Pleasing to All," *Chicago Ill. Journal of Commerce*, 10 March 1934.

20. George Ross, "So This Is Broadway: Sidney Kingsley, Back from Protracted Vacation Abroad, Works on New Play," *New York World-Telegram*, 13 February 1934.

21. Ibid.

22. "*Men in White*: Play Banned in Germany," *West Lancashire Evening Gazette* (Blackpool), 20 July 1934.

23. Atkinson, "Men of Medicine."

24. "Doctors Roused by Play Scene: Interne's Impetuous Act Causes Discussion," [*New York World-Telegram*?], 30 September 1933.

25. "Thank You, Doctor: The Author of *Men in White* Did His Research in a Hospital," *Post*, 28 October 1933; Whitney Bolton, "*Men in White* Does Drama and Surgery Proud in Deft Operation," *Morning Telegraph*, 28 September 1933.

26. Leo Fontaine, "Standing in the Broadway Wings: Therapeutic Drama New Cure-All," *New York World-Telegram*, 13 November 1933.

27. Letter from E. H. L. Corwin (Director, United Hospital Fund of New York, Hospital Information and Service Bureau) to Sidney Kingsley, 14 October 1933.

28. "*Men in White*," *Medical Record*, 7 February 1934.

29. "*Men in White*," *Weekly Bulletin of the St. Louis Medical Society*, 16 February 1934, pp. [336?]–38.

30. Charles A. Wagner, "Books: Machinery of Medicine," *New York Daily Mir-*

*ror,* 13 December 1934; John Chamberlain, "Books of the Times," *New York Times,* 18 December 1933.

31. Brooks Atkinson, "Pulitzer Prize Package," *New York Times,* 14 May 1934; Atkinson, "The Play: Sidney Kingsley's *Dead End:* A Realistic Drama of the East River Waterfront," *New York Times,* 3 October 1935; Mantle, *The Best Plays of 1933–34,* v; From the Pulitzer Prize awards program, Columbia University, 7 May 1934, p. [3].

32. William Lyon Phelps, "Introduction," in *The Pulitzer Prize Plays 1918–1934,* edited by Kathryn and William Cordell (New York: Random House, 1935), [vii, viii].

33. Whitney Bolton, "*Dead End* Abreast of *Men in White* in Brilliance, Strength and Force," [*Morning Telegraph?,* 29 October 1935?]; Joseph Wood Krutch, "Drama Sure Fire," *Nation,* 13 November 1935.

34. Arthur Pollock, "*Dead End:* The Most Striking of This Season's New Dramas, Opens Vividly at the Belasco Theater," [*Brooklyn Daily Eagle?,* 29 October 1935?]; Burns Mantle, "*Dead End:* As Alive as Steam: Gorgeous Setting for a Drama That Is Smothered with Realism," [*New York Daily News?,* 29 October 1935?]; Gilbert W. Gabriel, "*Dead End:* A Hugely Exciting Street Scene Brought Home to the Belasco," [*New York American?,* 29 October 1935?]; John Mason Brown, "Norman Bel Geddes Stages *Dead End* Excellently: Sidney Kingsley's Drama of Contrasts in an East Side Street Well Acted at the Belasco," *New York Evening Post,* 29 October 1935.

35. Brown, "Norman Bel Geddes Stages *Dead End* Excellently"; Percy Hammond, "Youth in the Slums of *Dead End,*" *New York Herald Tribune,* 10 November 1935.

36. Robert Garland, "Robert Garland's Ten Best Plays of 1935–1936," *New York World-Telegram,* 20 June 1936.

37. "How the Sergeant Wrote His Play," newspaper clipping, Sidney Kingsley scrapbook collection.

38. "Catholics Ban 7 N.Y. Plays," *New York American,* 24 January 1936.

39. George Haight, Mara Tartar, and Sidney Kingsley, transcript of WJZ radio interview by William Lundell, 9 February [1935?].

40. Mantle, "*Dead End:* As Alive as Steam"; Gilbert W. Gabriel, "*Dead End:* A Brave Show Bravely Done: Riverfront Drama Is Rasping Realism," *New York American,* 10 November [1935].

41. Atkinson, "Kingsley's *Dead End.*"

42. Mantle, "*Dead End:* As Alive as Steam."

43. John Anderson, "John Anderson Reviews *Dead End* at the Belasco: Kingsley and Bel Geddes Picture Slum in Play Covering Waterfront," [*New York Evening Journal?, ?* 1935?]; Gabriel, "*Dead End:* A Hugely Exciting Street Scene."

44. *Public Housing Progress,* 15 December [1935?].

45. "Mothers Threaten Baby Strike Here," *New York East Side News,* 9 October 1937.

46. *Summary of Hearings on the Wagner Housing Bill before the Committee on*

*Education and Later the United States Senate: April 20, 21, 22, 23, 24, 25 and 29 1936* (Chicago: National Association of Housing Officials, 1936), viii.

47. Sidney Kingsley, "On Lifting Washington's Periwig," [*New York Times*], 21 February 1943.

48. Thomas Jefferson, "First Inaugural Address March 4, 1801" in *Thomas Jefferson: Selected Writings*, ed. Harvey C. Mansfield, Jr. (Arlington Heights, Ill.: AHM Publishing Corp., 1979), 64.

49. Jacob Ernest Cooke, *Alexander Hamilton* (New York: Charles Scribner's Sons, 1982), 233.

50. Burns Mantle, *The Best Plays of 1942–1943* (New York: Dodd, Mead, 1943), v.

51. Kingsley, "Washington's Periwig."

52. Wharton, *Life among the Playwrights*, 121.

53. Mantle, *The Best Plays of 1942–1943*, 29.

54. Wharton, *Life among the Playwrights*, 121.

55. George Jean Nathan, *The Theatre Book of the Year 1942–1943: A Record and Interpretation* (New York: Alfred A. Knopf, 1943), 1.

56. Lewis Nichols, "The Play in Review: *The Patriots*," *New York Times*, 30 January 1943.

57. Louis Kronenberger, "A Vivid Chapter in U.S. History," *PM*, 31 January 1943.

58. John Anderson, "*The Patriots* Opens at National Theatre," *New York Journal American*, 30 January 1943.

59. Howard Barnes, "Thomas Jefferson," *New York Herald Tribune*, 30 January 1943.

60. Samuel Grafton, "I'd Rather Be Right," *New York Evening Post*, [? 1943].

61. *Congressional Record*, vol. 89, no. 68, 13 April 1943.

62. "Protest against *The Patriots!*: Excerpts from an Address on Alexander Hamilton by Ellis Chadbourne April 28th, 1943, at The Playgoer's Guild, Hotel Ambassador, New York City" (New York: The Hamilton Club), 2, 3.

63. Wharton, *Life among the Playwrights*, 122.

64. Ward Morehouse, "Sidney Kingsley's New Play, *The Patriots*, Offered at the National," *Sun*, 30 January 1943.

65. Burns Mantle, "*The Patriots* Finds Inspiring Moments in Our Political Past," *New York Daily News*, 30 January 1943.

66. Richard F. Shepard, "TV: Kingsley's *Patriots*: Hallmark Show Puts 11 Years into 90 Minutes—Heston Plays Jefferson," *New York Times*, 17 November 1963.

67. E. B. Radcliffe, "Out in Front: The Patriots, Cox," *Cincinnati Enquirer*, 18 January 1944.

68. Burton Rascoe, "Kingsley's Patriots Better than Before," *New York World-Telegram*, 21 December 1943.

69. Sidney Kingsley, *Detective Story*, Act III.

70. John Chapman, *The Burns Mantle Best Plays of 1948–49* (New York: Dodd, Mead, 1949), 148, 147; Robert Coleman, "*Detective Story* a Good Plug for

'The Finest,'" *New York Daily Mirror,* 24 March 1949; George Jean Nathan, *The Theatre Book of the Year 1948–1949* (New York: Alfred A. Knopf, 1949), 328; Chapman, *Burns Mantle,* 370.

71. Richard Watts, Jr., "Kingsley's Police Play Is Town's Newest Hit," *New York Post,* 24 March 1949; Robert Garland, "New Kingsley Play Better than Good," *New York Journal American,* 24 March 1949.

72. Brooks Atkinson, "*Detective Story* Sidney Kingsley Applies Naturalistic Method to New York Police Station," *New York Times,* [3?] April 1949; Ward Morehouse, "*Detective Story* Vivid Melodrama," *Sun,* 24 March 1949; John Chapman, "A Dandy Melodrama, *Detective Story,* Adds Zip to the Season," *New York Daily News,* 24 March 1949; Wolcott Gibbs, "Cops and Causes," *New Yorker,* 9 April 1949, 48.

73. "*Detective Story,*" [*Variety*], 26 September 1951.

74. Philip Yordan and Robert Wyler, *Detective Story,* excerpts from a film based on the play by Sidney Kingsley, directed and produced by William Wyler, associate producers Robert Wyler and Lester Koenig (Hollywood: Paramount, 1951).

75. "The Year's Best," *New York Times,* 20 December 1951.

76. Jack Gaver, "Bellamy Thinks New Play Gives Him Best Role Yet," newspaper clipping, Sidney Kingsley scrapbook collection.

77. See Watts, "Kingsley's Police Play"; Garland, "New Kingsley Play Better than Good"; Chapman, "A Dandy Melodrama, *Detective Story*"; and Coleman, "*Detective Story* a Good Plug."

78. Watts, "Kingsley's Police Play."

79. Brooks Atkinson, "First Night at the Theatre," *New York Times,* 24 March 1949.

80. Howard Barnes, "One of the Finest," *New York Herald Tribune,* 24 March 1949.

81. Gaver, "Bellamy Thinks New Play."

82. Seymour Peck, "Ralph Bellamy, Detective," *New York Times,* 10 April 1949.

83. Sidney Kingsley, interview with Nena Couch, Oakland, N. J., 27 April 1993.

84. See Watts, "Kingsley's Police Play"; Gibbs, "Cops and Causes."

85. See Barnes, "One of the Finest"; and Thomas Brailsford Felder, "New Plays on Broadway: Death of a Detective," *Cue,* 2 April 1949, 23.

86. Coleman, "*Detective Story* a Good Plug"; Ward Morehouse, "*Detective Story* Vivid Melodrama"; Nathan, *Theatre Book of the Year 1948–1949,* 332.

87. Watts, "Kingsley's Police Play"; Atkinson, "First Night at the Theatre."

88. Sidney Kingsley, private notes.

89. Ibid.

90. "*Darkness at Noon* on VOA," *New York Daily Mirror,* 17 April 1951.

91. "F.I.F.," *Saturday Review of Literature,* 2 December 1950.

92. Commercial Arbitration Tribunal, "In the Matter of the Arbitration between Arthur Koestler and Sidney Kingsley," Case No. C-9800, N.Y.C.-212-51, 27 February 1952.

93. "Senate Votes DP Extension, Backs Koestler Stay in U.S.," *Washington Post,*

22 June 1951; and "House OKs Koestler Stay in America," *Minneapolis Star,* 8 September 1951.

94. *Philadelphia Inquirer,* 24 August 1951.

95. Wharton, *Life among the Playwrights,* 193.

96. Henry T. Murdock, "*Darkness at Noon* Bows on Stage at the Forrest," *Philadelphia Inquirer,* 27 December 1950; Richard Watts, Jr., "Two on the Aisle: The Grim Tragedy of Revolution," *New York Post,* 15 January 1951; John Chapman, "*Darkness at Noon* Is a Powerful and Intellectual Modern Drama," *New York Daily News,* 15 January 1951.

97. Brooks Atkinson, "At the Theatre," *New York Times,* 15 January 1951. (See also Atkinson, "*Darkness at Noon:* Sidney Kingsley Makes a Drama from the Novel by Arthur Koestler," *New York Times,* 21 January 1951); William Hawkins, "*Darkness at Noon* Floodlights Reds," *New York World-Telegram and Sun,* 15 January 1951; Chapman, "*Darkness at Noon* Is a Powerful and Intellectual Modern Drama"; Elliot Norton, "Lash Communists in Broadway Hit *Darkness at Noon,*" *Boston Post,* 8 April 1951; Max Lerner, "Darkness in the Heart," *New York Post,* 16 January 1951; Hobe Morrison, "*Darkness at Noon,*" *Variety,* 17 January 1951.

98. Bob Lauter, "*Darkness at Noon,* Sidney Kingsley's Pompous Fraud," *Daily Worker,* 18 January 1951.

99. Howard Rushmore, "*Darkness at Noon:* Kingsley Replies to Reds," *New York Journal American,* 23 January 1951; Bob Lauter, "Sidney Kingsley Adopted by Hearst," *Daily Worker,* 26 January 1951.

100. Sidney Kingsley, interview with Nena Couch, Oakland, N.J., 27 April 1993.

101. "*Darkness at Noon* on VOA."

102. Chapman, "*Darkness at Noon* Is a Powerful."

103. Richard Watts, Jr., "The Grim Tragedy of Revolution," *New York Post,* 15 January 1951. See also Chapman, "*Darkness at Noon* Is a Powerful and Intellectual Modern Drama"; and Robert Coleman, "*Darkness at Noon* Points a Moral for Today," *New York Daily Mirror,* 15 January 1951.

104. See Hawkins, "*Darkness at Noon* Floodlights Reds"; John McClain, "Rains Is Effective in a Stark Drama," *New York Journal American,* 15 January 1951; and Howard Barnes, "Illuminated Shadows," *New York Herald Tribune,* 15 January 1951.

105. Coleman, "*Darkness at Noon* Points a Moral."

106. Jack Gould, "Anti-Red Broadcasts: Programs Stressing American Principles Pose a Challenge to Writers," *New York Times,* 11 February 1951.

107. Walter Winchell, *New York Daily Mirror,* 18 February 1951.

108. Stuart W. Little, "'Voice' Doing *Darkness at Noon,*" *New York Herald Tribune,* 25 March 1951.

109. "Colleges to Put on *Darkness at Noon,*" *New York Herald Tribune,* 11 March 1951.

110. *New York Socialist Call,* 26 January 1951.

111. "*Darkness at Noon* for Alger Hiss," *Atlanta Journal,* 13 March 1951.

112. Nelson Frank, "Labor Today: Stand on State Dept. May Be Poser for U.S. Unionists at World Parley: Issue Viewed as Biggest Problem," *New York World-Telegram and Sun,* 15 June 1951.

113. Ibid.

114. "Vogeler Returns," *New York Times,* 30 April [1951].

115. Earl Wilson, "It Happened Last Night," *New York Post,* 28 June 1951.

116. "What the Public Is Thinking," *Western Hospital Review* (January 1934): 12.

117. "Conversations with . . . Sidney Kingsley," 27.

# NOTE ON THE EDITING

IN WORKING on this volume of plays as editor, I have standardized the play format, including the punctuation and presentation of the texts. The original publication formats varied extensively from play to play. In addition, some other changes should be noted. For *Men in White*, footnotes describing medical practice, procedures, and illnesses, as well as identifying major medical practitioners, have been removed. The contents of many of these footnotes are now common knowledge or information that is easily obtained through standard reference sources.

Some spellings have been changed to reflect current practice, for example, "intern" rather than "interne." In *Dead End*, spellings of words have been standardized among the boys in the gang by choosing one of Kingsley's phonetic spellings. The exceptions are Milty and Angel, whose speech reflects their ethnic backgrounds. Where differences in the spelling of character names occurs between the acting and commercial editions, the latter has been followed.

The versions of the scripts chosen were the commercial editions rather than the acting editions because the former provided more description of the scene and action, reflecting Kingsley's realistic writing style. The editions on which this volume is based are: *Men in White* (New York: Covici-Friede, 1933), *Dead End* (New York: Random House, 1936), *The Patriots* (New York: Random House, 1943), *Detective Story* (New York: Random House, 1949), and *Darkness at Noon* (New York: Random House, 1951).

The publication history of these plays is extensive, with inclusion in anthologies and serials as well as individual commercial and acting editions.

# MEN IN WHITE

Now, ALMOST AT the end of my journey through life, searching back fifty years and meeting the young man who was myself—who wrote these plays—I hardly recognize him in myself or me in him. There is so much that he did and said that I would gladly disown. However, I must say I admire in that young man his prophetic vision and the passion to follow truth wherever it leads.

Now I am in my eighties and looking back with some sense of wonder at the young man who wrote *Men in White*. I worked and spent an enormous amount of time in the hospitals of New York and was so impressed with the study of the history of medicine and the achievements made in the previous decade. At that time (the 1930s), there was no further research being done in surgery. It was generally felt in medical circles that surgery had gone as far as it could. Examining the progress it had already made in the previous fifty years, I was convinced, being young and optimistic, that it had a great way yet to go, and thus I made the figures in my play about medicine two surgeons engaged in research. In the first scene, I refer to the great strides that had been made within the lifetime of the two doctors. And in the very last scene, when my young protagonist expresses despair and helplessness at the death of the young nurse, the older surgeon voices my own youthful hopes and vision of the future.

Only some six years after the play was written, research began again in surgery, and today the enormous strides in that art and the development of almost miraculous surgical techniques have justified my optimism. A number of my friends have, from time to time, suggested that this play, at the time of its production noted and reviewed in medical journals at home and abroad, played a part in renewing interest in surgical research. When we

3

look at the wonders that such investigations have developed, I would like to believe that my friends are correct and that in some small way, perhaps, *Men in White* encouraged the research that began again soon after the play was produced.

In a way, *Men in White* began in my early years, however, with two terrifying ghosts who haunted me as a child. I remember leaving New York for a miserable stay in Philadelphia, where my sister May and I were operated on for tonsils and adenoids, an operation that was a particularly traumatic experience. As the chloroform coming through the cones clamped over my nose began to take effect, I was still conscious of the doctors working over me.

After a brief convalescence, we moved to Schenectady, where my father found a nice, but haunted, house—an old-fashioned, two-story, wooden-framed structure in the suburban countryside. The first night there, something so horrendous happened as to influence my entire life. As I was about to fall asleep, two chalk-white, luminescent figures slowly appeared, floating high near the ceiling and then moving across the room and descending, ominously reaching for my throat. I began to scream! My father and mother and some guests they were entertaining came rushing up the stairs, and, as they entered the room, the ghosts vanished. My parents finally quieted me and tried to assure me it was a dream, but I was sure it was not. My mother turned up the lights and sat with me until I fell asleep. The next night, the ghosts reappeared, I screamed again, and, as my parents rushed upstairs to me, again the spectral figures reaching for me vanished. I thought it was the house, but several years later, when we moved back to New York, the ghosts came with me.

On the ground floor opposite us was a physician, Dr. Singer, who would bring out a chair and sit on the stoop and talk with my mother. He had the sweetest smile and gentlest manner I have ever known, and he was fond of me. He would gently pat me on the head and laughingly call me "Little Nemo"—a character in the comics of a Sunday newspaper, drawn in vivid colors, a boy who had the most horrendous and incredible dreams from which, at a horrifying climactic moment, he would awaken half out of bed in a tangle of sheets.

I had a similar assortment of wild dreams, sleeping and waking, which I carried around in my eyes, and Dr. Singer was a sharp enough physician to see them. One evening he took me aside, asked me many questions, and finally said, "You know, there are doctors who might help you, but that's a long, expensive process; and, in the long run, you have to help yourself. Some night, when you feel real strong and brave, turn out the light, let them come at you, and you take them by the throat, and you'll see, they'll disappear."

Several years later, old enough to be ashamed of my fears of the dark, I decided to try his advice. I turned out the lights and waited for the ghosts, and they came—closer and closer. When they came close enough, instead of screaming, I cursed them and reached out to hit them, and then in a flash I recognized them—they were the faces with the surgical masks of the anesthetist and the surgeon who had operated on me. I had to repeat that challenge again and again before they would go away. Occasionally, they came back and the hair of my neck bristled. That odd chill still ran up my spine, but I didn't scream. At last they grew dimmer and dimmer, and finally they left me forever . . . or almost. Those two ghosts came back to play an important, if now benign, role in my play.

A pal of mine, a young intern at Beth Israel Hospital, knowing I was deeply interested in medicine, encouraged me. Had the times been different, I think I might have well chosen to become a physician. But I had already picked one very difficult profession, and there were doctors then standing on the street corners selling apples to make a living.

I would visit my friend at the hospital, eat with the interns, sleep over at the hospital, double-date with nurses, drink a special brew the interns concocted with alcohol from the pathology lab, ginger ale, lemon, and a sprinkling of sugar (remember, those were the days of Prohibition). On many occasions I would go on rounds with the medical staff, wearing a white jacket, and sometimes a patient would call me over and describe his ailments. I would nod sympathetically and refer him to another "specialist." I read all the books I could find on the history of medicine.

Then, as part of the search for a play, I witnessed an operation and again experienced André Malraux's seminal idea—in the "scrub-up," the elaborate ritualistic, aseptic preparation for an operation, but more—much more: the tingling spine, the bristling of my hair, the urge to scream, but this time with delight, for suddenly my ancient ghosts became benign and shook me by both shoulders.

Edward Gordon Craig's pronouncement had already become my credo: that of all the arts that combine to make the theatre, the most important is the art of dance, the *mise-en-scène*. Now it was happening before me. There in the operating room were groups of men and women being helped into white masks and caps and gowns in a ritualistic, rhythmic pattern, against a surreal background lit by a great saucer of lights overhead, composing a ballet. Even more, this ballet was a demonstration of the history of surgery. What more could a playwright ask? I jotted down and made sketches of every movement; here was the ballet around which my play was to be designed.

The rhythmic scrubbing-up and the raising of their hands, some of them almost at the same time, others repeating it later as they allowed the soapsuds to dribble down the elbows—all part of the sterilization process; the entire procedure, with the unsterile nurses picking up the towels from the floor where they were thrown after being used, and the sterile nurses helping the doctors so carefully into the robes and sterilized gloves, the white caps and masks, the lighting—all to a choreographed rhythm—all so bizarre that I saw it clearly as a ballet. The same surgical caps and masks that in my childhood had created my own two ghosts and surrounded me in fear for so many years now heightened this spectral quality. The history of the "scrub-up" ritual I forecast in the play's first scene in a library, wherein the progress of medicine is discussed by one very old veteran and presented as a kind of prelude to the play.

Another searing first experience in my research was an autopsy I witnessed at the Bellevue morgue, when I saw a young girl who had died of a septic abortion being butchered for the autopsy. She had been a beautiful young girl. Subsequently in my studies, I was horrified to learn there were more than a million abortions being performed every year in this country—all illegal and mostly done by incompetents in septic, crude circumstances. Consequently, how many women died or were crippled by this, nobody could calculate, although certainly women who could not or did not want to have a child and were forced into abortions performed under such conditions often suffered those fates. It was the sight of that autopsy that provided me again with Malraux's seminal idea and led me to write a play espousing legalized abortion. Finally, forty years later, the laws were amended to correct this situation; however, to this day, these laws are being contested fiercely, in some cases paradoxically by asserting the right to life by indiscriminate murder.

In addition to the Pulitzer Prize, *Men in White* had another honor: the Nazis forbade both the play and the film with Clark Gable and Myrna Loy from being shown in Nazi Germany. It was, they said, "not consistent with the Nazi philosophy," and I quite agreed with them. I regarded that as a very special, if lopsided, honor.

S.K.

# MEN IN WHITE

"I swear by Apollo, the physician, and Aesculapius, and Hygieia, and Panacea and all the gods and all the goddesses—and make them my judges—that this mine oath and this my written engagement I will fulfill as far as power and discernment shall be mine. . . .

"I will carry out regimen for the benefit of the sick, and I will keep them from harm and wrong. To none will I give a deadly drug even if solicited, nor offer counsel to such an end; but guiltless and hallowed will I keep my life and mine art.

"Into whatsoever houses I shall enter I will work for the benefit of the sick, holding aloof from all voluntary wrong and corruption. Whatsoever in my practice, or not in my practice, I shall see or hear amid the lives of men which ought not to be noised abroad—as to this I will keep silent, holding such things unfitting to be spoken.

"And now, if I shall fulfill this oath and break it not, may the fruits of art and life be mine, may I be honored of all men for all time; the opposite if I transgress and be foresworn."

*—Excerpts from the Hippocratic oath, to which physicians have bound themselves since the days of antique Greece.*

Produced by The Group Theatre, and Sidney Harmon and James R. Ullman at the Broadhurst Theatre, New York, September 26, 1933, with the following cast:

| | |
|---|---|
| DR. GORDON | Luther Adler |
| DR. HOCHBERG | J. Edward Bromberg |
| DR. MICHAELSON | William Challee |

| | |
|---|---|
| DR. VITALE | Herbert Ratner |
| DR. MCCABE | Grover Burgess |
| DR. FERGUSON | Alexander Kirkland |
| DR. WREN | Sanford Meisner |
| DR. OTIS (SHORTY) | Bob Lewis |
| DR. LEVINE | Morris Carnovsky |
| DR. BRADLEY (PETE) | Walter Coy |
| DR. CRAWFORD (MAC) | Alan Baxter |
| NURSE JAMISON | Eunice Stoddard |
| MR. HUDSON | Art Smith |
| JAMES MOONEY | Gerrit Kraber |
| LAURA HUDSON | Margaret Barker |
| BARBARA DENNIN | Phoebe Brand |
| MRS. SMITH | Ruth Nelson |
| MR. SMITH | Sanford Meisner |
| DOROTHY SMITH | Mab Maynard |
| DR. CUNNINGHAM | Russell Collins |
| FIRST NURSE | Paula Miller |
| NURSE MARY RYAN | Dorothy Patten |
| ORDERLY | Elia Kazan |
| MR. HOUGHTON | Clifford Odets |
| MR. SPENCER | Lewis Leverett |
| MR. RUMMOND | Gerrit Kraber |
| DR. LARROW* | |
| MRS. D'ANDREA | Mary Virginia Farmer |
| SECOND NURSE | Elena Karam |
| Other hospital visitors and staff | |

Staged by Lee Strasberg
Setting by Mordecai Gorelik

*Although the role of Dr. Larrow does not appear in some early versions of the script, the character is included in published editions and later revisions of the play.

ACT ONE *Scene 1:* Staff Library, St. George's Hospital
        *Scene 2:* Mr. Hudson's Room
        *Scene 3:* Children's Ward
        *Scene 4:* George Ferguson's Room
ACT TWO *Scene 1:* Board Room
        *Scene 2:* Staff Library

## Scenes

The entire action takes place within the walls of St. George's Hospital.

*Advertising handbill for* Men in White. *Courtesy of the Jerome Lawrence and Robert E. Lee Theatre Research Institute.*

## ACT ONE
*Scene 1*

*The library of St. George's Hospital. The staff of the hospital gather here to read, to smoke, and to discuss many things—primarily Medicine.*

*This is a large, comfortable room flanked on the left by tall windows, on the right by ceiling-high bookcases crammed with heavy tomes. There is a bulletin board in one corner, on which various notices, announcements, advertisements, schedules, etc., are tacked; there is a long table, an abandon of professional magazines and pamphlets strewn upon it; there are many plump, leather club chairs, some of which are occupied at the moment by members of the staff. In a series of stalls against the back wall are a number of phones.*

*Niched high in the wall is a marble bust of Hippocrates, the father of Medicine, his kindly, brooding spirit looking down upon the scene. At the base of the bust is engraved a quotation from his Precepts: "Where the love of man is, there also is the love of the art of healing."*

*A number of the staff are smoking and chatting in small groups, the nucleus of each group being an older man in civilian clothes—an attending physician; the young men, interns, recognizable by their white short-sleeved summer uniforms, are doing most of the listening, the older ones most of the talking, the hush of the room on their voices.*

*One elderly, white-haired physician, seated well to the right, is straining his eyes over a thick medical volume. A number of other books and pamphlets are on a stool beside him. A middle-aged physician, his back to us, is searching the bookcase for a desired volume. A younger practitioner is standing by the window, looking out into the street.*

*Through a wide, glass-panelled double door, set in the rear wall, we see a section of the corridor alive with its steady cavalcade of nurses, interns, etc., all hurrying by to their separate tasks. The quick activity of the hospital outside contrasts noticeably with the classical repose of the library. The loudspeaker at the head of the corridor calls: "Dr. Ramsey! Dr. Ramsey! Dr. Ramsey!"*

*Phone rings. An intern crosses to the phones, picks one up, talks in low tones.*

*Enter* DR. HOCHBERG, *a short, vital man, whose large head is crowned by a shock of graying hair. He carries himself with quiet, simple dignity. There is strength in the set of his jaw; but the predominating quality expressed in his face is a sweet compassion—a simple goodness. That he is a man of importance is at once apparent in the respectful attention bestowed on him by the others.*

GORDON (*the middle-aged physician, who has just found his book*), *sees* HOCHBERG: Ah, Dr. Hochberg! I've been waiting for you. *He quickly replaces the volume and goes to* HOCHBERG.

*The young practitioner by the window wheels round at the mention of* HOCHBERG'S *name.*

GORDON: There's a patient I want you to see.

HOCHBERG: Certainly, Josh. We'll look at him in a minute. I just—*His eye sweeps the room.* George Ferguson isn't here, is he?

MICHAELSON (*one of the interns seated*), *looks up from his reading:* No, Dr. Hochberg. Shall I call him?

HOCHBERG, *nods:* Please.

*MICHAELSON rises and goes to a telephone.*

VITALE (*the young practitioner*), *leaves the window and approaches* HOCHBERG: Er . . . Dr. Hochberg.

HOCHBERG: Good morning, Doctor.

VITALE: I sent a patient of mine to your clinic yesterday. Did you have a chance to . . . ?

HOCHBERG, *recollecting:* Oh—yes, yes. *Reassuringly, knowing that this is perhaps* VITALE's *first private patient, and most likely a relative at that.* No rush to operate there. You try to cure him medically first.

VITALE, *relieved:* I see. All right, Doctor. Thank you. Thank you.

HOCHBERG: Not at all. Keep in touch with me. Let me know what progress you make.

VITALE: I will.

HOCHBERG: If we have to, we'll operate. But I think if we wait on nature this case will respond to expectant treatment.

VITALE: Right! *He goes.*

GORDON, *shakes his head, kidding* HOCHBERG: Fine surgeon you are—advising against operation!

HOCHBERG, *smiles and shrugs his shoulders:* Why not give the patient the benefit of the doubt? You can always operate! That's easy, Josh.

MICHAELSON, *returning from the phone:* Dr. Ferguson'll be right down, sir.

HOCHBERG: Thanks.

GORDON: I hear you've some interesting cases at your clinic.

HOCHBERG: Yes, yes—er—suppose you have dinner with me tonight. We'll talk, hm? I discovered a little place on Eighty-fourth Street where they serve the most delicious schnitzel and a glass of beer— *Measuring it with his hands.* —that high! . . . But beer!

GORDON: Sounds good. I'll just phone my wife and—

HOCHBERG: It won't upset her plans?

GORDON: Oh, no! *He crosses to the phone.*

HOCHBERG, *approaches the white-haired physician and places a hand gently on his shoulder:* And how is Dr. McCabe today?

McCABE: My eyes are bothering me! *He indicates the pyramid of books beside his chair.* Trying to read all of this new medical literature. It certainly keeps piling up! *He shakes his head.* Has me worried!

HOCHBERG: But, why?

McCABE, *nods toward interns:* These young men today—how can they ever catch up with all this?

HOCHBERG: These young men are all right. They're serious—hard-working boys. I've a lot of faith in them.

McCABE: But there's so much. *He shakes his head.* We've gone so far since I was a boy. In those days appendicitis was a fatal disease. Today it's nothing. These youngsters take all that for granted. They don't know the men who dreamed and sweated—to give them anesthesia and sterilization and surgery, and X-ray. All in my lifetime. I worked with Spencer Wells in London, and Murphy at Mercy Hospital. Great men. None of these youngsters will equal them. They can't. There's too much! I'm afraid it will all end in confusion.

HOCHBERG: Where the sciences *in general* are going to end, with their mass of detail—nobody knows. But, good men in medicine . . . we'll always have. Don't worry, Dr. McCabe . . . one or two of these boys may surprise you yet, and turn out another Murphy or another Spencer Wells.

McCABE, *shaking his head:* Not a Spencer Wells! No! Not a Spencer Wells! *HOCHBERG helps him rise.* Chilly in here, isn't it? *He walks slowly to the door.* I'm always cold these days. *He shakes his head.* Bad circulation!

*GORDON finishes his phone call, hangs up and crosses to* HOCHBERG.

HOCHBERG: All right for dinner, Josh?

GORDON: Oh, of course. Certainly!

*An intern,* GEORGE FERGUSON, *and an attending physician, DR. WREN, come up the corridor engaged in discussion. The intern stops outside the door to give some instructions to a passing nurse, who hastens to obey them.*

*He pauses in the doorway of the library, still talking to DR. WREN.*

GEORGE FERGUSON *is about twenty-eight; handsome in an angular, manly fashion, tall, wiry, broad-shouldered, slightly stooped from bending over books and patients; a fine sensitive face, a bit tightened by strain, eager eyes, an engaging earnestness and a ready boyish grin.*

FERGUSON: If we used Dakin tubes it might help. . . .

WREN: They're worth a trial!

FERGUSON: And, this afternoon, first chance I have, I'll take him up to the O.R. and debride all that dead tissue.

WREN: Good idea! *And he marches on down the corridor.*

*Dr. McCabe reaches the door. Ferguson holds it open for him. McCabe returns Ferguson's smile and nod. McCabe goes on. Ferguson enters and approaches Hochberg.*

MICHAELSON: They've been ringing you here, George.

FERGUSON: Thanks, Mike! *To Dr. Hochberg.* Good morning, Doctor Hochberg.

HOCHBERG: Good morning, George.

FERGUSON: I was down in the record room this morning. *He takes a pack of index-cards out of his pocket.* The first forty-five cases seem to bear you out. . . .

HOCHBERG, *smiles:* Uh, hm! . . .

FERGUSON: Some three hundred more charts to go through yet, but . . .

GORDON: What's this?

HOCHBERG: Oh, Ferguson and I are doing a little research. I have some crazy notions about modern surgical technique. Ferguson, here, is writing a paper to prove that I'm right!

FERGUSON: As a matter of fact, Dr. Hochberg is writing the paper. I'm just helping collect the data and arrange it.

HOCHBERG: Ah! You're doing all the hard work! How's 217?

FERGUSON: Pretty restless during the night, but her temperature's down to normal now.

HOCHBERG: Good! And Ward B—bed three?

FERGUSON: Fine! Asked for a drink of whiskey.

HOCHBERG, *smiles:* He'll be all right.

FERGUSON: He is all right! *He grins.* I gave him the drink.

HOCHBERG, *laughs:* Won't hurt him. . . .

FERGUSON, *becomes serious, turns to Dr. Gordon:* I wish you'd have another look at 401, Doctor.

GORDON: Any worse today?

FERGUSON: I'm afraid so. He's putting up a fight, though. He may pull through.

GORDON, *shaking his head dubiously:* Mm, I don't know.

FERGUSON: I hope so. He's a fine fellow. He's planning great things for himself—when he gets out of here.

GORDON, *significantly:* When he gets out. . . .

*The phone rings. A short intern crosses to phones and picks one up.*

HOCHBERG: Oh, by the way, George, we're sending Mr. Hudson home Tuesday.

FERGUSON, *suddenly excited:* Tuesday? Great! Does Laura know, yet?

HOCHBERG, *nods:* I phoned her this morning.

FERGUSON: She happy?

HOCHBERG: Naturally!

FERGUSON: I wish you had let me tell her.

HOCHBERG, *twinkling:* Ah—I should have thought of that!

SHORTY, *at phone:* One second. *Calls.* Ferguson! For you.

HOCHBERG: Go on! Call for you. *FERGUSON goes to phone. HOCHBERG beams at GORDON.* Good boy! Lots of ability! We're going to be proud of him some day.

*Enter a lean, shabby man who at first glance appears out of place here. His coat is rusty, and rough weather has left its stain on the hat he carries so deferentially. Tucked under one arm is a large envelope of the type used for X-ray pictures. He has a timid, beaten manner. He is a fairly young man, but worry has lined his forehead and prematurely grayed his hair, making him seem years older. He hesitates at DR. HOCHBERG's elbow, and finally ventures to touch it.*

HOCHBERG, *turns, looks at him. Politely, as to a stranger:* Yes? *Suddenly he recognizes the man.* Why . . . Levine! *He grips LEVINE's arms with both hands, almost in an embrace.* My dear Levine! . . . I didn't recognize you. . . .

LEVINE, *nods and smiles sadly:* I know.

HOCHBERG: Dr. Gordon! You remember Dr. Levine?

GORDON, *hesitates a moment:* Why, of course. *They shake hands.*

HOCHBERG: Such a stranger! Where have you been hiding all this time? Why it must be . . . five years since . . .

LEVINE: Six!

HOCHBERG: Six? My! Mm . . . *To GORDON.* We're getting old. *Then, affectionately.* Ah! It's good to see you again.

LEVINE: It's nice to get back, but . . . *He looks around.* Things here seem pretty much the same. New faces—that's all.

GORDON: Nothing much changes in a hospital.

LEVINE: Only people! We change . . . get old . . . break up so quickly. *The tragic quality in his voice affects the others. Pause.*

GORDON: Well . . . *To HOCHBERG.* I'm going up to look at that boy in 401. *HOCHBERG nods. GORDON turns to LEVINE.* I'm glad to have seen you again. *Exit GORDON.*

HOCHBERG: Tell me . . . how are things with you?

LEVINE: Oh . . . *He shrugs his shoulders.* Just about getting along.

HOCHBERG: And how is Katherine?

LEVINE, *his brow wrinkles:* Not so well.

HOCHBERG, *concerned:* What seems to be the trouble?

LEVINE: Her lungs. . . . She has a slight persistent cough! Some X-rays here. . . . *He opens the large envelope he is carrying and from it takes two*

*X-ray plates.* HOCHBERG *holds up the plates to the window and examines them.*

    FERGUSON *hangs up and returns to* HOCHBERG.

HOCHBERG, *holds the plates so that* FERGUSON *can see them:* George . . . ?

FERGUSON: That shadow there! The right apex.

LEVINE: Yes—I was afraid of . . .

HOCHBERG: Now, don't be an alarmist! *Sees something.* Mm! *Squints at the plate, and asks, gravely.* Have you examined the sputum? *Pause.*

LEVINE: I brought a specimen. *He takes out a bottle, wrapped in paper, and explains apologetically:* My microscope is broken.

HOCHBERG: We'll look at it here!

FERGUSON: Certainly! *He takes the bottle.* I'll have the path lab check up on this. Is it anything important?

LEVINE: My wife.

FERGUSON: Oh.

HOCHBERG: Er . . . Dr. Ferguson, Dr. Levine! *They shake hands and exchange greetings.*

FERGUSON: I'll tend to this at once, Doctor.

LEVINE: Thanks. Do you think if I came back this evening—?

FERGUSON: Oh, yes, the report will be ready then. Drop into my room— 106.

LEVINE: 106? *He turns to* HOCHBERG. *With nostalgia.* My old room.

FERGUSON: You interned here? Are you the—Oh, of course. Bellevue, aren't you?

LEVINE, *nods:* '23!

FERGUSON: Professor Dury mentions you quite often.

LEVINE: Dury? *To* HOCHBERG. He still remembers me. . . .

FERGUSON: He thinks a great deal of you.

HOCHBERG: George, here, is one of his prize pupils, too.

LEVINE: And does he want you to study abroad?

FERGUSON: Yes. I planned to go with Sauerbruch, but he has been forced to leave Germany. So, instead of that, I'm going to study under von Eiselsberg in Vienna.

HOCHBERG: Hm! I remember when I was a student in Berlin, one of my classmates came to an examination in military uniform . . . sabre and all. Virchow looked at him, and said, "You! What are you doing here in that monkey suit? Your business is with death! Ours is with life!" Virchow was a man of science. He knew. *He shakes his head.* I wonder what he would say to our beloved Germany today.

LEVINE: Yes. . . .

FERGUSON, *to* HOCHBERG: Well, Laura prefers Vienna, anyway, so . . . *To*
LEVINE. I'm going on my honeymoon too, you see.
LEVINE: You'll find it difficult mixing the two. I know von Eiselsberg.
HOCHBERG: It's going to be very difficult. You don't know Laura.
FERGUSON: After a year in Vienna I'm working with Dr. Hochberg. So the
real labor won't begin till I come back from Europe.
HOCHBERG: Oh, I'll drive you, George! With a whip, eh?
LEVINE: —Lucky! *Retrospectively.* Yes. . . . I once looked forward to all
that. *He sighs.*
HOCHBERG: Well, come, Levine. We'll go down to X-ray and read these
pictures properly.
FERGUSON, *holds up bottle:* And don't worry about this.
LEVINE: Thank you . . . thank you. *Exit* HOCHBERG. LEVINE *turns to* FERGU-
SON. Remember, there's only one Hochberg. Every minute with him is pre-
cious.
FERGUSON: I won't miss a second of it.
   LEVINE *goes.* FERGUSON *crosses to a long table at which* MICHAELSON
*and* SHORTY *are seated.*
MICHAELSON, *who has been watching* LEVINE *and* FERGUSON: He's telling
*you,* huh? FERGUSON *nods, smiles, and looks for a particular book in
the shelves.* Say, there's a damned interesting article on Hochberg in this
week's *A.M.A.*
FERGUSON: I know. *He finds the magazine and hands it over to* SHORTY, *a
small, chubby, good-natured, irresponsible, wise-cracking fellow, who
takes life in his stride.* Here it is. You want to read this, Shorty.
   SHORTY *sits down to read it.*
MICHAELSON: Yep. I wish I could get in with him for a year. . . .
FERGUSON, *to* SHORTY: What do you think of that first case? The way he
handled it? Beautiful job, isn't it? Beautiful!
PETE, *intern, a tall, gawky lad, slow-moving and casual about everything
but food, enters, fixing his stethoscope. He drawls:* Say, George . . .
SHORTY: Pete! Sweetheart! You're just the man I've been looking for.
PETE, *drily:* The answer is no.
SHORTY: Will you lend me your white tux vest for tonight? I've got . . .
PETE, *abruptly:* The answer is still no. *He turns to* FERGUSON. That little—
SHORTY, *sits down again:* Thanks!
PETE: You're welcome. *To* FERGUSON *again.* The little girl we just operated
on is coming out of her ether nicely. I was kind of worried about that pre-
op insulin.
FERGUSON: Why? How much did you give her?

PETE: Forty units.

FERGUSON: Twenty would have been enough.

PETE: I know.

FERGUSON: Then why the hell did you give her forty? You might have hurt the kid.

PETE: Dr. Cunningham ordered it.

SHORTY: That dope—Cunningham!

FERGUSON: You should have told me before you gave it to her. I'm not going to have any patients go into shock on the operating table! Understand?

PETE: O.K.

FERGUSON, *good-naturedly, slapping* PETE *on the head with a pamphlet:* If this happens again, Pete, you get your behind kicked in . . . and not by Cunningham!

PETE: O.K.

NURSE JAMISON, *passing by, carrying a tray of medication, halts in the doorway, looks in and calls:* Oh, Doctor Ferguson, that drink worked wonders. Bed three is sitting up and taking notice.

FERGUSON, *laughs:* A new school of therapy!

SHORTY: Say, Jamison, you're not looking so hot. You ought to stay home one night and get some sleep.

JAMISON: Oh, I'm doing all right. *She laughs and goes.*

SHORTY: Yeah? I'll bet you are.

    *The loudspeaker starts calling,* "Dr. Bradley! Dr. Bradley!"

PETE: Say, I'm hungry! Somebody got something to eat?

SHORTY: What, again? PETE *looks at him with scorn.* Lend me your white vest for tonight, will you, Pete? I'll fix up a date for you with that redhead. *Phone rings.*

PETE, *nodding at* FERGUSON: Fix him up.

    *Ferguson laughs.*

SHORTY: It'd do him good. That's the trouble with love—it kills your sex-life. . . . *Indicates the phone.* Pete! Phone!

PETE: I was once in love, myself. *He starts for phone.* But when it began to interfere with my appetite . . . Hell! No woman's worth that! *They laugh.*

FERGUSON: Thing I like about you, Pete, is your romantic nature.

PETE, *on phone:* Dr. Bradley! O.K. I'll be right up! *He hangs up.* Yep. At heart I'm just a dreamer.

SHORTY: At heart you're just a stinker!

PETE: Thanks!

SHORTY, *quickly:* You're welcome!

    *Pete goes toward the door.*

FERGUSON: Going upstairs, Pete?

PETE: Yep.

FERGUSON, *gives him the bottle of sputum:* Will you take this to the path lab? Ask Finn to examine it and draw up a report.

PETE: O.K.

   *Enter DR. GORDON.*

FERGUSON: Tell him to give it special attention! It's a friend of Hochberg's.

SHORTY, *follows PETE to door:* I take back what I said, Pete. You're a great guy, and I like you. Now, if you'll only lend me that white vest . . .

PETE: No!

SHORTY: Stinker! *They exit.*

   *GORDON comes over to FERGUSON.*

GORDON, *his face grave:* Well . . . I just saw 401. He's a mighty sick boy. He may need another transfusion.

FERGUSON: We'll have to go pretty deep to find a good vein.

GORDON: That's what I'm worried about. If it comes up tonight I want you to be here to do it.

FERGUSON: Tonight?

GORDON: There are three donors on call.

FERGUSON: This is my night out. . . . My fiancée has made arrangements. . . . So I'm afraid I won't be here.

GORDON: I'm sorry, Ferguson. When the House needs you . . .

FERGUSON: I'd like to, Doctor, but the same thing happened last week. I can't disappoint my fiancée again . . . or— *He smiles.* —I won't have any.

MICHAELSON: Er—Dr. Gordon, couldn't I do that transfusion?

GORDON: I'm afraid not—the superficial veins are all thrombosed. Ferguson has followed the case from the start; he knows the veins we've used.

FERGUSON: Laidlaw knows the veins. . . .

GORDON: Frankly, I don't trust any of the other men on this case. I know I'm imposing, but I want this boy to have every possible chance. . . . *Pause.* He's a sick boy, Ferguson. What do you say?

FERGUSON: All right! I'll stay.

GORDON: Thanks! *He starts to go—turns back.* And if your sweetheart kicks up a fuss, send her around to me. I'll tell her about my wife. Up at 4:30 this morning to answer the phone. Somebody had a bellyache. . . . *He laughs, nods and goes. FERGUSON remains, dejected.*

FERGUSON: Damn it! I wanted to be with Laura tonight.

MICHAELSON: That's tough, George. I'm sorry I couldn't help you out.

   *The loudspeaker starts calling:* "Dr. Manning! Dr. Manning!"

FERGUSON, *rises and walks about:* Laura's going to be hurt. You'd think they'd have a little . . .

NURSE, *comes quickly down the corridor, looks in, and calls, a bit breathless:* Dr. Ferguson? *She sees him.* Dr. Ferguson, a woman just came in on
emergency with a lacerated throat. She's bleeding terribly! Dr. Crane told
me to tell you he can't stop it.

FERGUSON: Get her up to the operating room. *He snaps his fingers.* Stat. *She
hurries off. He turns to* MAC. Drop that, Mac, and order the O.R.! Come
on! *MAC goes to a phone. To* MICHAELSON. Call an anesthetist, will you?
And locate Dr. Hochberg! Try the X-ray room!

MICHAELSON: Right! *He jumps to a phone. Exit* FERGUSON.

MAC: Operating room! . . . Emergency B! . . . Quick! . . . O.R.?
. . . Set up the O.R. right away! Lacerated throat! Dr. Ferguson! Yes!

*On*

*phones,*     MICHAELSON: Find Dr. Hochberg! Right away! Emergency! . . .

*simulta-*     *The loudspeaker, which has been calling, "Dr. Manning!"*

*neously*      *changes to a louder and more persistent, "Dr. Hochberg! Dr.
Hochberg, Dr. Hochberg!"* Well, try the X-ray room! . . .
And locate the staff anesthetist!

*In the back corridor we catch a glimpse of an orderly hurriedly pushing
a rolling stretcher on which the emergency patient is lying, crying hysterically. An intern on one side and the nurse at the other are holding pads to
her throat and trying to calm her.*

FADE OUT


**ACT ONE**
*Scene 2*

*The largest and the most expensive private room in the hospital. It is
luxuriously furnished in the best of taste and tries hard to drive all clinical
atmosphere out into the corridor. What the room can't eliminate, it attempts
to disguise; not, however, with complete success. For there, behind a large,
flowered screen, the foot of a hospital "gatch" bed peeps out, and in the
corner we see a table with bottles of medication on it.*

MR. HUDSON, *a large man, haunched, paunched, and jowled, clad in
pajamas and a lounging robe, is sitting up on a divan being shaved by the*
HOSPITAL BARBER. *He is talking to one of his business associates, a* MR.
MOONEY, *who is a smaller, nattier, less impressive, and, at the moment,
highly nervous edition of* HUDSON.

HUDSON, *through a face full of lather:* We'll get that property, Mooney!
And we'll get it now . . . on our own terms.

MOONEY, *marching impatiently to and fro:* How are you going to break that Clinton Street boom?

HUDSON: You get in touch with the real estate editor of every paper in town. Tell them we've decided to change the location of Hudson City from Clinton to . . . say Third Street. Map out a territory! Make it convincing!

*A nurse enters with a bowl of flowers, places it on a small table, arranges the flowers, and departs.*

MOONEY, *hesitantly:* Think they'll believe it?

HUDSON: Sure. . . . Got a cigar?

MOONEY, *produces one, then hesitates:* You're not supposed to smoke, you know.

HUDSON: I'm all right! Can't think without a cigar! *He takes it. The* BARBER *gives him a light. He puffs once or twice with huge relish.* Start negotiations with every realty owner in the new territory. Buy options! They'll believe that!

*The* BARBER *finishes, starts to powder* HUDSON's *face, but is waved away.*

MOONEY: Oh yes. . . .

HUDSON: In the meantime sell ten of our houses on Clinton Street—including corners. Sell low!

MOONEY: Hey! We want that stuff!

HUDSON: Get Henderson! Form two dummy corporations—and sell to them.

MOONEY: Oh! . . . Yes, I think it'll work . . . that ought to bring down those prices.

*The* BARBER *packs his shaving kit and exits.*

HUDSON: We'll wait till they're ready to take nickels . . . then our dummy corporations can grab all that property. . . . Mooney, we'll be excavating this Spring, yet.

*Enter DR.* HOCHBERG. *He sees* HUDSON *smoking, frowns, goes to him, takes the cigar out of his mouth, and throws it away.*

HOCHBERG: Didn't Dr. Whitman say no more cigars?

HUDSON, *startled, his first impulse one of extreme annoyance:* Hochberg, please. . . . *He controls himself, turns to* MOONEY.

MOONEY, *glances at* HOCHBERG, *picks up his coat and hat:* Well, I'll be going now.

HUDSON, *helps him into his coat:* Phone me!

MOONEY: I will. . . . Don't worry! *Shakes* HUDSON's *hand.* Take care of yourself! *To Hochberg.* Goodbye, Doctor! HOCHBERG *nods. Exit* MOONEY.

HOCHBERG *watches* MOONEY *go, then turns to* HUDSON *and shakes his head.*

HUDSON: Whitman's sending me home Tuesday, isn't he? What do you want to do? Make an invalid of me? *He goes to the phone.* Operator! Get me Vanderbilt 2-34— *He gasps, an expression of pain crosses his face, his free hand goes to his breast.*

HOCHBERG, *nods grimly:* Uh, huh! HUDSON *glances at* HOCHBERG *guiltily, controls himself, continues on the phone.*

HUDSON: 3471!

HOCHBERG, *goes to him, takes the phone out of his hand, puts it down, with an abrupt nod of the head toward the bed:* You better lie down!

HUDSON: It's nothing. Just a . . .

HOCHBERG, *softly:* I know. Get into bed.

   HUDSON *shakes his head and smiles to himself at* HOCHBERG'S *persistence. Then he goes to the bed and lies down.* HOCHBERG *feels his pulse.*

HUDSON: I tell you, I'm all right!

HOCHBERG: I don't understand people like you, John. Whitman is the best cardiac man in the country, but he can't give you a new heart! Don't you know that? Are you such a fool?

   *Enter* LAURA, *a spirited, chic young lady; lithe, fresh, quick, modern, a trifle spoiled perhaps, but withal eminently warm, lovable, and human.*

LAURA: What's he done now, Hocky?

HUDSON: Hello, honey!

HOCHBERG: Laura!

LAURA, *kissing* HUDSON: How's my dad, today?

HUDSON: I'm fine, dear, just fine.

LAURA, *takes* HOCHBERG'S *hand:* And Hocky, *wie gehts?*

HOCHBERG: Laura, my dear, can't you do anything with him?

LAURA: Why? . . . Smoking again?

HOCHBERG: Yes.

LAURA: Oh, Dad!

HUDSON: Now, don't you start, Laura!

LAURA: But it's so foolish.

HUDSON: I have an important deal on, honey. Besides I'm all right. Whitman's sending me home Tuesday.

LAURA: I know, dear, and that's great! But it isn't going to do any good if you act this way. Can't you forget the office? Close it up! I mean that.

HOCHBERG: She's right, John—absolutely.

LAURA: What good is your money, damn it! if you can't enjoy it?

HUDSON: Well, it can still buy my little girl a honeymoon.

LAURA: I could spend my honeymoon right here! And have a swell time. As long as it's with George. . . . *To* HOCHBERG. Where is that man?

HOCHBERG: Upstairs—busy!

LAURA: Oh! *To her father.* So, are you going to behave yourself, Dad?

HUDSON, *smiles and pinches her cheek:* Don't worry about me! I'm all right. . . . I'll live. *Deliberately changing the subject.* How was Doris's party last night?

LAURA: Noisy.

HUDSON: Not much fun, eh?

LAURA: Not much.

HUDSON: Too bad George couldn't be there.

LAURA: I spent most of the time upstairs with Doris's baby. It woke and wanted some attention. Babies are awfully human that way, aren't they? Do you know that Doris was going to let him cry himself to sleep? Can you imagine?! . . . Believe me, when I have my baby, it's going to get all the care and love and attention it can use.

HOCHBERG, *chuckles:* You have the right instincts, Laura.

LAURA: Have I? *Rises.* I haven't had a real kiss in days. . . . Can I get George on the phone, Hocky?

HOCHBERG: He'll be down soon.

LAURA, *goes to phone:* I want to see that man! *She picks up the phone.*

HOCHBERG, *brusquely:* Better wait! LAURA *looks at him, a bit resentfully.* He's in the operating room.

LAURA: Oh!

HUDSON: Er . . . while you're there, Laura, will you call the office like a good girl, and ask Henderson if . . .

LAURA: No! *She hangs up sharply.*

HUDSON: But this is on my mind.

HOCHBERG: Again? John, you're a madman!

LAURA, *quickly, with a tinge of bitterness:* And he's not the only one, Dr. Hochberg.

HUDSON, *looks up at her quizzically, sees what's eating her, then turns to* HOCHBERG: God, they make a slave of that boy. And he doesn't get a dime! I can't see it.

HOCHBERG, *smiles at that one:* He's not here for the money! He's here to learn. The harder he works, the more he learns. If he wanted to make money he wouldn't have chosen medicine in the first place. You know, when he comes with me, his pay is only going to be $20 a week, but there's a chance to work. The man who's there with me now works from sixteen to eighteen hours a day. He even has a cot rigged up in one of the laboratories, where he sleeps sometimes.

HUDSON: For $20 a week?

HOCHBERG, *nods vigorously:* Yes, yes. . . . *He turns to* LAURA. George is a fine boy with great promise. The next five years are crucial years in that boy's life. They're going to tell whether he becomes an important man or not.

LAURA: George is an important man right now, Hocky, to me.

HOCHBERG: To *you*. . . .

LAURA: Well . . . I don't count?

HOCHBERG: Of course you do, dear!

LAURA, *controls herself, turns to her father, abruptly changing the conversation:* What time shall I call for you Tuesday?

HUDSON, *to* HOCHBERG: When can I get out of here?

HOCHBERG: In the morning. Eight—nine o'clock.

HUDSON: Good! *To* LAURA. Have Martha prepare a big juicy steak—they've been starving me here.

HOCHBERG: No big steaks!

> *Hudson groans.*
> FERGUSON *enters, tired and upset.*

LAURA: George! *She goes to him.*

FERGUSON: Hello, darling! *He kisses her.*

LAURA: Why so glum, dear—toothache?

FERGUSON, *grins—looks at her hat:* Where did you get that hat?

LAURA: Don't you like it?

FERGUSON: Looks like a sailboat! LAURA *wrinkles her face, pretending to be on the verge of tears.* No, it's becoming! You look beautiful . . . doesn't she, Dr. Hochberg?

HOCHBERG, *disparagingly:* Hm—she looks all right.

LAURA, *laughs:* I'll kill that man.

HOCHBERG: You should have seen the brat when I delivered her. *The recollection is too much for him. He looks at* LAURA, *shakes his head, and chuckles.*

FERGUSON, *goes to the bedside:* And Dad—I guess we're going to lose our best patient Tuesday.

LAURA: Isn't it marvelous?

FERGUSON: Did you ever see him look so healthy?

HUDSON: I feel fine, George! Good enough to eat a big steak!

HOCHBERG, *grunts:* Mm!

HUDSON: Oh, by the way, George, my secretary's tending to the wedding invitations. Better get your list in to him. And see him about your visas, too. He'll tend to all that.

FERGUSON, *to* LAURA: You know—I still can't believe it's going to happen! I mean just happen!

LAURA: Neither can I.

FERGUSON: Vienna's going to be lots of fun.

LAURA: Fun? You don't know. Wait till you've seen the Prater. It's Coney

Island with a lift! Lights all over . . . and those lovely people all laughing and happy . . . and the whole place just tinkling with music.

FERGUSON: I've always had a yen to hear Strauss on his home grounds.

HOCHBERG, *softly:* When I visited von Eiselsberg his students spent all their time working—with an occasional glass of beer for relaxation. That's what George's Vienna is going to be, Laura.

GEORGE *and* LAURA *are brought up sharp. Enter a* NURSE *with a wheel-chair.*

NURSE: Time for your sunbath, sir.

HUDSON: Oh—go away!

HOCHBERG: Come on, Mr. Hudson, no nonsense.

HUDSON: Aw, hell, I can walk, I'm no cripple!

LAURA: Sit down, Dad.

HUDSON *sits in the chair. The* NURSE *tucks a blanket around him.*

HUDSON, *grumbles to himself:* Treat me like a goddamned baby! . . . *To* NURSE. Get me that report, will you?

HOCHBERG: John . . .

HUDSON: I can read, can't I? There's nothing the matter with my eyes. . . . For God's sake. . . . *He turns to* GEORGE *and* LAURA. Don't you listen to that old fogey! You kids enjoy yourselves. You're only young once.

*The* NURSE *wheels him out.* HOCHBERG *watches him go and nods.*

HOCHBERG: Yes, that's true enough! *He looks at* FERGUSON *and* LAURA, *a twinkle in his eyes, and sits down as if he were there to stay.*

FERGUSON: You don't need me yet, Dr. Hochberg, do you?

HOCHBERG: Why not?

LAURA, *threateningly:* Hocky!

HOCHBERG, *rises, grinning like a little boy who's had his joke:* All right! *To* FERGUSON. I'll call you when I want you. *He goes.*

LAURA, *softly:* Sweetheart! *She holds out her hands to him.*

FERGUSON, *taking them:* Darling! *He draws her up out of the chair to him.*

LAURA: How's my boy?

FERGUSON, *stares at her in adoration. He almost whispers:* You're lovely. . . . Lovely, Laura.

*Big hug.*

LAURA: If you knew how I've been aching for this. *Silence for a moment, as she clings to him.* Three months! *She sighs deeply.* I don't know how I can live till then.

FERGUSON, *tenderly:* Sweet! They're going to be long—those three months—terribly.

LAURA: Yes, I know—I hate to think of them! *She takes his hand, leads him to a huge easy-chair.* Come here and—

FERGUSON: Ah!

LAURA: Sit down! *She pushes him down into the chair and curls up on his lap. Then she takes his head in her hands and scrutinizes his face.* Let me look at you. *She shakes her head.* You're getting thin, young man! And your eyes are tired.

FERGUSON: I didn't have much sleep last night. It was a pretty sick house.

LAURA: You're overworked. . . . *Pulls his head over on her shoulder.* And I don't like it one bit. *Pause.* You know, you've spoiled everything for me. *FERGUSON raises his head, LAURA pushes his head back.* I was thinking last night, all the music and noise and fun . . . didn't mean a thing without you. I don't seem to get a kick out of life any more, unless you're around. *She pauses.* And that's not very often, is it?

FERGUSON: Darling, we'll make up for it all . . . later on. Honestly.

LAURA: I don't know if we can, George. Last night, for instance. If you had been there—perfect! Now's it's—gone. You see, dearest, the way I feel, if I had you every minute from now on, it wouldn't be enough. *FERGUSON starts to speak, she puts her hands over his lips.* I wish I'd lived all my life with you. I wish I'd been born in the same room with you, and played in the same streets.

FERGUSON, *smiles:* I'm glad you missed them. They were ordinary and gloomy. They might have touched you . . . changed you. . . . *He cups her face in his hands and looks at her.* About seven months ago there was a boy here who'd been blind from birth. We operated on him—successfully. One night I showed him the stars—for the first time. He looked at them a moment and began to cry like a baby, because, he said, they were so lovely, and—he might never have seen them. When I look at you, Laura, I get something of that feeling. I . . . I can't tell you how large a part of me you've become, Laura! You're . . . *The loudspeaker is heard calling,* "Dr. Ferguson! Dr. Ferguson. . . ." Oh, damn it! . . .

LAURA: Don't move! *She clutches him tightly.*

FERGUSON: It's no use, Laura! That's my call! Let me up!

LAURA: No!

FERGUSON: Come on! *He rises, lifting her in his arms, kisses her, sets her on her feet.*

LAURA: Oh! You spoiled it.

> *He goes to the phone, picks up the receiver.* LAURA *finds her vanity case . . . powder and lipstick.*

FERGUSON: Dr. Ferguson! . . . Yes! . . . Oh! Yes, sir! . . . Yes, Doctor! I'll be ready. . . . I'll tend to all that. Right! *He hangs up—turns to* LAURA.

LAURA: All right, go on—go to work!

FERGUSON: I won't be needed for half an hour yet.

LAURA: Well, I have to go to my hairdresser's and make myself beautiful for tonight.

FERGUSON: Laura, dear, I . . .

LAURA: And what a night we're to going to have! Doris asked us over there, but I want you to myself. I want to go to that cute little roadhouse where the food and the music were so good—then a long drive up the Hudson—and, darling, there's a full moon tonight!

FERGUSON: Laura, I've some bad news. You won't be upset, will you?

LAURA: Why?

FERGUSON: I can't make it tonight. I have to stay in. . . .

LAURA, *almost in tears:* Again?

FERGUSON: I'm so sorry, dear. I tried to duck out of it, but I couldn't. There's a transfusion I have to do.

LAURA: What time? I'll wait.

FERGUSON: Better not! It depends on the patient. I've just got to be around and ready!

LAURA:  Are you the only one here who can do that transfusion?

FERGUSON: Dr. Gordon seems to think so!

LAURA: George! They're overworking you. It's not fair. . . .

FERGUSON: I don't mind it so much for myself . . . only. . . .

LAURA, *dully:* No? Well, I do. *Pause. Then* LAURA *continues in a low voice, suddenly hoarse.* I was planning so much on tonight.

FERGUSON: Don't you think I was, Laura? All week I've been looking forward to it.

LAURA: Sure. I know.

FERGUSON: You're not sore?

LAURA: It's not your fault. I don't imagine it's much fun for you, either—

FERGUSON: Fun! If you knew how fed up I can be with this place sometimes . . .

LAURA: George, I'm so low—I've been this way for weeks.

FERGUSON: Damn Gordon! Laidlaw could have done that transfusion.

LAURA: Oh, George, what's our life going to be like?

FERGUSON, *gently:* Pretty grand, I should say.

LAURA: How can it be? How can it?

FERGUSON: Dear . . . we'll go out tomorrow instead. Mac promised to take my floor. And we'll have a swell time. Saturday's more fun anyway.

LAURA: It's not just tonight! It's all the nights.

FERGUSON: Darling! You're exaggerating! You're . . .

LAURA: No, I'm not.

FERGUSON: What do you expect me to do? I want to get out . . . I want to enjoy myself . . . but I can't, that's all. I can't.

LAURA: George, I know this is important to you . . . and if it's going to help you . . . I can go on like this for another three months . . . for another year and three months; but when we come back to New York, let's arrange our

lives like human beings. You can open up an office and have regular hours
. . . specialize!

FERGUSON: If I work with Hochberg, darling, I won't have the time to go
into practice.

LAURA: That's just it. I know Hocky. I'll never see you then, George.

FERGUSON: But, Laura . . . *He laughs nervously.* I've plugged all my life just
in the hope that some day I'd have a chance to work with a man like
Hochberg. . . . Why . . .

LAURA: I couldn't go on this way. I just couldn't. . . . I'd rather break off now,
and try to forget you. . . .

FERGUSON: Laura! Don't ever say a thing like that!

LAURA: I mean it—it would kill me. But I'd rather die quickly than by slow
torture. I can't . . . *The loudspeaker is calling him.* FERGUSON *and* LAURA
*stand there, both in anguish.* They're calling you.

FERGUSON: I know. *He hesitates a moment . . . goes to the phone.* Dr. Ferguson! Yes . . . who? South 218 . . . yes? . . . well, call Dr. Cunningham. It's
his case . . . let him. *Suddenly his voice becomes brittle.* When? What's
her temperature? . . . Pulse? . . . Is she pale? . . . Perspiring? . . . Did she
ask for food before she became unconscious? . . . No! No more insulin!
Absolutely. I'll be right down. *He hangs up.* I have to go now, Laura. And
please—please don't worry. *He bends down to kiss her. She turns her face
away. He straightens up and regards her with a worried expression.*

FERGUSON: As bad as that?

LAURA, *in a low voice—a bit husky with emotion:* Yes.

FERGUSON, *forcing a smile:* Things will straighten themselves out.

LAURA: No, they won't.

*Pause.* FERGUSON *pulls himself together, looks towards the door.*

FERGUSON: I'll see you tomorrow night, dear? Right?

LAURA: Yes. *She puts on her hat.* Think it over, George! We'll have to come
to some decision!

FERGUSON: Oh Laura, will you please . . .

LAURA: I mean it! Absolutely!

FERGUSON, *pauses for a moment in the doorway:* All right . . . all right!

FERGUSON *goes.* LAURA *stands there a moment, the picture of frustration
and woe, then she walks in a little circle, crying quietly.*

*BLACK OUT*

**ACT ONE**
*Scene 3*

*A bed, screened off from the others, in a corner of the children's ward. The entire wall, separating ward from corridor, is framed in glass panels, so that the nurse on duty out there can always keep a watchful eye over the youngsters.*

*A little girl of ten is lying back, eyes closed, skin pale and clammy. Her father stands at the foot of the bed, gazing fearfully at his little daughter. He is wan and unkempt, his hair disheveled, his eyes sunken, his collar open, tie awry—the picture of despair. His wife is standing beside the child, weeping.*

*At the phone is a young student nurse,* BARBARA DENNIN. *She is speaking rapidly into the phone.*

BARBARA: South 218! . . . Calling Dr. Ferguson! At once!

MRS. SMITH: She's so pale, Barney. . . . She's so pale!

MR. SMITH: Where's Cunningham? . . . Why isn't he here? *To* BARBARA. Miss Dennin! Can't you do something?

BARBARA: Dr. Ferguson will be right here, sir!

*Enter* DR. CUNNINGHAM, *a dignified, impressive-looking gentleman, immaculately attired, goatee, pince-nez, throaty voice—just a bit too much of the "professional manner," arrived at in this instance by a certain false philosophy which one occasionally finds in the profession.* CUNNINGHAM *believes that nine patients out of ten will be cured by nature anyway, and the tenth will die no matter what the physician does for him. This system of logic concludes that impressing the patient and assuaging his fears are more important than keeping up with medical journals and the march of treatment. The sad part of it is that* CUNNINGHAM *is a successful practitioner— successful, that is, in terms of bank account. True, most of his colleagues look down on him with scorn, but he has a magnificent Park Avenue office, with all the impressive equipment, wealthy patients, and political influence—which, although he is not a member of the staff, has gained him the "courtesy" of the hospital—meaning that he may bring his patients here for hospitalization.*

BARBARA: Dr. Cunningham! Thank God you're here!

MRS. SMITH: Dr. Cunningham! My baby! She's fainted! She's . . .

CUNNINGHAM: Now please . . . please, Mrs. Smith! *He takes off his coat, turns to* BARBARA. What's happened here?

BARBARA: Complete collapse . . . about two minutes ago. . . .

CUNNINGHAM: Let's see the chart! *She hands him the chart. He looks at it, frowns, shakes his head.* Hm! This is bad! *He takes* DOROTHY'S *wrist and feels the pulse, closing his eyes.*

NURSE: Pulse is barely . . .

CUNNINGHAM: Sh! Quiet, please! . . . *Silence*. Hm! . . . Let me have my stethoscope! *She takes his stethoscope out of his bag and hands it to him. He listens to* DOROTHY's *heart. His frown deepens*. Diabetic coma!

MRS. SMITH: Doctor! . . . you've got to save her!

MR. SMITH: Rose . . . come here!

CUNNINGHAM: Miss Dennin— *He indicates* MRS. SMITH *with a gesture of the head.*

BARBARA, *takes* MRS. SMITH's *arm:* You'll have to wait outside. . . . Just a moment. . . .

MRS. SMITH: Oh, my God!

   BARBARA *leads them out, then returns.*

CUNNINGHAM: Prepare some insulin! At once . . . forty units . . . with fifty grams of glucose.

BARBARA: But, sir, Dr. Ferguson advised against insulin. . . .

CUNNINGHAM: Ferguson? You please take your orders from me . . . forty units! Quick!

BARBARA: Yes, sir.

   FERGUSON *enters the room*. DR. CUNNINGHAM *glances at him, nods curtly, and turns to* BARBARA.

CUNNINGHAM: Please, hurry that!

FERGUSON, *looks at the patient, shakes his head:* I was afraid of shock!

CUNNINGHAM: This isn't shock! It's diabetic coma!

FERGUSON, *his brow wrinkled, looks at the patient again:* Her temperature's subnormal?

CUNNINGHAM, *impatiently:* Yes! *To* BARBARA. Is that insulin ready yet?

FERGUSON: I beg your pardon, Doctor, but isn't insulin contraindicated here?

CUNNINGHAM: No. It's our last chance.

   FERGUSON *bites his lips to restrain himself*. CUNNINGHAM *takes the hypo from* BARBARA *and presses out the air bubbles.*

FERGUSON: Doctor, I mean no offense, but I've studied this case history, and it looks like shock . . . not coma!

CUNNINGHAM, *pauses—looks at the patient, shakes his head:* No . . . no. . . .

FERGUSON: But, the clinical picture is so clear-cut. . . . Look at the patient! She's pale, cold, clammy, temperature subnormal. She's complained of hunger! Sudden onset!

CUNNINGHAM, *angrily:* Suppose you let me handle this case, young man. *To* BARBARA. Prepare that arm!

   BARBARA *swabs the arm*. CUNNINGHAM *leans over the patient*. FERGUSON *hesitates a moment, then goes to* CUNNINGHAM, *puts his hand on* CUNNINGHAM's *arm.*

FERGUSON: Please, Doctor! Call in one of the other men! . . . Ask them! Anybody!

CUNNINGHAM: There's no time! Take your hand off!

FERGUSON: That insulin's going to prove fatal.

CUNNINGHAM, *wavers a moment, uncertain, hesitant, then he turns on FER-GUSON:* Get out of here, will you? I don't want any interruption while I'm treating my patient! *He shakes FERGUSON's arm off. . . . Bends to administer the hypo, hesitates a moment, then straightens up . . . confused and worried. FERGUSON, with sudden resolve, takes the hypo from CUNNING-HAM's fingers and squirts out the insulin.* Here! What are you. . . Why did you do that, you fool?

FERGUSON, *ignores him, turns to BARBARA, his voice crisp and cool:* Shock position! *BARBARA goes to the foot of the bed, turns the ratchet that elevates the foot of the bed. FERGUSON dashes to the door, looks out, calls down the corridor.* Nurse! Nurse!

A NURSE, *answers from down the corridor:* Yes, sir?

FERGUSON: Sterile glucose! Quick! And a thirty-cc syringe.

BARBARA: Some glucose here, sir, all ready!

FERGUSON: How much?

BARBARA: Fifty grams!

FERGUSON: Good! Half of that will do! Apply a tourniquet . . . right arm!

BARBARA: Yes, sir!

FERGUSON, *calls down the corridor:* Never mind the glucose—a hypo of adrenalin!

   THE NURSE's *voice answers:* Yes, sir.

FERGUSON, *turns up the corridor:* Nurse, Nurse! Some hot packs . . . and blankets! Quick . . . come on . . . hurry! *He starts to return to the patient, but DR. CUNNINGHAM, who has sufficiently recovered from his shock, blocks FERGUSON's path.*

CUNNINGHAM: What do you think you're doing? I'll have you brought up before the medical board. . . . I'll have you thrown out of this hospital . . . you can't . . .

FERGUSON: All right! Have me thrown out! I don't give a damn! I don't care! I really don't . . . pardon me! *He brushes CUNNINGHAM aside and hurries to patient.*

CUNNINGHAM, *flustered and impotent:* I never heard of such a thing . . . why . . .

FERGUSON: Ready?

BARBARA: Yes, sir!

FERGUSON, *quickly:* Let's have that glucose. *BARBARA gives it to him.* Swab that arm! Never mind the iodine! Just the alcohol! *BARBARA swabs the arm.* Thank God! A good vein! *He administers the hypo.*

CUNNINGHAM: You'll pay for this, young man! . . . That patient's life is on
   your hands. . . .
   *NURSE enters with blankets and hot packs.*
NURSE: Blankets and hot packs, Doctor!
FERGUSON: Yes. . . . *He and* BARBARA *place the hot packs on* DOROTHY,
   *then* BARBARA *covers her with the blankets.*
   *Enter another* NURSE.
SECOND NURSE: A hypo of adrenalin!
FERGUSON: Here! *He takes it from her, administers it. Then straightens up,
   sighs, turns to two nurses.* That's all. Thank you! *They go.* FERGUSON,
   BARBARA, *and* CUNNINGHAM *watch the patient intently. There is no
   change in her condition.*
FERGUSON: That's about all we can do!
CUNNINGHAM: You report downstairs . . . at once!
   *They watch the patient, strained, tense. After a long moment* DOROTHY'S
   *arm, which has been hanging limp over the bedside, moves. She raises her
   hand to her forehead, opens her eyes. She looks at* FERGUSON.
DOROTHY, *faintly:* Dr. George . . .
FERGUSON: Yes, baby?
DOROTHY: I'm thirsty. . . . I want a drink. . . .
FERGUSON: You bet, sweetheart. *To* BARBARA. Water!
   BARBARA *gives the child a glass of water;* DOROTHY *sits up and sips it,
   still rubbing her eyes sleepily.*
DOROTHY: I feel so funny . . . Dr. George! Dizzy-like. . . .
FERGUSON: Drink that!
DOROTHY: What happened?
FERGUSON: Nothing! You just fell asleep, that's all. DOROTHY *has stopped
   sipping her water to stare at* FERGUSON *with huge blue eyes, wide open
   now. He grins at her and points to the glass.* Come on! Bottoms up! *She
   smiles back at him, and drains the glass.* Atta girl!
   BARBARA *lowers foot and raises head of bed.*
DOROTHY: Barbara!
BARBARA: Yes, dear?
DOROTHY: I want Mother. Where's Mother?
BARBARA: She's just outside, dear.
DOROTHY: I want Mother. . . .
BARBARA: I'm bringing her right in.
   FERGUSON *meanwhile has turned to face* CUNNINGHAM, *who is ner-
   vously fidgeting with his pince-nez.*
DOROTHY: Dr. George . . . my operation hurts me here. . . .
FERGUSON, *sympathetically:* Oh! We'll fix that up in a minute! *To* CUN-
   NINGHAM. An opium suppository, doctor?

CUNNINGHAM: No! *To* BARBARA. Morphine! A twelfth!

BARBARA: Yes, sir. *She goes.*

CUNNINGHAM, *turns his glance on* FERGUSON: I ought to report you, of course! You're a damned, meddling young puppy. . . . *He hesitates a moment.* However . . . under the circumstances, I guess I can afford to be lenient . . . this time. But if you ever dare interfere again in any of my cases . . . !

> MR. AND MRS. SMITH *enter. They rush to the bedside.*

MRS. SMITH, *crying and laughing:* Dorothy, my darling.

MR. SMITH: Dots! Dots!

MRS. SMITH: Are you all right, my baby? *She kisses* DOROTHY. My baby!

DOROTHY: Oh! . . . my operation, Mother. . . .

CUNNINGHAM: Careful, Mrs. Smith. . . .

MR. SMITH: Careful, Rose!

MRS. SMITH: Yes . . . yes . . . of course. Did I hurt my darling?

CUNNINGHAM: Now, the child's been through quite an ordeal. You mustn't excite her. I want her to have some rest . . . you'd better . . . *Indicating the door with his hand.*

MR. SMITH: Yes, come, Rose. . . . She's weak. . . . *To* DOROTHY. Go to sleep, darling.

MRS. SMITH: Goodbye, dear! *She kisses her.* Is there anything Mother can bring you, darling?

DOROTHY, *sleepily:* No, Mama. . . .

> MR. SMITH *kisses the child, takes his wife's arm and leads her away.*

CUNNINGHAM, *turns to* FERGUSON: Order a blood sugar! If there are any new developments, phone my secretary at once!

MRS. SMITH, *to* CUNNINGHAM: She'll be all right, Doctor?

CUNNINGHAM: Yes . . . yes. . . . You call me tonight!

> DR. CUNNINGHAM, MR. AND MRS. SMITH *start to go.*

MRS. SMITH, *as they exit, to* CUNNINGHAM: Doctor, how can I ever thank you enough for this?

FERGUSON, *goes to* DOROTHY: Well, young lady, how about getting some sleep?

DOROTHY: O.K., Dr. George!

FERGUSON: Close your eyes!

DOROTHY: But don't go away!

FERGUSON, *sits on bedside:* No. . . . I'll sit right here! Come on! DOROTHY *takes his hand, shuts her eyes, and dozes off. Enter* BARBARA *with hypo.* FERGUSON *whispers.* She won't need that!

BARBARA: Did Dr. Cunningham say anything to you?

FERGUSON: No. *He stares down at* DOROTHY. Pretty kid, isn't she?

BARBARA: I was scared we were going to lose her.

FERGUSON, *touches the sleeping child's hair, and murmurs:* She has hair like Laura's.

BARBARA: What, Doctor?

FERGUSON: Nothing. . . . Nothing. . . .

BARBARA: I think it was wonderful of you to stand up against Dr. Cunningham that way! I . . .

FERGUSON, *annoyed, turns to hypo, etc., and says a bit curtly:* Better clean up that mess.

BARBARA: Yes, sir. *She puts hypos, etc., on trays. Suddenly her trembling fingers drop the hypo. It splinters with a crash.*

FERGUSON, *angrily:* Here! *Glances over at the sleeping child.* What's the matter with you?

BARBARA: I'm sorry. I was just . . . nervous, I guess. . . .

FERGUSON, *looks at her a moment. She is a soft, feminine girl. . . . Her jet black hair and serious, large brown eyes are set off to pretty advantage by the blue and white student-nurse uniform. She has a simple, naive quality that lends her an air of appealing wistfulness. He sees how genuinely nervous she is . . . and smiles to reassure her:* Has Cunningham been treating you too?

BARBARA, *smiles:* No, sir. This is my first case with a sick child and I got to like her an awful lot. I guess that was. . .

FERGUSON: I see. What's your name?

BARBARA: Barbara Dennin.

FERGUSON: You're going to be a swell nurse, Barbara!

BARBARA: Thanks!

FERGUSON: Now, take my advice! I know just how you feel—nerves all tied up in a knot . . . want to yell! Feel the same way myself. . . . You get as far away from here as you can, tonight. Have a good time! Relax! Forget hospital! Tomorrow you'll be all right.

BARBARA: I . . . I can't. I have an exam in Materia Medica tomorrow.

FERGUSON: Materia Medica? . . . Hm! . . . I think I have some notes that may help you. . . . I'll leave them with the orderly on the first floor, and you can get them on your way down.

BARBARA: Thanks.

FERGUSON: May help you a bit. You won't have to cram all night, anyway.

    *The loudspeaker is calling* "Dr. Ferguson." MARY, *another and much older nurse, enters with a basin, etc.*

MARY: Your call, Dr. Ferguson?

FERGUSON, *listening:* Yes. Are you on duty here now?

MARY: Yes, sir.

FERGUSON: If she wakes with any pain, give her an opium suppository! If her temperature goes below normal, call me! I'll be in.

MARY: Tonight, too?

FERGUSON, *almost savagely:* Yes, tonight, too! *His name is called louder, more insistently. He turns to the door, mutters to the loudspeaker:* All right! All right! I'm coming! *He goes.* MARY *turns to stare after him, her eyebrows raised in surprise.*

MARY: Gee! Ain't he snappy today?

*BARBARA simply stares after him.*


*BLACK OUT*


**ACT ONE**
*Scene 4*

*A tiny, sombre, austere, cell-like room, with hardly enough space for its simple furnishings—a cot-bed, a bureau, a desk, a chair, a small bookcase, and a washbasin. On the bureau is a small radio—the one luxury in the room. On the walls are two framed diplomas—the sole decorations. The room is untidy—as all interns' rooms are; the bed is messed, it being customary for interns to use it as a lounge; the books are piled irregularly on the bookshelves, on the desk, on the bureau, and on the floor.*

*A moonlit night filters in through a single square window.* FERGUSON, *wearing spectacles, is at his desk, reading, by the light of a desk lamp, a ponderous medical tome. Occasionally he jots down a note.*

*A knock at the door.*


FERGUSON, *without looking up, in a tired voice:* Come in!

*Enter SHORTY in a stiff-bosom shirt, collar, white vest.*

SHORTY, *triumphantly:* Well, I got the vest. . . .

FERGUSON: That's good.

SHORTY: Can you lend me a tie, George? Mine is—er—

FERGUSON *rises and wearily goes to his dresser, finds a tux bow tie, hands it to SHORTY.*

FERGUSON: Here you are, Shorty. *He sits down again to his book.*

SHORTY: Thanks! Say, do you mind making a bow for me? I can never get these things straight.

FERGUSON: Come here! I'll try. *He starts to tie SHORTY's bow.*

SHORTY: Drink in my room . . . if you want one.

FERGUSON: I don't think so, Shorty!

SHORTY: Good drink! . . . Ginger ale, sugar and alcohol . . . out of the large jar in the path lab. . . .

FERGUSON: Stand still, will you? *After fumbling nervously with the tie, he makes a bad job of it.* Oh, hell! I can't do it! Sorry! *He undoes the tie.* Ask Laidlaw!

SHORTY, *looks askance at* FERGUSON: Nerves, young fellow! . . . Better see a doctor about that!

PETE, *pokes in his head:* Anything to eat in here?

FERGUSON: Some chocolate!

PETE: Good! *Enters—comes up to desk.*

FERGUSON: Here! *Gives him a chunk.* SHORTY *starts to go.* Have a good time, Shorty!

SHORTY, *confidently:* I will.

PETE, *stands there, eating chocolate:* Hope she gives in without a struggle.

SHORTY: No fun, you dope—without a struggle. *Exits.*

PETE: Oh yeah? *Calls after him.* Well, take off my vest before you start. I don't want any stains on it. *He returns to the desk and points to the chocolate.* Now can I have some of that myself! *He reaches over and breaks off a piece of chocolate.*

FERGUSON, *smiles:* Who was the first piece for?

PETE: Oh that? That was for my tapeworm. *He holds up the chocolate.* This is for me. *Pops it into his mouth.* FERGUSON *laughs a tired laugh, and hands him the rest of the large bar, anxious to get rid of him.*

FERGUSON: Here, take it all, Pete!

PETE: Thanks! What a lousy dinner we had tonight! Fish! . . . Oh, how I hate fish!

FERGUSON: Friday night.

PETE: Yeah! Say! What are you doing in?

FERGUSON: 401 may need a transfusion. . . .

PETE: A lot of good that'll do him! *Stuffs his mouth with chocolate.* For Christ's sake . . . he passed out. . . .

FERGUSON: No?

PETE: About ten minutes ago.

FERGUSON, *slowly:* Gee, that's too bad!

PETE, *jamming in a huge chunk of chocolate:* Yeah! Say, I'm hungry. . . . I'm going to run out to Fleischer's and grab a sandwich. Will you keep an eye on my floor till I get back?

FERGUSON: All right! Hurry it, will you? . . . I may be going out myself.

PETE: Be right back! *Exits.*

FERGUSON *sits there a moment, staring blankly at the wall. Finally he sighs, wearily closes the book, pushes it away, takes off his spectacles, puts them in a case, and reaches for the phone.*

FERGUSON: Outside wire, please! . . . Atwater 9-0032. . . . Yes. . . . Hello! Hello! Is Miss Hudson there? Dr. Ferguson calling. . . . Yes. . . . Hello,

Laura! . . . How are you dear? . . . Feeling better? . . . Oh! . . . Well, look
dear, I can make it tonight, after all. What? . . . Oh, don't be silly! . . . But
darling . . . we'll work that out! We'll find some . . . It's so far away,
yet. . . . Why talk about . . . ? Listen, Laura! That chance to work with
Hochberg is one of the best breaks I've ever had! You don't expect me to
throw it over, like that, at a moment's notice, simply because you have
some crazy idea that . . . No, no! I don't want to even talk about it, tonight. I'm tired, Laura. It's been a hell of a day! Three operations and . . .
I can't think! I can't make an important decision tonight . . . in a minute!
Oh, Laura! What the hell are you doing? Punishing me? . . . All right,
Laura. *A knock at the door.* All right. . . . I'll see you tomorrow night! . . .
Yes . . . yes . . . goodbye! *He hangs up, somewhat sharply, then wearily
goes to the door, opens it.* DR. LEVINE *is standing there.*

LEVINE: I'm sorry if I . . .

FERGUSON: Oh, no! Come on in, Dr. Levine!

   DR. LEVINE, *murmurs a hardly audible thanks and enters. He looks
about, touches the desk, smiles, nods, and murmurs almost to himself:*
Yes. . . . Yes . . . it certainly is nice! Six years . . . like yesterday. *Looks at his
watch.* Think that report is ready?

FERGUSON: I'll see. *Takes phone.*

LEVINE: Oh, don't trouble!

FERGUSON: That's . . . *Into phone.* Hello! Path lab, please! *To* DR. LEVINE.
   What did Dr. Hochberg find?

LEVINE: He left it for the X-ray man to read.

FERGUSON, *into phone:* Hello! . . . Dr. Finn? . . . Ferguson! What about that
   sputum? . . . Oh! *To* DR. LEVINE. Under the microscope, now. *Into phone.*
   Fine! Hurry that through, will you? . . . And send it down to my room!
   . . . Yes. Thanks! *He hangs up.* A few minutes . . . I hope it's nothing. . . .

LEVINE, *nods:* Poor Katherine! She's had so much. Things were so different
   when I was here . . . before I married.

FERGUSON: Yes . . . Professor Dury told me.

LEVINE: Dury? I know just what he says: Levine—the fool!—wealthy
   mother—chance to work with Hochberg—to be somebody. Threw it all
   away . . . for a pretty face. *He laughs to himself, sadly.* —Hm . . . Dury!

FERGUSON: Your mother? Hasn't she . . . ? DR. LEVINE *shakes his head.* Not
   yet? . . . Well, she'll come around to your way.

LEVINE, *shakes his head again:* No. When I married Katherine, a gentile,
   and my mother disowned me . . . it must have broken her heart. But still,
   she was doing the right thing from her point of view. . . . *He sighs.* Poor
   Katherine! I didn't count on that! East side! Tenements! Fifty-cent patients! Poverty! Dirt! Struggle! *He shakes his head.* I don't know. Maybe

it would have been better for her the other way . . . maybe. *He smiles sadly at* FERGUSON. Burnt offerings! Jehovah and Aesculapius! They both demand their human sacrifice. . . . *Pauses.* Medicine! Why do we kill ourselves for it?

FERGUSON: I don't know. I often wonder, myself, whether it was worth the grind of working my way through college and med school. . . .

LEVINE: Med school, too?

FERGUSON: Yes.

LEVINE: I don't see how you kept up with classes.

FERGUSON: I managed.

LEVINE: Terrific grind!

FERGUSON: It wasn't much fun . . . but, still . . . I guess it's the only thing I really want to do. . . . *Pause.* My dad used to say, "Above all is humanity!" He was a fine man—my dad. A small-town physician—upstate. When I was about thirteen, he came to my room one night and apologized because he was going to die. His heart had gone bad on him. He knew if he gave up medicine and took it easy he could live for twenty years. But he wanted to go right on, wanted to die in harness. . . . And he did. *Pause.* Above all else is humanity—that's a big thought. So big that alongside of it you and I don't really matter very much. That's why we do it, I guess.

LEVINE: You're right, of course! Ah . . . it's not good—too much suffering! Kills things in you. . . . A doctor shouldn't have to worry about money! That's one disease he's not trained to fight. It either corrupts him . . . or it destroys him. *He sighs.* Well . . . maybe someday the State will take over Medicine. . . .

FERGUSON: Before we let the State control medicine, we'd have to put every politician on the operating table, and cut out his acquisitive instincts.

LEVINE, *laughs:* That, I'm afraid, would be a major operation!

FERGUSON, *smiles:* Yes. . . . *Then he becomes serious again, working himself up, thinking of* LAURA. But, it *is* a danger! We can't allow outside forces, or things . . . or people to interfere with us. . . . We can't! And, if they do, we've got to bar them out . . . even if we have to tear out our hearts to do it. . . . LEVINE *looks puzzled. He can't quite follow this.* FERGUSON *suddenly realizes the personal turn his thoughts have taken, sees* LEVINE's *bewilderment, and stops short. He laughs, a bit self-conscious.* I'm sorry. I guess that's a bit off the track . . . just something personal.

LEVINE, *smiles:* Oh! Yes. . . .

*A knock at the door.* FERGUSON *goes to the door. An orderly is there.*

ORDERLY: Dr. Ferguson?

FERGUSON: Yes?

ORDERLY: Dr. Finn sent this down! *He hands* FERGUSON *a printed report.*

FERGUSON: Oh, yes, thanks! *Orderly goes.* FERGUSON *is about to hand it to* LEVINE. Doctor . . . FERGUSON *glances at it and suddenly stiffens.* One second!

LEVINE, *suddenly becomes tense, too:* Dr. Ferguson! Is that . . . ?

FERGUSON, *in a strained, brittle voice:* Wait! *He goes to the phone.* Path lab!

LEVINE: Is that for me?

  FERGUSON *doesn't answer him.*

FERGUSON: Path lab? . . . Dr. Finn . . . Ferguson! That report you just sent me . . . are you positive? . . . Make sure! Look again. . . .

LEVINE: Is that the finding on my . . . ?

FERGUSON, *over the phone:* Yes. . . . Yes. . . . Clear as that? *Slowly.* I'm afraid you're right. *He hangs up slowly, turns to* LEVINE, *hands him the card in silence.*

LEVINE, *takes it, reads it. He droops. His fingers tremble, the card falls to the ground. After a moment's silence he wets his lips and murmurs, almost inaudibly:* I knew it. . . . I knew it. . . .

FERGUSON: Gee, I wish I could tell you how sorry I . . .

LEVINE: Tuberculosis! Oh, my poor Katherine! *He sits down on the bed and stares vacantly ahead.* What are we going to do, now?

FERGUSON, *goes to the bed, sits down next to him, tenderly puts a hand on his shoulder:* She'll come through all right! You'll see. *A silence.* DR. LEVINE *pulls himself together.* Perhaps if you took her to a drier climate . . .

LEVINE: Maybe . . . maybe! *He rises.* That means . . . giving up the little practice I have . . . means starting all over again. I don't know if we can do it. We're not young, any longer. I don't know. . . .

  DR. LEVINE *turns toward the door.*

FERGUSON: Is there anything I can do?

LEVINE: No, thanks! Thanks! *Exit* DR. LEVINE.

  FERGUSON *stands there a moment, staring after him. Enter* PETE.

PETE, *sucking his teeth with great gusto:* Boy, what a roast-beef sandwich I had! Mm! *He sucks his teeth louder.* Have you got a . . . oh, yeah! *He reaches over and takes a tongue-depressor out of* FERGUSON'S *breast pocket.* PETE *splits the depressor and, using one of the splinters as a toothpick, continues to make an even greater noise with his lips.* FERGUSON, *pretty near the cracking point, turns his back on* PETE. PETE *goes to the radio, and tunes in on a loud jazz number. He flops down onto the bed— sucks his teeth.* Going out?

FERGUSON: No!

PETE: Change your mind?

FERGUSON: Yes.

PETE: Boy, you know that Miss Simpson down in the X-ray lab—She was over at Fleischer's. Next table to mine. Say—she's swell all dressed up in street clothes. I looked at her for ten minutes without recognizing her. I guess maybe it was because I wasn't looking at her face. *Sucks his teeth.* Luscious! She had one of those tight black silk dresses . . . absolutely nothing else on underneath—you could see that. And a pair of mammaries! Mm!

FERGUSON, *tensely:* Pete! I want to do some reading. Will you get the hell out?

PETE, *sits up, looks at* FERGUSON, *rises quickly:* Sure! *With a puzzled, backward glance at* FERGUSON, *he goes.* FERGUSON *switches off the radio, walks up and down the room, almost frantic, then throws himself face down on the bed. There is a timid little knock at the door.*

FERGUSON: Come in! *The knock is repeated.* FERGUSON *rises, calling impatiently.* Come in. Come in! BARBARA *opens the door and slips in, breathless with the adventure.* What . . . er?

BARBARA: I came down for those notes. . . .

FERGUSON: Oh! Of course. I forgot . . . stupid of me. Let's see—what was it? Materia Medica?

BARBARA: Yes.

FERGUSON, *looks through drawer in his desk:* I had them here someplace.

BARBARA: I suppose I oughtn't to have come in.

FERGUSON, *sorting notes:* Pathology, Histology—no—no.

BARBARA: I hope nobody saw me.

FERGUSON: Materia Medica. Here! *He takes a notebook out of the drawer, glances through it, hands it to her.* There you are!

BARBARA: Thanks!

FERGUSON: Not at all! . . . Hope they're some help. *He goes to the window, looks out—dismissing her. Still in his old mood.*

BARBARA, *stands there a moment, waiting. Finally, she asks timidly:* Is there . . . anything wrong?

FERGUSON: What?

BARBARA: Anything wrong?

FERGUSON: Oh! No! No! *He turns to the window again.* BARBARA *hesitates a moment—sees that he has already forgotten her in the intensity of his mood. She slowly turns, opens the door, looks out, and suddenly shuts it with an exclamation of fright.* What—

BARBARA, *breathless . . . frightened:* Head nurse! Outside!

FERGUSON: See you? Wait a minute! She'll be gone! Better sit down!

BARBARA: Thanks! *She watches him a moment.* Are you sure Dr. Cunningham didn't— FERGUSON *shakes his head.* Because . . . if it would mean anything . . . I'd go right down and tell them all—everybody—just what happened. . . .

FERGUSON: No, it's not Cunningham—

BARBARA: What is it, then?

FERGUSON: It's just— *With an effort he shakes off his mood.* Don't mind me tonight.

BARBARA: You work very hard, don't you?

FERGUSON, *almost savagely:* Work? Sure! What else is there *but* work— and work! *He suddenly realizes* BARBARA *is staring at him. He pulls himself together.* Let's see those notes! *She brings them to him. He places the book on the desk, leans over it, and turns the pages.* There! BARBARA *is next to him, leaning over the notes, her head near his.* These pages synopsize the whole business. Read through the notes carefully; memorize these pages—and you've got it! I think you'll find it lots easier that way.

BARBARA, *pointing to a word:* What's this?

FERGUSON: Calomel!

BARBARA, *her head almost touching his:* Oh, of course! It's a C.

FERGUSON, *hands her the book:* Clear?

BARBARA: Yes. *As she reaches for the book, her hand meets his, and she clings to it.* You know, when I thought Dots was going to die . . . I got the feeling like I . . . I . . . God! . . . I can't put it into words!

FERGUSON: I know. I know that feeling. . . .

BARBARA: You, too?

FERGUSON: Me, too? *Clutching his throat.* Up to here, Barbara! Right now! Christ! I'm tired of work, and blood and sweat and pain! And the chap in 401 is dead! And Levine's wife is going to die . . . and one begins to wonder where in Heaven's God, and what in Hell's it all about, and why on earth does anything make any difference.

BARBARA, *clutches his arm with her hand:* Yes, that's the feeling . . . and you get so lonely . . . and you feel . . . tomorrow it's me . . . and the only thing that matters is just being alive . . . just being alive. Now! . . . Isn't it? *She is very close to* GEORGE *now, clutching his arm with her hand.*

FERGUSON, *looks at her sympathetically:* You kids have a pretty tough time of it, don't you? Grind all day and lights out at ten o'clock.

BARBARA: And only one night out till twelve-thirty . . . and I haven't taken mine in two months. There's just nobody . . . *They are very close, now. She almost whispers the last words to him.*

FERGUSON: You're a sweet girl, Barbara. *Suddenly he takes her in his arms and kisses her. She clings to him for a moment. Then they separate. He is confused and upset.* I'm sorry, Barbara . . . I . . . *He goes to the notes, opens them—after a pause.* These diagrams here go with this page. Aside from that, I guess they'll be pretty clear. *He gives the book to her . . . grips her shoulder.* Please don't feel that I . . . just . . .

BARBARA: Oh! No! No!

FERGUSON: Thanks. *Goes to the door . . . opens it . . . looks out.* I'm going up to Ward C, to look around for a few seconds. The coast is clear— you'd better go now. *Exit FERGUSON.*

BARBARA *takes up the notes . . . walks slowly to the door . . . hesitates there a moment . . . is about to go out, suddenly stops . . . decides to stay. For a moment she leans against the door, breathless, then she goes back into the room, slowly drops the notes on the table, goes to the bed, sits down, takes off her cap, throws it on the bed, and sits there . . . waiting.*

*CURTAIN*

## ACT TWO
*Scene 1*

> *Three months later.*
> *A softly lit room, the main feature of which is a long table. Seated about it are the members of the Joint Committee—three laymen representing the Lay Board, and four doctors representing the Medical Board. Beyond them, we see mahogany panels, a huge fireplace and an oil portrait hanging over it, dark plush portieres drawn to conceal windows and doors—in effect, a rich boardroom of the same general conspiratorial appearance as the board-room of a railroad, a steel, oil, banking, or other big business institution.*
> *At rise:* MR. HOUGHTON, *short, stodgy, aggressive . . . the economist, has just finished reading a report.*

HOUGHTON: . . . 28,000—19,000—33,500, which adds up to a total deficit of 163,000 dollars so far, doctors. *He shakes his head.* You'll have to cut down those expenses, doctors.

GORDON: How?

WREN: We're to the bone, already. We've cut—

SPENCER, *presiding, gray-templed, sure, suave, six generations of Harvard! He gives* DR. WREN *the floor.* Dr. Wren!

WREN, *rises:* Everything—our staff, nurses, technicians, salaries, meals— telephones even! Our interns are allowed only two outside calls. . . .

HOCHBERG: An absurd economy!

HOUGHTON, *taking some papers out of his briefcase:* Mm! . . . It seems to me we've a lot of people in our laboratories. Couldn't we reduce—

HOCHBERG: No, no— *To the chairman.* Mr. Spencer!

SPENCER, *giving* HOCHBERG *the floor:* Dr. Hochberg.

HOCHBERG, *rises, and explains, very patiently:* Those laboratories, Mr. Houghton, *are* the hospital. Most of our *real* work is done in them. *He smiles and shakes his head.* Without that pathology lab and the chemistry lab and the X-ray lab we're helpless.

RUMMOND, *rather old and dim-witted, trying very hard to be a constructive part of this business, but not quite able to grasp it:* You are? . . . Really?

HOCHBERG: Absolutely.

RUMMOND: Hm. Interesting. I didn't realize they were that important.

HOCHBERG: Oh, yes.

GORDON: I should say so.

HOUGHTON: Well, then. . . . *He looks at his papers, and shakes his head.* I don't know. 163,000 dollars—these days! The Board of Trustees is—

SPENCER: Er . . . we'll come back to that later, Mr. Houghton. I want to clear away all . . . er . . . Dr. Gordon! Any reports from the Medical Board to this joint committee?

GORDON: Appointments! Two-year internships, gentlemen—recommended on the basis of competitive examinations. *Starts looking through some papers for the list.* Interns. . . . Ah, yes. *Finds his list and reads from it.* Aubert, Dickinson, Flickers, Frankey, Gordon, Kern, Monroe! The Medical Board awaits your approval of these men.

HOUGHTON, *quickly:* Where's Ten Eyck?

SPENCER: You still can't do anything for Ten Eyck?

GORDON: Ten Eyck? *He glances over his lists, murmuring.* Ten Eyck, Ten Eyck, Ten Eyck. Oh, yes—here it is. Gentlemen! Charles Arthur Ten Eyck finished fourth from the bottom—on a list of three hundred men examined.

HOUGHTON: Senator Ten Eyck's going to be sore as hell. . . .

LARROW, *pompous pedant, cut pretty much from the same pattern as DR. CUNNINGHAM:* I met the boy. Seems well-bred. Good family. . . .

WREN: He doesn't *know* anything. I gave him his oral in medicine. An ignoramus.

LARROW: Examinations! Bah! He graduated at an approved medical school, didn't he?

           WREN: How he managed it is a mystery to me.

*Together*    GORDON: We gave him special consideration, Mr. Spencer. But he just won't do.

SPENCER: Well—his uncle's kicking up a fuss, but if the boy's that bad. . . . After all, you know best. The appointments are in your hands. Which brings me to the real purpose of this special meeting. *He organizes his papers, clears his throat, and looks at them a moment. Then portentously.* Mr. Houghton has just . . . er . . . read the bad news.

WREN: We usually run up a much larger deficit.

SPENCER, *smiles at this naiveté, so typical of the doctor in business:* Yes . . . but these are unusual times, Doctor. As you, no doubt, have heard, there has been a depression.

GORDON: *Has* been? I like that. You try and collect some of my bills.

LARROW: Yes. People are too poor to get sick these days.

HOCHBERG: That's something no matter how poor a man is he can always get—sick!

    *GORDON and WREN enjoy a laugh at LARROW's discomfiture.*

SPENCER: Er . . . Doctors! Please! This is a very important matter! *They quiet down, and lean forward. There is no escaping the note of impending ill news in SPENCER's manner.* Two of our Trustees are very shaky, and may not be able to meet their usual subscription at all. They've already spoken to me about resigning. *The doctors look at each other. This* is *bad.* And so, I've been looking around carefully for a new Trustee—and believe me, doctors, it was a mighty hard search. But, finally— *He smiles.* —I found someone to underwrite our deficit. *Sighs of relief and approval from the doctors.* A man well known for his philanthropies, his generous soul, his civic and social services—John Hudson—the real estate Hudson. HOCHBERG *grunts.* A friend of yours, I believe, Doctor!

HOCHBERG: Yes. But I didn't recognize him by the description. *MR. SPENCER laughs.* He'll be useful. The only real estate man I heard of who's made money the last few years. Good business head. He'll put St. George's on a paying basis.

SPENCER, *laughs:* If he can do that, he's a wizard. Mr. Houghton will resign in favor of him tomorrow.

HOUGHTON: With pleasure.

SPENCER: I've talked the matter over with him, and he's definitely interested. *Chorus of approval from the committee.*

HOUGHTON: If we can get him to subscribe for . . .

SPENCER: Mr. Houghton! Please!

HOUGHTON: Sorry!

SPENCER: Now, it happens that one of our interns is marrying John Hudson's daughter—in a few weeks, I believe. Of course, Doctors, appointments lie completely in your hands, but we feel here is an opportunity. We suggest the Medical Board offer Dr. Ferguson an associateship. . . .

HOCHBERG: What? Impossible!

SPENCER: Impossible? A serious student, capable, going to study a year abroad under a well-known man—why impossible?

HOCHBERG: He won't be *ready* for the job!

SPENCER: Have you any personal prejudice against the boy?

HOCHBERG, *annoyed:* No . . . no! *He rises.* As a matter of fact, I'm very fond of that boy. I think he has promise of becoming a good surgeon, someday. But not overnight. He has years of intensive study ahead of him. I don't care what strength of character is native to a man—he will not work for something he can get for nothing—and Ferguson's no exception. An associateship here now simply means he'll go into practice and drop his studies.

LARROW: And why shouldn't he? He's marrying well. . . . With his wife's connections, he ought to . . . er . . . do very nicely.

HOCHBERG: If he doesn't continue his studies, he'll never be worth a damn as far as medicine goes.

SPENCER: After all, Dr. Hochberg, that's *his* concern, not ours.

*Together* 
> LARROW: Oh! *Dubiously.* He's all right. . . . But—*with conviction.*—he's no infant Cushing by any means.
> SPENCER: We must think of the hospital, Doctors! That's our job.

HOCHBERG, *losing his temper. To* DR. LARROW: You're wrong, Doctor. That boy has *unusual* ability. Yes, yes—another Cushing, perhaps! *Controls himself—to* MR. SPENCER *quietly.* Exactly, Mr. Spencer! The hospital! Do you realize the responsibility in precious human life that lies in an associate's hands? Ferguson doesn't know enough, yet; he's apt to make mistakes that will hurt not only himself, but the integrity of St. George's Hospital.

SPENCER: Oh, come now, Dr. Hochberg!

*Together*
> HOUGHTON: Oh, for Christ's sake. . . .
> RUMMOND: Nothing to be thrown away so lightly!

SPENCER: What do you think, Dr. Wren?

WREN, *slowly:* Well . . . he won't be ready for it, of course, but—er—we could see to it that he'd always be covered by an older man!

HOCHBERG: And give him nothing to do! Make a figurehead of him. Fine! That's fine!

HOUGHTON: What of it?

GORDON: Of course, we don't exactly approve of the appointment, however . . .

HOUGHTON, *exploding:* Approve! Approve!

SPENCER, *irritably:* Mr. Houghton! Please! HOUGHTON *subsides with a grunt.* Dr. Gordon! Go on!

GORDON: Of course, we don't exactly approve the appointment for such a young man; however, we do need Hudson. And Ferguson's not a fool, by any means.

SPENCER: Exactly, Dr. Gordon.

HOCHBERG: But, Josh, don't you see—?

GORDON: Leo, we've got to face the facts. There's hardly a hospital in this city that hasn't shut down on its charity wards. I know a dozen that have completely closed off entire floors and wings! If we have to economize any more, our wealthy patients will take care of themselves, but who's going to take care of all your charity cases? The wards upstairs are full, right now.

*Together*
> HOUGHTON: It takes money to run a hospital, Doctor!
> HOCHBERG, *to* GORDON: You're right, Josh . . . you're . . . *To* HOUGHTON. I know, Mr. Houghton, I know.

And, believe me, we're deeply grateful to you gentlemen for your help.

*Together*    RUMMOND: A good cause.
       SPENCER: I only wish I could subscribe more, Doctor! I would.
HOCHBERG: Yes. Deeply grateful. . . . Although it's a social crime, gentlemen, that hospitals should depend on the charity of a few individuals.
    *The trustees look at each other, not quite sure whether they've been attacked or flattered.*
LARROW: The fact remains that we can't afford to refuse Hudson's help.
HOCHBERG: I don't say that.
LARROW: We need him.
HOCHBERG: We do. And till hospitals are subsidized by the community and run by men in medicine, we'll continue to need our wealthy friends. I realize that. I say by all means make Hudson a Trustee. Take all the help he can give. And promise Ferguson an associateship as soon as he's *ready* to go into practice.
SPENCER: And that'll be—when?
HOCHBERG: In five or six years.
       HOUGHTON: Oh, for Christ's sake! You're dealing with a businessman there, not a child!
*Together*    RUMMOND: You can't expect the man to—
       SPENCER, *smiling wryly:* I'm very much afraid Hudson will tell us to come around ourselves in five or six years.
HOCHBERG, *to SPENCER:* How do you know?
SPENCER: He wants the boy to open an office and settle down.
HOCHBERG: He does? That's nice. Well, Ferguson won't be ready.
SPENCER: If we don't appoint the boy we can't expect Hudson to be interested.
WREN: There you are right, probably.
SPENCER: Well, that's—er—the important thing, after all, isn't it? Hudson's interest.
HOUGHTON: I should say it was his *capital!* HOUGHTON *roars with laughter at his own quip.*
SPENCER: Then you'll submit our recommendation to the Medical Board?
WREN: Yes. And they'll O.K. it, too. I'm pretty sure it'll go through.
    DR. HOCHBERG *throws up his hands.*
SPENCER: Fine! Fine! After all, Dr. Hochberg, as you say, we're here in a common cause—the hospital. *He smiles. Looks over his papers.* Mm! . . . Guess that's about all! *He glances around.* Anything else, gentlemen? Mr. Houghton? HOUGHTON *gathers his papers, shakes his head "No," puts papers in portfolio.* Dr. Wren?
WREN, *looks at his watch:* No. Nothing!

RUMMOND: What time have you there? *Compares watches, nods, rises, and gets his coat.*

SPENCER: Anybody? Then the meeting is—

GORDON: One second, Mr. Spencer! Since you're discussing this with Mr. Hudson, I think it would be a fine thing if we could extend our X-ray therapy department.

SPENCER: First give him the associateship, then we'll talk about equipment.

HOCHBERG, *rises:* Don't count your chickens, Josh!

GORDON: Oh, he'll get the appointment!

HOCHBERG: Yes. But he won't accept it.

SPENCER, *smiles:* What makes you say that?

HOCHBERG: I know the boy! He's too honest, too wise, to sacrifice his career for a nice office and an easy practice. Besides, he won't have the time. He's going to work with me! And . . . er . . . well . . . *He laughs.* It was perhaps a bit foolish to waste so much energy arguing the matter. *He starts for the door.*

SPENCER, *laughs:* As a matter of fact—I had dinner last night at the Hudsons' and I spoke to Ferguson about the appointment. He's delighted with the idea. . . .

HOCHBERG, *stops—returns—incredulous:* He said that?

SPENCER: Certainly! And why not? It's a fine opportunity for him. *Looks around.* Nothing else, gentlemen? No? . . . *Bangs his mallet on the table.* Meeting is adjourned!

All except HOCHBERG move toward the door. He stands there, stock-still, palpably hit.

BLACK OUT

**ACT TWO**
*Scene 2*

The library.
DR. McCABE is sitting in an armchair, reading. MICHAELSON is seated at the long table. Nearby, SHORTY is swinging an imaginary golf club.

SHORTY: My stance was all wrong, see? That's one reason I sliced so much. McCABE looks up, grunts, and goes back to his book.

MICHAELSON: I wouldn't even know how to hold a club any more.

SHORTY: You'd be surprised. A couple of games, and you're right back in form. Look at Ferguson! He hasn't played tennis in years—since high school, I think he said—and yet, last week he beat Laura two sets in a row. And that girl swings a mean racquet.

PETE, *enters, sour-faced:* That patient in 310! Boy, I'd like to give him two dozen spinal taps and bite the point off the needle to make sure he feels them.

MICHAELSON: Whoa! *Laughs.* Your gallbladder needs draining, Pete!

PETE: Ah! The smart alec! He invited me to share this special lunch with him. When I heard *lunch,* I accepted— *he snaps his fingers* —like that! *Then, morosely.* Smart alec!

SHORTY: Well, what's the matter with that?

PETE: Do you know what 310's here for? *Shrilly.* Rectal feeding!
*The others laugh.*

McCABE, *looks up, annoyed:* Sh! Sh! Quiet!
    *They glance over at him and quiet down. He goes back to his books.*
*They kid* PETE *in an undertone, muffling their laughter.*

CUNNINGHAM, *enters—looks around irritably:* Where's Ferguson?

SHORTY: Not here, Doctor.

CUNNINGHAM: I've been trying to find him since twelve o'clock. What kind of house-service is this? Where is he?

MICHAELSON: Why, you see, Doctor—Ferguson's being married next week, and he's at a ceremony rehearsal or something.

CUNNINGHAM: I told him not to let 327's bladder become distended.

MICHAELSON: 327? Ferguson catheterized him this morning.

CUNNINGHAM: Well, he needs another.

SHORTY: I'll get one of the juniors to do it, right away.

CUNNINGHAM: Never mind! I'll do it myself. *He goes to the door, grumbling.* Fine house-service you get around here. 327 is full of urine.

PETE: And so are you.

McCABE, *looks up:* What's that?

PETE: I'm sorry, Doctor.

McCABE: What for? You're quite right. He is. *The interns grin.* McCABE *looks at them quizzically. He turns to* SHORTY. Young man! How would you treat the different forms of acute pancreatitis?

SHORTY, *a study in blankness:* Er . . . acute pancrea . . .mm . . . Why, the same way. I'd—

McCABE: Wrong! *Pause, he shakes his head at* SHORTY. You play golf, huh? *He tosses a pamphlet to* SHORTY. Read that, and find out something about pancreatitis. *He suddenly draws his shoulders together and looks over at the windows.* There's a— *He turns to* MICHAELSON. Will you see if that window's open? There's a draft in here, someplace. MICHAELSON *crosses to the window.*

*Through the glass-paned door, we see* FERGUSON, *in civilian clothes, and* LAURA *coming up the corridor. They are in high spirits, joking and laughing.* FERGUSON *starts to enter the library, but* LAURA *hesitates in the doorway.*

PETE: How was it?

FERGUSON, *grinning:* Terrible.

MICHAELSON, *to* FERGUSON *and* LAURA: Ho' there! *To* MCCABE. They're all closed, Doctor.

FERGUSON, *to* LAURA: Come on in!

LAURA: Well—is it all right for me to—?

*The* INTERNS *assure her in chorus that it's quite all right.* FERGUSON *takes her arm and pulls her into the room.*

FERGUSON: Sure. Come on! *To others.* Any calls for me?

MICHAELSON: Yes. Quite a few, George.

LAURA: You should have seen my hero! He was scared to death.

FERGUSON: Who wouldn't be?

SHORTY: What was it like?

FERGUSON: Every step a major operation. Next time I take spinal anesthesia first. SHORTY *sings a funereal wedding march.* Exactly, Shorty! The last mile.

*They laugh.* MCCABE *looks up, very much annoyed. He snorts, shuts his book with a bang. The others stop laughing and glance at him.* MCCABE *reaches for his cane, rises rustily, and goes out mumbling.*

LAURA, *watches him go, then turns to the others, who grin:* Perhaps I shouldn't have come in here.

SHORTY: Nonsense!

MAC: It's perfectly O.K.

PETE: Don't mind old Doc McCabe! He thinks the world ended in 1917 when he retired.

LAURA: Retired!

FERGUSON: Yes, but he still comes around to talk, read, watch operations. Gives us hell for not knowing anything. Medicine's not just his profession—it's his life. *He shakes his head admiringly.* Great guy! If I live to be eighty, that's the way I want to grow old!

LAURA: Not I. When I'm too old to enjoy life firsthand I want to lie down, and say, "Laura, it was good while it lasted. Now, *fini!*"

SHORTY: My idea exactly. Why sit around and listen to your arteries hardening?

PETE: Don't worry, sweetheart! The chances are none of us will live to grow that old. *To* LAURA. Most doctors die pretty young, you know.

*LAURA looks pained.*

MICHAELSON: That's right. The strain gets them around forty-five. Heart goes bad.

LAURA, *glances at* FERGUSON *and grimaces:* There's a pleasant thought.

FERGUSON, *laughs:* Cheerful bunch!

PETE: So I say—eat, drink and be merry—for tomorrow you . . . *With a gesture.* Pht!

MICHAELSON: George! Better phone in! Cunningham's been looking for you!

FERGUSON: What's he want now?

SHORTY: His shoes shined, or something. I don't know.

PETE: 327 catheterized!

FERGUSON: Again? He'll wind up by— *Goes to phone.* —giving that patient a urethritis. *Picks up the phone.* Dr. Ferguson! I just came in. Any calls for me? Find him, will you? Library!

PETE: He's certainly been giving you all the dirty work lately.

MICHAELSON: Yes!

SHORTY: What'd you do? Kick his mother?

FERGUSON: What's the difference? Four more days and I'll be *aus* intern.

LAURA: Who is this charming fellow?

FERGUSON: He doesn't matter, darling! Nothing matters, now—except Vienna!

MICHAELSON: I bet you'll have a swell time over there.

FERGUSON: You bet right! *The phone rings.* FERGUSON *goes to it. On phone.* Yes, Dr. Cunningham? . . . Yes, Dr. Cunningham! . . . Yes. . . . Oh, you're quite right! . . . Yes. . . . Yes. . . . *He winks at the boys, who smile and shake their heads.* Uh, huh! . . . Yes . . . yes. . . . All right, Doctor! Sure.

MAC: Will you have lunch with us, Laura?

PETE: A lousy lunch.

LAURA, *laughs:* Just had one, thanks! George and I dropped into Rumpelmayer's after the rehearsal!

SHORTY: Rumpelmayer? At the St. Moritz?

LAURA: Yes.

PETE, *hungrily:* How was the food? Good?

LAURA: Delicious!

PETE: Oh? *Sighs enviously, then in a resigned tone.* Well—guess I'll go down and eat slop.

MAC: Sure we can't coax you?

LAURA: I'm full up to here! Thanks!

MAC: Sorry. So long.

    MAC, SHORTY, *and* PETE *go.*

FERGUSON, *still on the phone:* Yes. . . . Absolutely right, Doctor. I'll tend to it. *He hangs up, wrings the phone as if it were* CUNNINGHAM's *neck, and grins at* LAURA.

LAURA: Can I smoke in here?

FERGUSON: Sure.

LAURA, *puts a cigarette in her mouth and waits for a light:* Well?

FERGUSON: What? *She points to her cigarette.* Oh! *He laughs, fishes out a packet of matches and lights her cigarette.*

LAURA: Darling! You're marvelous this way. I've never seen you so high.

FERGUSON: I've never been so high! You know, dear, I love this old place, and yet, my God, I can't wait to get out of here.

LAURA: I was worried last night, after Mr. Spencer spoke to you—you looked so glum. I was afraid you might change your mind.

FERGUSON: Not a chance!

LAURA: Not bothered about that appointment?

FERGUSON: No. That'll be all right—if I get it.

LAURA: You'll get it.

FERGUSON: What do you know about it?

LAURA: I know you, you fish!

FERGUSON, *grins, then suddenly becomes serious:* I wonder if . . . Mr. Spencer spoke to the committee, yet?

LAURA: If he did, it's quick work.

FERGUSON: I hope he hasn't yet.

LAURA: Why?

FERGUSON: Well, I—want to talk to Dr. Hochberg first.

LAURA, *laughs:* Why are you so afraid of Hocky? He won't bite you! Or, do you think by delaying it you can change my mind—and work with Hocky when we come back?

FERGUSON: No, that's not it.

LAURA: Because if you do, I'm warning you! I'll just drop out of the picture, George. Even if we're married—you'll come home one day, and I just won't be there.

FERGUSON, *takes her in his arms. Tenderly:* Shut up, will you? It's just that I don't want to seem ungrateful.

LAURA: Oh, he'll probably find somebody else.

FERGUSON: Of course he will. *Smiles, somewhat wistfully.* There isn't a man I know who wouldn't give a right eye for the chance to work with Dr. Hochberg. You don't realize it, dear, he's an important man. He . . .

LAURA, *impatiently:* The important man, George, is the man who knows how to live. I love Hocky, I think an awful lot of him. But he's like my father. They have no outside interests at all. They're flat—they're colorless. They're not men—they're caricatures! Oh, don't become like them, George! Don't be an important man and crack up at forty-five. I want our lives together to be full and rich and beautiful! I want it so much.

FERGUSON, *fervently:* Oh, my dear, so do I. . . . And believe me, that's the way it's going to be. *He looks at her fondly.* And I once thought I could live without you.

LAURA: What? When?

FERGUSON: Never! *He kisses her.* NURSE JAMISON *enters, smiles, embarrassed.* FERGUSON *turns around, sees her, grins.* Yes?

JAMISON: Mrs. D'Andrea—the mother of that boy—the automobile accident that came in this morning—she's outside, raising an awful rumpus. Wants to see you.

FERGUSON: Take her to Michaelson!

JAMISON: I did! She wants to see you!

FERGUSON: There's nothing I can tell her now.

JAMISON: I know, Doctor, but she insists on seeing you.

FERGUSON: What for? We won't know till tomorrow whether he'll live or die. MRS. D'ANDREA *tries to enter.* NURSE JAMISON *restrains her.* All right! Let her in, Jamison! Let her in!

MRS. D'ANDREA: Dottore. . . . Dottore. . . . Heeza all right? Yes? Heeza all right?

FERGUSON: I'm sorry! There's nothing I can tell you now.

MRS. D'ANDREA: Heeza gonna . . . live? Dottore?

FERGUSON: Tomorrow! Tomorrow! You come back tomorrow! We'll know then—tomorrow.

MRS. D'ANDREA: Tomorrow?

FERGUSON: Yes.

MRS. D'ANDREA: Mamma mia! Tomorrow! . . . Oh, Dottore! Pleeza! Pleeza! Don't let my boy die! Pleeza! . . .

FERGUSON: I'll do everything I can, Mother. And you, try not to worry too much.

NURSE: Come! You'd better . . .

MRS. D'ANDREA *to* NURSE JAMISON: Oh, lady, heeza my boy. . . . *To* LAURA. Heeza my boy! Heeza besta boy I got. Heeza besta boy in the world. If he's gonna die I'm gonna die, too. . . . *She prays in Italian.*

NURSE: Come! Come! *She leads out* MRS. D'ANDREA.

*As they go to the door,* DR. HOCHBERG *enters, passing them. He pauses to watch them go, then turns to* FERGUSON.

LAURA: Hello, Hocky!

HOCHBERG: Hello, Laura! *To* FERGUSON. Who was that?

FERGUSON: Mrs. D'Andrea, mother of that case . . . automobile accident . . . this morning.

HOCHBERG: Oh, yes, yes, yes, I know—you gave him a shot of tetanus antitoxin?

FERGUSON: Dr. Michaelson took care of that.

HOCHBERG: He did? Good! *Glances at his watch.* Where have you been since twelve o'clock?

FERGUSON: I was gone a little longer than I expected to be.

LAURA: It was awfully important, Hocky.

HOCHBERG: It must have been.

FERGUSON: I left Michaelson in charge to cover me. I only meant to be gone half an hour. . . .

HOCHBERG: In the meantime it was two.

FERGUSON: Sorry, Doctor! This won't happen again.

HOCHBERG: I hope not. *He relaxes—becomes the old familiar again.* Watch it! A few more days to go. Your record is clean. Keep it that way! *There is a pause.* HOCHBERG *looks at* GEORGE *steadily for a moment.* GEORGE *becomes self-conscious and uneasy. Finally* DR. HOCHBERG *speaks.* George . . . I heard something this morning—I didn't know quite what to make of it. *Pause.* You still want to accomplish something in medicine?

FERGUSON: Certainly.

HOCHBERG: You mean that?

FERGUSON: Yes.

HOCHBERG, *to* LAURA: You love George, don't you, Laura?

LAURA: You know I do.

HOCHBERG: Of course you do and you want to help him—but that's not the way, Laura. Believe me, nobody can help George but himself—and hard work! He cannot buy this; he must earn it. *To* FERGUSON. That appointment they talked to you about, George . . . you won't be ready for it. . . .

FERGUSON: After a year with von Eiselsberg, I thought . . .

HOCHBERG: One year? *He shakes his head.*

FERGUSON: It's not as if I were going to drop my studies. I intend to keep on.
  HOCHBERG *shakes his head.*

LAURA: I don't see why not!

HOCHBERG, *to* LAURA: My dear child. . . .

LAURA: After all, George has worked so terribly hard till now, Hocky. If it's going to make things easier . . .

HOCHBERG: There are no easy roads in medicine.

FERGUSON: I didn't expect it to be easy. I counted on work. Hard work!

HOCHBERG: Ten years of it! Then . . . yes.

LAURA: I can't see how it's going to hurt George.

HOCHBERG: There are a great many things you can't see, Laura.

LAURA: If he goes into practice, we'll have some time for ourselves, Hocky.

HOCHBERG: Time? How? There are only twenty-four hours in a day. He's working with me and if— *He suddenly stops short as the truth strikes him. Or is he? To* FERGUSON. Are you?

FERGUSON: Doctor Hochberg, I haven't loafed yet, and I don't intend to start now. But Laura and I are young, we love each other. I want a little *more* out of life than just my work. I don't think that's asking too much.

HOCHBERG: I see. I see. *Pause.* So, you've decided not to come with me next year.

*There's a long silence. Finally* LAURA *answers apologetically.*

LAURA: After all, Hocky, we feel that we'll be happier that way—and . . .

HOCHBERG: Of course, Laura. It's George's life and yours. You've a right to decide for yourselves—what you're going to do with it. I didn't mean to meddle. . . .

LAURA: Oh, Hocky, you know we don't feel that way about you.

HOCHBERG: I'm glad you don't. . . . *Pause. Trying to hide his hurt, he continues.* How's Papa?

LAURA: So-so. . . . He still has an occasional attack.

HOCHBERG: Still smokes, I suppose.

LAURA, *nods:* When I'm not around. He's building again.

HOCHBERG: Well—don't let him work too hard!

LAURA: As if I have anything to say about that! You know Dad! He usually has his way.

HOCHBERG, *glances at* FERGUSON, *then nods significantly:* Yes. . . . DR. HOCHBERG *turns to* GEORGE *and says gently.* You'd better get into your uniform, George. We may have to operate shortly. A new case just came in on the surgical service. One of our own nurses. What's her name? That nice little girl up in Pediatrics? Oh yes—Dennin! Barbara Dennin! You remember her? Pediatrics.

FERGUSON, *embarrassed:* Oh, yes, yes. I remember her—an excellent nurse.

HOCHBERG: Poor child! Such a nice little girl, too. . . . Sepsis!

FERGUSON, *sympathetically:* Oh! That's awful! She bad?

HOCHBERG: Temperature 105, blood count way up.

FERGUSON: Tch! What was it—ruptured appendix?

HOCHBERG, *shakes his head:* Septic abortion!

FERGUSON: Abortion?

HOCHBERG: Yes. Poor girl—it's a shame. Well, we'll see what we can do. Meet me up there. *He starts towards the door.*

*FERGUSON stands there, his brow wrinkling.*

MICHAELSON, *entering:* That D'Andrea fellow is still unconscious. Seems to be something the matter with his lower jaw. . . .

HOCHBERG: What!

MICHAELSON: Protruding—somewhat rigid. Thought it might be tetanus.

HOCHBERG: No! Not so soon! Anyway, you gave him antitoxin, didn't you?

MICHAELSON: Why—er . . . *He shoots a quick glance at* FERGUSON. No!

HOCHBERG: What? *Angrily.* Don't you know yet that T.A.T. is routine in this hospital?

MICHAELSON: Yes, sir. . . . But I thought— *To* FERGUSON. You didn't tell me. I thought you gave it!

HOCHBERG, *to* FERGUSON: Dr. Ferguson!

FERGUSON: I intended to . . . mention it to him. I guess—I—forgot. . . .

HOCHBERG: Forgot? Is that a thing to forget? You should have given the antitoxin yourself!

LAURA: It's my fault, Hocky, I dragged him away—we were late.

HOCHBERG: That's no excuse. He's not supposed to leave the house at all! And a very sick house, too. You know that, Dr. Ferguson!

FERGUSON: Yes, sir.

LAURA: Oh, Hocky—it was important! Terribly important! It was a rehearsal of our wedding.

HOCHBERG: A rehearsal? Yes, Laura, that's nice. A rehearsal of your wedding. But do you realize, upstairs, there is a boy all smashed to bits. There'll be no wedding for him, if he develops tetanus. *To* FERGUSON. Dr. Ferguson! Inject that antitoxin at once!

FERGUSON: Yes, sir! *He goes.*

HOCHBERG, *turns to* LAURA, *looks at her a moment, then shakes his head and says slowly:* Laura, you deserve to be spanked! LAURA's *face becomes angry and defiant. Her jaw tightens, but she says nothing.* Don't you realize what that boy's work means?

LAURA: Of course I do, Hocky.

HOCHBERG, *very softly, almost to himself:* No . . . no, you don't! *Then, louder.* Would you like to see, perhaps?

LAURA: Yes . . . why not? . . .

HOCHBERG, *glances toward the corridor where* MICHAELSON *is standing, talking to a nurse:* Dr. Michaelson! MICHAELSON *enters.* Take Miss Hudson here upstairs, see that she gets a cap and gown, and have her in the operating room in about— *With a sharp jerk of his arm he bares his wrist watch and looks at it.*—twenty minutes! *Without so much as another glance at* LAURA, *he marches briskly out of the library.*

*BLACK OUT*

## ACT TWO
*Scene 3*

   *The end of the corridor. In the corner are the night desk and a medicine cabinet. To the left of them is a room, numbered 401.*

*To the right are the elevator doors. A* WOMAN *and a* BOY *are waiting for the elevator.*

*A* NURSE *carrying a basin, some towels, etc., enters from the left.* MARY *comes out of 401, crosses to the night desk—takes a hypodermic needle and some bottles from the chest. The* NURSE *with the basin enters 401. The elevator whirs, and the doors open with a clang. An aged* COUPLE *step out first, then* FERGUSON. *The* WOMAN *and the* BOY *enter the elevator. The door clangs shut, and the elevator whirs. The aged* COUPLE *cross to the left and disappear off.* FERGUSON *starts to go into 401, stops, turns to* MARY. MARY, *who has been eyeing him, looks away.*

FERGUSON: How is she? MARY *shakes her head. She is pale, grim, restrained.* Temperature?
MARY: 106.
FERGUSON: 106?
MARY: Yeah!
FERGUSON: Delirious?
MARY: She was—before—*Pause, as she lights a small alcohol lamp, and sterilizes a hypodermic needle by boiling it in a spoon held over the flame.* She kept calling—for you.
FERGUSON, *suddenly rigid:* For me?
MARY: Yeah!
FERGUSON, *stunned:* Oh! *He turns to enter the room.*
MARY: Better wait! Dr. Hochberg's in there. She's quiet, now. If you went in she might start talking again.

*The* NURSE *with the basin and towels comes out of the room, sees* FERGUSON, *smiles at him, and as she crosses left, throws a cheery hello to him over her shoulder. He doesn't answer.* NURSE, *puzzled, exits left.*

FERGUSON: God! I never dreamed this would happen.
MARY: Men don't—usually. . . .
FERGUSON: Why didn't she come to me? Why didn't she tell me? Why did she keep away?
MARY: I guess that was my fault. Long time ago I saw she was falling for you. I told her you were in love with someone else, and engaged to be married—and to keep away from you. I didn't know then, that she already . . .
FERGUSON: I see! I see! That's why she—I thought after that night . . . she'd just realized how crazy we'd both been. . . . Crazy! I thought she at least knew how to take care of herself. But when this happened . . . she should have told me! You should have told me! Why did you let her do this?

MARY: I didn't know . . . till last night. It was . . . too late, then! She was just a green kid! Didn't realize what it was all about!

FERGUSON: God! I wouldn't have let this happen! I wouldn't have let this happen. . . .

MARY: I suppose you'd have helped her—

FERGUSON: Yes! Yes! Yes . . . rather than this. . . .

HOCHBERG, *pokes his head out the door of 401:* Where's that hypo?

MARY: In a second, Doctor!

HOCHBERG, *to* FERGUSON: Did you tend to D'Andrea?

FERGUSON: Yes, sir! Gave him the T.A.T. He's conscious, now.

HOCHBERG: That business with his jaw?

FERGUSON, *mechanically:* Slight dislocation. Put it back into place. Bandaged it! No further evidence of internal injury. . . . Although there may be a slight fracture of the tibia or the fibula of the left leg. I'll have some X-ray pictures taken this afternoon!

HOCHBERG: Uh huh! Pain?

FERGUSON: Complained of slight pain . . . general.

HOCHBERG: Did you give him some morphine?

FERGUSON: No, sir. . . .

HOCHBERG: Why not?

FERGUSON: Accident case! Didn't want to mask any possible internal injuries.

HOCHBERG: Ah! Yes. Very good, very good. *To* MARY. Er . . . tell me . . . was this Miss Dennin a friend of yours?

MARY: Yeah . . . in a way. I sorta . . . liked her.

HOCHBERG: Well, she's a mighty sick girl. You'd better notify her relatives. . . .

MARY: Ain't none . . . that would be interested.

HOCHBERG: No? Her friends, then? MARY *shakes her head.* My . . . my! *To* FERGUSON. What a pity! Tch, tch! *He turns back into the room.* Oh, Wren, I want you to— *He disappears into the room.*

MARY: Nobody! Nobody to turn to!

FERGUSON: Her folks? Her people? At home! Surely there's—

MARY: Yeah!—a stepfather! And to top it all, she's going to be kicked out of here!

FERGUSON: They wouldn't do that!

MARY: Wouldn't they, though? Ask Miss Hackett! And she won't get into any other hospital, either. They'll see to that!

FERGUSON: Poor kid!

MARY: It might be a lucky break for her if she just passed out!

FERGUSON: What are you talking about? She can't die! She's got to pull through! She's got to!

MARY: And then, what? . . . She hasn't got a dime to her name.

    HOCHBERG *and* WREN *come out of the room.*

HOCHBERG: Tch! Poor girl! . . . Why do they go to butchers like that?

WREN: Well . . . she couldn't have come to us.

HOCHBERG: No . . . that's the shame! Ah, Wren, some of our laws belong to
the Dark Ages! Why can't we help the poor and the ignorant? The others
will always help themselves—law or no law.

FERGUSON: What are your findings on the case, Doctor?

HOCHBERG: Definite evidence of sepsis. . . . Better order the operating room,
at once! A hysterectomy!

FERGUSON: Don't you think operation is contraindicated?

HOCHBERG: Not in this case.

FERGUSON: If we put her in Fowler's position and . . .

HOCHBERG: You see, the infection is localized in the uterus . . . and it's been
my experience in cases like this . . . the only way to save the patient is to
remove the focus of infection. Otherwise she hasn't a chance. . . .

FERGUSON: The girl was up in the children's ward. She asked to be put there,
because she loves them. It seems a terrible shame to deprive her of the
chance of ever having any of her own.

HOCHBERG: It is. It is a terrible shame—yes. But it's future life or her life.
We'll save hers . . . if we can. Order the operating room!

FERGUSON: Yes, sir.

HOCHBERG, *to* MARY: And, the man, who—was responsible— FERGUSON
*stiffens.* Does he realize what's happened?

MARY: I suppose so.

HOCHBERG: Mmm, hmm! . . . Who is the man?

MARY: I don't know!

HOCHBERG: Well—if you can find out, he should be notified, at least. *To*
FERGUSON. What are you waiting for? Order the operating room!

FERGUSON: Yes, sir. *He goes to the phone.* Operating room! . . . Hello! . . .
How soon can you have the O.R. ready for a hysterectomy? Dr. Hochberg!
Yes. . . . *Turns to* HOCHBERG. Ready now.

HOCHBERG: Good! *To* MARY. Patient prepared?

MARY: Yes!

HOCHBERG: Fine! Er—give her that hypo!

MARY: Yes, sir! *Goes into* BARBARA's *room.*

HOCHBERG, *to* FERGUSON: Have her brought up at once.

FERGUSON, *into phone:* Patient ready! Send a rolling stretcher down to 401,
at once! *He hangs up.*

HOCHBERG: Call the staff anesthetist!

WREN: I'll give the anesthesia, if you want me to, Hochberg.

HOCHBERG: There's no one I'd rather have.

WREN: General?

HOCHBERG: No—no. I'm afraid to give her ether. . . . We can work better under spinal anesthesia.

WREN: Spinal?—Good!

HOCHBERG: Come! I'd like to take a quick look at that D'Andrea boy.

WREN: I want to prepare my—

HOCHBERG: A second! Come. *To* FERGUSON. You can start scrubbing, now. *Exit* HOCHBERG *and* WREN.

FERGUSON *stands there a moment.* MARY *comes out. She puts the alcohol and iodine back on the emergency shelf.*

MARY: Well, that's—

*The elevator begins to whine.* MARY *and* FERGUSON *glance over at the indicator dial over the elevator door. It slowly comes round from O.R. to 3, where it stops. The door opens with a clang. An* ORDERLY *steps out, backward, pulling a rolling stretcher after him. He turns to* MARY *and grins.*

ORDERLY: Well, here I am, sweetheart!

MARY, *suddenly bursts into tears:* Who the hell are you calling sweetheart? *She hurries into the room.*

ORDERLY, *puzzled:* What the— *He looks at* FERGUSON, *embarrassed, smiles, and shakes his head in bewilderment. Then he wheels the stretcher into the room.*

THE ELEVATOR MAN *who has kept the elevator door open, calls to* FERGUSON *in a monotone:* Going down?

FERGUSON, *slowly enters the elevator, then, in a low, harsh voice:* Up! Operating room! *The door clangs shut, the elevator whines siren-like, rising to a crescendo, as the indicator dial goes up.*


BLACK OUT


## ACT TWO
*Scene 4*

*The Operating Room.*

*A feeling of sharp, white, gleaming cleanliness! Back center, the huge, hanging, kettledrum lamp, with its hundreds of reflecting mirrors, throws a brilliant, shadowless light on the chromium operating table. All the nooks and corners of the room are rounded off to facilitate cleansing, and to prevent the accumulation of dust.*

*To the right is the sterilizing room, with its polished nickel autoclaves, bubbling and steaming.*

*To the left is a long north skylight, double-paned.*

*There is one* Sterile Nurse, *wearing cap and gown, mask and long rubber gloves; there are two* Unsterile Nurses, *similarly clothed but wearing no gloves. They move to and fro like so many pistons, efficiently, quickly, quietly—ghostlike automata.*

*In the right-hand corner nearest us, stands a row of half a dozen sinks, the faucets in them turned on and off by means of knee-stirrups attached underneath. Above, a shelf holds cans of sterile brushes, pans of liquid soap, and eight-minute glasses—one to each sink. Well apart from these sinks, and to the right, are two basins in a white-enamel stand; one contains blue bichloride, the other alcohol. Beyond them again stands a foot-pedal gown drum, scarred from its purifying baths of steam.*

*To the left is a long glove table, on which are the gloves wrapped in canvas "books," sterile powder can, and towels covered by a sterile sheet.*

Wren, *in cap and mask, is dipping his hands in the bichloride pan;* Pete, *at the washbasin, is cleaning his nails with an orange-stick, and* Michaelson *is scrubbing his hands with long, easy, rhythmic strokes of the brush. They are chatting quietly.*

*The* Sterile Nurse *goes to the glove table and folds over the sheet, uncovering the glove books, etc.*

*A* Nurse *comes from the sterilizing room, carrying a steaming tray of instruments to the instrument table at the foot of the operating table. The* Sterile Nurse *returns to the instrument table, and there is a clink of instruments as she arranges them.*

Wren *holds up his hands so that the bichloride rolls down the forearm and off the elbow; he repeats this once more in the bichloride, and twice in the alcohol pan, then walks away, holding his dripping hands high and away from him.*

*A* Sterile Nurse *gives him a sterile towel. He dries his hands, using the separate sides and ends of the towel for each hand, then he tosses the towel to the floor, and crosses to the glove table.*

*An* Unsterile Nurse *quickly crosses, picks up the towel, and takes it away.* Wren *powders his hands, opens a glove book, gingerly plucks out a glove, handling it by the cuff, careful not to touch the outside of the glove, as that might still soil it (since the hands themselves can never be completely sterilized) and slips it on. The second glove he slips on, careful not to touch his wrist with his already gloved hand. He then snaps the gloves over the cuffs of his jacket, wraps a sterile towel about his hands and walks over to the operating table.*

Pete *finishes scrubbing, goes to the bichloride basin, and dips his hands, using the same technique as* Wren. *When he is through with the alcohol, however, he turns to the gown drum. The* Sterile Nurse *crosses to the drum, steps on the pedal, which raises the lid, and deftly extracts a folded gown, without touching the drum itself. She releases her foot, and the lid clunks back. She hands the folded gown to him; he takes a corner of it, unrolls it, and slips into it. An* UNSTERILE NURSE *comes up behind, careful not to touch him, and ties the gown for him.*

*The whole effect is that of a smooth, well-oiled machine, a routine so studied that the people in the operating room can afford to be casual—as they are.*

*One of the* UNSTERILE NURSES *enters with* LAURA, *whom she has just helped into a cap and gown.*

NURSE: All right?

LAURA: Yes.

MICHAELSON, *to* LAURA: Well, you're all set, now!

LAURA, *smiles nervously:* Yes—thanks!

MICHAELSON: Not at all! A pleasure.

LAURA, *doubtfully:* Oh! The pleasure's all mine!

MICHAELSON, *laughs:* I'll bet it is.

LAURA: This gown seems awfully wrinkled.

NURSE: They're never pressed. That would unsterilize them.

LAURA: Oh! I see. *Enter* HOCHBERG *and* FERGUSON *in operating pajamas. They are putting on their masks.* Hello!

HOCHBERG: Oh, hello! *To* FERGUSON. We have a guest! *He turns over the eight-minute glass and begins to scrub up.*

FERGUSON, *stands stock-still for a moment:* Laura! What? . . . .

LAURA: Surprise! *She starts to go toward* GEORGE.

HOCHBERG, *warning her back with a quick gesture:* Uh, uh! *She stops.* Stand over there—in the corner! Don't come near us! We're getting clean! You're full of contamination.

LAURA: Oh—am I?

    FERGUSON *begins to scrub up.*

HOCHBERG: Yes. *A long pause while they scrub.* HOCHBERG, *still scrubbing, turns to* LAURA. Well—how do you feel?

LAURA, *trying to bluff off her nervousness:* Great!

HOCHBERG: Mm, hm!

LAURA: How do I look? *She holds out her gown at both sides.*

HOCHBERG: Very becoming!

LAURA: Think so, George?

FERGUSON: Yes—very!

HOCHBERG: You can look around, but keep out of the way! Don't touch anything! Put your hands behind your back! *A long silence, broken only by the rasping sound of scrubbing brushes.* LAURA *stares, fascinated.*

HOCHBERG: Oh, Nurse— *A* NURSE *comes over.* See that Miss Hudson here gets a mask before she goes in. Find a stool for her—and put it near the operating table! I don't want her to miss anything!

LAURA, *wryly:* Thanks, Hocky!

HOCHBERG: Don't mention it, Laura!

    DR. HOCHBERG *finishes scrubbing and goes through the same routine as the others. When he gets his gown he disappears to a corner of the operating room, hidden by the basins.* FERGUSON *also goes through the routine of gown and gloves, etc.*

WREN: Orderly! Orderly!

ORDERLY, *enters from anesthesia room:* Yes, sir?

WREN: Bring the patient in!

    BARBARA *is wheeled in by the* ORDERLY. *As she enters,* WREN *bends over to look at her.* FERGUSON *comes over.*

FERGUSON: How is she, Doctor?

BARBARA: George!

FERGUSON: Yes?

BARBARA: What are they going to do to me?

FERGUSON: There's nothing to be afraid of, Barbara!

BARBARA: You won't let them hurt me?

FERGUSON: No, of course not.

BARBARA: Will you be there? George, darling, please be there!

FERGUSON: I'll be there.

BARBARA: Thanks, dear. . . . I loved you. . . . I don't care. . . . *Her head goes back.*

WREN, *looks at* FERGUSON, *who is rigid. Then at* LAURA, *who is equally rigid. He turns to* ORDERLY *and says, sharply:* Come on! Come on!

    *The* ORDERLY *wheels* BARBARA *to the operating table.* WREN *follows. The patient is transferred to the operating table.*

LAURA: What was that all about?

FERGUSON: Laura, I'm sorry as hell—I wish I . . .

LAURA: George! Is it? *She clutches his arm.*

FERGUSON, *recoiling from her touch:* Don't! You mustn't! Stand away! Over there! You've unsterilized the gown! *He tears off his gown and gloves, throws them on the floor, and calls into the sterilizing room.* Nurse! Nurse! Sterile gown, gloves, towels! Quick! *He turns to* LAURA, *explains, apologetically.* We've got to be very careful. . . . You know . . . germs are . . .

    *A* NURSE *enters, picks up the gown and gloves. He dips his hands into the bichloride pan, and then the alcohol pan. A* STERILE NURSE *brings him a sterile gown, he unfolds it and slides into it. And the* UNSTERILE NURSE, *behind him, ties it. In the meantime, another* NURSE *returns with a sterile towel. He dries his hands, and throws the towel on the floor. The* UNSTERILE NURSE *picks it up and takes it away. The* STERILE NURSE *powders his hands, brings him a sterile glove book and opens it. He plucks out a glove, and puts it on, the* NURSE *helping him, in approved aseptic technique, by thrusting her fingers under the cuff, and pushing home the glove. In the meantime, the patient, concealed by the people around her, has been anaesthetized, and is being draped. All the time,* LAURA *has been staring at* FERGUSON. FERGUSON, *working the fingers of the gloves, looks at* LAURA. *Exit the* ORDERLY *with the rolling stretcher.*

LAURA: Did you . . . Did you have an affair with that girl—or what?

FERGUSON, *almost inaudibly:* Yes. . . .

LAURA: Oh! *A bitter little laugh.* That's a funny one!

HOCHBERG, *on a footstool, bends over the patient—calls:* Dr. Ferguson! . . . *The call is taken up by a number of voices. A* NURSE *crosses to* FERGUSON.

NURSE: Dr. Ferguson! The patient is draped and ready!

FERGUSON: All right! I'm coming! *He goes to the operating table.*

NURSE, *to* LAURA: If you want to watch—you'd better go over. I'll get a stool for you—mask!

LAURA: No, thanks! . . . I've had enough! . . . I've had enough!

A SECOND NURSE, *enters:* Here! Here! Get busy! *Notices* LAURA. You! What's the matter? You look so . . . Feel ill, dear? *To* FIRST NURSE. Take her out! Near a window! Give her some water!

LAURA: No! . . . No! . . . I'm . . . I'm fine! . . . Thanks! *She tears off the tight cap, begins to sob, and exits.*

  *The* NURSES *look at each other and grin.*

FIRST NURSE: Med student?

SECOND NURSE: Of course! First time! What else?

FIRST NURSE: She's got a long way to go, yet! *They laugh.*

  *Nurse and doctors about the table turn and say, "Sh! Sh!" The* NURSES *immediately hush.*

HOCHBERG: Ready, Dr. Wren?

WREN: All set!

HOCHBERG: Ready, Dr. Ferguson?

FERGUSON: Ready!

HOCHBERG, *reaching out his hand, without looking up:* Scalpel!

  *The* OPERATING NURSE *hands over the scalpel, cutting a gleaming arc through the air, then she clumps it into* HOCHBERG's *hand. He bends over the patient. There is a sudden burst of activity and gleam of clamps about the table.*

*The* UNSTERILE NURSES, *hands behind their backs, stand on tiptoe, and crane their necks to see over the shoulders of the* ASSISTANT.

*All lights dim down, except the operating light, which bathes the tableau in a fierce, merciless, white brilliance.*

### CURTAIN

**ACT THREE**
*Scene 1*

> FERGUSON's *room. The next morning. The shade is drawn, the room dark, except for the small lamp at the bed.* FERGUSON *is sitting on the bed, his head in his hands. His clothes are wrinkled—he hasn't changed them all night. His hair is mussed, his eyes red.*
>
> *A knock at the door.*
>
> FERGUSON *doesn't stir. The knock is repeated.* FERGUSON *still remains motionless. The door slowly opens.* HOCHBERG *enters.*

HOCHBERG: Good morning, George.

FERGUSON: Oh. Good morning. HOCHBERG *pulls up the shade. A great burst of sunlight streams in, blinding* GEORGE. *He turns his face away, rubs his eyes.* What time? *He picks up the clock.* Oh—I didn't know it was so late.

HOCHBERG: Lovely out, isn't it?

FERGUSON: Yes. . . . *He rises wearily, goes to the washbasin, washes himself, and combs his hair.*

HOCHBERG, *examining a brain in a jar on the desk:* Hm. . . . That's a fine specimen. Ah . . . yes . . . you've been doing some study on brain surgery?

FERGUSON: Yes. . . .

HOCHBERG: Fascinating work. Miss Dennin's temperature is down this morning. . . .

FERGUSON: I know.

HOCHBERG: The nurse tells me you watched the case all last night. That's very nice. . . . Hm. Excellent book—this. You should read all of Cushing's reports. How is—er—D'Andrea?

FERGUSON: Examined those pictures. He did have a fracture of the tibia of the left leg. No further evidence of internal injury. He'll be all right, I guess.

HOCHBERG: Good. Good. He's a lucky boy. He looked badly hurt.

FERGUSON: Dr. Hochberg. There's something I've got to tell you. . . .

HOCHBERG, *quickly:* I know. Wren told me. *Pause.* HOCHBERG *looks at the specimen.* Great field—brain surgery—for a young man.

FERGUSON: You must think it was pretty low of me.

HOCHBERG: George . . . George!

FERGUSON: I didn't know anything about it till yesterday. I wouldn't have let her . . . I swear I wouldn't have. . . .

HOCHBERG: It was a bad job. . . .

FERGUSON: Oh, that poor kid. God, I ought to be shot.

HOCHBERG: Did you force her to have an affair with you; or did she come to you of her own free will? Then why do you blame yourself so?

FERGUSON: That has nothing to do with it.

HOCHBERG: That has everything to do with it!

FERGUSON: Dr. Hochberg, you don't know what she's up against.

HOCHBERG: I know.

FERGUSON: It's not as if she were just a tramp. . . . She's a fine, sensitive girl! God. What a mess I've gotten her into! She can't bear any children. Thrown out of the hospital—nowheres to go—no one to turn to. What's she going to do?

HOCHBERG: Don't worry. We'll find something for her.

FERGUSON: Just giving her a job—isn't going to help her very much. There's only one decent thing . . . I'm going to . . . marry her . . . if she'll have me.

HOCHBERG: George! Stop talking like an idiot! Pull yourself together! What about Laura?

FERGUSON: She's through with me, Dr. Hochberg.

HOCHBERG: She knows?

FERGUSON: Yes. I kept phoning her all day yesterday—all last night. She wouldn't come to the phone . . . wouldn't even talk to me, Dr. Hochberg.

HOCHBERG: Hm . . . that's too bad. Yet you know, George, in a way—that's not the worst that could have happened to you. . . .

FERGUSON: No! Don't say that!

HOCHBERG: Well, now there's work, my boy. Remember that's the master word—work.

FERGUSON: I'm going to marry that girl.

HOCHBERG: What for?

FERGUSON: I have to take care of her, don't I?

HOCHBERG: I see. You've saved some money then?

FERGUSON: Out of what?

HOCHBERG: Then how are you going to help her? How are you going to take care of her?

FERGUSON: I'm going into practice. . . .

HOCHBERG: Mid-Victorian idealism won't solve this problem, George. . . .

FERGUSON: That girl is human, isn't she? She needs me.

HOCHBERG: If you think you can provide for both of you by first starting practice—then you just don't know. . . .

FERGUSON: I'll manage somehow. I'm not afraid of that.

HOCHBERG: Remember Levine? I got a letter from him yesterday. Colorado. He's trying to build up a practice. . . . *The loudspeaker in the corridor starts calling "Dr. Hochberg."* They're starving, George. He begs me to lend him twenty dollars.

FERGUSON: I don't see what that has to do with me.

HOCHBERG: You didn't know him six years ago. He wouldn't *let* me help him, then. He was sure! So confident! And better equipped for practice than you are.

FERGUSON: Possibly!

HOCHBERG: I won't answer for Levine . . . at least he loved Katherine. But you don't love this girl. It was an accident—and for that you want to ruin yourself—the rest of your life—destroy your ambition, your ideals—fill yourself with bitterness, live day and night with a woman who will grow to despise you. . . .

FERGUSON: Dr. Hochberg. Please—it's no use. I've thought of all that! It doesn't make any difference. There's only one decent thing to do—and I'm going to do it.

HOCHBERG, *picks up the phone:* Yes? . . . Dr. Hochberg. . . . Yes, hello. . . . That's all right. Wait for me down in the—no . . . Come up here to 106, 106. Yes. Is the man there at the desk? Yes. Hello, Arthur. Please ask one of the orderlies to show this young lady up to 106. Yes, thank you.

FERGUSON: Is that Laura?

HOCHBERG: Yes.

FERGUSON: I can't see her now! I can't talk to her.

HOCHBERG: Don't be a child! You've got to see her and have this out. *Pause.*

FERGUSON: Dr. Hochberg, I want you to know that . . . I appreciate all you've done for me.

HOCHBERG: What have I done?

FERGUSON: I mean yesterday. I . . . I must have seemed very ungrateful. But it's just because there are so many other things that I thought I wanted.

HOCHBERG: I know. It's our instinct to live, to enjoy ourselves. All of us.

FERGUSON: I love Laura so much. She's so full of life and fun, and all the things I've missed for so many years. I just didn't have the guts to give them up. I kidded myself that I could have that, and still go on. And last night, I realized I kidded myself out of the most important thing that ever happened to me, a chance to work with you. . . .

HOCHBERG: Do you still want to? You can, if you do.

FERGUSON: No—not now.

HOCHBERG: But why? If you realize, now, what you really want . . .

FERGUSON: I'm going into practice, I told you. . . .

HOCHBERG: Now, George, calm down. Give yourself a chance to think it over.

FERGUSON: I've thought it over.

HOCHBERG: I warn you, George. You'll be sorry.

FERGUSON: I can't just ignore this!

HOCHBERG: In that case, you're through—you're finished—you're . . .

FERGUSON: All right! Then I am. Why not? What good's a profession that can't give you bread and butter after you've sweated out ten years of your life on it? And if I can't make a go of practice, I'll find a job at something else—and to hell with medicine! I won't starve. I'll always make a living. . . .

*LAURA appears in the doorway, accompanied by an ORDERLY.*

ORDERLY: Right here, miss.

FERGUSON: Good morning, Laura.

LAURA, *deliberately ignoring GEORGE, looking only at HOCHBERG, clipping every word:* Hello, Hocky. . . . Did you want me up here?

HOCHBERG: Yes. Come in, Laura.

LAURA: Sorry to call you so early, but . . .

HOCHBERG: It isn't early for me, Laura. . . . *She's still standing in the doorway, tense and hard. Impatiently.* Come in, come in. . . . *She wavers a moment, then enters.* Sit down.

LAURA: No. I'm in a hurry, Hocky. I just wanted to see you for a minute . . . alone.

HOCHBERG: Sit down, Laura.

LAURA: I suppose you wondered why I disappeared, yesterday.

HOCHBERG: No. . . . I heard all about it. . . .

LAURA: Oh, you did? A laugh, isn't it?

HOCHBERG: Not particularly.

LAURA: Well, you spanked me all right.

HOCHBERG: Harder than I meant, Laura. . . . Forgive me.

LAURA: Oh, that's all right. Better now than later, Hocky.

HOCHBERG: Will you please sit down, Laura? *LAURA, suddenly limp, sits down. HOCHBERG, scrutinizing her face closely.* Sleep much last night?

LAURA: Sure. Why not? *She puts a cigarette into her mouth, searches for a match. GEORGE's hand automatically goes to his pocket, to find a match for her.* Light, Hocky? *HOCHBERG gives her a light. She exhales a huge puff of smoke.* I'm washed up with the whole business, Hocky.

HOCHBERG: Yes, of course you are . . . of course.

FERGUSON: I'm sorry you feel so bitter about it, Laura. . . .

LAURA: How did you expect me to feel?

FERGUSON: I don't blame you. I . . .

LAURA: Thanks. That's sweet of you.

HOCHBERG: Neither do I blame him, Laura.

LAURA: There's no excuse for a thing like that—you know it, Hocky. None at all. . . .

HOCHBERG: I know nothing—except the human body, a little. And I haven't met the wise man or woman, Laura, whom impulse couldn't make a fool of. . . .

LAURA: If you want to reason that way, there isn't anything you couldn't justify.

HOCHBERG: I'm not trying to, Laura. It's so far beyond that. . . . *FERGUSON starts for the door.* Where are you going?

FERGUSON: Upstairs.

HOCHBERG: Wait, George! Wait a minute!

FERGUSON: There's nothing more to be said, Dr. Hochberg. Laura's perfectly right.

LAURA, *rises:* Don't leave on my account. I've got to go now, anyway. I've got to pack. I'm sailing on the Olympic, tonight. Going to get as far away from all this as I can. *She laughs.* Humph! I was making plans. I was worried all the time. . . . God! What a fool I was. . . .

HOCHBERG: Do you think he's having such an easy time of it?

LAURA: Oh, he'll take care of himself.

HOCHBERG: Maybe you'd better go home now, Laura.

LAURA: I think it was a pretty rotten trick.

HOCHBERG: Stop it! Laura, stop it!

LAURA: He had no time for me—he was too busy for me—but he did find time to . . . That's what hurts, Hocky! Hurts like the devil!

HOCHBERG: Don't you think I know how you feel, Laura?
   *The loudspeaker is calling,* "Dr. Hochberg."

LAURA: You think I still care? Well, I don't!

HOCHBERG: That's fine! Then it doesn't make any difference to you that right now he's throwing his life away. *Goes to the phone, picks it up, speaks into it.* Yes? Dr. Hochberg! *To* LAURA. He's going to marry her, Laura.

LAURA: No?

FERGUSON: Dr. Hochberg! Please!

HOCHBERG: Yes. And go into practice, and starve, and give up his studies, and maybe get out of medicine altogether. The thing he's meant for! And worked so hard for. *Into the phone, suddenly tense.* Yes! What! Prepare a hypo of caffeine, and adrenaline, long needle! At once! *He hangs up and hurries to the door.*

FERGUSON: Do you want me— ?

HOCHBERG: No . . . no . . . no. . . . You stay here! *He hurries out.*
   LAURA *stands there a moment looking at* GEORGE, *then starts to go.*

FERGUSON: Laura!

LAURA: What?

FERGUSON: I don't want you to go away feeling like this. . . .

LAURA: What difference does it make how I feel?

FERGUSON: A great deal . . . to me.

LAURA, *pause:* You love her, don't you?

FERGUSON: I love you, Laura.

LAURA, *laughs bitterly:* Yes, I'm sure you do.

FERGUSON, *grasps both of* LAURA's *arms tightly:* I don't care whether you believe it or not, Laura, it just happens that I do.

LAURA: Let go—let go my arm! You're . . .

FERGUSON: Sorry! *He turns from her and sinks down despondently on the bed.*

LAURA, *after a pause:* Then how? I don't quite understand. . . . I didn't sleep a wink last night, George. I was trying to figure this out. But it doesn't make sense . . . except that . . . I don't know. If you cared for me, how could you do that?

FERGUSON: I don't know myself, Laura. Everything had gone wrong that day. Six long operations. I had a battle with Cunningham, I lost a patient. . . . Things sort of kept piling up till I thought I'd bust . . . this kid came to my room for some notes . . . she was sympathetic and lonely herself, and . . . well . . . But after that I didn't see her around, and . . . I just forgot about it. You'd think she'd come to me when this happened. But she didn't. I know I should have looked her up. I know I was pretty small and rotten. I thought . . . I thought it didn't mean very much to her. But it did, Laura! Now she's up against it, and . . .

LAURA: If we meant anything at all to each other, you'd have come to me. I don't give a damn about ceremony! But the point is you didn't really care about me, George. Not for a minute.

FERGUSON: I wanted you more than anything else in the world that night, Laura. But we'd quarrelled and—you wouldn't even go out with me.

LAURA: It was that night?

FERGUSON: Yes.

LAURA: Oh!

FERGUSON: I didn't want to give up Hocky . . . and I didn't want to give you up . . . and I was fighting you . . . and . . .

LAURA: Through her?

FERGUSON: Yes. . . .

LAURA, *laughs bitterly:* And you say you loved me!

FERGUSON: If I hadn't, I'd have called quits then and there, Laura. I'd have gone to Vienna and worked my way through. That's what I was planning to do . . . before I met you. Alone in Vienna I'd really accomplish something. . . .

LAURA: Well, why don't you go on? Go on and do it, now. If it's so important

to you. I won't be around to distract you! Go on! . . . But you're not, you
see. You're going to marry a girl you say you don't care for. You're going
to let a casual incident rob you of all the things you say are important.

FERGUSON: It's not a casual incident, *any more*, Laura.

LAURA: All right, make your beautiful gestures. Marry her!

FERGUSON: I'm going to.

LAURA: Go ahead! And inside of a year you'll be hating the sight of each
other.

FERGUSON: That's a chance I'll have to take.

LAURA: You think you're being brave and strong, I suppose. But you're not.
You're a coward. You're doing it because it's the easiest way out. Because
you're afraid people'll say things about you. You have no backbone.

FERGUSON: Yes, Laura. You're right. I had no backbone when I let myself
be talked out of a chance to work with Hocky. And maybe to do something fine someday. But right now I have no choice. I'm not doing this
because I give a good Goddamn what anybody says or thinks; I'm doing
it because that girl's life is smashed, and I'm responsible, and I want to try
and help her pick up the pieces and put them together again. *He stops
short. LAURA is weeping quietly.* Oh, Laura! . . . Don't!

LAURA: I knew how you felt about Hocky and I shouldn't have . . . insisted.
I've been selfish, but it was only because I loved you so much. And . . . I
still do. That's the way I am, George. I can't help it. I . . .

*Enter HOCHBERG, slowly, his face drawn and grave, something tragic
written on it. He looks at FERGUSON.*

FERGUSON, *sensing HOCHBERG's look:* What is it, Doctor?

HOCHBERG: Miss Dennin died.

FERGUSON, *dazed:* What? . . .

LAURA: Oh, God!

HOCHBERG: A few minutes ago.

*FERGUSON looks blankly at DR. HOCHBERG, glances, as if for corrobora-
tion, at LAURA, and suddenly starts for the door. HOCHBERG catches his arm
and holds it tightly.*

HOCHBERG, *softly:* There's nothing you can do, George. Embolism! Went
into collapse! Died instantly.

FERGUSON, *almost inaudibly:* Oh! *He sinks down on the bed, his back to
them.*

HOCHBERG: George!

LAURA: Darling!

FERGUSON: Only a few hours ago . . . she was pleading with me for a chance
to live. . . . She was so young. She didn't want to die. . . .

LAURA: Stop it, George! Stop torturing yourself. Please! These things happen. It might have happened to anybody.

FERGUSON: Couldn't you do anything, Dr. Hochberg?

HOCHBERG: I tried . . . everything. Caffeine intravenously. Adrenaline directly into the heart. Useless! That little blood clot in the lung . . . and we're helpless. Forty years I've spent in medicine . . . and I couldn't help her.

FERGUSON: Then what's the use? What good is it all? Why go on? It takes everything from you, and when you need it most it leaves you helpless. We don't know anything. . . . We're only guessing.

HOCHBERG: We've been doing a little work on embolism . . . getting some results. It's slow, though . . . slow. Maybe, someday, George. . . .

FERGUSON: Someday? . . .

HOCHBERG: There isn't a man in medicine who hasn't said what you've said and meant it for a minute—all of us, George. And you're right. We are groping. We are guessing. But at least our guesses today are closer than they were twenty years ago. And twenty years from now, they'll be still closer. That's what we're here for. Mm . . . there's so much to be done. And so little time in which to do it . . . that one life is never long enough. . . . *He sighs.* It's not easy for any of us. But in the end our reward is something richer than simply living. Maybe it's a kind of success that world out there can't measure . . . maybe it's a kind of glory, George. *Pause.* Yes, question as much as we will—when the test comes we know—don't we, George?

FERGUSON: Yes. . . .

HOCHBERG, *goes slowly to the door, pauses there:* Er . . . we'll reduce that fracture at ten. Schedule the appendix at three . . . the gastric ulcer immediately afterwards.

FERGUSON: Yes, sir.

    HOCHBERG *goes.* LAURA *turns to* FERGUSON.

LAURA: Oh, darling! I'm so sorry! *Pause.* George, let's get away from here. Let's go someplace where we can talk this thing over quietly and sanely.

FERGUSON: No, Laura. This is where I belong!

LAURA: Yes. . . . *Pause.*

FERGUSON: You see . . .

LAURA: I understand. . . . *Pause.* Well . . . when you come back from Vienna, if Hocky'll let you off for a night, give me a ring! I'll be around. And maybe someday we'll get together, anyway.

    *The loudspeaker is heard calling,* "Dr. Ferguson!"

LAURA, *smiles wryly:* They're calling you.

FERGUSON: Yes.

LAURA: Work hard.

FERGUSON: So long, Laura. LAURA *tears herself away, and hurries out.* FERGUSON *stares after her till she disappears. The loudspeaker calls him back.*

*He goes to the phone, slowly, a bit stunned. He picks up the phone.* Yes?
Dr. Ferguson! . . . Who? . . . Oh, Mrs. D'Andrea? Sure! Your boy's all
right! Yes. Now, you mustn't cry, Mother! You mustn't! He's all right!
*With his free hand he is brushing the tears from his own eyes and nose,
for he is beginning to weep, himself. But you could never tell it by his
voice, which is strong with professional reassurance.* We'll fix his leg this
morning, and he'll be home in a week. Yes . . . he's going to live . . .
don't cry!

  *He is still reassuring her as the curtain descends.*

    *CURTAIN*

# DEAD END

THE NIGHT *Men in White* closed, I walked home slowly, alone, fully aware that a hit like this came once in a lifetime, and wondering would I ever do it again. I was living at 442 East 52nd Street; and after a restless night, I walked around to 53rd Street and sat on the wharf, watched the kids swimming in the filthy East River, glanced over at the posh River Club, recalled a quotation from Thomas Paine: "The contrast of affluence and wretchedness is like dead and living bodies chained together"—and I had my next play.

As I looked at the kids swimming in the East River, other ideas that had been waiting a long time began crowding in on my thoughts. There was a study I had made at Cornell in biology of the environment and its influences on the species; a similar study of slum environments, in economics. J. B. S. Haldane in England had given me a number of his books, and in them I had come across some further ideas about evolution and retrogressive evolution, and with that came a whole flock of those dreams we call memories, of myself as a kid on the East Side. I reached into my memory for all of the vivid language that kids in the city street use. Much of it fell into place immediately. I had been "cockalized" and participated in the gang effort of doing it to others. And so these ideas working on each other began to take form. In nine months, I was delivered of the play. Most of my other plays took much longer.

Language! At one of the readings, Garson Kanin and Martin Gabel, who were friends of mine, had invited George Abbott. At the end of the reading, Abbot had said, "Frankly, I'm shocked." But later on, after I had directed the play, he flattered me by inviting me to direct a play for him.

I of course clung to my faith in the Edward Gordon Craig concept of the dance element being the most important of the arts in the production. Craig dreamed that someday one man would come along and combine the play-

77

wright, the scene designer, and the director in one production. I now decided I would combine all three and reach for Edward Gordon Craig's ideal—no less.

I devised my own special *mise-en-scène* chart, each actor being represented by a map-pin of a certain color, tracing the movements of each actor with a thread from pin to pin. With one of these charts, it is quite possible today, over fifty years later, to duplicate the precise movements of the actors for the actions on three pages of the script.

Casting was a series of unusual experiences. Casting the "kids" was a problem. I wanted real "dead end kids." A few professionals came in—Gabe Dell; and Billy Halop, a star on radio then. We then toured about a dozen boy clubs in New York, and in Huntz Hall I found "Dippy." He was missing two front teeth and had a hopelessly goofy look. The three little kid brothers from up the block we found easily, particularly one very talented little kid who turned out to be Sidney Lumet. One young boy came in with the face of an angel, but was indeed an evil little bastard—"Spit," no question about it. Later, he proved so troublesome that we had to replace him with his understudy, Leo Gorcey. Gorcey looked even more like "Spit" than his predecessor, but he was a nice kid and quite independent. One day, I found him sitting on the wharf, looking very morose. He told me he was quitting because: "Acting is so boring. Same thing every night, same time, same spot, same words . . . boring. What I want to be is a plumber. There's always a fresh challenge and a new adventure, different people, different problems."

I told him that Sam Goldwyn had bought the film, and if he got the part, he would find making films less boring and more filled with variety than the stage, more of an exciting career. When I finally talked him into that, I walked away feeling guilty, but Gorcey had something.

Many years later, after he had become a star and been successful as one of the "Dead End Kids" in films, he wrote in his autobiography that had he followed his original inclination, he would have made more money and kept it because he would have had fewer wives and been much happier as a plumber. Forgive me, "Spit," wherever you are.

Working with the kids presented a number of difficulties. They had to be kept disciplined, something not in my nature, but I developed it. When the play opened, they were so good that a number of critics seemed to feel that I had just thrown a lot of kids loose on the stage and let them take over. Of course, nothing could have been further from the truth: I had to work twice as hard to discipline them and exercise great ingenuity to solve each one's separate problem.

When Samuel Goldwyn bought the play, he told me that he intended casting the boys from the regular supply of Hollywood child actors. I thought that was a mistake. I had spent many months working with these kids, and they were as close to the real thing as he could find; and although they had individual problems, they were gifted and precisely the characters—nobody could play them as well. Finally, with Willy Wyler's help, we persuaded Samuel Goldwyn to use them; he never regretted it. The film was a great hit. Then Mervyn LeRoy said that he would like to use the kids in a series of other films, calling them the Dead End Kids. I gave him permission, and they found a lifelong career.

Casting the others in the play went quite swiftly. Marjorie Main, her hair in wisps, her housedress soiled and shabby, auditioned for the gangster's mother. I talked to her one minute, listened to that strange, whiny voice, and I said, "Alright, you've got the part." What I didn't know till much later was that if I had said no, she would have been dead within an hour. She was down to a few dollars and no prospects. She was determined as a routine thing to go about casting calls that day, and then she would have gone home, turned on the gas, and joined her dead husband. Goldwyn used her in the film, and the qualities I saw in Marjorie Main were caught on the screen. She became a star with her own feature film.

Martin Gabel, who was a friend of mine, was cast as Hunk. I had him in mind for that role before I wrote the part. It was no accident that he did so well in it that, on his death, the *New York Times* still praised Martin Gabel in *Dead End* as having given one of the best performances of his distinguished career.

The part of the gangster was cast, believe it or not, from the actor's rear end. One night in Grand Central Station, walking to the train with Martin, who was going off to Chicago for the road company of *Three Men on a Horse,* suddenly, from the back, I noticed a lean figure with a strange, fascinating walk, as if he had a broken hip. I could see my gangster walking that way. I asked Martin if the man was an actor and, if so, a good one, and Martin told me he was. So I ran down way ahead and walked back leisurely to see what he looked like. His face was perfect. It was lean, bony, ferret-faced, dark—perfect. A few days later, I invited him to come to the office. We talked. He read. Perfect.

The girl came in, recommended by Gabel. She looked ideal. She had a sharp, bony face and crimson, crinkly hair. She read the part. She was just right. Sammy Levine was a friend, and his girl, Elspeth Eric, belonged to our group, so I invited her in. She read with raw power; she was splendid. A number of people read for "Gimpty," and one fellow I rejected never let me forget it. Over the years to come, whenever I met him, he would say, "You sorry now you didn't cast me in that part?" and I would invariably say, "No, Danny, you're still wrong for the part." He was Danny Kaye.

During rehearsals, Joe Downing, who played the gangster, and Sheila Trent, who played the prostitute, were extraordinarily good, but they both had one curious trait in common that, in tandem, made for a circus. When

Sheila would go up on a line, she would compulsively scream, "Ooh, ooh, ooh, ooh," four times and hit her head. When Downing went up on a line, he would say, "Ah, ah, ah," three times and slap his thigh! When they both went up on their lines together, the chorus of exclamations and gestures that went with it were excruciatingly funny.

One postscript: A number of years later, I was walking past the Belasco Theatre, which was dark; the restaurant next door had been burnt out, and the street looked as if it had been bombed. As I was thinking of *Dead End,* I heard, very distinctly, the prostitute's lines ringing out in the street, "Who the hell are you? What'd you send for me fer? What do you want?" The sounds were so real that I couldn't believe it was just memory. I turned, and across the street I saw Sheila Trent, dressed shabbily as she was in the play, stockings wrinkled, swinging her bag exactly as she had in the play; and she staggered down the block, drunk. A few months later, she died of alcoholism. It broke my heart. Sheila was such a splendid talent.

Originally, Geddes and I were going to coproduce the play, but I finally chose not to get involved in that phase of it, although I did have an ironbound contract that I was to cast the play, direct it without any interference, and that the set was to be designed according to my specifications. When we came to designing the set, Geddes wanted to design a series of levels as he had done with *Lysistrata.* I insisted that I wanted a superrealistic set. Geddes had never designed a realistic set, and he was afraid of it.

However, he did design a realistic set, which was great but had some serious defects. When we went to look at the Belasco Theatre, I saw the deep musicians' pit, and I knew at once what the defects were and how to correct them. The set had to be turned around 180 degrees so that the River, instead of being an upstage backdrop, was out front in the pit. This solved all my directorial problems. The actors would now sit downstage facing front (the River), as one normally did sitting on a wharf. The cyc upstage would no longer catch all the light and throw the characters upstage into silhouette.

Geddes refused. He called Jo Mielziner to design it, but Mielziner was too busy. I sat down with pencil and paper and demonstrated what I wanted, and finally Geddes agreed to do it, all the while protesting that it wouldn't work; but since our contract was ironbound, he had to design it my way. He did, but when he gave it to the builders, Cirker and Robbins, he told them that I was "a young man and crazy, stubborn—but this is what he wants, so build it; but I am going on record, saying it won't work."

He was wrong. It worked. The set was magnificent; more important, it was the most functional, working set. I managed to use all the areas not only on the stage floor, but all three-dimensional space above and below, using the pit as the River. It worked so well that it became his most famous set, and deservedly.

*Dead End*, now a fact accomplished, became a bigger hit than *Men in White*. It turned out to be the tenth-longest run on Broadway at the time, and it now established me, as one admirer so elegantly put it, as "no splash in the bedpan."

In fact, *Dead End* had an honorable influence. The Boys' Clubs of America tripled their contributions received, and there was a vast social and political reaction to the play. I recall the excitement in the theatre when Mrs. Roosevelt came to see the play three times and appeared backstage and spoke to the cast. Following that, the play was the first command performance in the White House presented at the request of the president. Subsequently, the president appointed a slum study commission. In the report of the commission, the play was quoted, and Senator Robert Wagner, who proposed the first slum-clearance legislation in the Congress of the United States, publicly credited the play with being responsible for that legislation.

S.K.

*Sculpture of the Dead End Kids by Sidney Kingsley. Courtesy of Sidney Kingsley.*

# DEAD END

The contrast of affluence and wretchedness is like dead and living bodies chained together.

> —*Thomas Paine*

Presented by Norman Bel Geddes at the Belasco Theatre, New York, on
October 28, 1935, with the following cast:

| | |
|---|---|
| GIMPTY | Theodore Newton |
| T.B. | Gabriel Dell |
| TOMMY | Billy Halop |
| DIPPY | Huntz Hall |
| ANGEL | Bobby Jordan |
| SPIT | Charles R. Duncan |
| DOORMAN | George Cotton |
| OLD LADY | Marie R. Burke |
| OLD GENTLEMAN | George N. Price |
| 1ST CHAUFFEUR | Charles Benjamin |
| "BABY-FACE" MARTIN | Joseph Downing |
| HUNK | Martin Gabel |
| PHILIP GRISWALD | Charles Bellin |
| GOVERNESS | Sidonie Espero |
| MILTY | Bernard Punsly |
| DRINA | Elspeth Eric |
| MR. GRISWALD | Carroll Ashburn |
| MR. JONES | Louis Lord |
| KAY | Margaret Mullen |

82

| | |
|---|---|
| JACK HILTON | Cyril Gordon Weld |
| LADY WITH DOG | Margaret Linden |
| THREE SMALL BOYS | Billy Winston, |
| | Joseph Taibi, |
| | Sidney Lumet |
| 2ND CHAUFFEUR | Richard Clark |
| SECOND AVENUE BOYS | David Gorcey, |
| | Leo Gorcey |
| MRS. MARTIN | Marjorie Main |
| PATROLMAN MULLIGAN | Robert J. Mulligan |
| FRANCEY | Sheila Trent |
| G-MEN | Francis de Sales, |
| | Dan Duryea, |
| | Edward P. Goodnow, |
| POLICEMEN | Francis G. Cleveland, |
| | William Toubin |
| PLAINCLOTHESMAN | Harry Selby |
| INTERN | Philip Bourneuf |
| MEDICAL EXAMINER | Lewis L. Russel |
| SAILOR | Bernard Zaneville |

A CROWD: Inhabitants of East River Terrace, ambulance men and others

Staged by Sidney Kingsley
Setting by Norman Bel Geddes

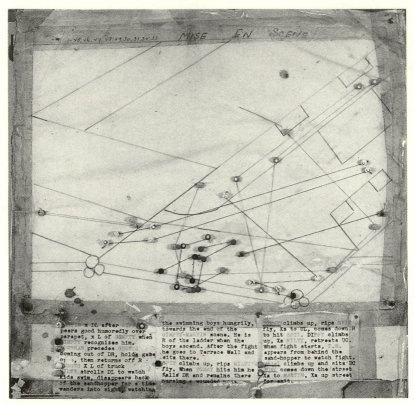

*Sidney Kingsley's* mise-en-scène *from act 1 of* Dead End, *actors designated by pins with colored heads. Courtesy of Sidney Kingsley.*

**ACT ONE**

*Dead End of a New York street, ending in a wharf over the East River. To the left is a high terrace and a white iron gate leading to the back of the exclusive East River Terrace Apartments. Hugging the terrace and filing up the street are a series of squalid tenement houses.*

*Beyond the wharf is the East River, covered by a swirling scum an inch thick. A brown river, mucky with floating refuse and offal. A hundred sewers vomit their guts into it. Uptown of the wharf as we float down Hell Gate, the River voices its defiant protest in fierce whirlpools and stumbling rapids, groaning. Further down, we pass under the arch of the Queensboro Bridge, spired, delicate, weblike in superstructure, powerful and brutal in the stone and steel which it plants like uncouth giant feet on the earth. In its hop, skip, and jump over the River it has planted one such foot on the Island called Welfare, once the home of hospital, insane asylum, and prison, now being dismantled, an eyesore to the fastidious who have recently become its neighbors. And here on the shore, along the Fifties, is a strange sight. Set plumb down in the midst of slums, antique warehouses, discarded breweries, slaughterhouses, electrical works, gas tanks, loading cranes, and coal-chutes, the very wealthy have begun to establish their city residence in huge, new, palatial apartments.*

*The East River Terrace is one of these. Looking up this street from the vantage of the River, we see only a small portion of the back terrace and a gate; but they are enough to suggest the towering magnificence of the whole structure. The wall is of rich, heavy masonry, guarded at the top by a row of pikes. Beyond the pikes, shutting off the view of the squalid street below, is a thick edging of lush green shrubbery. And beyond that, a glimpse of the tops of gaily colored sun umbrellas. Occasionally, the clink of glasses and laughter filter through the shrubs. The exposed sidewall of the tenement is whitewashed and ornamented with an elaborate, ivy-covered trellis to hide its ugliness. The gateposts are crowned with brass ship lanterns, one red, one green. Through the gateway is a catwalk which leads to a floating dock, where the inhabitants of this apartment moor their boats and yachts.*

*Contrasting sharply with all this richness is the mis-eased street below, filthy, strewn with torn newspapers and garbage from the tenements. The tenement houses are close, dark, and crumbling. They crowd each other. Where there are curtains in the windows, they are streaked and faded; where there are none, we see through to hideous, water-stained, peeling wallpaper, and old, broken-down furniture. The fire escapes are cluttered with gutted mattresses and quilts, old clothes, breadboxes, milk bottles, a canary cage, an occasional potted plant struggling for life.*

*To the right is a huge, red sand hopper, standing on stilts of heavy timber several stories tall. Up the street, blocking the view, is a Caterpillar steam shovel. Beyond it, way over to the west, are the sky-scraping parallelepipeds of Radio City. An alleyway between two tenements tied together by droop-ing lines of wash gives us a distant glimpse of the mighty Empire State Build-ing, rearing its useless mooring tower a quarter of a mile into the clouds.*

*At the juncture of tenement house and terrace is a police callbox; at the juncture of the street and wharf is a police stanchion bearing the warning "Dead End."*

*The boards of the wharf are weather-beaten and deeply grained; the piles are stained green with algae to where the water licks, and brown above. A ladder nailed to the beams dips down into the river. The sunlight tossed from the waves dances across the piles to the musical lap of the water. Other river sounds counterpoint the orchestration: the bells and the whistles, the clink and the chug of passing boats.*

*A gang of boys are swimming in the sewerage at the foot of the wharf, splashing about and enjoying it immensely. Some of them wear torn bathing trunks, others are nude. Their speech is a rhythmic, shocking jargon that would put a truck driver to blush.*

*There are a few onlookers. A fat, greasy woman leans out a tenement window. She is peeling an orange and throwing the peels into the street. A sensitive-faced young man, in a patched, frayed shirt, open at the neck, is sitting on one of the piles. In his lap is a drawing board. Occasionally he will work feverishly, using pencil and triangular ruler, then he will let the pencil droop, and stare out over the river with deep-set eyes, dream-laden, moody.*

*A tubercular-looking boy about sixteen is up near the hopper, pitching pennies to the sidewalk. There is a splash of water, a loud derisive laugh, and up the ladder climbs a boy, lean, lithe, long-limbed, snub-nosed, his cheeks puffed with water. Reaching the top of the ladder, he leans over and squirts out the water. A yelp below. He laughs again and cries:*

"Gotcha dat time!"

*Two boys come running down the street toward the wharf. One, a tiny Italian with a great shock of blue-black hair, is dangling a shoe box almost as big as himself; the other, a gawky Polack, head shaven, cretinous, adenoi-dal, is slapping his thigh with a rolled newspaper as he runs. They shout:*

"Hi ya, Tommy?"

TOMMY: H'lo Angel! H'lo Dippy! ANGEL *unslings his box, and starts tearing off his clothes. A squat boy with a brutish face, snot bubbling from his nostrils, climbs up after* TOMMY. *As he reaches the top and sees the others, he shouts in a mocking singsong,* "Dopey Dippy, dopey Dippy, dopey Dippy!"

DIPPY: Shat ap, will ya, Spit!

SPIT, *spitting through his teeth at* DIPPY, *who is stripping his jersey over his head:* Right inna belly-button! *Laughs and climbs onto the wharf to sprawl next to* TOMMY. DIPPY *mumbles and wipes out his navel with his finger.*

TOMMY: Lay off 'im, why doncha?

SPIT: I'll knock 'im innis eye!

TOMMY: Wassamattuh? Yuh a wise guy er a boy scout? C'mon in, Dippy!

ANGEL: Howza wawda, Tommy?

TOMMY: Boy! Duh nuts!

SPIT: Geeze, great!

ANGEL: Cold?

TOMMY: Nah. Swell. Jus' right. *Wiping off some of the river filth that has clung to him.* Boy, deah's a lot a junk inna wawda tuhday!

DIPPY, *pointing to some dirt on* SPIT's *back:* Wat's 'at? *He touches* SPIT, *smells his finger and makes a wry face.* Pee—ew, whadda stink! SPIT *plucks off a huge gob of filth and throws it at* DIPPY. DIPPY *whines.* What yuh wanna do dat fuh?

SPIT: Aw, I'll mobilize yuh!

TOMMY: Leave 'im alone! *To* DIPPY. Whyn't yuh keep yuh trap shut, huh?

DIPPY: He trew dat crap on me! I wuz . . .

TOMMY: O.K. O.K. O.K. *Pointing at some imaginary object near the sand hopper.* Hey, felluhs, look! *All look off.* TOMMY *sticks his forefinger next to* SPIT's *averted nose.* Hey, Spit! SPIT *turns his head and bumps his nose on* TOMMY's *finger. The boys laugh.* Nex' time leave 'im alone, see?

*The cadaverous-looking lad picks up his pennies, and comes down to the others, boasting,* "Boy, I git a crack all a time!"

TOMMY, *rising:* Yeah? Aw right, T.B., I'll pitch yuh.

T.B.: O.K. C'mon.

TOMMY: Lemme a couple.

T.B.: Yuh ain't got 'ny?

TOMMY: Come on! I'll pay yuh back. TOMMY *and T.B. go up to the hopper and pitch pennies to the sidewalk.*

SPIT, *turning to* DIPPY, *makes a swipe at him.* DIPPY *backs away:* Two fuh flinchin' . . . two fuh flinchin'!

DIPPY: I di' not.

SPIT: Yuh did so.

DIPPY: I di' not.

ANGEL: Whyn't cha choose? Choose 'im! Choose fer it!

SPIT, *scrambling to his feet:* O.K. Odds!

ANGEL: Go on!

DIPPY: Evens! *SPIT and DIPPY match fingers.* Once fuh me. See? Cheatin' shows!

SPIT: Come on! Once fuh me. Twice fuh me. An' tree fuh me. Cheatin' shows? Yeah. Boy, ahl knock yuh fer a loop!

ANGEL: Go on, Dippy, yuh lost. Yuh git yer lumps.

DIPPY, *whining:* Hey, Tommy. . . .

SPIT, *grabbing DIPPY's rolled newspaper:* Come on! *He bangs DIPPY twice on the head.*

DIPPY: Ow! . . . Ow! . . . Ow! Ah, yuh louse. Yuh didn't have tuh hit me so hahd. Wid' all his might he hit me. Wid' all his might, duh son uva bitch!

TOMMY, *still absorbed in pitching pennies with T.B.:* Whyn't yuh pick on a kid who kin fight back?

SPIT: Aw-w-w!

TOMMY: Ah!

The DOORMAN, *a giant in powder-blue uniform with gilt buttons and braid, opens the gate of the apartment house, crosses to the end of the side-walk and blows a whistle, then signals to someone up the street to come down. He turns to speak to an aristocratic* OLD GENTLEMAN *and* OLD LADY *who appear in the gateway of the East River Terrace.*

DOORMAN: I'm so sorry, ma'am, but it'll only be for a day or two.

OLD LADY: That's quite all right.

OLD GENTLEMAN, *arthritic, grumpy, walking slowly and with effort:* It isn't at all. There's no reason why we should have to walk half a block to the car.

A *colored man in chauffeur's uniform comes down the sidewalk.*

DOORMAN: I'm so sorry, sir.

OLD LADY: That's quite all right. *She pauses a moment, surveying the boys.* Look at this!

OLD GENTLEMAN: Humph! I've seen it from the balcony.

ANGEL: Hey, look, guys! Dey usin' a back daw.

TOMMY: I wonduh why.

DIPPY, *familiarly, to the young man who is sketching:* Duh yuh know, Gimpty? Hey, Gimpty?

GIMPTY: What?

DIPPY: Duh yuh know why?

GIMPTY: Why what?

DIPPY: Why dey usin' a back daw.

GIMPTY: Are they?

DIPPY: Yeah.

GIMPTY: No . . . no, I don't.

*The* COLORED CHAUFFEUR *salutes the* OLD MAN *and offers him an arm to lean on.*

CHAUFFEUR: Good afternoon, sir, I'm sorry I couldn't drive the car around the . . .

OLD LADY: That's all right, Jordan. Look at these youngsters! Aren't they sweet?

OLD GENTLEMAN: Sweet? Yes . . . from a distance!

*They walk up the street, out of sight. A passing tug blasts the air with its foghorn.* TOMMY, *having won at penny-pitching, puts the pennies in the pocket of his trousers, which are hanging on the hopper. T.B., disconsolate, goes to* ANGEL.

T.B.: Dat cleans me. I dunno. I kin always git a crack when I'm playin' by myself. *He watches* ANGEL, *who is fussing with a scrap of newspaper and some strange, brown substance.* Watcha got deah?

ANGEL: It's a dried up hawse-ball.

T.B.: Watcha doin'?

ANGEL: I'm gonna make some cigarettes. Some guy tole me—yuh kin make cigarettes outa dem.

T.B.: Yeah?

ANGEL: Yeah. I'm gonna try it.

T.B.: I never hoid a dat.

ANGEL: It's good. Some guy tole me.

TOMMY: Aw, yuh crazy.

ANGEL: Naw . . . it's good.

T.B.: Deah wuz a guy at rifawn school once used tuh smoke marywanna. Yuh know what dat is? Dope. It's like dope. It's dope. It gives yuh dreams.

ANGEL: Didja try it?

T.B.: Nah. I can't smoke on accoun' a my T.B. It gits me. I cough like anyt'ing.

ANGEL, *rises and crosses to* GIMPTY: Hey, Gimpty, got a match?

T.B., *murmurs:* My pratt and your face. Dat's a good match! *Laughs to himself.*

GIMPTY: What for?

DIPPY: He's makin' cigarettes outa hawse-balls.

GIMPTY: Out of what?

ANGEL: Hawse-balls.

GIMPTY: Throw it away, you crazy fool. You want to get sick?

ANGEL: I kin smoke. Whadda yuh t'ink I yam?

GIMPTY: Listen. I read about a guy once who smoked that stuff. You know what happened to him.

ANGEL: What?

GIMPTY: Great big things grew right out of his head.

ANGEL, *turning away from* GIMPTY, *with disgust:* Aw-w-w, go wan.

GIMPTY: Listen . . . if I give you a good one, will you throw that away?

ANGEL, *turning back eagerly:* Sure!

GIMPTY *appropriates* ANGEL's *horrible cigarette and throws it into the water; then takes a sack of tobacco from his pocket, adeptly rolls a cigarette and holds it out to* ANGEL: Here! Stick out your tongue. ANGEL *licks the paper.* GIMPTY *completes rolling the cigarette and gives it to him.* There you are! Now don't try that again. You'll get sick as a dog. Remember . . . I'm tellin' you.

ANGEL, *proudly exhibiting his cigarette:* Boy! Hey, felluhs, look! Gimpty gimme a butt. *To* T.B. Gimme a light, T.B. T.B. *fishes some matches from his pocket and lights* ANGEL's *cigarette.*

DIPPY, *dashing over to* GIMPTY: Me too, Gimpty! Gimme! Yew know me! Yew know me! DIPPY, TOMMY, *and* SPIT *descend on* GIMPTY, *swarming over him like a horde of locusts. They hold out their hands and beg plaintively.* "Give us one! Yew know us, Gimpty."

GIMPTY: No! No! No more! Beat it! That's all! *They only plead the louder.* I said that's all. Don't you understand English? You want a boot in the behind?

*Two men come down the street. One, tall, young, rather good-looking in a vicious way; the other, older, shorter, squat, a sledgehammer build. The first has thin nervous lips, narrow agate eyes, bloodshot. A peculiarly glossy face, as if the skin had been stretched taut over the cheekbones, which are several sizes too large for the lean jaw underneath. Here is a man given to sudden volcanic violences that come and are gone in a breath. His movements are sharp, jerky; his reflexes exaggerated, those of a high-strung man whose nerves are beginning to snap under some constant strain. He covers it, though, with a cocky swagger. He walks leaning forward, hips thrown back, almost as if out of joint. He wears a gray, turned-down fedora, an expensive suit, sharpy style, the coat a bit too tight at the waist, pleated trousers, and gray suede shoes. His squat companion is dressed almost identically, but was not designed to wear such clothes. His trousers hang on his hips, revealing a bulge of shirtwaist between vest and trouser-top, his barrel of a chest is too thick for his jacket, his arms too long for the sleeves. His huge fingers you notice at once! Thick stubs sticking out of the shapeless bags of his hands like the teats of a cow. The two men come down almost to the edge of the wharf. The tall one lights a cigarette, looks about, smiles, shakes his head, and talks* sotto voce *to his companion.*

TOMMY, *to* GIMPTY: Aw, ta hell wid' yuh! Cheap skate!

*The boys walk away, disgusted.* GIMPTY *rolls another cigarette, lights it, and returns to his drawingboard.*

SPIT: Yeah, ta hell wid' im!

DIPPY: Yeah, ta hell wid' im!

SPIT, *crosses to his clothes, which are hanging from a nail on the hopper:* I dun need hisn. I gotta stack a butts I picked up I'm savin'.

TOMMY: Give us one.

DIPPY: Yeah! Give us one!

SPIT: Nah. I'm savin' 'em.

TOMMY: Don' be a miser. SPIT *takes out a tobacco tin, opens it, exposing a rare collection of cigarette ends gleaned from the streets. Grudgingly he hands* TOMMY *and* DIPPY *a butt each, then selects a choice one for himself.* Gimme a light, T.B. *They all light up and puff away with huge satisfaction.*

ANGEL, *suddenly aware of the two strangers:* Shine, mistah? *The tall fellow shakes his hand and turns away.* A good shine. Come on! *To the other.* Yew? *The squat man glares at him and growls,* "Yuh cockeyed? Can't yuh see we got one?"

ANGEL, *turns away, muttering:* Aw . . . call 'at a shine?

*The* DOORMAN *comes to the gate and holds it open. A* GOVERNESS, *accompanied by a well-dressed, delicate-featured little boy, comes out of the Terrace Apartments. The* GOVERNESS *talks with a marked French accent. She nods to the* DOORMAN.

GOVERNESS: Good afternoon.

DOORMAN: Good afternoon, ma'am.

GOVERNESS: But . . . where is our chauffeur?

DOORMAN: I think he's on the corner with the cabdrivers. Shall I get him?

GOVERNESS: Never mind. *To the little boy.* Wait here. *Attends moi ici, mon cheri.*

*The* DOORMAN *goes in, closing the gate behind him. The little boy, surveying the curious scene, answers, a bit distracted,* "All right, I'll . . ." *When he opens his mouth, he shows a shiny, gold orthodontic brace.*

GOVERNESS: *Mais, Philippe! En français!*

PHILIP, *obediently: Oui, mademoiselle, j'attendrai.*

GOVERNESS: *Très bien. J'y reviendrai de suite . . . dans deux minutes.*

PHILIP: *Oui, oui, mademoiselle.*

*She hurries up the sidewalk and out of sight.*

TOMMY: Wee-wee! He's godda go wee-wee! *All the boys shout with laughter.*

DIPPY: Do a swan-dive, Tommy. 'At's wad I like.

TOMMY: OK. Hole my butt. *He hands his cigarette to* DIPPY. Hey, kid! Hey, yew! Hey, wee-wee! PHILIP *looks at him.* Yuh wanna see sumpm? A swan-dive. Watch! TOMMY *dashes off, under the hopper. We hear his* "Whe-e-e" *and a splash. The boys cluck approval.*

PHILIP: What's so wonderful about that?

ANGEL: Aw, yuh fat tub a buttuh, it's more'n yew kin do.

PHILIP: That shows how much you know.

T.B.: I bet a dollar he can't even swim.

PHILIP: I can too.

T.B.: Ah, balonee!

PHILIP: Balonee yourself! We've a pool in there and I swim every day . . . with instruction.

SPIT: Aw, bushwah! TOMMY *appears on the ladder.* DIPPY *hands him his cigarette.*

DIPPY: He sez dey godda pool in 'ere.

TOMMY: How wuzat swan-dive?

DIPPY: He sez it wuz lousy.

TOMMY, *climbing over the parapet and crossing to* PHILIP, *belligerently:* Oh yeah? What wuza mattuh wid' it? Kin yew do betta?

PHILIP: A trillion times.

TOMMY: Awright. Lessee yuh.

PHILIP: Where?

TOMMY: Heah!

PHILIP: Here?

TOMMY: Yeah, heah. Yew hoid me. Yew ain't deef. *Turns to the others.* His eahs ovuhlap, dat's it! *They roar with laughter.*

PHILIP: I wouldn't swim here.

T.B.: He's yelluh, dat's what! Dat's what! He's godda yelluh streak up 'is back a mile wide.

PHILIP: It's dirty here.

DIPPY, *shocked:* Doity!

T.B., *very indignant:* Doity! He sez doity. He sez it's doity! I'll sock 'im!

ANGEL: Lil fairy!

SPIT: Wassamattuh? Yuh sca'd yuh git a lil doit on yuh?

PHILIP: Besides, I haven't got my suit.

TOMMY: Well, go in bareass.

T.B.: Yeah, wassamattuh wid' bareass?

PHILIP: And besides, I'm not allowed to.

DIPPY, *singsong:* Sissy, sissy, sucks his mamma's titty!

PHILIP: Sticks and stones may break my bones, but names will never hurt me. *The boys crowd him back against the gate.*

TOMMY: Ah, ahl spit in yuh eye an' drown yuh. Hey, what's 'at junk yuh got in yuh mout . . . like a hawse?

PHILIP: It's a brace, to make my teeth straight.

TOMMY: Wha-a-at? I could do dat wid' one wallop! *The gang roars with laughter.*

PHILIP: You try and you'll be arrested.

SPIT: Yeah?

TOMMY, *contemptuously:* Look who's gonna arrest us!

PHILIP: My uncle's a judge.

TOMMY: Balonee!

PHILIP: Did you ever hear of Judge Griswald?

ANGEL: So what? So I know a guy whose brudduh's a detective. He'll git us out.

T.B.: Yeah? Did yuh evuh hear a Judge Poikins! Well, he's a frien' a mine, see? He sent me to rifawm school once.

DOORMAN, *appears, bellowing:* What's the matter? Get away from here, you! *They scatter, razzing him. He turns to* PHILIP. Were they bothering you?

PHILIP: No, I don't pay any attention to them.

 *The* DOORMAN *opens the gate and both he and* PHILIP *go in. The boys laugh and mock them.* DIPPY, *preoccupied with the phenomena of his body, suddenly discovers a lone hair on his chest.*

DIPPY: Boy! Gee! Hey, I godda hair! *He caresses it, proudly. T.B. comes over, inspects the hair, admires it, then suddenly plucks it out, and runs away laughing and holding up the trophy.* DIPPY *yips, first with pain, then with rage.* TOMMY *finds an old discarded broom in the litter under the hopper. He balances it skillfully on the palm of his hand.*

SPIT: Gese, I'm hungry!

TOMMY: Me too!

ANGEL: Boy, I'm so hungry I could eat a live dog.

DIPPY, *looks up from his wounded chest:* Boy, I could eat a hot dog.

ANGEL: Wid' sour-kraut!

DIPPY: Yeah.

ANGEL, *licking his lips and patting his belly:* Yum.

SPIT: Hey, should we go tuh Schultzie's 'n' see if we kin snitch sumpm?

TOMMY, *balancing the broom:* Nah, Schultzie's wise tuh us.

ANGEL: We could try some udduh staws.

TOMMY, *still balancing the broom:* Nah, dey're all wise tuh us. Duh minute we walk in 'ey ask us wadda we want. If we had some dough, while one uv us wuz buyin' sumpm de udduh guys could swipe some stuff, see? I got faw cents, but 'at ain' enough. *He drops the broom, and becomes the man of action.* Anybody got any dough heah? Hey, yew, Angel, yuh got some?

ANGEL: No, I ain'.

TOMMY: Come on! Don' hole out!

ANGEL: Honest! I didn' git no customuh dis mawnin'.

TOMMY: Weah's 'is pants? Look in 'is pants! *T.B. and SPIT rush to the hopper, grab ANGEL's pants, and start rifling the pockets. ANGEL follows them, yelling.*

ANGEL: Hey! Git outa deah! Git outa deah!

T.B.: Nuttin' but a couple a stamps 'n' a boy-scout knife.

SPIT, *taking the knife himself:* Oh baby, kin I have dis?

ANGEL, *follows SPIT:* No, I need it.

SPIT: No, yuh don't.

ANGEL: Aw, Spit, gimme my knife!

SPIT, *mocking his accent:* Watsa ma'? Piza Taliana? *He spits at him.* Right inee ear! Ha!

ANGEL *backs a step and wipes out his ear with a finger:* Ah, yuh louse! Ast me fuh sumpm sometime 'n' see watcha git.

TOMMY: Giv'im 'is knife!

SPIT: Da hell I will!

ANGEL: Aw, Spit, gimme my knife! Tommy, make 'im, will yuh?

TOMMY: Gimme dat knife!

SPIT: What fuh?

TOMMY, *makes a fist and waves it in front of SPIT's nose:* Fuh dis . . . right in yuh bugle! *He grabs the knife and examines it.* Gese, dat's a knife! Five blades! Boy, I'd like one like 'at.

*Enter from the lower tenement door, a young boy of about twelve, a bit timid, neatly dressed, obvious Semitic features.*

ANGEL: Aw, Tommy, I need it. I godda use it. Honest!

TOMMY, *gives him his knife:* Here! Stop squawkin'! Don' say I nevuh gave yuh nuttin'!

ANGEL: Tanks, Tommy. Dat's white.

TOMMY, *good-naturedly:* Ah, shat ap! *To DIPPY, who sits reflectively picking his nose.* Hey, Dippy! Pick me a big juicy one! *DIPPY grins, rolls the resinous matter into a little ball, and flicks it at TOMMY. TOMMY laughs, and trots up the street to join the others who are seated on a tenement stoop. The TALL MAN turns from his conversation with his companion, and calls to DIPPY, "Hey, you!"*

DIPPY: What?

THE TALL ONE: Wanna run a errand fuh me?

THE SQUAT ONE: *offers:* I'll go, chief. What is it?

DIPPY: Sure. Wheah?

THE TALL ONE, *points to a tenement house up the block:* 418 . . . fourth floor . . . Mrs. Martin. Tell her a friend a hers wants a see her here.

DIPPY: O.K. 418? O.K. *He trots off.*

GIMPTY, *who has looked up at the sound of the TALL ONE's voice:* Don't

I know you from somewhere? *The stranger's lips compress—*"no." I could've sworn I . . .

SQUAT MAN, *comes over and mutters in a thick voice full of threat:* He said no, didn' he? *The other restrains him with a touch on the arm.*

GIMPTY: Sorry. *He looks down at his drawing. The two walk away, and stand leaning against the wall, talking in low tones. The boys on the stoop suddenly notice the little Jewish boy who is peering over the wharf.*

T.B.: Hey, look! Deah's 'at new kid 'at moved aroun' a block.

SPIT: 'At's 'at Jew kid! *They rise and come down toward him.*

TOMMY: Hey, kid!

ANGEL: Hey, kid!

MILTY, *looks up:* Wadda yuh want?

SPIT: Come heah, Ikey! Come on! Don' be so slow. *He comes over, eager to join them, yet scared.*

TOMMY: Yew da noo kid onna block, aintcha?

MILTY: Yeah.

TOMMY: Watsya name?

MILTY: Milton. Milton Schwartz.

TOMMY: Yuh wanna belong tuh are gang?

MILTY, *eagerly:* Yeah. Shuah.

TOMMY: Got 'ny dough? Yuh godda be ineetiated.

MILTY: I god tree sants.

TOMMY: Gimme it!

SPIT, *prodding him in the ribs:* Give it tuh 'im!

T.B., *prodding him harder and pulling him around:* Go on!

TOMMY, *pulling him back:* Come on! Don' hole out! MILTY *fishes out three cents and hands them to* TOMMY. 'At's all yuh got?

MILTY: Yeah.

SPIT: Sure?

MILTY: Hones'.

TOMMY: Soich 'im! *They start to go through his pockets.*

MILTY, *turns his pockets inside out:* Don'! Yuh don' haf tuh. Look!

SPIT: Ah, you punk!

TOMMY: Listen, yew! If yuh wanna belong to dis gang, yuh godda git a quatuh.

MILTY: A quatuh? Wheah ahm gonna git a quatuh fum?

SPIT: Fum yuh ole lady.

MILTY: She woodn gimme no quatuh.

SPIT: Yuh know wheah she keeps huh money, doncha?

MILTY: Dat's a sin tuh steal.

SPIT, *mocking his accent:* Wassamattuh, Ikey?

MILTY: Don' make fun on me. I can' help it.

SPIT, *contemptuously:* Yuh scared tuh snitch a quatuh? Gese, she won' fin' out.

MILTY: Yes, she would.

SPIT, *still mocking him:* Oh, she counts huh money all a time, huh, Jakey Ikey?

MILTY: Stop dat! Gimme back my tree sants. I don' wanna hang out wid' youse.

TOMMY, *to SPIT:* Yuh godda watch-pocket, aincha?

SPIT: Yeah.

TOMMY: Guard dis dough! *He hands the money to* SPIT, *who puts it in his pocket. They walk away, completely ignoring* MILTY.

MILTY, *follows them, murmuring tremulously:* Gimme back my tree sants!

SPIT, *whispers to the others:* Let's cockalize him!

ANGEL: Wadda yuh say, Tommy?

TOMMY: O.K.

T.B.: Come on!

ANGEL *crosses nonchalantly behind* MILTY, *then crouches on his hands and knees, unnoticed. The others turn and slowly approach him. Suddenly* TOMMY *pushes* MILTY, *who stumbles backward and trips over* ANGEL, *feet flying up. They all pounce on the prostrate boy, pin his arms and legs to the ground, unbutton his pants, pull up his shirt.*

TOMMY: Gimme some a dat doit!

SPIT *scoops up a handful of dirt:* Heah! *They rub it into* MILTY's *groin. He kicks and screams, hysterically laughing at the sensation. When he's through rubbing in the filth,* TOMMY *coughs up a huge wad of saliva and spits on* MILTY's *organ. Each of them spit, once round the circle. The* TALL ONE *and the* SQUAT ONE *laugh. A tattoo of heels running down the street! A whirlwind hits the group, and the boys are dispersed right and left. The whirlwind is a girl not much bigger than* TOMMY, *with a face resembling his—pushed-up nose and freckles. She slaps and pulls and pushes the boys, who scatter away, laughing and shouting. She stands there, eyes blazing.*

TOMMY: Aw scram, will yuh, Drina! Scram!

DRINA: Shut up! *She helps the sobbing* MILTY *to his feet, brushes him off, and wipes his face, comforting him. On second glance she is not the child she seemed. Her simple dress, her hair combed back of the ears and held in place with a cheap celluloid clasp, her lithe, boyish figure combine to create the illusion of a very young girl. When she comforts* MILTY, *however, it is apparent in the mature quality of her solicitude that she is much older—in her earlier twenties. The* TALL ONE *grins at her. She throws him a contemptuous side-glance and rebukes him sharply.*

DRINA: You ought to be ashamed of yourself, standing there and letting them pile up on this kid.

TOMMY: Aw, Drina, will yuh butt outa dis?

DRINA, *to the snivelling boy:* Are you hurt? *To the* TALL ONE. Why didn't you stop 'em?

THE TALL ONE: What fer? It'll do 'im good.

DRINA, *furiously:* Oh, yeah? I suppose it'll do you good if I crack your face, huh?

THE TALL ONE: Oh, lady, yuh scare me!

DRINA: Fresh guy, huh?

THE SQUAT ONE, *walks over to her, his face screwed up in disgust:* Shut yuh big mouth or I'll . . .

THE TALL ONE, *sharply:* Hunk! Cut it! HUNK *obeys instantly. They walk away to the bulwark.*

TOMMY: Aw, Drina, why dontcha butt outa my business?

DRINA: Wait till I get you home, I'll show you butt out of . . . TOMMY *scratches his head. She places her hands on her hips and frowns.* What are you scratchin' your head for? Are you buggy again? *Her authoritative, maternal concern gives her the air of a little girl playing house.*

TOMMY: Aw, git out a heah or I'll bust yuh one!

DRINA: That's fine talk, Tommy . . . bust you one! *He scratches again.* There you go again! Scratchin'! *She crosses to him.* Come on home! I'm gonna wash your head.

TOMMY: Aw, lemme alone. All a time yuh bodderin' me. . . . *Runs away from* DRINA *and climbs up the hopper like a monkey, out of her reach.*

DRINA, *to* GIMPTY: Pete, why didn't you stop 'em?

GIMPTY: I'm sorry, Drina. I didn't notice what was happenin'. I was thinkin' about somethin'.

DRINA: Yeah? *She turns to* TOMMY, *dangling high on his perch.* Tommy, did you go to school today?

TOMMY: Sure.

DRINA: If you're lying, Tommy, I'll kill you.

TOMMY, *wiggling his toes at her:* Aw, nuts!

DRINA, *to* MILTY, *who is still sobbing:* What's the matter? Did they hurt you?

MILTY: Dey took my money.

DRINA: They did? How much?

MILTY: Tree sants.

DRINA: Tommy!

TOMMY: What?

DRINA: Did you take this boy's three cents?

TOMMY: Nope.

DRINA: You did so!

TOMMY: I di' not!

DRINA: You did so!

TOMMY: Well, I ain't got it.

DRINA: Who has? Who's got it? *To* ANGEL. You?

ANGEL: Not me.

   DRINA *looks accusingly to T.B.*

T.B., *walks away, indignantly:* Don' look at me!

TOMMY: Go on, Spit, giv 'im back 'is tree cents.

DRINA, *turns on* SPIT: Oh, so you're the one! Come on!

SPIT, *thumbs his nose:* Like hell I will.

DRINA: Come on!

SPIT: Frig you!

DRINA, *flaring:* I'll crack you . . . you talk like that!

SPIT: Ah, I'll sock yuh inna tit. *She smacks him. He clenches his fist and draws it back ready to swing.*

TOMMY, *jumps from the hopper and rushes at* SPIT, *fists clenched, arms raised in fighting position:* Cut dat out, yuh louse!

SPIT: Well . . . she smacked me foist. She smacked me foist. No dame kin smack me foist an' get away wid' it.

TOMMY: Give 'er dat dough.

SPIT: What fuh?

TOMMY: Give 'er da dough. Dat's what fuh.

SPIT: Yeah?

TOMMY: Yeah.

SPIT: Ah, yuh mudduh's chooch!

TOMMY: Ah, yuh fadduh's doop!

DRINA: Keep quiet, Tommy! *To* SPIT. Come on! *Come on!*

TOMMY: Hurry up! Give 'er dat dough! *Pause.* SPIT *grudgingly gives her the money.* TOMMY *drops his hands and returns to the hopper, whistling.* DRINA *hands the money back to* MILTY.

DRINA: Here.

MILTY: Tanks!

DRINA: That's all right. You look like a nice boy. Stay away from them. They're no good. They're bums.

SPIT, *sullen, but seeking an ally:* Come on, Angel. Y'ain' bin in yet. Wanna go in?

ANGEL: OK.

SPIT: Last one in's a stinkin' rotten egg! *They rush off and jump into the water with great splashes. T.B. remains near the hopper, watching.*

   *Off right, voices are heard.* PHILIP's *father, a tall, lean, soft-spoken gen-*

*tleman, middle-aged, wearing shell-rimmed glasses and carrying a pipe, appears at the gate. He is followed by a plumpish man of about the same age.* PHILIP *opens the gate for them, smiling.*

PHILIP: Hello, Daddy!

GRISWALD: Hello, Son. Shoulders back! PHILIP *straightens.* Attaboy. Where's Jeanne?

PHILIP: She went to find Charles.

GRISWALD: Oh? And where's he?

PHILIP: I don't know.

GRISWALD, *goes up the street, looks into the tenement hallway. He shakes his head in disapproval and turns to his companion:* Say, Jones! Look at this at our back door! JONES *nods.*

DRINA, *to* GIMPTY: You let them take his money without even interfering. Shame on you!

GIMPTY: I told you I didn't notice what was happening. My mind was on somethin' else.

DRINA: Ah, you're always sticking up for them. *To* TOMMY. Tommy! I'm gonna get some kerosene and clean your head right away.

TOMMY: Aw-w-w.

DRINA: Don't aw-w-w me! *She walks up the street.* TOMMY *jumps down from the hopper and dives into the water.*

GRISWALD: Hm! Whose property is this?

JONES: I think J. and J. I'm not sure, Griswald.

GRISWALD: Why don't they keep it in repair?

JONES: What for? It's valuable stuff as it is. No upkeep.

GRISWALD, *gasps at the stench that comes out of the building:* Phew! What do they do? Use this hallway as a latrine?

JONES: Probably.

GRISWALD: Hm! Terrible!

JONES: Well, these people have to live someplace.

GRISWALD, *groping in his coat pockets:* Hm. Forgot my tobacco pouch. Will you run up and get it for me, son?

PHILIP: Sure, Daddy! Where is it?

GRISWALD: Now, let me see. I think it's . . . I'd better go myself. *Turns to* JONES.

JONES: I'll go up with you.

GRISWALD: We'll be down in a minute. Ask Charles to wait for us.

PHILIP: Certainly, Daddy.

GRISWALD: Thanks, son. *They go off into the apartment house.* DIPPY *comes running down the sidewalk.*

DIPPY: I fuhgot. Wot wuzat name? Moitle?

THE TALL ONE: Martin!

   *HUNK cautions him with a tug. GIMPTY's head jerks up. He stares at the TALL ONE.*

HUNK: Maybe I better go.

THE TALL ONE: O.K. 418, fourth floor. *To DIPPY.* Nevuh mind, kid. *To HUNK.* And while yuh at it, look in 'at tailor's I tole yuh.

HUNK, *nods:* Check! *Exit HUNK up the sidewalk.*

DIPPY: I'll go. I'll go git her.

THE TALL ONE: Beat it!

DIPPY: Don' I git nuttin'? I went part a da way.

THE TALL ONE: Nuttin' fer nuttin'. Beat it!

DIPPY: Ah, dat's a lousy trick tuh play on a kid.

THE TALL ONE, *raises his foot to kick DIPPY:* Come on! . . . *DIPPY runs to the ladder, grumbling, climbs over, yells.*

DIPPY: Hey! Yew! *The TALL ONE turns to look.* Go tuh hell! *And he quickly jumps into the water. The TALL ONE laughs, comes down to the edge of the wharf, and watches DIPPY splash away.*

GIMPTY, *snaps his fingers. Sudden recollection:* Martin! Baby-face Martin!

THE TALL ONE, *wheels to face GIMPTY, one hand reaching under his coat for a shoulder holster:* I ain't Martin, you bastard!

GIMPTY: Don't you remember me?

MARTIN: OK. Yew asked fer it an' yuh git it!

GIMPTY: I'm Gimpty. . . . Remember?

MARTIN: Gimpty?

GIMPTY: Sure, Baby-face. I . . .

MARTIN: Sh! Shat ap! My name's Johnson. Git it? Johnson.

GIMPTY: We were kids here. Don't you remember? I was one of the gang.

MARTIN, *squints at him carefully for a long time:* Yeah.

GIMPTY: You don't have to worry about me.

MARTIN: I ain't worryin' about you. I'm worryin' about me. *His hand emerges slowly from under his coat.* You wuz dat funny kid who used to mind my clothes when I went swimmin'.

GIMPTY: Yeah.

MARTIN: Yeah. 'At's right. Kin yuh still keep yer lips buttoned up?

GIMPTY: I guess so.

MARTIN: Yuh guess so! Yuh better find out. And Goddamn quick!

GIMPTY: You know me, Marty, I . . . *A man comes out of the East River Terrace.*

MARTIN: Sh! *MARTIN waits till the man is out of hearing, then relaxes.* O.K. Ony, I'm tellin' yuh, if it wuz anybody else, so help me God, I'd . . . *Gestures with thumb and forefinger, as if reaching for his gun.*

GIMPTY: Thanks. . . . What did you do to your face?

MARTIN: Operation. Plastic, dey call it.

GIMPTY: Oh! And you dyed your hair, too.

MARTIN: Yeah. I guess yuh read about me.

GIMPTY: Sure. You're the headliner these days.

MARTIN: Goddamn right! *Pauses. Looks around reminiscently and nods toward the East River Terrace Apartments.* Hey, dat's somethin' new, ain't it?

GIMPTY: No. It's been up a couple of years.

MARTIN: Yeah? What is it?

GIMPTY: One of the swellest apartment houses in town.

MARTIN: Yuh don' tell me! Well, what do yuh know!

GIMPTY: Yeah. You have to have blue blood, a million bucks, and a yacht to live in there, or else you have to . . . *Breaks off, moodily.*

MARTIN: What?

GIMPTY: Oh nothin'.

MARTIN: Come on! I don' like 'at. If you're gonna say it, say it.

GIMPTY: It's nothin'. You see over there? They got a floatin' dock.

MARTIN: Yeah. . . . What's it doin' there? Right by de ole wharf. We used to pee over deah . . . remember?

GIMPTY: Yeah.

MARTIN: Uh-huh. *Regards GIMPTY quizzically.* What's your racket?

GIMPTY: I'm an architect.

MARTIN: What's dat?

GIMPTY: I design houses.

MARTIN: Yuh don' say! What do yuh know! Little Gimpty, an' look at 'im! An architect! Well, I always knew yuh'd come trew. Yuh had somethin' here, kid! *Taps his head.* Yep. Well, I'm glad tuh see yuh doin' O.K., Gimpty. Not like dese udder slobs. Yuh must be in a big dough, huh?

GIMPTY, *laughs:* Nine out of ten architects are out of work.

MARTIN: Yeah?

GIMPTY: Yeah.

MARTIN: So what da hell's a good?

GIMPTY: That's the question. Don't ask me. I don't know. . . . Strictly speakin', I'm not even an architect. You see, before you're an architect, you got to build a house, an' before anybody'll let you build 'em a house, you got to be an architect.

MARTIN: Sounds screwy.

GIMPTY: Yeah, I guess it is. Besides, nobody's building any more, anyway.

MARTIN: An' fer dat yuh had tuh go tuh high school?

GIMPTY: College, too.

MARTIN: College? Yuh went tuh college?

GIMPTY: Six years.

MARTIN: Six years? Why, yuh son uva bitch, yuh're marvelous!

GIMPTY: Well, I won a scholarship, and Mom worked like hell . . . and here I am. I was doin' a little work for the government, but . . .

MARTIN: Oh, yeah?

GIMPTY: No . . . don't get excited. . . . On a slum clearance project. But that folded up. I'm on home relief now.

MARTIN: Oh!

   A MAN *comes down the street and enters the tenement. He bangs the door.* MARTIN *starts and looks back jerkily.*

GIMPTY: Say, is it so smart for you to come here? With that big reward.

MARTIN: I ain' here. I'm out West. Read da papers.

GIMPTY: Have you seen your mother yet?

MARTIN: No. Dat's one reason why I come back. I ain' see dee old lady 'n seven years. I kind a got a yen. Yuh know?

GIMPTY: Sure. . . . I saw her here day before yesterday.

MARTIN: Yeah? I taught she might be aroun'. How's she look?

GIMPTY: All right.

MARTIN: Gese. Seven years! Since a day I come out a reform school. Say, yew came down 'ere wid' her tuh meet me, didn' cha?

GIMPTY: Yeah.

MARTIN: Sure. 'At's right.

GIMPTY: Well, you've gone a long way since then.

MARTIN: Yeah.

GIMPTY: You know, Marty, I never could quite believe it was you.

MARTIN: Why not?

GIMPTY: To kill eight men?

MARTIN: Say, what ta hell a yuh tryin' tuh do? Tell me off, yuh bastard. Why, I'll . . .

GIMPTY: No, Marty. . . .

MARTIN: Say, maybe yuh changed, huh? Maybe yuh become a rat. Maybe yuh'd like tuh git dat faw grand 'at's up fuh me. . . .

GIMPTY: You know better.

MARTIN: I'm not so sure. Fawty-two hundred bucks is pretty big dough fer a joik like yew.

GIMPTY: You can trust me.

MARTIN: Den don' gimme any a dat crap! What ta hell did yuh t'ink I wuz gonna do, hang aroun' 'is dump waitin' fer Santa Claus tuh take care a me, fer Chris' sake? Looka yew! What a yew got? Six years yuh went tuh college an what da hell a yuh got? A lousy handout a thoity bucks a

month! Not fer me! I yain't like yew punks . . . starvin' an' freezin' . . . fuh
what? Peanuts? Coffee an'? Yeah, I got mine, but I took it. Look! *Pulls at
his shirt.* Silk. Twenty bucks. Look a dis! *Pulls at his jacket.* Custom tai-
lored—a hunderd an' fifty bucks. Da fat a da land I live off of. An' I got
a flock of dames 'at'd make yew guys water at da mout'. 'At'd make yew
slobs run off in a dark corner when yuh see dere pichure an play pocket-
pool.

GIMPTY: Ain't you ever scared?

MARTIN: Me? What of? What ta hell, yuh can't live fa'ever. Ah, I don' know.
Sure! Sometimes I git da jitters. An' sometimes I git a terrific yen tuh stay
put, an' . . . Ah, ta hell wid' it! Say, do yew remember dat kid Francey?

GIMPTY: Francey?

MARTIN: She wuz my goil when we were kids.

GIMPTY: Oh, yeah. She was a fine girl. I remember.

MARTIN: Yew bet. 'Ey don' make no more like her. I know. I had 'em all.
Yuh ain't seen her around, have yuh?

GIMPTY: No.

MARTIN: Hoid anythin' about her?

GIMPTY: No.

MARTIN: Gee, I got a terrific yen tuh see dat kid again. 'At's why I come
back here. I wonder what she's doin'. Maybe she got married. Nah, she
couldn'! Maybe she died. Nah, not Francey! She had too much on a ball,
too much stuff . . . guts. Yeah, she wuz like me. Nuttin' kin kill Baby-face
Martin an' nuttin' kin kill her. Not Francey. Gese, I wonder what's become
a her?

GIMPTY: She's the girl whose uncle owns a tailor shop around the corner,
isn't she?

*MILTY strolls over to the parapet and stands looking into the water.*

MARTIN: Yeah. Yuh remember her now.

GIMPTY: Sure I remember her, all right.

MARTIN: I tole Hunk, he's one a my boys, tuh look in 'ere an' see if he could
git her address. Gese, I gotta see dat kid again!

*SPIT climbs out of the water, goes to MILTY, and in one sweep of his
arm, tears MILTY's fly open.*

SPIT: Tree bagger!

MILTY: Stop dat!

SPIT, *threatening him:* What?

TOMMY, *follows SPIT over the parapet:* Aw, cut it out, Spit. We gave 'im
enough fuh one time.

SPIT: I'll knock 'im intuh da middle a next week!

TOMMY, *tearing open SPIT's fly:* Home run!

*The rest of the kids climb out of the water.* MILTY *joins them in laughing at* SPIT's *discomfiture.*

SPIT, *turning on* MILTY: Whadda yuh laughin' at?

DIPPY: Yeah, what?

SPIT: Sock 'im, Dippy.

DIPPY: Aw, I could lick 'im wid' one han' tied behin' my back. *Taps* MILTY's *shoulder with his clenched fist in rhythm to:* Tree, six, nine, da fight is mine, I kin lick yew any ole time. Tree, six, nine, da . . .

MILTY: Git outa heah. Lemme alone. *He swings at* DIPPY, *who retreats frightened.*

SPIT, *grabbing* MILTY *roughly by his shirt:* Oh . . . a tough guy, huh?

TOMMY: I said leave 'im alone. We give 'im enough fuh one time.

SPIT, *releases* MILTY *and goes to* TOMMY, *threateningly:* Wheah da hell a yuh come off, all a time tellin' me what tuh do?

TOMMY: I'll put yew out like a light.

SPIT, *spitting at* TOMMY: Right inna nose!

TOMMY, *ducks, and the wad of saliva flies over his head:* Miss! Now yuh git yer lumps!

SPIT: Try it! Wanna make somethin' out uv it? Come on! Come on! *He starts dancing in front of* TOMMY, *waves his fists and mutters dire threats.* TOMMY *suddenly gives him one terrific blow, and* SPIT *collapses, his nose bleeding.*

GIMPTY: Hey!

TOMMY: Hay fuh hosses! It wuz comin' tuh him. *To* MILTY, *patting his back.* O.K., kid! Yew kin stick aroun'.

*HUNK enters down the sidewalk.*

T.B.: Hey, Tommy, len' me a couple a my pennies. I wanna practice pitchin'.

TOMMY: O.K. *They pitch pennies from the hopper to the sidewalk.*

MARTIN, *to* GIMPTY: Da kids aroun' here don' change! *Turns, meets* HUNK's *suspicious stare at* GIMPTY; *to* HUNK. He ain' nuttin' tuh worry about.

HUNK: It's your funeral as well as mine.

MARTIN: Did yuh git huh address?

HUNK: Yuh mudder's out. Deah wuz no answer.

MARTIN: Francey. What about huh?

HUNK: Dee old joker said ee didn' know, but ee gimme da address of her aunt in Brooklyn. She might know.

MARTIN: Well, hop a cab an' git it.

HUNK, *making a wry face:* Brooklyn?

MARTIN: Yeah.

HUNK: Oh, hell!

MARTIN: Come on! Stop crappin' aroun'.

HUNK: Awright. *Exit up the sidewalk.*

SPIT, *to* PHILIP, *who has appeared on the terrace to watch the fight:* Whadda yuh lookin' at, huh? Yuh nosey li'l . . .

PHILIP: Nosey nothing. It's a free country, isn't it?

TOMMY: Hey, wee-wee, what ah yuh, a boy 'r a goil?

T.B.: He's a goil, cantcha see?

PHILIP: I'm a man!

    *T.B. razzes him loudly.* PHILIP *razzes loudly back.*

T.B.: Wassamattuh? Yew a wise guy?

PHILIP: Yes, I am.

T.B.: Oh, yeah?

PHILIP: I can name all the presidents of the United States. Can you?

T.B.: What? Tommy kin . . .

PHILIP: Ah-h-h!

TOMMY: I used tuh be able tuh.

T.B.: Ah, I bet yuh. I bet yuh a dolluh ee kin. I bet yuh. . . .

PHILIP: All right.

T.B.: Awright what?

PHILIP: I'll bet you a dollar.

T.B.: What?

PHILIP, *takes a dollar bill from his pocket and proudly waves it aloft:* Put up your dollar!

DIPPY: Gese, a buck!

T.B., *slaps his cheek in amazement:* A whole real live dollar . . . my gawd!

    ANGEL *and* SPIT, *impressed, exclaim and whistle.*

PHILIP: Aw, you haven't even got a dollar.

T.B.: Yeah, well . . . show 'im, Tommy, anyway. Show 'im! Jus' show 'im up, will yuh?

PHILIP: Washington, Adams, Jefferson. Go on! Name the next three!

TOMMY: Madison . . . Harrison . . . no . . .

PHILIP: Wrong!

TOMMY: Well, I used tuh know 'em. I fergit.

PHILIP: Aw-w.

TOMMY: Well, who cares, anyway? Yuh li'l sissy! Let's cockalize 'im! Whadda yuh say? Come on! *Chorus of approval. They start climbing up the wall, but the* DOORMAN *appears just in time.*

DOORMAN: Get out of here! *He gives them a dirty look, then exits, closing the gate.*

TOMMY: Wait till I git yew . . . I'll fix your wagon! Come heah, guys. We gotta git dat kid away from deah. We gotta git him. . . .

    *The gang all huddle about* TOMMY, *whispering. Three* SMALLER BOYS *straggle down the street and sit on the curb. They try to insinuate their way into the conclave.*

TOMMY, *to the three* SMALLER BOYS: Hey, whadda yew want? *The three* SMALLER BOYS *don't answer, but are ready for a fight.* Angel, tell yuh kid brudder tuh git da hell outa heah!

ANGEL: Beat it!

TOMMY: Go home and tell yuh mudduh she wants yuh!

ANGEL, *rises, rushes the kids. The smallest stops to fight him, but* ANGEL *routs them and they flee up the sidewalk:* Dat crazy brudduh a mine!

*DRINA enters down the street, carrying a can of kerosene.*

MARTIN: Well, keep yer nose clean, Gimpty, an' yer lips buttoned up tight, see?

GIMPTY: Forget it!

*MARTIN exits up the sidewalk, eyeing DRINA as she passes him.*

DRINA: Come on, Tommy.

TOMMY: Not now, I'm busy.

DRINA: Tommy, don't be like that, will you? You can't go around with a head full of livestock.

TOMMY: I ain't got no bugs.

DRINA, *grabbing him, as he pulls away:* Let me see . . . come here! *She examines his head.* Whew! You ain't! You got an army witha brass band. Come on home.

TOMMY: Wassamattuh wid' tuhnight?

DRINA: Tonight I got a strike meetin' . I don't know what time I'll be home.

TOMMY: Aw, yew an' yuh lousy meetin's.

DRINA: It ain't no fun for me, Tommy. Come on an' let's get you cleaned up.

TOMMY: Aw, Drina!

DRINA: I don't like it any more than you do.

TOMMY: Gese, look it! *He points up the street, and* DRINA *relaxes her hold on him.* TOMMY *rushes off under the hopper and dives into the water with a "Whee-ee." The other kids laugh and then straggle up the street to sit in a huddle on the doorstep of a tenement house.*

DRINA: Tommy!

GIMPTY, *laughs.* DRINA *looks at him. He smiles understandingly:* You've got a tough job on your hands, Drina.

DRINA, *peering over the wharf, following* TOMMY *with her eyes:* He's really a good kid.

GIMPTY, *also watches* TOMMY, *whom we can hear thrashing the water with a clockwork, six-beat crawl:* Sure.

DRINA: Just a little wild.

GIMPTY: Hey . . . Tommy's got a good crawl-kick!

DRINA, *calling:* Tommy! Come on! TOMMY *shouts under the water, making a noise like a seal.* DRINA *laughs, against her will.* What are you gonna do with a kid like that?

GIMPTY, *laughs:* I don't know.

DRINA, *seating herself on the parapet, next to* GIMPTY: It's not that he's dumb, either. I went to see his teacher yesterday. She said he's one of the smartest pupils she's got. But he won't work. Two weeks he played hookey.

GIMPTY: I don't blame him.

DRINA: I can't seem to do anything with him. It was different when Mom was alive. She could handle him . . . and between us we made enough money to live in a better neighborhood than this. If we win this strike, I'm gonna move, get him outa here the first thing.

GIMPTY: Yeah. That's the idea.

DRINA, *noticing his drawings:* What've you got there? More drawings?

GIMPTY: Couple a new ideas in community housing. Here! See? *He passes the drawing pad to her.*

DRINA, *studies them and nods admiration:* Yeah. They're beautiful houses, Pete. But what's the good? Is anybody going to build them?

GIMPTY: No.

DRINA, *handing back the drawings:* So what?

GIMPTY: All my life I've wanted to build houses like these. Well . . . I'm gonna build 'em, see? Even if it's only on paper.

DRINA: A lot of good they'll do on paper. Your mother told me you've even given up looking for a job lately.

GIMPTY, *suddenly bitter and weary:* Sure. What's the use? How long have you been on strike now?

DRINA: A month.

GIMPTY: Picketin' an' fightin' an' broken heads. For what?

DRINA: For what? For two dollars and fifty cents a week extra. Eleven dollars a month, Pete. All toward rent. So's Tommy an' I can live in a decent neighborhood.

GIMPTY: Yeah. You're right there. I've seen this neighborhood make some pretty rough guys. You've heard about Baby-face Martin? He used to live around here.

DRINA: Yeah. I read about it.

GIMPTY: I used to know him.

DRINA: You did? What was he like?

TOMMY *climbs up out of the water, breathless. He lies on the parapet, listening.*

GIMPTY: As a kid, all right . . . more than all right. Yeah, Drina, the place you live in is awfully important. It can give you a chance to grow, or it

can twist you— *He twists an imaginary object with grim venom.*—like
that. When I was in school, they used to teach us that evolution made men
out of animals. They forgot to tell us it can also make animals out of
men.

TOMMY: Hey, Gimpty.

GIMPTY: Yeah?

TOMMY: What's evilushin? *He clambers along the parapet and lies on his
stomach in front of* DRINA.

GIMPTY, *looks at* TOMMY *a moment, smiles, and comes out of his dark
mood:* What's evolution, Tommy? Well, I'll tell you. A thousand million
years ago we were all worms in the mud, and that evolution made us men.

DRINA: And women!

GIMPTY: And women.

TOMMY: An' boys and goils?

GIMPTY: And boys and girls.

TOMMY: Ah, I wuzn't even born a tousan' million years ago.

GIMPTY: No, but your great, great, great, great grandfather and mother
were; and before them their great, great, great, great, great grandfather
and mother were worms.

TOMMY: Blah-h-h!

DRINA, *impressed:* It's like God!

GIMPTY: It is God! Once it made dinosaurs—animals as big as that house.

TOMMY: As big as 'at?

DRINA: Sure.

TOMMY: Wow!

GIMPTY: Then it didn't like its work, and it killed them. Every one of them!
Wiped 'em out!

TOMMY: Boy! I'd like tuh see one a dem babies.

GIMPTY: I'll show you a picture sometime.

TOMMY: Will yuh?

GIMPTY: Sure.

TOMMY: 'At'll be swell, Gimpty.

   SPIT *appears on the ladder and stops to listen, hanging from the top
rung.*

GIMPTY: Once evolution gave snakes feet to walk on.

TOMMY: Snakes? No kiddin'!

SPIT, *sings in mockery:* Te-da-da-da-da-bushwah, te-da-da bushwah!

TOMMY: Shat ap! Right innee eye! *He spits.* SPIT *jumps back into the water.*

DRINA: Tommy, cut that out! See? You're like an animal.

TOMMY: Well . . . he does it tuh all ee udduh kids. . . . Anyhow, what happened tuh duh snakes' feet?

GIMPTY: Evolution took 'em away. The same as ostriches could once fly. I bet you didn't know that.

TOMMY: No.

GIMPTY: Well, it's true. And then it took away their power to fly. The same as it gave oysters heads.

TOMMY: Oysters had heads?

GIMPTY: Once, yeah.

TOMMY: Aw-w!

DRINA: Sh, listen!

GIMPTY: Then it took them away. "Now men," says Evolution, "now men"— *Nods to* DRINA, *acknowledging her contribution.* —"and women . . . I made you walk straight, I gave you feeling, I gave you reason, I gave you dignity, I gave you a sense of beauty, I planted a God in your heart. Now let's see what you're going to do with them. An' if you can't do anything with them, then I'll take 'em all away. Yeah, I'll take away your reason as sure as I took away the head of the oyster, and your sense of beauty as I took away the flight of the ostrich, and men will crawl on their bellies on the ground like snakes . . . or die off altogether like the dinosaur."

KAY, *a very attractive, smartly groomed young lady in a white linen suit comes out of the gate. She brings a clean coolness into this sweltering street. She has a distinctive, lovely face; high forehead, patrician nose, relieved by a warm, wide, generous mouth and eyes that shut and crinkle at the corners when she smiles—which she is doing now.*

TOMMY: Gee!

GIMPTY: That scare you?

TOMMY: Wow!

ANGEL, *who has been sitting on the tenement steps up the street, watching T.B. and* DIPPY *climb the tractor, notices the woman come out of the gate:* Hey, Gimpty, heah's yuh goil friend!

GIMPTY: Oh, hello, Kay!

KAY: Hello, Pete. *Her manner is simple, direct, poised and easy. She is a realist; no chichi, no pretense. And she is obviously very fond of* GIMPTY.

DIPPY, *to T.B.:* Hey, Gimpty's goil fren come outa deah.

T.B., *rising:* No kid! No kid!

ANGEL: Gee whiz! *The* THREE BOYS *saunter down to* KAY.

DIPPY: Do yew live in deah?

GIMPTY, *embarrassed:* Hey!

KAY, *laughs:* Yes.

ANGEL: Have dey really got a swimmin' pool in 'at joint?

KAY: Yes. A big one.

DIPPY: Ah yew a billionairess?

KAY: No.

DIPPY: Millionairess?

KAY: No.

GIMPTY: Hey-y-y!

ANGEL: Den what a yuh doin' comin' outa deah?

DRINA: Angelo! *To* KAY. Don't mind him!

KAY, *smiling:* Oh, he's all right.

DIPPY: I got it. She's a soivant goil.

T.B.: Nah, she's too swell-dressed all a time.

    KAY *laughs.*

GIMPTY, *squirming with embarrassment:* Look! Will you kids beat it? Scram! Get outa here! Go on!

DRINA: Come on, Tommy! I'm gonna wash your head.

TOMMY, *crawling over to the ladder:* Nah! Hey, Gimpty . . .'at evilushin guy . . .

GIMPTY: What about him?

TOMMY: Did he make everything?

GIMPTY: Yeah.

TOMMY: Bugs too?

GIMPTY: Yeah.

TOMMY, *to* DRINA: Deah yuh ah! God makes bugs an' yew wanna kill 'em. *Gently chiding her as if she were a naughty child.* Is 'at nice? *He dives off the ladder into the water.* Whee-e-e!

KAY: He's very logical.

DRINA: Yeah. That part's all right, but he's very lousy too, an' that part ain't. *She calls.* Tommy! Come on! *More splashing of the water from* TOMMY.

DIPPY: Whee! Look! He's a flyin' fish! Do dat again, Tommy! Wait, I'm comin', Tommy! *He mounts the parapet.* Look a me! I'm divin' . . . a back-jack! *He stands poised for a backjack, then looks back and downward, fearfully.* It's awfully high. Wait a minute! Wait . . . wait! *He climbs two rungs down the ladder. Looks down. Nods. This is better.* I'm divin' a backjack! Watch out, Tommy! *He jumps sprawling out of sight. A tremendous splash.* KAY *looks over the parapet, laughing.* DIPPY *calls up:* How wuz 'at?

KAY: Beautiful!

T.B.: Stinks! *He walks off toward the hopper, arm-in-arm with* ANGEL. *Two* GIRLS *come out of the Terrace, and walk up the street, chattering.* T.B. *and* ANGEL *follow them, mimicking their mincing walk, and making indecent remarks. One of the* GIRLS *stops and turns to slap* ANGEL. *The* BOYS *laugh and run off behind the hopper. The Two* GIRLS *go up the street, one indignant, the other giggling.*

KAY *has picked up* GIMPTY's *drawings and is admiring them.* DRINA *stares enviously at* KAY, *at her modish coiffure, at her smart suit, at her shoes.* KAY *becomes conscious of the scrutiny and turns.*

DRINA, *embarrassed, drops her eyes, then calls to* TOMMY: Tommy! Coming?

TOMMY, *from the water:* No-o-o!

DRINA: Well, I'm goin' home. I can't wait here all day. *She goes.*

GIMPTY: They're using the back entrance today. . . .

KAY, *handing him the drawing pad:* Yes. There's some trouble in front. They've ripped up the whole street. *She looks out across the River, and breathes deep.* It's a grand day, isn't it?

GIMPTY: Yeah.

KAY: Oh! . . . I was talking to some of Jack's friends last night. I thought they could find something for you. *Produces a business card from her pocket.* Here's a man who said you might come up and speak to him. Here's his card.

GIMPTY, *takes the card from her, and reads it:* Del Block. Oh, yeah . . . he's a good man. Thanks! Gee! Thanks!

KAY: I don't know if it'll help much.

GIMPTY: This is swell of you! *He looks at her a moment, lost in admiration. Then shyly, with a good deal of hesitation and groping for the right words:* I was telling Mom about you last night. I been kind of going around the house like a chicken with its head chopped off . . . and Mom asked me why. So I told her.

KAY: What?

GIMPTY: Oh, just a little about you. How we'd got to talking here, and meeting every day, and what great friends we've become. How you've been trying to help me. And . . . that I worship you!

KAY: You didn't!

GIMPTY: Well, I do. Do you mind?

KAY, *deeply touched:* Mind? You fool! What'd she say?

GIMPTY: She said you sounded like a very real, good person.

KAY: Good? Did you tell her all about me? About Jack?

GIMPTY: Yeah.

KAY: Your mother must be a sweet woman. I'd like to meet her sometime.

GIMPTY, *enthusiastically:* She'd be tickled. Will you?

KAY: Right now, if you like.

GIMPTY: Well, she's out for the afternoon.

KAY: Oh!

GIMPTY: Maybe I can get her down here day after tomorrow, huh?

KAY, *pauses, then, a bit depressed:* I may not be here then. I may leave tomorrow.

GIMPTY: Tomorrow?

KAY: Night. Jack's going on a fishing trip. He wants me with him.

GIMPTY: Isn't that sudden?

KAY: He's been planning it for some time.

GIMPTY: How long will you be gone?

KAY: About three months.

GIMPTY: That's a long time.

KAY: Yes.

*Down the street strides* JACK HILTON, *a well-dressed, rather handsome man in his early forties, hard lines around the eyes. At the moment he is hot and uncomfortable. He eyes the tenements curiously as he passes them. The* DOORMAN *appears as he starts to enter the gate. He asks the* DOORMAN *in a cultured, quiet voice,* "What happened in front?"

DOORMAN: I'll tell you, Mr. Hilton. You see, the gas mains . . .

KAY, *rises:* Hello, Jack!

HILTON, *turns around, sees* KAY. *Surprised:* Hello! What're you doing here? *He crosses to her.*

KAY: Oh, I just came out.

HILTON, *takes off his panama, wipes the sweatband and mops his brow with a handkerchief:* Phew! It's been a hell of a day, arranging things at the office. Well, I've made the plans for the trip. Everything's set. The boat's in shape. I've talked to Captain Swanson.

*DIPPY climbs up over the parapet, talking to himself.*

DIPPY: Hooray fuh me! I did a backjack! *To* GIMPTY: Wuz 'at good, Gimpty?

GIMPTY: All right!

DIPPY, *to* KAY: Hey, Gimpty's goil friend, wuz 'at good?

KAY: Beautiful.

*DIPPY, patting his chest and gloating* "Attaboy, Dippy!" *goes back into the water.* HILTON *is puzzled and annoyed. He looks at* KAY.

HILTON: What's all this about?

KAY: Nothing.

HILTON, *his voice begins to rasp:* Come on. Let's go in.

KAY: It's nice out. I'd like to take a walk first.

HILTON: You'll do that later. Come on.

KAY: I have a little headache. I want to stay out a few minutes more.

HILTON: Take an aspirin and you'll be all right. Come on!

KAY: Please!

HILTON: We've a million things to do.

KAY: You go ahead. I'll be right in.

HILTON, *casts a glance at* GIMPTY: What's the big attraction out here?

KAY: Nothing.

HILTON: Then stop acting like a prima donna and come on in.

KAY: Please don't make a fuss.

HILTON, *suddenly loses his temper and snaps:* It's not me . . . it's you! Damn it, I've been tearing around all day like a madman, and I come home and find you behaving like a cheap . . .

KAY: Jack!

HILTON, *bites his lip, controls himself, and mutters curtly:* All right! Stay there! *He goes in.* KAY *follows him to the gate, pauses there, uncertain. Then indulges in a momentary flash of temper, herself.*

KAY: Oh . . . let him! *She returns slowly.*

GIMPTY: Is that the guy?

KAY: Yes. *Then, not to be unfair.* Don't judge him by this. He's really not so bad. He's going to be sorry in a few minutes. He's so darn jealous. His wife gave him a pretty raw deal. You can't blame him for . . .

GIMPTY, *suddenly inflamed:* All right! If it were anybody else, all right! But you? He can't treat *you* like that!

KAY, *sits there a while in silence, thinking. Finally, she speaks, slowly, almost in explanation to herself:* I've been living with Jack a little over a year now. He isn't usually like this. You see, he really loves me.

GIMPTY: He has a funny way of showing it.

KAY: He wants me to marry him.

GIMPTY: Are you going to?

KAY: I don't know.

GIMPTY: Do you love him?

KAY: I like him.

GIMPTY: Is that enough?

KAY: I've known what it means to scrimp and worry and never be sure from one minute to the next. I've had enough of that . . . for one lifetime.

GIMPTY, *intensely:* But Kay, not to look forward to love . . . God, that's not living at all!

KAY, *not quite convincingly:* I can do without it.

GIMPTY: That's not true. It isn't, is it?

KAY, *smiles wryly:* Of course not.

A *very stout* LADY, *with much bosom, comes out of the gate, fondling a tiny, black dog.*

TOMMY, *clambering over the parapet, sees the dog and chuckles:* Look a dat cockaroach, will yuh? Hey, lady, wheah didja git dat cockaroach?

FAT LADY: Well, of all the little . . . ! TOMMY *starts to bark. The dog yaps back and struggles to escape. The other* BOYS *climb up and bark in various keys. The three* SMALLER BOYS *appear and join in the medley. The*

*stout* LADY *is distraught. She shouts at them, but to no avail.* Get away
from here, you little beasts!

SPIT: In yuh hat, fat slob! *And he continues barking.*

FAT LADY: Wha-a-at? Doorman! *To the frantic dog.* Quiet, Buddy darling!
Quiet! Doorman!

  *The* DOORMAN *comes out on the run and chases the boys away. They
run en masse to the hopper.* TOMMY *climbs up on it. The* SMALLER BOYS
*retire to the steps of an upper tenement doorway.* MR. GRISWALD, PHILIP,
*and* MR. JONES *come out of the East River Terrace Apartments.*

GRISWALD: What's the matter?

DOORMAN: Those kids! They're terrible, sir.

PHILIP: They wanted to hit me, too, Daddy!

GRISWALD: Oh, yes? Why? What did you do to them? *Smiles at* JONES.

PHILIP: Nothing.

GRISWALD: Sure?

PHILIP: Honest, Daddy, I didn't say anything to them.

DOORMAN: It's all their fault, sir.

FAT LADY: They're really horrible brats. And their language . . . !

TOMMY, *hanging from the hopper:* Ah, shat ap, yuh fat bag a hump!

GRISWALD: You touch him again and I'll break your necks.

TOMMY: Balls to yew, faw eyes!

GRISWALD, *to* PHILIP, *as he takes his arm and walks him up the street:* The
next time you hit them back.

PHILIP: But they all pile up on you, Daddy.

GRISWALD: Oh, is that so? Well, I think I'm going to buy you a set of gloves
and teach you how to box. *They continue up the sidewalk, followed by*
JONES.

PHILIP: Will you, Daddy?

  THE GOVERNESS *and a young* CHAUFFEUR *in maroon livery meet them.*

GOVERNESS: *Bonjour, monsieur!*

CHAUFFEUR, *saluting:* I'm sorry to keep you waiting, sir, but . . .

GRISWALD, *waves them ahead:* That's all right. Never mind. *To* PHILIP. The
next time someone attacks you, you'll be able to defend yourself.

MR. JONES: That's the idea!

TOMMY, *shouts up the street after them:* Yeah! Wid' ee army an' navy behin'
'im! *Gang laughs and shouts.* TOMMY *jumps down from the hopper. The*
FAT LADY *waddles across to* KAY.

TOMMY: Come 'ere, guys, I got a scheme how we kin git dat kid an' cockalize
'im. *They gather in a huddle.*

ANGEL: How?

TOMMY, *subsiding to a whisper:* Foist we git 'im inna hallway, an' . . .

FAT LADY: The little Indians! They oughtn't to be allowed in the street with decent people.

*Exit the* DOORMAN, *closing the gate.*

GIMPTY: No? What would you do with them?

FAT LADY: Send them all away.

GIMPTY: Where?

FAT LADY: I'm sure I don't know.

GIMPTY: Huh!

*Great outburst of laughter from the huddle.*

T.B.: Dat'll woik! You'll see! Dat'll git 'im!

TOMMY: Wait! Shat ap! I got maw! . . .

*The conclave becomes a whispered one again.*

FAT LADY: The little savages! They're all wicked. It's born in them. They inherit it.

GIMPTY, *suddenly bursts out, a bitter personal note in his passion:* Inheritance? Yeah. You inherit a castle thirty stories over the river, or a stinkin' hole in the ground! Wooden heads are inherited, but not wooden legs . . . nor legs twisted by rickets!

*The* FAT LADY *is completely taken aback by this unexpected antipathy. She looks at* KAY, *gasps, and walks away, head high, patting her animal.* KAY *smiles at* GIMPTY *sadly, sympathetically.*

GIMPTY: I'm sorry.

KAY, *touches his hand:* Oh, Pete!

*Another outburst. The three* SMALLER BOYS *have crept down and joined the fringe of the huddle.*

TOMMY: Dey're back again! Angel, will yuh tell yuhr kid brudduh tuh git tuh hell outa heah?

ANGEL *swings at the tiniest of the* BOYS, *who kicks him in the shin, spits at him, and runs away, thumbing his nose.* ANGEL *chases the* BOYS *part of the way up the street, then returns, rubbing his shin and shaking his head.*

ANGEL: 'At crazy kid brudduh a mine, I'm gonna kill 'im when I git 'im home!

*The huddle reorganizes.*

GIMPTY: Gosh, I wish we could be alone for a minute!

KAY: Pete, I've thought of that so many times. I've wanted to invite you inside, but . . .

GIMPTY: You couldn't, of course.

KAY: Cock-eyed, isn't it? Couldn't we go to your place?

GIMPTY: Gee, I . . . ! No, you wouldn't like it.

KAY: Why not?

GIMPTY: It's an awful dump. It would depress you.

KAY: Oh!

GIMPTY: I'd love to have you, Kay, but I'm ashamed to let you see it. Honestly.

KAY, *rises and offers him her hand:* Oh, Pete, that's silly. I wasn't born in a penthouse. Come on! *With the aid of a cane, he rises. They walk up the street. For the first time we notice that one of his legs is withered and twisted—by rickets.*

*MILTY rises and crosses to within a few steps of the huddle.*

MILTY, *timidly:* Hey.

TOMMY: What?

MILTY: Look, I . . . *He approaches* TOMMY *slowly.* If yuh want, I t'ink I kin snitch 'at quatuh fuh yuh.

*The chug of an approaching tugboat is faintly heard.*

TOMMY, *thinks it over:* O.K., Milt! O.K. Den yuhr inna gang, see? *Turns to the others.* Anybody gits snotty wid' Milt, gits snotty wid' me, see? *To* MILTY: Now git dat quatuh. Come on, git duh lead outa yuh pants!

*The chug-chug grows louder.*

MILTY, *jubilant:* O.K., Tommy! *Runs off into the tenement house.*

*The chug-chug grows louder.*

TOMMY: See? He's a good kid. He loins fast. Remember da time I moved aroun' heah? I wuz wearin' white socks an' I wouldn't coise, so yuh all taught I wuz a sissy.

*The chug-chug grows louder.*

DIPPY: 'Cept me, Tommy.

TOMMY: Yeah, 'cept yew. Everybody else I hadda beat da pants off a foist. *Down to business again.* Now here's how we git wee-wee. Yew, T.B. . . . *His voice is drowned out by the chug-chug-chug-chug—*

*CURTAIN*

**ACT TWO**

SCENE: *The same, the following day, lit by a brilliant afternoon sun. The boys are playing poker with an ancient deck of cards, greasy and puffed, inches thick. Matchsticks are their chips. Their faces are grave and intense. They handle their cards familiarly, caressing them like old gamblers.*

MARTIN *lounges against the terrace wall and watches them with grim nostalgia.*


ANGEL, *throwing two matchsticks into the pot:* I'll open fuh two. Hey, Spit, it's rainin'. Come on, decorate da mahogany!
T.B., *adds his two:* O.K. I'm in.
SPIT, *follows suit:* Heah's my two. Dippy.
DIPPY, *tosses in his matchsticks, deliberately, one at a time:* I'm in.
ANGEL, *slapping down two cards:* Gimme . . . two.
SPIT, *deals:* Aw, he's got tree uva kin'.
T.B., *throws away one:* Gimme one. Make it good. SPIT *deals him one.*
ANGEL: Ah, yuh ain' got nuttin'.
SPIT: He's got a monkey. I ain' takin' any. How many fuh yew, Dippy?
DIPPY, *studies his hand with grave deliberation:* I'll take five.
SPIT: Yuh can' take five.
DIPPY, *the mental effort contorts his face:* Faw.
SPIT: Yuh kin ony take tree.
DIPPY, *after considerable hesitation:* Gimme one!
ANGEL, *inclining his head toward T.B.:* Say, T.B., feel 'at bump I got. Feel it!
T.B., *explores* ANGEL's *head with a finger:* Wow! Feel 'at bump Angel's got!
DIPPY, *leans over and feels the bump:* Boy! 'At's like 'n egg!
SPIT: Wheah juh git it?
ANGEL: Me ole man give it tuh me.
DIPPY: Fuh what?
ANGEL: Fuh nuttin'. Just like 'at, fuh nuttin'. Last night me ole man cum-zin drunk.
SPIT, *impatiently:* Cum on, cum on . . . whadda yuh do?
ANGEL, *raps his knuckles on the sidewalk:* I blow.
T.B., *raps:* I blow.
SPIT, *raps:* I blow, too. Dippy?
DIPPY, *raps:* I blow.
T.B.: Watcha got?
ANGEL, *reveals a pair of jacks:* A pair of Johnnies. You?
T.B., *exhibits two pair, twos and threes:* Two pair. Deuces and trays. *He reaches for the pot.*

ANGEL: Aw hell!

SPIT: Wait a minute! *Lays down three tens.* Read 'em an' weep! Judge
    Shmuck . . . thoity days!

DIPPY: I guess I ain't got nuttin'.

  *SPIT gleefully rakes in the matchsticks. Enter* TOMMY, *kicking a tin can
before him. The* BOYS *greet him.*

TOMMY: Hi yuh, guys. Howza wawda?

SPIT: Cold.

TOMMY: Whatcha playin' fuh?

SPIT: Owins. Wanna play?

TOMMY, *starts undressing:* Deal me inna next han'. Who's winnin'?

T.B.: I yam.

TOMMY: How much?

T.B.: Twenty-eight matches.

TOMMY: Twenty-eight cents . . . boy, 'at's putty good! Hey, didja heah
    about it?

|             | SPIT: What?        |
| *Together*  | ANGEL: About what? |
|             | DIPPY: What, Tommy? |

TOMMY: Dincha heah? Boy, deah wuz a big fight at da Chink laundry las'
    night.

ANGEL: No kiddin'!

TOMMY: Yeah.

DIPPY: How did it staht, Tommy?

TOMMY: Oh . . . a couple handkuhchifs got snotty. *They all roar with laugh-
    ter.* Did wee-wee show up yet?

DIPPY: No, Tommy.

ANGEL: Don' worry. I bin on a lookout furrim.

DIPPY: Yeah, we bin on a lookout furrim.

ANGEL: So, like I wuz tellin' yuh, las' night me old man comes in stinkin'
    drunk. So he stahts beatin' hell outa me ole lady. Boy, he socks 'er all ovah
    da place!

  *SPIT laughs.*

TOMMY: What da hell a yuh laughin' at? Dat ain' so funny.

ANGEL: No, dat ain' so funny. Cause den ee picks up a chair and wants a
    wallop me wid' it.

DIPPY: Whatcha do den?

ANGEL: So I grabs a kitchen knife . . . dat big . . . an' I sez, "Touch me, yuh
    louse, an' I give yuh dis."

T.B.: Yeah?

ANGEL: Yeah, yeah, I did. So he laughs, so he laughs, so he falls on a flaw, an' he goes tuh sleep . . . so he snores— *imitates a rasping snore* —like 'at. Boy, wuz ee drunk! Boy, he wuz stinkin'!

*Enter* MILTY *down the sidewalk.*

MILTY: Hello, Tommy!

TOMMY: Hi yuh, Milty! How's evyting?

MILTY: Swell.

TOMMY: Attaboy.

*MILTY goes to* MARTIN.

MARTIN: Well?

MILTY: She wuz deah. I tole huh. She said not tuh come up. She said tuh meet huh down heah.

MARTIN: O.K. Heah, kid, buy yerself a Rolls Royce. *He gives* MILTY *a half-dollar.*

MILTY: Gee!

SPIT: Whatcha git?

MILTY: Oh, momma! Haffa buck!

SPIT, *shouting quickly:* Akey! Akey! Haffies!

MILTY, *also shouting quickly, topping* SPIT *and holding up crossed fingers:* Fens! No akey! No akey!

SPIT, *throws down his cards and rises threateningly:* I said akey. Come on, haffies.

MILTY: Yuh didn' have yuh finguhs crossed.

SPIT: Don' han' me dat balonee! Gimme two bits.

MILTY: Yuh didn't cross yuh finguhs.

SPIT, *thrusting his face into* MILTY's: Gimme two bits 'r I kick yuh ina slats.

MILTY: Yeah?

SPIT: Yeah.

MILTY: Ah, yuh mudduh's chooch!

SPIT: Ah, yuh fadduh's doop!

MILTY: Hey, Tommy, do I gotta givim?

TOMMY: Naw. He didn' have 'is finguhs crossed.

SPIT: I'll choose yuh fer it.

MILTY: Whadduh yuh t'ink I yam, a dope?

SPIT: Ah, yuh damn jip ahdist!

MILTY: Look who's talkin'!

SPIT: Ah, yew stink on ice!

TOMMY: Stan' up tuh him, Milty! Stan' up tuh him.

MILTY, *suddenly thrusts his jaw forward:* Watsamatteh? Yew wanna fight?

SPIT: Yeah.

MILTY: Join ee ahmy! . . . Ha!

*The boys roar at* SPIT.

SPIT, *raising a fist and twisting his face fiercely:* Ah!
MILTY, *raising his fist and returning the grimace:* Ah!
SPIT, *fiercer in grimace and growl:* Mah!
MILTY, *tops him:* Wah!

They stand there a moment, glaring at each other in silence, fists raised, faces almost touching, then SPIT turns in disgust and sits down again to his cards.

TOMMY, *grins at* MILTY'S *triumph:* Kimmeah, Milty! Yuh wanna play?
MILTY: I dunna how.
TOMMY: Kimmeah, watch me. I'll loin yuh.

Two strange, tough-looking BOYS come down the street. They pause, watch a moment, confer, then wander over to the group.

FIRST BOY: Hey, which one a youse guys is a captain a dis gang?
TOMMY, *doesn't even deign to look up:* Who wantsa know?
SECOND BOY: Weah fum da up da blocks.
TOMMY: Second Avenoo gang?
FIRST BOY: Yeah.
TOMMY, *assorting his cards:* Yeah? Well, go take a flyin' jump at ta moon!
SECOND BOY: Whoza leaduh?
TOMMY: Me. What about it? I pass. *Throws down his cards, rises, turns to the enemy.* Wanna make sumpm out uv it?
SECOND BOY, *a bit frightened:* Yew tell 'im.
FIRST BOY: Yuh wanna fight are gang?
TOMMY: Sure. *Turns to his gang.* O.K. felluhs? Yuh wanna fight da Second Avenoo gang? *They approve raucously.* TOMMY *turns back to the emissaries.* Sure!
FIRST BOY: O.K. On are block?
TOMMY: Yeah. O.K.
SECOND BOY: Satiday?
TOMMY, *asks the gang:* O.K., Satiday, felluhs? *They shout approval.* Faw o'clock. *A little bickering about time, but they agree.* O.K. We'll be up deah Satiday faw o'clock an' boy, we'll kick the stuffin's outa youse!
SECOND BOY: Yeah?
TOMMY: Yeah! No bottles 'r rocks, jus' sticks 'n' bare knucks. Flat sticks. No bats.
SECOND BOY: Sure.
TOMMY: O.K.?
SECOND BOY: O.K.!
TOMMY: O.K. Now git da hell out a heah befaw I bust yuh one! Scram!
The two BOYS run off. From a safe distance they yell.
FIRST BOY: Nuts tuh yew! Son uva bitch! Son uva bitch!

SECOND BOY: Satiday! We be waitin' faw yuh. We kick da pants offa yuh!
> TOMMY *picks up a rock, hurls it after them.* DIPPY *rises, does the same.*
MARTIN *laughs.*
ANGEL, *first noticing* MARTIN: Shine, mistuh?
MARTIN: O.K., kid.
> ANGEL *moves his box down to* MARTIN *and begins to shine his shoes.*
SPIT, *sneers at* DIPPY: Look at 'im trow, will yuh? Like a goil. Yuh godda
     glass ahm? Cantcha trow a rock even?
DIPPY: Yeah. Kin yew trow bettuh?
SPIT, *picks up a rock, rises, looks for a target. He spots a flowerpot on a fire
     escape:* Watch! See 'at flowuh pot? *He throws the rock and breaks the pot.*
TOMMY: Pot shot! Pot shot!
MARTIN: Say, 'at wuz good pitchin'. Yew kids like tuh git some dope on
     gang fightin'?
ANGEL: Sure! Hey, felluhs, come heah! *They crowd about* MARTIN.
MARTIN: Foist ting is tuh git down ere oiliuh' an yuh . . . GIMPTY *enters
     down the sidewalk, whistling cheerfully.* Hello, Gimpty!
GIMPTY: Hello.
MARTIN, *continues the lesson.* GIMPTY *stops and listens:* Oiliuh an yuh said,
     see? Dey won't be ready fuh yuh. En I tell yuh kids what yuh wanna do.
     Git a lot of old electric bulbs, see? Yuh trow 'em, an den yuh trow a couple
     a milk bottles . . . an' some a dee udder kids git hoit, an' den yuh charge
     'em.
TOMMY: Yeah, but we made up no milk bottles, ony bare knucks an' sticks.
MARTIN: Yuh made up! Lissen, kid . . . when yuh fight, dee idee is tuh win.
     It don' cut no ice how. An' in gang fightin' remember, take out da tough
     guys foist. T'ree aw faw a yuh gang up on 'im. Den one a yuh kin git
     behin' 'im an' slug 'im. A stockin' fulla sand an' rocks is good fuh dat. An'
     if 'ey're lickin' yuh, pull a knife. Give 'em a little stab in ee arm. 'Ey'll yell
     like hell an' run.
TOMMY: Yeah, but we made up no knives. Gese, 'at ain' fair. . . .
GIMPTY: What's a matter with you? What are you trying to teach these kids?
MARTIN: Yew shut yer trap. *To* TOMMY. Lissen. If yuh wanna win, yuh gotta
     make up yer own rules, see?
TOMMY: But we made up dat . . .
MARTIN: Yuh made up . . .
TOMMY: We kin lick 'em wid' bare knucks . . . fair and square.
MARTIN: Lissen, kid . . . Ere ain' no fair an' ere ain' no square. It's winnah
     take all. An' it's easier tuh lick a guy by sluggin' 'im fum behin' 'en it is by
     sockin' it out wid' 'im toe tuh toe. Cause if yuhr lickin' 'im, en he pulls a
     knife on yuh, see? En wheah are yuh?

TOMMY: Den I pull a knife back on him.

MARTIN: Yeah, but what's a good unless yuh got one an' know how tuh use it?

TOMMY: I know how tuh.

GIMPTY: Don't pay any attention to him, guys!

MARTIN: Yew lookin' fer a sock in a puss?

GIMPTY: If you kids listen to that stuff, you'll get yourselves in Dutch.

TOMMY: Aw, shat ap.

   *The boys razz* GIMPTY.

MARTIN: Git out a heah, yuh monkey! GIMPTY, *angry but impotent, walks away.* MARTIN *turns to the boys again.* See what I mean?

TOMMY: Yeah, well, if I had a knife . . .

MILTY: Angel's godda knife.

ANGEL: Aw, I need it.

   MARTIN *hands* ANGEL *a dime for the shine.*

TOMMY: Yuh kin jus' loan it tuh me. I'll give it back tuh yuh.

ANGEL: No, yuh won't. Honest, I need it.

SPIT: Give it tuh him! Go on, or I'll crack yuh one!

ANGEL: No!

TOMMY: Nevuh mind . . . tuh hell wid' 'im!

T.B., *to* ANGEL: Ah, yuh stink on ice!

ANGEL: Aw, shat ap!

T.B.: Shat ap yuhself!

MILTY: Look, Angel, I tell yuh what. Ahl give yuh a quatuh fuh it. Whadda yuh say?

ANGEL: Sure!

MILTY, *to* MARTIN: Change, Misteh?

MARTIN: Yeah. . . . *He gives* MILTY *two quarters in exchange for the half, then rises. A newspaper in the gutter catches his attention. He frowns, picks it up, reads it, wandering off to the tenement stoop, where he sits on a step, absorbed in the newspaper item.* ANGEL *runs to the hopper, finds his trousers, fumbles in the pocket, produces the knife, and returns with it. He completes the transaction with* MILTY, *who hands the knife to* TOMMY.

MILTY: Heah, Tommy.

TOMMY, *rises:* Wha' faw?

MILTY: Fuh a present.

TOMMY: Yuh mean yuh givin' it tuh me?

MILTY: Yeah. Yuh kin keep it.

TOMMY: Gee, t'anks, Milty! Gese, 'at's swell . . . t'anks!

MILTY: Aw, dat's nuttin'.

TOMMY: Aw, dat's a whole lot. T'anks! Gee!

CHARLES, *the chauffeur, enters from the gate of the East River Terrace, followed by* PHILIP.

T.B.: Hey, Tommy . . . ! *He points to* PHILIP. *The gang gathers under the hopper, in huddled consultation.*

PHILIP: I think I'll wait here, Charles.

CHARLES: Wouldn't you rather come with me to the garage?

PHILIP: No.

CHARLES: But your mother said . . .

PHILIP: I'll wait here for them.

CHARLES: Yes, sir.

*Exit* CHARLES *up the street.* PHILIP *examines his wristwatch ostentatiously.* KAY *appears on the terrace, finds a space in the shrubbery, leans over the balustrade, and signals to* GIMPTY.

KAY: Pete!

GIMPTY, *rising and crossing toward her, beaming:* Hello, Kay! How are you feeling?

KAY: All right. And you?

GIMPTY: Like a million dollars!

KAY: I'll be down in a second. *She disappears behind the shrubs.*

*The conclave finished, all the boys saunter off in different directions, pretending disregard of* PHILIP. TOMMY, *whistling a funeral dirge, signals* T.B. *with a wink and a nod of the head.* T.B. *approaches* PHILIP *casually.*

T.B.: Hello, what time is it?

PHILIP: Half past four.

T.B.: T'anks. Gee, dat's a nice watch yuh got deah. What kine is it?

PHILIP: A Gruen.

T.B.: Boy, 'at's as nice as 'n Ingersoll. *Coughs, then proudly tapping his chest, boasts* —T.B. I got T.B.

TOMMY, *on the tenement stoop:* Hey, felluhs, come on inna hall heah. I got sumpm great tuh show yuhs. Come on, T.B. *They all whip up loud, faked enthusiasm.*

T.B.: O.K. *To* PHILIP. Yuh wanna come see?

TOMMY: Nah, he can't come. Dis is ony fuh da gang.

*The others agree volubly that* PHILIP *can't join them in the mystery.*

T.B.: Aw, why not? He's a good kid.

TOMMY, *supported by a chorus of "Nahs":* Nah, he can't see dis. Dis is ony fuh da gang.

PHILIP: What is it?

T.B.: Gee, I can't tell yuh . . . but it's . . . gese, it's sumpm great!

TOMMY, *to* T.B.: Come on! Git da lead outa yuh pants!

T.B.: Too bad dey won' letcha see it. Boy, yuh nevuh saw anyting like dat.

PHILIP: Well, I don't care. I can't anyway. I'm waiting for my father and mother. We're going to the country.

T.B.: It'll ony take a minute. . . . Hey, felluhs, let 'im come 'n' see it, will yuh? He's O.K.

TOMMY, *consenting with a great show of reluctance:* Well . . . awright. Let 'im come. TOMMY *enters the tenement, followed by the others.*

T.B.: Come on.

PHILIP: I don't know. I expect my . . .

T.B.: Awright, it's yuhr loss!

    *T.B. starts up the sidewalk.*

PHILIP: Wait! Wait! I'm coming! *Runs to catch up with T.B. As they reach the steps and enter, T.B. pushes him in the doorway, spits on his hands, and follows him in.*

    *KAY enters.*

GIMPTY, *beams. He is very happy:* Hello!

KAY: Hello, darling. *There is a slight strain in her voice and attitude, which manifests itself in over-kindness and too much gentleness, as if she were trying to mitigate some hurt she is about to give him. They sit on the coping.*

GIMPTY: Well . . . I got up early this morning and went down to a stack of offices looking for a job.

KAY: That's swell. Did you find one?

GIMPTY: Not yet. But I will. Wait and see.

KAY: Of course you will.

GIMPTY: Thanks to you.

    *SPIT runs from the hallway, stops a second on the sidewalk, looking about, then grabs a large barrel stave, whacks his hand with it, whistles, and runs back into the tenement hallway.*

KAY: Did you see Del Block?

GIMPTY: Yep.

KAY: Didn't he have anything for you?

GIMPTY: Oh, we had a nice talk. He's a very interesting guy. He showed me some of his work. He's done some pretty good stuff. *Grins.* He asked me if I knew where *he* could find a job. *They both have to laugh at this.* He thinks you're pretty swell, too.

KAY: Pete . . . you've got to get something.

GIMPTY: I will.

KAY: I didn't know how important it was until yesterday.

GIMPTY: Hey, there!

KAY: I used to think we were poor at home because I had to wear a made-over dress to a prom. Yesterday I saw the real thing. If I hadn't seen it, I couldn't have believed it. I dreamt of it all night . . . the filth, the smells, the dankness! I touched a wall and it was wet. . . . *She touches her fingertips, recalling the unpleasant tactile sensation. She shivers.*

GIMPTY: That house was rotten before I was born. The plumbing is so old and broken . . . it's been dripping through the building for ages.

KAY: What tears my heart out is the thought that you have to live there. It's not fair! It's not right!

GIMPTY: It's not right that anybody should live like that, but a couple a million of us do.

KAY: Million?

GIMPTY: Yeah, right here in New York . . . New York with its famous sky-line . . . its Empire State, the biggest Goddamned building in the world. The biggest tombstone in the world! They wanted to build a monument to the times. Well, there it is, bigger than the pyramids and just as many tenants. *He forces her to smile with him. Then he sighs, and adds, hopelessly:* I wonder when they'll let us build houses for men to live in? *Suddenly annoyed with himself.* Ah, I should never have let you see that place!

KAY: I'm glad you did. I know so much more about you now. And I can't tell you how much more I respect you for coming out of that fine, and sweet . . . and sound.

GIMPTY, *his eyes drop to his withered limb:* Let's not get started on that.

PHILIP *can be heard sobbing in the tenement hallway. He flings open the door and rushes out, down the street into the apartment, crying convulsively, his clothes all awry. The gang follows him from the hallway, yelling and laughing.*

TOMMY, *holding* PHILIP's *watch:* Come on, let's git dressed an' beat it!

SPIT: Let's grab a quick swim foist.

TOMMY: Nah!

SPIT: Come on!

MILTY: Betteh not. . . .

SPIT, *rushes off under the hopper and dives into the water:* Las' one in's a stinkin' rotten egg!

TOMMY, *throws the watch to T.B.:* Guard 'at watch and lay chickee!
    *All the boys except T.B. dive into the water.*

GIMPTY: When I see what it's doing to those kids I get so mad I want to tear down these lice nests with my fingers!

KAY: You can't stay here. You've got to get out. Oh, I wish I could help you!

GIMPTY: But you have. Don't you see?

KAY: No. I'm not that important.

GIMPTY: Yes, you are!

KAY: I mustn't be. Nobody must. For your own good, you've got to get out of here.

GIMPTY: I will, damn it! And if I do . . . maybe I'm crazy . . . but will you marry me?

KAY: Listen!

GIMPTY: Don't get me wrong. I'm not askin' you to come and live there with me. But you see, if . . .

KAY: Listen! First I want you to know that I love you . . . as much as I'll allow myself to love anybody. Maybe I shouldn't have gone with you yesterday. Maybe it was a mistake. I didn't realize quite how much I loved you. I think I ought to leave tonight.

GIMPTY: Why?

KAY: Yes, I'd better.

   *The chug of a small boat is heard.*

GIMPTY: Why?

KAY: I'd better get away while we can still do something about this.

GIMPTY: How will that help?

KAY: If I stay, I don't know what will happen, except that . . . we'll go on and in the end make ourselves thoroughly miserable. We'd be so wise to call it quits now.

GIMPTY: Gee, I don't see it.

KAY: I do, and I think I'm right. *Pause. She looks out over the river.* There's the boat.

GIMPTY, *pauses. Turns to look:* Is that it?

KAY: Yes.

GIMPTY, *irrelevantly, to conceal his emotion. In a dull monotone:* It's a knockout. I'm crazy about good boats. They're beautiful, because they're designed to work. That's the way houses should be built . . . like boats.

KAY: Pete, will you be here . . . tonight . . . before I leave?

   MARTIN *looks up from his newspaper to eye* KAY.

GIMPTY: Don't go, Kay. I'll do anything. Isn't there some way . . . something?

KAY, *hopelessly:* What? *Rises.* I guess I'll go in now, and get my things ready. . . . I'll see you later? *She presses his shoulder and exits.*

   MARTIN *rises, throws down his newspaper and approaches* GIMPTY.

MARTIN, *sucks his lips, making a nasty, suggestive sound:* Say . . . dat's a pretty fancy-lookin' broad. High class, huh? How is she? Good lay? *GIMPTY glares at him.* MARTIN *laughs.* Well, fer Chris' sake, what's a matter? Can't yuh talk?

GIMPTY: Cut it out, Martin. Just cut it out!

MARTIN: Lissen, kid, why don' yuh git wise tuh yerself? Dose dames are pushovers, fish fuh duh monkeys!

GIMPTY, *half-rising, furious:* I said cut it out!

MARTIN, *roughly pushes him back:* Sit down, yew! *A chuckle of contempt.* Look what wansa fight wid' me! Little Gimpty wansa fight wid' me! Wassamattuh, Gimpty? Wanna git knocked off?

HUNK *slouches down the street, followed in a painfully weary shuffle by a gaunt, raw-boned, unkempt woman, sloppy and disheveled. Her one garment, an ancient housedress retrieved from some garbage heap, black with grease stains. Her legs are stockingless, knotted and bulging with blue, twisted, cord-like veins. Her feet show through the cracks in her house slippers. In contrast to the picture of general decay is a face that looks as if it were carved out of granite; as if infinite suffering had been met with dogged, unyielding strength.*

HUNK: Hey!

*She comes to a dead stop as she sees* MARTIN. *There is no other sign of recognition, no friendliness on her lips. She stares at him out of dull, hostile eyes.*

MARTIN'S *face lights, he grins. He steps rapidly toward her:* Hello, Mom! How are yuh? *Pause.* It's me. *No recognition.* I had my face fixed. *There is a moment of silence. She finally speaks in an almost inaudible monotone.*

MRS. MARTIN: Yuh no-good tramp!

MARTIN: Mom!

MRS. MARTIN: What're yuh doin' here?

MARTIN: Aintcha glad tuh see me? *She suddenly smacks him a sharp crack across the cheek.*

MRS. MARTIN: That's how glad I am.

MARTIN, *rubs his cheek, stunned by this unexpected reception. He stammers:* 'At's a great hello.

MRS. MARTIN: Yuh dog! Yuh stinkin' yellow dog yuh!

MARTIN: Mom! What kin' a talk is 'at? Gese, Mom . . .

MRS. MARTIN: Don't call me Mom! Yuh ain't no son a mine. What do yuh want from me now?

MARTIN: Nuttin'. I just . . .

MRS. MARTIN, *her voice rises, shrill, hysterical:* Then git out a here! Before I crack yuh goddam face again. Git out a here!

MARTIN, *flaring:* Why, yuh ole tramp, I killed a guy fer lookin' at me da way yew are!

MRS. MARTIN, *stares at him and nods slowly. Then, quietly:* Yeah. . . . You're a killer all right. . . . You're a murderer . . . you're a butcher, sure! Why don't yuh leave me ferget yuh? Ain' I got troubles enough with the cops and newspapers botherin' me? An' Johnny and Martha . . .

MARTIN: What's a mattuh wid' 'em?

MRS. MARTIN: None a yer business! Just leave us alone! Yuh never brought nothin' but trouble. Don't come back like a bad penny! . . . Just stay away and leave us alone . . . an' die . . . but leave us alone! *She turns her back on him, and starts to go.*

MARTIN: Hey, wait!

MRS. MARTIN, *pauses:* What?

MARTIN: Need any dough?

MRS. MARTIN: Keep yer blood money.

MARTIN: Yuh gonna rat on me . . . gonna tell a cops?

MRS. MARTIN: No. They'll get yuh soon enough.

MARTIN: Not me! Not Martin! Huh, not Baby-face Martin!

MRS. MARTIN, *mutters:* Baby-face! Baby-face! I remember . . . *She begins to sob, clutching her stomach.* In here . . . in here! Kickin'! That's where yuh come from. God! I ought to be cut open here fer givin' yuh life . . . murderer!!! *She shuffles away, up the street, weeping quietly.* MARTIN *stands there looking after her for a long time. His hand goes to his cheek.* HUNK *comes down to him, clucking sympathetically. A boat whistle is heard.*

HUNK: How da yuh like 'at! Yuh come all away across a country jus' tuh see yer ole lady, an' what da yuh git? Crack inna face! I dunno, my mudder ain' like dat. My mudder's always glad tuh see me. . . .

MARTIN, *low, without turning:* Shut up! Gese, I must a been soft inna head, so help me!

HUNK: Yuh should a slugged 'er one.

MARTIN: Shut up! I must a bin crazy inna head. I musta bin nuts.

HUNK: Nah! It's jus' she ain't gota heart. Dat ain' . . .

MARTIN, *turns on* HUNK, *viciously, barking:* Screw, willyuh? Screw! *Exit* HUNK *up the sidewalk.* MARTIN *turns, looking after his mother. Turns slowly onto the sidewalk, then notices* GIMPTY. Kin yuh pitchure dat?

GIMPTY: What did you expect . . . flags and a brass band?

MARTIN, *suddenly wheels and slaps* GIMPTY: Why—yew—punk!

GIMPTY: What's the idea?

MARTIN: Dat's ee idea . . . fer shootin' off yer mout'. I don' like guys 'at talk outa toin. Not tuh me!

GIMPTY: Who the hell do you think you are?

MARTIN, *claws his fingers and pushes* GIMPTY's *face against the wall:* Why, yuh lousy cripple, I'll . . .

GIMPTY, *jerks his head free of* MARTIN's *clutch:* Gee, when I was a kid I used to think you were something, but you're rotten . . . see? You ought to be wiped out!

MARTIN, *his face twitching, the veins on his forehead standing out, kicks* GIMPTY's *crippled foot and shouts:* Shut up!

GIMPTY, *gasps in pain, glaring at* MARTIN. *After a long pause, quietly, deliberately:* All right. O.K., Martin! Just wait!

MARTIN: What? *Reaches for his shoulder holster.* What's 'at?

GIMPTY: Go on! Shoot me! That'll bring 'em right to you! Go on!

MARTIN, *hesitates. He is interrupted by the excited voices of* GRISWALD *and* PHILIP. *Cautiously he restrains himself and whispers:* I'll talk to yuh later. I'll be waitin' right up thuh street, see? Watch yuh step.

GRISWALD *appears behind the gate with* PHILIP, *who is sobbing. The* GOVERNESS *tries to quiet* PHILIP *while she dabs his face with her handkerchief.* MARTIN *goes up the street.*

GRISWALD: It's all right, Son! Now stop crying! What happened? Stop crying! Tell me just what happened?

GOVERNESS: *Attends, mon pauvre petit . . .* 'ere, let me wipe your face . . . *attends, attends!*

PHILIP: They hit me with a stick!

GRISWALD: A stick!

PHILIP, *spread-eagling his arms:* That big!

GRISWALD, *furious:* I'll have them locked up . . . I swear I'll send them to jail. Would you know them if you saw them?

PHILIP: Yes, Daddy.

GRISWALD, *to the* GOVERNESS: You should have been with him. After yesterday . . .

GOVERNESS: I told him to stay in the garden. Madame said it was all right and she asked me to help Clara with the curtains in his room.

SPIT *starts up the ladder, followed by the other boys.* DIPPY *is frozen. He is blue and shaking with cold. His teeth are chattering.*

DIPPY: Look, I'm shiverin'. My teet' 'r' knockin'.

TOMMY: Yeah. Yuh lips 'r' blue! Yuh bettuh git dressed quick, aw yuh'll ketch cold. *Looks down at* MILTY, *who is climbing the ladder, behind him.* How do yuh like it, Milty?

MILTY, *grins from ear to ear:* Swell!

As the boys appear over the parapet, T.B. *rises from under the hopper, points to* GRISWALD, *and calls the danger-cry.*

T.B.: Chikee! Putzo! Hey, felluhs! Chikee! Tommy!

PHILIP *sees the boys and points them out to* GRISWALD.

PHILIP: There they are! They're the ones. *Points out* TOMMY. He's the leader!

GRISWALD: That one?

PHILIP: Yes.

SPIT, DIPPY, MILTY, *and* ANGEL *dash to the hopper, all yelling "Chikee!" They gather up their clothes and run madly up the street, followed by* T.B. TOMMY, *stooping to pick up his clothes, trips, falls, and is grabbed by* GRISWALD, *who shakes him violently.*

GRISWALD: What right did you have to beat this boy? What makes you think you can get away with that?

TOMMY, *struggling to escape:* Lemme go! Lemme go, will yuh? I didn' do nuttin' . . . lemme go!

PHILIP, *jumping up and down with excitement:* He's the one! He's got the watch, Daddy!

TOMMY, *tries to break away and get at* PHILIP: I have not, yuh fat li'l bastid!

GOVERNESS, *frightened, screams:* Philippe, come 'ere!

GRISWALD, *jerks* TOMMY *back:* Oh, no! Not this time! I'll break your neck!

PHILIP: He's the one!

GRISWALD: Give me that watch!

TOMMY: I yain't got it!

PHILIP: He has! He's got it!

GRISWALD, *turns to the* GOVERNESS, *peremptorily:* Jeanne! Call an officer! *To* TOMMY *again.* Give me that watch!

TOMMY, *frightened by the police threat:* I yain't got it. Honest, I yain't! *Suddenly shouts up the street for help.* Hey, felluhs!
    *The* GOVERNESS *stands there, paralyzed.*

GRISWALD: Jeanne, will you call an officer! Come on! Hurry!

GOVERNESS: *Oui, oui, monsieur!*
    *She runs up the sidewalk in a stiff-legged trot.*

TOMMY, *stops struggling for a moment:* Aw, mister, don't toin me ovuh tuh da cops, will yuh? I won' touch 'im again. We do it to allee udduh kids, an 'ey do it tuh us. Dat ain' nuttin'.

GRISWALD: No? I ought to break your neck.

TOMMY: Oh, yeah? *He suddenly pulls away, almost escaping.* GRISWALD *puts more pressure on the arm.* TOMMY *calls to the gang.* Hey, felluhs! GRISWALD *twists his arm double.* TOMMY *begins to cry with pain, striking at* GRISWALD. Yuh joik! Ow, yuh breakin' my ahm! Hey, Gimpty!

GIMPTY: Have a heart! You're hurting that kid. You don't have to . . .

GRISWALD: Hurt him! I'll kill him!
    MILTY *runs down the street, holding out the watch.*

MILTY: Heah yuh ah! Heah's duh watch! Leave 'im go, misteh! He didn' do nuttin'! Leave 'im go! *He starts pounding* GRISWALD. TOMMY *frees his hand.* GRISWALD *hooks his arm around* TOMMY *in a stranglehold, and with the free arm pushes* MILTY *away.*

GRISWALD, *to* MILTY: Get out of here, you . . .

TOMMY: Hey, yer chokin' me! Yer chokin' me! *Both hands free, he gropes in the trousers he has clung to. Suddenly he produces an open jackknife and waves it.* Look out! I gotta knife. I'll stab yuh! GRISWALD *only holds him tighter, trying to capture the knife. A flash of steel!* GRISWALD *groans and clutches his wrist, releasing* TOMMY. TOMMY *and* MILTY *fly up the street.* GRISWALD *stands there stunned, staring at his bleeding wrist.*

PHILIP: Daddy! Daddy! Daddy! *He begins to sob at the sight of blood.*
   *The* DOORMAN *comes out of the gateway and is immediately excited.*
DOORMAN: What's the matter?
GRISWALD, *jerking his head toward the fleeing boys:* Catch those boys! *The*
   DOORMAN *lumbers up the street in pursuit.* GRISWALD *takes a handker-*
   *chief from his breast pocket and presses it to his wrist. Blood seeps*
   *through.* GRISWALD, *self-controlled now, tries to quiet the sobbing* PHILIP.
   It's all right, son, it's all right! No, no, no! Now stop crying. Let me have
   your handkerchief!
GIMPTY: Are you hurt?
GRISWALD: What do you think?
GIMPTY: Can I help?
GRISWALD: It's a little late for that now.
PHILIP, *fishes out a crumpled handkerchief and hands it to his father:* Here.
GRISWALD: Haven't you a clean one?
PHILIP: No.
GIMPTY: You can have mine.
GRISWALD: Never mind. *To* PHILIP, *who puts his own handkerchief back.*
   You should always carry two clean handkerchiefs. Put your hand in my
   pocket. You'll find one there. No, the other pocket.
   PHILIP *finds the handkerchief. The* GOVERNESS *comes down the side-*
*walk with a policeman,* MULLIGAN.
MULLIGAN: What's the matter?
GRISWALD: Plenty.
GOVERNESS, *sees the blood and shrieks:* Oh! He's bleeding! *To* PHILIP.
   *Qu'est-ce qui se passe, mon petit?*
PHILIP: That boy stuck him with a knife!
GOVERNESS, *to* GRISWALD: *Mon Dieu!* Are you hurt, *monsieur?*
   GRISWALD *ignores her and tightens the bandage.*
MULLIGAN: Is it deep?
GRISWALD: Deep enough.
MULLIGAN: Better let me make a tourniquet.
GRISWALD: Never mind.
MULLIGAN: Who did it?
GRISWALD: One of these hoodlums around here. I want that boy arrested.
MULLIGAN: Sure. Do you know who he was?
GRISWALD: No.
GOVERNESS: Can I help you, *monsieur?*
GRISWALD: Yes. Go up and call Dr. Merriam at once. I'm afraid of infection.
   *The* DOORMAN *returns, empty-handed, puffing, and mopping his brow.*
   GRISWALD *frowns.* Where is he?

DOORMAN, *panting:* Phew . . . I couldn't catch them.

GRISWALD, *angry:* You let them go?

DOORMAN: I tried, sir. They were like little flies . . . in and out. . . . Just when I thought I had one of them. . . . he ran down the cellar. . . . I went after him, but he got away. . . .

GRISWALD: Officer, I want you to find that boy and arrest him. Understand?

MULLIGAN, *takes out a notebook and pencil:* Well, that ain't gonna be so easy, you know.

GRISWALD: Never mind. That's your job! It's pretty serious that a thing like this can happen on your beat in broad daylight.

MULLIGAN: Well, I can't be everywhere at once.

GRISWALD: Before he stabbed me, he and some others beat up my boy and stole his watch. You should have been around some of that time.

MULLIGAN, *annoyed at his officiousness. Brusquely:* Well . . . what's your name?

GRISWALD: My name's Griswald . . . I live here. *Nods toward the East River Terrace.*

MULLIGAN: What did the boy look like?

GRISWALD: He was about so high . . . black hair . . . oh, I don't know. I didn't notice. Did you, son?

PHILIP: One of them coughs.

MULLIGAN: Didn't you notice anything else?

PHILIP: No.

GRISWALD: Jeanne?

GOVERNESS: Let me see . . .

MULLIGAN: How was he dressed?

GOVERNESS: They'd been in swimming here. They were practically naked . . . and filthy. And their language was 'orrible.

GRISWALD, *irritated:* He knows that, he knows that! What were they like, though? Didn't you see?

GOVERNESS: It all happened so quickly, I didn't have a chance to, *monsieur.*

PHILIP: He hit me with a stick.

MULLIGAN: Hm!

GRISWALD, *suddenly a bit faint:* These men can tell you better. They saw it. Jeanne, will you please call Dr. Merriam right away? I'm feeling a little sick.

GOVERNESS: *Oui, monsieur!* Come, Philippe! *She goes in, accompanied by* PHILIP.

GRISWALD: I don't want to make any trouble, Officer, but I want that boy caught and arrested. Understand?

MULLIGAN: I'll do the best I can. *Exit* GRISWALD. MULLIGAN *mutters:* I wonder who the hell that guy thinks he is. . . .

DOORMAN, *impressively, rolling the sound on his tongue:* Mr. Griswald.
  CHARLES, *the chauffeur, saunters down the sidewalk.*
MULLIGAN: What of it?
DOORMAN: Don't you know? He's Judge Griswald's brother.
MULLIGAN, *his attitude changes:* Oh!
DOORMAN, *to the CHAUFFEUR, who has reached the gate:* Oh, I don't think
  Mr. Griswald'll be using the car now. He was just hurt.
CHARLES: Wha-a-at? What happened?
DOORMAN: He was stabbed. It's a long story. I'll tell you later.
CHARLES, *concerned:* Well, will you call him and see if he wants me?
DOORMAN, *starting off:* Yeah.
MULLIGAN: Hey, wait!
DOORMAN: I'll be right out, Officer. Mr. Griswald may need him.
MULLIGAN: Oh, all right.
  DOORMAN *and* CHARLES *go in through the gate.*
CHARLES: What happened?
DOORMAN: These kids around here have been raising an awful rumpus all
  day, and just now one of them . . .
  *Their voices die off.*
MULLIGAN, *to* GIMPTY: Did you see the kids who did this?
GIMPTY: I didn't notice them.
MULLIGAN: You come around here often?
GIMPTY: Yes.
MULLIGAN: Didn't you recognize any of 'em?
GIMPTY: No.
MULLIGAN: Can you describe 'em?
GIMPTY: Not very clearly.
MULLIGAN, *annoyed:* Well, what were they like?
GIMPTY: About so high . . . dirty an' naked. . . .
MULLIGAN, *impatiently:* And they socked that young jalopee in the eye.
  Yeah. I got that much myself. But that might be any kid in this neighbor-
  hood. Anything else?
GIMPTY: No.
MULLIGAN, *slaps his book shut:* Why the hell didn't I learn a trade? *He starts
  toward the gate.* DRINA *comes down the street and approaches* GIMPTY.
  *She looks tired and bedraggled. She has an ugly bruise on her forehead.*
GIMPTY, *to* DRINA: Hey, what's the matter with your head?
DRINA, *looking at* MULLIGAN *and raising her voice:* We were picketing the
  store, an' some lousy cop hit me.
MULLIGAN, *wheels around, insulted:* What's that?
DRINA, *deliberately:* One a you lousy cops hit me.
MULLIGAN: You better watch your language or you'll get another clout!

DRINA: Go on and try it!

GIMPTY, *urging discretion:* Sh!

MULLIGAN: Listen! I'm in no mood to be tampered with. I'm in no mood! . . . Not by a lousy Red.

DRINA, *quietly:* I ain't no Red.

MULLIGAN, *thick-skulled:* Well, you talk like one.

DRINA: Aw nuts!

MULLIGAN: You were strikin', weren't you?

DRINA: Sure. Because I want a few bucks more a week so's I can live decent. God knows I earn it!

MULLIGAN, *who has had enough:* Aw, go on home! *He turns and goes in the gate, addressing someone.* Hey, Bill, I wanna see you . . . *Pause.*

DRINA, *to* GIMPTY: We were only picketing. We got a right to picket. They charged us. They hit us right and left. Three of the girls were hurt bad.

GIMPTY: I'll give you some advice about your brother.

DRINA: I was just lookin' for him. Did you see him?

GIMPTY: Tell him to keep away from here . . . or he's in for a lot of trouble.

DRINA, *sits down, exhausted, and sighs:* What's he done now?

GIMPTY: Plenty.

DRINA: What?

GIMPTY: Just tell him to keep away.

DRINA: Gosh, I don't know what to do with that boy! *A passing boat hoots twice.* DRINA *ponders her problem a moment.* There's a feller I know . . . is always askin' me to marry him. . . . Maybe I ought to do that, hm? . . . For Tommy . . . he's rich. . . . What should I do?

GIMPTY, *disinterested, too absorbed in his own problem:* That's up to you.

DRINA: Most of the girls at the store are always talkin' about marryin' a rich guy. I used to laugh at 'em. *She laughs now at herself.*

GIMPTY: Maybe they're right.

DRINA, *looks at him:* That doesn't sound like you.

GIMPTY: No? How do you know what goes on inside of me?

DRINA, *shakes her head and smiles sadly:* I know.

GIMPTY, *curtly:* Smart girl!

DRINA, *very tender and soft. She knows he's suffering:* What's the matter?

GIMPTY: Nothing.

DRINA: I understand.

GIMPTY: You can't.

DRINA: Why can't I? *Suddenly exasperated.* Sometimes, for a boy as bright as you, with your education, you talk like a fool. Don't you think I got a heart too? Don't you think there are nights when I cry myself to sleep? Don't you think I know what it means to be lonely and scared and to want somebody? God, ain't I human? Am I so homely that I ain't got a right to . . .

GIMPTY: No, Drina! I think you're a swell girl. You are.

DRINA, *turns away, annoyed at his patronage:* Oh, don't give me any of that taffy! You don't even know I'm alive!

GIMPTY: Why do you say that?

DRINA: What's the difference? It don't matter. . . . Only I hate to see you butting your head against a stone wall. You're only going to hurt yourself.

GIMPTY: What're you talking about?

DRINA: You know. . . . Oh, I think that lady's beautiful . . . and I think she's nice. . . .

GIMPTY, *angry:* Look! Will you be a good girl and mind your own business?

DRINA: She's not for you!

GIMPTY: Why not?

*MULLIGAN comes out of the East River Terrace, notebook and pencil in hand. He goes to GIMPTY.*

MULLIGAN: Well, I got something to work on, anyway. . . . Do you know a kid named Tommy-something around here?

*DRINA starts, but checks herself.*

GIMPTY: No.

MULLIGAN: They heard the others call him Tommy. *Jerks his head toward the gate.* You know what he's liable to do? With his pull? Have me broke, maybe. The first thing I know, I'll be pounding a lousier post than this! Harlem, maybe. Get a knife in my back. . . . *Looks up from his notebook, to DRINA.* Hey, you!

DRINA: What?

MULLIGAN: You live around here?

DRINA, *very docile, frightened:* Yes.

MULLIGAN: Know a kid named Tommy-something?

DRINA: No . . . no, I don't.

MULLIGAN, *studying his notes:* I'll catch him. I'll skin him alive!

DRINA, *finally ventures:* What'd he do?

MULLIGAN: Pulled a knife on some high muck-a-muck in there.

DRINA: No!

MULLIGAN: Yeah. Ah, it don't pay to be nice to these kids. It just don't pay.

DRINA: Was the man hurt?

MULLIGAN: Yeah. It looks like a pretty deep cut. Lord, he's fit to be tied! I never seen a guy so boined up! *DRINA turns and goes up the street, restraining her impulse to run. MULLIGAN jabbers on, complainingly.* This is a tough enough precinct . . . but Harlem?—There's a lousy precinct! A pal of mine got killed there last year Left a wife and a couple a kids.

GIMPTY: Is that so?

MULLIGAN: Yeah.

GIMPTY: Too bad! *As the idea begins to take form.* Well . . . maybe you can catch Baby-face Martin or one of those fellows, and grab off that forty-two-hundred-dollar reward.

MULLIGAN: Yeah.

GIMPTY: Then you could retire.

MULLIGAN: Yeah, you could do a lot on that.

GIMPTY: Yeah, I guess you could. . . . Say . . . tell me something. . . .

MULLIGAN: What?

GIMPTY: Supposin' . . . supposin' a fellow knew where that . . . er . . . Baby-face Martin is located. How would he go about reporting him . . . and making sure of not getting gypped out of the reward?

MULLIGAN: Just phone police headquarters . . . or the Department of Justice direct. They'd be down here in two minutes. *He looks at* GIMPTY *and asks ironically:* Why? You don't know where he is, do you?

GIMPTY, *smiles wanly back at him:* Colorado, the newspapers say. . . . No, I was just wonderin'.

MULLIGAN: Well, whoever turns that guy in is taking an awful chance. He's a killer.

GIMPTY: Well . . . you can't live forever.

*A passing tug shrieks its warning signal. And shrieks again.* MARTIN *walks, cat-footed, down the street.*

MULLIGAN: That's right.

GUMPTY *turns, sees* MARTIN, *and rises.*

GIMPTY, *to* MULLIGAN: Excuse me.

MULLIGAN: Sure.

GIMPTY *crosses to the other side of the street and walks away, pretending not to notice* MARTIN.

MARTIN: Hello, Gimpty! GIMPTY *accelerates his pace and hobbles off.* MARTIN *sucks his teeth for a second, thinking. Then he adopts an amiable smile and approaches* MULLIGAN. Kinda quiet today, ain' it, Officer?

MULLIGAN: Not with these kids around.

MARTIN, *jerks his head in* GIMPTY's *direction:* Dat's a nice feller. Friend a mine.

HUNK *has entered from up the street just after* GIMPTY's *exit. He is lighting a cigar, when he sees* MARTIN *in friendly conversation with the arch-enemy. He stands there, transfixed, match to cigar.*

MULLIGAN: I had quite a talk with him.

MARTIN, *fishing:* What about?

MULLIGAN: Oh . . . about these kids here.

MARTIN: Zat all?

MULLIGAN: Say, that's plenty! *He puts his notebook in his pocket.* You don't happen to know a kid around here named Tommy-something, do you?

MARTIN, *shakes his head:* Uh-uh!

MULLIGAN: Well, I'll catch him, all right! *He strides up the sidewalk.* MARTIN *watches him, then laughs. The match burns* HUNK's *fingers. He drops it.*

HUNK: Jesus!

MARTIN, *laughing:* A pal a mine.

HUNK: Dat's crazy.

MARTIN: Dey don' know me . . . wid' dis mug.

HUNK, *sighs. This is too much for him. Then he remembers his errand:* Say, dat dame is heah.

MARTIN: Who?

HUNK: Er . . . Francey, or whatevah yuh call huh.

MARTIN: She is?

HUNK: Yeah. I got 'er waitin' on a corner. *Puzzled.* I dunno what yuh wanna bodder wid' a cheap hustluh like dat fuh.

MARTIN, *sharply:* Wha da yuh mean? Francey ain' no hustluh!

HUNK, *skeptical:* No?

MARTIN: No.

HUNK, *smiles weakly:* O.K. My mistake. We all make mistakes, boss. Dat's what dey got rubbuhs on ee end a pencils faw. *Laughs feebly.*

MARTIN: Pretty cute, ain' cha? Maybe yuhr a mistake. Maybe yuhr liable tuh git rubbed out yuhself.

HUNK, *frightened:* I'll git huh now. *He starts off. A young girl comes down the street, an obvious whore of the lowest class, wearing her timeless profession defiantly. A pert, pretty little face still showing traces of quality and something once sweet and fine. Skin an unhealthy pallor, lips a smear of rouge. Her mop of dyed red hair is lusterless, strawy, dead from too much alternate bleach and henna. She carries herself loosely. Droopshouldered. Voluptuous S-shaped posture. There are no clothes under her cheap, faded, green silk dress, cut so tight that it reveals the nipples of her full breasts, her navel, the "V" of her crotch, the muscles of her buttocks. She has obviously dressed hastily, carelessly; one stocking streaked with runs dribbles down at the ankle. She accosts* HUNK, *impatiently.*

FRANCEY: Hey, what ta hell's ee idear, keepin' me standin' on a corner all day? I'm busy. I gotta git back tuh da house. Yuh want Ida tuh break my face?

MARTIN *looks at her.*

MARTIN: Francey! Jesus, what's come over yuh?

FRANCEY, *turning sharply to Martin:* How do yew know my name? Who are yew? *Impatiently.* Well, who th' hell . . . *Then she recognizes him, and gasps.* Fuh th' love a God! Marty!

MARTIN, *never taking his eyes off the girl:* Yeah. Hunk . . . scram!

 HUNK *goes up the street, stops at the tenement stoop, and lounges there, within earshot.*

FRANCEY, *eagerly:* How are yuh, Marty?

MARTIN: Read duh papers!

FRANCEY: Yuh did somethin' to yuh face.

MARTIN: Yeah. Plastic, dey call it.

FRANCEY: They said yuh wuz out aroun' Coloradah—th' noospapuhs! Gee, I'm glad to see yuh! MARTIN *slips his arm around her waist and draws her tight to his body. As his lips grope for hers,* FRANCEY *turns her face away.* MARTIN *tries to pull her face around. She cries furiously:* No . . . don' kiss me on a lips!

MARTIN, *releasing her, puzzled:* What? What's a matter? *He can't believe this. He frowns.* I ain't good enough for yuh?

FRANCEY, *quickly:* No. It ain't dat. It ain't yew. It's me. I got a sore on my mouth. Fuh yuhr own good, I don't want yuh to kiss me, dat's why.

MARTIN: I ain't nevuh fuhgot da way yew kiss.

FRANCEY, *wistfully:* I ain't niethuh. *She laughs.* Go on! You wit all yer fancy dames. Where do I come off?

MARTIN: Dey don't mean nuttin'.

FRANCEY: Dat chorus goil . . . what's 'er name?

MARTIN: Nuttin'. She ain't got nuttin' . . . no guts, no fire. . . . But yew been boinin' in my blood . . . evuh since . . .

FRANCEY: An' yew been in mine . . . if yuh wanna know.

MARTIN: Remembuh dat foist night . . . on a roof?

FRANCEY: Yeah, I remembuh . . . da sky was full a stars, an' I was full a dreamy ideas. Dat was me foist time. I was fourteen, goin' on fifteen.

MARTIN: Yeah. It wuz mine too. It wuz terrific. Hit me right wheah I live . . . like my back wuz meltin'. An I wuz so sca'd when yuh started laffin' an' cryin', crazy-like. . . . *They both laugh, enjoying the memory, a little embarrassed by it.*

FRANCEY: Yeah.

MARTIN: Gee, I nevuh wuz so sca'd like 'at time.

FRANCEY: Me too.

MARTIN, *draws her to him again, more gently:* Come eah! Close to me!

FRANCEY, *acquiescing:* Ony don' kiss me on a lips!

MARTIN: Closuh! *They stand there a moment, bodies close, passionate.* MARTIN *buries his face in her hair.*

FRANCEY, *eyes closed, whispers:* Marty!

MARTIN: Dose times unduh da stairs . . .

FRANCEY: A couple a crazy kids we were! We wuz gonna git married. I bought a ring at da five an' dime staw.

MARTIN: Yeah. Ony we didn' have money enough fuh de license. Gee, it seems like yestiddy. We wuz talkin' about it right heah.

FRANCEY: Yestiddy! It seems like a million yeahs!

MARTIN, *as voices are heard coming from the East River Terrace:* Wait! *They separate. He draws his hat over his eyes and turns away as a young couple come out of the gate and walk up the street.*

GIRL: So many people standing around. What's all the excitement? What's happened?

MAN: The elevator man said someone was stabbed.

GIRL: Really? Who was it, do you know?

MAN: Mr. Griswald, I think he said. Twelfth floor.

GIRL: Oh! Yes? Did he say who did it?

MAN: He said one of the kids around here somewhere. . . .

*When they are well out of sight,* FRANCEY *clutches* MARTIN'S *arm.*

FRANCEY: Marty, listen! Yuh got ta take care a yuhself. Yuh gotta go way an' hide. I don' wan' 'em to git yuh! I don' wan' 'em to git yuh!

MARTIN: Whatsa diffrince wheah I go? Ey got thuh finger on me everywheah. Ah, frig 'em.

FRANCEY: Dey won't reco'nize yuh. Dey won't! Even I didn't.

MARTIN: Yeah, but yuh can' change 'ese, Francey. Look! *He holds up his fingers. The tips are yellow and scarred.* Tree times I boined 'em wid' acid an' t'ings. No good. Dere are some t'ings yuh can't change. But I'll tell yuh what . . . I'll scram outta heah. I'll scram . . . if yew come wid' me.

FRANCEY: Ah, what do yuh want me fer? A broken-down hoor.

MARTIN: Shut up!

FRANCEY: I wouldn' be good fuh yuh.

MARTIN: I know what I want.

FRANCEY, *laughs, crazily:* Yeah. Dis is a swell pipe dream I'm havin'! I'm Minnie de Moocher kickin' a gong aroun'!

MARTIN: Listen! I got de dough now, kid. We kin do it now.

FRANCEY: But I'm sick, Marty! Don't yuh see? I'm sick!

MARTIN: What's a matter wid' yuh?

FRANCEY, *almost inaudibly:* What do yuh think?

MARTIN *looks at her for a long time. He sees her. The nostalgic dream is finished. His lips begin to curl in disgust.*

MARTIN: Why didncha git a job?

FRANCEY: Dey don grow on trees!

MARTIN: Why didncha starve foist?

FRANCEY: Why didnchou?

> MARTIN *makes no effort to conceal his growing disgust. Turns away.*

FRANCEY, *suddenly shouts, fiercely, at the top of her lungs:* Well, what ta hell did yuh expect?

MARTIN: I don' know.

> *A passing tug shrieks hoarsely. The echo floats back.*

FRANCEY, *quietly, clutching at a hope:* Maybe . . . if yuh got da dough . . . yuh git a doctuh an' he fixes me up . . .

MARTIN: Nah. Once at stuff gits in yuh . . . nah! *Again the tug shrieks and is answered by its echo. He reaches into his inner breast pocket, extracts a fat roll of bills, peels off several, and hands them to her.* Heah. Buy yerself somethin'.

FRANCEY, *her eyes suddenly glued to the money:* Baby! Dat's some roll yuh got. Yuh cud choke a hoss wid' dat.

MARTIN, *thrusting it at her:* Heah!

FRANCEY, *takes the money:* Is it hot?

MARTIN: Yeah. Bettah be careful where yuh spend it.

FRANCEY: Sure.

MARTIN: An' keep yuh lips buttoned up!

FRANCEY: I wouldn' tell on yuh, Marty. Not if dey tied me ta wild hosses, I wouldn't.

MARTIN: Bettuh not.

FRANCEY, *folds her money, still fascinated by the huge roll of bills in his hand. Her voice takes on a peculiar whining, wheedling quality:* Honey!

MARTIN: Yeah?

FRANCEY: Cud yuh spare another twenty bucks? I godda . . .

MARTIN: No!

FRANCEY: Aw, come on, dearie!

MARTIN: No!

FRANCEY: Don't be a tightwad!

MARTIN, *reaching the limit of his disgust:* What ta hell do yuh t'ink I am? Some guy yuh got up in yuh room? I'll . . . *He raises his hand, ready to slap her. Again the shriek of a tug, and the echo.*

FRANCEY, *quickly, frightened:* Nah, ferget it, Marty! I wuz just . . .

MARTIN: Awright! Awright! Now beat it!

FRANCEY: O.K., Marty. *She starts to go, pauses, turns back.* Fer old times' sakes, will yuh do me a favor? Please?

MARTIN, *shoves the money back into his pocket:* No!

FRANCEY: Not dat.

MARTIN: What?

FRANCEY: Will yuh kiss me! Heah? Ona cheek? Jus' fuh old times' sakes? Come on. *He hesitates. She comes close, presses her cheek against his lips. He pecks her cheek, and turns away, scowling. She laughs, a low bitter laugh, at his obvious disrelish.* Thanks! *She goes up the street slowly, her purse swinging carelessly, her body swaying invitation, the tired march of her profession. The shriek of the tug is drawn out and distant now. The echo lingers.* MARTIN *spits and wipes the kiss off his lips with a groan of distaste.*

HUNK, *comes down the sidewalk, slowly:* Well?

MARTIN: Huh?

HUNK: See?

MARTIN: Yeah. Yeah!

HUNK: Twice in one day. Deah yuh ah! I toldja we shouldn' a come back. But yuh wouldn' lissen a me. Yuh nevuh lissen a me.

MARTIN: Yeah.

HUNK, *trying to console him:* I know how yuh feel, Marty. Les go back to St. Louis, huh? Now dat dame yuh had deah—Deedy Cook—Now dat wuz a broad. Regaler. Bet she's waitin' fuh yuh . . . wid' welcome ona doormat.

MARTIN: Awright! Don' talk about dames, Hunk, will yuh? Fuhget 'em. All cats look alike inna dahk. Fuhget 'em.

*A little girl comes out of the gate, bouncing a rubber ball.* MARTIN *looks at her, thinks a moment, turns to watch her go up the street. He sucks his teeth a moment, thinking.*

HUNK: Listen, Marty. . . . Let's git outa heah. Too many people know yuh heah. Whaddaya say?

MARTIN: Sh! I'm thinkin'. *Pause.*

HUNK: Well, guess I'll go shoot a game a pillpool. *Starts to go up the street.*

MARTIN, *motions him back, turns to stare at the Terrace Apartments:* Wait a minute. . . . HUNK *returns.* Yuh know, Hunk. *He shakes a thumb at the Apartment.* Der's a pile a tin in 'ere.

HUNK: Yeah.

MARTIN: Didja see what dese kids did heah today?

HUNK: No.

MARTIN: 'Ey got one a dese rich little squoits in a hallway, slapped him around, an' robbed his watch.

HUNK: So what?

*A man appears on the terrace, watches them for a second, and then slips away. Two men come down the street talking casually, one of them goes into the tenement, the other, waiting for him, wanders over back of the hopper and is hidden from view.*

MARTIN, *glances at them, lowers his voice:* Maybe we kin pull a snatch . . . kidnap one a dese babies.

HUNK: We're too hot. Foolin' round wid' kids ain' our racket.

MARTIN: Scared?

HUNK: No . . . ony . . . I . . .

MARTIN: Stop yuh yammerin'! Git a hold a Whitey. See wot he knows about duh mugs in heah! *HUNK hesitates.* Come on, Hunk, git goin'!

HUNK: O.K. Yuh duh boss! *He goes reluctantly.*

*The tap of* GIMPTY's *cane on the sidewalk is heard approaching, its rhythmic click ominous.* GIMPTY *appears, tight-lipped, pale, grim.* MARTIN *smiles out of one corner of his lips, and throws him a conciliatory greeting.*

MARTIN: Hello, Gimpty!

GIMPTY *turns away without answering.* MARTIN, *amused, laughs. He is suddenly in a good mood. The man who spied on him from the terrace appears in the gateway and catches* GIMPTY's *eye.* GIMPTY *points his cane at* MARTIN. *The good mood passes.* MARTIN's *eyebrows pull together in one puzzled line.*

MARTIN: What's eatin yuh, wise guy?

*The man behind the gate draws a revolver, comes quickly up behind* MARTIN, *and digs the gun in his back.*

G-MAN: Get 'em up, Martin! The Department of Justice wants you!

MARTIN: What ta hell . . . ! *Tries to turn, but the revolver prods him back.*

G-MAN: Come on, get 'em up!

MARTIN, *hands up:* I ain't Martin. My name's Johnson. Wanna see my license? *He slides his hand into his breast pocket.*

G-MAN: If you're smart, you'll behave yourself!

MARTIN, *wheels around, draws his gun, and fires in one motion:* No, yuh don't . . . *The G-MAN drops his gun, crumples onto the sidewalk, holding his belly and kicking.* MARTIN *turns to face* GIMPTY, *who has backed away to the hopper.* MARTIN, *his face black and contorted, aims at* GIMP-TY. So yuh ratted, yuh . . .

*From behind the hopper and the tenement doorway, guns explode. Two other G-MEN appear and descend on* MARTIN, *firing as they come.* MARTIN *groans, wheels, and falls, his face in the gutter, his fingers clawing the sidewalk. One of the G-MEN goes to aid his wounded comrade. The other G-MAN stands over* MARTIN's *body, pumping bullet after bullet into him, literally nailing him to the ground. The G-MAN kicks him to make sure he's dead. No twitch!* MARTIN *lies there flat. The G-MAN takes out a handkerchief, picks up* MARTIN's *gun gingerly, wraps it in the handkerchief, puts it in his pocket.*

SECOND G-MAN: Where'd he get you, Bob? Come on, sit up here! *Helps him to sit against the coping.* FIRST G-MAN *presses his hand in agony to his wound. From the street there is a rising babble of voices. Tenement windows are thrown up, heads thrust out; the curious crowd to the edge of the terrace, come to the gate, run down the street, collect in small groups, discussing the macabre scene in excited, hushed murmur. A* LADY *comes out of the gate, sees the dead man, screams hysterically, and is helped off by the* DOORMAN. MULLIGAN *comes tearing down the street, revolver drawn. He forces his way through the crowd.*

MULLIGAN: Outa my way! Look out! *To the* THIRD G-MAN. What's this?

THIRD G-MAN, *taking out a badge in a leather case from inside his coat pocket and holding it up:* It's all right, officer. Department of Justice! *Replaces the badge.*

MULLIGAN: What happened? Who's this guy?

THIRD G-MAN: Baby-face Martin.

MULLIGAN: Is that him?

THIRD G-MAN: Yep.

MULLIGAN: Gese, I was talkin' to him a couple of minutes ago.

SECOND G-MAN: Get an ambulance, quick! Will you?

MULLIGAN, *crosses to the police box, opens it:* Box 10 . . . Mulligan. Send ambulance! Make all notifications! Baby-face Martin was just shot by Federal men. He winged one of 'em. . . . I don't know . . . yeah . . . here. Gese, I was talking to him myself a few minutes ago. . . . Hell, Sarge, I couldn't recognize him. His face is all made over. *He hangs up. The shrill siren of a radio car mounts to a crescendo, mingles with the screech of brakes, and is suddenly silent. Two more policemen dash on, forcing their path through the crowd. They are followed by* SPIT, *wearing a single roller skate. He edges his way to the front of the crowd.*

SECOND POLICEMAN: Hi, Mulligan. What have yuh got here?

MULLIGAN: Baby-face Martin!

THIRD POLICEMAN: Did you git him?

MULLIGAN: No such luck. The Federal men got him. He winged one of them. *Gestures toward the wounded G-MAN.*

SECOND POLICEMAN: Did you notify the house?

MULLIGAN: Yeah. I gave 'em everything. . . . Lend us a hand, will yuh. Git rid of this crowd. MULLIGAN *stands by* MARTIN's *body, writing in a notebook. The other* POLICEMEN *push back the crowd.* SPIT *slips through, and looks at the dead man with scared curiosity.*

SECOND POLICEMAN, *pushing the crowd:* Break it up! This is no circus. Come on, break it up!

GIRL IN THE CROWD: Don't push me!

SECOND POLICEMAN: Well, go on home! Go on, break it up!

SECOND G-MAN, *to the wounded agent:* How you feelin', Bob?

FIRST G-MAN: Lousy.

SECOND G-MAN: You'll be O.K.

FIRST G-MAN: I don't know . . . I don't know! I should've plugged him right away . . . in the back. You don't give a snake like that a break. . . . Anyway, we got him! That's something!

SECOND G-MAN: Sure you did, Bob. You'll get cited for this.

FIRST G-MAN: That's dandy! That's just dandy! Give the medal to my old lady for the kids to play with . . . an' remember they once had an old man who was a . . . hero!

THIRD G-MAN: Aw, cut it, Bob. You'll be O.K. Don't talk like that!

DOORMAN, *pushing through the crowd:* Officer! Officer!

MULLIGAN: Get outa here! You with the rest of them. Come on, get back!

DOORMAN: Officer, this is important! That's one of the boys . . . there, that one! He's one of the gang!

MULLIGAN: What boy? What the hell are you talkin' about?

DOORMAN: The one who stabbed Mr. Griswald.

MULLIGAN: What? Oh, where?

DOORMAN, *pointing:* That one there! He's one of the gang.

MULLIGAN: Are you sure?

DOORMAN: Yes . . . yes . . . I'll swear to it!

MULLIGAN: Come here! Hey you! *Runs over to* SPIT, *grabs his arm. The murmur of the crowd rises.*

SPIT: Lemme go! I didn' do nuttin'. Lemme go!

SECOND POLICEMAN: What is this kid got to do with it?

MULLIGAN: That's somethin' else.

   *The clang of an approaching ambulance comes to a sudden halt. Enter, pushing their way down the street, an* INTERN *carrying a doctor's bag, followed by an* AMBULANCE MAN *carrying a folded stretcher, which encloses a pillow and a rolled blanket. The murmur of the crowd hushes.*

INTERN: Hello, Mulligan.

MULLIGAN: Hello, Doc. *To* SECOND POLICEMAN. Hold this kid a minute.

   SECOND POLICEMAN *grabs* SPIT's *arm and drags him back to the crowd on the sidewalk.*

INTERN: What's up? *He comes down to the body.*

MULLIGAN: Just got Baby-face Martin!

   *The murmur rises again as the news is spread.*

INTERN: You did? *He glances at the body.* He won't need me!

SECOND G-MAN: Hey, Doc, look at this man! *The* INTERN *kneels to the wounded man, examines his wound, sponges it, places a pad over it.* It's not bad, is it, Doc?

INTERN, *cheerfully:* Not very bad, but we'd better rush him off to the hospital. Here, somebody help get him on the stretcher.

*The* AMBULANCE MAN *opens the stretcher, places the pillow at the head.* SECOND G-MAN *and* MULLIGAN *lift the wounded* G-MAN *carefully and lay him on the stretcher with words of encouragement. The* AMBULANCE MAN *unrolls the blanket over him.* SECOND G-MAN *and the* AMBULANCE DRIVER *carry the wounded man up the sidewalk, calling "Gangway!" The* THIRD G-MAN *accompanies them, holding the wounded man's hand and talking to him. The crowd open a path, and stare, their murmur silenced for a moment.*

MULLIGAN, *pointing to* MARTIN: Want to look at this guy, Doc?

INTERN *kneels by the body, rips open the coat and vest, cursorily inspects the wounds, rolls back the eyelid, applies a stethoscope to the heart:* Phew! They certainly did a job on him! Nothing left to look at but chopped meat. God, they didn't leave enough of him for a good P.M.! *Rises, takes pad and pencil from his pocket, glances at* MULLIGAN's *shield, writes:* Mulligan . . . 10417 . . . 19th Precinct. Have you got his pedigree?

MULLIGAN, *reading from his own notebook:* Joe Martin. 28. White . . . U.S. 5 ft., 9 in. 170 lbs. Unmarried. Occupation . . . *Shrugs his shoulders.*

INTERN: All right. Dr. Flint. Mark him D.O.A.!

MULLIGAN, *writing:* Dead . . . on . . . arrival. . . .

*Enter, pushing their way through the crowd, the* MEDICAL EXAMINER, *followed by the* POLICE PHOTOGRAPHER. *The* PHOTOGRAPHER *opens his camera, adjusts it, and photographs the body from several angles.*

INTERN, *as the* EXAMINER *approaches:* Hello, Doc!

EXAMINER: Hello, Doctor. So they finally got him, did they?

INTERN: Yes, they sure did.

EXAMINER: It's about time. What have you got on him?

INTERN: Twelve gunshot wounds. Five belly, four chest, three head. *Picks up his bag and goes.*

*The* EXAMINER *inspects the body.*

MULLIGAN *to the* DOORMAN: Hey, find something to cover this up with. *The* DOORMAN *nods and disappears through the gateway.* MULLIGAN *turns to the* THIRD POLICEMAN, *who is still holding back the crowd.* Hey, Tom! Stand by while I go through this bum! *He kneels and goes through* MARTIN's *pockets, handing his findings to the* THIRD POLICEMAN *who jots them down in his notebook.* MULLIGAN *takes a ring off* MARTIN's *finger.* Diamond ring. Look at that rock! *He hands it to the* THIRD POLICEMAN, *who pockets it and makes a note.* MULLIGAN *extracts* MARTIN's *wad of bills.* And this roll of bills! What a pile! You count it!

EXAMINER: Through with him, boys?

MULLIGAN, *rising:* Yeah.

PHOTOGRAPHER: One second! *Takes a last photograph.*

EXAMINER: Well, as soon as the wagon comes, send him down to the morgue. I'll look him over in the morning. Mulligan, you report to me there first thing in the morning, too.

MULLIGAN: Yes, sir.

> The EXAMINER *goes. The* PHOTOGRAPHER *folds his camera and follows.*

WOMAN IN THE CROWD *to the* SECOND POLICEMAN, *who is holding* SPIT: Officer! What did this boy have to do with it? Why are you holding him?

SECOND POLICEMAN: Never mind. Stand back!

SPIT: Lemme go! I didn't do nuttin'! Whadda yuh want?

MULLIGAN, *goes to* SPIT: You're one of the gang who beat up a boy here today and stabbed his father, ain't you?

SPIT: No, I yain't. I did'n 'ave nuttin' tuh do wid' it. It wuz a kid named Tommy McGrath.

> *The murmur of the crowd fades as they all listen.*

MULLIGAN: Tommy McGrath! Where does he live?

SPIT: On Foist Avenoo between Fifty-toid and Fifty-fawt.

MULLIGAN: Sure?

SPIT: Yeah.

MULLIGAN, *to the* SECOND POLICEMAN: Take this kid around there, will yuh? Get ahold a Tommy McGrath. He's wanted for stabbin' some guy. I got to wait for the morgue wagon.

SECOND POLICEMAN: O.K. *Drags* SPIT *through the crowd.* Come on! You show us where he lives and we'll let you go. *As they go off, the murmur of the crowd rises again.*

> *The* THIRD G-MAN *crosses to* GIMPTY, *who is leaning against the hopper, white and shaking. The* DOORMAN *comes out with an old discarded coat, the gold braid ravelled and rusty, the cloth dirty and oil-stained.* MULLIGAN *takes it from him.*

THIRD G-MAN, *to* GIMPTY: Good work, Mac. Come over to the office and pick up your check. *He makes his way up the street.* MULLIGAN *throws the coat over* MARTIN's *body. The murmur of the crowd rises high. A boat horn in the river bellows hoarsely and dies away.*

*CURTAIN*

**ACT THREE**

*The same scene. That night. A very dark night. From the dock, the sounds of a gay party, music, babble, laughter. GIMPTY, a bent silhouette, sits on the coping, leaning against the terrace wall. There's a lamp shining up the street. The lights from the tenement windows are faint and yellow and glum. The lanterns on the gateposts, one red, one green, are lit and look very decorative. There's a blaze of fire crackling out of an old iron ash can in the center of the street. The boys hover over it, roasting potatoes skewered on long sticks. Their impish faces gleam red one minute and are wiped by shadows the next as they lean over the flames.*

ANGEL, *gesturing wildly:* All uv a sudden da shots come . . . bing . . . bing . . . bam . . . biff . . .

T.B., *superior:* I hoid da shots foist. I wuz jus walkin' up. . .

ANGEL, *angrily:* Yuh di'not.

T.B.: I did so.

ANGEL: Yuh tought it wuz a rivitin' machine, yuh said.

T.B.: I di'not.

ANGEL, *tops him:* Yuh did so.

T.B., *tops him:* I di'not.

ANGEL, *tops him:* Yuh did so.

T.B., *tops him:* Ah, yuh mudduh's chooch!

ANGEL, *tops him:* Yeah, yuh fadduh's doop!

T.B., *crescendo:* Fongoola!

*DIPPY runs down the street, waving two potatoes.*

DIPPY: Hey, guys, I swiped two maw mickeys. Look!

ANGEL: Boy, 'at's good!

SPIT: O.K. Put 'em in.

DIPPY: Wheah's Tommy?

SPIT: Put 'em in!

DIPPY: Dis big one's mine, remembuh!

SPIT: Put 'em in, I said!

DIPPY: Don' fuhgit, dis big one's mine!

SPIT: Shat ap!

DIPPY: Yeah . . . yew . . . yew shat ap!

SPIT: Wha-a-at?

DIPPY, *cowed, moves away from* SPIT: Wheah's Tommy?

ANGEL: I dunno. He didn' show up yet.

T.B., *reflectively, referring to* MARTIN: Da papuhs said dey found twenty gran' in 'is pockets.

ANGEL: Twenty G's. Boy 'at's a lot a dough!

SPIT: Boy, he must a bin a putty smaht guy.

T.B.: Baby-face? Sure! He wuz a tops. Public enemy numbuh one. Boy, he had guts. He wasn' a scared a nobody. Boy, he could knock 'em all off like dat . . . like anyt'ing! Boy, like nuttin'!

DIPPY *takes a stick from the can and holds it against his shoulder, pointed at* ANGEL, *maneuvering it as if it were a machine gun.*

DIPPY, *makes a rapid, staccato bleating sound:* Ah-ah-ah-ah-ah! Look, I godda machine gun! Ah-ah-ah-ah!

ANGEL, *pointing his kazoo at* DIPPY: Bang Bang!

DIPPY, *sore:* Nah, yuh can't do dat. Yuh'r dead. I shot yuh foist.

ANGEL, *ignores that salient point, raises the kazoo again, takes dead aim at* DIPPY: Bang!

DIPPY, *lets loose with his improvised machine gun:* Ah-ah-ah-ah! Deah. Now I gotcha! Now yuh dead!

ANGEL: Bang.

DIPPY, *disgusted:* Aw-w-w! *He throws the stick into the fire and turns away.*

T.B.: Gese . . . what I could do wid' twenty G's!

ANGEL: What?

SPIT: Snot!

T.B.: Yeah, I bet I could buy a boat like dat, huh? *He points off toward the dock.*

ANGEL: Look! Dey got lights an' flags an' music!

SPIT: Dey got some hot party on, hey guys?

DIPPY: Look! Look! Dey're dancin'! *Cavorts about with an imaginary part-ner, making ribald gestures and singing.* Yuh're da top, yuh're da coli-seum. Hey! I'm dancin'! Look, felluhs! Look on me! I'm dancin'! Look on me! *He whirls around and looks at them for approval.*

T.B., *sour-faced:* Sit down! Yew stink!

DIPPY *stops grinning and dancing simultaneously. He sits down, squelched.*

ANGEL: Twenty grand! . . .

SPIT: Yeah . . . so what's it got 'im?

ANGEL: Yeah. Yuh see duh pitchuh uv 'is broad inna papuhs? Deedy Cook aw sumpm . . .

T.B.: Boy, some nice nooky, huh?

SPIT: Boy, she's got some contrac's now! I heah she's gonna do a bubble dance in a boilesque, I t'ink.

ANGEL: Yeah. My fadduh took one look at huh pitchuh. So 'ee said 'ee'd let 'em shoot 'im too, fuh half an hour wid' a fancy floozy like dat. So my mudduh gits mad. So she sez dey wouldn' haf tuh shoot cha. Haf an hour wid' 'at cockamamee, yuh'd be dead! *They all laugh.* So she spills some boilin' watuh on 'im. So 'ee yells like a bastid an' runs outa da house mad. *MILTY comes down the sidewalk, breathless with excitement.*

MILTY: Hey, felluhs, yuh know what?

ANGEL: What?

SPIT: Snot!

MILTY: Balls tuh yew!

SPIT: Ah, I'll mobilize yuh!

MILTY: Yuh know what, guys? Duh cops ah wise tuh Tommy.

ANGEL: Gese!

T.B.: No kid! No kid!

SPIT: Aw, bushwah!

MILTY: No bushwah! Deah' lookin' fuh 'im. He tole me hisself. *To SPIT.* Fot smelleh! Dey went up tuh his house. Some guy snitched.

T.B.: No kid!

SPIT: Did dey git 'im?

MILTY: Nah. Tommy's too wise fuh dem. Dey come in tru de daw. He goes out tru de fire escape, down a yahd, oveh de fence, tru de celleh, up de stayuhs, out dee udduh street.

SPIT: Wheah's he now?

MILTY: He's hidin' out.

SPIT: Wheah?

MILTY: Wheah duh yuh t'ink, wheah? Wheah dey don' ketch 'im, dat's wheah.

SPIT: Ah, dey'll ketch 'im.

MILTY: Dey don' ketch Tommy so quick.

SPIT, *nervously, looking into the fire:* How're de mickeys comin'?

T.B.: Gese, I bet a dollah dey sen' 'im tuh rifawm school.

SPIT: Sure. Dat's what dey do.

DIPPY: Yeah, dat's what. Ain' it, T.B.?

T.B.: Yeah. Dey sent me tuh rifawm school fuh jus' swipin' a bunch of bananas. An' 'ey wuz all rotten too, most a dem.

MILTY: I pity duh guy who snitched. Tommy's layin' fuh him, awright.

DIPPY: Does 'ee know who?

SPIT, *trying to change the subject:* Hey, guys, duh mickeys ah awmost done!

ANGEL, *fishing out his potato and poking it with his kazoo:* Nah, not yet. Look, dis one's hard inside.

DIPPY, *reaches to feel ANGEL's mickey:* Yeah. Like a rock. . . . Ouch! Dat's hot! *Licks his fingers.*

ANGEL, *dipping the mickey back into the embers:* Gese, poor Tommy! If dey ketch 'im, he don' git no maw mickeys like dis fer a long time.

DIPPY: Dey git mickeys in rifawm school, don' dey?

T.B.: Slop dey git, slop . . . unless dey git some dough tuh smeah da jailies wid'.

SPIT: Aw, shat ap! All a time yuh shoot yuh mout' off about rifawm school . . . like yew wuz 'ee on'y one who evuh went.

DIPPY: Yeah. Yew wuz on'y deah six mont's.

ANGEL: Tom'll git two yeahs.

DIPPY: T'ree, maybe, I bet.

MILTY: Gese, dat's lousy.

SPIT: Ah, shat ap, will yuh?

T.B.: Yeah, nevuh mind. Yuh loin a barrel a good t'ings in rifawm school.

*The* DOORMAN *comes out of the gate, exasperated.*

DOORMAN: Now I'm not going to tell you again!

*Simulta-*                SPIT: Ah, go frig!
*neously*                  T.B.: Deah're awmost done.
                          ANGEL: Jus' a li'l while.

DOORMAN: No! Get away from here . . . all of you . . . right now!

GIMPTY, *approaches the* DOORMAN *and addresses him in a voice tight and hoarse, hardly recognizable:* Did you give her my note?

DOORMAN: Yes. She said she'd be out in a moment.

GIMPTY: Thanks. *He retires to sit again in the shadows.*

DOORMAN: If you kids don't beat it, I'm going to call a cop! *Turns to the gate.*

SPIT: Aw, hold yuh hawses!

DOORMAN, *wheels about, threateningly:* Wha-a-at?

SPIT, *scared:* Nuttin'.

*A* LADY *in evening gown and a* MAN *in tuxedo come down the street, talking quietly. The* WOMAN *laughs. As they reach the gate, the* DOORMAN *touches his hat.*

DOORMAN: Good evening.

MAN AND WOMAN: Good evening.

*The* DOORMAN *follows them through the gateway.*

SPIT, *when the* DOORMAN *is well out of earshot:* Ah, yuh louse, I'll mobilize yuh!

*The boys all roar.*

ANGEL: Hey, de fire's dyin' down.

T.B.: Yeah, we need maw wood.

SPIT: Let's scout aroun' an' soich out some maw wood. I'll stay heah an' guard de mickeys.

T.B.: Me too.

SPIT: Yew, too, balls!

T.B.: Whatsa mattuh wid' me?

SPIT: Whatsa mattuh wid' yew? Yew stink on ice, 'at's what's a mattuh wid' yew!

T.B.: Yeah, well, yew ain' no lily a da valley.

SPIT: Go on now, or yuh git dis mickey . . . red-hot . . . up yuh bunny!

T.B.: Yeah? *He begins to cough.*

SPIT: Yeah! Wanna make sumpm otov it?

T.B.: If it wasn't fuh my T.B. . . .

SPIT: Ah, dat's a gag. Anytime yuh put it straight up tuh 'im, he goes . . . *Imitates the cough.* My T.B. . . . Balls!

T.B.: Oh, yeah? . . . Look, smart guy! *He has been holding his hand to his lips. He coughs again, spits, opens his hand, holds it out and displays a bloody clot in the palm. Proudly:* Blood! *The boys gasp.*

ANGEL: Wow!

T.B.: Smart guy!

SPIT: Ah, I could do dat. Yuh suck yuh mout'!

DIPPY, *sucks his mouth audibly, spits into his hand:* I can't . . . I can't. How do yuh do it?

    DRINA *comes down the street, sees the boys and hurries to them.*

MILTY: Hello, Drina.

DRINA: Did you see Tommy? *There is a tired, desperate quality in her tone.*

MILTY: No.

DRINA, *to DIPPY:* Did you?

DIPPY: Nope.

DRINA: Did anybody see him? He hasn't been home at all.

MILTY: No. Nobody saw 'im, Drina.

DRINA, *tired, very tired:* Thanks. Thanks, Milty. *She notices GIMPTY and approaches him.*

ANGEL, *in a whisper:* Whyn't yuh tell huh?

MILTY, *also whispering:* No. Tommy said no.

SPIT, *aloud:* Ah, balonee!

MILTY, *whispers:* Sh! Shat ap!

SPIT, *deliberately loud:* Who fuh! I'll give yuh yuh lumps in a minute.

DRINA, *to GIMPTY:* Pete, did you see Tommy?

GIMPTY: What?

DRINA: My brother? Have you seen him at all?

GIMPTY: Oh! No.

DRINA: Gee, he hasn't showed up yet. The cops are looking for him. I'm scared to death.

GIMPTY: I'm sorry.

SPIT: Hey, Drina! Milty knows, but he won't tell!

DRINA, *turns quickly:* Does he?

MILTY: No.

SPIT: He does.

MILTY, *quietly to* SPIT: Ah, you louse! *Aloud to* DRINA. I do not!

SPIT, *to* MILTY: I'll mobilize yuh! *To* Drina. He does so.

>    DRINA *takes* MILTY *by both shoulders and shakes him.*

DRINA: Milty, please tell me if you know . . . please! I'm half crazy.

MILTY: Tommy said not tuh tell.

DRINA, *pleading:* But I wouldn't hurt him. You know that. It's for his good. I've got to talk to him. I've got to find out what we're gonna do. *Pause.* Milty, you've gotta tell me . . . please!

MILTY, *reluctantly:* Aw right! Come on. . . .

DRINA, *as they go up the street:* How is he? Is he all right? Is he hurt or anything?

MILTY: Nah!

DRINA: Why didn't he come home?

MILTY: Don' worry, Drina. Dey won' catch 'im.

>    *They're out of sight and the voices fade off.*

SPIT: Hey, Angel. You stay heah wid' me. Youse guys git some wood. Go on!

DIPPY: O.K. Watch my mickey.

T.B.: Mine too.

>    DIPPY *and* T.B. *exit up the sidewalk.*

DIPPY: Me, I'm goin' ovuh on Toid Avenoo.

T.B.: I'm goin' ovuh tuh Schultzie's.

DIPPY: Naw, whyn't cha go ovuh on Second Avenoo? *Their voices fade away.*

SPIT: Hey, Angel, yew stay heah an' guard dose mickeys.

ANGEL: Wheah yuh goin'?

SPIT: I'm gonna trail Milty an' fin' out wheah Tommy is.

ANGEL: What faw?

SPIT: None a yuh beeswax! *He lopes up the street.*

>    ANGEL *watches him for a while, puzzled, then fishes his kazoo from a pocket, relaxes by the fireside, and hums into the instrument. A shadow detaches itself from the hopper and creeps stealthily toward* ANGEL. *It whispers* "Psst! Hey! Angel!" ANGEL *wheels around, startled.*

ANGEL: Tommy! Gese!

TOMMY, *his face glowing red as he leans over the fire toward* ANGEL: Sh! Shat ap! *In a hoarse whisper.* Wheah ah da guys? *They both talk in whispers.*

ANGEL: Dey went tuh look fuh wood.

TOMMY: What?

ANGEL: Fuh wood. Maw wood. Milty jus' took yuh sistuh . . .

TOMMY: Is Spit wid' de guys?

ANGEL: Yeah.

TOMMY: O.K.

ANGEL: Milty jus' took yuh sistuh tuh yer hideout.

TOMMY: He did? De louse!

ANGEL: Whatcha gonna do, Tommy?

TOMMY: Run away . . . so de bulls don' git me.

ANGEL, *impressed:* Gese!

TOMMY, *quietly:* But foist I'm gonna ketch de guy who snitched. Do yuh know who it wuz?

ANGEL: Me? No.

TOMMY, *flaring:* Don' lie tuh me . . . I'll kill yuh!

ANGEL: Yew know me, Tommy.

TOMMY: O.K. I t'ink I'm wise tuh who done it.

ANGEL: who?

TOMMY: Spit.

ANGEL: Yuh t'ink so?

TOMMY: Yeah.

ANGEL: Gese!

TOMMY: Now I'm gonna hide, see? Right back a deah. *Points up behind the hopper.* If yuh let on I'm heah . . . *Ominously.* I'll put yuh teet' down yuh t'roat!

ANGEL: Aw, Tommy, yuh know me . . . yuh know me!

TOMMY: O.K. Den do like I tell yuh. When Spit comes back, yew tell 'im like dis . . . Duh guy I stabbed wuz down heah lookin' fuh Spit tuh giv'im five bucks fuh snitchin' on who done it. Yuh got dat straight?

ANGEL: Duh guy what he got stabbed . . . wuz down heah lookin' fuh Spit . . . tuh giv'im five bucks fuh snitchin' on who done it.

TOMMY: Right.

ANGEL: O.K.

TOMMY: An' remembuh . . . yew let on I'm heah, I'll . . .

ANGEL: Aw, Tommy, yew know me.

TOMMY: Aw right. Jus' do like I tole yuh.

ANGEL: Whadda yuh gonna do tuh Spit if 'ee done it? TOMMY *takes a knife from his pocket and nips open the blade. The firelight runs along the blade. It looks bright and sharp and hard.* TOMMY *grimly draws it diagonally across his cheek.* ANGEL *grunts.* Mark a de squealuh?

TOMMY, *snaps the blade home and pockets the knife:* Right.

ANGEL: Gese!

TOMMY: Now, go on playin' yuh kazoo like nuttin' happened . . . like I wuzn't heah.

*Footsteps and voices from the gate.* TOMMY *ducks and melts into the shadows of the hopper.* ANGEL *plays his kazoo a bit ostentatiously. The*

DOORMAN *opens the gate.* KAY *appears in a shimmering evening gown, lovely and scented.*

GIMPTY, *his voice dull and tired:* Hello, Kay!

KAY: Hello, Pete! GIMPTY *looks past* KAY *at the* DOORMAN. Yes?

DOORMAN: Ma'am?

KAY: Anything you want?

DOORMAN: Oh no . . . no, ma'am. Excuse me. *Exit.*

GIMPTY: I sent you a note this afternoon. Did you get it?

KAY: Yes, I was out. I didn't get back till late. I'm so sorry, Pete. Forgive me.

GIMPTY: Forget it!

Two couples in evening clothes come down the street. They are all hectic, gay, and a trifle drunk. They greet KAY merrily. She laughs and jests with them, tells them she'll join them shortly, and in the gate they go. Not, however, without one or two backward glances at GIMPTY. Their chatter, off, ends in a burst of laughter that fades away. KAY turns to GIMPTY.

KAY: What a brawl that's turning into!

GIMPTY: Yeah. It seems like quite a party.

KAY: Yes, it is.

GIMPTY, *after a pause, in a voice so low it can scarcely be heard:* Kay . . . did you hear what happened here this afternoon?

KAY: What do you . . . ?

GIMPTY: The shooting.

KAY, *making talk. Evading:* Oh, yes. And we just missed it. It must have been exciting. I'm . . .

GIMPTY: I didn't miss it.

KAY: No? . . . Oh, tell me . . . was it very . . . ?

GIMPTY, *begins to give way to the terror and remorse pent up in him:* It was pretty horrible.

KAY: Oh . . . of course.

GIMPTY: Horrible!

KAY, *realizing by his tone that something dreadful lies in all this, she becomes very tender and soothing:* Pete, give me your hand. Come here. *She leads him to the edge of the wharf.* Sit down. . . . Now, what happened?

GIMPTY: I'd rather not talk about it for a minute.

KAY: If it upsets you, let's not talk about it at all.

GIMPTY: Yes, I've got to . . . but not for a minute. . . .

KAY: All right.

Underneath them, the River plashes against the bulwark. Off, on the yacht, the band is playing a soft, sentimental melody. The chatter and the laughter from the party float faintly over the water. They sit there for a long time, just staring across the river, at its lights, at the factories and signs on *the opposite shore, at the bridge with its glittering loops, at the string of ghostly barges silently moving across the river. For a long time. Then she speaks, quietly.*

KAY: I love the river at night. . . . It's beautiful . . . and a bit frightening.

GIMPTY *stares down at the black water swirling under him. He begins to talk, faster and faster, trying to push back into his unconscious the terror that haunts him, to forget that afternoon if only for a few seconds:* It reminds me of something. . . . What is it? . . . Oh, yeah . . . when I was a kid. In the spring the sudden sun showers used to flood the gutters. The other kids used to race boats down the street. Little boats: straws, matches, lollipop-sticks. I couldn't run after them, so I guarded the sewer and caught the boats to keep them from tumbling in. Near the sewer . . . sometimes, I remember . . . a whirlpool would form. . . . Dirt and oil from the street would break into rainbow colors . . . iridescent. . . . *For a moment he does escape.* Beautiful, I think . . . a marvel of color out of dirty water. I can't take my eyes off it. And suddenly a boat in danger. *The terror in him rises again.* I try to stop it. . . . Too late! It shoots into the black hole of the sewer. I used to dream about falling into it myself. The river reminds me of that. . . . Death must be like this . . . like the river at night. *There is no comfort in her big enough for his needs. They sit in brooding silence, which is finally interrupted by the* DOORMAN's *voice, off.*

DOORMAN: Miss Mitchell came out here only a moment ago. Yes, there she is now.

*The* DOORMAN *and a* SAILOR *come out of the gate.*

SAILOR: Miss Mitchell?

KAY: Yes?

SAILOR: Mr. Hilton says we're ready to cast off. We're waiting for you, ma'am.

KAY: Tell him I'll be there in a minute.

SAILOR: Yes'm.

*Exit* SAILOR.

DOORMAN, *turns to* ANGEL, *who is still hovering over the fire:* Why don't you kids beat it?

ANGEL: Aw-w!

DOORMAN: All right! I'll fix you! *He strides off up the street.*

GIMPTY, *desperately:* Kay, there's still time. You don't have to go.

KAY, *finality in her quiet voice:* I'm afraid I do.

GIMPTY: Listen . . . I knew where Martin was. And I told the police.

KAY: You? How did you recognize him?

GIMPTY: I used to know him when I was a kid.

KAY: Oh!

GIMPTY: I know it was a stinkin' thing to do.

KAY: No. It had to be done.

GIMPTY: There was a reward.

KAY: Yes, I know. I read about it. That's a break for you, Pete. You can help your mother now. And you can live decently.

GIMPTY: How about you?

KAY: This isn't the miracle we were looking for.

GIMPTY, *after a long pause:* No. I guess you're right.

KAY: How long would it last us? Perhaps a year, then what? I've been through all that. I couldn't go through it again.

GIMPTY: I guess it's asking too much.

KAY, *softly, trying to make him see the picture realistically, reasonably:* It's not all selfishness, Pete. I'm thinking of you too. I could do this. I could go and live with you and be happy— *And she means it.* —and then when poverty comes . . . and we begin to torture each other, what would happen? I'd leave you and go back to Jack. He needs me too, you see. I'm pretty certain of him. But what would become of you then? That sounds pretty bitchy, I suppose.

GIMPTY: No . . . no, it's quite right. I didn't see things as clearly as you did. It's just that I've been . . . such a dope.

KAY: No! It's just that we can't have everything . . . ever. *She rises.*

GIMPTY: Of course.

KAY: Good-bye, darling.

GIMPTY, *rises:* Good-bye, Kay. Have a pleasant trip.

KAY, *one sob escaping her:* Oh, Pete, forgive me if I've hurt you. Please forgive me!

GIMPTY: Don't be foolish. You haven't hurt me. It's funny, but you know, I never honestly expected anything. I didn't. It was really just a . . . whimsy I played on myself.

KAY: Pete.

GIMPTY: Yes?

KAY: Will you stay here and wave good-bye to me when the boat goes?

GIMPTY: Naturally. I expected to.

KAY: Thanks. *She kisses him.* Take care of yourself! *She goes quickly.* GIMP-TY *follows her to the gate, standing there, peering through the bars, catching a last glimpse of her.* SPIT *trots down the street.*

SPIT: He wuzn't deah.

ANGEL: No?

SPIT: Nah. Milty's a lot of bushwah. I tole yuh. *He looks at the fire. Spits into it.* ANGEL *glances backward at the shadows under the hopper.*

ANGEL: Hey, Spit!

SPIT: What?

ANGEL: Dey wuz a guy heah . . .

   *T.B. appears, dragging an egg crate.*

T.B.: Look what I got! Whew! Boy, dat'll go up like wildfire!

SPIT: Babee! Dat's good!

ANGEL: Yeah! Dat's swell!

   *They smash up the crate by jumping on it. They they tear off the slats and break them across the curb. The noise of the crashing and splintering exhilarates them. They laugh and chatter. DIPPY enters, puffing and grunting, dragging an old discarded automobile seat by a rope.*

DIPPY, *proud of his contribution:* Hey, yuh t'ink dis'll boin? I t'ink it'll boin, don' chew? Boy, like a house afire, I bet.

ANGEL: Nah, dat'll stink up da place.

DIPPY, *disappointed:* Aw gese, I dragged it a mile. I dragged it fuh five blocks. It wuz way ovuh by Toid Avenoo.

   *The BOYS throw some of the wood into the fire. It flares up with a great crackling. Tongues of flame shoot up out of the can. The band on the boat plays "Anchors Aweigh!" There is much laughter and shouting of "Bon Voyage!" "Have a pleasant trip," etc. from the party who have disembarked. The bells and the whistles of the boat blow, the engines throb, and the propellers churn the water. GIMPTY stands strained and tense, looking off, through the gate.*

T.B.: Hey, look! Look! Duh boat! She's goin' like sixty. Babee! *They rush over to the gate.*

ANGEL: Boy, dat's some boat! Dat's a crackerjack.

DIPPY: Yeah. *He imitates the sound of the bells, the foghorn, the engine.* Clang, clang! Oooh! Ch, ch, ch! Poo! Poo! I'm a boat! Look, felluhs! I'm a boat. Ch! Ch! Ch! *He shuffles around, hands fore and aft.*

ANGEL, *points at the departing boat:* Lookit duh dame wavin' at us.

DIPPY, *waves vigorously:* Yoo, hoo! Yoo hoo!

T.B.: She ain't wavin' at us, yuh dope.

SPIT: At Gimpty.

T.B.: How'd yuh like tuh be on 'at boat?

DIPPY: Boy! I bet yew cud cross 'ee ocean in 'at boat. Yuh cud cross 'ee ocean in 'at boat, couldn't yuh, Gimpty?

GIMPTY: What?

DIPPY: Yuh cud cross 'ee ocean in 'at boat, couldn't yuh?

   *ANGEL returns to the fire and pokes around in it.*

GIMPTY: Oh, yeah, I guess you could.

T.B.: A cawse yuh could, yuh dope, anybody knows 'at.

SPIT, *sees* ANGEL *fishing out a mickey:* Hey, watcha doin'?

ANGEL, *testing his mickey:* My mickey's done. Dey're done now, felluhs!
*The sounds of the yacht die off in the distance.*

SPIT: Look out! Look out! Wait a minute!
*They all rush to haul out their mickeys.* SPIT *pushes them aside, and spears the biggest potato with a stick.*

DIPPY: Hey, Spit, dat big one's mine. Remembuh . . . I swiped it!

SPIT: Shat ap, yuh dope! *He punches* DIPPY, *who begins to snivel.*

DIPPY: If Tommy wuz heah, yuh wouldn't do dat.

SPIT: Nuts tuh yew! Who's got da salt?

ANGEL, *takes a small packet of newspaper from his shoe-shine box:* Heah,
I got it! *The salt is passed around. They eat their mickeys with much smacking of the lips.*

DIPPY, *who has gotten the smallest mickey:* Ahl git even witcha!

SPIT: Nuts!

DIPPY: Yew wait till yuh ast me tuh do sumpm fuh yew some day. Jus' wait.
See whatcha git!

SPIT, *spits at* DIPPY: Right innee eye!

DIPPY, *wiping his eye:* Ah, yuh louse!

ANGEL, *remembering the conspiracy. Slowly and deliberately, between
munches:* Hey, Spit.

SPIT: What?

ANGEL: Dey wuz a guy heah . . . yuh know da guy what Tommy stabbed?
. . . Well, he wuz heah.

SPIT: What fuh?

ANGEL: He wuz lookin' fuh yew.

SPIT: Fuh me?

ANGEL: Yeah.

SPIT: What faw?

ANGEL: He said he wuz gonna give yuh five bucks fuh snitchin' on who
done it.

SPIT: Wheah izee? Wheah'd ee go?

DIPPY: Did yew snitch on Tommy?

SPIT: Sure. Sure I did. *A chorus of disapproval follows this confession.* SPIT
*rises and doubles up his fists. To* DIPPY. What's it to yuh?

DIPPY: Nuttin'! SPIT *looks at* ANGEL.

ANGEL: Nuttin'!

T.B.: Yew snitched on Tommy! Gese!

SPIT: Aw, shat ap, 'r I'll give yuh yuhr lumps! *He turns, looking for the
benefactor.* Wheah'd he go? Which way? I want dat five bucks.

TOMMY *runs from behind the hopper, leaps onto* SPIT's *back, bearing him to the ground.*

TOMMY, *sits astride* SPIT, *his knees pinning* SPIT's *arms down:* Yuh'll git it, yuh stool pigeon! In a pig's kapooch yuh will!

*Simulta-*     DIPPY: Tommy!
*neously*      ANGEL: Gese!
               T.B.: Wow!

TOMMY: Ahl give yuh sumpm yuh won' fuhgit so easy. Say yuh prayuhs, yuh louse!

SPIT: Lemme go! Lemme go!

TOMMY: Oh, no, yuh don't!

SPIT: Aw, Tommy, I didn' mean tuh. Dey had me! De cops had me! What could I do?

TOMMY: Yuh know watcha gonna git fuh it? *He takes out his knife.* SPIT *squeals with terror.* TOMMY *jams his hand over* SPIT's *mouth.* Shat ap!

DIPPY: What's 'ee gonna do?

ANGEL: Gash his cheek fum heah tuh heah!

T.B.: No kid!

ANGEL: Yeah.

DIPPY: Gee whiz! Wow!

SPIT, *crying and pleading:* Tommy, don't, will yuh? I'll give yuh dose bike wheels I swiped. I'll give yuh me stamps. I'll give yuh me immies. I'll give yuh dat five bucks. Ony lemme go, will yuh?

TOMMY: Dis time yuh don' git away wid' it so easy, see?

SPIT: Hey, felluhs! Hey, Gimpty! He's godda knife!

GIMPTY, *notices for the first time what's happening:* Stop that, you crazy kid!

TOMMY: No!

GIMPTY, *starts toward* TOMMY: Let him go, Tommy!

TOMMY: Come near me, Gimpty, an' I'll give it tuh yew. Stay back, or I'll give it tuh 'im right now! *He places the knife point at* SPIT's *throat.* GIMPTY *stops short.*

GIMPTY: Getting easy, isn't it?

TOMMY: Yeah, it's a cinch.

GIMPTY: Let him up, Tommy!

TOMMY: No!

GIMPTY: Tommy, give me that knife!

TOMMY: No!

GIMPTY: Sell it to me! I'll buy it from you!

TOMMY: No!

GIMPTY: What's a matter? You a yellow-belly, Tommy?

TOMMY: Who's a yeller-belly?

GIMPTY: Only a yellow-belly uses a knife, Tommy. You'll be sorry for this!

TOMMY: Well, he squealed on me!

    *MILTY and DRINA come down the street.*

MILTY: I dunno. He wuz heah befaw . . . honest! *Seeing the fight, he rushes to* TOMMY *and* SPIT. Wassamatteh, Tommy?

DRINA, *rushing to* TOMMY *and* SPIT: Tommy! Tommy! Where've you been?

SPIT: Drina! Drina, he's godda knife! He wants a stab me!

TOMMY, *slaps* SPIT: Shat ap!

DRINA: Tommy! . . . Give me that knife! . . . What's the matter with you? Aren't you in enough hot water now? Don't you understand what you're doing? *Screams.* Give me that knife!

GIMPTY: Go on, Tommy! *Pause.*

TOMMY, *reluctantly hands the knife to* DRINA: Heah! *He rises, releasing* SPIT. *As* SPIT *scrambles to his feet,* TOMMY *kicks him in the rump, yelling.* Beat it, yuh son uva . . . SPIT *runs up the sidewalk.*

DRINA, *sharply:* Sh, Tommy!

SPIT, *from a safe distance, turns:* Tuh hell witcha, yuh bastid! *Then he redoubles his speed, disappearing around the corner.*

TOMMY: I'll kill yuh! *He starts after* SPIT, *but* DRINA *grabs his arm and pulls him back.*

DRINA: Tommy, behave yourself!

TOMMY: But 'ee squealed on me, Drina!

DRINA: That's no excuse for this. Now it's knives! *She snaps the blade shut.* What'll it be next? What's happening to you, Tommy?

TOMMY: I wuz ony gonna scare 'im.

DRINA, *grasps him by the shoulders and shakes him to emphasize what she's saying:* Listen to me! The cops came up to the house ten minutes ago. They were lookin' for you. You stabbed some man! Why! *Why!* TOMMY *turns away.* Don't you see what you're doing? They'll send you to jail, Tommy!

TOMMY, *all the fight gone:* No, dey won't. Dey gotta ketch me foist.

DRINA: What do you mean?

TOMMY: I'm gonna run away.

DRINA: Run away? Where to?

TOMMY: I dunno.

DRINA: Where?

TOMMY: Dere a plenty a places I kin hitch tuh. Lots a guys do.

DRINA: And what are you gonna eat? Where you gonna sleep?

TOMMY: I'll git along.

DRINA: How?

TOMMY: I dunno. Some way. I'll snitch stuff. I dunno. *Belabored and uncertain.* Aw, lemme alone!

DRINA: I can see what's gonna happen to you. *Fiercely.* You'll become a bum!

TOMMY: Aw right! I'll become a bum, den!

DRINA, *hurls the knife onto the sidewalk and screams:* That's fine! That's what Mamma worked her life away for! That's what I've worked since I was a kid for! So you could become a bum! That's great!

TOMMY, *shouting back:* Aw right! It's great! Well, gese, whadda yuh want me tuh do? Let da cops git me an' sen' me up the rivuh, Drina? I don' wanna be locked up till I'm twenty-one. Izzat what yuh want me tuh do?

DRINA, *suddenly very soft and tender, maternally:* No, darling, no. I won't let that happen. I won't let them touch you, Tommy. Don't worry.

TOMMY: Well, what else kin we do?

DRINA: I'll run away with you, Tommy. We'll go away, together, someplace.

TOMMY: No, Drina, yuh couldn't do dat. Yer a goil. *Pause.* Yuh know what? Maybe, if I give myself up, an' tell em I didn' mean tuh to do it, an if I swear on a Bible I'll nevuh do it again, maybe dey'll let me go.

DRINA: No, Tommy, I'm not gonna let you give yourself up. No!

TOMMY: Yeah, Drina.

    *Enter* DOORMAN *with* MULLIGAN.

DOORMAN, *pointing to the boys:* There!

MULLIGAN, *roars:* Get ta hell outa here! Go wan home!

T.B.: Chickee da cop! *The* BOYS *scatter.* DIPPY *and* T.B. *duck into the tenement doorway.* ANGEL *and* MILTY *scramble under the hopper.*

MULLIGAN, *to the* DOORMAN: Get some water! Put this out. MULLIGAN *turns to the cringing figures under the hopper.* Yuh wanna set fire to these houses? Lemme ketch you doin' this again and I'll beat the b'jesus outa you! *He slaps the blazing can with his nightstick to punctuate the warning. Sparks fly up.*

TOMMY, *slowly:* Yuh know, Drina, I t'ink 'at's what I ought tuh do.

DRINA, *holding him tight, terrified. In a hoarse whisper:* No. I won't let you do that.

TOMMY: Yeah. *He detaches her arm, and goes to* MULLIGAN. Hey, mister!

MULLIGAN: What do you want? Come on, beat it!

TOMMY: Wait a minute! I'm Tommy McGrath.

MULLIGAN: What of it? *The other* BOYS *creep back.*

TOMMY: I'm da kid dat stabbed dat man today.

MULLIGAN: What!!! *He grabs* TOMMY's *arm. The* DOORMAN *comes running over to verify this.*

TOMMY, *his voice shrill and trembly:* Yeah. He wuz chokin' me an breakin' my ahm . . . so I did it.

MULLIGAN: So, you're the kid. I bin lookin' fuh you.

DOORMAN, *who has been staring at* TOMMY, *suddenly elated:* That's him, all right. That's him! Wait, I'll call Mr. Griswald. He'll tell you! *He rushes off through the gateway.*

MULLIGAN: All right. I'll keep him here. Don't you worry.

DRINA, *goes to* MULLIGAN, *pleading:* Tommy! No, no, they can't take him, let him go, Officer! Please!

MULLIGAN: I can't do that, miss.

DRINA: He didn't know what he was doing. He's only a baby.

MULLIGAN: You tell it to the judge. Tell it to the judge.

DRINA, *trying to wrench* TOMMY *free:* No! Let him go! Let him go!

MULLIGAN, *pushes her away roughly:* Get away. Don't try that! *To* GIMPTY. You better take her away or she'll get hurt.

GIMPTY: Drina, come here.

DRINA: No.

MULLIGAN: In a minute I'll take her to the station house, too.

TOMMY: Aw, Drina, cut it out, will yuh? Dat ain' gonna help.

GIMPTY: He's right, you know.

T.B., *sidles over to* TOMMY, *whispering:* Hey, Tommy, if yuh go tuh rifawmatory, look up a guy named . . .

MULLIGAN, *shoving T.B. away:* Git outa here! *T.B. flies across the street.*

DRINA: Yes, of course he's right. I'm so . . . I just don't know what I'm . . .

DOORMAN, *enters with* MR. GRISWALD: Yes, Mr. Griswald, I'm sure it's the boy.

   GRISWALD *pushes him aside and walks briskly to* MULLIGAN.

GRISWALD: So you've caught him.

MULLIGAN: Yes, sir.

DRINA: He gave himself up!

GRISWALD: Let me look at him. *He looks searchingly at* TOMMY's *face and nods.* Yes, this is the boy, all right.

MULLIGAN: Good.

DRINA: He gave himself up.

GRISWALD, *turns to her:* What's that?

DRINA, *trying desperately to be calm:* I'm his sister!

GRISWALD: Oh. Well . . . a fine brother you've got.

MULLIGAN, *to* ANGEL *and* MILTY, *who have crept to the foreground:* Come on, get outa here! Beat it! *They scramble back again under the hopper.*

DRINA: Listen, mister! Give him another chance. . . . *She clutches his arm. He winces and draws his breath in pain.* Please, will you?

GRISWALD: Careful of that arm!

DRINA: Oh! I'm sorry. . . . Give him another chance! Let him go!

GRISWALD: Another chance to what? To kill somebody?

TOMMY: I won' evuh do it again. Yew wuz chokin' me an' I wuz seein' black aready, an' I . . .

DRINA: Have a heart, mister! He's only a kid. He didn't know what he was doing.

GRISWALD: No?

DRINA: No.

GRISWALD: Then you should have taught him better.

DRINA, *her impulse is to fight back, but she restrains herself:* Listen! He's a good boy. And he's got brains. Ask his teacher . . . Miss Judell, P.S. 59. He used to get A, A, A . . . all the time. He's smart.

GRISWALD: Then I can't see any excuse at all for him.

DRINA, *flaring:* All right! He made a mistake! He's sorry! What's so terrible about that?

GIMPTY: Sh! Drina!

GRISWALD: I have a gash half an inch deep in my wrist. The doctor is afraid of infection. What do you say to that?

DRINA, *with such an effort at self-control that she trembles:* I'm sorry! I'm awfully sorry!

GRISWALD: Sorry! That won't help, will it?

DRINA: Will it help to send him to reform school?

GRISWALD: I don't know. It'll at least keep him from doing it to someone else.

DRINA: But you heard him. He swore he wouldn't ever do it again.

GRISWALD: I'm afraid I can't believe that. He'll be better off where they'll send him. They'll take him out of the gutters and teach him a trade.

DRINA, *explodes again:* What do you know about it?

GRISWALD: I'm sorry. I've no more time. I can't stand here arguing with you. *To* MULLIGAN. All right, Officer! I'll be down to make the complaint. *Starts to exit.*

GIMPTY, *stepping in front of* GRISWALD *and blocking his path:* Wait a minute, mister!

GRISWALD: Yes?

GIMPTY: May I talk to you a moment?

GRISWALD: There's no use, really.

GIMPTY: Just a moment, please?

GRISWALD: Well, what is it?

GIMPTY: You know what happened here today? A man was shot . . . killed.

GRISWALD: You mean that gangster?

GIMPTY: Yes.

GRISWALD: What about it?

GIMPTY: I killed him.

GRISWALD: You what?

MULLIGAN: He's crazy. *To* GIMPTY. What are you trying to do?

GIMPTY: It was I who told them where to find him.

GRISWALD: Well, that may be so. Then you were doing your duty. It's simple enough. And I'm doing mine.

DRINA, *hysterically:* No! It ain't the same! Martin was a butcher, he was like a mad dog. He deserved to die. But Tommy's a baby . . .

GIMPTY: Please! That's not the point!

DRINA: It is!

MULLIGAN, *to* ANGEL *and* MILTY, *who are back again:* How many times have I gotta tell you! . . . *They retreat.*

GIMPTY: Yes, maybe it is. Anyway, I turned him over for my own selfish reasons. And yet the thing I did, Griswald, was nothing compared to what you're doing. . . . Yeah . . . Martin was a killer, he was bad, he deserved to die, true! But I knew him when we were kids. He had a lot of fine stuff. He was strong. He had courage. He was a born leader. He even had a sense of fair play. But living in the streets kept making him bad. . . . Then he was sent to reform school. Well, they reformed him all right! They taught him the ropes. He came out tough and hard and mean, with all the tricks of the trade.

GRISWALD: But I don't see what you're driving at.

GIMPTY: I'm telling you! That's what you're sending this kid to.

GRISWALD: I'm afraid there's no alternative.

DRINA: Are you so perfect? Didn't you ever do anything you were sorry for later? *Screams.* God! Didn't anybody ever forgive you for anything?

GRISWALD, *looks at her in silence for a moment. Then, gently, and sympathetically:* Of course. I'm sorry. I'm very sorry. Believe me, I'm not being vindictive. I'm not punishing him for hurting me. As far as this goes— *touches his bandaged wrist.* —I would forgive him gladly. But you must remember that I'm a father . . . that today he, unprovoked, beat my boy with a stick and stole his watch. There are other boys like mine. They've got to be protected, too. I feel awfully sorry for you, but your brother belongs in a reformatory. *To* MULLIGAN. All right, Officer! *He shakes his head and disappears in the gateway.*

DRINA, *with a cry of despair:* What?

MULLIGAN: All right! Let's go! *To* TOMMY. Come along.

T.B. *edges over to* TOMMY: Hey, Tommy, wait! Look up a guy named Smokey! . . .

MULLIGAN: Get away from here. I'll bounce one off your head!

TOMMY, *looking back to* DRINA: Don' worry, Drina. I ain' scared.

DRINA, *trying to smile for* TOMMY: Of course not, darling. I'm coming with you. *Starts up.*

MULLIGAN: Yeah, I think you better. Come on! *He calls over his shoulder to the* DOORMAN. Put out that fire!

DOORMAN: Oh, yes . . . yes, Officer! *Hurries off, through the gate.*

> MULLIGAN *and* TOMMY *go up the street.* DRINA *starts to follow.* T.B. *catches her arm.*

T.B.: Drina! Drina! Wait!

DRINA: No, I can't, I gotta . . .

T.B.: It's important. It's about Tommy!

DRINA, *turns:* What?

T.B., *very knowing and very helpful. He's been through this before:* Look, Drina, dere's a guy at rifawm school named Smokey . . . like dat, Smokey, dey call him Smokey. Yew tell Tommy tuh be nice tuh him and give im t'ings like cigarettes an dat. Cause dis guy Smokey, he knows a lot a swell rackets fuh Tommy when 'ee gits out . . . cause Tommy's a wise kid an' . . .

DRINA, *scared, helpless, begins to sob:* Oh, Mom, why did you leave us? I don't know what to do, Mom. I don't know where to turn. I wish I was dead and buried with you.

T.B., *puzzled by this unexpected reaction to his good advice:* What's a mattuh? What'd I say? I didn' say nuttin'. What'd I say?

GIMPTY: Sh! Shut up! *He goes to* DRINA, *who is sobbing her heart out, and puts a protective arm around her:* You poor kid! You poor kid. Stop crying. Stop crying now.

DRINA: I'm all right. I'll be all right in a minute.

GIMPTY: Now, you stop crying and listen to me. Tomorrow morning you meet me right here at half past nine. We're going downtown. We're going to get the best lawyer in this city, and we'll get Tommy free.

DRINA: But that'll cost so much!

GIMPTY: Don't worry about that. We'll get him out.

DRINA: Do you really think so?

GIMPTY: I know so.

DRINA: Oh, God bless you . . . you're so . . . *She breaks into sobs again.*

GIMPTY: Now, now. You go along now and stick by Tommy.

DRINA, *controlling herself:* You've been so awfully good to us, I . . . I hate to ask for anything else, but . . .

GIMPTY: Sure, what is it?

DRINA: I wish you'd come along with us now. I know if you're there . . . they wouldn't dare touch . . . *Her voice catches.* Tommy!

GIMPTY: Me? I'm nobody. I can't . . .

DRINA: I wish you would. Please?

GIMPTY, *softly:* All right. *They go up the street, his arm still around her, his cane clicking on the sidewalk even after they've disappeared from sight. Awed by the scene, the kids gather about the fire again.*

ANGEL: Gese, wadda yuh tink'll happen tuh Tommy?

MILTY: Dey'll git 'im off. Dey'll git 'im off. Yuh'll see.

T.B.: Even if dey don't, yuh loin a barrel a good tings at rifawm school. Smokey once loined me how tuh open a lock wid' a hairpin. Boy! It's easy! It's a cinch! I loined one-two-three, but now I fuhgit. . . .

*The* DOORMAN *appears, uncoiling a garden hose. He pushes* ANGEL *aside, points the nozzle into the can, and releases the stream. The fire hisses, spits, and dies. A thick pillar of smoke ascends skyward out of the can.*

ANGEL, *looks upward, entranced:* Holy smokes!

DIPPY: Whee!

ANGEL: Look a dat!

T.B.: Boy! Right up tuh duh sky!

ANGEL: Right up tuh duh stahs!

DIPPY: How high ah dey? How high ah duh stahs?

DOORMAN, *turning back at the gate:* And you rats better not start any more trouble, if you know what's good for you! *He goes in. The* BOYS *wait till he is out of earshot, then they hurl a chorus of abuse.*

|  | MILTY: Gay cock of'm yam! |
|---|---|
| *Simulta-* | ANGEL: Fongoola! |
| *neously* | DIPPY: Nuts ta yew! |
|  | T.B.: In yuhr hat! |

ANGEL *plays a mocking tune on his kazoo.*

T.B., *sings the lyrics:* Te da da da da bushwah. Te da da bushwah.

ANGEL: Ahl goul him!

DIPPY, *laughs:* Yeah.

*After this outburst, there is a long pause. They watch the smoke coiling upward.*

MILTY, *softly:* Gee! Looka dat smoke!

T.B.: Dat reminds me—all a time at rifawm school Smokey usta sing a song about Angel—"If I had de wings of a Angel."

*They laugh.*

MILTY: Angel ain't got no wings.

DIPPY: Real ones got wings. I saw it in a pitcha once.

ANGEL *starts playing "If I Had the Wings of an Angel" on his kazoo.*

T.B.: Dat's right. Dat's it! *In a quavery voice, he accompanies* ANGEL. If I had de wings of a angel. Ovuh dese prison walls I wud fly. . . . *The others join in, swelling the song.* Straight tuh dee yahms a my mudduh. Ta da da, da da. . . *A passing tramp steamer hoots mournfully. The smoke continues to roll out of the can, as their cacophony draws out to a funereal end.* Da . . . da . . . da . . . dum.

*CURTAIN*

# THE PATRIOTS

IF THERE WAS a play that was written out of the questions raised by the fearful epoch of World War II through which we were passing, it was *The Patriots*. Hitler was rising, threatening the concept of democracy and so, on the other hand, was Stalin. There were some who felt that the coming struggle for world domination was between fascism and communism, and democracy was pushed aside as a vital world force.

In April 1934, during my visit to France with Lee Strasberg on the way to see the splendid production of *Men in White* in Budapest, I had occasion to lunch with several French playwrights who expressed the fear that apparently was very important in the French mind then: that, any day, clouds of German planes would be overhead bombing them. This fear was in the atmosphere everywhere in the world, and it raised the question being discussed by many in this country and in England as to the very survival of democracy. Thus, it occurs to me that the seeds of *The Patriots* were sown then in the days of *Men in White* and my first visit to France. There was a serious question as to whether our country or its principles would survive. I felt an impelling urgency to search for some answers to the doubts and questions raised. I knew, if only as a matter of blind faith, I had to find some concrete and specific answers for myself. I decided to write a play, searching for an answer.

I set out to write a play about democracy. I intended it to be a contemporary play; but in the searching for first principles, I found that a study of the American Revolution provided me with a more specific answer to the questions raised by the terror that was in the air. I answered my need to search for answers—not to rewrite history but to dramatize the significant meaning of events.

169

During this time, Robert Sherwood and Maxwell Anderson prevented a very serious takeover of the Dramatists Guild. Lillian Hellman had, in fact, proposed that the Dramatists Guild declare the war a "phoney war," that is, until the Nazis turned on the Soviet Union and attacked Russia. Then suddenly it became a holy war, and Lillian, along with the American Communists, was screaming for a second front. I was in the army, still wearing World War I puttees, and they wanted a second front; but it was coming.

So I was facing the challenge not only of being a soldier, but of simply trying to find a place to write *The Patriots*. There was no place on the army base, not even the attic of the barracks. I knew the apartment on 58th Street had no area in which I could work. Hearing me talk about this one day, Sherman Billingsley at the Stork Club, said, "Why don't you come here when you come to the City from the army? This is very quiet in the late afternoon, no one, no how. Sit down at one of the tables and work here." Well, believe it or not, a good part of *The Patriots* was written in sergeant's uniform at the Stork Club.

Through Max Anderson's good efforts, the Playwrights Company produced my play, but not without difficulty. After writing, but before production, I suffered a blow from which it took some time to recover. Elmer Rice had, without my awareness, voted and protested against the Playwrights Company doing my play. He claimed he was working on a play about Thomas Paine and therefore thought my play would be a conflict. The only difference was that, as I learned much later, Elmer had not written the play, and I, of course, had completed the full play. Nevertheless, the ayes prevailed and the Playwrights Company did *The Patriots*.

There were problems other than Elmer Rice, however. The first director we chose died before rehearsals began. The new director was bored and would leave rehearsals early. The dress rehearsals proved a disaster. We gave a special dress rehearsal performance for my battalion. The production was a near disaster: poor, stumbling direction, heavy, elaborate sets, and the interminable waits between scenes. Since that rehearsal was also a special performance for my army battalion, it was a double disaster for me. I wangled a two-week leave of absence. Working on the physical production day and night, I took on the direction, redesigned the set, threw half the production in the alley. Our wonderful angel, Rowland Stebbins ("Roley"), a great gentleman, a very important stockbroker as well as a patron of the arts (he had also backed and produced Marc Connelly's *Green Pastures*), said, "That's what theatre alleys are for—discarded scenery."

Back in the army, a meeting of the whole battalion at the assembly hall was ordered. At the meeting, my name was called, "front and center." An officer summoned one of my fellow soldiers, who presented me with a special, beautifully illuminated manuscript on parchment, which one of our gifted soldiers had designed and drafted, congratulating me on the play and thanking me for the special performance, and signed by all the members of my battalion.

The support of the soldiers and officers of my battalion during *The Patriots* was very meaningful to me as, I hope, the issues the play addressed were meaningful for them at a difficult time. In fact, they were quite interested in the play. After the Pulitzer Prize was announced, and I didn't win it, came a terse communiqué from the commanding officer: "Explain your actions in not winning the Pulitzer Prize"!

Casting was very difficult. There seemed to be no good actors around at this point, and Elmer Rice, the one dissenting member of the Playwrights Company, urged me to put off the production of the play. My big triumph, though, was in finally persuading my wife, actress Madge Evans, to act in the play. We had had quite a battle before when I did *The World We Make*. Madge would have been wonderful in it, and it was the kind of thing she needed to do, but Madge had a will of iron, too, and she was determined not to be in any play of mine . . . ever. In *The Patriots,* however, she relented and accepted a part largely because it was not a major role, although she was absolutely splendid and beautiful in it. It wasn't very much of a part, certainly nothing comparable to what I would have liked to see her do, but she did it cheerfully and loved doing it. In a way, it was a godsend for her.

The old phrase "Break a leg" came true when the actor who was playing George Washington slipped on the ice and broke his leg following the opening night performance. He insisted he could play the role in a wheelchair. When we refused, he stuck his nose in the air and said, "Then you will just have to find somebody else." Since we already had a very good understudy, that didn't frighten us; but we placated him with assurances he would heal more quickly this way and would be paid full salary during the convalescence. We inserted a plaque on the sidewalk reading, "George Washington slipped here."

The play opened on January 29, 1943, to fine notices and did very well. The play was heartily received. Even John Mason Brown, my dedicated critical opponent, praised it and voted "aye" when it won the Critics Prize, a surprise and a very special award to me because the critics had formed the Critics Circle after some of them had been very rough on me for winning the Pulitzer Prize with *Men in White*.

After the play was successfully produced, Philip Barry one day approached me and said that all his life he had wanted to write a play about

Thomas Jefferson and couldn't do it, and complimented me on the play and the dramatic invention which had enabled me to make a play out of the Jefferson/Hamilton conflict. That dramatic invention was in the third act, and the play itself turned on it. It was a perfect example, I think, of a dramatic device in which historic invention was, in essence, truer than the fact. The fact is that, when Jefferson was running for president of the United States, he and Burr had been elected and the electoral process then called for the Congress of the United States to choose the president and the vice president. Aaron Burr, as Alexander Hamilton knew, was a sinister and Machiavellian figure. Hamilton had enough friends in the Congress to control the vote, so he had it in his power to ensure that the man of his choice would be selected as president. In order to keep many of his friends in office, Hamilton wanted to make a deal with Jefferson. Since he and Jefferson were not on speaking terms at that moment, all of this discussion took place between Jefferson and a friend and Hamilton and a friend. The two friends, thus, carried forward the discussion—all in a series of letters.

As I read the letters, I realized that here was a critical, dramatic situation that could be translated into drama only if the discussions in the letters were made a direct confrontation between the two men. This scene was the dramatic tour de force of the play, and yet, historically, it never took place— only in that series of correspondences with a third and fourth party. Actually, it was one of the most moving moments for me.

I was attacked later by the Hamilton Club for besmirching Hamilton: after all, I was only a "non-commissioned upstart" and Hamilton had been "an intrepid Major-General of the Army of the Revolution." That he had died several hundred years ago didn't seem to matter! But perhaps most important of all, the scene really gave Hamilton great stature. It pictured him as so colorful, an extraordinarily brilliant patriot, loyal to causes and principles that he finally never fully grasped. One thing I can affirm—there was hardly one word of dialogue in the scene between Hamilton and Jefferson that cannot be verified in their correspondence relating to that issue.

As with *Men in White* and *Dead End*, *The Patriots*'s influence went beyond that of a Broadway play. Two months after we opened, I received a request from the Chief Librarian of the Library of Congress, the distinguished poet Archibald MacLeish, to produce the play at the Library of Congress to open its celebration of the bicentennial of the birth of Thomas Jefferson, an honor that I gratefully accepted. Not only did *The Patriots* play the Library of Congress, but at the same time I was invited to sit in the President's Box at the inauguration of the Jefferson Memorial. I was particularly pleased because I had previously been invited by the sculptor Rudolph Evans (no relation to Madge) to be photographed with the sculpture while it was being made and still in clay. Evans, knowing that I was a bit of a sculptor myself, gave me one of his tools and invited me to smooth out a deep gouge in the clay of the Jefferson foot. I not only smoothed it out—I left my thumbprint on it—but I was able to see its inauguration, in the company of President and Mrs. Roosevelt in their private family box!

S.K.

# THE PATRIOTS

DEDICATION

*To my friend and brother, Tom Evans, U.S.N., who, in this war-torn March 1943, gave his life to the flag which is the undying symbol of hope for all men.*

Presented by The Playwrights Company in association with Rowland Stebbins at the National Theatre, New York, on January 29, 1943, with the following cast:

| | |
|---|---|
| CAPTAIN | Byron Russell |
| THOMAS JEFFERSON | Raymond Edward Johnson |
| PATSY | Madge Evans |
| MARTHA | Frances Reid |
| JAMES MADISON | Ross Matthew |
| ALEXANDER HAMILTON | House Jameson |
| GEORGE WASHINGTON | Cecil Humphreys |
| SERGEANT | Victor Southwick |
| COLONEL HUMPHREYS | Francis Compton |
| JACOB | Thomas Dillon |
| NED | George Mitchell |
| MAT | Philip White |
| JAMES MONROE | Judson Laire |
| MRS. HAMILTON | Peg La Centra |
| HENRY KNOX | Henry Mowbray |
| BUTLER | Robert Lance |
| MR. FENNO | Ronald Alexander |
| JUPITER | Juano Hernandez |
| MRS. CONRAD | Leslie Bingham |
| FRONTIERSMAN | John Stephen |

Thomas Jefferson Randolph    Billy Nevard
Anne Randolph    Hope Lange
George Washington    Jack Lloyd
   Lafayette
Sailors, voices of the signers of the Declaration of Independence, others

Staged by Shepard Traube
Setting by Howard Bay
Costumes by Rose Bogdanoff and Toni Ward
Lighting by Moe Hack
Musical arrangement by Stanley Bate

## Scenes

Prologue  The deck of a schooner—1790

Act One New York—1790
        *Scene 1:* The presidential mansion
        *Scene 2:* A smithy of an inn on the outskirts of New York
Act Two Philadelphia—1791–1793
        *Scene 1:* Hamilton's home
        *Scene 2:* Jefferson's rooms
        *Scene 3:* The same. A few days later
Act Three Washington—1801
        *Scene 1:* Jefferson's rooms at Conrad's boardinghouse
        *Scene 2:* The Senate Chamber

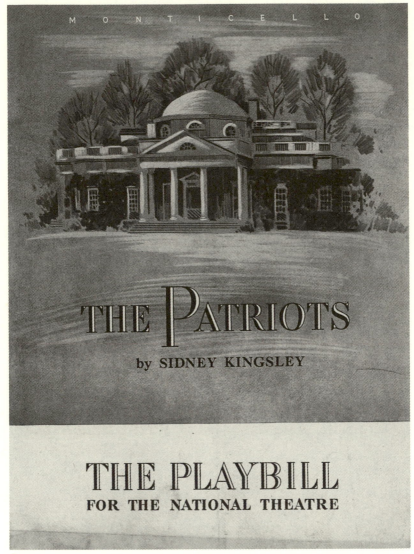

*Program cover for* The Patriots. *Courtesy of the Jerome Lawrence and Robert E. Lee Theatre Research Institute.*

**PROLOGUE**

 1790. *A section of the deck of a schooner. A star-lit night, wind in the sails, rushing water, the creak of tackle.*

 *A middle-aged man and a girl lean on the ship's rail and gaze out over the ocean:* JEFFERSON *and his daughter* PATSY. *He is tall and thin, his face too sensitive, a gentleness almost womanish written on it. He has dispensed with the wig of the period. His hair, ruffled by the winds, is reddish, streaked with gray. The girl is in her late teens, vibrant, lithe, handsome. Above them a helmsman, in shadow, steers the ship.*

 *The* CAPTAIN *approaches them.*

CAPTAIN: Evening, sir.
JEFFERSON: Good evening, Captain.
PATSY: Are we nearing land, Captain?
CAPTAIN: If we hold to our course. Gittin' impatient? *PATSY laughs.*
JEFFERSON: Tell me, does the voyage home always take forever?
CAPTAIN: Longer'n that, sometime. *Looks at the sky.* May blow up a bit, sir.
  Better think a goin' below. *He salutes, goes off.* PATSY *and* JEFFERSON *stare out over the ocean.*
PATSY: I wonder will the house be the way I remember it.
JEFFERSON: Not as large, perhaps. You were only a little lady when we left.
PATSY: How long ago that seems!
JEFFERSON: Doesn't it?
PATSY: It's odd. Now that we're coming home again, all those years in Paris
  suddenly seem so unreal, don't they, Papa?
JEFFERSON: Yes.
  *She sighs.* JEFFERSON *looks at her, smiles.*
PATSY: Are we going to New York first?
JEFFERSON, *shakes his head:* Direct to Monticello.
PATSY: I thought you might want to see President Washington at once.
JEFFERSON: We'll go home first and arrange your wedding.
PATSY: Won't the president be waiting your answer?
JEFFERSON: Not particularly—no. *Pause.*
PATSY: Papa?
JEFFERSON: Yes, dear?
PATSY: I've been wondering.
JEFFERSON: What?
PATSY: Do you think we should put it off? My wedding?
JEFFERSON: Put it off?

*Sidney Kingsley (in uniform) viewing the statue of Thomas Jefferson with sculptor Rudolph Evans. Courtesy of Sidney Kingsley.*

PATSY: If you accept the president's offer, you'll have to live in New York. You'll be alone for the first time in your life. You'll be utterly miserable. I know you too well.

JEFFERSON: But I have no intention of accepting.

PATSY: You haven't?

JEFFERSON: He's given me the option of refusal. And I certainly mean to take advantage of it.

*Sidney Kingsley accepting the New York Drama Critics Circle Award for* The Patriots. *Courtesy of Sidney Kingsley.*

PATSY, *vastly relieved:* Why didn't you tell me?

JEFFERSON: It never occurred to me. *Pause.* You see, dearest, I discovered a long time ago that Nature didn't make me for public office. I accepted the French post only because—at the time—your mother's death had left me so blank. . . . I fancied a change of scene would . . . *He breaks off.*

PATSY: I know, Father. *A long pause as they both stare into space.* Strange out there.

JEFFERSON: Time and space seem to disappear.

PATSY: I wish she were waiting for us at home.

JEFFERSON: Your mother?

PATSY: Yes. I never think of Monticello without thinking of her. She used to love to tell me about *your* wedding night.

JEFFERSON: Did she?

PATSY: In the garden cottage, midst such a clutter of your drawings and your books and your inventions, you could hardly move about.

JEFFERSON, *smiles:* That's right.

PATSY: And how you lit a fire, and found half a bottle of wine a workman had left behind some books. And mother played the pianoforte and you your violin, and you sang old songs. *The wind rises.* JEFFERSON *draws his cloak tighter.*

JEFFERSON: It is blowing up a bit. Excuse me. *He starts off.*

PATSY: Where are you going?

JEFFERSON: I want to take a look at your sister.

PATSY: She's asleep, Father.

JEFFERSON: She'll have kicked off her blanket. She might catch a chill. We don't want her coming home with the sniffles. *He goes off.*

PATSY, *calls after him:* Father!

JEFFERSON, *off:* Yes?

PATSY: I'll go. You wait here.

JEFFERSON: All right, dear. *Reenters.*

PATSY: I'll be right back.

    *PATSY goes.* JEFFERSON *stares off toward the horizon. The hypnotic surge of the water . . . The moonlight fades until he and the ship become a single silhouette in the night. Soft music dimly heard . . . Slowly, dancing as if on the ocean, the exterior of an enchanting house materializes. Monticello! Snow is falling and has piled deep around it.*

    *Laughter is heard offstage.* TOM JEFFERSON, *a young man, and* MARTHA, *a young woman, radiantly beautiful, appear, shaking the snow off their cloaks.*

MARTHA: Was there ever such a wedding night? I declare, Tom Jefferson, those last few miles the horses fairly flew through the snow.

JEFFERSON, *points to the house:* There it is, Martha.

    MARTHA *turns, gasps.*

MARTHA: Oh, Tom!

JEFFERSON: You like it?

MARTHA: I never dreamed it would . . . You really designed this, yourself?

JEFFERSON: For you, Martha. *Takes her hand.*

MARTHA: It's incredibly lovely.

JEFFERSON: Your hand is like ice. Come!

MARTHA: No! I want to stand here and look at it a minute more. Please!

JEFFERSON: It'll be ready for us to move into by April. Till then we'll use the garden cottage. *Apologetically.* It's only one room.

MARTHA, *laughs:* Like a couple of dormice. We won't stir till spring. *Looks about, enchanted. Points offstage.* Your Blue Ridge Mountains are out there?

JEFFERSON, *nods:* There's one peak, Martha, the sun tips with pure gold. And from here Nature spreads a magic carpet below—rocks, rivers, mountains, forests . . .

MARTHA: I can't wait for morning.

JEFFERSON: When stormy weather's brewing, you can look down into her workshop and see her fabricating clouds and hail and snow and lightning—at your feet.

MARTHA: Tom, dearest?

JEFFERSON: Yes, Martha?

MARTHA: I can't tell you what you've done for me.

JEFFERSON: What I've done for you?

MARTHA: Before I met you, circumstances and the intolerance of little men had begun to make me lose faith. The earth had begun to shrink. Living had become something quite unimportant. Then, the night we met, after the gay chatter, when you began to talk gravely, I suddenly fell in love, not only with you. I fell in love with the possibilities of the whole race of man. *She stops short. He is gazing at her, laughing.* Now, what are you laughing at, Mr. Jefferson?

JEFFERSON: If I live to be a thousand and close my eyes—this is the way I'll see you, my love. With snow on your face and your eyes shining!

MARTHA: Oh, Tom, I'm only trying to say I'm happy.

JEFFERSON: Are you?

MARTHA: And I want to be bussed. *He kisses her tenderly.*

JEFFERSON: "When we dwell on the lips of the lass we adore,
> Not a pleasure in nature is missing.
> May his soul be in Heaven
> He deserved it, I'm sure,
> Who was first the inventor of kissing." *She laughs. They embrace.*

MARTHA: Will you love me so forever, Tom?

JEFFERSON: Forever and ever—and ever. . . . *She shivers.* You shivered? You are cold. *The light begins to fade.*

MARTHA: A bit!

JEFFERSON: Come, Mrs. Jefferson. *He sweeps her up in his arms.* We'll light a fire that will warm you to the end of time! *He carries her off. Suddenly the roar of a rising wind. Men's voices far off.*

CAPTAIN'S VOICE, *offstage:* Port quarter!

    *Monticello fades and vanishes.* CAPTAIN *enters, approaches the dreaming silhouette of* JEFFERSON.

CAPTAIN: Runnin' into a patch of ugly weather. Better go below, sir. *The sudden roar of wind. The wheel spins.* Watch the helm, Higgins! Bring the wind on the port quarter!

VOICE *offstage:* "Aye, sir." *Many voices offstage. Exit* CAPTAIN. *The babble of men's voices raised in argument.*

*Another vision appears in space. Young* JEFFERSON, *seated at a desk, a manuscript before him. As the voices are heard, he looks from one antagonist to another.*

FIRST VOICE: Georgia votes nay.

SECOND VOICE: This document is a mass of glittering generalities.

THIRD VOICE: Carolina votes nay. I move to strike out the clause condemning the slave traffic. It has no place here. Georgia and Carolina object.

FOURTH VOICE: Motion to strike out clause condemning the slave traffic. Hands! For? JEFFERSON *looks about, dismayed, counting the votes.* Against? JEFFERSON *raises his hand.* Motion carried. You will please strike out that clause. JEFFERSON *bitterly scratches out the offending clause.*

GEORGE READ'S VOICE: That second sentence. Don't like it.

JEFFERSON: But this is the heart of it, man. Are we going to have to creep up on liberty, inch by inch?

VOICE: Where does this lead? No wonder we're driving all our men of property into the arms of the loyalists.

JEFFERSON: I was asked to write the declaration and I wrote it. I haven't tried to be original. This is a simple expression of the American mind. Our people want this.

READ'S VOICE: From a legalistic viewpoint . . .

JEFFERSON: The men who migrated to America, who built it with their sweat and blood, were laborers, not lawyers.

READ'S VOICE: Plague on't, boy! You want some precedent. Where can you show me anything like this in history?

JEFFERSON: Where in history do we see anything like this new world or the man of this new world? Where have we ever seen a land so marked by destiny to build a new free society based on the rights of man? Precedent? Let's make precedent! Better to set a good example than follow a bad one.

READ'S VOICE: Are you aware, sir, of the consequences?

JEFFERSON, *controls his emotion, rises, steps from behind the desk, appeals to the assembly:* There is not a man in the whole empire who wished conciliation more than I. But, by the God that made me, I would have sooner ceased to exist than yield my freedom. And, in this, I know I speak for America. I am sorry to find a bloody campaign is decided on. But, since it is forced on us, we must drub the enemy and drub him soundly. We must teach the sceptered tyrant we are not brutes to kiss the hand that scourges us. But this is not enough. We are now deciding everlastingly our future and the future of our innocent posterity. Our people have already been fighting a year—for what? *He picks up the document.* For this. Let us give it to them—in writing—now. Now is the time to buttress the liberty we're fighting for. It can't be too strongly emphasized! *Now,* while men are bleeding and dying. Tomorrow they may grow tired and careless, and a new despot may find in the old laws an instrument to rob their liberty again. Now is the time to build a free society. Now! Not later.

READ'S VOICE: I'll debate this point all day.

JEFFERSON, *fiercely:* No member of this Congress is more eager than I to settle the business on hand and go home. My wife is ill and bearing me a child, and while I stay here she's doing all my work at home. I'm half mad with anxiety, but I'll stay on all summer, if necessary, to fight for this one sentence. *Pause.*

READ'S VOICE: Well—er—Read it again. Let's examine it again!

JEFFERSON, *sits. Reads from the document, his voice rich with deep emotion:* We hold these truths to be self-evident: that all men are created equal; that they are endowed by their Creator with certain inalienable rights; that among these are life, liberty, and the pursuit of happiness; that to secure these rights, governments are instituted among men, deriving their just powers from the consent of the governed.

*The Liberty Bell begins to peal. Young* JEFFERSON'S *face is transfigured by an almost sacred light, which grows brighter, then fades and vanishes. Total darkness obscures even the shadowy ship and the dreaming silhouette of* JEFFERSON. *In the darkness the Liberty Bell peals louder and louder, then fades off—Soft, sweet, ghostly music . . . The image of* MARTHA *appears, smiling sadly. The dreamer on the ship becomes visible again. He reaches out his hand.*

JEFFERSON, *murmurs:* Forgive me, Martha! It was such a price to ask of you. Forgive me! I wanted a happy world—for us; and, reaching for it, I lost you. *The ghost of* MARTHA *smiles sadly and shakes her head.* Oh, my darling, in every picture I ever painted of the future you were the foreground. Without you, there's no picture. There's . . .

PATSY'S VOICE, *off:* Father!

*The ghost of* MARTHA *reaches out her hand, then fades and vanishes.* PATSY *appears.*

PATSY: Father! *The light comes on slowly. The ship again.* PATSY *is at his side.* Maria's all right, Father.

JEFFERSON: Hm?

PATSY: She's sound asleep—Maria.

JEFFERSON: Oh! Good. Did she kick off the blanket?

PATSY: Yes, but I tucked her in again. Tight.

JEFFERSON: Good.

PATSY: You were so deep in meditation. What were you thinking?

JEFFERSON: Oh—nothing, dear. Just thinking.

   *From above, the watch suddenly cries out,* "Land ho!" *The cry is re-peated below. From above,* "Two points to the starboard! Land ho!"

PATSY: Father! There it is! Do you see?

JEFFERSON: No. Where, Patsy? Where?

PATSY: That light! There!

JEFFERSON, *peering off, his face working with emotion:* Yes, yes, it's land! It's America, Patsy.

PATSY: We're home, again.


                            *CURTAIN*

**ACT ONE**
*Scene 1*

New York, Spring 1790. The MacComb mansion on lower Broadway, the presidential residence. PRESIDENT WASHINGTON, *tight-lipped and grave, is listening to scholarly, prematurely wizened* JAMES MADISON *and* ALEXANDER HAMILTON, *a short, handsome, young man of flashing personality and proud carriage.* COLONEL HUMPHREYS, *foppish and affected, stands by, his face a mirror reflecting Hamilton's lightning changes of mood.*


MADISON, *vehemently:* If Colonel Hamilton's treasury bill is reintroduced, Congress will kill it again.
HAMILTON, *drily:* Mr. Madison, I am tempted to seize your Congress by their separate heads and knock them together into a collective jelly.
MADISON: What would that achieve?
HAMILTON: Unity! Of some kind.
MADISON: Yes, but what kind? That's the question.
HAMILTON: You cry, "Speculation!" That's not the issue at all, and you know it.
MADISON: I know nothing of the sort. On the contrary.
HAMILTON: You deny your South is afraid the North will profit a little more?
MADISON: And will they? Will they?
HAMILTON: That's beside the point. Yes, they will. What of it? *He turns to* WASHINGTON, *pleading.* The crying need of this infant government *now* is confidence in its financial policy.
MADISON: Exactly. And is this the way to achieve it?
HAMILTON: Question? Can the wise and learned congressman from Virginia propose any better plan?
MADISON: Colonel Hamilton! Personalities are not the . . .
WASHINGTON: Gentlemen! Gentlemen! Thank you, Mr. Madison, for your views. Of course it is not in this office to interfere with the people's legislature.
MADISON: Thank you!
HAMILTON: But, Mr. President! You . . .
WASHINGTON: Congress must decide the merits of your bill.
MADISON: Good day, Mr. President. *Bows to* HAMILTON, *who is almost bursting with fury.* Colonel Hamilton.
HAMILTON: My congratulations! You've won a noble victory over unity and honor. MADISON *smiles, shakes his head, goes.* HAMILTON *turns to* WASHINGTON. I warn you, sir . . .
WASHINGTON: Slow, Colonel. Slow but sure. That must be our political maxim.

HAMILTON: I'm afraid I may have to resign.

WASHINGTON: Now, my boy!

HAMILTON: I can't build a treasury out of thin air.

WASHINGTON: I know, my boy. I know. *He hands* HAMILTON *some papers.* Check these figures for me. *He ruffles some other documents.* These we'll go over this evening. Mrs. Washington is expecting you and your lady.

HAMILTON: Mrs. Hamilton is confined to bed.

WASHINGTON: She is? Anything wrong?

HAMILTON: On the contrary.

WASHINGTON: Another?

HAMILTON: On the way.

WASHINGTON: By God! You little men! My congratulations.

HAMILTON, *laughs:* Thank you, sir. I'll check these, now. Is there anything else?

WASHINGTON: No.

> HAMILTON *turns to go. A* SERGEANT *enters.*

SERGEANT: His Excellency's Ambassador to the Court of France, Mr. Jefferson!

WASHINGTON: Oh! Good! Show him in.

SERGEANT: Yes, sir.

> SERGEANT *exits.* HAMILTON *wheels around.*

HAMILTON: Mr. Jefferson in New York?

HUMPHREYS: He arrived last night. HAMILTON *glares at him.* HUMPHREYS *whines.* I thought you knew, Alec. . . . I . . .

HAMILTON, *suddenly very excited, to the president:* Providence is with us. Mr. Jefferson could easily persuade the South to vote for my treasury bill. I have never met him, so if you'd speak to him . . .

WASHINGTON: I can't do that.

HAMILTON: Why not?

WASHINGTON, *groans:* Again? Must we go over the ground again, and again, and again, and again, and again?

HAMILTON: It seems nothing but a catastrophe will make any impression. *Sweetly.* But I am optimistic. I expect very shortly we will see a colossal catastrophe. *He smiles ironically, bows, and goes.* COLONEL HUMPHREYS *follows.* WASHINGTON *stares after him, a shadow of a smile on his grim face.* JEFFERSON *enters.*

JEFFERSON: General Washington!

WASHINGTON, *rises:* Mr. Jefferson! Welcome home. Let me look at you. *The two men study each other.* Six years!

JEFFERSON: Six. A long time.

WASHINGTON, *sighs:* Yes. How was Patsy's wedding?

JEFFERSON: Beautiful. *He hands* WASHINGTON *some parcels.* For Mrs. Washington. For you.

WASHINGTON: Oh! You shouldn't have. *Goes to his desk, picks up a knife, slits the seals of the parcels and opens them.*

HUMPHREYS, *entering:* Jefferson, *mon vieux!*

JEFFERSON: David Humphreys! How are you?

HUMPHREYS: *Assez bien! Assez bien! Et notre charmante Paris? Comment va-t-elle?*

JEFFERSON: Changed. Everybody in Paris now talks politics. And you know how the French love to talk.

HUMPHREYS: Ha! *Laughs—a high, affected cackle. Et la chère reine? Et le roi?* How are they? *Daintily pinches some snuff into his nostrils.*

JEFFERSON: The king hunts one half the day, drinks the other half.

HUMPHREYS, *slyly:* La! La!

JEFFERSON: The queen weeps, but sins on.

HUMPHREYS: Ho, ho! *Mechante . . .*

WASHINGTON, *opens his package, takes out some lily bulbs:* By God! Lily bulbs!

JEFFERSON: The loveliest species I've ever seen. Magnificent flower. Found them in the south of France.

WASHINGTON: And rice seed.

JEFFERSON: Italy!

WASHINGTON: Beautiful grain.

JEFFERSON: Look at the size!

WASHINGTON: Mm. Beautiful! Sit here! *Moves a chair for him.*

JEFFERSON: Thank you. *Sits.*

WASHINGTON, *crosses to a cabinet, takes out decanter and glasses, pours wine:* And you found Virginia?

JEFFERSON: Ah!

WASHINGTON: Mm!

JEFFERSON: Yes!

WASHINGTON: Crops?

JEFFERSON: Rye's splendid. Wheat's good. It's going to be an excellent harvest.

WASHINGTON, *sighs:* So I hear.

JEFFERSON: Of course, my own lands are almost ruined.

WASHINGTON: These damnable overseers! Ignorant. Careless. *Hands him a glass of wine.*

JEFFERSON: Mine complained the rabbits always ate the outside row of cabbages.

WASHINGTON: Humph! What'd you tell him?

JEFFERSON: Told him to remove the outside row.

WASHINGTON, *laughs:* Good! *He draws up a chair and sits close to JEFFERSON.*

HUMPHREYS: Your Excellency, I believe you have an appointment. . . .

WASHINGTON, *dismisses HUMPHREYS with a gesture:* All right, Colonel Humphreys, later.

HUMPHREYS: *Monsieur l'Ambassadeur!* Your Excellency! *He makes several exaggerated bows and backs off.*

JEFFERSON, *stares after HUMPHREYS, amused:* Tell me, don't the little boys in the street run after him? *WASHINGTON looks after HUMPHREYS, turns to JEFFERSON, nods gravely. JEFFERSON laughs. They raise their glasses.*

WASHINGTON: The Republic! *They drink. JEFFERSON sips the wine appreciatively, holds it up to examine the color.* Recognize it? *JEFFERSON nods.* Excellent Madeira!

JEFFERSON: Patsy and I shopped all over Paris for it.

WASHINGTON: Mr. Adams is very pleased with the wines you sent him. But—er—*He looks gravely at JEFFERSON.* His daughter is disappointed in the purchase you made for her.

JEFFERSON: Mrs. Smith? Now, what did she . . .? The Paris corset? *WASHINGTON nods.* It didn't fit?

WASHINGTON: No! *He gestures with his hands, indicating the outlines of an ample bosom.*

JEFFERSON: Oh, what a tragedy!

WASHINGTON: It's very pretty, too. Mrs. Adams showed it to Mrs. Washington. Pink ribbons. The ladies are heartbroken.

JEFFERSON: They mustn't despair. Tell Mrs. Smith to put it aside. After all, there are ebbs as well as flows in this world. When the mountain didn't go to Mohamet, Mohamet went to the mountain.

WASHINGTON, *smiles, drains his glass, puts it on the sideboard:* So Lafayette is trying to establish a republic in France?

JEFFERSON: Slowly, by constitutional reform. In my rooms in Paris he drew up the first bill of rights for France. The people are all looking to our experiment. It's a heart-warming thought that, in working out the pattern of our own happiness, we are inadvertently working for oppressed people everywhere. There's a great danger there, though. I toured France, incognito. Visited the peasants in their hovels. The poverty and ignorance! Appalling! If they should ever lose Lafayette . . . *Shakes his head, finishes his drink.*

WASHINGTON: Anarchy?

JEFFERSON: Yes.

WASHINGTON, *sighs heavily:* Yes.

JEFFERSON, *studying him:* Mr. President, you look tired.

WASHINGTON, *rising:* I'm not accustomed to this indoor life. I need activity.

JEFFERSON: Long walks. The best exercise.

WASHINGTON: It's not permitted. The dignity of the State forbids it, I'm told. When we lived on Cherry Street, I couldn't go down the street without a parade. But I can tell you since we moved here to Broadway, it's a Godsend. Now, occasionally, I can steal out that door to the back yard, across the meadow, and down to the river.

JEFFERSON: What do you do down at the river?

WASHINGTON: Go fishing.

JEFFERSON: Ah!

WASHINGTON, *rises, fetches a dish of biscuits:* I've had two attacks of illness this year. I doubt if I'd survive a third. Oh, well, tomorrow or twenty years from now, we are all in the hands of a Good Providence. Try one of these biscuits.

JEFFERSON: Thank you.

WASHINGTON, *goes to his desk:* I'm organizing the ministers of the various departments into a cabinet to advise me. As our secretary of state, you're . . .

JEFFERSON: General Washington.

WASHINGTON: Mm?

JEFFERSON: In your letter you did give me the option of refusal.

WASHINGTON: You can't mean to refuse?

JEFFERSON: I must.

WASHINGTON: Why?

JEFFERSON: I've been away so long. I know none of the duties of this office. I may bungle it. I have forebodings.

WASHINGTON: We're all groping. This will be a government of accommodation.

JEFFERSON, *shakes his head:* I'm sorry. I want you to understand. Whatever spice of political ambition I may have had as a young man has long since evaporated. *He rises, places the half-nibbled biscuit on a dish.* I believe every man should serve his turn. I think I've done my share. Now I want to go home. I must complete my house. Twenty years it's waited. Patsy and her husband have come to stay with me at Monticello. The truth of the matter is, I've lived with my children so long, I've come to depend on their affection and comfort.

WASHINGTON: Tom, have you ever thought of marrying again?

JEFFERSON: No.

WASHINGTON: She was a wonderful woman, your Martha.

JEFFERSON: Yes. *Pause.* When I came home—she was in every room. *Pause.*

I've learned one thing. For me there's no peace anywhere else in the world but Monticello. You understand why I must refuse your offer?

*HUMPHREYS enters.*

HUMPHREYS: Excuse me, Sire.

WASHINGTON: Yes, Humphreys?

HUMPHREYS: The theatre box and the guard of honor are arranged.

WASHINGTON, *drily:* Good.

HUMPHREYS: And I've discovered the ambassador of the sultan of Turkey is going to be present.

WASHINGTON, *with a notable lack of enthusiasm:* Mm, mm.

HUMPHREYS: A suggestion, Excellency?

WASHINGTON: Yes?

HUMPHREYS: Wouldn't it be advisable to return to six horses on the coach?

WASHINGTON: I thought we compromised on four.

HUMPHREYS: When I was at the court of Louis . . .

WASHINGTON, *slowly, making a great effort to contain his impatience:* Colonel Humphreys, I recognize the importance of these forms to the dignity of a state, particularly one so young as ours. Understand, I know nothing of these matters. I've never been to the courts of Europe. I'm just an old soldier. I leave the ceremonies in your hands. *The impatience wears thin and he growls.* But it seems to me four horses and that canary coach with the pink and gilt angels will be enough to impress even the ambassador of the sultan of Turkey.

HUMPHREYS: But, Sire . . .

WASHINGTON: Four will do—that's final. *He ruffles some papers, frowns.* On second thought, I won't be free to go to the theatre tonight. Cancel it!

HUMPHREYS: Sire, if I may . . .

WASHINGTON, *rises, thundering:* Don't "sire" me! How many times must I tell you? By the Eternal! I am not a king! I am the elected head of our people. This is a republic. Can you get that through your skull? *He controls himself. Wearily.* All right! Go!

HUMPHREYS: Very well, Mr. President. *He goes.* WASHINGTON *sighs heavily.*

WASHINGTON: I was offered the crown.

JEFFERSON: The crown!

WASHINGTON: Twice. *Pause.* I don't want to be a king, Tom. *He crosses to the cabinet, takes up a pipe, fills it with tobacco from a jug.*

JEFFERSON: I know you don't, Mr. President.

WASHINGTON: You've no idea. *He touches a taper to the flame of a burning candle.* Every eye is on this office. A number of our people suspect me. As God is my judge, I would rather live and die on my farm than be emperor of the world. *He lights his pipe, puffing angrily.*

JEFFERSON, *pause:* I know. And yet—since I've been back—particularly here in New York—I find alarming yearnings. Our fashionable folk appear to be looking wishfully for a king and a court of our own.

WASHINGTON: Yes. I suppose so. *He sighs, exhales a huge puff of smoke, extinguishes the taper.* On the other hand, there is the equal danger of anarchy. We came close to it while you were away! *He puffs nervously at his pipe.* We walk between those two pitfalls. Our people don't take to discipline. But, without it—we shall be lost. We've yet to see how large a dose of freedom men can be trusted with. Tom, from the earliest days in Virginia, you were close to them, you seemed always to understand them. In this office I find myself far removed from direct contact with them. I need your agency. I need their faith in you. This is the last great experiment for promoting human happiness. I need the hand that wrote, "All men are created equal." I can't let you go home yet! I need you here.

*A long pause.* JEFFERSON *turns to the desk, pours back the rice seed he has been fondling, turns to* WASHINGTON.

JEFFERSON: It's for you to marshal us as you see fit.

WASHINGTON, *goes to him, grips his shoulder:* Good!

JEFFERSON: It's a great honor. I hope I can be worthy of it.

*HUMPHREYS enters.*

HUMPHREYS: Mr. President?

WASHINGTON: I don't wish to be disturbed. . . .

HUMPHREYS: His Excellency, the minister of the king of Spain is arrived to pay his respects. It had already been arranged, sir. Just the courtesies!

WASHINGTON: All right. *Sighs. Beckons to the reception room.* I'll see him. *To* JEFFERSON. You'll excuse me? It will be a few minutes. There are some journals.

JEFFERSON, *holds up his portfolio:* I have my tariff reports to study.

WASHINGTON, *escorted by* HUMPHREYS, *goes up corridor.* HAMILTON *drifts into the room, some papers in his hand. The two men look at each other.*

HAMILTON: You're Jefferson?

JEFFERSON: Yes.

HAMILTON: I'm Hamilton.

JEFFERSON: *The* Hamilton?

HAMILTON, *bows:* Alexander.

JEFFERSON: Your servant.

HAMILTON: Yours.

JEFFERSON: I read your Federalist papers while I was in France. Brilliant! You've given me a great deal of pleasure.

HAMILTON: Thank you. HAMILTON *looks at his papers, groans, shakes his head, throws the papers on the president's desk.*

JEFFERSON: Troubles?

HAMILTON, *groans again:* God! Yes. You have a pleasant voyage home?

JEFFERSON: It seemed forever.

HAMILTON, *smiles:* Of course. *He arranges papers on desk.* Have you accepted the secretary of state?

JEFFERSON: Yes.

HAMILTON: My congratulations. We must work in concert.

JEFFERSON: I'm such a stranger here, I shall lean on you.

HAMILTON: No, I'm afraid—it's—I who need your help. *Suddenly agitated, emotional.* Mr. Jefferson, it's enough to make any man who loves America want to cry. Forgive me! I really shouldn't burden you with this. It's a matter of my own department.

JEFFERSON: If I can be of any assistance . . . ?

HAMILTON: It's often been remarked that it's given to this country here to prove once and for all whether men can govern themselves by reason, or whether they must forever rely on the accident of tyranny. An interesting thought, Mr. Jefferson.

JEFFERSON: God, yes. We live in an era perhaps the most important in all history.

HAMILTON: An interesting thought! An awful thought! For, if it is true, then we dare not fail.

JEFFERSON: No.

HAMILTON: But we are failing. The machinery is already breaking down. *He snaps his fingers.* We haven't that much foreign credit. The paper money issued by the States is worthless. We are in financial chaos. *He paces to and fro.* The galling part is I have a remedy at hand. The solution is so simple. A nation's credit, like a merchant's, depends on paying its promissory notes in full. I propose to pay a hundred cents on the dollar for all the paper money issued by the States. Our credit would be restored instantaneously.

JEFFERSON, *worried:* Mr. Madison spoke to me very briefly of your bill last night. It seems there's been some speculation in this paper, and he fears . . .

HAMILTON: Madison! I loved that man. I thought so high of that man. I swear I wouldn't have taken this office—except I counted on his support. And now, he's turned against me.

JEFFERSON: Mr. Madison has a good opinion of your talents. But this speculation . . .

HAMILTON: I don't want his good opinion. I want his support. Will you use your influence?

JEFFERSON: You understand I've been away six years. I've gotten out of touch here. I'll need time to study the facts.

HAMILTON: There is no time.

JEFFERSON: Well, three or four weeks.

HAMILTON: Three or four . . . ? For God's sake, man, can't you understand what I'm trying to tell you? The North is about to secede!

JEFFERSON: Secede?

HAMILTON: Hasn't the president told you?

JEFFERSON: No.

HAMILTON: Unless my bill is passed, there is every prospect the Union will dissolve.

JEFFERSON: I'm aware there's a great deal of tension here, but . . .

HAMILTON: Walk in on a session of Congress tomorrow.

JEFFERSON: I see evils on both sides. *A long pause.* However, it seems to me—if the Union is at stake—reasonable men sitting about a table discussing this coolly should arrive at some compromise. *He comes to a sudden decision.* Have dinner with me tomorrow night?

HAMILTON: Delighted.

JEFFERSON: I'll invite a friend or two.

HAMILTON: Mr. Madison?

JEFFERSON: I can't promise anything. He's bitterly opposed to your plan.

HAMILTON: I have a way to sweeten the pill. The cost of living in New York has become so unreasonable there's talk of moving the capital.

JEFFERSON: Yes.

HAMILTON: It's already been promised temporarily to Philadelphia. Give me my bill and I can promise Madison the nation's capital will go to the South. Permanently. I was born in the West Indies—I have no local preference. However, for the sake of the Great Man, I'd like to see it go to Virginia.

JEFFERSON, *pauses:* Well, I'll bring you together, and sit at the table to see you don't shoot each other.

HAMILTON, *laughs:* Fair enough.

JEFFERSON, *takes out his fan-shaped notebook, jots down the appointment:* You see, Colonel Hamilton, we must never permit ourselves to despair of the republic.

HAMILTON: My dear Jefferson, if I haven't despaired of this republic till now, it's because of my nature, not my judgment. JEFFERSON *laughs.* Your address?

JEFFERSON: Twenty-three Maiden Lane.

HAMILTON: Twenty-three Maiden Lane. At seven?

JEFFERSON: Make it seven-thirty.

*Washington enters.*

WASHINGTON: You two gentlemen have met?

HAMILTON: Yes. What impression did the Spanish ambassador leave with you?

WASHINGTON: Like all the rest. They regard us as a contemptuous joke.

HAMILTON: Well . . . *Looks at* JEFFERSON, *smiles.* We shan't despair. Seven-thirty? *He bows to* WASHINGTON. Excellency. *He goes.*

JEFFERSON: Remarkable young man.

WASHINGTON: They call him the Little Lion.

JEFFERSON: Little Lion! I can see it. *Picks up his portfolio.* Shall I review my report on the French tariff situation?

WASHINGTON: Yes, yes, do.

JEFFERSON: Just before I left France, I had conversations with Monsieur Neckar on the matter of fishing rights. During the last year, some 23,000 francs . . . WASHINGTON *heaves a huge sigh.* JEFFERSON *looks up. The president is staring out the window.* Nice day out, isn't it?

WASHINGTON, *distracted, turns:* Hm? Oh, yes—yes.

JEFFERSON, *grins:* Have you a fishing pole for me?

WASHINGTON, *looks at* JEFFERSON, *goes to a closet, takes out two fishing poles:* How'd you know? *Hands one to* JEFFERSON. You don't mind, now?

JEFFERSON, *laughs:* I can't think of a better way to discuss the affairs of a republic.

   *Washington removes his jacket, takes an old one from the closet, calls gruffly.*

WASHINGTON: Sergeant! JEFFERSON *helps him on with the jacket.* Sergeant! *Sergeant enters.*

SERGEANT: Yes, sir?

WASHINGTON: I'm not to be disturbed. By anyone. I'm in conference with my secretary of state.

SERGEANT, *knowingly:* Yes, sir. *Exits.*

WASHINGTON, *whispers to* JEFFERSON: If Humphreys caught me in these clothes, I'd never hear the end. WASHINGTON *removes his wig, sets it on a stand, claps on a disreputable, battered old hat, picks up his pole and some documents, opens the door, starts out, sees someone off, draws back, signaling* JEFFERSON *to wait.* One of the servants.

JEFFERSON: Don't they approve of democracy?

WASHINGTON, *looks at* JEFFERSON, *shakes his head sadly:* No! *He peers out again. The coast is clear, now. He signals* JEFFERSON *to follow him.* Come! *Stealthily, they exit.*


*CURTAIN*

**ACT ONE**
*Scene 2*

*The smithy of an inn in New York. Through the large open door, a glimpse of the courtyard of the inn.* JACOB, *the smith, is hammering out a horseshoe.* MAT, *his apprentice, is pumping the bellows. Burst of laughter and men's voices from the inn courtyard.* NED, *the potboy, crosses doorway, clutching several foaming tankards.*


JACOB: Pump her, Mat! *His hammer comes down with a clang.* MAT *pumps the bellows. The fire glows.* NED *enters.*

NED: Colonel Hamilton wants his horse saddled right off.

JACOB: He in a hurry? *Clang.*

NED: Yep.

JACOB: Leavin' his party? So soon?

NED: Yep.

MAT: Why, they ain't hardly started a-belchin' yet.

JACOB: Fire's gettin' cold, Mat.

MAT. I'm a-pumpin'!

NED: Wants her saddled right off, he said.

MAT: We heard you.

NED, *irritably:* I'm only tellin' yuh what . . .

MAT, *sharply:* Awright.

JACOB: Here! Kinda techy, you two, today. Ain't you? *Pause. He looks at them both, shakes his head, hammers away at the horseshoe.*

NED, *apologetically:* Standin' by, listenin' to that Tory talk out there! Gets me mad.

JACOB: Git the saddle on, Mat!

MAT: Awright. *Fetches saddle.*

NED: Braggin' about the millions they made in paper money! I keep thinkin' of my sister.

MAT: And me! Don't fergit me! Three hundred dollars—whish!—right out-a me pocket. *Laughter off. He spits.*

NED: Know what one was a-sayin'? "President" ain't a good title for the head of the United States. Ain't got enough distingay.

MAT: French words!

NED: 'At's what he said. There are presidents of cricket clubs and fire companies, he said.

MAT: What the plague do they want? Royal Highness?

NED: Yep. That's it.

*JACOB looks up, a frown on his face.*

JACOB: You mean that?

NED: 'At's what they said.

MAT: Fer cripes sake! *He goes. Just outside the door he greets newcomers—* "Good afternoon, sir." *JEFFERSON's voice:* "Afternoon, Mat." *JEFFERSON enters with MONROE and MADISON.*

JEFFERSON, *to MADISON:* You tell my children they're to write me more often, will you, Jemmy?

MADISON: I'll do that.

JEFFERSON: I want to hear about everything at Monticello from Patsy to Grizzle.

MONROE: Who's Grizzle?

JEFFERSON: Our pet pig. *MONROE and MADISON laugh.*

JACOB: Afternoon, Mr. Jefferson!

JEFFERSON: How are you today, Jacob?

JACOB: Middlin'. I forged them fittin's you ordered. They're right over there on that tool bench.

JEFFERSON: Fine.

MONROE: Smith, my horse is limpin' on the off-front foot.

JACOB: Picked up a pebble?

MONROE: May have.

JEFFERSON: Looks to me as if she's sprung a shoe, James.

MONROE: Think so?

JACOB: Find out fer yuh in a minute.

MADISON: Give my nag a good going-over too, will you, smith? I'm off on a long journey.

JACOB: Where to, Mr. Madison?

MADISON: Home.

JEFFERSON, *sits on a keg examining the fittings:* Virginia.

JACOB: Oh! Nice weather.

MADISON: Ideal.

JEFFERSON: The lilacs'll be in full bloom, and the golden willows and the almond trees.

JACOB: Not so early.

JEFFERSON: Oh, yes. In Virginia.

JACOB: That so?

*A burst of laughter, offstage.*

MADISON: A festive board out there!

JACOB: Some a Colonel Hamilton's friends givin' him a party.

MONROE: Celebrating the passage of his bill, I suppose.

JACOB: Yep. *He goes off.*

MONROE, *bitterly:* Yes.

JEFFERSON: Now, James.

MONROE: Well, plague on it, Mr. Jefferson!

MADISON: I have to agree with Mr. Jefferson. *Ad necessitatus rei.*

MONROE: No matter how many fine Latin names you call it—"a pig is a pig."

MADISON: This was the lesser of two evils.

MONROE: You honestly think so?

MADISON, *without conviction:* I do. Yes.

MONROE: And you, Mr. Jefferson?

JEFFERSON, *doubtfully:* I don't know. I—hope so. I'm . . .

    *Laughter offstage.* MONROE *growls in disgust.* JEFFERSON *looks up at him, smiles wryly at* MADISON, *picks up the fittings* JACOB *has forged for him, examines them.*

MONROE: You've seen the newspapers, of course?

JEFFERSON: Yes, I've seen them.

MAT, *enters. To* MADISON: Wants a feedin', your mare does. She's askin' for it.

MADISON: All right. Some oats, please. MAT *pours some oats in a bag.*

MAT: Senator Monroe?

MONROE, *looks at his watch:* Yes. It's her dinnertime.

MAT: Mr. Jefferson?

JEFFERSON, *rises:* I just fed my horse, Mat, thank you. A couple of carrots, though. So he doesn't feel neglected.

MAT, *laughs:* Got some in the kitchen. *Hands* MADISON *and* MONROE *bags of oats.* MADISON *exits with bag of oats.* MAT *exits.* JACOB *enters, holding a horseshoe in his nippers.*

JACOB: Sprung it, awright.

MONROE: Did, hm? Shoe her at once, will you, smith?

JACOB: Yes, sir.

    MONROE *exits with bag of oats.* JACOB *puts the horseshoe in the furnace and proceeds to pump the bellows.* JEFFERSON *examines the metal fittings* JACOB *has forged for him.*

JEFFERSON: You've done an excellent job on these.

JACOB: They awright?

JEFFERSON: Good. You know your craft!

JACOB: Ought to. Twenty years a-doin' it. JEFFERSON *places some of the metal bits together.* Makin' another one of your inventions, are you?

JEFFERSON: A "convenience."

JACOB: What is it this time?

JEFFERSON, *crosses to* JACOB: A sort of closet on pulleys that will come up from the kitchen to the dining room—carry the food hot and the wine cold right in, without people running up and down stairs.

JACOB: Now, say, that's a purty good invention.

JEFFERSON: You think so?

JACOB: Told my wife about the collapsible buggy top you invented. Kinda useful idea, she said. But this'll catch her fancy. What do you call this here invention?

JEFFERSON, *smiles:* A "dumbwaiter."

JACOB: Dumbwaiter? *He puzzles it out.* Oh, yeah! *Gets it.* Oh, yeah! *Roars with laughter.* A dumbwaiter. Purty good. JACOB, *chuckling, extracts a horseshoe from the fire and begins to shape it on the anvil.*

JEFFERSON: Jacob!

JACOB, *intent on his work:* Yes?

JEFFERSON: I need your advice.

JACOB: What about?

JEFFERSON: This money bill we've just passed.

JACOB: Oh! *Looks up for a moment.*

JEFFERSON: What do you think of it?

JACOB: Don't like it much.

JEFFERSON: You don't?

JACOB: Nope. *Frowns, hammers the shoe.*

JEFFERSON: Because of the speculators?

JACOB: Yep.

JEFFERSON: I see. Still, it's done the country considerable good?

JACOB: Mebbe.

JEFFERSON: What do your friends think of it, generally?

JACOB: Don't like it much.

JEFFERSON: I see.

  *Ned pokes in his head.*

NED: Saddled yet? He's waitin'!

JACOB: Tell Mr. Jefferson, Ned. He's askin' about the money bill.

NED: A blood-suckin' swindle, Mr. Jefferson. *He is suddenly all aflame.* Look at my sister! Her husband was killed at the battle of Saratoga. Left her two little ones and some paper money they paid him. She's been savin' that for years. Two months ago the speculators told her it would be years more before she got anything on it, if ever. Got her to sell it for forty dollars. Six hundred dollars' worth! 'N they got Jacob's savin's. MAT *enters.*

JEFFERSON: They did?

JACOB: Nine hundred.

NED: From the Revolution. His pay.

JACOB: That ain't what we fit the Revolution fer.

JEFFERSON, *rises, restlessly:* No.

MAT: I tell you it's gettin' time we . . . HAMILTON *enters.*

HAMILTON: Is my horse ready, Jacob? Mr. Jefferson! I thought I saw you in the courtyard. I've some very good reports for you.

    NED *exits.*

JEFFERSON: Splendid.

JACOB: Mat?

MAT: She's ready. *Exits.*

JACOB: Your horse is ready, Colonel Hamilton.

HAMILTON: Thank you! Fine day, Jacob!

JACOB, *grunts:* Yep. *Exits.*

HAMILTON, *to* JEFFERSON: A little soured this morning, isn't he? Liver?

JEFFERSON, *shakes his head:* Speculators.

HAMILTON: Jacob? JEFFERSON *nods.* A shame.

JEFFERSON: And Mat. And the potboy.

HAMILTON: Why didn't they hold on to their paper?

JEFFERSON: Apparently they did. For almost seven years.

HAMILTON: Tch! Too bad. They should have had more faith in their government.

JEFFERSON: They had no way of knowing the bill was about to redeem that paper. I'm very disturbed by this.

HAMILTON: You are?

JEFFERSON: Very. Apparently, a handful of speculators, many of them in high places, have taken advantage of their knowledge of the bill to feather their own nests.

HAMILTON: Oh, now! Don't paint it worse than it is.

JEFFERSON: There's a good deal of bitter talk.

HAMILTON: Idle gossip!

JEFFERSON: Hardly.

HAMILTON: The treasury can't ask every man who submits a paper note how he came by it. At least in this way these people received something.

JEFFERSON: There must have been a means to avert this speculation.

HAMILTON: Look here—I don't quite understand your attitude. *Burst of laughter, offstage.* If we want to develop this country we've got to create great personal fortunes. Those men out there are building manufactories and industry. They're building America!

JEFFERSON: Good. Let's encourage them! But not at the expense of the people!

HAMILTON: You and Madison! The people whisper—you tremble. MONROE *and* MADISON *enter, stand silently listening.*

JEFFERSON: That's as it should be, isn't it?

HAMILTON: I am determined this country's happiness shall be established on a firm basis. I think its only hope now lies in a moneyed aristocracy to protect it from the indiscretions of the people.

JEFFERSON: I see. And this bill is to lay the foundation for such an aristocracy?

HAMILTON: Exactly.

JEFFERSON: I wasn't aware of that. You said nothing of that to me. I must be quite honest with you. I regret that I have been made a party to your bill.

HAMILTON: Made? Made, you say? You've been in politics twenty-one years. Don't play the innocent with me! Are you dissatisfied with your bargain? Is that it?

JEFFERSON: Bargain?

HAMILTON: The capital of the nation is going to *your* state—not mine.

JEFFERSON: Oh, for God's sake!

HAMILTON: Frankly, these alarms smell of hypocrisy. One minute you say you know nothing of Treasury matters; the next you set yourself up as an authority.

MONROE: What do you propose, Colonel? Shall we scrap the Constitution at once?

HAMILTON, *turns, sees* MONROE *and* MADISON, *murmurs, in disgust:* The Constitution!

JEFFERSON: You supported it.

HAMILTON, *flaring:* I had no choice. I couldn't stand by and see the country go down in convulsions and anarchy. *Pause. He controls himself.* I must confess it's my opinion this government won't last five years. However, since we've undertaken this experiment, I'm for giving it a fair trial. But, be certain of this: while it lasts it will be an aristocratic republic. If any man wants a democracy, let him proceed to the confines of some other government. Good day, gentlemen. *He goes.*

JEFFERSON, *to* MONROE: My apologies. I was wrong. *To* MADISON. Forgive me, Jemmy. I shouldn't have asked you to compromise.

MADISON: Tom, we can't escape it. He's trying to administer the Constitution into something it was never intended to be.

MONROE: I have a statement from a man who swears that Hamilton gave him money out of the public treasury to speculate with.

JEFFERSON: That I don't believe.

MONROE: There are also some letters in Hamilton's hand.

JEFFERSON: Don't believe it! He's personally honest. I'll vouch for that.

MONROE: Will you at least confront him with these letters? Ask him to explain them?

JEFFERSON: I can't.

MONROE: Why not?

JEFFERSON: Oh, for God's sake, James!

MONROE: You fight fire with fire.

JEFFERSON: I'm no salamander. Fire's not my element.

MONROE: His bill has made the fortunes of half the prominent men in the Federalist Party. It's a ring he's put through their nose. And it's clear enough, God knows, where he intends to lead them. You can't allow that. You've got to fight him. You've got to wrest the leadership of the Federalist Party away from him!

JEFFERSON, *a surge of revulsion:* If there's one thing makes me sick to death—it's the whole spirit of party politics. James, if the only way I could enter heaven was on the back of a political party, I'd rather burn in purgatory.

*Jacob appears in the doorway, adjusting saddle.*

JACOB: Your horse is ready, Mr. Jefferson.

JEFFERSON, *looks at him, pauses:* Oh, thank you, Jacob.

JACOB: Ready your horses, gentlemen?

MADISON: Yes, please.

*Jacob exits.*

JEFFERSON, *staring after JACOB, his voice harsh and lifeless:* You're wrong about the letters, James. For the rest, his bill has values. But it's hurt our people. Through it, he's created a corrupt squadron. Naturally, if he does try to pervert the Constitution, I shall oppose him. But I must do it in my own way. I'm not a brawler; I'm not a politician. *Crosses to MADISON.* Say howdya to all my neighbors for me. *MADISON nods.* The matter I spoke to you of . . . ? *Hands a paper to MADISON.*

MADISON, *nods:* I'll tend to this first thing on my arrival.

JEFFERSON: Thanks, Jemmy.

MADISON: I know how important it is to you.

JEFFERSON: Very. Pleasant journey, Jemmy. Hurry back. *To MONROE, gently.* A game of chess tonight? *MONROE nods. JEFFERSON goes.*

MONROE, *looking after him:* Blast it! This isn't the Jefferson we knew.

MADISON: No.

MONROE: The country's red-hot. It's being shaped, *now.* What does it need to wake him again?

MADISON: The tears Christ wept before the tomb of Lazarus.

MONROE: You talk of Tom as if he were dead.

MADISON, *holds up the paper JEFFERSON gave him:* He asked me to order a new stone for Martha's grave. *Unfolds paper.* Do you understand Greek?

MONROE: No. Translate it!

MADISON, *translates:* Roughly . . .
"If in the shades below,
The fires of friends and lovers cease to glow,
Yet mine, mine alone
Will burn on through death, itself."

MONROE: After nine years?

MADISON: After nine years!

   JACOB *and* MAT *enter, go to hearth.*

JACOB: Horses ready!

MONROE: Thank you, Jacob.

   NED *enters.* MADISON *and* MONROE *exit.*

NED, *raging as he tears off his apron:* I'll be damned if I'll serve on them any
   more! Know what they're saying now? Dukes and lords we oughta have!

MAT: Dukes and lords?

NED: Ay! The blood-suckin' swindlers!

JACOB: Pump her, Mat! Pump her!

MAT: What do they want to do? Make serfs outa us?

NED: Is that what we fought Lexington and Bunker Hill for? Is this the
   freedom my brother and my sister's husband died for? Where's your goddamn revolution now?

JACOB, *between his teeth, grimly:* Pump her, Mat! Come on, pump her!

   MAT *pumps. The forge glows, highlighting the taut and angry faces.* JA-
COB *hammers the hot iron with mighty, ringing blows.*

*CURTAIN*

**ACT TWO**
*Scene 1*

    *Hamilton's home. Candlelight.* HAMILTON, HUMPHREYS, *and* KNOX *are having coffee.* MRS. HAMILTON *is pouring coffee.* HAMILTON *is opening a package of cigars.*


MRS. HAMILTON, *seated on sofa:* When I think of Louis and Marie in jail!

HUMPHREYS: I haven't slept a wink since the palace fell. Dreadful! Did you read Fenno's piece in the *Gazette* today?

MRS. HAMILTON: I never miss Fenno. Brilliant, wasn't it?

HUMPHREYS: *Un chef-d'oeuvre!*

MRS. HAMILTON: Veritable!

KNOX: The situation seems to be growing worse, too. What do you think, Alec, of this French Republic?

HAMILTON: Dangerous. Highly dangerous. I'm particularly disturbed by the effect it may have on some of our inflammables. *He places the cigars on a tray.*

HUMPHREYS: You certainly lashed Mr. Jefferson on that score! *Ma foi!* Gave it to him. But proper!

MRS. HAMILTON, *to* KNOX: Sugar?

KNOX: Please.

MRS. HAMILTON: Mr. Jefferson isn't really one of these filthy Democrats?

HAMILTON: I'm afraid so, my dear.

MRS. HAMILTON: Does he *really* believe every man is as good as every other man?

HAMILTON: Even better. *They laugh.* HUMPHREYS *applauds.*

MRS. HAMILTON: Cream?

KNOX: Please.

HAMILTON: And our people seem so convinced of it. They can't wait to cut each other's throats. *Offers cigars to* KNOX. Try one of these.

KNOX: Yes. You saw it so clearly during the war. In the army.

HAMILTON: Army? *He offers cigars to* HUMPHREYS. Colonel Humphreys?

HUMPHREYS, *takes a cigar, examines it apprehensively:* So this is one of these new "cigars"?

HAMILTON, *crosses to table, sets down cigars, lights a taper:* From the Spanish Islands. . . . Army? It was no army, it was a mob. Only one man held it together. *He holds the lighted taper to* KNOX's *cigar.*

KNOX: The Chief. *Lights his cigar with huge puffs.*

HAMILTON, *nods:* Washington. *Lights* HUMPHREYS's *cigar.*

KNOX, *examines his cigar:* Very interesting leaf.

HUMPHREYS, *puffing away:* Mm! Good! Good!

HAMILTON, *to* KNOX: I hope you like them, Henry. I've ordered a packet for you.

KNOX: Why, thank you, Alec.

HAMILTON: Not at all. *Selects and lights a cigar for himself.*

KNOX: Yes. The Chief made an army out of a rabble, all right. There's no doubt of that.

HAMILTON: Ah! But to accomplish it, even he had to resort to the gallows and the lash. As with an army, so with a nation. You need one strong man.

KNOX: The Chief's getting old, though.

HAMILTON: Exactly. Sometimes I lay awake nights wondering how we can ever hold this country together when he's gone.

KNOX: Personally, I think it's his character alone that does it. I wouldn't give a penny for the Constitution without him.

HAMILTON, *sits:* Well, it's real value is as a stepping-stone. *Purring over his cigar.* Wonderful flavor?

KNOX: Mm!

HUMPHREYS, *wryly:* A bit strongish. *They laugh. He disposes of his cigar in tray beside chair.* I agree with Alec. A monarchy would have been our best salvation.

MRS. HAMILTON: Only today I was talking to some of the ladies of our court on this subject. You go out in the streets. It's frightening. We're all agreed, the time is ripening for us to have a *real* king.

BUTLER, *entering:* Senator Monroe is calling, sir.

HAMILTON: Monroe? What's he want? *Rises.* Show him in.

BUTLER: Yes, sir. *BUTLER exits.*

HUMPHREYS, *rises:* Now, there's a country bumpkin! James Monroe. *Pas d'élégance!*

KNOX: He's a good soldier! Fought in almost every important battle of the war.

HAMILTON: The soul of a clerk, though. I can't abide that.

HUMPHREYS: He was, you know. He was a clerk in Jefferson's law office ten years ago.

HAMILTON: Still is, as far as I'm concerned. *They laugh.* I'll wager ten to one he's here on some errand for Mr. Jefferson! Mark! You'll see!

   *BUTLER enters.*

BUTLER: Colonel Monroe.

MONROE, *enters, bows:* Gentlemen! Colonel Hamilton.

   *KNOX rises, bows briefly, and sits again.*

HAMILTON: Colonel Monroe. This is an unexpected pleasure. You've met my lady.

MONROE: Mrs. Hamilton. *He bows.* I was reluctant to intrude on you in your home.

HAMILTON, *crosses to pick up tray of cigars:* Quite all right.

MONROE: However, I've been trying to make an appointment with you at your office for several weeks.

HAMILTON, *crosses to* MONROE, *offers him cigars:* My office has been so busy. . . . The new taxes. Cigar?

MONROE: No, thanks.

HAMILTON: From the Spanish Islands.

MONROE: No, thanks. I should like to speak with you alone, if I may.

MRS. HAMILTON: My dear, it sounds ominous.

KNOX, *rises:* Well—er . . .

HUMPHREYS: I have an engagement with my wig-maker.

HAMILTON, *restrains them:* No. Stay, gentlemen. Pray. *To* MONROE. What's on your mind?

MONROE, *grimly:* I said alone.

HAMILTON, *curbs his annoyance, smiles:* I'm sorry. I've had an exhausting day. I refuse to discuss business now. I'll see you at my office. Tomorrow at four-thirty, if you wish.

MONROE: I'm seeing the president at four.

HAMILTON: Next week, perhaps.

MONROE: I'm seeing him on a matter that concerns you.

HAMILTON: Me? Indeed! Well, I wish you luck. You're sure you won't have one of these cigars—to smoke on the way?

MONROE: No, thanks.

HAMILTON: You'll excuse us, I'm sure. *To* BUTLER, *who is waiting at the door.* Chandler!

BUTLER, *steps forward:* Yes, sir.

MONROE: Very well. I have some papers I intend to submit to the president. I wanted to give you a chance to explain.

HAMILTON: Give me a chance to . . . ? I don't like your tone. I don't like it at all.

MONROE: I think you should be informed. There have been charges leveled against you.

HAMILTON: What charges?

MONROE: Of appropriating Treasury funds.

HAMILTON: What! *Moves toward* MONROE. You dare to come into my house and accuse me of . . . ?

MONROE: *I'm* not accusing you. I'm inquiring into the facts.

HAMILTON: General Knox, will you act as my second?

KNOX: Your servant.

HAMILTON: Sir, you will name your friend to this gentleman. They can arrange weapons, time, and place. Good night.

MONROE: I'll be very happy to oblige you.

HAMILTON, *to* SERVANT: Show him out.

MONROE, *takes some letters out of his pocket:* But I must first demand you explain these letters. . . .

HAMILTON, *raging—moves down, facing* MONROE: Any man who dares call me thief . . .

MONROE: To Mr. Reynolds.

HAMILTON, *stops short:* Reynolds?

MONROE: Yes.

HAMILTON: I see. May I . . . ? *He puts out his hand.* MONROE *gives him one of the letters. He glances at it, returns it.*

MONROE: Is that your writing?

HAMILTON: It is. This puts the matter on a different footing. I have no objection to a fair inquiry. And I think you are entitled to a frank answer.

KNOX: We'll go, Alec. KNOX *starts to go,* HAMILTON *restrains him.*

HAMILTON: I want you as a witness to this.

KNOX: Of course.

HAMILTON, *to* MONROE: If you will be at my office tomorrow evening, I . . .

MONROE, *stubbornly:* I'm seeing the president at *four.*

HAMILTON: In the morning, then. It happens, fortunately, I can supply you with all the letters and documents in this instance.

MONROE: Mr. Reynolds charges you gave him money from the public treasuries to speculate with in your behalf.

HAMILTON: Where is Mr. Reynolds now?

MONROE: I've no idea.

HAMILTON: He's in jail. Subornation of perjury in a fraud case. You take the word of such a character?

MONROE: Did you give him this money?

HAMILTON: I did. But it was my own.

MONROE: And why did you give money to such a character? *A long pause.*

HAMILTON: He was blackmailing me.

MRS. HAMILTON: Alec!

MONROE: What for?

HAMILTON: A personal matter which has nothing to do with the Treasury. I'll prove that to your full satisfaction.

MONROE: Under any circumstances, I shall ask for an accounting to Congress.

HAMILTON: As a senator, that is your privilege. And I shall oblige you. I will invite all America to look into the window of my breast and judge the purity of my political motives. Not one penny of the public funds have I ever touched. I would sooner pluck out my eye by the roots.

*MONROE remains stonily unmoved. HAMILTON's smile becomes cynical.*

MONROE: At your office. Tomorrow at ten.

HAMILTON: Ten will do.

MONROE: If it's as you say, the matter will, of course, be kept confidential.

HAMILTON, *ironically:* Yes, I'm sure it will. *MONROE bows, turns to go.* Tell him for me, Colonel Monroe, it would have been more manly, at least, to have come here, himself.

MONROE: Who are you referring to?

HAMILTON: Who sent you, Colonel Monroe?

MONROE: No one sent me, Colonel Hamilton.

HAMILTON: No one?

MONROE: No one!

*MONROE goes.*

HUMPHREYS: *Quelle folie!*

HAMILTON: Henry! Humphreys! Will you gentlemen . . . ?

KNOX: Of course, Alec. We were just leaving. If there's anything we can do? Anything at all, call on us. All your friends will be at your disposal.

HAMILTON: Thank you. It's not as serious as that, believe me.

HUMPHREYS: Ridiculous, of course. A bagatelle! When I was at the court, there was such an incident. . . .

KNOX: Come, Humphreys!

HUMPHREYS: Hm? Oh, yes, yes! *Bows.* Your servant, my lady. *To HAMIL- TON. Votre cher ami,* Colonel.

KNOX, *bows:* Mrs. Hamilton! Alec! *They go.*

HAMILTON: Betsy, I tried to spare you this.

MRS. HAMILTON, *rises:* We'll go to Father. He'll help you, darling. I know he will. You mustn't worry.

HAMILTON: It's not a question of money. Good God, Betsy, do *you* think I'm an embezzler?

MRS. HAMILTON: I only know you're in trouble and I want to help you.

HAMILTON: Thank you, my dear. Thank you. *He kisses her.* You've been a wonderful wife, Betsy. Far better than I deserve.

MRS. HAMILTON: What was this man blackmailing you for? What have you done, Alec?

HAMILTON: I've been very foolish, Betsy.

MRS. HAMILTON: Please, Alec. Tell me!

HAMILTON: When I wooed you, do you remember I said I wanted a wife who would love God but hate a saint?

MRS. HAMILTON: Don't jest with me now, Alec.

HAMILTON: I'm not.

MRS. HAMILTON: What was this man blackmailing you for?

HAMILTON: Philandering with his wife.

MRS. HAMILTON: Oh! I see. *Turns away—sits, controlling herself.* Who is she? Do I know her?

HAMILTON: No. It was a game they were playing together. She and her husband. He suddenly appeared one night, claimed I'd ruined his life, and threatened to inform you, unless I gave him a thousand dollars. He's been bleeding me dry ever since. Now, he's gotten himself in jail, and wants me to use my influence to release him. I refused. This is his revenge. *Contritely.* Forgive me, dearest. I would do anything . . . *He sits beside her.*

MRS. HAMILTON: Let's not discuss that, Alec. The question is, what shall we do now to clear you?

HAMILTON: My accounts will do that, Betsy. Congress will clear me.

MRS. HAMILTON: Oh! *Pause.* Good, then. *She turns to* HAMILTON. Why didn't you tell me this before?

HAMILTON: I didn't want to hurt you.

MRS. HAMILTON, *suddenly rises, moves away:* Then I wish to Heaven you hadn't told me at all.

HAMILTON, *rises:* I'm forced to it, Betsy. Jefferson obviously wants to destroy my position as leader of the party. As long as these letters in his hands go unexplained—by insinuation, he could undermine belief in my honesty. I must be prepared to *publish* the facts, if necessary. *He goes to her, takes her arm.* Betsy . . .

MRS. HAMILTON, *drawing arm away:* Please, Alec!

HAMILTON: You understand, don't you?

MRS. HAMILTON: Oh, yes.

HAMILTON: Believe me, I love you.

MRS. HAMILTON, *her indignation explodes with an icy blast:* And slept with a harlot! Don't insult me, Alec! You never loved me.

HAMILTON, *gently:* Why did I marry you?

MRS. HAMILTON: Was it because my father was General Schuyler?

HAMILTON, *flaring:* And I the illegitimate son of a Scotch peddler? I married you for your wealth and your position! Is that what you believe?

MRS. HAMILTON, *wearily:* I don't know what to believe.
    *Butler enters.*

BUTLER: Excuse me, sir. Mr. Fenno calling on you, sir.

HAMILTON: Tell him to go away!

MRS. HAMILTON: Show him in, Chandler. *The* BUTLER *hesitates.* Show him in!

BUTLER: Yes, Ma'am. *Exits.*

HAMILTON: Betsy, I want to talk this out with you.

MRS. HAMILTON, *presses her fingers to her temples:* I don't care to discuss this any more.

HAMILTON, *takes her by shoulders:* Listen to me, Betsy! You must listen. . . .

MRS. HAMILTON: Alec, please! *She draws away from him.* I don't care to hear any more, now. I'm—tired. *As she turns and goes, her handkerchief falls to the floor. He stares after her a moment, sees the handkerchief, picks it up.*

BUTLER: Mr. Fenno.

ENTER MR. FENNO, *a dandified gentleman; at the moment, however, he is in a lather of perspiration.*

FENNO: My dear Alec. I had to rush here and tell you. We have just received some shocking news. I—I'm trembling so, I can hardly talk.

*The BUTLER exits.*

HAMILTON, *turning to FENNO, wearily:* What is it, Fenno?

FENNO: The king and queen of France have been executed.

HAMILTON: They've . . . ?

FENNO: Guillotined.

HAMILTON: Monstrous!

FENNO, *sinks into a chair, mops his forehead with his kerchief:* The mobs in France are utterly out of hand. Burning, looting, killing. A bloodbath! Unbelievable, isn't it? Simply unbelievable!

HAMILTON: I was afraid of this.

FENNO: Worse. I've heard ugly rumors here. I passed a house yesterday, and I heard a group of men down in the cellar, singing *"Ça Ira"!* Rufus King told me he'd heard open threats against us. Even against General Washington.

HAMILTON: I've no doubt of it.

FENNO: I fear this is going to spread like the smallpox.

HAMILTON: Yes. And who've we to thank? Jefferson! Jefferson!

FENNO: Oh, no, I don't think he would dare . . .

HAMILTON, *pacing furiously:* I tell you, yes! The man's a lunatic. He's been encouraging our people to all sorts of wild illusions. Bill of rights! Freedom! Liberty! License! Anarchy! This is the fruit of his disordered imagination. That man will stop at nothing to achieve chaos. But there'll be no more of him here! I promise you. I will see to it. *Looks at BETSY's handkerchief, smooths it, a note of savage heartbreak in his voice.* There's no longer any room in this country—in this world, for both me and that—fanatic!

*CURTAIN*

**ACT TWO**
*Scene 2*

> *The wild strains of "Ça Ira." As the music fades away, the harsh, discordant voices of a crowd chanting it are heard.*
> *Philadelphia. 1793. Evening.*
> *A room in a house rented by JEFFERSON. A mist hangs outside the window. Under the window, on the table, a row of potted plants. On a large table in the center of the room, books and papers piled high; a vise, some tools, a machine in process of construction. A kettle of water on a Franklin stove. The noise of the crowd in the street faintly heard.*
> *JEFFERSON enters, hat in hand. He goes to the window, looks out. The sound of the crowd fades. He strikes flint and tinder and lights an oil lamp. Its light only serves to reveal the cheerlessness of the room. He extracts a journal from his pocket, sits, studying it, frowning.*
> *JUPITER, his body servant, enters. A Negro with a good, intelligent face.*

JUPITER: Evenin', Mister Tom!

JEFFERSON: Good evening, Jupiter.

JUPITER, *goes about lighting the lamps:* You come in so quiet. Didn't hardly hear you. We have a busy day, Mister Tom?

JEFFERSON: Mm, hm.

JUPITER: Supper's ready soon as you say.

JEFFERSON: I'm not very hungry, Jupiter.

JUPITER: But yuh got to tuck sumpin' in yuh.

JEFFERSON: Later, perhaps. *With an exclamation of disgust, JEFFERSON rises, throws the newspaper on the chair. JUPITER looks up, surprised at this unusual outburst. JEFFERSON walks over to the potted plants, examines them. JUPITER picks up the newspaper, looks at it quizzically, places it on the table. JEFFERSON examines the potted plants, nips off a few dead leaves.*

JUPITER *wheedles:* Good supper. We got basted puddin' an' chicken.

JEFFERSON, *shakes his head:* Thanks. *Picks up a little watering pot near by and waters the plants.*

JUPITER: You just come fum one a dem cabinet meetin's?

JEFFERSON, *nods, smiles:* Yes!

JUPITER: Mm, mm! *Nods knowingly.* Funny weather outside. Sticky! That yeller fog hanging all over Philadelphia. I heard today ten white folk died o' the fever.

JEFFERSON: More than that.

JUPITER: Don't like it none. *Turns to go. JEFFERSON notices JUPITER's hand is roughly bandaged with a blood-stained handkerchief.*

JEFFERSON: What's happened to your hand?

JUPITER: Oh, it's nothin'.

JEFFERSON: Let me look at it! Come here. *He removes the bandage.* A nasty gash. Sit over here! *JUPITER sits. JEFFERSON goes to the stove, pours some water into a cup, selects a bottle of wine and cruet of oil from the cupboard.* How did you do that, Jupiter?

JUPITER: When I do my marketin' this afternoon, Mister Tom.

*JEFFERSON sets the cup, the wine and the oil on the table, opens a drawer, and takes out some cloth. He opens JUPITER's hand, examines it.*

JEFFERSON: This is going to sting a bit. *Tears cloth into strips.*

JUPITER: That's all right, Mister Tom.

JEFFERSON, *dips the cloth in the water and starts to clean the wound. He soaks the cloth with wine, dabs the wound. JUPITER winces:* Hurt you? *JUPITER stoically shakes his head.* How did you do this?

JUPITER: Down outside Bainbridge Market. Just as I came out.

JEFFERSON: Yes?

JUPITER: Three men was talkin'. "Mr. Jefferson's a devil," they say. Colonel Hamilton tell dem you gonna bring the French Revolution here. Murder everybody. I don't like that. I told them that ain't true. "Ain't you Jefferson's nigger?" they say. They say they was gonna kill me. One of 'em tried to hit me on the head with a stick. I put my hand up. The stick had a nail in it.

JEFFERSON: Oh, Jupiter! Haven't you learned yet?

JUPITER: They talk bad about you. What I'm gonna do?

JEFFERSON: When an angry bull stands in your path, what do you do?

JUPITER: What I do?

JEFFERSON: A man of sense doesn't dispute the road with such an animal. He walks around it. *He smiles. JUPITER laughs and nods.*

JUPITER: Yeah, I guess so.

JEFFERSON: What happened then, Jupiter?

JUPITER: Then a crowd came down the street, yellin'! Dey's a lot a crowds in de street, Mister Tom.

JEFFERSON: I know.

JUPITER: De men see dat crowd. Dey get scared an' run away. Mister Tom— dem crowds in de street—dey're talkin' wild. Yellin', "Kill de aristocrats! Break dere windows! Burn dere houses!" Singin' French songs.

JEFFERSON, *bandages the hand:* Hurt? Too tight?

JUPITER, *shakes his head:* Dey talkin' bad about President Washington.

JEFFERSON: Washington?

JUPITER: Yes, Mister Tom. *JEFFERSON frowns as he bandages the hand.* Dat get me all mixed up. I know he fight for liberty. I remind me you tell me General Washington try to free my people.

JEFFERSON: That's right. He did.

JUPITER: I remind me, how you try, Mister Tom. I like to see my little Sarah free some day. An' I remind me how you say we gotta some day open all that land in the Northwest and ain't gonna be no slaves there. An' how we gotta git my people education, an' we gotta git 'em land, an' tools.

JEFFERSON: Some day, Jupiter. It's written in the book of fate. Your people will be free.

JUPITER: Mister Tom. Dat crowd. Git me mixed up. Git me all mixed up. I don' like it. Dey jus' gonna make trouble.

JEFFERSON: I'm afraid you're right, Jupiter. You see, the men who beat you—they're monarchists. They want a king here. The others—the crowd—they're mixed up. It's what's happening in France now. It's gone wild. *Finishes bandaging JUPITER's hand.* How's that feel?

JUPITER: Fine, Mister Tom. *He tries his hand.* Fine.

JEFFERSON: Don't use that hand for a while.

JUPITER: No, Mister Tom.

>   *The bell tinkles.*

JEFFERSON: The door-pull!

> JUPITER *goes to answer it.* JEFFERSON *picks up the wine, returns it to cupboard.*

JUPITER, *appears in the doorway, excited and laughing:* Mister Tom! Looka here! Look who's here.

>   *PATSY enters.*

PATSY: Father!

JEFFERSON: Patsy? Darling.

>   *They rush to each other and embrace.*

PATSY: Oh, Father. It's so good to see you.

JEFFERSON: My dearest. What in the world . . . ?

PATSY: I wanted to surprise you.

JEFFERSON: It's a wonderful surprise. Jupiter, kill the fatted calf! Two for supper.

JUPITER: It's chicken.

>   *They laugh.*

JEFFERSON: Kill it, anyway.

JUPITER, *laughs:* He got his appetite back! Looka his face. You shore good medicine, Mrs. Patsy.

JEFFERSON: Where's your trunk?

PATSY: The coachman left it outside.

JUPITER: I get it right away. *Starts off.*

JEFFERSON: I'll fetch it, Jupiter. Your hand is . . .

JUPITER, *holds up his good hand:* That's all right, Mister Tom. I kin manage.

PATSY, *goes to JUPITER:* Your wife sends you her love, Jupiter. And Sarah.

JUPITER, *stops and turns:* Dey all right?

PATSY, *nods:* I've brought you some presents they made for you.

JUPITER: Thanks, Mrs. Patsy! It's sure good to have you here, Mrs. Patsy! *He exits.*

JEFFERSON: How's little Jeff, and my sweet Anne, and Maria? And Mr. Randolph? Here! Give me your cloak.

    *JEFFERSON takes her cloak, places it on a chair.*

PATSY: Jeff has two new teeth.

JEFFERSON: Two? Wonderful!

PATSY: He's beginning to talk. Anne's growing so. You'd hardly recognize her.

JEFFERSON: Does she still remember me, Patsy?

PATSY: Of course. She's always playing that game you taught her—I love my love with an A. She's forever chattering about you. "Where's Grandpapa? When's Grandpapa coming home? What presents is Grandpapa going to bring me?"

JEFFERSON, *chuckles:* Mm, hm!

PATSY: Maria sends love, squeezes, and kisses. We both adored the hats and veils.

JEFFERSON: Did they fit?

PATSY: Perfectly. And the cloaks were beautiful.

JEFFERSON: The style was all right?

PATSY: Oh, yes.

JEFFERSON: And how's your good husband?

PATSY: Mr. Randolph's well, working hard. Doing the best he can with the overseer. . . . Is it always so close in Philadelphia?

JEFFERSON: This is very bad weather. A contagious fever's broken out here.

PATSY, *looks about:* So this is where you live?

JEFFERSON: Do you like my quarters?

PATSY: A little gloomy, isn't it?

JEFFERSON, *laughs:* You must be exhausted. A glass of sherry?

PATSY: I'd love it. *JEFFERSON crosses to wine cabinet.* Father! Coming here— the coach had to stop. There was such a crowd of people up the street.

JEFFERSON: The French ambassador's been haranguing them lately. There have been some disorders. This epidemic of fever here seems to bring a moral contagion with it. *He selects several bottles, holds them up.* Dry or sweet?

PATSY: Dry, please. *She toys with a mechanical device on the table.* What's this? Another "convenience" of yours?

JEFFERSON: That's a copying machine. Very handy. It makes duplicate copies of letters. I'll show you how it works.

PATSY, *laughs:* Oh, Father. You and your inventions! Sometimes I . . . *Her eye is caught by the journal on the table. She stops laughing, frowns, picks it up, reads it. Her face sets in anger.*

JEFFERSON, *pouring sherry:* Has Maria learned to baste a pudding yet? In her last letter she said Aunt Eppes was teaching her . . .

PATSY: Father!

JEFFERSON: Hm? *Turns, sees her with the newspaper.* Oh! You don't want to read that! *Crosses to take it from her.*

PATSY: Oh, my God!

JEFFERSON: Now don't get upset, dear!

PATSY: What sort of a newspaper is this?

JEFFERSON: The "court" journal. The snobs nibble it for breakfast. Here, drink your sherry.

PATSY: I'd heard what they were doing to you here, but this is worse than I could have possibly imagined.

JEFFERSON: It's very flattering. Especially that bit about the harem! A harem! At my age! Pretty good. . . .

PATSY: I don't see any humor in it! You'll answer these charges?

JEFFERSON: Answer one lie, they print twenty new ones.

PATSY: Then what are you going to do?

JEFFERSON: Let's ignore it, dear, hm?

PATSY: Who wrote it? Who's Pacificus?

JEFFERSON: I don't know. It's a pseudonym.

PATSY, *pauses. She looks at him, almost in tears; finally, very bitterly:* You must enjoy being the secretary of state very much to put up with such abuse.

JEFFERSON: It's my job, dear.

PATSY: Job? *Rises, walks to the window, agitated.* Father?

JEFFERSON: Yes, dear?

PATSY: Don't you think you've sacrificed enough?

JEFFERSON: I haven't sacrificed anything.

PATSY: You haven't?

JEFFERSON: No. *Pause.*

PATSY: A few weeks ago I found a pamphlet Mother had written during the Revolution to the Women of Virginia on the necessity for them— *Bitterly.* —to make sacrifices to help win the war. I remember Mother so ill she could hardly walk, doing ten men's work at home. I remember, after she died, sitting on the cold floor outside your door, listening to you sob till I thought you, too, must die. I remember hearing you cry out you'd sacrificed her to the Revolution.

JEFFERSON, *sinks into a chair:* Patsy . . .

PATSY: The morning and afternoon of your life you sacrificed. Wasn't that enough?

JEFFERSON: Patsy, dear! Please!

PATSY: No. If you won't think of yourself, what of us? A child of twelve and a baby of four, torn from our home, from all we loved, taken to a foreign land, seeing you only on occasion, longing always for home and security and . . . Why? For what? Is there no end . . . ?

JEFFERSON: Patsy, I beg of you!

PATSY: Don't you owe anything to yourself? Don't you owe anything to us? I tell you, Father, everything at home is going to pieces. If you don't come back soon, there'll be nothing left. Nothing!

JEFFERSON, *rises, in agony:* Patsy! Will you, for God's sake, stop!

PATSY, *crosses to him, overcome with remorse:* Father! Oh, Father, I didn't mean to . . .

JEFFERSON, *takes her in his arms:* I know. I know.

PATSY: Forgive me.

JEFFERSON: Of course.

PATSY: I've been so confused and unhappy. I had to come and talk it out with you.

JEFFERSON: Of course you did. I should have been very hurt if you hadn't.

PATSY: It's the business of running Monticello and the farms. We try! Lord knows we try! But Mr. Randolph has no talent for it. And his failure makes him irritable. And I worry so. I'm afraid you may lose everything you own.

JEFFERSON: I see, my dear. I see. *He strokes her hair.* I haven't been altogether insensible to this. It's weighed on me very heavily, the trouble I put your good husband to.

PATSY: I shouldn't have said anything. I know what your work here means to you.

JEFFERSON, *a sudden surge of bitterness:* I have never loathed anything as much in my life. You've no idea, Patsy, of the rank and malignant hatreds here. Politics destroys the happiness of every being in this city! I'm surrounded here by hate and lies. Lately I've seen men who once called themselves my friends go so far as to cross the street to avoid tipping their hats to me.

PATSY: You, of all people! Why?

JEFFERSON: There are a gang of king-jobbers here who are bent on changing our principle of government—by force, if necessary. Since Mr. Madison and Mr. Monroe have left, I'm alone against them. I can't contend with them, Patsy.

PATSY: What of the president?

JEFFERSON: Only his strength and his stubborn purity oppose them. But he's old, and he's sick. *Sits.* I work from morning till night. They undo everything. This isn't spending one's life here. It's getting rid of it.

PATSY: Oh, my poor father! *PATSY goes to him, kneels at his feet. He draws out a locket hanging around his neck.*

JEFFERSON: Do you know, dear, my only pleasure? For an hour or so every evening I sit and dream of Monticello. I find myself more and more turning to the past and to those I loved first. Your mother . . . *He opens the locket, studies it.* She was a beautiful person, Patsy. She loved you all so dearly. *Closes the locket.* You're right, Patsy. If I hadn't neglected my duties at home during the war, she would have been alive today. It's true. I sacrificed your mother to the Revolution. And now I'm doing the same to you. Darling, your happiness is more important to me than my life. And, like a fool, I've been jeopardizing it. For the privilege of being— *Rises, picks up the newspaper.* —called in the public prints "lecher, liar, thief, hypocrite!" *He throws down the newspaper.* But no more! You mustn't worry, dearest. Everything's going to be all right. I promise you. I'm tending to my own from now on. *Grim-faced, he takes down a portable writing-desk from the mantelpiece, sits, places it on his lap, opens it, extracts paper and pen, and begins to write furiously.* Patsy!

PATSY: Yes.

JEFFERSON: Will you ring for Jupiter? The bellpull's there. *PATSY pulls the cord. A tinkle is heard, offstage.* I have a job for you tomorrow.

PATSY: Good. What is it?

JEFFERSON, *as he writes:* I want you to help me select what furniture and articles suit Monticello, and pack and ship them to Richmond.

PATSY: To Richmond?

JEFFERSON: I'll be busy here the next few weeks, but we'd better get them off at once while the shipping lanes are still seaworthy. *He sands the letter, blows it, reads it a moment.*

 *JUPITER enters.*

JUPITER: Yes, Mister Tom?

JEFFERSON: You know where the president's home is?

JUPITER: Yes.

JEFFERSON: Please deliver this letter there at once.

JUPITER: After supper?

JEFFERSON, *rises:* No, now, Jupiter.

JUPITER: My supper's gonna get spoiled.

JEFFERSON: At once, Jupiter. *To PATSY.* We're going home, together. To stay, Patsy. I'm resigning. *He places the open portable desk on the table.*

JUPITER: You goin' home, Mister Tom?

PATSY: Yes, Jupiter.
   *Jupiter stares at* JEFFERSON.
JUPITER: Mister Tom goin' home . . . ?
PATSY: Oh! I'm so happy, Father, I . . . *The faint noise of a crowd outside.*
   PATSY *breaks off, listens. The noise grows.*
JEFFERSON: The crowd again. *He crosses to the window and looks out.* This
   is good fuel for the Federalists!
   *The chanting of the mob suddenly becomes loud and ominous.*
PATSY: What are they chanting?
JEFFERSON: I can't make it out.
   *The chanted words:* "Down with . . ." *become distinguishable.*
PATSY: Down with—who?
JEFFERSON, *as the last word becomes clearly* "Washington": Washington?
   Wash—! *He and* PATSY *look at each other. A moment of shocked silence.*
   He's all that stands between them and their enemies. *Pause.* Patsy! When
   all our names are sponged from the records, his will burn brighter, wher-
   ever men fight for freedom. *Irritably, to* JUPITER *who is standing there as if
   rooted to the spot.* All right, Jupiter. Run along! What are you waiting for?
JUPITER *goes.* PATSY *looks at* JEFFERSON *questioningly.* No, darling. It isn't
   going to make any difference. If our people won't deserve their liberty, no
   one can save it for them. I'm going home. *He picks up the portable desk,
   slams it shut, and places it back on the mantel.*

CURTAIN

## ACT TWO
*Scene 3*

   *The same, a few days later. Most of the furnishings are now gone, leaving
noticeably naked areas in the room. There are several bundles of books, etc.,
on the floor.* PATSY *is wrapping pictures and the more fragile articles in several layers of cloth, and packing them carefully in a barrel.* JEFFERSON, *sitting at his desk, is writing furiously, disposing rapidly of a great mass of
documents piled before him. Clouds of smoke hang over the room, fed by
several braziers.*

   JUPITER *enters, his face sick with apprehension. He picks up a bundle of
books, starts to take them out. The ominous rumbling of a cart is heard
outside.* PATSY, JEFFERSON, *and* JUPITER *straighten up, listening.*

JUPITER: De death cart! *He goes to the window.* It's piled full, Mister
   Tom. . . . *He crosses to the braziers.* Dis yellow fever everywhere! White

folks droppin' like flies, Mister Tom! *He pours some nitre into the braziers. Fresh ribbons of smoke spiral up.*

JEFFERSON, *to* PATSY: You hear that?

*PATSY stubbornly continues her wrapping.*

JUPITER: I never seen nuttin' like dis.

JEFFERSON: Jupiter! Take Mrs. Randolph at once to Germantown.

PATSY: I shan't go.

*The door-pull tinkles. JUPITER goes to answer it.*

JEFFERSON: Patsy! I'll pick you up there in a few days, and then we'll go on home together.

PATSY: I shan't leave you here alone.

JEFFERSON: I have work to finish.

PATSY: Then I'll stay, too.

JEFFERSON: You're a stubborn child.

PATSY: I come by it honestly.

*Enter JUPITER and HAMILTON.*

JUPITER: Mister Tom, you have a visitor.

JEFFERSON, *rises:* Colonel Hamilton.

HAMILTON: Has the president arrived yet? *JUPITER exits.*

JEFFERSON: Not yet. My daughter, Mrs. Randolph. Colonel Hamilton. *PATSY curtsies. HAMILTON bows.*

HAMILTON: He asked me to meet him here. I'll wait in my carriage.

JEFFERSON: You're welcome to sit here.

HAMILTON: Thank you!

PATSY: Excuse me, Father! Colonel Hamilton! *She curtsies, goes.*

HAMILTON: There's a fellow lying on the sidewalk, dead of the plague. *JEFFERSON goes to the window.* Not a pleasant sight. I sent my driver to fetch the death cart.

JEFFERSON: A bad business!

HAMILTON: Getting worse by the minute. *Looks about.* You moving?

JEFFERSON: Yes. You'll have to pardon our appearance. *Sits, picks up his pen.* Excuse me! I . . . *Indicates his work.*

HAMILTON: Quite all right. Please! Don't let me disturb you.

*JEFFERSON goes back to his writing.*

JEFFERSON: The president should have left the city immediately.

HAMILTON: You may be sure I ordered him out. The great man's a stubborn warrior, though. Can't budge him. Never could.

*JEFFERSON concentrates on his writing.*

*HAMILTON glances at several magazines on a table near his chair, selects one with great surprise, glances toward JEFFERSON with uplifted brows, then, smiling mischievously:* The Gazette?

JEFFERSON *looks up from his work, searches* HAMILTON *with a cold glance, murmurs drily.*

JEFFERSON: Yes.

HAMILTON: I notice an article referring to you. Have you read it?

JEFFERSON, *stops writing, looks up:* I have. *There is a pause. He goes back to his writing.*

HAMILTON, *smiles, enjoying the game immensely:* Well phrased.

JEFFERSON: Brilliantly. And thoroughly untrue, Colonel Hamilton. Thoroughly.

HAMILTON: Oh, come now, Mr. Jefferson—you do well with the ladies?

JEFFERSON, *writes on:* So I see in the *Gazette.*

HAMILTON: When I read this article I . . .

JEFFERSON: Read it? It's commonly supposed, Mr. Hamilton, that you wrote it.

HAMILTON: It's written by some person called— *Peers at journal mockingly.* —Pa—ci—fi—cus.

JEFFERSON, *savoring the irony, smiles wryly:* Pacificus. Peaceful! A proper pen name. Colonel Hamilton, almost since our first cabinet meeting—you and I have been thrown at each other like cocks in a pit. The cockfight is over. "Peaceful" will soon have the cabinet to himself.

HAMILTON: How is that?

JEFFERSON: Hasn't the president informed you?

HAMILTON: No.

JEFFERSON: I've resigned.

HAMILTON: Oh! I'm sorry to hear that.

JEFFERSON: I'm not. I'm very happy, Colonel.

HAMILTON, *rises, moves to window:* In that event, I rejoice with you.

JEFFERSON: Colonel Hamilton, you're going to your home in the country, now, to wait out the plague?

HAMILTON: Yes.

JEFFERSON: I, too, will be gone in a few days. We may never see each other again. *Crosses to mantel; places portable writing-desk on it.*

HAMILTON: Quite probably we won't.

JEFFERSON: I should like to ask you as man to man, without rancor or warmth— *He picks up the newspaper.* —is this fitting to the dignity of a minister of state?

HAMILTON, *bitterly:* Was it fitting the dignity of your high office to send your henchmen prying into my private life?

JEFFERSON: I never did that.

HAMILTON: You thought I would keep silent, did you? You thought sooner than risk my personal happiness I'd let you call me thief? Well! You see what you've done? Congress has cleared my public name, and I'm all the stronger for it! I didn't run away! However, in your case, I think it wise for you to go home and sit on your mountain-top. The philosophic experiment is over. Your Democracy is finished.

JEFFERSON: You really think that?

HAMILTON: I know it. I knew it six years ago. *The bellpull tinkles.* My God, aren't the omens clear enough, even to a Utopian? What do you think of your people now? Your fellow dreamer, Lafayette, in irons, rotting in a German jail, his only refuge from the very ones he sought to free. At that, he's lucky. If he hadn't escaped in time, even now his head would be lying in the basket, his blood flowing in the gutters, running into a river of the noblest blood of France—for your drunken swine, the people, to swill in. I tell you—it nauseates me to the very heart. And now, the same rioting mobs here, and next, the same terror!

JUPITER, *enters:* General Washington.

WASHINGTON, *enters:* Gentlemen! *He is getting very old. His face is tired and bewildered, but a bulwark of grim, stubborn determination.* JUPITER *exits.*

JEFFERSON: Mr. President. *Moves to* WASHINGTON; *takes his hat and stick.*

HAMILTON: No asafoetida pad? *Produces a spare pad and hands it to the president.* In these times, Mr. President, we can't afford to lose you. I beg of you!

WASHINGTON: Very well. *Accepts pad.* Thank you! *Sits down heavily, silent for a moment, as he broods, all the while tapping the arm of the chair as if it were a drum. The death cart outside rumbles by.* More than two thousand dead already. This plague is worse than a hundred batteries of cannon. *Sighs, taps.*

HAMILTON: You should have left the city immediately, sir.

WASHINGTON: I think I almost prefer to be in my grave than in the present situation. *Taps, sighs heavily. A long pause.* What does it mean? *Silence; taps.* Incredible. Aren't men fit to be free? Is that the answer? Have you spoken to the French minister?

JEFFERSON: Yes. One can't reason with him. He's a lunatic! I've demanded his recall.

WASHINGTON: They're all lunatics. Lafayette fleeing for his life? Lafayette? And here now, mobs rioting! What does this mean? *Pause.* We must do what we can to help Lafayette.

JEFFERSON: I've already despatched a letter to Ambassador Morris, urging him to make every solicitation in his power.

WASHINGTON: I don't know if it'll help. I doubt it. WASHINGTON *nervously picks up the* Gazette, *glances quickly at* JEFFERSON. *To* HAMILTON, *with a touch of sternness.* Do you mind waiting below? I should like to talk with you.

HAMILTON, *glances a bit guiltily at* JEFFERSON, *then smiles ironically:* I'll wait in your carriage. WASHINGTON *nods.* Your servant, Mr. Jefferson.

JEFFERSON: Mr. Hamilton.

HAMILTON *goes.*

WASHINGTON: I shall have to speak to him again. He's very difficult. He's always been that way, though. Once, during the war, when he was my aide, he kept me waiting two hours. When I rebuked him, he resigned. Sulked like a little boy. *Softens, with evident love of* HAMILTON. Finally I gave him what he wanted—a command in the field. He was a very good soldier. Led his troops in the first assault on Yorktown. He's an invaluable man. Why can't you two work together?

JEFFERSON: Our principles are as separate as the poles.

WASHINGTON: Coalesce them!

JEFFERSON: It can't be done.

WASHINGTON: Let me be the mediator.

JEFFERSON: You've tried before.

WASHINGTON: Let me try again.

JEFFERSON: It's no use. Believe me. Neither of us could honestly sacrifice his belief to the other.

WASHINGTON, *sighs, taps:* Well, I'm ordered back home. Any messages to Albemarle County?

JEFFERSON, *sits next to* WASHINGTON: My best regards to Mr. Madison. And you might look at my new threshing machine. If it interests you, the millwright's in Richmond now. He'd be very happy for any new commissions. You get eight bushels of wheat an hour out of two horses.

WASHINGTON: Hm! I'll certainly examine it.

JEFFERSON: Tell Madison next spring we'll be planting our gardens together.

WASHINGTON: No, Tom. I'm afraid you won't.

JEFFERSON: Why not?

WASHINGTON, *rises. Takes out a paper, lays it on desk:* Your resignation. I can't accept it.

JEFFERSON, *rises:* I'm sorry, Mr. President. You'll have to.

WASHINGTON: Where can I find anyone to replace you?

JEFFERSON: I don't flatter myself on that score. I've failed.

WASHINGTON: Let me be the judge of that.

JEFFERSON: I've spent twenty-four years in public life. I'm worn down with labors that I know are as fruitless to you as they are vexatious to me. My personal affairs have been abandoned too long. They are in utter chaos. I must turn to them and my family.

WASHINGTON: And the good esteem of your fellow men?

JEFFERSON, *moves away:* There was a time when that was of higher value to me than anything in the world. Now I prefer tranquillity. Here, for everything I hate, you ask me to give up everything I love. I'm sorry, no! I want a little peace in my lifetime.

WASHINGTON: I know. I know. I'm sick, Tom, and I'm getting old, and I catch myself dreaming of the Potomac and Mount Vernon. *He almost shouts.* Don't you think I hate this, too? Don't you think I yearn for the peace of my own farm? Don't you think all this—all this . . . *Controls himself. There is a long silence. He murmurs.* Peace in our life? Where. . . ? *His memories turn back as he searches for the phrase.* Oh, yes. . . . Paine wrote it. Was it in *The Crisis?* "These are the times that try men's souls. The summer soldier and the sunshine patriot will, in this crisis, shrink . . ." *JEFFERSON sinks into a chair; unwittingly, the president has dealt him a stunning blow.* How that brings back the picture! As if it were yesterday. My men starved, naked, bleeding. I read Paine's essay. You know, it lent me new strength. I had it read to my men through trumpets. Nailed it on trees for them to read. It helped them. Gave them sore-needed courage. Do you remember the passage on the Tory innkeeper who was opposed to the war because— *He finds the phrase he's been searching for.* —that's it—"He wanted peace in his lifetime"? And Paine looked down at the innkeeper's children crawling on the floor and thought, "Were this Tory a man, he would say: If there must be conflict with tyranny, let it come in my time. Let there be peace and freedom in my children's time." Yes. That's the answer, I suppose. The only answer. *Suddenly, desperately, he grips JEFFERSON's arm.* Tom! The fabric is crumbling. Our Republic is dying. We must bolster it, somehow—some way. *Fiercely, a grim, stubborn warrior fighting a ghost. He pounds the table.* It must have a chance. It will, I say. It will, it will, it will! I'll defend its right to a chance with the last drop of my blood. *The fierceness vanishes. Again he becomes a tired, sick, old man.* You'll stay on a few days more? Till I find someone else?

JEFFERSON: Yes.

WASHINGTON: Good! You see, I'm like a man about to be hanged. Even a few days' reprieve makes me rejoice. *Sighs heavily, starts to go, turns.* I wouldn't stay here. Take your papers, go to the country. You can work there. *Bows.* Mr. Jefferson.

JEFFERSON, *rises:* Mr. President.

WASHINGTON *goes. Outside, the death cart rumbles by.* JEFFERSON, *torn and tortured, drops back into his chair.* JUPITER *enters, pours more nitre into the braziers.* PATSY *enters, holding up a music box.*

PATSY: Father! Look! I found this little music box inside. May I . . . Father! You're not ill?

JEFFERSON: No, Patsy.

PATSY: You look so pale. Are you sure, Papa?

JEFFERSON: Yes, dear.

PATSY: Can I get you something? A drink of water?

JEFFERSON: No, dear. I'm all right. *Pause. JUPITER exits.*

PATSY: May I take this home to Anne?

JEFFERSON: Yes, dear.

   *She turns a knob. The music box plays a tinkling melody.*

PATSY: Anne will love it. Can't you just see her face?

JEFFERSON: Mm. *Pause.*

PATSY: Did the president accept your resignation?

JEFFERSON: Yes.

PATSY: I spoke to him in the hallway. He looks so old, doesn't he? *JEFFERSON nods. PATSY shuts off the music box.* Oh, Father, please! Please don't torment yourself so!

JEFFERSON, *rising:* He's a dying man, Patsy. He's dying. And, when he's gone, they'll take the reins. And that'll be the end, Patsy. That'll be the end of the Republic.

PATSY: Perhaps we weren't ready for it, Father.

JEFFERSON, *moves about, restlessly:* If not here and now, where, then? Where will men ever have such a chance again? This was my dream, Patsy! From my earliest youth.

PATSY: You've done your best, Father.

JEFFERSON: Not good enough, apparently. Summer soldier. *Pause.* It was seventeen years ago, *here in Philadelphia,* I wrote the Declaration of Independence. That's how I dreamed of America, Patsy. A beacon for all mankind. *Pause.* Patsy! It's not our people who've failed us. It's we who've failed them. Yes. I see that now. *Paces about the room.* These fermentations are a healthy sign. Our people are groping. They're jealous of their rights? Good! They want a larger share in their government. Most of them today haven't even the privilege of voting. It would take so little education to make them understand these disorders are not to their advantage. That's where we've failed them, Patsy. It's not enough to create the form of a Republic. We must *make* it work. We must see that our people get the right to vote. We must educate them to use it and be worthy of it. We must give them free schools, and universities, and a liberal press. Only an enlightened people can really be free. Till now, the genius of the common people has been buried in the rubbish heap. We must rescue that! I'm convinced of it! We must make war on ignorance and poverty. We must go into the streets and the squares and the smithies. . . .

JUPITER, *entering:* Mister Tom.

   *HAMILTON appears in the doorway.*

HAMILTON: I beg your pardon. I didn't mean to . . .
  JEFFERSON *faces* HAMILTON. JUPITER *exits.*
JEFFERSON: It's quite all right. Come in!
HAMILTON: The president asked me to speak to you. He's greatly distressed.
JEFFERSON: Yes, I know he is.
HAMILTON: He asked me to make an effort to coalesce our differences. There's no reason why we shouldn't.
JEFFERSON: You think we can?
HAMILTON: If you will only stop regarding the Constitution as something handed down from Mount Sinai.
JEFFERSON: I see.
HAMILTON: If we're to work together, you'll . . .
JEFFERSON: We're not!
HAMILTON: Oh!
JEFFERSON: We are natural enemies.
HAMILTON: Well, I offered peace.
JEFFERSON: The wolves offered the sheep peace.
HAMILTON: You don't flatter me!
JEFFERSON: It is not an American art.
HAMILTON: I am an American by choice, not by accident.
JEFFERSON: Yet you bring here a lie bred out of the vices and crimes of the old world.
HAMILTON: Lie?
JEFFERSON: The lie that the masses of men are born with saddles on their backs, and a chosen few booted and spurred to ride them legitimately, by the grace of God.
HAMILTON: It's laughable! You, born to wealth and land and slaves, driveling about the common people!
JEFFERSON: Search your own birth, Mr. Hamilton, and you'll . . .
HAMILTON: Don't say it! *Trembling with rage.* I must warn you.
JEFFERSON: Say what? That you as a boy were poor? That you came to this country and it gave you honor and wealth? I believe every boy in this land must have that opportunity.
HAMILTON: Why do you think I want the country strong?
JEFFERSON: It can only be strong if its people govern it.
HAMILTON: You think the peasants on my farm can make it strong?
JEFFERSON: There are no peasants in America.
HAMILTON: Words! What do I care for them! Call them yeomen! Call them what you will! Men cannot rule themselves.
JEFFERSON: Can they then rule others? Have we found angels in the forms of kings and dictators to rule them?

HAMILTON: I've made my last gesture. Go! Run back to your hill! From here on, I promise you, you will never again dare raise your head in this party.

JEFFERSON: I hate party. But if that's the only way I can fight you—then I'll create another party. I'll create a people's party.

HAMILTON: Now it comes out. You want two parties! You want blood to flow! At heart you, too, are a Jacobin murderer.

JEFFERSON: That's another lie you believe because you wish to believe it. It gives you the excuse you need to draw your sword! I'm sick to death of your silencing every liberal tongue by calling "Jacobin murderer."

HAMILTON: Well, aren't you? Confess it!

JEFFERSON: Go on! Wave the raw head and the bloody bones! Invent your scares and plots! We were asleep after the first labors, and you tangled us and tied us, but we have only to awake and rise and snap off your Lilliputian cords.

HAMILTON: Very well. Let it be a fight, then. But make it a good one. And, when you stir up the mobs, remember—we who really own America are quite prepared to take it back for ourselves, from your great beast, "The People."

JEFFERSON: And I tell you, when once our people have the government securely in their hands, they will be strong as a giant. They will sooner allow the heart to be torn out of their bodies than their freedom to be wrested from them by a Caesar!

HAMILTON, *bows:* Good day, Mr. Jefferson.

JEFFERSON: Good day, Colonel Hamilton. *HAMILTON exits.*

JEFFERSON *turns to* PATSY: Patsy, this is a fight that may take the rest of my life. . . .

PATSY: Yes.

JEFFERSON: But I have to! I hate it, but I have to, Patsy. I want Anne and Jeff and their children to grow up in a free republic. I have to, Patsy.

PATSY: Of course you do. *Rises. Crosses to* JEFFERSON. Of course you do, Father. *She takes his hand impulsively, kisses it.*

## *CURTAIN*

## ACT THREE
*Scene 1*

> The new city of Washington, 1801. JEFFERSON's rooms in Conrad's Boarding House.
>
> JEFFERSON seated at his desk, writing. His grandchildren, a little boy and a girl, playing on the floor at his feet. PATSY seated, crocheting. Outside, in the hallway, the excited babble of many voices. JUPITER is placing a tray on the desk. Prominently set on the mantel is a marble bust of Washington.
>
> A knock at the door. PATSY starts up. JUPITER turns to the door.

PATSY: I'll take it, Jupiter. *She hurries to the door, opens it. A* MESSENGER *hands her a message. A crowd of boarders surrounds him, asking questions.*

MESSENGER: Twenty-seventh ballot just come up.

PATSY: Thank you. *The crowd assails her with questions.* In a minute. *She hands the message to her father.* JEFFERSON *reads it, while she waits anxiously.* JEFFERSON *crumples it, throws it away, smiles, shakes his head.*

JEFFERSON: The same.

PATSY: Oh, dear! *She goes to the door.* No. I'm sorry. Congress is still deadlocked.

> *The crowd in the hallway becomes persistent.*

FIRST MAN: We heard Mr. Burr lost a vote to your father.

PATSY: That's not true, as far as I know.

MESSENGER, *shakes his head:* No. I told them. *To others.* I told you. *He goes.*

SECOND MAN: We elected Mr. Jefferson to be president. What's Congress fiddling around for, anyway? What are they up to, Mrs. Randolph?

THIRD MAN: Is it true the Feds are going to try and just make one of their own men president?

PATSY: I can't say. . . .

> *Suddenly, a high-pitched voice is heard, and a little lady comes pushing through the crowd. She is* MRS. CONRAD, *the proprietress of the boardinghouse.*

MRS. CONRAD: In the parlor, please! All my boarders. Downstairs! In the parlor! You'll get the returns there as soon as you will up here. Now, stop a pesting Mr. Jefferson! Give a man a little privacy, will you? Downstairs in the parlor! *She enters, apologetically, in a whisper.* Everybody's so worked up, you know.

PATSY: It's all in the family.

MRS. CONRAD: Well, I can't have the other boarders disturbing your father at a time like this.

PATSY: Thank you.

*A husky voice is heard singing* "Outa my way." "One side!" *The boarders are tumbled aside. A man in frontier outfit, armed to the teeth, appears in door.*

FRONTIERSMAN: Tom Jefferson here?

PATSY: What is it?

FRONTIERSMAN: Message from Governor Monroe of Virginia.

JEFFERSON: Here!

FRONTIERSMAN: You're Tom Jefferson?

JEFFERSON: Yes.

FRONTIERSMAN, *hands him message:* Governor Monroe said to deliver it to you personal.

JEFFERSON: Thank you! *Opens it. Reads it.* Sit down.

FRONTIERSMAN: Don't mind astandin'. Rid my horse hard all a way from Richmond. She's got a mean jog. Governor's waitin' on your answer.

JEFFERSON: No answer, yet.

FRONTIERSMAN: Nothing settled yet on the election?

JEFFERSON: No. You'd better stand by.

FRONTIERSMAN: Yep.

JEFFERSON: Mrs. Conrad, will you see this gentleman gets something warm to eat? Jupiter, will you saddle a fresh horse?

JUPITER: Yes, Mr. Tom. *Exits.*

MRS. CONRAD: I'll tend to it right away, Mr. Jefferson. *Goes to door, calls.* Nathan!

VOICE, *offstage:* Yes, Mrs. Conrad.

MRS. CONRAD: Fix up some vittles right off!

PATSY: Perhaps you'd like a drink?

FRONTIERSMAN: Why, thank you, ma'am. Now that's a Christian thought.

*PATSY smiles, fetches brandy bottle. MRS. CONRAD returns.*

JEFF: Gramp! Play with me.

PATSY, *pouring drink:* Jeff, Grandpapa's busy.

JEFF: Come on, Gramp. . . .

JEFFERSON: Later, Jeff. I've a new game to teach you.

JEFF: A new one?

JEFFERSON: A good one.

JEFF: Is it like riding a horse to market?

ANNE: Oh, goody, Grandpapa! Shall I get the broom?

PATSY, *hands the drink to the FRONTIERSMAN:* Children! Go inside.

JEFFERSON: No, no. They don't disturb me. I want them here.

*Patsy beckons the children away from the desk, seats them in the corner by her side.*

FRONTIERSMAN, *tosses down the drink:* Hm! That washes the dust down!

*A knock at the door. PATSY hurries to it. MADISON is there. Crowded behind him in the hall is the group of boarders. They are asking him questions. MADISON is saying, "That's the latest balloting. I've just come from the Capitol."*

MADISON, *enters, worn, breathless, almost crumbling with fatigue:* I've just come from the House of Representatives. I had to push my way here. The streets are jammed with people. I've never seen so many human beings.

JEFFERSON, *rising:* Jemmy, you look like a dead one.

MADISON, *sits and groans:* I am. The twenty-seventh ballot came up.

JEFFERSON: We just got the message.

MADISON: You should see Congress! What a spectacle! They fall asleep in their chairs, on their feet. Red-eyed, haggard!

JEFFERSON: Mr. Nicholson's fever any better?

MADISON: Worse. He's resting in a committee room. He has about enough strength to sign his ballot.

JEFFERSON: Who's attending him?

MADISON: His wife's by his side, giving him medicine and water.

JEFFERSON: He should be removed to a hospital.

MADISON: He won't budge. Insists he'll vote for you till he dies. I doubt whether he'll survive another night. *JEFFERSON shakes his head.* Tom, there's an ugly rumor going around. The crowds are getting angry.

JEFFERSON: Yes, I know. May be more than a rumor, I'm afraid. *He hands MADISON a communication.*

MADISON: Gad! How's this going to end?

MRS. CONRAD: I been talkin' to my husband, Mrs. Randolph, and we both decided the whole way of votin' now just ain't right.

MADISON: Agreed. Agreed.

MRS. CONRAD: Take my husband. He wanted your father for president, Mr. Burr for vice-president. Well, he should be allowed to put that down on the ballot instead of just the two names and lettin' Congress decide. Stands to reason, don't it? See what happens? We beat the Federalists, and then the old Congress, most of 'em Feds themselves, don't know who to pick. Deadlocked six days now. They might like as not go on being deadlocked four years, and we'll have no president at all. Now, I say, it's deliberate. Everybody's sayin' that!

JEFFERSON: They are?

MRS. CONRAD: Stand to reason. *She nods vigorously and scurries off, having said her piece.*

MADISON: We should have foreseen this difficulty. We certainly bungled the electoral system.

FRONTIERSMAN: Constitution's gotta be changed so a man can put down who he wants for president.

JEFFERSON: Well, it can be amended. That's the great virtue of the Constitution. It can grow.

MADISON: If we ever have the chance to amend it. I'm worried sick by this, Tom.

*A young man,* LAFAYETTE, *appears in the doorway.*

LAFAYETTE: Does Monsieur Jefferson live here?

MRS. CONRAD, *appears:* In the parlor! Down in the parlor!

PATSY: It's all right, Mrs. Conrad.

MRS. CONRAD: Oh, excuse me. I thought he was one a my boarders. *She goes.*

LAFAYETTE: Monsieur Jefferson?

JEFFERSON: Yes, young man.

LAFAYETTE: You do not remember me? Twelve years ago. Paris?

JEFFERSON: You're . . . ? Of course, you're Lafayette's boy.

LAFAYETTE, *nods:* Your servant.

JEFFERSON: I was expecting you. I'd heard you were in America. You remember Patsy? *To* PATSY. George Washington Lafayette.

PATSY: Of course.

*LAFAYETTE bows and PATSY curtsies.*

LAFAYETTE: She has not changed one little bit. Only more beautiful, if possible.

PATSY, *laughs:* He's Lafayette's son, all right.

JEFFERSON: He has the gift. And these are my grandchildren.

PATSY, *proudly:* My daughter, Miss Anne Randolph.

ANNE, *curtsies:* Monsieur Lafayette.

LAFAYETTE, *bows:* Miss Randolph.

PATSY: Monsieur George Washington Lafayette . . . *Brings the little boy forward.* My son . . . *(Proudly)* Thomas Jefferson Randolph.

*The little boy makes a deep bow.* LAFAYETTE *smiles at* JEFFERSON, *who beams.*

JEFFERSON: My friend, Mr. Madison.

LAFAYETTE: The father of your immortal Constitution? *Bows.* My veneration!

MADISON, *drily:* Immortal? It's running a high fever now. The next few days, the next few hours, may tell whether it's going to live at all, or die in hemorrhage. *To* JEFFERSON. Tom! I'm as nervous as a cat. I haven't slept a wink in three nights.

JEFFERSON: Lie down inside.

MADISON: No, no.

JEFFERSON: Go on! Patsy, make up the bed for Jemmy.

MADISON: No! I couldn't. Please! Just let me sit here. *Sits.*

JEFFERSON, *moves chair for* LAFAYETTE: We're passing through a terrible storm here.

LAFAYETTE, *sits:* I am sorry to come in the midst of all this, but as soon as I arrive I hurry to you.

JEFFERSON, *to* LAFAYETTE: Tell me! How is your father?

LAFAYETTE: He is out of prison now.

JEFFERSON: I'd heard. I haven't written him because things here, too, have been so bad these last years, my letter would never have reached him. *Pause.* How does he look?

LAFAYETTE: Six years in prison.

JEFFERSON: They didn't break his spirit?

LAFAYETTE: That they will never break.

JEFFERSON: No.

LAFAYETTE: He asked me to explain he dare not write. Bonaparte watches him. He is only free on—a string.

JEFFERSON, *sighs:* I had hoped, at first, Bonaparte would value the real glory of a Washington as compared to that of a Caesar. *He glances at bust of Washington.*

LAFAYETTE, *follows his glance:* When we heard he died, my father wept like a child. *Pause.*

JEFFERSON: A great man fell that day. America now must walk alone.

LAFAYETTE: Here—forgive me. This isn't the America I expected. This is like when Bonaparte came to us.

JEFFERSON: There is an ominous note in this dissension. You've sensed it. Our own little Bonaparte may step in with his comrades at arms and force salvation on us in his way.

LAFAYETTE, *rises:* That must not be. This is the message my father asked me to deliver. Tell Jefferson, he says to me, tell him the eyes of all suffering humanity are looking to America. It is their last hope on earth.

*A knock at the door.* JEFFERSON *opens the door. A* COURIER *stands there.*

COURIER: Mr. Jefferson?

JEFFERSON: Yes?

COURIER: Message!

JEFFERSON: Thank you!

COURIER *goes.* JEFFERSON *takes message, opens it, reads it, becomes grave.*

MADISON, *rises:* What is it, Tom?

JEFFERSON: A group of the Federalists are meeting tonight.

MADISON: To set aside the election?

JEFFERSON: Possibly. *Hands the message to* MADISON. MADISON *reads it, groans.*

FRONTIERSMAN: Like hell they will! Nobody's gonna take my Republic from me.

JEFFERSON, *to the* FRONTIERSMAN: That's right, my friend. *He crosses to his desk, picks up the letter he has been writing, folds it.* I'm afraid there's no time for that meal now. Will you see if your horse is ready?

FRONTIERSMAN: Yep. *Goes.*

JEFFERSON, *seals letter. To* PATSY: I think you had better plan on going home.

PATSY: Very well, Father.

JEFFERSON: I don't know how long this will keep up. I don't know how it will end.

   FRONTIERSMAN *returns.*

FRONTIERSMAN: Horse is saddled and out front.

JEFFERSON, *hands letter to him:* To Governor Monroe, with my compliments.

FRONTIERSMAN: Yes, sir.

JEFFERSON: Give your horse the spur!

FRONTIERSMAN: Ride him like the wind, Mr. Jefferson. No fear! *He goes.*

PATSY: When do you want us to leave?

JEFFERSON: Now. *Looks at his watch.* After dinner.

PATSY: So soon?

JEFFERSON: Please.

PATSY: There's going to be serious trouble?

JEFFERSON: I don't know, Patsy.

PATSY: General Hamilton? Again? Is there no end to that man's malevolence?

LAFAYETTE: Hamilton? *He looks about at a loss.* But, during the war, he was my father's friend, too. My father often speaks of him.

PATSY: People changed here after the war, Monsieur Lafayette. The real revolution has been fought in the last six years.

MADISON: And our people have won, Monsieur Lafayette. Through the ballot they've taken the government into their own hands. But now the Federalists intend to drag everything down with them, rather than admit defeat. *There is a knock at the door.*

PATSY: They've turned President Adams completely against my father—one of his oldest friends!

LAFAYETTE: This shocks me. I cannot believe it.

PATSY: Do you know why he didn't write your father all these years? He couldn't! They opened his mail! They twisted phrases he used in his letters, and printed them against him.

*The knock is repeated.*

JEFFERSON: These are things, Patsy, that are best forgotten.

PATSY: Father, there are men in the streets with guns. They're expecting Hamilton and his troops. They say there'll be shooting.

*The doors open.* HAMILTON *stands there. A long, stunned silence.*

HAMILTON: Mr. Jefferson.

JEFFERSON: General Hamilton.

PATSY: You dare . . . !

JEFFERSON: Pat! Go inside, please.

PATSY: Yes, Father. Come, children! *She steers the children off.*

JEFFERSON: General Hamilton, Monsieur George Washington Lafayette.

HAMILTON: Lafayette? You're his son?

LAFAYETTE: Yes.

HAMILTON: Of course. I knew your father well. He was my friend.

LAFAYETTE: He often speaks of you. He was yours.

MADISON, *picks up his hat and starts to leave:* Gentlemen!

LAFAYETTE: I go with you, if I may.

MADISON: Come along.

JEFFERSON: You'll dine with us? LAFAYETTE *nods.* JEFFERSON *looks at his watch.* In twenty-three minutes.

LAFAYETTE: Twenty-three.

JEFFERSON: On the dot. Mrs. Conrad runs her boardinghouse along democratic lines. The early birds get the choice cuts.

LAFAYETTE *smiles, turns to* HAMILTON, *bows.*

LAFAYETTE: Monsieur Hamilton.

HAMILTON *bows.* LAFAYETTE *goes.* JEFFERSON *and* HAMILTON *survey each other.*

JEFFERSON: What can I do for you, General Hamilton?

HAMILTON: Nothing! But I can do something for you. I'm not going to equivocate, Mr. Jefferson. My sentiments toward you are unchanged. I still despise you and everything you represent.

JEFFERSON, *moves to desk. Indicates a chair:* Chair, General?

HAMILTON: Is that understood?

JEFFERSON: I think pretty widely. *Points to chair.* Chair?

HAMILTON, *sits:* Thank you. *Pause. They survey each other.* You've grown leaner.

JEFFERSON: And you stouter.

HAMILTON: Not at all. It's this waistcoat. . . . A few pounds, perhaps. *Pause.*

HAMILTON *glances out the window.* So this is your city of Washington. A mud hole!

JEFFERSON: A few trees and some sidewalks and it will do.

HAMILTON: The first day we met this was born.

JEFFERSON: Yes.

HAMILTON: You remember?

JEFFERSON: Oh, yes.

HAMILTON: The presidential mansion appears not bad.

JEFFERSON: Not bad.

HAMILTON: Large enough.

JEFFERSON: Large enough for two emperors and a rajah.

HAMILTON: Who's it to be—Aaron Burr or you?

JEFFERSON: Congress will decide.

HAMILTON, *rises:* I have some friends in that body. I can influence this decision for or against you, I believe.

JEFFERSON: I'm certain of that.

HAMILTON: Certain? I'm not. You'd be astonished, Mr. Jefferson, at the number of gentlemen who, no matter what I counsel, would vote for the devil himself in preference to you.

JEFFERSON: Yes. That's quite probable.

HAMILTON: Not that I approve of it. I don't. I deplore it. In the matter of the public good, men must consult their reason, not their passions. I believe I can swing Congress over to you, *if* you accede to certain conditions.

JEFFERSON: I see.

HAMILTON, *moves to desk:* One: I want your solemn assurance that you will continue all my friends in the offices they now fill. Two: I want . . .

JEFFERSON, *smiles, shakes his head:* I'm sorry.

HAMILTON: You refuse?

JEFFERSON: This time, no bargains. I appreciate your motives . . .

HAMILTON, *in a rage, shouting:* Bargains? What puny channels your mind runs in!

JEFFERSON: No need to shout, General.

HAMILTON, *pacing furiously:* I'll raise the roof if I please.

JEFFERSON, *nods toward the next room:* My grandchildren . . .

HAMILTON: Excuse me.

JEFFERSON: This is like old times, General.

HAMILTON: Do you realize how dangerous this situation has become?

JEFFERSON: Yes.

HAMILTON: I came here to compromise. I hoped to avert the more drastic alternative. But the years have made you even more pigheaded, if possible. I might have spared myself this trouble.

JEFFERSON: I couldn't enter the presidency with my hands tied.

HAMILTON: Don't concern yourself. You won't enter it at all! My friends are meeting tonight. You oblige them to act to set aside this election altogether and choose their own man.

JEFFERSON, *grimly:* They would be smashing the Constitution.

HAMILTON: Stretching it!

JEFFERSON, *rises:* Smashing it, I say. HAMILTON *shrugs his shoulders, turns to go.* Have you seen the crowds about the Capitol Building?

HAMILTON: A pistol-shot and they'd disperse.

JEFFERSON: Don't deceive yourself! Our people will not be *"put aside."* *Hands him a letter.* From Maryland. Fifteen hundred men met last night. Resolved: If anyone dares usurp the presidency, they will come here in a body and assassinate him. *He picks up several letters.* From Governor McKean of Pennsylvania . . . From Governor Monroe of Virginia. Their militia are ready to march at a moment's notice. If you put aside this election tonight, tomorrow morning there will be blood in the streets.

HAMILTON: I am an old soldier, Mr. Jefferson. If you give us no alternative . . .

JEFFERSON: But you have an alternative. End this deadlock at once! Use your influence with your friends. I shall use mine. Make Aaron Burr president.

HAMILTON: Aren't you being whimsical?

JEFFERSON: No. I should honestly prefer that.

HAMILTON: So you want Aaron Burr to be president?

JEFFERSON: He's a superior man, energetic, sharp, believes in our people.

HAMILTON: God! You're gullible! I know the man. He despises your Democracy more than I. Yet he has chimed in with all its absurdities. Why? Because he is cunning, and audacious, and absolutely without morality—possessed of only one principle, to get power by any means and keep it by all.

JEFFERSON: That's an opinion.

HAMILTON: That's a fact. He has said it to me to my face. A dozen times.

JEFFERSON: He has sworn the contrary to me.

HAMILTON: Burr has been bankrupt for years. Yet he spent vast sums of money on this campaign. Where do they come from?

JEFFERSON: I don't know.

HAMILTON: What do you think has been the sole topic of conversation at his dinner table? To whom are the toasts drunk? Can you guess?

JEFFERSON: No.

HAMILTON: The man who supplies his funds, the man with whose agents he is in daily conference.

JEFFERSON: What man?

HAMILTON: Bonaparte.

JEFFERSON: Bonaparte? I can hardly . . .

HAMILTON, *extracts some documents from his pocket and places them on the desk:* Proofs, if you wish them. Burr is the Cataline of America. He'll dare anything. You may as well think to bind a giant by cobwebs as his ambition by promises. Once president, he'd destroy all our institutions. Usurp for himself complete and permanent power. Make himself dictator.

JEFFERSON: I know you have no faith in them, but do you think the American people would stand idly by?

HAMILTON: No, I have no faith in them. But they'd fight. I grant you that. There'd be bloody civil war! And that's all Bonaparte would need. He would swoop down on us— *Slams his fist on the desk.* —Like that! *Long pause.* JEFFERSON *picks up the "proofs," studies them.* Now you know my motive. I'm afraid, I'm profoundly afraid for the happiness of this country. HAMILTON *examines the bust of* WASHINGTON. Cerracchi?

JEFFERSON, *looks up from the "proofs":* Yes.

HAMILTON: Excellent! I've commissioned him to sculpt one of the Great Man for me. JEFFERSON *looks up, sighs.* Well? JEFFERSON *lays down the papers. He is tired and confused.* You've been duped, my friend.

JEFFERSON, *smiles feebly:* I suspected only you.

HAMILTON: Of what?

JEFFERSON: Planning to be our Bonaparte.

HAMILTON: When Washington died, I could have. Why didn't I?

JEFFERSON: Why?

HAMILTON: Burr asked me that question. Contemptuously. This may be difficult for you, but try to grasp it. I happen to love this country, too. I have fought for it in field and council. Above every small, selfish, personal desire, I want to see it peaceful and prosperous and strong. *Triumphant.* Well? Will you meet my terms? *Pause.*

JEFFERSON, *miserably:* I can't.

HAMILTON, *moves to desk:* My conscience is clear. I know how to proceed.

JEFFERSON: If you do this, it can only lead to the very thing you condemn.

HAMILTON, *reaches for papers:* Perhaps. Perhaps that is the only hope for us in a world of Bonapartes and Burrs.

JEFFERSON: Then what will we have gained?

HAMILTON: Good day, Mr. Jefferson. *Goes to the door.*

JEFFERSON, *rising:* I warn you, there will be bloodshed tomorrow.

HAMILTON: Oh, no, there won't. You see, I'm counting on you. You will prevent it.

JEFFERSON, *with sudden newborn fierceness:* You're wrong, my friend.

HAMILTON, *pauses, turns:* You'd condone it?

JEFFERSON, *crosses to* HAMILTON: I'd be part of it.

HAMILTON: You?

JEFFERSON, *growls:* I.

HAMILTON, *returns, looks at him, surprised:* You really mean it.

JEFFERSON: By the God that made me, I mean it. I'd open my veins and yours in a second.

HAMILTON: You amaze me.

JEFFERSON: Why? Isn't the blood of patriots and tyrants the natural manure for liberty?

HAMILTON: You've become a tough old man.

JEFFERSON: Who made me tough?

HAMILTON, *laughs ironically:* Then I haven't lived in vain.

JEFFERSON: That's right. *HAMILTON is staring at JEFFERSON.* Listen to me, Hamilton!

HAMILTON: This is a strange . . .

JEFFERSON: Listen to me! I know you love this country. But you have never understood it. You're afraid of Bonaparte? Well, there's no need to be. Bonaparte will die and his tyrannies will die, and we will be living, and we will be free. You're afraid of Burr? If Burr tries any quixotic adventures, he will smash himself against the rocks of our people. You see, this is the mistake you have always made. You have never properly estimated the character of the American people. You still don't understand them. At this moment. *There is a long silence.*

HAMILTON: I confess it. I don't. *Sits.*

JEFFERSON, *standing over him. Gently:* This is not the way, Hamilton. Believe me. If you really love this country, this isn't the way. Our people who fought the revolution from a pure love of liberty, who made every sacrifice and met every danger, did not expend their blood and substance to change this master for that. *His voice grows strong.* But to take their freedom in their own hands, so that never again would the corrupt will of one man oppress them. You'll not make these people hold their breath at the caprice, or submit to the rods and the hatchet, of a dictator. You cannot fix fear in their hearts, or make fear their principle of government. I know them. I place my faith in them. I have no fears for their ultimate victory.

HAMILTON, *wavering:* I wish I had such faith. *Shakes his head.* I don't know. I frankly don't know. I find *myself lost here.* Day by day, I am becoming more foreign to this land.

JEFFERSON: Yet you helped build it.

HAMILTON: There is a tide here that sweeps men to the fashioning of some strange destiny, even against their will. I never believed in this—and yet, as you say, I helped build it. Every inch of it. *Pause. He rises.* And still, I must admit it has worked better than I thought. If it could survive—if . . .

JEFFERSON: It can. And it will. This tide is irresistible. You cannot hold it back. This is the rising flood of man's long-lost freedom. Try as you will, you cannot stop it. You may deflect it for a moment. But in the end you will lose. Try the old way of tyranny and usurpation, and you *must* lose. Bonapartes may retard the epoch of man's deliverance, they may bathe the world in rivers of blood yet to flow, and still, still, in the end, they will fall back exhausted in their own blood, leaving mankind to liberty and self-government. No, General Hamilton, this way you lose. Believe me. *He crosses to his desk, crisp and final.* I shall not compromise, General Hamilton. You do whatever you choose. I cannot compromise on this.

HAMILTON, *holds out his hand. It is shaky:* Since the fever took me, I can't hit the side of a barn with a pistol. Burr is cool as a snake, and one of the best shots in America. I've fought him for five years now. If I cross him in this—he will challenge me. I have no doubt of that. I am a dead man, already. But at least you are honest. I shall urge my friends to break the deadlock. You will be president. Your victory is complete.

JEFFERSON: There is no personal victory in this for me. I didn't *want* this for myself. I still don't. If it will give you any satisfaction, my own affairs have been neglected so long . . . In another office, with time to mend them, I might have saved myself from bankruptcy. As president, I am certain to lose everything I possess, including Monticello, where my wife and four of my children lie. Where all the dreams of my youth lie. No matter! I thank you—for a glorious misery.

HAMILTON *bows, goes.* JEFFERSON *turns, stares at the statue of Washington.*

CURTAIN

**ACT THREE**
*Scene 2*

The interior of the Senate Chamber.
JEFFERSON, *hand raised, is taking the oath of office from* CHIEF JUSTICE MARSHALL.

JEFFERSON: I do solemnly swear that I will faithfully execute the office of President of the United States, and will, to the best of my ability, preserve, protect, and defend the Constitution of the United States.

JUSTICE MARSHALL *waves* JEFFERSON *to assembled audience. Nervously, hesitantly,* JEFFERSON *steps forward to the audience, looks about. His glance rests on* PATSY, *standing proudly with* ANNE *and* JEFF. PATSY *smiles and nods.* JEFFERSON *faintly smiles. He turns to the audience, begins to speak in a voice hesitant and uncertain.*

JEFFERSON: Friends and fellow citizens: Called upon to undertake the duties of the first executive of our country, I will avail myself of the presence of that portion of my fellow citizens which is here assembled to express my grateful thanks for the favor with which they have been pleased to look upon me. A rising nation spread over a wide and fruitful land, advancing rapidly to destinies beyond the reach of mortal eye—when I contemplate these transcendent objects and see the honor, the happiness and the hopes of this beloved country committed to the issue of this day, I—I shrink before the magnitude of the undertaking. Utterly, indeed, should I despair if not for the presence of many whom I see here. To you, then, I look for that guidance and support which may enable us to steer with safety the vessel in which we are all embarked amid the conflicting elements of a troubled world.

This is the sum of good government. Equal and exact justice to all men, of whatever state or persuasion, a jealous care of the right of election, absolute acquiescence to the decisions of the majority, the vital principle of republics, from which is no appeal but to *force,* the vital principle and parent of despotism. . . . Freedom of religion, freedom of press, freedom of person, and trial by juries impartially selected. These form the bright constellation which has gone before us and which has guided us in an age of revolution and reformation. The wisdom of our sages and the blood of our heroes have attained them for us. They are the creed of our political faith, the touchstone of our public servants. Should we wander from them in moments of error or alarm, let us hasten to retrace our steps and to regain this road which alone leads to peace, liberty and safety. During the present throes and convulsions of the ancient world, during these agonizing spasms of blood and slaughter abroad, it was not strange that the agitation of the billows should reach even this distant and peaceful shore. That this should be more felt and feared by some than by others. I know, indeed, that some honest men fear that a republic cannot be strong, that this government is not strong enough. But would the honest patriot, in the full tide of successful experiment, abandon a government which has so far kept us free and firm, on the theoretic fear that it may possibly want energy to preserve itself? I trust not. I believe this, on the contrary, the only government where every man would fly to the standard and meet invasions of the public order as his own personal concern. I believe this the strongest government on earth. I believe, indeed, I know, this government is the world's best hope . . .

*CURTAIN*

# DETECTIVE STORY

WHILE RESEARCHING *Men in White,* I met two New York detectives who invited me to visit their precinct. I was intrigued by their life and I realized that though the police station had been exploited perhaps more than any other background in literature—in thousands of whodunits—there had never been a completely honest picture. I suddenly recognized the locale for my next play. I saw that the measure of a free society can be taken right there in a police station, in the relation of police activity to constitutional law.

I was privileged to do most of my research on *Detective Story* at New York City's 17th Precinct. The detectives I met there were themselves a varied group, each one interesting in his own way and all of them kind of special. In discussing *Detective Story,* I have to confess that some of the same saucy toughness that I had as a young man, I found waiting for me in the detective squad room.

And then there were the criminals. I met at the precinct the two burglars I used as models for *Detective Story.* There was, particularly in the relationship between the police and the criminals, a strange manner not dissimilar to the manner of the reporters in *The Front Page.* If a criminal was whining, there was one detective who would say to him, "Come on. You wanted to be a thief? OK, you're a thief, so be a good one. You knew sooner or later you'd get dropped, so be a good thief. You'll meet all your friends in jail."

Much of my research did not end up in the play. In particular I remember some of the kidding around, clowning, and amusing situations. For instance, a burglar who had been picked up was complaining because the elevator man had crept up behind him as he broke into an apartment and hit him on the head with a flashlight. The burglar felt that was unfair.

One, more serious, situation occurred down the block from where I lived

241

on 58th Street while I was doing research. Walking by one day, I saw a crowd gathered round and discovered there had been a holdup with shooting, in the course of which the holdup man had been shot dead. Later, over at the station house, the detective who had done the shooting was standing by talking, and the captain muttered to me, "Look at his face, watch him." Slowly, the man's face began to turn pale and greenish. The captain looked at his watch and said, "In about ten minutes!" And sure enough, in about ten minutes the detective was very sick and could hardly stand. According to the captain, this usually happened when a detective shot and killed someone—there was a delayed reaction and then, in about an hour or an hour and a half, it would get to the detective, and he would always get a little sick. I did not use this particular item in the play, but I have never forgotten it. Such gravity and anguish were reality and were the elements with which the play dealt.

In doing my research, visiting police stations, the district attorney's office, and accompanying detectives on their rounds, I filled thirty notebooks. Then I decided it was time to quit, get away somewhere and boil it down. I spent almost a year on my farm near Oakland, where I tried to capture a new kind of violent rhythm in the play. I believe this play moves faster than other plays contemporary with it.

On the surface, *Detective Story* is an exciting melodrama about cops, dealing with the events of four hours in the detective squad rooms of a New York police station. Actually, however, it's an attempt to investigate a basic problem, the case of the tough and violent perfectionist, the "good" fascist on the side of the angels who divides everything into good and bad and wants to destroy everything he considers bad. In 1949 I believed that a new form of society would emerge, that by the turn of the century man would be evolving a new government, a single world government, but what kind of a single world government? The world is changing rapidly, and it is imperative that some of our present institutions be preserved—constitutional protection of the freedom of the individual, for instance. Men like McLeod constitute a serious threat, for such men may well rule the world state of the future.

In writing *Detective Story*, I was influenced by General George C. Marshall's speeches in 1947 in which he used the phrase "the police state." Thinking of the police state, I felt convinced that we must eventually have a single world government. What will its principles be? Will it be a free or an ant society? My feeling is that there can be happiness for the people of the world only if a firm protection for human rights is incorporated in the world government. Police power is a symbol, a measuring rod, of freedom in a society. When the police power answers to a democratic code of human rights, you have a free society.

When I started this play I was in a searching mood. I wanted to do a play that expressed the fears and tensions we were experiencing. I felt a moral responsibility to help alleviate the awful tedium of our time and, in doing so, excite and stimulate the audience. This was the first level of my play.

The second level, which may not be apparent to audiences, went much deeper. I took as my premise "Judge not, but ye be judged" from the Sermon on the Mount, and I used the classic form with the unities of time, place, and action. The action is within four hours. The central figure is of heroic proportions, though a slightly romantic one. He is a moralist, wanting to bolster a collapsing civilization by turning back the clock.

The first act of the play does not state a problem, but gives people an emotional undercurrent that something is going to happen. From first to last, I attempted to give the audience an impression of looking at a slice of life—tragic and comic, brainless and thoughtful, ribald and innocent, all the aspects of life seen in a police station. From that, I hope, I have evoked in audiences a feeling and understanding of the very great need to keep police power out of the hands of dangerous men.

I gave the audience a chance to sit behind the scenes of a detective squad room. It was the first authentic picture of routine life of a police station. No big murders take place, nothing spectacular, nothing in the traditionally romantic sense. I tried to make a virtue out of the trivial cases rather than the extraordinary. I tried, of course, to evoke that germinal idea. But I wanted to evoke the idea, rather than state it.

Everything in the play is so integrated, like a symphony. All the action takes place on one big set, the inside of the police station. Several stories are being told at once. An episode of one story is presented, then part of another. Actors are quiet on one side of the stage while action is taking place on the other side. A fine job of ensemble acting is required in *Detective Story*.

Professor Alexander Drummond, with whom I studied directing at Cornell, always emphasized the importance of Edward Gordon Craig's theories and the elements of movement. Certainly, in this play I experimented with movement. It requires split-second timing. It is like a ballet—a challenge with 30+ characters. The challenge to a director is that he is using a wide-angle lens. The theatre is based on a narrow focus, and the modern tendency has been to narrow it more to produce a hypnotic effect. Directorially, *Detective Story* was a much more creative job than anything else I have ever done.

I believe that artists help to shape events—for example, *Dead End* figured in the debates over slum clearance. So in *Detective Story*, I tried to write a play that would stir people to feel the necessity for keeping public control over police power. When I named my police station the Twenty-first Precinct, I hoped some of the audience might ask themselves whether we will be living in a police state in the twenty-first century, or whether we will be getting the protection of the police in accord with the rules of a free society. My rough cop, McLeod, thinks democracy is not efficient in its war against evildoers. He wants to achieve efficiency by taking the law into his own hands, by making people abide by right as he sees it, or by personally bringing them to account if they do not. Of course, the inefficiency comes from our checks and balances, so that no man is to be trusted with absolute power. The answer to McLeod is that the inefficiency of humankind is a really a higher efficiency, since it permits the human spirit to breathe.

S.K.

# DETECTIVE STORY

Presented at the Hudson Theatre by Howard Lindsay and Russel Crouse on March 23, 1949, with the following cast:

| | |
|---|---|
| DETECTIVE DAKIS | Robert Strauss |
| A SHOPLIFTER | Lee Grant |
| DETECTIVE GALLAGHER | Edward Binns |
| MRS. FARRAGUT | Jean Adair |
| JOE FEINSON | Lou Gilbert |
| DETECTIVE CALLAHAN | Patrick McVey |
| DETECTIVE O'BRIEN | John Boyd |
| DETECTIVE BRODY | James Westerfield |
| ENDICOTT SIMS | Les Tremayne |
| DETECTIVE MCLEOD | Ralph Bellamy |
| ARTHUR KINDRED | Warren Stevens |
| PATROLMAN BARNES | Earl Sydnor |
| 1ST CAT BURGLAR (CHARLEY) | Joseph Wiseman |
| 2ND CAT BURGLAR (LEWIS) | Michael Strong |
| HYSTERICAL WOMAN (MRS. BAGATELLE) | Michelette Burani |
| DR. SCHNEIDER | Harry Worth |
| LT. MONOGHAN | Horace McMahon |
| SUSAN CARMICHAEL | Joan Copeland |
| PATROLMAN KEOGH | Byron C. Halstead |
| PATROLMAN BAKER | Joe Roberts |
| WILLY | Carl Griscom |
| MISS HATCH | Maureen Stapleton |

245

| | |
|---|---|
| MRS. FEENEY | Sarah Grable |
| MR. FEENEY | Jim Flynn |
| CRUMB-BUM | Archie Benson |
| MR. GALLANTZ | Garnay Wilson |
| MR. PRITCHETT | James Maloney |
| MARY MCLEOD | Meg Mundy |
| TAMI GIACOPPETTI | Alexander Scourby |
| PHOTOGRAPHER | Michael Lewin |
| LADY | Ruth Storm |
| GENTLEMAN | John Alberts |
| MR. BAGATELLE | Joseph Ancona |
| INDIGNANT CITIZEN | Jacqueline Paige |

And a stream of others who come and go . . . ceaselessly.

Staged by Sidney Kingsley
Setting by Boris Aronson
Costume supervision by Mildred Sutherland

## Scenes

ACT ONE    A day in August. 5:30 P.M.
ACT TWO    7:30 P.M.
ACT THREE  8:30 P.M.

TIME: The Present.
The entire action of the play takes place in the detective squad room of a New York precinct police station.

*Program cover for* Detective Story. *Courtesy of the Jerome Lawrence and Robert E. Lee Theatre Research Institute.*

## ACT ONE

*The 21st Detective Squad, second floor of the 21st Precinct Police Station, New York City. The major area of the stage is occupied by the squad room; to the right, separated by a door and an invisible wall, we glimpse a fragment of the LIEUTENANT's office. Severe, nakedly institutional, ghost-ridden, these rooms are shabby, three-quarters of a century old, with an effluvium of their own, compounded of seventy-five years of the tears and blood of human anguish, despair, passion, rage, terror, and violent death. The walls are olive green to the waist and light green above. In the wall upstage, two ceiling-high windows guarded by iron grillwork. The entrance, stage left, is surrounded by an iron railing with a swinging gate. Tacked to the wall, a height chart; next to it, a folding fingerprint shelf; above that, a green-shaded light. Adjoining, a bulletin board, upon which are tacked several notices, photographs of criminals, etc. In the center of the room is the phone desk, on which are two phones. Downstage left is another desk, on it a typewriter. High on the main wall, a large electric clock; beneath it, a duty board with replaceable celluloid letters, reading "On Duty—Det. Gallagher, Det. Dakis, Lt. Monoghan." In the segment of the LIEUTENANT's office, a desk, a swivel chair, several small chairs, some files, a watercooler, a coatrack, etc. A small window in the LIEUTENANT's office looks out upon an air shaft. Through it we catch a glimpse of the window of the washroom, the door to which is upstage right.*

*The light is fading. It is late afternoon, five-twenty by the clock on the wall. Through the main windows, a magnificent view of the city and its towering skyscrapers; dominating the panorama are a General Motors sign, a church spire, and a cross.*

*At the curtain's rise, NICHOLAS DAKIS is seated at the typewriter desk, making out a form and interrogating a young woman who has been picked up for shoplifting. At the phone desk his partner, GALLAGHER, is writing up some "squeals," and sipping Coca-Cola from the bottle. A traffic policeman in uniform pauses momentarily in the doorway to murmur a greeting to another uniformed policeman; then they vanish. DETECTIVE GALLAGHER is a young man, third-grade, a novice about 27 years of age, and good-looking in spite of a broken nose. The heat has him a little down: he is sweating profusely and every once in awhile he plucks at his moist shirt, which clings to his body. He and his partner, DETECTIVE DAKIS, are in their shirtsleeves, their collars open.*

*DAKIS is a bull of a man, as wide as he is high. He has a voice like the roll of a kettledrum. He is a middle-aged Greek American. He tackles his job efficiently and unemotionally, in an apparently offhand, casual manner—as indeed do most of the detectives.*

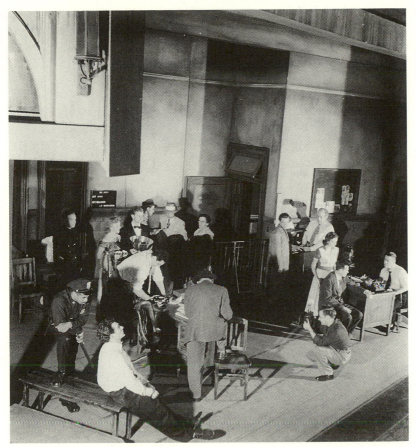

*The squad room at the beginning of act 3, from the touring production of* Detective Story. *Courtesy of Sidney Kingsley.*

The SHOPLIFTER *is a shapeless, moronic little creature with a Bronx accent. Her voice is the blat of a moose calf, and, in spite of her avowed guilt, she has all the innocence of ignorance.*

DAKIS: Hair? *Squints at her frazzled hair.*
SHOPLIFTER: Brown.
DAKIS, *typing, hunt-and-peck system:* Brown. *He squints at her eyes.* Eyes?
SHOPLIFTER: Blue.
DAKIS, *types:* Blue.
   *The phone rings.* GALLAGHER *picks up the receiver.*

GALLAGHER: 21st Squad Detectives, Gallagher. Yes, Madame, what is your name, please? *He reaches for a pencil and pad, glances at the clock, writes.* Address? Phone number? Plaza 9-1855 . . .

DAKIS: Weight?

GALLAGHER, *as the other desk phone rings:* One second, please. *He picks up the other receiver, balancing the first on his shoulder.* 21st Squad Detectives, Gallagher.

SHOPLIFTER: 109, I think.

DAKIS, *types:* 109 will do. . . . *He squints at her potato sack of a figure.* Height?

SHOPLIFTER: I don't know. About . . .

DAKIS: Stand up against the wall! *He waves her to the height chart.* Over there.

GALLAGHER, *on phone:* Hello, Loot. No, nothing. A shoplifter. Best's. A pocketbook. *He calls to* DAKIS. Hey, Nick, what was the price on that purse she lifted?

SHOPLIFTER, *mournfully:* Six dollars.

DAKIS, *to the* SHOPLIFTER: Five-foot-one. All right, come back. *The* SHOPLIFTER *returns to the desk.*

GALLAGHER, *on the phone:* Six bucks.

DAKIS: Age?

SHOPLIFTER: Twenty-seven. *Corrects herself, quickly.* Twenty-two.

DAKIS, *squints at her, types:* Twenty—seven.

GALLAGHER, *on the phone:* Right, Loot. It come in too late. Night court. Right, chief. *He hangs up, applies the other receiver.* Sorry, Mrs. . . . *Glances at his pad.* Andrews. Yes. Have you a list of just what's missing? It would help. Any cash? You do? One of the servants? All right. I'll be there. Yes, Madame. *Hangs up, makes some notes on the scratch pad, sips at the Coca-Cola bottle.*

SHOPLIFTER: My God, the times I spent twice as much for a pocketbook.

DAKIS, *matter of fact, no animus:* Well, you took it.

SHOPLIFTER: I don't know why. It was crazy.

DAKIS, *shrugs it off:* It's your first offense. You'll get off on probation.

SHOPLIFTER: I didn't need it. I didn't ever like it. Crazy!

    *A burst of song offstage: an overmellow baritone pouring out Canio's heartbreak from* I Pagliacci, *making up in vigor all that it lacks in sweetness:* "Ma il vizio alberga sol ne l' alma tua negletta." *The* SHOPLIFTER, *puzzled, glances about, hunches her shoulders at* DAKIS *inquisitively, but he is absorbed in his work and he does not even glance up. The singing comes closer. More heartbreak!* "Tu viscere non hai . . . sol legge." *Enter* GUS KEOGH, *a uniformed policeman with a normally smiling, smooth, white Irish face, twisted for the moment with the agony of the tragic song he is pouring forth.*

KEOGH: *"è 'l senso a te . . ." Breaks off, beaming.* Got any 61's?

GALLAGHER: A couple: You're off-key today, Gus. *Hands him several slips.*
   KEOGH *studies them; his face contorts again with the emotion of the song as he goes off.*

KEOGH: *"vo' ne lo sprezzo mio schiacciarti . . ."— And fades off down the hall with a sob. —"sotto piè."*

DAKIS, *rises, crosses to fingerprint board, rolls ink on pad, beckons to the* SHOPLIFTER: Come here! *The* SHOPLIFTER *crosses to* DAKIS. *He takes her hand. She stiffens. He reassures her gently—in the interests of efficiency.* Take it easy, girlie. Let me do the work. You just supply the finger.

SHOPLIFTER: Ooh!!

DAKIS: This finger. Relax, now, I'm not going to hurt you. Just r-r-r-roll it. . . . *He presses her finger down on the sheet.*

GALLAGHER, *glances up, toward door into hallway at someone approaching:* Uh, uh! Here comes trouble. *To* DAKIS. Look at the calendar!

DAKIS, *glances at the calendar on the wall:* A full moon tonight.

GALLAGHER, *groans:* It never fails. *Enter an elderly, aristocratic-looking woman, dressed in the style of a bygone era.* GALLAGHER, *rises gallantly.* Come in, Mrs. Farragut! Are those people still bothering you?

MRS. FARRAGUT: Worse than ever, Officer. If I hadn't awakened last night and smelled that gas coming through the walls, I'd be gone—we'd all be gone.

GALLAGHER, *solicitously:* Have a chair.

MRS. FARRAGUT: Why haven't you given me protection? I demand protection.

GALLAGHER, *conning her:* I got twelve men on duty guarding you.

MRS. FARRAGUT: But whose side are they really on? Are you sure you can trust them?

GALLAGHER, *wounded:* Mrs. Farragut! One of them is my own *brother.*

MRS. FARRAGUT: Oh, I'm sorry! I didn't mean to offend you. *She sits, leans toward him, confidentially.* Only it's so important. You see, they know I know all about it—Atom bombs! GALLAGHER *nods sagely.* They're making them—these foreigners next door and they blow this atomic vapor through the wall at me. And they have a man watching me from the top of the Empire State Building . . . with radar. . . .

GALLAGHER: That man we got covered.

MRS. FARRAGUT: You have?

GALLAGHER: Day and night.

MRS. FARRAGUT: Does the president know about this?

GALLAGHER: I talked to him only an hour ago.

MRS. FARRAGUT: That's important, very important. These foreigners know I have electronic vision. I can see everything around us vibrating with electricity. . . . Billions of atoms like stars in a universe, turning, vibrating, vibrating. Out there in the streets ten million living dynamos—coming and going. . . . They create crosscurrents; and those great tall skyscrapers draw all this human electricity to the top of the Empire State Building, where that man sits, and he turns it back and shoots it down on us. It's a terrifying situation . . . terrifying!! Do something!—Or it's the end of the world!! *She rises, having worked herself into a frenzy of terror.*

JOE FEINSON, *police reporter, enters, leans his head on the rail watching; a tiny man, a few inches more than five feet, exaggerated nose, crooked features, JOE's superficially wisecracking police-reporter attitude is only the persona with which he cloaks a genuine, philosophic, humanistic outlook. Nothing escapes his humorous, beady, birdlike eyes.*

GALLAGHER, *rises, crosses around to her, takes her arm reassuringly:* Now, Mrs. Farragut, I'm watching it, every second; and I got it all under control. Tell you what—I'm going to *double* the men I got guarding you. Twenty-five picked men day and night. How's that?

MRS. FARRAGUT, *calms down:* Oh, that's better. Much better. Thank you.
      *Exit MRS. FARRAGUT.*

GALLAGHER, *plucking at his damp shirt:* Get out the butterfly net.

JOE: You give the customers a good massage.

GALLAGHER: Hell, this job is ninety percent salesmanship!

DAKIS, *finishes the fingerprints:* O.K., girlie, wash your hands. In there! *He points to the washroom door. The SHOPLIFTER crosses to the washroom, dangling her lamp-blacked fingers before her so as not to soil her dress.*

JOE: What's new?

GALLAGHER: It's quiet. *Knocks wood.*

JOE: The town's dead as Kelcey's. *He saunters over to GALLAGHER's desk.*

SHOPLIFTER, *opens the door, frowning, calls out:* There isn't any lock on the door.

DAKIS: Just wash your hands, girlie.

SHOPLIFTER, *indignant:* A fine howdoyoudo! *She slams the door.*

JOE: Story for me?

GALLAGHER: No. Shoplifter.

JOE: She anybody?

GALLAGHER: Nobody at all.

JOE: Any angles?

GALLAGHER: Nah! Just a slob.

*Two detectives enter. One of them, CALLAHAN, is very exuberant and high-spirited, Tenth Avenue in his speech, dressed in a yellow polo shirt and baggy trousers, which do not match his wrinkled jacket. The other, DETECTIVE O'BRIEN, is an older man, spectacled, neatly dressed, soft-spoken. CALLAHAN, tears off his jacket, revealing the full splendor of his polo shirt—*

*Hawaiian in motif, with brilliant foliage woven into the pattern:* Hi, Tom,
Nick, Joe! Phew, it's hot out! Sweat your kolonjas off!

JOE: What the hell are you dressed up for? Must be Halloween?

CALLAHAN: I wonder what he means?

O'BRIEN: Saks Fifth Avenue pays Mike to advertise their clothes.

CALLAHAN: Geeze, were we given a run around! We tailed a guy for two
hours, from Fifty-thoid to Ninety-foist and back. I thought for sure, "This
one belongs to us."

O'BRIEN: Looked like a good man.

CALLAHAN: Then the jerko took a bus. *Glances at the schedule hanging on
the wall.* Moidèr! Sunday again! What the hell am I?—a Sunday detective?
My kids'll grow up, they won't even know me. *To JOE.* Say, Joe, there's a
big story on Thoid Avenue. You get it? The brewery truck?

JOE: No, what about it?

CALLAHAN: A brewery truck backed up into the sidewalk, and a barrel of
beer fell right out inna baby carriage.

JOE, *rising:* Was the baby in it?

CALLAHAN: Yeah.

JOE: Was it killed?

CALLAHAN: No, it was light beer! Boyeeng! *He doubles over, holding his
sides with laughter.* Ha, ha, ha!

JOE, *groans and sinks back into his chair:* You're a cute kid. What's your
name, Berle?

    *The SHOPLIFTER returns from the washroom. As she crosses, CALLAHAN
studies her face, squinting his eyes professionally.*

O'BRIEN: Busy day?

GALLAGHER: Quiet.

O'BRIEN: Good. *He knocks wood.*

GALLAGHER: Too quiet.

O'BRIEN: We're due. We're ripe for a homicide.

GALLAGHER: Ssh. Wait till I get out of here. *The desk phone rings, GAL-
LAGHER groans.* Can't you keep your big mouth shut? *He picks up the
receiver.* 21st Squad Detectives, Gallagher. Yes, Madame. That's right.
Where? Now what is it you lost?

JOE: Her virginity.

GALLAGHER: In a taxicab?

JOE: Hell of a place!

GALLAGHER: Did you get his number? Can you describe it?

JOE: This is going to be educational.

*Simulta-*   GALLAGHER: What's your name? Address? Yes, Madame. I'll
*neously*    check that for you. Not at all.
       JOE: I got a squeal for you. I lost something. My manhood.

CALLAHAN: We don't take cases *that* old, Joe.

GALLAGHER, *hanging up:* Outlawed by the statute of limitations.

DETECTIVE LOU BRODY *enters with several containers of coffee, Coca-Colas, and a bag of sandwiches.* BRODY *is a huge man, deceptively obese and clumsy in appearance; bald-headed, ugly, carbuncled face, lit up, however, by sad, soft, gentle eyes. He hands one bag to* DAKIS.

BRODY: Here you are, Nick!

DAKIS: I appreciate that.

BRODY: My pleasure. Here you are, Miss.

SHOPLIFTER: With Russian Dressing? *Standing up, searching in her purse.*

BRODY: They ran out. *He crosses, places the remaining sandwiches and coffee on the long table, then goes into the* LIEUTENANT'S *office, hangs his hat and jacket on the coat-tree.*

SHOPLIFTER: How much do I owe you?

DAKIS: It's on the house.

SHOPLIFTER: You're all awful decent, really, awful decent.

DAKIS: Well, you didn't kill anyone.

A *man carrying a briefcase enters, stands at the gate a moment, taps on it impatiently. He is about thirty-five, erect in bearing, sharply chiseled features, self-possessed, apparently immune to the heat; he is crisp and cool, even to the starched collar. When he speaks, his voice is equally crisp and starched, and carries considerable authority.*

GALLAGHER: Yes, sir?

*The man fishes a card out of his wallet and presents it.*

SIMS: My name is Sims, Endicott Sims. I'm an attorney.

GALLAGHER: What can we do for you, Counselor?

SIMS: I represent Mr. Kurt Schneider. Your office has a warrant out for him?

DAKIS: Hey, Lou! This is Jim's squeal, ain't it? Kurt Schneider?

BRODY: Yeah, I'll take it. *Crosses to* SIMS. This is my partner's case. What about Schneider, Counselor? Where is he?

SIMS: He's ready to surrender himself into your custody.

BRODY: Fine, bring him in.

SIMS: First, however, I have here some photographs. . . . *He takes some pictures from his briefcase, and hands them to* BRODY. He had these taken half an hour ago.

BRODY, *examines them, makes a face:* Nudes? Ugly, ain't he?

SIMS, *smiles wryly:* He's no Mr. America.

BRODY: No, that he ain't.

SIMS: The purpose is not aesthetic. I don't want any rubber hoses used on him.

BRODY: Counselor, how long have you been practicing law? We don't assault our prisoners.

SIMS: Who's handling this case here?

BRODY: My partner.

SIMS: A man named James McLeod?

BRODY: Yeah.

SIMS: I've heard a good deal about him. A law unto himself. You will please tell him for me . . .

BRODY: Wait a minute. Tell him for yourself. Here he is.

JAMES MCLEOD *enters, his big hand gripping the arm of a stunned, sensitive-looking young man, whom he guides into the room.* JAMES MCLEOD *is tall, lean, handsome, has powerful shoulders, uncompromising mouth, a studied, immobile, masklike facies, betrayed by the deep-set, impatient, mocking eyes, which reveal the quick flickers of mood, the deep passions of the man possessed by his own demon.*

BRODY: Oh, Jim, this is your squeal. *To* SIMS. This is Detective McLeod, Mr. Sims.

MCLEOD: How do you do, sir? *Takes out a handkerchief, mops his brow, wipes the sweatband of his hat.*

SIMS: How do you do?

BRODY: Mr. Sims is an attorney.

MCLEOD: And very clever. I've seen him in court.

SIMS: Thank you.

BRODY: He's here for Kurt Schneider.

MCLEOD, *the quick flicker of mockery in his eyes:* Oh, yes. *To* SIMS. I had the pleasure of arresting your client a year ago.

SIMS: So I am informed.

MCLEOD: He's changed his lawyer since, if not his business.

SIMS: Kurt Schneider is a successful truck farmer from New Jersey.

MCLEOD: With a little abortion mill in New York for a sideline. Nothing fancy, just a quick ice-tong job. I've a considerable yen for your client.

SIMS: I'm aware of that. *To* BRODY. Show him those pictures! BRODY *hands the photographs to* MCLEOD.

MCLEOD, *looks at the pictures, grimaces:* There's no doubt the process of evolution is beginning to reverse itself.

SIMS: You understand, Officer, that my client has certain rights. I am here to see that those rights are respected.

MCLEOD, *urbanely:* One second, Counselor. I'll be right with you. Have a chair. *He guides the young man into the squad room.*

GALLAGHER: Jim, call your wife!

MCLEOD: Thanks, Tom. *He searches the young man for weapons; the quick "frisk," ankles, legs, thighs, front and rear.* All right, Buster. Sit down over there. *To* GALLAGHER. When'd she phone?

GALLAGHER: Twenty minutes ago. *The phone rings.* 21st Squad Detectives, Gallagher. Yes, sir. *He hands the phone to* MCLEOD. The Lieutenant.

MCLEOD, *takes the phone and it is evident from his grimace at the phone that he has no great love for his* LIEUTENANT. *He sits on the desk:* Yes, Lieutenant? I just got back.

JOE, *crosses down, drapes himself on the chair next to* MCLEOD: Hiya, Seamus!

MCLEOD, *smothers the mouthpiece of the phone, murmurs quickly:* Oh, Yussel, Yussel! You're supposed to be an intelligent reporter.

JOE: What's the matter, Seamus?

MCLEOD: That Langdon story!

JOE: Didn't I spell your name right?

MCLEOD: It's the only thing you did get right. *On the phone.* Yes, Lieutenant. I just brought him in. *To the young man,* ARTHUR. Arthur, were you arrested before?

ARTHUR: I told you.

MCLEOD: Tell me again.

ARTHUR: No.

MCLEOD, *back to phone:* Says no. We'll check his prints. Yes, sir. Yes, sir. *He covers the mouthpiece.* You're degenerating into a real sob sister, Yussel. Grrrim grray prrrison walls! Wish you'd have seen Langdon in the bull pen. "Yiha, Jack! Yiya, Charley!" Smiling. He was happy! He was home again! *On phone.* Yes, Lieutenant. Yes, sir.

JOE: The mortal God—McLeod! Captain Ahab pursuing the great gray Leviathan! A fox with rabies bit him in the ass when he was two years old, and neither of them recovered. Don't throw water on him. He goes rabid!

MCLEOD, *hangs up, pulls* JOE's *bow tie:* You apple-headed member of the fourth estate, to look natural you should have a knife and fork sticking out of the top of your head. City College is going to be proud of you yet! *Rises, talks Yiddish. Mir daft ihr dihagginun!*

JOE, *laughs, ties his tie:* Is this story worth a picture?

MCLEOD: Mm . . . possibly. *To* ARTHUR. Don't try running for it, Buster. You'd just about reach that door and suddenly you'd put on weight. Bullets are supersonic.

ARTHUR: Don't worry.

MCLEOD: I won't. Either way.

   BRODY, *at the sound of the young man's voice, stops and turns quickly. He comes over, scrutinizes the young man's face.*

MCLEOD: Know him?

BRODY: No. . . . No. . . . I . . . *Shakes his head.*

McLeod, *calls across the room to* Mr. Sims: One second, Counselor. *He crosses to the* Lieutenant's *office, comes face-to-face with* Callahan. *He pauses to survey* Callahan's *sartorial splendor. Shakes his head.* Strictly Pier 6!

Callahan: I ain't no friggin' barber-college detective with pleats in my pants.

McLeod, *sardonically:* No, you *ain't.* . . . *Goes into* Lieutenant's *office, closes the door, dials a number.*

Callahan, *miffed:* Remind me to get that college graduate a bicycle pump for Christmas to blow up that big head of his.

*O'Brien and* Gallagher *laugh.*

O'Brien: He needling you again?

Callahan: Mm! Big needle-man from sew-and-sew.

McLeod, *on the phone:* Hello, darling. *His voice at once takes on warmth and tenderness; his eyes, his smile, his whole being seem to undergo a metamorphosis.* What did the doctor say? . . . Thank God! Nothing organic? Sure, now, Mary? . . . How does he explain those palpitations? . . . Psychosomatic? Mm! And how does he explain that? . . . What tensions? *Laughs.* What'd he prescribe, short of a new world? Phenobarbital and Vitamin B1? The history of our time. *He laughs.* Oh, Mary! You're wonderful! I love you! Of course, I was worried *sick.* Mm. Yes. . . . Thank you, my angel. I'll call you later. Good-bye.

*In the squad room,* Arthur's *face turns gray; he clutches his stomach and bites his lip.* Brody, *who has been studying him, crosses to him.*

Brody: What's the matter, sonny?

Arthur: Nothing.

Brody *points to the washroom.* Arthur *crosses to it, quickly. Once inside, alone, his bravado falls away. He is a sick and desperate boy. He dry-retches over the sink for a moment. Breathing heavily, he looks about in sudden panic.*

Brody *glances toward the washroom, goes to his files, takes out a bottle, goes to the washroom, props open the door, stands there, watching.* Arthur *controls himself, turns on the water in the sink, buries his face in it.* Brody *takes a paper cup, pours out a drink, offers it to him:* Have a bomb?

Arthur: No, thanks. *Dries his face.*

Brody *tosses off the drink, himself. They return to the squadroom. The desk phone rings.* Gallagher *reaches for it.*

Brody, *glances at the clock:* O.K., Tom. I'll take over now. Go on home. *Picks up the phone.*

Gallagher: Home? I got a squeal. *Goes off into the next room.*

BRODY, *on the phone:* 21st Squad, Detective Brody. Yeah? Get his license number? . . . *He glances at the clock, scribbles data on a pad.*

MCLEOD, *enters the squad room, crosses to* MR. SIMS: Now, Counselor?

SIMS, *presents him with the photographs again:* You will observe there are no scars or lacerations of any kind! *Points to photos.* This is the way I'm delivering my client to you, and this is the way I want him back.

MCLEOD, *studies them gravely:* I should think that any change whatsoever would be an improvement, Counselor.

SIMS: I want you to know I'm not going to allow you to violate his constitutional rights. You're not to abuse him physically or degrade his dignity as a human being, do you understand?

MCLEOD, *bites this off sharply:* Counselor, I never met a criminal yet who didn't wrap himself in the Constitution from head to toe, or a hoodlum who wasn't filled to the nostrils with habeas corpus and the rights of human dignity. Did you ever see the girl your client operated on last year—in the morgue—on a marble slab? Wasn't much human left of her, Counselor—and very little dignity!

SIMS: My client was innocent of that charge. The court acquitted him.

MCLEOD: He was guilty.

SIMS: Are you setting yourself above the courts of the land?

MCLEOD: There's a higher court, Counselor.

SIMS: I'm sure there is, Officer. Are you qualified to speak for it? I'm not. God doesn't come down and whisper in my ear. But when it comes to the man-made law on terra firma, I know it, I obey it, and I respect it.

MCLEOD: What do you want to do?—Try the case here? This isn't a court. Save it for the judge. Now, Counselor, I'm busy. Your client will be treated with as much delicacy as he is entitled to. So bring him in—or get off the pot.

SIMS: I've heard about you. You're quite an anomaly, McLeod, quite an anomaly. It's going to be a real pleasure to examine you on the witness stand.

MCLEOD: Anything to give you a thrill, Counselor.

SIMS: We may have a thrill or two in store for you.

MCLEOD: Meaning?

SIMS: For over a year you personally have been making my client's life a living hell. Why?

MCLEOD: I beg your pardon.

SIMS: Why?

MCLEOD, *sardonically:* Because I'm annoyed by criminals that get away with murder. They upset me.

SIMS: You're easily upset.

McLEOD: Oh, I'm *very* sensitive. *Dismissing him.* To me your client is just another criminal. *Turns away.* O.K., Arthur! In there! *He indicates the* LIEUTENANT'S *office.* ARTHUR *rises, enters the office.*

SIMS: That's your story. At considerable expense we have investigated and discovered *otherwise.*

*McLEOD turns to stare at him.* SIMS *smiles knowingly and goes.*

BRODY: What the hell's he driving at?

McLEOD: A fishing expedition. That's a shrewd mouthpiece. I've seen him operate. *He enters the* LIEUTENANT'S *office. To* ARTHUR. Empty your pockets! Take everything out! Put it on the desk! ARTHUR *empties the contents of his pockets on the desk.* That all?

ARTHUR: Yes.

McLEOD: Turn your pockets inside out. ARTHUR *obeys.* Sit down! Over there! What'd you do with the money?

ARTHUR: I spent it.

McLEOD, *examines the articles one by one, very carefully:* All of it?

ARTHUR: Yes.

McLEOD, *picks up a book of matches:* When were you at the Stork Club?

ARTHUR: Wednesday night.

McLEOD: Been doing the hot spots?

ARTHUR: Some.

McLEOD: Any of the money left?

ARTHUR: How far can you go with four hundred dollars?

McLEOD: Four hundred and eighty.

ARTHUR: Was it four-eighty?

McLEOD: So your employer claims.

ARTHUR: He ought to know.

McLEOD: Arthur, why'd you take the money?

ARTHUR: What's the difference? I took it, I admit it, I took it!

McLEOD: Where'd you spend last night?

ARTHUR: In my room.

McLEOD: I was there. Where were you? Under the bed?

ARTHUR: I sat in the park.

McLEOD: All night?

ARTHUR: Yes.

McLEOD: It rained.

ARTHUR: Drizzled.

McLEOD: You sat in the drizzle?

ARTHUR: Yes.

McLEOD: What were you doing?

ARTHUR: Just dreaming.

McLeod: In the park at night?—Dreaming?

Arthur: Night is the time for dreams.

McLeod: And *thieves! He examines the articles in* Arthur's *pockets. . . . The phone in the squad room rings.* Brody *answers.*

Brody: 21st Squad, Detective Brody. . . . Callahan, for you!

Callahan, *crosses to phone, throws a parking ticket on the desk:* A kiss from Judge Bromfield. *Into phone:* Callahan, 21st.

Joe, *examines the ticket:* You get a parking ticket?

Dakis, *morosely:* I got one, too. In front of the Criminal Court Building. You're such a big shot, Joe, why don't you thrown a little weight around?

Joe: Mind if I use the phone?

Brody, *nods:* The outside one.

*Joe dials a number.*

O'Brien: Some of these judges haven't the brains God gave them. They refrigerate them in law school.

Dakis: It ain't enough we use our own cars to take prisoners to court, and our own gas—we can't even deduct it from our income tax. Where's your justice?

Joe, *into phone:* Hello, Jerry—this is Joe Feinson. *Suddenly yelling at the top of his lungs.* Who the hell does that Judge Bromfield think he is? . . . He's persecutin' cops, that's what! Parkin' tickets on duty. I'm going to stir up the goddamndest hornet's nest! . . . All right! All right! . . . *Calmly.* Yeah. Fine. Sure. I got one here. Yeah. *He hangs up, take the ticket.* O.K. Forget it. It's fixed. *Crosses to get* Dakis's *ticket.*

O'Brien: You frighten him?

Joe: I frightened myself. *Holds up his trembling hand.* Look at my hand! Shaking!

*Dakis laughs—a bellow that makes the room vibrate.*

Callahan: A cop's got to get a reporter to fix a ticket for him. I seen everything now.

Joe: That's the way it should be. A free press is the tocsin of a free people. The law keeps you in line, we keep the law in line, the people keep us in line, you keep the people in line. Everybody kicks everybody else in the ass! That way nobody gets too big for his britches. That's democracy! *Crosses to the gate.*

Dakis: You have the gall to call that yellow, monopolistic sheet—a free press? Ha! Ha! *Bellows again.* You kill me!

*Exit* Joe, *waving the ticket triumphantly.*

Shoplifter: So.

Dakis: So what?

Shoplifter: So what happens to me now?

DAKIS: We wait here till night court opens. Nine o'clock. Then the magistrate will probably set bail for you.

O'BRIEN: Have you got a lawyer? You might save the bail bond.

SHOPLIFTER: My brother-in-law's a lawyer.

DAKIS, *belches:* Excuse me. Call him up. . . .

SHOPLIFTER: Gee, I hate to. He's kind of a new brother-in-law. If my sister finds out, oh, God! she'll die! And she's in the fourth month, too.

O'BRIEN: It's up to you.

DAKIS: Suit yourself. The court'll appoint you one.

SHOPLIFTER: Gee, I don't know what to do!

MCLEOD, *completes his examination of the articles in* ARTHUR's *pockets:* Ever been arrested before, Arthur?

ARTHUR: I told you no.

MCLEOD: You sure?

ARTHUR: Yes.

MCLEOD: It would help your case if you returned the money.

ARTHUR: I know. But I can't. I told you it's gone.

> BRODY *enters the* LIEUTENANT's *office and listens to the interrogation.*

MCLEOD: What's this pawn ticket for?

ARTHUR: Textbooks.

MCLEOD: Where did you get them?

ARTHUR: College.

MCLEOD: Graduate?

ARTHUR: No

MCLEOD: What stopped you?

ARTHUR: World War Two, the first time.

MCLEOD: And the second time?

ARTHUR: World War Three.

MCLEOD: Foolish question, foolish answer. *Examining contents of AR-THUR's pockets.* Have you any identifying marks on you, Arthur? Any scars? . . . Roll up your sleeves. . . . ARTHUR *obeys. On his left wrist is a tattoo mark.* A tattoo mark. A heart. And what's the name? J—O—Y! Who's Joy?

ARTHUR: A girl.

MCLEOD: Your girl?

ARTHUR: No.

MCLEOD: Whose girl?

ARTHUR: What's the difference?

MCLEOD: What branch of the service were you in?

ARTHUR: Navy.

MCLEOD: How long?

ARTHUR: Five years.
McLEOD: What rank?
ARTHUR: Chief petty officer.
McLEOD: You married?
ARTHUR: No.
McLEOD: How old are you?
ARTHUR: Twenty-seven.
McLEOD: How long you been in New York?
ARTHUR: A year.
McLEOD: Where you from?
ARTHUR: Ann Arbor, Michigan.
McLEOD: What's your father's business?
ARTHUR: My father's dead.
McLEOD: What *was* his business?
ARTHUR: He was a teacher. Music. History of music.
McLEOD: History of music? He must've been proud of you. Where's your
    mother?
ARTHUR: She's dead.
McLEOD, *looking through* ARTHUR's *address book:* Ah! Here's Joy again—
    Joy Carmichael. Maybe I better give her a ring.
ARTHUR: What for? Why drag her into this? She doesn't know anything
    about it.
McLEOD, *mockingly:* You wouldn't lie to me, would you, Arthur?
ARTHUR: Why should I lie?
McLEOD: I don't know. Why should you steal? Maybe it's because you're
    just no damn good, hm, Arthur? The judge asks me and I'm going to
    throw the book at you.—Tattoo *that* on your arm! McLEOD *rises.*
BRODY: Admission?
McLEOD: Yes.
BRODY: Get the money?
McLEOD: No. He doesn't milk easily. A superman. I've got an angle. *Crosses
    into the squad room, dials phone.*
BRODY, *to* ARTHUR: Sonny, you look like a nice boy. How'd you get into
    this mess?
ARTHUR, *rises:* What is this? Are you going to give me a sermon?
BRODY: Don't get funny with me, son. I'll knock you right through the floor!
    Sit down! ARTHUR *sits.* How'd you get into this mess, son?
ARTHUR: I don't know. You get trapped.
BRODY: Where's the money?
ARTHUR, *shakes his head:* Gone! It's gone.
BRODY: What did you do with it?

ARTHUR: Spent it.

BRODY, *pauses, takes out a cigarette, offers* ARTHUR *one, lights them:* You went to college? What did you study?

ARTHUR: Majored in history.

BRODY: History? What for?

ARTHUR: To teach. I wanted to be a teacher.

BRODY: Much of a career in that?

ARTHUR: I used to think so.

BRODY: You're a long way from home?

ARTHUR: Yes.

BRODY: Why didn't you finish?

ARTHUR: No time. The war washed that up. There's no time. You can't start from scratch at twenty-five.

   BRODY *studies him, shakes his head. The sudden babble of voices is heard, off.*

McLEOD, *looks up from phone:* Uh-uh! Here comes trouble! A couple of customers.

   *A uniformed* POLICEMAN, *Negro, enters, herding in front of him two burglars handcuffed to each other. They are followed by other* POLICEMEN, *a* HYSTERICAL WOMAN, *and, at the tail of the parade,* WILLY, *the janitor, with broom, pail, and inquisitive look.*

   *The Negro policeman,* BARNES, *is a big man of erect carriage, with a fine, intelligent face. The two burglars are a study in contrasting personalities. The first burglar,* CHARLEY, *is nervous, thin, short, wiry, with long expressive hands that are never still, forever weaving in and out. He has jet-black hair, which keeps falling over his forehead in bangs, tiny black eyes, an olive complexion, and a slight Italian accent. He is protesting his innocence with percussive indignation. He is wearing an expensive suit and a pink shirt with no tie. The second burglar,* LEWIS, *is a chunky, sandy-haired young fellow, slow-moving, slower-thinking, who is inclined to take this arrest as a minor nuisance at worst. He is wearing a "zoot suit" with extremely narrow cuffs on the trousers. He moves slouching slowly, swaying from side to side. There is something "off-beat," something disturbing about both these men.* WILLY, *the janitor, is a thin, sour, grizzled man with a pockmarked face and a moth-eaten toothbrush moustache. He wears a worn black shirt and old, torn trousers. The* HYSTERICAL WOMAN *is a short, dumpy, elderly Frenchwoman, whose hair is in disarray and whose slip is showing. She is wringing her hands, crying and gabbling half in French, half in English. As they enter, they are all talking at once.* CHARLEY's *percussive cries and the* WOMAN's *wails dominate the hubbub.*

   BRODY, *hearing the noise, crosses back into squad room.*

McLeod: What have you got there?

Barnes: Burglars. Caught 'em red-handed. Forcible entry.

Woman, *in a French accent:* I come up to my apartment. The door was open. The lock was burst wide open. The jamb was broken down. They were inside. I started to run. This one grabbed me and choked me.

Charley: It's a lie! It's a pack of lies! I don't know what she's talking about. . . .

Barnes: I was right across the street when I heard her scream. They come running down the stairs. I collared them. . . . This one put up a struggle.

Charley, *screaming:* I was walkin' down the stairs mindin' my own business—the cop jumps on me and starts beatin' the crap outa me. . . .

McLeod, *roars:* All right! Charley *stops screaming, pantomimes his innocence.* We'll come to you. *He takes his revolver out of his holster, puts it in his pocket.* Brody *takes out his revolver, places it in the desk drawer.* Dakis *does likewise. This is official routine, which* Callahan *alone neglects to observe.*

Charley, *softly:* Think I'm crazy to do a thing like this?

Brody: Sh! You'll get your turn to talk. Sit down.

Barnes: On this one I found this jimmy, and this . . . *Takes out a jimmy and a revolver, hands them to* McLeod.

Brody: Twenty-two?

McLeod, *nods:* Loaded. *He unloads the cylinder, places the cartridges on the desk.*

Brody, *to* Charley: What's your name? Stand up! *Searches him more thoroughly.*

Charley: Gennini. Charles Gennini. And I don't know nothin'. I don't even know this guy. Ask him! *To the 2nd* burglar, Lewis. Do I know you? *To* Brody. No!

Brody: Take it easy, Charley. Sit down! *To* Lewis. What's your name?

Lewis: Lewis Abbott.

Brody, *brandishes revolver and jimmy:* Were you carrying these, Lewis?

Lewis, *thinks for a moment, nods, unemotionally:* Ya.

Woman, *begins to cry:* By the throat he grabbed me! How can this happen in New York?

McLeod, *gently:* Take it easy, Madame. You're all right, now. Sit down, Madame. I'll get you a glass of water.

Woman: Oh, please, please!

   McLeod *crosses to the watercooler.*

Brody, *searches* Lewis: You're a bad boy, Lewis, and what's more you're a bad thief. Don't you know a good thief never carries a loaded pistol? It means five years added to your sentence, Lewis.

LEWIS: I'd never use it.

BRODY: That's what you think, Lewis. But it'd happen. You're lucky you were picked up. Probably saved you from a murder rap. Just once you'd walk in, a woman, she'd scream, resist, you'd get scared . . .

CALLAHAN: Boom! Boom! *Sings a funeral dirge.* Ta da de da da de da de da de dum . . .

BRODY: You like the smell a burning flesh? Your own?

LEWIS, *thinks, shakes his head:* Na.

McLEOD *returns with the glass of water, hands it to the* HYSTERICAL WOMAN.

BRODY: Getting dropped today was the luckiest thing ever happened to you, Lewis. *Turns to* CHARLEY. Now, *you!*

CHARLEY *rises;* BRODY *searches him more carefully.*

CHARLEY, *his hands weaving:* I got nothing to do with this, I swear. You think I got rocks in my head?

BRODY, *producing a large wad of bills from* CHARLEY'S *pockets:* Look at this!

McLEOD: Quite a bundle! How much is here, Charley?

CHARLEY: Fourteen hundred bucks.

McLEOD, *digs into his own pocket, takes out a slim roll of bills:* Eleven! Why is it every time one of you bums comes in, you've got fourteen hundred dollars in your kick and I've got eleven in mine?

BRODY: You don't live right.

McLEOD: No, evidently not. *To* CHARLEY. Where'd you get this?

CHARLEY: I saved it. I worked.

McLEOD: Where?

CHARLEY: I was a bricklayer.

McLEOD, *hands the money to the* PATROLMAN: Count it! This goes to the custodian. We don't want Charley suing us. *To* CHARLEY. Let's see your hands! *He feels them.* The only thing you ever "laid," Charley, was a two-dollar floozy.

CALLAHAN: Do you always carry so much money around?

CHARLEY: Yeah.

McLEOD: What's the matter, Charley, don't you trust the banks?

BRODY: When were you in stir last, Charley?

CHARLEY: Me? In jail? Never! I swear to God on a stack of Bibles!

McLEOD: What's your B number?

CHARLEY: I ain't got none.

McLEOD: You sure?

CHARLEY: On my mother's grave, I ain't got no B card.

CALLAHAN: You're stupid.

McLeod, *looks at the others, shakes his head, and laughs softly:* You just
  gave yourself away, Charley. How do you know what a B card is if you
  never had one?
Charley: I . . . heard. I been around.
McLeod: I'll bet you have. You've been working this precinct since October.
Charley: No. I swear . . .
McLeod, *laughs in his face:* Who the hell do you think you're kidding?
  *Charley glares at him.* I know that face. This is a good man. He's been
  in jail before.
Charley: Never, so help me God! What are you tryin' to do, hang me? I
  wanta call my lawyer.
McLeod: Shut up! Print him. You'll find he's got a sheet as long as your arm.
Charley: I don't know what you're talkin' about. I swear to God! I get
  down on my knees. . . . *He falls to his knees, crying.* What do you want
  me to . . .
McLeod: Get up! Get up! I can smell you. He's a cat burglar. A real mur-
  derer!
Callahan: How many women you raped? *Callahan stands nearby, his
  back to the prisoner, his revolver sticking out of the holster. Charley
  looks at it, licks his lips.*
McLeod, *to Callahan:* Watch the roscoe! What's the matter with you?
  *Callahan takes his revolver out of his holster, puts it in his pocket. To
  Charley.* Sit down! Over there.
Woman: Isn't anybody going to take care of me?
McLeod: Look Madame! You're very upset. We don't need you here. Why
  don't you go home and rest up?
Woman: No, no, no! I am afraid to go back there now. I'm afraid even to
  go out in the street.
McLeod, *laughs:* Now, come on! You've got nothing to be afraid of.
Woman: No, no! I am! I am afraid.
McLeod: Suppose I send a policeman with you? . . . What time do you
  expect your husband back?
Woman: Seven o'clock.
McLeod: I'll send a policeman home with you to keep you company. A nice,
  handsome Irish cop. How's that?
Woman, *thinks it over, giggles at him, nods:* That would be fine. Thank you,
  very much!
McLeod, *turns her over to Keogh:* Gus, see that this lady gets home safely.
  *Gus, grinning, takes her in tow. Exit Gus and the Woman, giggling.*
Shoplifter: I think I better call my brother-in-law.
Dakis: What's the number?

SHOPLIFTER: Jerome 7-2577.

*DAKIS crosses to phone, dials the number.*

BRODY, *moves a chair center, turns to* LEWIS: Now, Lewis, sit down! *LEWIS sits.* You're in trouble.

McLEOD, *steps close to* LEWIS: You help us, we'll help you. We'll ask the D.A. to give you a break.

BRODY: Tell us the truth. How many burglaries you committed here? *LEWIS is silent.* BRODY *hands him a cigarette.*

CALLAHAN, *comes in from behind, lights his cigarette:* Be a man. You got dropped! Face it!

O'BRIEN, *closes the circle around* LEWIS: Why not get the agony over with?

CALLAHAN: If you don't, we're gonna get the D.A. to throw away the key.

DAKIS, *to* SHOPLIFTER, *holding out the phone:* Here you are, girlie! Come and get it.

SHOPLIFTER, *crossing rapidly:* Oh, God, what'll I tell her? What should I say? *She takes the phone and assumes her most casual singsong.* Hello, Milly! . . . Yeah! . . . Nothin'! I just didn't have any change. How are you? Yeah? Fine! How was the party? You went to Brooklyn? In your delicate condition? Milly! *She laughs feebly.* Say, Milly, is Jack there, by any chance? Could I talk to him? Oh, nothin'! Some friend of mine wants some advice on somethin'. I don't know what. *She puts phone down.* He's there. What should I tell him? I don't know what to tell him.

DAKIS: Tell him to meet you at night court, 100 Center Street.

SHOPLIFTER: Shall I tell him to bring hard cash?

DAKIS: He'll know better than we.

SHOPLIFTER, *whispers hoarsely into phone:* Hello, Jack? Listen—can Milly hear me? I don't want her to know, but I'm in a jam. I need your help. So don't let on. Make out like it's nothing. I can't give you all the details. I'm at the police station. Yeah. I took a bag. Best's. *Blatting.* I had to admit it, Jack, it was on my arm. Thanks, Jack! 100 Center Street. If Milly asks, tell her . . . Gee, Jack, you're a . . . *she hangs up slowly, sighs with relief to* DETECTIVE DAKIS. Boy! Am I relieved!

*ENDICOTT SIMS appears with KURT SCHNEIDER, and they stand within the gate, talking softly. SCHNEIDER is gaunt, neatly attired, with a dark, sullen, narrow, ferret-like face, bulging eyes, and well-trimmed, waxed moustache.*

McLEOD, *coming out of the* LIEUTENANT's *office, crosses to them:* Hello, Kurt! Come on in.

SIMS, *to* McLEOD: I have advised my client of his legal rights. He will answer no questions other than his name and address. Remember, Kurt! Name and address, that's all. Is that understood?

McLeod: As you say, Counselor.

Sims: When are you going to book him?

McLeod: In a couple of hours, when we get around to it.

Sims: I want to arrange his bail bond.

McLeod: You'll have to get Judge Crater to stand bail for him.

Sims: Suppose you tend to your business and I'll tend to mine.

McLeod: I'll be glad to, if you'll get the hell out of here and let me.

Sims: Remember, Kurt! Name and address, that's all. *Exit.*

McLeod: Sit down, Kurt. Over here! How've you been?

Kurt: So-so.

McLeod: You look fit. That farm life agrees with you. Some coffee, Kurt?

Kurt: You got enough?

McLeod: There's plenty. *Pours some.* Here you are! Sandwich?

Kurt: I just ate.

McLeod: Cruller?

Kurt: I'm full—

McLeod: Be right with you. *Hands him a newspaper, crosses to the phone, looks up a number in his notebook, dials it.*

Brody, *to* Patrolman Barnes, *pointing at* Charley *and indicating the washroom:* Steve!

Barnes, *nods:* Come on, Charley, in here! *Takes* Charley *off into the washroom.*

Brody, *to Lewis:* Charley let *you* carry the gun and the jimmy. . . . You're the one that's going to burn. Don't you see how he's crossed you?

Callahan: You ever hear of the guy who sold his buddy up the river for thirty pieces of silver?

Lewis: Ya. *The ring of men closes around* Lewis.

O'Brien: Well? Think!

Brody: When were you in jail last? *Silence.*

McLeod: Look, Lewis, we're gonna fingerprint you. In half an hour we'll know your whole record, anyway.

Brody: Make it easy for yourself. How many burglaries you committed in New York, Lewis?

Lewis: What'll I get?

Callahan: Were you in jail before?

Lewis: Ya. Elmira. I got out in March.

Brody: How long were you in?

Lewis: Three and a half years.

Brody: What for?

Lewis: Burglary.

BRODY: Well, I'd say, seven and a half to ten; maybe less, if you cooperate, if not—fifteen to twenty!

LEWIS: What do you want to know?

BRODY: How many burglaries you committed in New York?

LEWIS: Nine or ten.

CALLAHAN: That's better.

BRODY: What'd you do with the stuff?

LEWIS: Gave it to Charley.

CALLAHAN: He was in on it, then?

LEWIS: Ya.

BRODY: You sell it?

LEWIS: Ya.

BRODY: Where?

LEWIS: In Boston . . . I think.

BRODY: You *think?* Didn't he tell you?

LEWIS: Na.

CALLAHAN: You're a bit of a shmuck, ain't you, Lewis?

BRODY: No, Lewis is regular. He's cooperating. *To* LEWIS. How much did he give you altogether?

LEWIS: Half. Four hundred dollars.

CALLAHAN: Wha-a-t?

BRODY: This stuff was worth thirty to forty thousand dollars.

LEWIS: Charley said it was mostly fake.

BRODY: Look! Here's the list! See for yourself!

    LEWIS *looks at it, his face drops.*

McLEOD: Lewis, you've been robbed!

LEWIS: Ya.

BRODY: Where does Charley live?

LEWIS: 129th Street, West. I know the house. I don't know the number. I can show it to you.

BRODY: Fine.

    DAKIS *crosses to the toilet, opens the door, nods to* PATROLMAN BARNES, *who brings* CHARLEY *back into the room.*

CALLAHAN: That's using your . . . *Taps* LEWIS's *head* . . . tokas, Lewis.

    LIEUTENANT MONOGHAN *enters. He is an old-time police officer, ruddy, moonfaced, a cigar always thrust in the jaw, gray hair, muscle gone a bit to fat; his speech, crude New Yorkese interlarded with the vivid thieves' vernacular, crackles with authority.*

O'BRIEN: Hello, Chief!

BRODY: Hi, Lieutenant!

LIEUTENANT, *looking around:* Busy house!

O'BRIEN: Yes, sir, we're bouncin', all of a sudden.

CALLAHAN: John! Got your car here? *O'BRIEN nods.* Run us over? We're gonna hit this bum's flat, Chief.

LIEUTENANT, *squints at LEWIS:* What's your name?

LEWIS: Lewis Abbott.

CALLAHAN, *shows LIEUTENANT the jimmy:* Look at this. . . . *Shows him the gun . . .* and this.

LIEUTENANT: Loaded?

CALLAHAN: Yeah.

BRODY, *indicating CHARLEY:* The other burglar.

LIEUTENANT: What's your name?

CHARLEY: Gennini. I don't know nothing about this, Lieutenant. I was . . .

LIEUTENANT, *snorts, turns his back on CHARLEY:* Print him!

CALLAHAN: Yes, sir.

LIEUTENANT: Who made the collar?

BRODY: Uniform arrest. Patrolman Barnes.

LIEUTENANT, *to BARNES:* Nice goin'!

McLEOD, *indicating KURT to LIEUTENANT:* Kurt Schneider. Turned himself in.

LIEUTENANT: That mouthpiece of his got hold of me downstairs, chewed my ear off. I wanna have a talk with you. *Beckons him inside.*

DAKIS: Charley, on your feet! Let's go. *Leads CHARLEY over to the finger-print board and "prints" him.*

McLEOD, *in the LIEUTENANT's office, indicates ARTHUR:* Kindred. The Pritchett complaint.

LIEUTENANT: Admission?

McLEOD: Yes.

LIEUTENANT: Step inside, lad.—In there. *He indicates an anteroom, off right. ARTHUR exits, off right. To McLEOD.* Shut the door. *McLEOD shuts door to the squad room. The LIEUTENANT takes off his hat and jacket, tosses them onto the coatrack.* On Schneider—what's your poisenal angle?

McLEOD, *subtly mimics the LIEUTENANT's speech:* Poisenal angle! None. Why?

LIEUTENANT, *looks up sharply:* His mouthpiece hinted at something or other.

McLEOD: Fishing expedition.

LIEUTENANT: You sure?

McLEOD: Sure, I'm sure. What did Mr. Sims imply?

LIEUTENANT, *takes off his shoulder holster, hangs it on the rack, transferring the revolver to his hip pocket:* Just vague hints.

McLEOD: You can write those on the air!

LIEUTENANT: What've you got? *Takes off his shirt, hangs it up.*

McLEOD: Girl—Miss Harris in the hospital. Critical. I called the D.A.'s office. I'm taking Schneider over to the hospital for a positive identification. I've got a corroborating witness. I phoned her. She's on her way over here. And I want to get a signed statement from Schneider.

LIEUTENANT: How?

McLEOD: "Persuasion."

    JOE *saunters into the outer office.*

LIEUTENANT: Keep your big mitts off. That's an order.

McLEOD: Were you ever in those railroad flats of his? Did you ever see that kitchen table covered by a filthy, bloodstained oilcloth on which Kurt Schneider performs his delicate operations?

LIEUTENANT, *crosses to desk, opens drawer, takes out shaving articles and towel:* This is an impoisonal business! Your moral indignation is beginning to give me a quick pain in the butt. You got a messianic complex. You want to be the judge and the jury, too. Well, you can't do it. It says so in the book. I don't like lawyers coming in here with photos. It marks my squad lousy. I don't like it—and I won't have it. You understand?

McLEOD: Yes, sir.

LIEUTENANT: Can't you say, "yes, sir," without making it sound like an insult? *Pause.*

McLEOD, *the sting still in his voice:* Yes, sir.

LIEUTENANT, *furious:* You're too damn superior, that's your trouble. For the record, I don't like you any more'n you like me; but you got a value here and I need you on my squad. That's the only reason you're not wearing a white badge again.

McLEOD, *reaches in his pocket for his shield:* You wouldn't want it back now, would you?

LIEUTENANT: When I do, I'll ask for it.

McLEOD: Because you can have it—with instructions.

LIEUTENANT, *controls himself:* Get what you can out of Schneider, but no roughhouse! You know the policy of this administration.

McLEOD: I don't hold with it.

LIEUTENANT: What the hell ice does that cut?

McLEOD: I don't believe in coddling criminals.

LIEUTENANT: Who tells you to?

McLEOD: You do. The whole damn system does.

LIEUTENANT: Sometimes, McLeod, you talk like a maniac.

McLEOD, *starts to speak:* May I . . .

LIEUTENANT: No! You got your orders. That's all.

McLEOD: May I have the keys to the files, *sir?*

LIEUTENANT: You got to have the last word, don't you? *Tosses the keys on the desk, stalks off right.*

DAKIS, *finishes fingerprinting* CHARLEY, *waves him to the washroom:* Charley, wash up! In there!

JOE, *to* BRODY: How many burglaries?

BRODY: Nine or ten.

*A tall, slender girl enters and stands at the gate. Her face is handsome with a bony, freckled, intelligent, scrubbed handsomeness; wide, soft, generous lips, huge clear eyes, at the moment very troubled, indeed.*

JOE: Any important names? Any good addresses?

BRODY, *moans:* We don't know yet. You'll get it. Don't rush us, will you, Joey?

YOUNG GIRL: Is Detective McLeod here?

CALLAHAN, *crosses up to gate:* Yes, Miss?

YOUNG GIRL: May I see Detective McLeod?

CALLAHAN: He's busy. Anything I can do for you? *He scrutinizes her, grins, a little "on the make."* I seen your face before?

YOUNG GIRL: No.

CALLAHAN: I never forget a face.

*JOE looks at her, then wanders into the* LIEUTENANT'S *office.*

YOUNG GIRL: You probably saw my sister.

CALLAHAN: Who's your sister?

YOUNG GIRL: Please tell him Miss Susan Carmichael is here.

CALLAHAN: Yes, Miss. Just a minute. *Replaces the cards in the files.*

McLEOD, *in the* LIEUTENANT'S *office, examining burglary sheets, still fuming at his* LIEUTENANT: Ignorant, gross ward-heeler!! Why don't you print the truth for once, Yussel?

JOE: Which truth?—Yours, his, theirs, mine?

McLEOD: *The* truth.

JOE: Oh, that one? Who would know it? If it came up and blew in your ear, who would know it?

CALLAHAN, *pokes his head into the doorway, addresses* McLEOD: Kid outside for you! *Returns to his files.*

JOE: A nice, tall, long-stemmed kid. *He sits down, picks his teeth, rambles on, almost to himself.* McLEOD, *who is going through the files and grinding his teeth in anger, pays no heed to* JOE's *reflections.* I love these tall kids today. I got a nephew, seventeen, six-foot-three, blond hair, blue eyes.

*Sucks his teeth.* Science tells us at the turn of the century the average man and woman's going to be seven foot tall. Seven foot! That's for me. We know the next fifty years are gonna be lousy: war, atom bombs, whole friggin' civilization's caving in. But I don't wake up at four A.M. to bury myself, any more. I got the whole thing licked—I'm skipping the next fifty years. I'm concentrating on the twenty-first century and all those seven-foot beauties. . . .

McLEOD, *impatiently:* I've no time for a philosophic discussion today, Yussel. *Starts for outer office.*

JOE, *following, murmurs:* Don't throw water on McLeod. He goes rabid.

BARNES, *to* CHARLEY *as he comes out of washroom:* O.K., Charley. Come with me. *They exit through gate.*

McLEOD, *calls to* O'BRIEN, *who is about to exit with* LEWIS *in tow:* Hey, John, I need eight or ten fellows up here for a lineup. Ask a couple of the men downstairs to get into civvies!

O'BRIEN: Lineup? Sure. *Exit.*

McLEOD, *coming down to the desk, addressed the young lady at the gate:* Miss Carmichael?

SUSAN: Yes. I'm Susan Carmichael.

McLEOD: Come in, please!

SUSAN, *enters through the gate, crosses down to the desk facing* McLEOD: Are you the officer who phoned?

McLEOD: Yes. I'm Detective McLeod.

SUSAN: Where's Arthur? What happened to him? What's this about?

McLEOD: Did you contact your sister?

SUSAN, *hesitating:* N . . . no!

McLEOD: Why not?

SUSAN: I couldn't reach her.

McLEOD: Where is she?

SUSAN: Visiting some friends in Connecticut. I don't know the address. Where's Arthur? Is he all right?

McLEOD: Yes. He's inside. How well do you know Arthur Kindred?

SUSAN: Very. All my life. We lived next door to each other in Ann Arbor.

McLEOD: Kind of a wild boy, wasn't he?

SUSAN: Arthur?? Not at all. He was always very serious. Why?

McLEOD: Did he give your sister any money?

SUSAN: My sister earns $25 an hour. She's a very successful model. She averages $300 to $400 a week for herself. Will you please tell me what this is about?

McLEOD: Let me ask the questions. Do you mind?

SUSAN: Sorry!

McLeod: Arthur was in the navy?

Susan: Five years.

McLeod: He got a dishonorable discharge.

Susan: What are you talking about?

  Brody *becomes interested, edges over, listening.*

McLeod: That's a question.

Susan: You didn't punctuate it.

McLeod: Correction. *He smiles.* Did he?

Susan: Arthur was cited four times. He got the Silver Star. He carried a
  sailor up three decks of a burning ship. He had two ships sunk under
  him. He floated around once in the Pacific Ocean for seventeen hours with
  sharks all around him. When they picked him up, he was out of his head,
  trying to climb onto a concrete platform that wasn't there. He was in the
  hospital for ten weeks after that. Any more questions?

McLeod: What is his relationship to your sister?

Susan: I told you, we all grew up together.

McLeod: Is he in love with her?

Susan: My sister is one of the most beautiful girls in New York. A lot of
  men are in love with her. May I talk to Arthur now, please?

McLeod: He didn't give her any money, then?

Susan, *impatiently:* No.

McLeod: Did he give it to you?

Susan: Are you kidding?

McLeod: I'm afraid not. Your sister's boyfriend is in trouble.

Susan: What trouble?

McLeod: He's a thief.

Susan: Who says so?

McLeod: He does.

Susan: I don't believe you.

McLeod: Sit down. *He calls through door of the Lieutenant's office, off
  right.* Arthur! In here! Arthur *enters, sees* Susan, *stops in his tracks.*

Susan: Jiggs! What happened?

Arthur: Suzy! *He glares indignantly at* McLeod. Did you have to drag
  children into this?

McLeod, *ironically:* Now, Jiggs!

Arthur: Susan, you shouldn't have come here.

Susan: What happened?

Arthur: I took some money.

Susan: Who from?

Arthur: The man I worked for.

Susan: But why, Jiggs, why?

ARTHUR: None of your business.

BRODY, *scanning a list:* Say, Jim!

MCLEOD: Yes?

> BRODY *beckons to him.* MCLEOD *turns up, talks to* BRODY *sotto voce.*
> ARTHUR *whispers to* SUSAN, *urgently.*

ARTHUR: Suzy, go home—quick—go home—get out of here.

SUSAN, *whispers:* Jiggs, what happened? Have you got a lawyer?

ARTHUR: No!

SUSAN: I'll phone Joy and tell her.

ARTHUR: Do you want to get her involved? There are newspapermen here.
   You want to ruin her career?

SUSAN, *whispering:* But, Jiggs—

ARTHUR, *whispering:* Get out of here, will you?

> MCLEOD *returns.*

MCLEOD: Well, young lady—satisfied?

SUSAN: How much did he take?

MCLEOD: $480.

ARTHUR: What's the difference? Will you please tell her to go home, Officer?
   She's only a kid.

SUSAN, *indignantly:* I'm not. I wish you'd . . .

ARTHUR: She shouldn't be here. She's got nothing to do with this.

MCLEOD: All right, young lady. I'm sorry to have bothered you. Have your
   sister get in touch with me as soon as you hear from her.

ARTHUR: What for? Don't you do it, Suzy—you don't have to. *To* MCLEOD.
   You're not going to get her involved in this.

MCLEOD: You shut up! *To* SUSAN. O.K. *Motions* SUSAN *to go. She bites her
   lip to keep from crying, and goes.*

BRODY, *comes down to* ARTHUR: Is it true that you carried a wounded sailor
   on your shoulders up three decks of a burning ship?

ARTHUR: Yes.

BRODY: Pretty good.

ARTHUR: Could I have that drink now? Please!

BRODY: Sure. *Crosses up to his files, takes out a bottle of whiskey, cleans a
   glass, pours a drink.* MCLEOD *ambles down to* KURT, *sipping coffee from
   a container.*

MCLEOD: You're looking pretty well, Kurt.

KURT: Could be better.

MCLEOD, *sits at typewriter, inserts a sheet of paper:* How's the farm?

KURT: All right!

MCLEOD: Wasn't there a drought in Jersey this year? *Starts to type
   statement.*

KURT: I irrigate my crops. I've got plenty of water.

McLEOD: What do you raise?

KURT: Cabbage . . . lettuce . . . kale! Truck stuff!

McLEOD, *typing:* That's the life. Picturesque country, North Jersey. Nice hills, unexpected!

KURT: Yes. How're things with you?

McLEOD: This is one business never has a depression. *Drinks—surveys his container.* They make a pretty good cup of coffee across the street.

KURT: Mm! So-so.

BRODY, *comes down, hands drink to* ARTHUR: Here you are, son! *Crosses up again to replace bottle in his file.* ARTHUR *tosses down the drink.*

McLEOD, *types:* When I retire I'm going to buy myself a little farm like yours, settle down. Does it really pay for itself?

KURT: If you work it.

McLEOD: How much can a man average a year? *Types.*

KURT: Varies. Two thousands a good year.

McLEOD: Clear? That's pretty good. *Types.*

KURT: Sometimes you lose a crop.

McLEOD, *types:* How long you had that farm?

KURT: Eleven years.

McLEOD: And you average two thousand a year? *Stops typing, fixes him with a sharp, searching glance.*

KURT: What's . . . ?

McLEOD: Then how'd you manage to accumulate $56,000 in the bank, Kurt? Hm? *Silence.* Hm, Kurt? How?

KURT: Who says I have?

McLEOD: I do. I checked. $56,000. That's a lot of kale. *Takes out a notebook from his pocket.* You got it in four banks. Passaic—Oakdale—two in Newark. Here are the figures. How'd you get that money, Kurt?

KURT: I got it honestly.

McLEOD: How? How?

KURT: I don't have to tell you that.

McLEOD: Oh, come on, Kurt. How? *Kurt shakes his head.* Make it easy for yourself. You're still running that abortion mill, aren't you?

KURT: My name is Kurt Schneider—I live in Oakdale, New Jersey. That's all I have to answer.

McLEOD: You operated on Miss Harris, didn't you?

KURT: No, I did not!

McLEOD: She identified your picture. *He rips the sheet of paper out of the typewriter and sets it down before* KURT. Sign that, Kurt!

KURT: What is it?

McLeod: An admission.

Kurt: You think I'm crazy.

McLeod: We've got you dead to rights. Make it easy for yourself.

Kurt: I'm not saying anything more on advice of counsel!

McLeod: I'm getting impatient! You better talk, Kurt.

Kurt: I'm standing on my constitutional rights!

McLeod, *rising nervously, moving above the desk and down to* Kurt: Hold your hats, boys, here we go again. *Looking down on* Kurt *from behind him, murmurs softly.* You're lucky, Kurt. You got away with it once. But the postman rings twice. And this time we've got you, Kurt. Why don't you cop a plea? Miss Harris is waiting for you. We're going to visit her in the hospital. She's anxious to see you. And what you don't know is . . . there was a corroborating witness, and she's downstairs, ready to identify you, right now. . . . You're getting pale, Kurt. Kurt *laughs softly to himself.* What are you laughing at?

Kurt: Nothing.

McLeod: That's right! That's just what you've got to laugh about—nothing. You're on the bottom of this joke.

Kurt: Maybe I am. Maybe I'm not. Maybe somebody else is.

McLeod: What's that mean?

Kurt: I know why you're out to get me.

McLeod: Why? . . . Kurt *shakes his head.* Why, Kurt? This is your last chance. Do you want to talk?

Kurt: My name is Kurt Schneider. I live in Oakdale, New Jersey. That's all I'm obliged to say by law.

McLeod: You should have been a lawyer, Kurt. A Philadelphia lawyer. *Crosses to the rail, shouts downstairs.* Lineup, Gus! Gus, *offstage, shouts up:* "Coming!" *He can be heard approaching singing the melody of "The Rose of Tralee."*

McLeod, *to* Dakis: Nick, put on your hat and coat for a lineup.

*Brody crosses down to* Arthur *again.* Arthur *hands him the glass.*

Arthur: Thanks.

*A pause. As* Brody *looks at the boy, something of agony creeps into his face.*

Brody: My boy was in the navy, too. The *Juneau.* Know her?

Arthur: She was a cruiser.

Brody: Yeah.

Arthur: Didn't she go down with all hands? In the Pacific?

Brody: There were ten survivors. He wasn't one of them.

Arthur: Too bad.

Brody: Yeah! He was my only boy. It's something you never get over. You never believe it. You keep waiting for a bell to ring . . . phone . . . door. Sometimes I hear a voice on the street, or see a young fellow from the back, the set of his shoulders—like you—for a minute it's him. Your whole life becomes like a dream . . . a walking dream.

ARTHUR: Maybe he was one of the lucky ones.

BRODY: Don't say that!

ARTHUR: Why not?

BRODY: Because it wouldn't make sense then.

ARTHUR: Does it?

BRODY, *fiercely:* Yes, damn it! Yes.

McLEOD: Say, Lou! Will you put on your hat and coat for a lineup?

*Enter policemen in civilian clothes, and detectives putting on hats and coats, joking and laughing.*

BRODY: Yeah.

McLEOD: John, Nick, hat and coat!

*The men line up.*

DAKIS, *to* CHARLEY: Sit over there, Charley. *Indicates the bench.*

McLEOD, *coming down to* KURT: Kurt. Put on your hat and coat. Pick your spot. End, middle, anyplace. No alibis later. KURT *finds a place in the line and stands there stiffly.* McLEOD *calls off.* Come in, Miss Hatch. *Enter* MISS HATCH, *a hard-looking young woman, with hair bleached a lemon yellow. She wears an elaborate fur stole.* How do you do, Miss Hatch?

MISS HATCH: I'm fine, thank you. *Crosses down to* McLEOD. McLEOD *scrutinizes her, frowns.* What's the matter?

McLEOD, *indicating the fur piece:* Rushing the season, aren't you?

MISS HATCH, *laughs nervously:* Oh!

McLEOD: New?

MISS HATCH: Yes.

McLEOD: Mink?

MISS HATCH: Uh, uh! Dyed squirrel! Looks real though, doesn't it?

McLEOD: Mmm. It was nice of you to come down and help us. We appreciate that.

MISS HATCH: Don't mention it. Let's just get it over with, huh? I got an engagement. What do I—*She looks about for an ashtray in which to deposit her cigarette.*

McLEOD: Throw it on the floor. *She obeys. He steps on it.* You have your instructions?

MISS HATCH: Yeah. I look at them all, then touch the one on the shoulder. *He nods. She walks slowly down the line, nervously scrutinizing the faces, a little too quickly to be convincing. She turns to* McLEOD. He isn't here.

McLEOD: You haven't looked.

MISS HATCH: I looked. Of course I did.

CALLAHAN: It's the new look.

McLEOD: Just look, will you. Not at me. Over there.

MISS HATCH: I don't recognize anyone. I never saw any of them in my life before.

McLEOD: You identified a picture of one of these men.

MISS HATCH: What are you trying to do . . . make me give you a wrong identification? Well, I ain't gonna do it.

McLEOD, *rubs his thumb and forefinger together, suggestively:* Do you know what this means?

MISS HATCH, *sharply:* Yeah. That's your cut on the side.

McLEOD: You're fresh! *Phone rings.* BRODY *answers it.*

BRODY: 2–1 Squad. Brody. *Conversation sotto voce.*

McLEOD: I've a good mind to prefer charges against you.

MISS HATCH, *screams at him:* That's what I get for coming all the way downtown to help you. You cops are all the same. Give you a badge and you think you can push the world around.

McLEOD: You identified one of these men. Now point him out or I'm going to throw you in the clink.

MISS HATCH: You'll do *what?*

BRODY *hangs up the phone, calls him to one side.*

BRODY: Jim!

McLEOD: Yes?

BRODY, *in subdued tones:* That was the D.A.'s office. The Harris girl died.

McLEOD: When?

BRODY: A couple of hours ago.

McLEOD: Why weren't we informed?

BRODY: I don't know.

McLEOD: There goes the case.

BRODY: The D.A. says just go through the motions. He can't get an indictment now. Just book him and forget it, he says.

McLEOD: Sure, forget it. Let him fill the morgues! *Crosses over to* KURT. Congratulations, Kurt! The girl died. Sit down over there, Kurt. All right, Miss Hatch. You've earned your fur piece. I hope you'll enjoy it.

MISS HATCH, *flaring:* You can't talk to me that way. I'm no tramp that you can talk to me that way. Who the hell do you think you are, anyway?

McLEOD: Get out! Take a couple of drop-dead pills! Get lost!

MISS HATCH, *exits, murmuring:* Big cheese! See my lawyer about him.

McLEOD: All right, men, thank you.

*As they go, we hear snatches of the following conversations from the men.*

GUS: I was waiting for her to put the finger on you, boy.

DAKIS: Me? Do I look like an ice-tong man?

O'BRIEN: Regular Sarah Heartburn.

CALLAHAN: One minute more we'd have gotten the witches' scene from *Macbeth*. *Exit.*

    WILLY, *the janitor, has entered during the above.*

WILLY, *sweeping vigorously, muttering all the while:* Now look at this joint, will you? You filthy slobs. You live in a stable. *To* SHOPLIFTER. Come on, get up. *She rises. He sweeps right through her.* Wouldn't think I swept it out an hour ago. Boy, I'd like to see the homes you bums live in. Pigpens, I bet. *Exit.*

McLEOD, *crosses up to the duty chart, takes it off the wall, crosses down to the desk with it, murmuring for* JOE'S *benefit:* Why am I wasting my life here? I could make more driving a hack. I like books, I like music, I've got a wonderful, wonderful wife—I could get a dozen jobs would give me more time to enjoy the good things of life. I should have my head examined. All this work, these hours! What for? It's a phony. *He removes the letters spelling out* GALLAGHER *and* DAKIS, *places them in the drawer, takes out other letters, inserts his name and* BRODY'S.

JOE, *comes down:* Was she reached, you think?

McLEOD: What do *you* think?

JOE: I don't know.

McLEOD, *groans:* Oh, Yussel.

JOE: I don't know.

McLEOD: This is a phony. The thieves and murderers could have written the penal code themselves. Your democracy, Yussel, is a Rube Goldberg contraption. An elaborate machine a block long—you set it all in motion, 3,000 wheels turn, it goes PING. *He crosses up again, replaces the chart on the wall.*

JOE: That's what's great about it. That's what I love. It's so confused, it's wonderful. *Crosses to* McLEOD. After all, Seamus, guilt and innocence!— The epistemological question! Just the knowing . . . the mere knowing . . . the ability to ken. Maybe he didn't do it. Maybe she can't identify him. How do you know?

    BRODY *enters, sits at desk.*

McLEOD: How do you know anything? You've got a nose, you can smell; you've got taste buds, you can taste; you've got nerve endings, you can feel; and, theoretically, you've got intelligence . . . you can judge.

JOE: Ah, ha! That's where it breaks down!

McLEOD, *to* BRODY: Got an aspirin?

    BRODY *hands him a box of aspirin,* McLEOD *takes the box and crosses over into the* LIEUTENANT'S *office.* JOE *follows him.*

JOE: I was talking to Judge Mendez today. He just got on the bench last year,

Seamus. Twenty-nine years a successful lawyer. He thought this would be a cinch. He's lost forty pounds. He's nervous as a cat. His wife thinks he has a mistress. He has:—The Law. He said to me, "Joe! I've got to sentence a man to death tomorrow. How can I do it? Who am I to judge? It takes a god to know!—To really know!"

McLeod, *in* Lieutenant's *office, draws a glass of water, tosses the aspirin into his mouth:* Bunk!

Joe: I'm quoting Judge Mendez.

McLeod: Then he's a corrupt man, himself. All lawyers are, anyway. I say hang all the lawyers, and let justice triumph. *Washes down the aspirin with a drink, sits, takes off his tie, rolls up his sleeve, then slowly, with mounting bitterness.* Evil has a stench of its own. A child can spot it. I know . . . I know, Yussel. My own father was one of them. No good he was . . . possessed. Every day and every night of my childhood I saw and heard him abuse and maliciously torment my mother. I saw that sadistic son-of-a-bitch of a father of mine with that criminal mind of his drive my mother straight into a lunatic asylum. She died in a lunatic asylum. *He controls himself.* Yes, I know it when I smell it. I learned it early and deep. I was fourteen and alone in the world. I made war on it. Every time I look at one of these babies, I see my father's face!

*Phone rings in the outer office.* Brody *answers.*

Brody: 2–1 Squad. Brody. *Pause.* Lock the door. Don't let him out! I'll be right over. *Hangs up, rushes into the inner office, grabs his hat and coat.* Say, Jim, there's a guy at O'Donovan's bar with a badge and gun, arresting a woman. Claims he's a cop. Might be, might be a shakedown. I'll be right back. Catch the phone for me! *Takes his gun out of the drawer and runs off.*

Joe, *runs after him:* Could be some shooting. Wait for me, baby! *Exit.*

McLeod *comes out of* Lieutenant's *office, his face grim, black, the veins in his temple standing out.*

McLeod, *to* Kurt: You're a lucky man, Kurt. Kissed in your cradle by a vulture. So the girl died, Kurt.

Kurt: That's too bad.

McLeod: What have you got, Kurt, in place of a conscience? Kurt *starts to speak.* Don't answer!—I know—a lawyer. I ought to fall on you like the sword of God.

Kurt: That sword's got two edges. You could cut your own throat.

McLeod, *takes out a cigarette, turns away to light it, his face twitching neurotically:* Look! The gate's open! While I'm lighting my cigarette— why don't you run for it? One second, you'll be out in the street.

Kurt: I'll go free, anyway. Why should I run?

McLeod: Give me the little pleasure— *Touching his gun.* —of putting a hole in the back of your head.

Kurt: You wouldn't do that. Talk!

McLeod: Is it?

Kurt: You're an intelligent man. You're not foolish.

McLeod: Try me, Kurt. Why don't you? Go ahead, dance down that hall!

Kurt, *smiles and shakes his head:* Soon as you book me, I'm out on bail. When I go to trial, they couldn't convict me in a million years. You know that. Even if I were guilty, which I'm not. . . . The girl is dead. There are no witnesses. That's the law.

McLeod: You've been well briefed. You know your catechism.

Kurt: I know more than my catechism!

McLeod: What, for example? *Kurt smiles and nods.* What, Kurt? What goes on under that monkey-skull of yours, I wonder! *Kurt is silent.* On your feet! *Kurt looks up at McLeod's face, is frightened by its almost insane intensity. McLeod roars at him.* Get up!! *Kurt rises.* Go in there! *Points to the Lieutenant's office. Kurt goes into the Lieutenant's office. McLeod follows him, shuts the door.* Sit down, Kurt. *Kurt sits.* I'm going to give you a piece of advice. When the courts and the juries and the judges let you free this time, get out of New York. Go to Georgia. They won't extradite criminals to us. So, you see, Kurt take my advice, go to Georgia, or go to hell, but you butcher one more girl in this city, and law or no law, I'll find you and I'll put a bullet in the back of your head, and I'll drop your body in the East River, and I'll go home and I'll sleep sweetly.

Kurt: You have to answer to the law the same as I. You don't frighten me. Now, I'll give you some advice. I've got plenty on you, too. I know why you're so vindictive. And you watch your step! Because I happen to have friends, too, downtown . . . with pull, lots of pull!

McLeod: Have you? What do you know? Aren't you the big shot! *Pull!* Have you got any friends with *push!* Like *that! Kicks him; Kurt goes over, chair and all.*

Kurt: Cut that out! You let me alone now. . . . *McLeod grabs him by the lapels, pulls him to his feet.* You let me go! Let me go!

McLeod: No, Kurt! Everybody else is going to let you go. You got it all figured . . . exactly. The courts, the juries, the judges— *He slaps him.* —Everybody except *me. He slaps him again. Kurt starts to resist, growls, and tries to push McLeod away. McLeod hits him in the belly. Kurt crumples to the floor. McLeod's rage subsides. He sighs, disgusted with himself for losing his temper.* Why didn't you obey your lawyer and keep your mouth shut? All right! Get up, Kurt! Come on! Get up!

KURT, *moaning and writhing:* I can't . . . I can't. . . . Something inside . . . broke! *He calls feebly.* Help! *He screams.* Help!

McLEOD: Get up! You're all right. Get up!

> KURT's *eyes roll up, exposing the whites.*
>
> LIEUTENANT MONOGHAN *enters quickly, wiping shaving lather off his face with a towel.*

LIEUTENANT: What's going on? *He sees* KURT, *goes to him, bends down.*

KURT: Inside! It broke. He hurt me. . . .

> DAKIS *rushes in.*

LIEUTENANT: Take it easy, son, you'll be all right.

KURT: I feel terrible.

LIEUTENANT: Nick! Quick! Get an ambulance.

DAKIS: Yes, sir. *Goes to the phone, puts in a call.*

LIEUTENANT: Did he resist you?

> GALLAGHER *enters on the double.*

McLEOD: No.

LIEUTENANT: No? You lunatic! Didn't I just get through warning you? *To* KURT *who is on the floor, moaning in agony.* What happened?

KURT, *gasping for breath:* He tried to kill me!

LIEUTENANT: Why should he do that?

KURT: Tami Giacoppetti! . . . Same thing! . . . She got him after me too. . . . Tami Giacoppetti . . . KURT's *mouth opens and closes with scarcely any further sound emerging.*

LIEUTENANT: What? Tami Giacoppetti? Who's he? What about him? *Puts his ear to* KURT's *mouth.* A little louder! Just try and talk a little louder, lad. KURT's *eyes close, his head falls back. To* GALLAGHER. Wet some towels! GALLAGHER *rushes to the washroom.* DAKIS *loosens* KURT's *collar, tries to restore him to consciousness. The* LIEUTENANT *rises, confronts* McLEOD, *glaring at him.* Who's Tami Giacoppetti?

McLEOD: I've no idea.

LIEUTENANT: What's the pitch here, McLeod?

McLEOD: He needled me. He got fresh. He begged for it, and I let him have it. That's all.

> GALLAGHER *returns with several wet towels.* DAKIS *takes them from him, applies them to* KURT's *head.*

LIEUTENANT: Don't con me! That ain't all. Come on! Let's have it! What about this Tami Giacoppetti?

McLEOD: I never heard of him.

GALLAGHER: Giacoppetti? I know him. A black-market guy. Runs a creep joint in the Village.

*Kurt groans.*

McLeod: He's putting on an act, Lieutenant. Can't you see . . .

*Kurt groans.*

Lieutenant: This could be a very hot potato. If this man's hurt, the big brass'll be down here throwin' questions at me. And I'm going to have the answers. What plays between you two guys? What's he got on you? What's the clout?

McLeod: Nothing.

Lieutenant: Then what was his mouthpiece yellin' and screamin' about?

McLeod: Red herring. Red, red herring!

Lieutenant: That I'm gonna goddamn well find out for myself. There's something kinky about this. McLeod, if you're concealing something from me, I'll have your head on a plate. *To* Gallagher. This Giacoppetti! Find him and bring him in!

Gallagher: Yes, sir. *Goes.*

Lieutenant, *calls after him:* My car's downstairs. Use it.

Gallagher: Yes, sir.

*The* Lieutenant *bends down to* Kurt. McLeod, *grim-faced, lights another cigarette.*

*CURTAIN*

**ACT TWO**

*The scene is the same, fifty-four minutes later by the clock on the wall.*
*At rise, the lawyer,* ENDICOTT SIMS, *is closeted in the* LIEUTENANT's *office, scolding the* LIEUTENANT *and* McLEOD. *In the squad room the* SHOP-
LIFTER *is reading the comics.* ARTHUR *is seated quietly, his head bowed in thought.* DAKIS, *the* JANITOR, *and* GUS *are in a huddle, whispering, glancing over toward the* LIEUTENANT's *door.* BRODY *is talking sotto voce to an excited man and woman, who are glaring at a tough-looking specimen. The setting sun is throwing long and ominous shadows into the darkening room.*

SIMS, *fulminating at* McLEOD, *who pointedly ignores him by focusing attention on a hangnail:* How dare you take the law in your own hands? Who are you to constitute yourself a court of last appeal?
LIEUTENANT, *oil on the surging waters:* Nah, Counselor . . .
   *The phone rings in the squad room.* BRODY *crosses to answer.*
BRODY: 21st Squad, Detective Brody . . . Yeah! . . . The hospital! Yeah. How is he? *Jotting notation.*
SIMS: No, Lieutenant! This is a felony. *Wheels back to* McLEOD. I'm going to press a felonious assault here. So help me, I'm going to see you in jail!
McLEOD, *calmly, biting the hangnail:* On which side of the bars, Counselor?
SIMS: Be careful. I'm an attorney and an officer of the court, and I don't like that talk.
McLEOD: I'm an officer of the peace, and I don't like collusion.
SIMS: What do you mean by that?
McLEOD, *looks up, sharply:* By that I mean *collusion.* Subornation of witnesses, Counselor.
SIMS: What the devil are you talking about?
McLEOD: I'm charging you with subornation.
SIMS: Your lips are blistering with lies.
McLEOD, *sardonically:* Praise from an expert. I had a witness here today you bought off, Counselor.
SIMS: That's so absurd, I'm not even going to answer it.
McLEOD: I'll prove it!
LIEUTENANT: All right! Cut it! Cut it out. Enough's enough.
SIMS, *to* LIEUTENANT: I intend to carry this to the commissioner.
LIEUTENANT, *pushes the phone across the desk toward* SIMS: Call him now. That's your privilege.
SIMS: And don't think *you're* entirely free of blame in this, Lieutenant.
LIEUTENANT: Me? What have I . . .
SIMS: I warned you personal motives are involved in this case. I was afraid

this was going to happen. You should have taken the necessary steps to prevent it. Luckily, I came armed with photos and affidavits.

LIEUTENANT: Mystery! Mystery! *What* motives?

McLEOD, *rises:* Yes. Why don't you tell us? Let's get it out in the open! What are these motives?

SIMS: It is not to my client's interests to reveal them at this moment.

McLEOD: Legal bull.

LIEUTENANT: I'm beginning to think so, myself.

SIMS: Sure. One hand washes the other.

   BRODY *knocks at the door.*

LIEUTENANT: Come in!

BRODY: Phone, Lieutenant.

LIEUTENANT, *picks up the phone:* 21st Squad, Lieutenant Monoghan. . . . Yeah. . . . Yeah . . .

   BRODY *returns to the squad room, hangs up the phone.*

SIMS, *softly, to* McLEOD: On what evidence do you make these serious charges?

McLEOD, *taunting him:* The evidence of my intelligent observation.

SIMS: Insufficient, incompetent, and irrelevant.

LIEUTENANT, *looks up, annoyed:* Sh! Sh! *Turns back to the phone.*

SIMS: You're pretty cagey, McLeod, but your tactics don't fool me for a second. You're not going to duck out of this so easily. You're in a position of responsibility here, and you have to answer for your actions. You can't use your badge for personal vengeance. That doesn't go. The public isn't your servant; you're theirs. You're going to be broken for this.

McLEOD, *roaring back at him:* Go ahead! Break me! You're worse than the criminals you represent, Counselor. You're so damn respectable. Yet, look at you! The clothes you wear, your car downstairs, your house in Westchester, all bought with stolen money, tainted with blood.

LIEUTENANT: Shut up! I got the hospital.

SIMS: How is he? *They listen attentively.*

LIEUTENANT, *on phone:* Yes. Yes. I see. Keep in touch with me. Let me know right away. *Hangs up.* See, Counselor, it always pays to wait the event. There are no external lacerations on your client that would warrant a felony assault. They're now making X-rays and tests to see if there are any internal injuries. So far you haven't got a leg to stand on.

McLEOD: Let him, let him! *To* SIMS. Bring your felony charge. It'll give me a chance to get your client on the stand and really tear his clothes off. And yours, too, Counselor.

LIEUTENANT: McLeod! Step outside!

   McLEOD *crosses out of the* LIEUTENANT'S *office, shuts the door.*

BRODY, *murmurs to* McLEOD: What's the score?

McLEOD: Tempest in a teapot. *Turns to his personal file.*

SIMS: What kind of an officer is that?

LIEUTENANT: Detectives are like fingerprints. No two alike. He has his quoiks.

SIMS: The understatement of the year.

LIEUTENANT: We all got 'em. He has a value here. He's honest. He ain't on the take. I stand up for him on that. Got no tin boxes.

SIMS: I wasn't saying he had.

LIEUTENANT: I thought you was, maybe.

SIMS: No . . .

LIEUTENANT: Then what was you saying? I guess I fumbled it.

SIMS: I can't discuss it with you.

LIEUTENANT, *sarcastically:* I'd love to discuss it with someone. Who do you suggest?

SIMS: McLeod.

LIEUTENANT: Nah, Counselor!

SIMS: Or his wife!

LIEUTENANT, *looks up sharply:* His wife? What do you mean by that?

SIMS: Never mind! Skip it!

LIEUTENANT: You mentioned his wife. What do you mean by that? Look! I got to get a clear-up here. A little cooperation would go a long way.

SIMS: When it serves my client's interests . . . not before.

LIEUTENANT: Four years ago I threw my radio set the hell outta the window. You know why? Because, goddamn it, I hate mysteries.

SIMS, *smiles, shakes his head:* Lieutenant, I'm not free to discuss this, yet. *Looks at his watch.* Gouverneur Hospital?

LIEUTENANT: Yeah.

SIMS: I want to see my client. Will I be allowed in?

LIEUTENANT: Yeah, yeah.

SIMS: I'll be back. *He leaves the* LIEUTENANT'S *office. In the squad room, he pauses to confront* McLEOD. I'll be back. I'm not through with you.

McLEOD: I can't wait.

*Exit* SIMS.

BRODY, *to* McLEOD, *indicating the tough, surly-looking character:* This creep was impersonating an officer.

MRS. FEENEY: I didn't know. I thought he might be a policeman. His badge looked real.

BRODY: A shakedown. After he got you outside he'd a taken all your money and let you go. You see, Mrs. Feeney, that's how we get a bad reputation. Now you will appear in court in the morning, won't you?

MRS. FEENEY: Oh, yes.

MR. FEENEY: Tomorrow morning? Hey! . . . I've got a job.

MRS. FEENEY: You'll explain to your boss. You'll just take off, that's all.

MR. FEENEY: But, Isabel . . .

MRS. FEENEY: He'll be there. Don't you worry. Thank you. Thank you. *They go off, arguing.*

BRODY, *to* MCLEOD: I'm going down to book this crumb-bum.

CRUMB-BUM, *aggressively:* What did you call me?

BRODY: A crumb-bum. Come on! *Exit* BRODY *and the glowering* CRUMB-BUM.

LIEUTENANT, *inside, squints at his cigar a moment, rises, bellows:* McLeod!

MCLEOD, *crosses to the* LIEUTENANT'*s door, opens it:* Yes, sir?

LIEUTENANT: What the hell is this about? What's he driving at? I want the truth.

MCLEOD: Lieutenant, I give you my solemn word of honor . . .

LIEUTENANT, *pauses, studies him, sighs, waves him out:* Shut the door!

MCLEOD *shuts the door and crosses to the desk. A sad-looking man appears at the gate.*

MCLEOD: Yes, sir? What can I do for you?

MAN: I want to report someone picked my pocket.

MCLEOD, *sitting at the desk:* Come in!

MAN, *exposes his backside, revealing a patch cut out of his trousers:* Look! They cut it right out.

MCLEOD: They work that way, with a razor blade. Sit down! Did you see the man?

MAN: No. First I knew I was in a restaurant. *Sits down.* I ate a big meal, reached in my pocket to pay the check. Boy, I almost dropped dead. I'm lucky I'm not here under arrest, myself.

MCLEOD, *smiles:* Yes. What's your name?

MAN: Gallantz, D. David.

MCLEOD: Address?

WILLY, *pail in one hand, broom in the other, taps* GALLANTZ *on the shoulder with the broom:* Git up!

GALLANTZ, *rises, staring at* WILLY: 419 West 80th Street.

WILLY, *bends down to the basket under the desk, empties the contents into his pail, muttering under his breath, rises heavily, paying no attention to anyone as he crosses off:* Look at this room, will you? Wouldn't think I cleaned up an hour ago! Detectives! The brains of the department?! Ha! Couldn't find a Chinaman on Mott Street. *Exit.*

MCLEOD: What did you lose?

GALLANTZ: My wallet.

McLeod, *writing:* Can you describe it?

GALLANTZ: Black leather.

McLeod, *picks up the phone:* Lost property. McLeod.

SHOPLIFTER, *lays down the newspaper, addresses* DAKIS: Have you got one of them two-way radio wristwatches like Dick Tracy?

DAKIS: No.

SHOPLIFTER: Behind the times, ain't you?

DAKIS: Yeah, behind the behind.

SHOPLIFTER, *feels her pulse:* Gee, I think I'm getting a reaction. Emotions are bad for me. I got diabetes. I'm not supposed to get emotions.

DAKIS, *belches, then, indignantly:* I got ulcers—I'm not supposed to eat sandwiches. A hot meal was waiting for me at home. Do me a favor!— Next time get yourself arrested before four o'clock. Let a fellow eat a home-cooked meal.

SHOPLIFTER, *genuinely contrite:* I'm sorry.

DAKIS: Do you realize this is on my own time? *With mounting anger.* Look at all these forms I had to type up. And when we get to court, what'll happen? The judge'll probably let you off. I won't even get a conviction. You cause me all this work for nothin'.

SHOPLIFTER: I'm sorry.

DAKIS: That's a big help.

*In his office the* LIEUTENANT *fishes an address book out of his desk drawer, thumbs through it for a number, reaches for the phone, dials.*

McLeod, *hangs up. To* GALLANTZ: Sorry. Nothing yet. We'll follow it up. If we hear anything, we'll let you know.

GALLANTZ: Thanks! *As he goes, he looks mournfully at his exposed derrière.* My best pants, too. *Exit.*

LIEUTENANT, *on the phone:* Hello. Mrs. McLeod? This is Lieutenant Monoghan of the 21st. No, no! He's all right. Nothing like that!

*The rest of his conversation is drowned out by the entrance of* CALLAHAN, POLICEMAN BARNES, BRODY, *and* CHARLEY, *the burglar, all talking at once.* CALLAHAN *and* BARNES *are carrying two suitcases and several pillowcases filled with loot from* CHARLEY'S *apartment.* BRODY *completes the parade, carrying more loot.* CALLAHAN *knocks at the* LIEUTENANT'S *door.*

LIEUTENANT: Come in!

CALLAHAN, *opens the* LIEUTENANT'S *door, holds up the loot:* Look what we found, boss. And by a strange coincidence—in Charley's apartment. *The* LIEUTENANT *covers the phone, nods approval.*

BARNES, *unlocks* CHARLEY'S *handcuffs:* Sit down! There!

CHARLEY *sits in the designated chair.*

CALLAHAN: O'Brien is taking Lewis around to identify the houses.

LIEUTENANT: Good! *Waves him out.* Shut the door!

*CALLAHAN slams the door with his knee; then aided by MCLEOD and BRODY and DAKIS, he begins unloading the stolen goods.*

CALLAHAN, *holding up some loot:* Look at this! These jockeys sure get around! . . . *The LIEUTENANT picks up his phone and continues his conversation, which is drowned out by the racket in the squad room as the men proceed to lay out and examine the stolen goods. CALLAHAN holds up an expensive clock, shakes it.* This worth anything?

MCLEOD, *examines it:* Very good piece—Tiffany, Where'd you get this, Charley?

CHARLEY: I bought it.

MCLEOD: Where?

CHARLEY: Outside the jewelry exchange. On the street.

MCLEOD: Who from?

CHARLEY: Some guy—

MCLEOD: What's his name?

CHARLEY: I don't know. I never saw him again.

MCLEOD: Or before?

CHARLEY, *nods:* Yeah.

MCLEOD: Or at all. The little man that wasn't there.

SHOPLIFTER, *feeling her pulse:* I am getting a reaction. Emotions are bad for me.

DAKIS, *checking a stolen article against a list:* Girls with diabetes shouldn't steal pink panties.

SHOPLIFTER: It wasn't pink pants.

DAKIS, *sighs:* I know.

SHOPLIFTER: It was a bag . . .

DAKIS, *closes his eyes, sighs:* I know.

SHOPLIFTER: Alligator.

DAKIS: I know.

SHOPLIFTER: Imitation alligator.

DAKIS, *sorry he started it all:* I know.

BRODY, *holds up a piece of jewelry:* This any good?

MCLEOD, *examines it:* Junk! Wait! Here's something! Monogrammed: J. G. *Checks with list.* Sure. This is some of the Gordon stuff. Where'd you get this, Charley?

CHARLEY, *hangs his head, disgusted:* I ain't talking.

BRODY: Where?

*CHARLEY shakes his head.*

CALLAHAN: Where'd you get it, Charley? *Takes out a "billy."* Know what this is? A "persuader." *Bangs it on the desk.*

CHARLEY: Go ahead! Beat me! Beat me unconscious. Go ahead!
  *The janitor enters.*
CALLAHAN, *laughs, puts the "persuader" away:* You're too eager, Charley.
  Some-a them creeps like it, you know. Gives 'em a thrill. Look at that
  kisser! I'm a son-of-a-bitch, I'm right.
BRODY, *holding up a piece of silver:* Where'd you get this, Charley?
  CHARLEY *hangs his head.*
DAKIS, *annoyed, walks over to him:* Why don't you be professional, Charley.
  He's talking to you. . . . What's the matter? What are you hanging your
  head for? What are you ashamed of? Nobody made you be a burglar. You
  wanted to be a burglar—you're a burglar. So be a good one! Be proud of
  your chosen profession! Hold your head up. DAKIS *lifts* CHARLEY'S *head
  up by the chin.* That's better. You're a good thief, Charley. You're no bum.
  They wear sweaters. Not you!—You got a hundred-dollar suit on. You
  . . . Wait a minute! *Opens* CHARLEY'S *coat, looks at label.* Take it off, you
  bum. Stolen! The name's still in it. Where'd you get it?
CHARLEY, *takes off the coat, talking fast:* You mean it's stolen? O.K. O.K.
  I'll tell you the whole story . . . may I drop dead on this spot.
CALLAHAN: On this one? Be careful, Charley.
CHARLEY, *faster and faster, the nervous hands weaving in the air:* Honest!
  The truth! But don't tell Lewis!—He'll kill me. He makes out like he's a
  dummy, don't he? He ain't. He's smart. Ooh, he's as smart as they come.
  Look . . . I just been in New York two weeks. I came here from Pittsburgh
  two weeks ago. So help me. I lose my valise in the station. I meet this guy,
  Lewis, in a poolroom. . . .
CALLAHAN: Where? What poolroom?
CHARLEY: 14th Street, corner of 7th Avenue. . . . Look it up! Check it! I'm
  telling you the truth, so help me. I shoot a game of pool with him. He says
  to me, "You got a place to stay?" I says, "No." He says, "Share my flat."
  I say, "O.K." My suit's all dirty. He lends me this one. Says it belongs to
  his brother who's in Florida. *Pause. He looks up at the unbelieving faces
  circling him, smiles feebly.* So help me.
CALLAHAN: Charley, my boy—I could tell you a story would bring tears to
  your eyes. Get in there and take off your pants! *He pushes* CHARLEY *into
  the washroom.*
BRODY: Willy! Got an old pair of pants?
WILLY: Yeah, I got some downstairs! *Exit.*
BRODY: Not even smart enough to take out the label. The name's still in it.
  Jerome Armstrong . . .
CALLAHAN, *examining his list:* Wait! I got that squeal right here. I think
  there was a rape connected with this one.

BRODY: I wouldn't be surprised. *Leaves the door of the toilet for a second. Goes to the desk, picks up the lists.*

LIEUTENANT, *calls:* Dakis!

*DAKIS hurries to the LIEUTENANT's door, opens it.*

DAKIS: Yes, sir?

LIEUTENANT, *beckons him in; then, softly:* Wait downstairs for Mrs. McLeod. When she gets here, let me know foist.

DAKIS, *startled, murmurs:* Right, Chief.

LIEUTENANT: And . . . a . . . Nick . . . *Touches his lips.* Button 'em up.

DAKIS: Yes, sir.

*As he crosses to the gate, he glances at MCLEOD, his forehead furrows. Exit. The LIEUTENANT studies his cigar, frowns, goes off. Through the little window we see CHARLEY throw up the bathroom shade and tug at the iron grillwork. MCLEOD crosses to the washroom door, calls in.*

MCLEOD: The only way you can get out of there, Charley, is to jump down the toilet and pull the chain.

*JOE FEINSON comes in, tense and disturbed. He glances at MCLEOD curiously, comes over to BRODY.*

JOE: Lot of loot. They do the Zaza robbery?

BRODY, *calls in to CHARLEY:* You robbed that Zaza dame's flat, Charley?

CHARLEY, *calls out:* I don't know nuttin'!

BRODY: He don't know from nuttin'!

CALLAHAN: He's ignorant and he's proud of it.

JOE: Any good names?

BRODY: Don't know yet—

JOE: Any good addresses?

BRODY: They're taking the other bum around. He's identifying the houses. We'll crack it in an hour.

JOE, *saunters over to MCLEOD:* What's with Kurt Schneider?

MCLEOD: No story.

JOE: He left here twenty-five minutes ago in an ambulance. What happened? He trip?

MCLEOD: Yes.

JOE: Over his schnozzola?

MCLEOD: Could have. It's long enough.

JOE: No story?

MCLEOD: No.

JOE: His lawyer's sore as a boil. What happened?

MCLEOD: You tell me. You always have the story in your pocket.

JOE: Look, Seamus! There are angles here I don't feel happy about.

MCLEOD: What angles?

JOE: I don't know . . . yet. Come! Give! Off the record.

MCLEOD: You can print it if you want to. Kurt Schneider was a butcher who murdered two girls and got away with it. High time somebody put the fear of God in him. The law wouldn't, so I did. Print it, Yussel. Go ahead. You don't like cops. Here's your chance.

JOE: I don't like cops? For a smart guy, Seamus, you can be an awful schmoe. If I got fired tomorrow, you'd still find me here, hanging around, running errands for you guys, happy as a bird dog! I'm a buff from way back. I found a home. You know that.

MCLEOD: Sentimental slop, Yussel.

*A short, stout, timid man enters and looks about apprehensively.*

JOE: My sixth sense is still bothering me, Seamus.

MCLEOD: Have a doctor examine it. *To the newcomer.* Yes, sir? *The nervous man looks about, moistens his lips with his tongue, mops his brow, starts to speak.* MCLEOD *recognizes him.* Oh! Come in, Mr. Pritchett. We've been waiting for you.

MR. PRITCHETT: Did you get my money back?

MCLEOD: I'm afraid not.

MR. PRITCHETT: What'd he do with it?

MCLEOD: Women and plush saloons.

MR. PRITCHETT: Cabarets? I wouldn't have thought it. He seemed such an honest boy. I don't make many mistakes. I'm a pretty good student of human nature . . . usually.

MCLEOD: You'll be in court tomorrow morning?

MR. PRITCHETT: Oh, yes.

MCLEOD: We can count on you?

MR. PRITCHETT: When I make my mind up, I'm like iron.

MCLEOD: Fine! Thank you, Mr. Pritchett.

MR. PRITCHETT: Like iron.

MCLEOD: Arthur, on your feet! ARTHUR *rises.* Is this the boy?

MR. PRITCHETT, *with a huge sigh:* I'm afraid it is.

MCLEOD: Arthur, over here. ARTHUR *crosses to them. The phone rings.* MCLEOD *goes to the desk, picks up the receiver.* 21st Squad! McLeod!

BARNES, *at the washroom door:* All right, Charley. *He leads* CHARLEY *back into the squad room.* CHARLEY *is now wearing an ill-fitting, torn, and filthy pair of trousers, at which the eloquent hands pantomime disgust.*

MR. PRITCHETT: Well, Arthur, is this your journey's end?

ARTHUR: I guess so.

MR. PRITCHETT: Did I treat you badly?

ARTHUR: No, Mr. Pritchett.

MR. PRITCHETT: Did I pay you a decent salary?

ARTHUR: Yes.

MR. PRITCHETT: Then why did you do this to me?

    *SUSAN appears at the gate.*

SUSAN, *catches* MCLEOD's *eyes:* May I? *He nods. She enters, fumbling in her purse.*

MR. PRITCHETT, *to* ARTHUR: You spent my money on fast women?

ARTHUR: Just a second . . .

MR. PRITCHETT: No! I didn't grow my money on trees. I built up my business from a hole in the wall where I sold neckties two for a quarter. Thirty years I built it. By the sweat of my brow. I worked darn hard for it. I want my money back.

SUSAN: And you'll get it. I promise you. *She takes some money out of her purse.* The bank was closed. All I could scrape together tonight, was $120. *She hands the money to* MR. PRITCHETT. I'll have the rest for you tomorrow.

ARTHUR: Susan! Take that back!

SUSAN: Let me alone! Don't interfere, Jiggs!

MR. PRITCHETT: Who is this? Who are you, Miss?

SUSAN: I'm an old friend of Mr. Kindred's family. And I'd like to straighten this out with you, Mister . . . What is your name?

MR. PRITCHETT: Pritchett, Albert J. Pritchett.

SUSAN: Mr. Pritchett. How do you do? I'm Susan Carmichael.

MR. PRITCHETT: How do you do? You say you're prepared to return the rest of my money, young lady?

SUSAN: Yes. I'll sign a promissory note, or whatever you suggest.

MCLEOD, *into the phone:* One second! *To* SUSAN. Where'd you get that cash, Miss Carmichael?

SUSAN: I had some and I pawned some jewelry. Here are the tickets. Do you want to see them?

MCLEOD: If you don't mind. *Takes them, examines them.* Anything of your sister's here?

SUSAN: Nothing. Not a bobby pin.

MR. PRITCHETT: Is this the young lady who . . .

ARTHUR: No. She doesn't know anything about it.

SUSAN: I know all there is to know. *To* MR. PRITCHETT. Mr. Pritchett, this whole mess you can blame on *my sister.*

ARTHUR: What's the matter with you, Suzy? What are you dragging Joy into this for? She's got nothing to do with it.

SUSAN: Hasn't she?

ARTHUR: No.

SUSAN: I've got news for you. I just spoke to her on the phone. *Pause.*

ARTHUR: You didn't tell her?

SUSAN: Of course I did.

ARTHUR: What'd she say?

SUSAN: She was upset.

ARTHUR: Naturally, she would be. You shouldn't have . . .

SUSAN: Naturally! My blue-eyed sister was in a tizzy because she didn't want to get involved in your troubles. You know where I called her? At Walter Forbes's in Connecticut. She's afraid this might crimp her chances to be the next Mrs. Forbes. . . . Big deal!

ARTHUR: I know, Suzy. That's not news to me. I know.

SUSAN: Till ten minutes ago, I thought my sister was the cherub of the world. There wasn't anything I wouldn't have done for her. But if she can do this to you—to you, Jiggs—then I don't want any part of her. And I mean that. I'm through with her. I loathe her.

ARTHUR: Suzy! Take it easy.

SUSAN: All my life everything I wanted Joy got. All right! I didn't mind. I felt she was so special. She was entitled to be Queen. But now I'm through.

ARTHUR: Suzy, maybe you don't understand. Like everybody else, Joy is frightened. She wants to grab a little security. Don't blame her for it. I don't.

SUSAN: Security? You've seen Walter Forbes. He's had four wives. He gets falling-down drunk every single night of his life. Some security!

ARTHUR: He's very rich. You can't have everything.

SUSAN: Jiggs! Don't! Don't you be disgusting, too. *To* MR. PRITCHETT. Should I make out a note for the rest?

MCLEOD: Wait a minute. *He hangs up the phone, crosses to* MR. PRIT-CHETT, *takes the money from him, and hands it back to* SUSAN. We don't run a collection agency here! This man is a thief. We're here to prosecute criminals, not collect money.

*Detective* DAKIS *enters, crosses into the* LIEUTENANT's *office.*

SUSAN: He's not a criminal.

MCLEOD: Miss Carmichael, you seem like a very nice young lady. I'm going to give you some advice. I've seen a thousand like him. *He's no good!* Take your money and run.

DAKIS, *to the* LIEUTENANT: She's downstairs.

LIEUTENANT, *grunts, rises, goes to the door, calls:* McLeod!

MCLEOD: Yes, sir?

LIEUTENANT: Get me the old files on that Cottsworth squeal!

MCLEOD, *thinks:* 1938?

LIEUTENANT: Yeah.

MCLEOD: March 12th . . . LIEUTENANT *nods.* That'll be buried under a pile inside, I'll have to dig them up.

LIEUTENANT: Dig 'em up! Do it now!

McLeod: Yes, sir. *As he crosses off left, he throws his judgment at* Arthur *and* Susan. He spells one thing for you—*misery* the rest of your life. He's no good. Believe me, I know! *Exit.*

Susan, *indignantly:* That isn't true! *To* Mr. Pritchett. That isn't true. I've known Arthur all my life. He never did anything before that was dishonorable. He was the most respected boy in Ann Arbor.

*The* Lieutenant *nods to* Dakis, *who goes off to bring up* Mrs. McLeod. Brody *crosses down, listening to* Susan *and* Mr. Pritchett.

Mr. Pritchett: Little lady, once I saw a picture, *Less Miserables.*—A dandy! That was before your time. This Gene Valjeane—his sister's nine children are starving. He steals a loaf of bread. He goes to jail for—I don't know—twenty years. I'm on Gene Valjeane's side there. Impressed me very much. I gave a little talk on it at my lodge. . . . But this? I don't go along with. He wasn't starving. He had a good job. He went cabareting . . . with my money. Heck, I don't go to them, myself!

Brody: Mr. Pritchett, maybe once a year we get someone in here steals because he's actually hungry. And we're all on his side. I'd do the same, wouldn't you?

Mr. Pritchett: Absolutely. I always say self-preservation is the first law of nature.

Brody: But that's one in a thousand cases.

Mr. Pritchett: Exactly my point! And what did *he* do it for?

Arthur, *softly:* I did it because I was hungry.

Mr. Pritchett: What?

Arthur: Hungry. You can be hungry for other things besides bread. You've been decent to me, Mr. Pritchett. You trusted me, and I let you down. I'm sorry. . . . It's hard to explain, even to myself. I'd been separated from my girl for five years—five long, bloody years! The one human being in the world I loved. She's very beautiful, Mr. Pritchett. Tall, a silvery blonde girl, warm, understanding.

Susan: Jiggs, don't!

Arthur: At least she was. She was, Susan. We all change. When I came back from the war, I tried going back to school, but I couldn't get settled. I came to New York just to be near her. She'd moved on into a new world. She was out of my reach. I should have accepted that. I couldn't. To take her out to dinner and hold her hand cost a month's salary. I hung on, anyway. Last Wednesday I had to face it. I was going to lose my girl. She told me she wanted to marry someone else. I made a final grandstand play for her. Late collections had come in. Your money was in my pocket. I blew the works on her. I didn't give a damn about anything except holding on to her. It was my last chance. I lost anyway. . . .

BRODY: You admit you did wrong?

ARTHUR: Yes, God, yes!

BRODY: You're willing to make restitution?

ARTHUR: If I get the chance.

SUSAN: Tomorrow morning. I promise you!

BRODY: That's in his favor. How do you feel, Mr. Pritchett?

MR. PRITCHETT: Well . . .

BRODY: This kid has a fine war record, too, remember.

MR. PRITCHETT: I know.

BRODY: He took a lot of chances for us. Maybe we ought to take one for him. You see, these kids today got problems nobody ever had. We don't even understand them. New blood. We're varicosed. If a new world is gonna be made outa this mess, looks like they're the ones gotta do it.

MR. PRITCHETT: It's funny you should say that. I was talking to my brother-in-law only the other night about my nephew, and I made exactly that point. I was saying to him . . .

BRODY: Mr. Pritchett, do you mind stepping over here a minute?

MR. PRITCHETT: Not at all! *Rises, follows him.*

BRODY: You, too, Miss!

*SUSAN follows BRODY off left.*

CHARLEY, *stamps his foot:* Give me another cigarette.

BARNES: What do you do? Eat these things?

CHARLEY: Give me a cigarette!

*BARNES gives him another cigarette.*

*DAKIS enters, leading MRS. McLEOD to the LIEUTENANT's office. MARY McLEOD is a pretty young woman, with blonde hair, big gray, troubled eyes, a sweet mouth, and delicate nose. She is inexpensively but attractively dressed. There is something immediately appealing about her. She is very feminine and very soft, and at the moment her evident terror augments these qualities.*

JOE, *sees her, is startled, rises, stops her:* How do you do, Mrs. McLeod! Remember me? I'm Joe Feinson, the reporter.

MARY, *disturbed and overwrought, studies him for a split second, then recalls him:* Oh, yes, of course. I met you with my husband. *Her mouth trembles.* JOE *smiles, nods.* What's happened to Jim?

JOE, *grins, reassuringly:* Nothing. He's all right. He's in there.

MARY: Mr. Feinson, please tell me!

JOE: I am.

DAKIS: This way, please. . . . *She follows him into the LIEUTENANT's office.*

LIEUTENANT: How do you do, Mrs. McLeod?

MARY: Lieutenant Monoghan?

LIEUTENANT: Yes, ma'am.

MARY: What is this about, Lieutenant?

LIEUTENANT: Have a seat?

MARY: Where's my husband?

LIEUTENANT: He'll be back in a few minutes.

MARY: He hasn't been *shot?*

LIEUTENANT, *reassuringly:* No!

MARY: I had a terrible feeling that he . . .

LIEUTENANT: Nothing like that. He's all right.

MARY: You're sure? You're not trying to break it easy?

LIEUTENANT: Nothing like that! I give you my word. You'll see him in a
few minutes.

MARY: Then, what is it? What's wrong?

LIEUTENANT: A certain situation has come up, and you might be able to help
us out.

MARY: Me? . . . I'm all at sea, Lieutenant!

LIEUTENANT: Mrs. McLeod, your husband and I never got along too well,
but I want you to know that right now I'm sticking my neck out a mile to
save him. I'm not doing it because I like him—I don't. I'm doing it because
he has a value here and I need him on the squad. So, like I say, I'm going
to help him, if you help me.

MARY: What kind of trouble is Jim in?

LIEUTENANT: A prisoner here was assaulted, maybe injured, by your
husband.

MARY: Jim wouldn't do that.

LIEUTENANT: He did. You'll have to take my word for it.

MARY: Then there must have been a reason. A very good reason.

LIEUTENANT: That's what I have to find out.

MARY: Jim is kind and gentle.

LIEUTENANT: That's one side of him.

MARY: It's the only side I know. I've never seen any other. *Pause.*

LIEUTENANT: Please sit down!

MARY: Is this man badly hurt?

LIEUTENANT: I don't know yet. This could become serious, Mrs. McLeod.
This might cost your husband his job. He could even wind up in jail.

MARY, *sinks into the chair:* How can I help?

LIEUTENANT: By answering some questions. By telling me the truth. Are you
willing to go along?

MARY: Yes, of course.

LIEUTENANT: Did you ever run into a man named Kurt Schneider?

MARY, *hoarsely:* No. *Coughs.*

LIEUTENANT: My cigar bothering you?

MARY: No. I love the smell of a cigar. My father always smoked them.

LIEUTENANT: Did you ever hear your husband mention that name?

MARY: What name?

LIEUTENANT: This prisoner's name. Kurt Schneider.

MARY, *shakes her head:* Jim made it a rule never to discuss his work with me.

LIEUTENANT: It's a good rule. We don't like to bring this sordid stuff into our homes.

MARY: I'm well trained now. I don't ask.

LIEUTENANT: How long you been married?

MARY: Three years.

LIEUTENANT: It took me ten years to train my wife. It's a tough life—being married to a cop.

MARY: I don't think so. I'm happy.

LIEUTENANT: You love your husband?

MARY: Very much.

LIEUTENANT: Where did you live before you were married?
    *The phone in the squad room rings.*

DAKIS, *picks up the receiver:* 21st Squad—Detective Dakis.

MARY: New York.

LIEUTENANT: You don't sound like a native. Where you from? Upstate?

MARY: Highland Falls. You've got a good ear.

LIEUTENANT: It's my business.

DAKIS, *knocks at the* LIEUTENANT'S *door, opens it:* Captain on the phone, Lieutenant.

LIEUTENANT, *nods to* MRS. McLEOD: Excuse me! ... *He picks up the phone, turns away from her, and talks into the mouthpiece sotto voce. In the squad room, the* SHOPLIFTER *rises and stretches.*

SHOPLIFTER, *coyly to* CALLAHAN, *who is at the desk, typing:* You don't look like a detective.

CALLAHAN: No? What does a detective look like?

SHOPLIFTER: They wear derbies. *She giggles archly.* You're a nice-looking fellow.

CALLAHAN: Thanks.

SHOPLIFTER: Are you married?

CALLAHAN: Yes.

SHOPLIFTER, *disgusted—this is the story of her life:* Ya-a-a!
    *She slaps the paper on the chair, sits down again.*

LIEUTENANT: Thanks Captain! *Hangs up, turns to* MRS. McLEOD, *resumes his interrogation.* When'd you leave Highland Falls?

MARY: The spring of 1941. I got a job in a defense plant.

LIEUTENANT: Where?

MARY: In Newark.

LIEUTENANT: This doctor was practicing in Newark at about that time.

MARY: Doctor?

LIEUTENANT: Schneider.

MARY: Oh, he's a doctor?

LIEUTENANT: Yes. You never met him? Around Newark, maybe?

MARY: No. I don't know him.

LIEUTENANT: He knows you.

MARY: What makes you think that?

LIEUTENANT: He said so.

MARY, *avoids his probing stare:* I'm afraid he's mistaken.

LIEUTENANT: He was positive . . . Kurt Schneider! Ring any bells?

MARY: No. I'm afraid not.

LIEUTENANT: You averted my gaze then. Why?

MARY: Did I? I wasn't conscious of it.

LIEUTENANT: Are you sure a Dr. Schneider never treated you?

MARY, *indignantly:* Certainly not. I just told you, "No."

LIEUTENANT: Why are you so indignant? I didn't say what he treated you for.

MARY: Did this man tell my husband he treated me?

LIEUTENANT: If you'll tell the truth, Mrs. McLeod, you'll help your husband. You'll save me time and trouble. But that's all. In the end, I'll get the correct answers. We got a hundred ways of finding out the truth.

MARY: I don't know what you're talking about, Lieutenant. I'm not lying.

   DETECTIVE GALLAGHER *enters with* TAMI GIACOPPETTI, *handsome, swarthy, on the sharp, loud side, very sure of himself, very sure.*

GIACOPPETTI: Can I use the phone, Champ?

GALLAGHER: Not yet, Tami. *Knocks at the* LIEUTENANT'S *door.*

GIACOPPETTI: O.K., Champ.

LIEUTENANT: Yeah! GALLAGHER *enters and hands a note to the* LIEUTENANT. *The* LIEUTENANT *glances at it, pockets it, and dismisses* GALLAGHER *with a gesture.* Mrs. McLeod, I'm going to ask you a very personal question. Now, don't get angry. I would never dream of asking any woman this type of question unless I had to. You must regard me as the impersonal voice of the law. Mrs. McLeod, did Dr. Schneider ever perform an abortion on you?

MARY: You've no right to ask me that.

LIEUTENANT: I have to do my job—and my job is to find out the truth. Let's not waste any more time! Please answer that question!

MARY: It seems to me I have some rights to privacy. My past life concerns nobody but me.

LIEUTENANT: You have the right to tell the truth. Did he?

MARY: No, Lieutenant Monoghan, he did not.

LIEUTENANT: Does this name mean anything to you: Tami Giacoppetti?

MARY: No.

*The* LIEUTENANT *goes to the door, beckons.* GALLAGHER *nudges* TAMI, *who walks inside, sees* MARY, *stops in his tracks. The smile on his face fades.*

GIACOPPETTI, *very softly:* Hello, Mary. *She withers, all evasion gone; her head droops as she avoids their glances.*

LIEUTENANT, *to* MRS. MCLEOD, *indicating the anteroom:* Would you mind stepping in here a minute! *To* GIACOPPETTI. Be right with you. *He leads her into the anteroom.*

*Whistling a gay tune,* DETECTIVE O'BRIEN *enters the squad room, followed by the burglar* LEWIS *and a* COP.

BARNES: Here's your boyfriend, Charley!

DAKIS: How'd you do?

O'BRIEN: We got the addresses and most of the names.

DAKIS: How many?

O'BRIEN: Nine. *To* LEWIS. Sit down! Over here! Lewis has been very cooperative.

CALLAHAN *has taken off his coat and puts his gun in his holster again. As he bends down over the desk,* CHARLEY *eyes the gun, tries to edge over, stands up.*

CALLAHAN: Whither to, Charley?

CHARLEY: I got to go.

CALLAHAN: Again? This makes the sixth time.

CHARLEY: Well, I'm noivous.

BARNES: Sit down, Charley!

CALLAHAN: He's noivous, poor kid.

O'BRIEN: He needs a vacation.

DAKIS: He's gonna get one. A long one. At state expense.

CALLAHAN, *dialing a number:* Nuttin's too good for Charley. *On phone.* Hello, Mrs. Lundstrom? This is Detective Callahan of the Twenty-foist Precinct. We got that property was burglarized from your apartment. Will you please come down and identify it? Yeah! Yeah! We got 'em. Right. Yes, ma'am. *Hangs up, looks at the squeal card, dials another number.*

O'BRIEN, *on phone, simultaneously:* Hello, Mr. Donatello, please. . . . Mr. Donatello? This is Detective O'Brien of the 21st Squad. Yes, sir. I think we've caught them. Yes. I have some articles here. Not all. Would you mind coming down to the station house and identifying them? Right. *He hangs up.*

CALLAHAN, *on phone:* Hello! Mrs. Demetrios? This is Detective Callahan.

Remember me? Twenty-foist Squad. Yeah. I'm still roarin'! How are you, Toots? *Laughs.* Retoin match? Where's your husband tonight? Okay. *McLeod enters with an ancient bundle of records wrapped in a sheet of dusty paper and tied with twine. He is blowing off clouds of dust.* I'll be off duty after midnight. *Starts to hang up, suddenly remembers the purpose of the phone call.* Oh, by the way, we got that stuff was boiglarized from your apartment. Come down and identify it. O.K., yuh barracuda! *Hangs up.* A man-eater.

O'BRIEN: You watch it!

CALLAHAN: What I don't do for the good of the soivice. I should be getting foist-grade money.

McLEOD, *undoing the package:* You'll be getting a "foist"-grade knock on the head.

CALLAHAN, *disdainfully:* Brain trust. *He walks away.*

BRODY, *approaches McLeod:* Say, Jim. I had a long talk with Mr. Pritchett, and he's willing to drop the charges.

McLEOD: He is? *Turns to Mr. Pritchett.* What's this about, Mr. Pritchett?

MR. PRITCHETT: I decided not to bring charges against . . . *Nods toward* ARTHUR.

McLEOD: I thought you were going to go through with this.

MR. PRITCHETT: I'd like to give the boy another chance.

McLEOD: To steal from someone else?

MR. PRITCHETT: I wouldn't want this on my conscience.

McLEOD: Supposing he commits a worse crime. What about your conscience then, Mr. Pritchett?

MR. PRITCHETT: I'll gamble. I'm a gambler. I bet on horses—this once I'll bet on a human being.

McLEOD: Stick to horses—the percentage is better.

BRODY: Wait a minute, Jim. I advised Mr. Pritchett to do this. I thought . . .

McLEOD, *harshly:* You had no right to do that, Lou. This is my case. You know better.

BRODY: I didn't think you'd mind.

McLEOD: Well, I do.

BRODY, *angrily:* Well, I'm sorry!!

SUSAN: But I'm going to return the money. And if he's satisfied, what difference does it make to you?

McLEOD: It isn't as easy as that. This isn't a civil action: this is a *criminal* action.

GUS, *enters with sheet in his hand:* Jim! Look at this sheet on Charley! *McLeod takes it, studies it.* As long as your arm. *To Barnes.* Keep your eye on that son-of-a-bitch!

MᴄLᴇᴏᴅ, *studying the sheet grimly:* Hm! *He crosses with* Gᴜs *to the gate, exits into the hallway.*

Mʀ. Pʀɪᴛᴄʜᴇᴛᴛ, *to* Bʀᴏᴅʏ: But you said . . .

Bʀᴏᴅʏ: I'm sorry. I made a mistake. It's his case. The disposition of it is up to him.

Sᴜsᴀɴ: But if everybody concerned is . . .

Bʀᴏᴅʏ: I'm sorry, girlie. You gotta leave me outa this. I got no right to inter-fere. Take it up with him. *Walks off left, leaving* Sᴜsᴀɴ *and* Pʀɪᴛᴄʜᴇᴛᴛ *suspended in mid-air.* Sᴜsᴀɴ *sinks into a chair, awaiting* McLᴇᴏᴅ's *return, glancing off despairingly in his direction.* Pʀɪᴛᴄʜᴇᴛᴛ *walks up to the gate, leans on it, looking off into the hallway. The* Lɪᴇᴜᴛᴇɴᴀɴᴛ *returns to his office from the anteroom.*

Gɪᴀᴄᴏᴘᴘᴇᴛᴛɪ, *rises:* What's this about, Champ?

Lɪᴇᴜᴛᴇɴᴀɴᴛ: Sit down, Tami! *Picks up* Tᴀᴍɪ's *hat from the desk, looks at the label in it.* Dobbs Beaver? *Impressed.* A twenty-buck hat. You must be rolling. *Hands* Tᴀᴍɪ *his hat.*

Gɪᴀᴄᴏᴘᴘᴇᴛᴛɪ, *taking it:* Forty bucks. I'm comfortable. No complaints. What's on your mind, Champ?

Lɪᴇᴜᴛᴇɴᴀɴᴛ: The woman you just said hello to.

Gɪᴀᴄᴏᴘᴘᴇᴛᴛɪ: Mary! What kind of trouble could she be in?

Lɪᴇᴜᴛᴇɴᴀɴᴛ: I'd just like a little information.

Gɪᴀᴄᴏᴘᴘᴇᴛᴛɪ, *frowns:* That girl's a hundred percent. I wouldn't say a word against her.

Lɪᴇᴜᴛᴇɴᴀɴᴛ: You don't have to. She ain't in no trouble.

Gɪᴀᴄᴏᴘᴘᴇᴛᴛɪ: No. That's good. What do you want from me, Champ?

Lɪᴇᴜᴛᴇɴᴀɴᴛ: Mr. Giacoppetti, all this is off the record.

Gɪᴀᴄᴏᴘᴘᴇᴛᴛɪ: When I talk, it's always for the record, Champ. I only say something when I got something to say, Champ.

Lɪᴇᴜᴛᴇɴᴀɴᴛ: Look, Giacoppetti, I'm Lieutenant Monoghan. I'm in charge here. Keep your tongue in your mouth, and we'll get along.

Gɪᴀᴄᴏᴘᴘᴇᴛᴛɪ: Mind if I phone my lawyer?

Lɪᴇᴜᴛᴇɴᴀɴᴛ: It ain't necessary.

Gɪᴀᴄᴏᴘᴘᴇᴛᴛɪ: My lawyer gets mad.

Lɪᴇᴜᴛᴇɴᴀɴᴛ: Nothing you say here will be held against you, understand? I give you my woid.

Gɪᴀᴄᴏᴘᴘᴇᴛᴛɪ: I won't hurt that girl.

Lɪᴇᴜᴛᴇɴᴀɴᴛ: I don't want you to. She's only a witness. It's someone else.

Gɪᴀᴄᴏᴘᴘᴇᴛᴛɪ: O.K. Shoot!

Lɪᴇᴜᴛᴇɴᴀɴᴛ: Married?

Gɪᴀᴄᴏᴘᴘᴇᴛᴛɪ: Yeah.

Lɪᴇᴜᴛᴇɴᴀɴᴛ: How long?

GIACOPPETTI: Fifteen years. What a racket that is!

LIEUTENANT: You're an expert, ain't you?

GIACOPPETTI: On what? Marriage?

LIEUTENANT: Rackets.

GIACOPPETTI: I'm a legitimate businessman. Take it up with my attorney.

LIEUTENANT: Look, Mr. Giacoppetti. We've got a sheet on you. We know you're in black market up to your neck. But we don't operate in the state of New Jersey. And what went on there ain't none of our business. Unless you make it so. Kapish?

GIACOPPETTI: Yeah, I kapish.

LIEUTENANT: Got any kids?

GIACOPPETTI: No.

LIEUTENANT: I got five. You don't know what you're missing, Tami.

GIACOPPETTI, *rises, furious:* Don't rub salt in! I know. I got a wife as big as the Sahara Desert—and twice as sterile. I got nine brothers, four sisters . . . all on my payroll. None of 'em worth anything. They got kids—like rabbits they got 'em—nephews, nieces, all over the lot. But a guy like me, I should become a nation, and I got no kids. Not one. So don't rub salt in, eh?

LIEUTENANT, *laughs:* O.K. I guess I know how you feel.

GIACOPPETTI, *controls himself, smiles sheepishly:* You're a sharpshooter, Champ. You hit me right on my spot.

LIEUTENANT: When did you know this girl?

GIACOPPETTI: Seven years ago.

LIEUTENANT: You like her?

GIACOPPETTI: I was crazy about her. She was my girl. I'd a married her, if I could a gotten a divorce.

LIEUTENANT: What broke it up?

GIACOPPETTI: I don't know.

LIEUTENANT: What do you think?

GIACOPPETTI: I think maybe I better call my lawyer.

LIEUTENANT: Come on, Giacoppetti. What the hell—you've gone this far. It's off the record.

GIACOPPETTI: Aah, she give me the air! She got "caught" . . . and that soured her on me. Dames! Who can understand them?

LIEUTENANT: Send her to a doctor?

GIACOPPETTI: To a doctor? Me? I wanted that kid. I told her: "Give me a son—anything goes." Anything she wants. The moon out of the sky . . . I'd get it for her. Dames! Who can understand them? She goes off. That's the last I see of her. Next thing I know I hear she went to some doctor. I

went looking for her. If I'd'a' found her, I'd'a' broken her neck. I found
him, though. I personally beat the hell out of him. Sent him to a hospital.

LIEUTENANT: What was his name?

GIACOPPETTI: A Dutchman. Schneider . . . something.

LIEUTENANT: Kurt Schneider.

GIACOPPETTI: That's it.

LIEUTENANT, *rises:* Thank you, Tami!

GIACOPPETTI: That all?

   LIEUTENANT *opens the door of the anteroom, beckons to* MARY.

LIEUTENANT: Almost.

GIACOPPETTI: Now will you tell me what this is about?

LIEUTENANT: Just a minute. MARY *enters.* Mrs. McLeod, Mr. Giacoppetti
has told me everything.

MARY: He has?

GIACOPPETTI: In a case like this, they find out, anyway. It's better to . . .
   MARY *begins to weep.*

LIEUTENANT: Now, now! . . . *Pause.* I'm sorry, Mrs. McLeod. Would you
like a glass of water?

MARY, *nods:* Please! *He fetches her a glass of water.*

LIEUTENANT: Mr. Giacoppetti! *Nods toward the anteroom. They both exit.*
   *Outside, night perceptibly lowers over the city. The squad room grows*
ominously dark. MCLEOD *enters,* CHARLEY's *sheet in his hand.*

MCLEOD: So you didn't done it, Charley? *He switches on the lights.*

CHARLEY, *weeping and wringing his hands:* No! No! On my mother's grave!

MCLEOD: And you never been in jail?

CHARLEY, *wailing:* May I drop dead on this spot! What do you guys want
from me?

MCLEOD, *to* MR. PRITCHETT: Heartbreaking, isn't it? *Crosses to* CHARLEY.
These are your fingerprints, Charley. They never lie. *He reads the sheet.*
Burglary, eight arrests. Five assaults. Seven muggings. Three rapes. Two
arrests for murder. Six extortions. Three jail sentences. One prison break!
Nice little sheet, Charley? *To* BARNES. He's a four-time loser. You have a
club. If he makes one false move—you know what to do with it—hit him
over the head.

BARNES: Don't worry, I will.

MCLEOD: Book him! *Nods in* LEWIS's *direction.* This bum, too. LEWIS *rises.*

CHARLEY, *abandons his weeping act abruptly, looks at* MCLEOD, *and begins
to grin:* Got a cigarette?

MCLEOD, *furiously:* What do you want—room service?

CHARLEY, *laughing:* It's the green-light hotel, ain't it?

McLEOD: Take him away!

BARNES: O.K., Charley. *To* LEWIS. Come on.

*Exit* BARNES, LEWIS, *and* CHARLEY, *the latter laughing raucously at* McLEOD.

McLEOD, *turns to* PRITCHETT: Don't invest these criminals with your nervous system, Mr. Pritchett. Sure! They laugh, they cry; but don't think it's your laughter or your tears. It isn't. They're a different species, a different breed. Believe me, I know.

*JOE FEINSON enters.*

SUSAN, *shrilly:* My God—didn't you ever make a mistake?

McLEOD: Yes. When I was new on this job we brought in two boys who were caught stealing from a car. They looked like babies. They cried. I let them go. Two nights later—two nights later—one of them held up a butcher in Harlem. Shot him through the head and killed him. Yes, I made a mistake, and I'm not going to make it again.

SUSAN: But, Officer, you . . .

McLEOD, *harshly:* Young lady, I don't want to discuss this with you. Now don't interrupt me!

ARTHUR, *rises:* Don't talk to her like that. She has a right to speak.

McLEOD, *his face goes black with anger. He roars at* ARTHUR: Shut up! Sit down! *ARTHUR sits.* McLEOD *controls himself, lights a cigarette, his hand trembling.* When you're dealing with the criminal mind, softness is dangerous, Mr. Pritchett.

MR. PRITCHETT: But if it's a first offense . . .

McLEOD: It's never a first offense: it's just the first time they get caught.

SUSAN: Why are you so vicious?

McLEOD: I'm not vicious, young lady. I didn't steal this man's money. *Extinguishes the match violently and hurls it in* ARTHUR's *direction.* He did. *To* MR. PRITCHETT. This is a war, Mr. Pritchett. We know it, they know it, but you don't. We're your army. We're here to protect you. But you've got to cooperate. I'm sick and tired of massaging the complainant into doing his simple duty! You civilians are too lazy or too selfish or too scared or just too indifferent to even want to appear in court and see the charges through that you, yourselves, bring. That makes us—street cleaners. They have a stick, sweep out the streets; we have a stick, sweep out the human garbage; they pile it in wagons, dump it in the East River; we pile it in wagons, dump it in the Tombs. And what happens?—The next day . . . all back again.

MR. PRITCHETT: But if I get paid . . .

McLEOD, *impatiently:* I don't care about that. This is a criminal action. Are you or aren't you going through with it? Because I'm not going to let him go.

MR. PRITCHETT: If I don't bring charges?

McLEOD: Then I'm going to book him, anyway, and *subpoena you* into court.

MR. PRITCHETT: Well . . . I . . . I . . .

McLEOD: It's my duty to protect you, in spite of yourself.

MR. PRITCHETT: I guess I've got to leave it up to you, Officer. Whatever you say.

McLEOD: I say, "Prosecute"!

MR. PRITCHETT: All right! You know best. *To SUSAN.* I'm sorry. But he had no right to rob me in the first place. That was a terrible thing to do.

McLEOD, *takes him by the arm, leads him to the gate:* We won't take up any more of your time. I'll see you in court tomorrow morning at ten.

MR. PRITCHETT *goes.*

SUSAN: Mr. Pritchett . . . *She rises and runs after him.*

McLEOD, *witheringly:* There goes John Q. Public, "a man of iron."

JOE: Humble yourself, sweetheart, humble yourself!

McLEOD: What?

JOE: Seamus, Seamus, why must you always make everything so black and white? Remember, we're all of us falling down all the time. Don't be so intolerant.

McLEOD: You're out of line.

JOE: Listen to me, Seamus. Listen! I love you, and I'm trying to warn you.

McLEOD: What about? What's on your mind?

JOE: You're digging your own grave. A bottomless pit, baby. It's right there in front of you. One more step and you're in. Humble yourself, sweetheart, humble yourself!

McLEOD: You're very Delphic today, Yussel. What's the oracle of CCNY trying to tell me?

There's a long pause. JOE *examines his face. All friendship is gone out of it. It's hard as granite, now, the jaw muscles bulging. JOE smiles sadly to himself, shakes his head.*

JOE: Nothing. Forget it. *He goes.*

LIEUTENANT, *returns to his office, followed by* GIACOPPETTI. MARY *rises.* Feel better now?

MARY: Yes. Thank you.

LIEUTENANT: Are you ready to tell me the truth?

MARY: Yes.

LIEUTENANT: Your husband's been persecutin' Schneider for over a year because of this?

MARY: No.

LIEUTENANT: Schneider's attorney says so.

MARY: I don't care what he says. Jim never knew. He never knew. I'm sure
of that.

LIEUTENANT: Careful now! Weigh your words. This is very important. Any
minute that phone'll ring. If Schneider is critically hurt, it's out of my
hands. The next second, this case'll be with the homicide squad. The
Commissioner'll be here, the District Attorney. If that happens, I gotta
have all the facts.

MARY: Jim didn't know.

LIEUTENANT: That's the question I gotta be sure of . . . now. *Thinks a moment, goes to the door, calls.* McLeod!

MCLEOD: Yes, sir? *The* LIEUTENANT *motions him in.* MCLEOD *enters, sees*
MARY, *stops short.* Mary! What are you doing here? What's this, Lieutenant? What's my wife . . .

LIEUTENANT: I sent for her.

MCLEOD: Why?

LIEUTENANT: This is Mr. Giacoppetti.

GIACOPPETTI: Hi, Champ!

MCLEOD: What's this about, Lieutenant?

LIEUTENANT: Schneider! Why'd you lie to me?

MCLEOD: I didn't lie to you.

MARY: May I . . . may I . . . please.

LIEUTENANT: Yes. Go ahead. *Watching* MCLEOD.

MARY: Jim, the lieutenant won't believe me that you knew nothing about
this. . . .

MCLEOD: About what, Mary?

MARY: Dr. Schneider.

MCLEOD: What's he got to do with you?

MARY: This man you struck, this Dr. Schneider . . .

MCLEOD: Don't keep saying that, Mary. He's no doctor.

MARY: He isn't? I thought he was. I . . . had occasion to see him once. I went
to him once when I needed help.

MCLEOD: You *what? After a long pause, studies her, murmurs to himself.*

MARY: A long time ago, Jim. *To the* LIEUTENANT. I told you he didn't . . .

MCLEOD: Wait a minute! *Turns to* GIACOPPETTI. What's he got to do with
this?

MARY: We were going together.

MCLEOD: I see.

MARY: I . . .

McLEOD: O.K. Diagrams aren't necessary. I get the picture.

GIACOPPETTI: I beat the hell out of this Schneider myself. *He touches McLEOD on the arm. McLEOD, with a growl, slaps his hand.* Geez! *Holds his hand in agony.*

LIEUTENANT: Cut that out!

GIACOPPETTI: I don't have to take that from you, Champ!

McLEOD: Touch me again and I'll tear your arm out of the socket.

LIEUTENANT, *to McLEOD:* You cut that out! In one second I'm going to flatten you, myself. *There is a long pause.*

McLEOD: Do you mind if I talk to my wife . . . alone?

> *The LIEUTENANT looks at MARY.*

MARY: Please!

LIEUTENANT: All right, Tami. You can go.

> *GIACOPPETTI goes. The LIEUTENANT walks into his anteroom, slams the door.*

MARY: I'm terribly sorry, Jim. Please forgive me. *She touches him; he moves away to avoid her touch.* Is this man badly hurt?

McLEOD: No.

MARY: Then you're not in serious trouble, Jim?

McLEOD: He's only acting. Nothing will come of it.

MARY: You're sure?

McLEOD: Yes.

MARY: Thank God for that.

McLEOD: My immaculate wife!

MARY: I never said I was.

McLEOD: You never said you weren't! Why didn't you tell me?

MARY: I loved you and I was afraid of losing you.

McLEOD: How long did you go with him?

MARY: A few months.

McLEOD: How many?

MARY: About four.

McLEOD: Four isn't a few.

MARY: No, I suppose not.

McLEOD: Did he give you money?

MARY: No.

McLEOD: But he did give you presents?

MARY: Yes. He gave me some presents, of course.

McLEOD: Expensive ones?

MARY: I don't know.

McLEOD: What do you mean you don't know?

MARY: I don't know. What difference does it make?

McLEOD: This difference. I'd just as soon Schneider died. I'd sooner go to jail for twenty years—than find out this way that my wife was a whore.

MARY: Don't say that, Jim.

McLEOD: That's the word, I didn't invent it. That's what they call it.

MARY: I don't care about "they." I only care about you, Jim, and it isn't true. You know it isn't true.

McLEOD: Why didn't you tell me?

MARY: I wanted to, but I didn't dare. I would have lost you.

McLEOD: I thought I knew you. I thought you were everything good and pure. . . . And with a pig like that! Live dirt!

MARY: Jim, don't judge me. Try and understand. Right and wrong aren't always as simple as they seem to you. I was on my own for the first time in a large city. The war was on. Everything was feverish! I'd only been out with kids my own age until I met this man. He paid me a lot of attention. I was flattered. I'd never met anyone like him before in my whole life. I thought he was romantic and glamorous. I thought I was in love with him.

McLEOD: Are you trying to justify yourself in those terms?

MARY: Not justify! Just explain. It was wrong. I know it. I discovered that for myself.

McLEOD: When? Just now?

*The phone rings. DAKIS answers it.*

MARY: I'm trying to make my life everything you want it to be. If I could make my past life over, I'd do that, too, gladly. But I can't. No one can. I made a mistake. I admit it. I've paid for it . . . plenty. Isn't that enough?

DAKIS, *crosses to the LIEUTENANT's office, enters:* Where's the lieutenant?

McLEOD: Inside.

DAKIS, *shouting off:* Lieutenant!—Hospital's on the phone.

LIEUTENANT, *enters and picks up the phone:* Yeah! . . . Put him on! . . . Yeah? You're sure? O.K., Doc. Thank you. *He hangs up.* The devil takes care of his own! . . . It looks like Schneider's all right. They can't find anything wrong with him.

*There is a long pause.*

MARY: May I go now?

LIEUTENANT: Yes, Mrs. McLeod.

*Exit LIEUTENANT.*

MARY: Jim, I beg you. Please understand.

McLEOD: What's there to understand? . . . You got undressed before him. . . .

MARY: Jim!

McLEOD: You went to bed with him.

Mary: Jim! I can't take much more of this.

McLeod: You carried his child awhile inside you . . . and then you killed it.

Mary: Yes. That's true.

McLeod: Everything I hate . . . even murder . . . What the hell's left to understand!

Mary, *completely stunned, looks at his face, swollen with anger, the face of a madman. She backs up to the door, suddenly opens it, turns, flees.*

*CURTAIN*

## ACT THREE

*The scene is the same, eight-thirty by the clock on the wall. Night has fallen. The black, looming masses and the million twinkling eyes of "the city that never sleeps," the flashing General Motors sign, the church spire and cross seem to enter into and become a part of this strange room.*

*At rise, the* LIEUTENANT's *office is dark and empty. The squad room, however, is crowded and humming like a dynamo. Half a dozen civilians, under the guidance of* DAKIS *and* CALLAHAN, *are identifying the stolen property piled high on the table.* BRODY *is fingerprinting* LEWIS. CHARLEY *is sitting, pantomiming to himself, the colored officer watching him closely.* MCLEOD *is seated at the typewriter tapping off* ARTHUR's *"squeal";* AR-THUR *is seated to the right of the typewriter desk, his eyes registering the nightmare.* SUSAN, *behind* ARTHUR's *chair, hovers over him, staring down at him like some impotent guardian angel. Near the same desk the* SHOPLIFT-ER's *big, innocent calf-eyes are busy watching, darting in all directions at once, enjoying the Roman holiday. A very chic lady and gentleman in formal evening attire, who are here to claim stolen property, are being photographed by a newspaper photographer.* JOE *weaves in and out of the throng, gleaning his information and jotting it down in a notebook.*

PHOTOGRAPHER, *to the chic lady in the evening gown, who is posing for him, holding a stolen silver soup tureen:* Hold up the loot! Little higher, please! *She holds it higher. Flash!* Just one more, please!
MCLEOD, *at the desk, to* ARTHUR: Hair?
ARTHUR: Brown.
MCLEOD: Eyes?
ARTHUR: Eyes? I don't know . . . greenish?
MCLEOD, *peering at* ARTHUR: Look brown.
SUSAN: Hazel. Brown and green flecked with gold.
    *Photographer's flash!*
MCLEOD: Hazel. *Types.*
PHOTOGRAPHER: Ankyou! *Reloads his camera.*
DAKIS, *to the* GENTLEMAN: Sign here. *He signs.* That's all. We'll notify you when to come down to pick up the rest of your property.
GENTLEMAN, *plucks out some tickets from his wallet, hands them to* DAKIS: Excellent work, Officer, excellent! My compliments.
    *Exit* GENTLEMAN *and* LADY.
PHOTOGRAPHER, *to* JOE: Did you get the name?
JOE, *writing story in notebook:* I got it, I got it.
PHOTOGRAPHER: Park Avenue?
JOE: Spell it backwards.

PHOTOGRAPHER: K-R-A-P.

JOE: You got it.

*The* PHOTOGRAPHER *chortles.*

DAKIS, *examines the tickets with a slow, mounting burn. To* CALLAHAN: How do you like that jerk? Two tickets for the flower show yet! There are two kinds of people in this precinct—the crumbs and the eelite; and the eelite are crumbs.

    CALLAHAN *laughs through his nose.* DAKIS *sits down and checks through his "squeals."*

MCLEOD, *typing:* You might as well go home now, young lady; as soon as we finish this we're through.

SUSAN: A few minutes more. . . . Please!

MCLEOD, *sighs. To* ARTHUR: Weight?

ARTHUR: A hundred and fifty-two.

MCLEOD: Height?

ARTHUR: Five-eleven.

MCLEOD: Identifying marks? Scars? Come here! *Pulls* ARTHUR'S *face around.* Scar on the left cheek. *Types.* And a tattoo. Which arm was that on? ARTHUR *raises his left hand.* Left? A heart and the name "Joy."

    *The phone rings.* CALLAHAN *answers it.*

CALLAHAN: 21st Squad Detectives, Callahan. Yeah? A jumper? Fifty-thoid Street? MCLEOD *stops typing, listens.* Her name? Mc . . . what . . . ? Geez!

MCLEOD, *calls across the room, sharply:* What was that name?

CALLAHAN, *on the phone:* Wait a minute! . . . *To* MCLEOD. What's 'at, Jim?

MCLEOD, *tense with sudden apprehension:* You got a jumper?

CALLAHAN: Yeah.

MCLEOD: Woman?

CALLAHAN: Yeah.

MCLEOD: She killed?

CALLAHAN: Sixteenth floor.

MCLEOD: Who is it?

CALLAHAN: What's with you?

MCLEOD: Who is it?

CALLAHAN: Name is McFadden. Old lady. Her son just identified her. Why?

MCLEOD, *mops his brow with his handkerchief, mumbles:* Nothing. That's my street. 53rd.

    CALLAHAN *looks at* MCLEOD *with puzzlement, concludes his phone conversation sotto voce.*

SUSAN, *smiling sadly at* ARTHUR: A tattoo?

ARTHUR, *sheepishly:* The others all had them. It made me feel like a real sailor. I was *such* a kid. Seven years ago.

SUSAN: Seven? It was yesterday, Jiggs.

ARTHUR: Seven years. Another world.

BRODY, *finishes fingerprinting* LEWIS: All done, Lewis! Go in there and wash your hands. Next . . .

     LEWIS, *dumb bravo, walks to the washroom, slowly, nonchalantly, his head lolling from side to side as if it were attached to his spine by a rubber band.*

McLEOD: Arthur!

     ARTHUR *rises, walks slowly to* BRODY *at the fingerprint board. They exchange glances.*

BRODY, *softly:* This hand, son. Just relax it. 'A-a-at's it. This finger. Roll it toward me.

DAKIS, *rises:* Well, three old squeals polished off. I'm clean. *He crosses, replaces the cards in the file.*

CALLAHAN: There's one here I'm sure they did. . . . *Propels himself in the swivel chair over to* CHARLEY. Charley, did you burglarize this apartment? CHARLEY *sniffs a contemptuous silence!* Why don't you give us a break? You do us a favor we might help you.

CHARLEY: How the hell you gonna help me? I'm a four-time loser. I'm gone to jail for life. How the hell you gonna help me?

CALLAHAN: You lived a louse, you wanta die a louse?

CHARLEY: Yaa!

CALLAHAN: You quif!

CHARLEY: Careful! De sign says "courtesy."

CALLAHAN: Coitesy? For you? You want coitesy? Here! *Tears off the sign, hits him on the head with it.* CHARLEY *laughs.* LEWIS *comes swaggering out of the washroom.*

BRODY, *finishes fingerprinting* ARTHUR: That's all, son. Go inside and wash your hands.

     ARTHUR *goes into the washroom.* SUSAN *holds onto herself tightly.*

SHOPLIFTER, *rises—to* SUSAN, *comforting her:* It don't hurt. You roll it. *Demonstrates.* Like that. It just gets your hands a little dirty. It washes right off. It's nothing. SUSAN *crumples into a chair.* What's a matter? Did I say something? SUSAN *shakes her head.* Are you married? SUSAN *shakes her head.* Me neither. Everybody tells you why don't you get married. You should get married. My mother, my father, my sisters, my brother—"Get married!" As if I didn't *want* to get married. Where do you find a man? Get me a man, I'll marry him. *Anything!* As long as it's got pants. Big, little, fat, thin . . . I'll marry him. You think I'd be *here?* For a lousy crocodile bag? I'd be home, cooking him such a meal. Get married! It's easy to talk! *She sits again, wrapped up in the tragedy of her spinsterhood.*

McLEOD, *at the main desk—to* LEWIS: Sign your name here, Lewis!

LEWIS *signs. The* PHOTOGRAPHER *signals* JOE.

JOE, *to* BARNES: O.K., Steve! Get 'em over here.

BARNES, *elbowing* LEWIS *over, nudges* CHARLEY *with his stick:* Rise and shine, Charley. *They line up in front of the desk.*

PHOTOGRAPHER, *to* BARNES: Stand on the end! PATROLMAN BARNES *obeys.*

BARNES: Stand here, Lewis.

LEWIS, *comes close to* CHARLEY, *murmurs in his ear:* You louse! I ought to kill you.

CHARLEY, *mutters:* Me? The thanks I get.

JOE, *to* PHOTOGRAPHER: Wait a minute! I want to line up those bullets. I want 'em in the shot. *He stands the bullets on end.* Can you get 'em in? *McLeod picks up* ARTHUR's *"sheet," and crosses to the desk.*

PHOTOGRAPHER: Yeah! Ready?

LEWIS: Thirty grand.

CHARLEY: Thirty bull!

LEWIS: I saw the list.

PHOTOGRAPHER, *to* BARNES, *posing them for the shot:* Grab that one by the arm!

CHARLEY, *mutters:* Lists? It's a racket! People get big insurance on fake stuff. They collect on it.

BARNES, *smiling for the photo, mutters through his gleaming teeth:* Sh! You spoil the picture. *Flash. The picture is taken.* BARNES *drops the smile.* Over there! *He waves them to a seat with his club, turns to the photographer to make sure his name is spelled correctly.*

LEWIS: What about that fourteen hundred dollars?

CHARLEY, *indignantly:* I had it on me for your protection. If this flatfoot had any sense, he was supposed to take it and let us go. . . . Dumb cop! Can I help it?

LEWIS, *pushes his face into* CHARLEY's, *threateningly:* I want my share.

CHARLEY: All right, Lewis. I'm not gonna argue with you. If it'll make you happy, I'll give you the whole fourteen hundred. Satisfied?

LEWIS, *thinks it over:* Ya.

CHARLEY: Good.

BARNES, *crosses over to them:* No talking—you!

McLEOD, *to* ARTHUR: Your signature. Here! ARTHUR *glances at the card, hesitates.*

SUSAN: Shouldn't he see a lawyer first?

McLEOD: It's routine.

SUSAN: Anyway a lawyer should . . .

McLEOD *presses his temples, annoyed.*

ARTHUR: Susan! *Shakes his head.*

SUSAN: Excuse me. *She forces a wan smile, nods, puts her fingers to her lips.* MCLEOD *hands* ARTHUR *the pen.* ARTHUR *looks about, seeking a depository for his cigarette butt.*

MCLEOD: On the floor. ARTHUR *throws it on the floor.* Step on it! ARTHUR *steps on butt.*

ARTHUR: Where do I sign?

MCLEOD: Here. *Indicates the line on the card.* ARTHUR *signs.* SUSAN *rises.*

SUSAN: I believe in you, Arthur. I want you to know. Deep inside—deep down, no matter what happens—I have faith in you.

JOE, *to* PHOTOGRAPHER: Now, this one. *To* MCLEOD. You want to be in this?

MCLEOD, *pressing his temples:* No! Got an aspirin, Yussel?

JOE, *curtly:* No. *Walks away.*

PHOTOGRAPHER, *to* ARTHUR: You mind standing up?
  *The flash, as he snaps the picture, galvanizes* SUSAN.

SUSAN, *hysterically:* No! No! They don't have to do that to him! They don't have to . . . *To* BRODY. Officer Brody. They're not going to print that in the papers, are they?

ARTHUR, *goes to her:* It's all right, Suzy! Stop trembling. Please. I don't care. . . .

BRODY, *beckons* JOE *and* PHOTOGRAPHER *out through the gate:* Joe! Teeney! *They follow him off.*

SUSAN: I'm not . . . really . . . It was the sudden flash! *She buries her head in her hands, turns away to control herself.* CHARLEY *laughs softly.*

DAKIS, *putting on his hat and jacket, glances at the clock:* Well, quarter to nine. Night court'll be open by the time we get there.

SHOPLIFTER, *rising, picking up her bag and scarf:* What do I do?

DAKIS: They'll tell you. Your brother-in-law's gonna be there, ain't he?

SHOPLIFTER: Yeah. All I can do is thank goodness my sister's sexy. Well . . . *She looks about.* So long, everybody! You been very nice to me. Really very nice. And I'm sorry I caused you all this trouble! Good-bye! *She and* DAKIS *go.*

MCLEOD, *to* SUSAN: You better go home now, young lady. It's all over.

SUSAN: May I talk to Arthur? For two minutes, alone? Then I'll go. I won't make any more trouble, I promise.

MCLEOD: All right. *He handcuffs* ARTHUR *to the chair.* Two minutes. *He goes into the* LIEUTENANT'S *office, sits in the darkened room.*

SUSAN, *to* ARTHUR, *her lips trembling:* Jiggs . . .

ARTHUR, *quickly:* Don't!

SUSAN, *dragging a chair over to him:* I'm not going to cry. This is no time for emotionalism. I mean we must be calm and wise. We must be realists.

*She sits down, takes his hand.* The minute I walk out of here I'm going to call Father.

ARTHUR: No, Susan, don't do that!

SUSAN: But he likes you so much, Arthur. He'll be glad to help.

ARTHUR: I don't want him to know. I'm ashamed. I'm so ashamed of myself.

SUSAN: Jiggs, it's understandable.

ARTHUR: Is it? God Almighty, I don't understand it! I stole, Suzy. I stole money from a man who trusted me! Where am I? Am I still floating around in the middle of the Pacific, looking for concrete platforms that aren't there? How mixed up can you get?

SUSAN: But, Jiggs, everybody gets mixed up, some time or other.

ARTHUR: They don't steal. *Pause.* Delirium, isn't it?

SUSAN: O.K. So it is delirium, Jiggs. So what? You're coming out of it fine.

ARTHUR, *shakes his head:* Look around, Susan. Look at this. *Studies the handcuffs.* The dreams I had—the plans I made . . . to end like this?

SUSAN: This isn't the end of the world, Jiggs.

ARTHUR: It is for me. *He rattles the handcuffs.* All I ever wanted was to live quietly in a small college town . . . to study and teach. No! *Bitterly.* This isn't a time for study and teachers . . . this is a time for generals.

SUSAN, *passionately:* I hate that kind of talk, Jiggs. Everywhere I hear it. . . . I don't believe it. Whatever happens to you, you can still pick up and go on. If ever there was a time for students and teachers, this is it. I know you can still make whatever you choose of your life. *She pauses, aware of his black anguish.* Arthur! Do you want Joy? Would that help? Would you like to see her and talk to her?

ARTHUR: No.

SUSAN: I'll go to Connecticut and bring her back?

ARTHUR: I don't want her.

SUSAN: I'll get her here. Say the word. I'll bring her here, Arthur. She'll come. You know she will.

ARTHUR: I don't want her, Suzy. I don't want Joy.

SUSAN: You're sure?

ARTHUR: Yes. *Pause.* For five years I've been in love with a girl that doesn't exist. I wouldn't know what to say to her now. *The noises of the city outside rise and fall.* That's finished. Washed up.

SUSAN: Oh, Arthur! Why couldn't you have fallen in love with me?

ARTHUR, *looks at her for a long time, then, tenderly:* I've always loved you, Suzy. You were always . . . my baby.

SUSAN: I've news for you. I voted for the president in the last election. I'm years past the age of consent.

ARTHUR: Just an old bag?

SUSAN: Arthur, why didn't you fall in love with me? I'd have been so much better for you. I know I'm not as beautiful as Joy, but . . .

ARTHUR: But you are. Joy's prettier than you, Susan, but you're more beautiful.

SUSAN: Oh, Jiggs, you fracture me! Let us not . . . *She almost cries.*

ARTHUR: Let us not be emotional. We were going to be "realists." Remember?

SUSAN: Yes.

ARTHUR: Suzy, when I go to jail . . . *Her lip quivers again.* Now . . . "Realists"??

SUSAN: I'm not going to cry.

ARTHUR: Be my sensible Susan!

SUSAN: Jiggs, I can't be sensible about you. I love you.

ARTHUR: Suzy, darling . . .

SUSAN: Jiggs, whatever happens, when it's over—let's go back home again.

ARTHUR: That would be wonderful, Suzy. That would be everything I ever wanted.

CHARLEY, *pretends to play a violin, humming "Hearts and Flowers." Then he laughs raucously, nudging* LEWIS: Hear that, Lewis? He's facin' five to ten? Wait'll the boys go to work on him. ARTHUR *and* SUSAN *look at him. To* SUSAN. What makes you think *he'll* want *you* then?

SUSAN: What?

CHARLEY: A kid like this in jail. They toss for him.

SUSAN: What do you mean?

CHARLEY: To see whose chicken he's gonna be!

SUSAN: What does that mean? What's he talking about?

ARTHUR: Don't listen to him. *To* CHARLEY. Shut up! Who asked you to . . .

CHARLEY: After a while you get to like it. Lots a guys come out, they got no use for dames after that.

ARTHUR: Shut up!

CHARLEY: Look at Lewis, there. He's more woman than man, ain't you, ain't you, Lewis? LEWIS *grins.*

ARTHUR, *rises in a white fury, goes for* CHARLEY, *dragging the chair to which he's handcuffed:* Shut up! I'll crack your goddam skull!

> BARNES *runs over to* CHARLEY.

SUSAN: Stop it! Stop! BRODY *enters quickly.* Officer Brody, make him stop! Make him stop!

BRODY, *to* ARTHUR: Take it easy! Sit down! *Kicks* CHARLEY *in the shins.* Why don't you shut up?

SUSAN: Oh, Officer Brody, help us! Help us!

BRODY: Take it easy. He ain't convicted yet. The judge might put him on probation. He might get off altogether. A lot of things might happen.

CHARLEY, *bending over, feeling his bruised shin:* Yak! Yak!

BRODY: One more peep outta you! One! *He slaps* CHARLEY, *turns to* BARNES, *irritated.* Take them inside!

BARNES *waves* CHARLEY *and* LEWIS *into the next room. As they pass* ARTHUR, LEWIS *eyes* ARTHUR *up and down, grinning and nodding.* CHARLEY *hums his mockery,* "*Hearts and Flowers.*" BARNES *prods* CHARLEY *with his nightstick, muttering,* "We heard the voice before." *They exit.*

BRODY, *to* SUSAN: If the complainant still wants to give him a break, that'll help. You got a good lawyer? *She shakes her head.* I'll give you the name of a crackerjack! I'm not supposed to, but I'll call him myself. There are a lot of tricks to this business.

SUSAN: Don't let it happen!

BRODY: Here's your picture. *Crumples up the photographic plate, tosses it into the wastebasket; goes to his locker, fishes out his bottle of liquor.* SUSAN *begins to weep.*

ARTHUR: Susan! Susan! The rest of my life I'm going to find ways to make this up to you. I swear. Whatever happens . . . *He puts his arms around her, pulls her down into the chair alongside him, holds her tight.*

SUSAN, *clinging to him:* Arthur, I . . .

ARTHUR: Sh! Don't say anything more, Suzy. We've a minute left. Let's just sit here like this . . . quietly. SUSAN *starts to speak.* Sh! Quiet! *She buries her head in his shoulder, and they sit there in a gentle embrace. After a second's silence, she relaxes.* Better?

SUSAN, *nods:* Mm!

BRODY, *goes into the* LIEUTENANT's *office, looking for* McLEOD: What are you sitting here in the dark for? *He switches on the light.* Want a drink, Jim?

McLEOD: No.

BRODY, *pours himself a stiff one:* Jim, I've been your partner for thirteen years. I ever ask you for a favor?

McLEOD, *pressing his hand to his temples:* What is it, Lou?

BRODY: That kid outside. McLEOD *groans.* I want you to give him a break.

McLEOD: You know better. I can't adjudicate this case.

BRODY: And what the hell do you think you're doing?

McLEOD: What makes him so special?

BRODY: A lot. I think he's a good kid. He's got stuff on the ball. Given another chance . . . *Pause.* Jim, he reminds me of my boy.

McLEOD: Mike?—was a hero.

BRODY: Why? Because he was killed? If Mike'd be alive today, he'd have the same problems this kid has.

McLEOD: Lou, Lou—how can you compare?

BRODY: Thousands like 'em, I guess. New generation, a screwed-up world.

We don't even understand them, Jim. I didn't Mike, till he was killed. *Pause.* Too late then. *He swallows his drink.* How about it?

McLeod: Don't ask me, will you?

Brody: But, I am.

McLeod: I can't. I can't do it, Lou. I can't drop the charges.

Brody: Louder, please! I don't seem to hear so good outta this ear.

McLeod: This fellow and Mike—day and night—there's no comparison.

Brody: Jim, this is me, Lou Brody. Remember me? What do you mean, you can't drop it? You coulda let him go two hours ago. You still can. The complainant left it up to you. I heard him.

McLeod: Be logical, Lou.

Brody: To hell with logic. I seen you logic the life out of a thing. Heart! Heart! The world's crying for a little heart. *Pause.* What do you say?

McLeod: No, Lou. No dice!

Brody: My partner! Arrest his own mother.

McLeod: I'm too old to start compromising now.

Brody: There's a full moon out tonight. It shows in your puss.

McLeod: You shouldn't drink so much, Lou. It melts the lining of your brain.

Brody, *pushes the bottle to him:* Here! You take it. Maybe that's what you need. Maybe it'll melt that rock you got in there for a heart.

McLeod, *a moan of anguish:* For Christ's sake, stop it, Lou, will you? My nerves are like banjo strings.

Brody: Well, play something on them. Play "Love's Old Sweet Song."

McLeod: Shut up! Lay off! Goddamn it! I'm warning you. Lay off! *Silence.*

Brody, *studies him, then . . . softer:* What's the matter?

McLeod: I'm drowning, Lou. I'm drowning. That's all. I'm drowning in my own juices.

Brody: I wish I could understand what makes you tick.

McLeod: I don't expect you to understand me, Lou. I know I'm different than the others. I think differently. I'm not a little boy who won't grow up, playing cops and robbers all his life, like Callahan; and I'm not an insurance salesman, like you, Lou. I'm here out of principle!! Principle, Lou. All my life I've lived according to principle! And, Goddamn it, I couldn't deviate even if I wanted to.

Brody: Sometimes you gotta bend with the wind . . . or break! Be a little human, Jim! Don't be such a friggin' monument!

McLeod: How, how? How do you compromise? How do you compromise—Christ!—convictions that go back to the roots of your childhood? I hate softness. I don't believe in it. My mother was soft; it killed her. I'm no Christian. I don't believe in the other cheek. I hate mushiness. You ask me to compromise for this kid? Who the hell is he? Now, right now, Lou, I'm faced with a problem of my own that's ripping me up like a .22 bullet bouncing around inside, and I can't compromise on that. So what do I do? What do I do?

*A long pause.* JOE *has entered quietly and has been standing in the doorway, listening.*

JOE: Try picking up that phone and calling her.

McLEOD: Who?

JOE: Mary. *Tosses an aspirin box onto the desk.* Here's your aspirin.

McLEOD: What are you talking about?

JOE: This ".22 bullet" of yours.

McLEOD: You don't know anything about it.

JOE: It's one story I had in my pocket years before it happened.

McLEOD: Listening at keyholes, Yussel?

JOE: No, I'm prescient. *Pause.* I met Mary years before you did. The spring of '41,—I was on the Newark *Star.* She didn't remember me. I never forgot her, though. It's one of those faces you don't forget. She's one in a million, your Mary. I know. She's a fine girl, Seamus. She could have had anything she wanted—materially—anything. She chose you instead. Why? What'd you have to offer her? Buttons!—These crazy hours, this crazy life? She loves you. You don't know how lucky you are. I know. I'm little and ugly— and because I'm a lover of beauty I'm going to live and die alone. But you? . . . The jewel was placed in your hands. Don't throw it away. You'll never get it back again!

CALLAHAN *reenters the squad room, crossing to the files. He pauses to light a cigarette.*

BRODY, *softly:* You know what you were like before you met Mary? You remember?

McLEOD: Yes.

BRODY: Like a stick!—Thin.

McLEOD, *his voice hoarse with emotion:* Yes.

BRODY: Dried-up, lonely, cold.

McLEOD: Yes.

BRODY: And you know what tenderness and warmth she brought to your life?

McLEOD: I know. I know better than you.

BRODY: So what the hell you asking me what to do? Pick up the phone! Get on your knees. Crawl!

MARY *enters the squad room, stands within the gate, pale, worn.* CALLAHAN *clears his throat, approaches her, adjusting his tie, a little "makey."*

CALLAHAN: Yes-s-s, Miss?

MARY: Is Detective McLeod here?

CALLAHAN: He's busy, Miss.

MARY, *wearily:* It's *Mrs.*, Mrs. McLeod.

CALLAHAN: Oh! Yes, ma'am. I'll tell him you're here. *Crosses. Pokes his head into the* LIEUTENANT's *office, to* McLEOD. Your wife is out here. McLEOD *rises at once, comes out to* MARY. JOE *and* BRODY *follow him out, and discreetly vanish into the washroom.*

MARY, *digs into her purse to avoid his eyes. Her voice is low and brittle:* I'm leaving now, Jim. I thought I'd come up and tell you. Here are the keys.

McLEOD, *softly:* Come inside.

MARY: My taxi's waiting.

McLEOD: Send it away.

MARY: No. My things are in it.

McLEOD: What things?

MARY: My valises and my trunk.

McLEOD: Oh, Mary, be sensible.

MARY: I intend to. Let's not drag it out, Jim! Please! I don't want any more arguments. I can't stand them. *Her voice becomes shrill.* CALLAHAN *passes by. She clamps the controls on, becoming almost inaudible.* It's only going to make things worse.

McLEOD: Come inside! I can't talk to you here.

MARY: The meter's ticking.

McLEOD, *firmly:* Let it tick! Come! *She obeys, follows him into the* LIEU- TENANT's *office. He shuts the door, turns to her.* Mary, this isn't the time or place to discuss our lives, past, present or future. I want you to take your things and go home. I'll be back at eight A.M. and we'll work this out then.

MARY: You think we can?

McLEOD: We'll have to.

MARY: I don't. I don't think it's possible.

McLEOD: Wait a minute! Wait one minute! I don't get this. What are *you* so bitter about? Who's to blame for tonight? You put me in a cement mixer. And now you're acting as if I were the . . .

MARY: The whore?

McLEOD: Don't say that!

MARY: I didn't invent the word, either, Jim.

McLEOD: I wasn't myself.

MARY: You were never more yourself, Jim. *Pause.*

McLEOD: I'm sorry, Mary.

MARY: It's all right. I'm beyond feeling. I'm nice and numb.

McLEOD: You're certainly in no condition to discuss this, tonight.

MARY: I've thought everything over and over and over again, and I don't see any other way out. Our life is finished. We couldn't go on from here.

McLEOD: You're married to me. You can't just walk out. Marriage is a sacrament, Mary. You don't dissolve it like that.

MARY: You once told me, when you bring a married prostitute in here, if she's convicted, her marriage can be dissolved just like that! Well, I've been brought in and I've been convicted.

McLEOD: I don't like that talk. Stop that talk, will you, Mary? I'm trying, I'm trying . . .

MARY: To what?

McLEOD: To put all this behind me.

MARY: But you can't do it?

McLEOD: If you'll let me.

MARY: Me? What have I got to say about it? I know the way your mind works. It never lets go. The rest of our days, we'll be living with this. If you won't be saying it, you'll be thinking it. *Pause.* It's no good. It won't work. I don't want to live a cat-and-dog existence. I couldn't take it. I'd dry up. I'd dry up and die.

McLEOD: Why didn't you ever tell me? If you'd come to me once, just once . . .

MARY: How could I? What good would it have done? Would you have understood? Would you have been able to forgive me?

McLEOD: Wasn't I entitled to know?

MARY: Yes, yes!

McLEOD: Why didn't you tell me?

MARY: Jim, I can't go over this again and again and again. I refuse to.

McLEOD: If I didn't love you and need you so, it'd be simple, you understand?

MARY: I understand.

McLEOD: Simple. You go home now and wait till morning.

MARY: That won't help us. Please, I'm so tired. Let me go now, Jim.

McLEOD: To what? What'll you go to? You, who turn on every light in the house when I'm not there!

MARY: Let me go, Jim.

McLEOD: You, who can't fall asleep unless my arms are around you! Where will you go?

MARY: Jim, I beg you . . .

McLEOD: No, Mary, I'm not going to. *He grasps her by the arm.*

MARY: You're hurting my arm. Jim!

McLEOD: I'm sorry . . . I'm sorry. *He lets her go.*

MARY: You ripped my sleeve.

McLeod: You'll sew it up.

Mary: The taxi's waiting. Please, Jim, let me go, without any more razor-slashing. I hate it.

McLeod: You'd go without a tear?

Mary: I wouldn't say that. One or two, perhaps. I haven't many left.

McLeod: Mary, I . . . Callahan *enters the* Lieutenant's *office, leaves paper on his desk, and goes.* Mary, you just don't stop loving someone.

Mary: I wouldn't have thought so. I wouldn't have believed it could happen. But, there it is. I suppose in this life we all die many times before they finally bury us. This was one of those deaths. Sudden, unexpected, like being run over by a bus. It happens.

McLeod: Who do you think you're kidding?

Mary: No one! *Begins to cry.* Least of all, myself.

McLeod, *takes her in his arms:* Mary, I love you.

Mary, *clinging to him, sobbing:* Then help me! I'm trying to be a human being. I'm trying to bundle myself together. It took every bit of strength to go this far. Help me, Jim!

McLeod, *caressing her:* It's no use, sweetheart, it's no use. I couldn't go home if you weren't waiting for me with the radio going and the smell of coffee on the stove. I'd blow out my brains. I would, Mary, if I went home to an empty flat—I wouldn't dare take my gun with me. *He gives her his handkerchief. She dries her eyes.* Now powder your nose! Put on some lipstick. *She kisses him.* Sims *appears at the gate, outside.*

Callahan, *crosses to* Sims: Yes, Counselor?

Sims: I want to see Detective McLeod.

Callahan: All right, Counselor. Come in. *Knocks on the door.*

McLeod: Come in!

Callahan: Someone outside to see you.

Mary: I'll go home now.

McLeod: No. Wait a minute.

Mary, *smiling now:* That taxi bill is going to break us.

McLeod, *grins back at her:* Let it break us. What do we care? *He goes off, sees* Sims, *his face goes grim again. He crosses to* Sims. You see, Counselor? I told you your client was acting.

Sims: He's still in shock.

McLeod: He'll be okay in the morning.

Sims: No thanks to you. When he's brought back here tomorrow, though, he'd better remain okay. This is not to happen again! You're not to lay a finger on him. If you do . . .

McLeod: Then advise him again to keep his mouth shut. And see that he does.

Sims: You're lucky you're not facing a murder charge yourself right now.

McLeod: I could always get you to defend me.

Sims: And I probably would. That's my job, no matter how I feel personally.

McLeod: As long as you get your fee?

Sims: I've defended many men at my own expense.

McLeod: That was very noble of you.

Sims: Nobility doesn't enter into it. Every man has a right to counsel, no matter how guilty he might seem to you, or to me, for that matter. Every man has a right not to be arbitrarily judged, particularly by men in authority; not by you, not by the Congress, not even by the president of the United States. The theory being these human rights are derived from God himself.

McLeod: I know the theory, Counselor.

Sims: But you don't go along with it? Well, you're not alone. There are others. You've a lot of friends all over the world. Read the headlines. But don't take it on yourself to settle it. Let history do that.

McLeod: Save it for the Fourth of July, Counselor.

Sims: I'll save it for the Commissioner. I intend to see him about you. I'm not going to let you get away with this.

McLeod: As long as Schneider gets away with it, Counselor, all's well. Why do you take cases like this, if you're so high-minded? Schneider killed the Harris girl—he's guilty. You know it as well as I do.

Sims: I don't know it. I don't even permit myself to speculate on his guilt or innocence. The moment I do that, I'm judging . . . and it is not my job to judge. My job is to defend my client, not to judge him. That remains with the courts. *He turns to go.*

McLeod: And you've got that taken care of, Counselor. Between bought witnesses and perjured testimony . . . *Sims stops in his tracks, turns suddenly white with fury.*

Sims: If you're so set on hanging Schneider, why don't you ask Mrs. McLeod if she can supply a corroborating witness? *McLeod is stopped in turn, as if he'd been hit by a meat-ax. Sims goes. Charley, Lewis, and Barnes enter.*

Barnes: Charley, sit over there. Over there for you, Lewis.

   *McLeod looks a little sick. He lights a cigarette slowly. He returns to the Lieutenant's office, his face twitching. Mary is just finishing powdering her face and removing the traces of the tears.*

Mary: What's the matter, dear?

McLeod: Nothing.

Mary: This has been our black day.

McLeod: Yes.

MARY, *puts her vanity case back into her bag:* I'm sorry, darling. And yet, in a way I'm glad it's out in the open. This has been hanging over my head so long. I've had such a terrible feeling of guilt all the time.

McLEOD, *mutters:* All right! All right!

MARY, *ignores the storm warnings:* I needed help and there was no one. I couldn't even go to my parents.

McLEOD: They didn't know?

MARY: No.

McLEOD: You didn't tell them?

MARY: I didn't dare. I didn't want to hurt them. You know how sweet and simple they are.

McLEOD: You didn't go home, then? After?

MARY: No.

McLEOD, *acidly:* Where'd you go?

MARY: That's when I came to New York.

McLEOD: And how long was that before I met you, Mary?

MARY: Two years.

McLEOD: Who'd you go with, then?

MARY: No one.

McLEOD: How many others were there, Mary?

MARY: Others?

McLEOD, *all control gone:* How many other men?

MARY: None. *Alarmed now.* What's the matter with you, Jim?

McLEOD: Wait a minute! Wait a minute! *He turns away, trying to control the insane turbulence inside.*

MARY: No! What's the matter with you?

McLEOD: At an autopsy yesterday I watched the medical examiner saw off the top of a man's skull, take out the brain, and hold it in his hand— *He holds out his hand.* —like that.

MARY, *horrified:* Why are you telling me this?

McLEOD: Because I'd give everything I own to be able to take out my brain and hold it under the faucet and wash away the dirty pictures you put there tonight.

MARY: Dirty pictures?

McLEOD: Yes.

MARY: Oh! I see. *A long pause. The brakes of a truck outside the window suddenly screech like a horribly wounded living thing.* I see. *To herself.* Yes. That would be fine, if we could. *She straightens, turns to him, wearily.* But when you wash away what I may have put there, you'll find you've a rotten spot in your brain, Jim, and it's growing. I know, I've watched it. . . .

McLEOD, *hoarsely:* Mary! That's enough.

MARY, *stronger than he, at last:* No, let's have the truth! I could never find it in my heart to acknowledge one tiny flaw in you because I loved you so—and God help me, I still do—but let's have the truth, for once, wherever it leads. You think you're on the side of the angels? You're not! You haven't even a drop of ordinary human forgiveness in your whole nature. You're a cruel and vengeful man. You're everything you've always said you hated in your own father.

McLEOD, *starts to throw on his jacket:* I'm not going to let you wander off in the streets this way. I'm going to take you home, myself.

MARY: What for? To kill me the way your father killed your mother!! *His hands drop to his side. He stares at her dumbly, stricken. She puts the keys down on the desk, turns to go.*

McLEOD: Where are you going? *Pause. She looks at him sadly.*

MARY: Far away . . . you won't find me. I'm scorching my earth . . . burning my cities.

McLEOD: When will I see you?

MARY: Never. . . . Good-bye. . . . *She goes.* McLEOD, *dazed, walks slowly back to the squad room.* BRODY *sees him from the washroom and enters with* JOE.

BRODY: How'd it go?

McLEOD, *almost inaudibly:* Fine.

BRODY: I mean Mary.

McLEOD: Fine. Dandy. *To* SUSAN. All right, young lady, your two minutes are up. *The* LIEUTENANT *enters.*

LIEUTENANT, *to* McLEOD: What the hell's the matter with you?

McLEOD: Nothing. . . .

LIEUTENANT: Don't you feel well?

McLEOD: Yes, sir. Feel all right.

LIEUTENANT, *to* BRODY: Am I crazy? Look at him.

BRODY: You've gone all green, Jim.

McLEOD: I've got a headache.

LIEUTENANT: You better go home. Buzz your doctor.

McLEOD: I've got a squeal to finish off, Lieutenant.

LIEUTENANT: Brody! You finish it off.

BRODY, *reluctantly:* Yes, sir.

McLEOD: I'd rather do it myself.

LIEUTENANT: You go home. That's an order.

McLEOD: Yes, sir.

LIEUTENANT: Callahan! You catch for Jim tonight.

CALLAHAN: Yes, sir. *He crosses up to the duty chart, takes it off the wall.*

BRODY, *to* MCLEOD: What happened, Jim? What's wrong?

MCLEOD, *sits heavily:* Mary left me. Walked out. We're finished.

BRODY: Too bad. She'll come back.

MCLEOD: No. This was for keeps.

*The* LIEUTENANT *crosses.*

LIEUTENANT: What are you sitting there for? Why don't you go home? *Exit* LIEUTENANT.

MCLEOD: Because I haven't *got* any.

JOE, *comes down to him:* You drove her away, didn't you? Why? MCLEOD *doesn't answer.* I tried to warn you, you damn fool. Why?

MCLEOD: I don't know. Why? Why do we do these things, Yussel? Who knows? . . . I built my whole life on hating my father—and all the time he was inside me, laughing—or maybe he was crying, the poor bastard, maybe he couldn't help himself, either.

*An excited woman enters, rattles the gate.*

CALLAHAN: Yes, Miss? *He is at the desk now, reaching into the bottom drawer for the celluloid letters to replace the name on the duty chart.*

WOMAN: Someone snatched my purse. . . .

CALLAHAN: Come in, Miss. We'll take care of you. *He bends over to pick up a letter.*

WOMAN: This happened to me once before . . . on 72nd Street. . . .

CHARLEY *lunges for* CALLAHAN'S *exposed gun, grabs it, hits* CALLAHAN *on the head with the butt, knocking him to the floor.* BARNES *raises his club.*

CHARLEY: Drop that club! *He aims at* BARNES.

BRODY: Drop it! He's a four-time loser. He'll kill you. BARNES *drops his club.*

CHARLEY: Goddamn right! Rot in jail the rest of my life? I take five or six a you bastards with me first. BARNES *makes a movement.*

BRODY: Take it easy! He can't get by the desk.

CHARLEY: Shut up! One word! One move! Anybody! MCLEOD, *seated center, laughs softly.*

MCLEOD: I was wondering when you'd get around to it, Charley.

CHARLEY: None of your guff, you!

MCLEOD, *rises:* Give me that gun!

CHARLEY: In the gut you'll get it. One step! I'm warnin' you. One!

BRODY: Easy, Jim. He can't get by the desk.

MCLEOD, *lunges for the gun:* You evil son-of-a-bitch!

CHARLEY *fires point-blank at* MCLEOD. *One, two, three quick shots.* MCLEOD *is hurled back and whirled around by the impact.* BARNES *goes into action, knocks the gun out of* CHARLEY'S *hand, and starts beating him over the head with his billy. Several of the others rush in and swarm all over* CHARLEY. *He screams twice and is silent.* MCLEOD *staggers, clutching his stomach.*

BRODY, *rushes to him, puts his arms around him, supporting him:* Jim! Did he get you? Are you hurt?

MCLEOD: Slightly. . . . *He unbuttons his coat. His shirt is a bloody rag. The sight stuns and sickens him.* God! *A little boy for one second.* Oh, Mary, Mary, Mary . . . *He wraps the coat tightly about him as if to shut in the escaping stream of life. He looks up, smiles crookedly.* Slightly killed, I should say. . . .

The LIEUTENANT *comes running in, a number of policemen crowd in through the gate.*

LIEUTENANT: What's happened?

BARNES: That son-of-a-bitch shot Jim!

LIEUTENANT: Take him inside! Get him into bed, quick.

BRODY, *to* MCLEOD: Easy, baby. Come, I'll carry you to bed. . . .

MCLEOD: Wait a minute.

BRODY: Now, Jim.

MCLEOD: No, don't! Don't pull at me. . . . *He sinks back into a chair.*

JOE: You got to lie down, Seamus.

MCLEOD: No. Once I lie down I'm not going to get up again. No.

LIEUTENANT: Notify the Communication Bureau! Get an ambulance. Quick!

MCLEOD: Never mind the doctor. Get a priest.

BRODY: Feel that bad, Jim?

GALLAGHER *goes to the phone.*

GALLAGHER, *on the phone:* Communication Bureau.

LIEUTENANT: Why don't you lie down, Jim?

MCLEOD: Get me a drink. *He gasps, unable to speak.* BRODY *starts for the watercooler.*

LIEUTENANT, *whispers to* BRODY: With a belly wound . . . ?

BRODY, *whispers:* What difference does it make? . . . Look at him!

MCLEOD: Don't whisper, Lou. I can hear you.

The LIEUTENANT *goes for a glass of water.*

BRODY: Sure you can. You're all right, baby. They can't hurt you. You're one of the indestructibles, you're immortal, baby.

MCLEOD: Almost, Lou, almost. Don't rush me. Give me your hand, Lou. Squeeze! Harder!

SUSAN *begins to sob.*

ARTHUR: Don't cry, Suzy. Don't cry!

MCLEOD, *glances up at* ARTHUR, *studies him, turns to* BRODY: Give me Buster's prints! I don't know. I hope you're right, Lou. Maybe he'll come in tomorrow with a murder rap. I don't know any more. Get me his prints. BRODY *goes for them.* CHARLEY *is dragged off, half-unconscious, moaning.*

JOE: How're you feeling, Seamus?

MCLEOD: Yussel! Find her! Ask her to forgive me. And help her. She needs help . . . will you?

JOE: Sure. Now take it easy.

BRODY, *hands* ARTHUR'S *fingerprint sheet to* MCLEOD.

MCLEOD: Tear it up! BRODY *tears it*. Unchain him, Lou. The keys are in my pocket. We have no case here, Lieutenant. The complainant withdrew. *He crosses himself.* In the name of the Father and of the Son and of the Holy Ghost. On, my God, I am heartily sorry for having offended Thee and I detest all my sins because I dread the loss of Heaven. . . . *He falls.* BRODY *catches him, eases him to the ground, feels for his pulse.* JOE *kneels to help him. After an interminable pause.*

BRODY: He's gone!

JOE: He's dead.

LIEUTENANT, *completes the Act of Contrition:* I firmly resolve with the help of Thy Grace to confess my sins, to do penance and to amend my life. Amen. *Crosses himself.*

BRODY, *murmurs:* Amen. BARNES *uncovers, crosses himself.* BRODY *crosses himself, rises clumsily, goes to* ARTHUR, *unlocks his handcuffs.* All right, son. Go on home! Don't make a monkey outa me! If I see you— BRODY *is crying now.* —up here again, I'll kick the guts outa you. Don't make a monkey outa me!

ARTHUR: Don't worry! I won't.

SUSAN: He won't.

BRODY: Now get the hell outa here! SUSAN *takes* ARTHUR'S *hand. They go. At the door* ARTHUR *pauses to look back.* BRODY *has turned to watch him go. They exchange glances.*

GALLAGHER, *on the phone:* St. Vincent's? Will you please send a priest over to the 21st Precinct Police Station to administer last rites?

LIEUTENANT, *on the phone:* Communication Bureau? Notify the Commissioner, the D.A., the homicide squad . . . 21st Precinct . . . Detective shot . . . killed.

BRODY, *his face twisted, glances down at* MCLEOD. JOE *rises, slowly, taking off his hat.*

*CURTAIN*

# DARKNESS AT NOON

WHEN I READ Arthur Koestler's novel *Darkness at Noon,* after my experience in the Soviet Union, I thought the book an essential statement for our time. It seemed an almost impossible play to write, but I hit upon a device very early that made it, I thought, possible to dramatize the conversations between the prisoners, to wit, the tapping messages through the stone walls by employing a code. The germinal idea! I recalled that in psychology we had learned that thought very often shapes itself in our mind with literal sentences and that the muscles of the throat really move as if we were silently speaking. With that in mind, I devised dialogue so that, as the prisoners were tapping out thoughts to each other, they uttered them. If you test this out yourself, sometime when you are thinking, you will find that unconsciously you are stating your thoughts silently and that your throat moves as if you were uttering your thoughts. When I tried it out, it did not seem outlandish at all—it worked—and with this device, I was able to convey the dialogue between the prisoners so that as they tapped the messages out they spoke them, ostensibly to themselves.

When I told this scheme to Koestler, he said it wouldn't work. He had another—that the words be projected onto the sets—a solution I felt was undramatic. A great deal of the success or failure of the play was obviously going to depend on whether this device of mine worked. Fortunately, it worked very well, as I knew it would. I acted it out myself, and felt that it was the only legitimate way in which I would preserve the sense of the actors reliving dramatic events and confronting each other through the solid walls as human beings.

The next problem in the play was, of course, the multiple scenes that took place in the mind of Rubashov. Because the play was a play about the

333

mind and thought, it had to move with the speed of thought within the stone walls and iron bars of a prison. And finally, when I had worked out the pattern for the production, I asked Freddie Fox to come in. He agreed with the plan. I then suggested we start constructing a model immediately. I had prepared cardboard and wood, paint and brushes, all the elements necessary to construct a model set. In my office I had a model stage with lighting which I had purchased from Jo Mielziner, the scene designer. It was a beautiful model stage. And, by cutting out some figures representing the actors in scale, we could design the scenes in scale. Freddie and I worked on it all that night. In the morning we had completed a scale model of the scene design for the play. Freddie was a beautiful artist, and he painted a beautiful and powerful series of designs. The result, I must say, delighted me when we built the sets and started to light them. It was a very pragmatic scheme, and worked beautifully for the play. And with Freddie's sensitive lighting, the sets projected Rubashov's fleeting emotions and thoughts perfectly.

The little set was made with a scrim for the back wall of Rubashov's cell. The scrim is a magical theatrical device that, when properly used, can make what seems to be a solid cell wall disappear, so that we can see through it into any scene beyond it. Thus, when Rubashov lies on the cot, the wall behind him seems solid. But as his mind turns to memories of Luba, his love, the scrim is lit behind; the wall disappears and Luba appears, apparently lying in bed with him. Similarly, when the lights are thrown on the wall from the front, Luba disappears and the wall becomes solid again. And the other scenes could be set behind it to wait for their cue.

One scene designer came in with a solution that used a revolving stage. I rejected it. A revolving stage makes a great deal of noise, which must be covered by music or some sound effects. More important, it takes a minute or more to revolve, which in a play with thirty scenes can cost thirty minutes—defeating the instantaneity that I was seeking. This could be arrived at only by translating the speed of thought into the speed of light. That, I decided, would be the method to give us what was essential.

I combined the scrim with a series of drops on stage left, painted after Freddie Fox's designs. With this scheme, it was possible to stage this play of thirty-odd scenes, reflecting the many thoughts and moods of Rubashov with the instantaneity of thought.

The special, strange character and nature of Arthur Koestler became known to me during our time in Paris. I recall particularly his drunkenness and his black gloves and his statement that he had patterned much of his life on Von Stroheim, whom he rather idolized. This quickly gave me a clue to the effectiveness of Koestler's villains. He sympathized with his villains, and they were so effective thereby. Often one identifies a writer with his heroes, but Koestler was rather fond of his villains and very often modeled his behavior in a most villainous way.

Working on *Darkness at Noon,* I met many times with Angelica Balabanoff, one of the original Bolsheviks, a fierce little lady, built like a cube, 81 years old, with the physical desires of a young woman, as she confided suggestively, to my terror, that she had fallen in love with me. She had been coeditor of *Avanti* with Mussolini. I was consulting her about *Darkness at Noon,* and she urged me to do a play about Mussolini. She gave me some interesting insights into the man's character when he was still a dedicated marxist and editor of the *Avanti* and she was having an affair with him. Despite his bravado, he was a coward, fearful of the dark, and he insisted on her walking him home every night.

I found Edward G. Robinson's comments in his autobiography about the role of Rubashov amusing because they are lies. I really wrote the part for Claude Rains and didn't even know Edward G. Robinson at that point. He claims I wrote the part for him, but he turned it down, and so it went to Rains. The truth is that Rains had been selected by Warner Brothers to play Alexander Hamilton in *The Patriots,* which they had purchased, but which they never made.

Rains had made a trip from his farm in Bucks County to my place in Oakland, New Jersey, to meet me; and we became warm friends. I weighed the possibility of Rains playing the lead in *Detective Story,* but he was much too short. I could have corrected that by casting everybody else much shorter, but it would aggravate the difficulty of casting the play properly. However, after *Detective Story,* I determined to find a part for Claude, and in *Darkness at Noon* I did. So, when Robinson says the part was written for him, it is, of course, a bit of nonsense designed to cover up his foolish professional pride about following Rains in the role in the road company. He also contended that he did not take the role as a way of answering the charges that he was a communist sympathizer, when in fact that was precisely why he took the role.

Claude played the role, a little terrified at coming back to the stage after such a long absence in films, but he had a wonderful quality that exudes authority, and he played the role with great sensitivity. Our friendship lasted until the play, when Claude had a double problem of hating direction and being fearful of coming back to the stage, needing direction every moment. It was a dilemma that ended in the destruction of our friendship.

*Darkness at Noon* marked a change in the way at least one critic viewed my work. John Mason Brown had been harshly critical of *Men in White,* and in *Dead End* had attributed the direction to Norman Bel Geddes, an error on which I had corrected him. I met him subsequently one day at '21.

He and a group of other critics were seated with George Jean Nathan. Nathan summoned me over, so I joined them. John Mason Brown, sitting next to me, confided that he would never give me a good review because he didn't like my choice of subjects. He said they were all so unpleasant. I tried to point out to him that many really great plays such as *Lear, Macbeth,* the Greek tragedies, were unpleasant in that sense and that I hoped some day to write a play that would please him. Then along came *Darkness at Noon,* and he wrote that Koestler was a genius and that I was ingenious. He had thought it impossible to make a play out of the Koestler book but that somehow I had achieved it. This represented a great triumph over his strong prejudice.

S.K.

# DARKNESS AT NOON

*Darkness at Noon* was first presented by The Playwrights Company at the Alvin Theatre on January 13, 1951, with the following cast:

| | |
|---|---|
| RUBASHOV | Claude Rains |
| GUARD | Robert Keith, Jr. |
| 402 | Philip Coolidge |
| 302 | Richard Seff |
| 202 | Allan Rich |
| LUBA | Kim Hunter |
| GLETKIN | Walter J. Palance |
| 1ST STORM TROOPER | Adams MacDonald |
| RICHARD | Herbert Ratner |
| YOUNG GIRL | Virginia Howard |
| 2ND STORM TROOPER | Johnson Hayes |
| IVANOFF | Alexander Scourby |
| BOGROV | Norman Roland |
| HRUTSCH | Robert Crozier |
| ALBERT | Daniel Polis |
| LUIGI | Will Kuluva |
| PABLO | Henry Beckman |
| ANDRÉ | Geoffrey Barr |
| BARKEEPER | Tony Ancona |
| SECRETARY | Lois Nettleton |
| PRESIDENT | Maurice Gosfield |
| Soldiers, Sailors, Judges, and Jurors | |

Staged by Sidney Kingsley
Setting and Lighting by Frederick Fox
Costumes by Kenn Barr

## Scenes

ACT ONE     First Hearing: A prison—March 1937
ACT TWO     Second Hearing: The same—Five weeks later
ACT THREE Third Hearing: The same—Several days later

The action of the play oscillates dialectically between the Material world of a Russian prison during the harsh days of March 1937 and the Ideal realms of the spirit as manifested in Rubashov's memories and thoughts moving freely through time and space.

*Rendering of* Darkness at Noon *by Frederick Fox for which he received the Donaldson Award. Reprinted by permission of Margery Fox.*

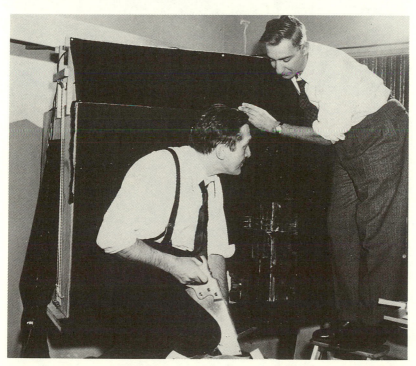

*Sidney Kingsley and Frederick Fox working on the stage model for* Darkness at Noon. *Courtesy of Sidney Kingsley.*

*The realized design for* Darkness at Noon, *Rubashov at left. Courtesy of Sidney Kingsley.*

## ACT ONE

*March 1937.*

*Granite and iron! The corridor of an ancient Russian prison, buried deep underground. To the left, set into a soaring, Byzantine arch, is a thick iron portcullis. Beyond it, visible through the bars, a steep flight of stone steps curves up out of sight. To the right, a tier of cells forms an ominous column of sweating granite, towering up to vanish in the shadows above. A GUARD with rifle and bayonet paces the corridor. He halts as the iron portcullis slides up to the clangor of chains, revealing an OFFICER and a prisoner. The prisoner, N. S. RUBASHOV, is a short, stocky, smooth-shaven, bespectacled man in his early fifties. His head is large beyond the proportions of his body, and characterized by an expanse of forehead. His eyes are set far apart and Mongoloid in cast. He carries himself very erect and with fierce authority. The GUARD opens the door of a cell, throws a switch in the corridor, which turns on the light, and the prisoner is pushed inside. The door clangs behind him. The heavy metallic sound of bolts being closed and a key turned. The prisoner surveys his cell slowly: a solid, windowless cubicle with an iron bed and a straw mattress, nothing else. There is no day here, no night; it is a timeless dank grave for the living corpse. He reaches into his pocket automatically for cigarettes, then he remembers, turns to the judas hole and observes the eye of the GUARD staring at him.*

RUBASHOV: Comrade guard! *He turns his empty pockets inside out.* They've taken away my cigarettes, too! Can you get me a cigarette?

GUARD, *harshly:* It's late, go to bed.

RUBASHOV: I've been dragged out of a sickbed. I have a fever. I need some cigarettes.

GUARD, *mutters:* Your mother! *Turns out the light in the cell, leaving the prisoner lit only by the light streaming through the judas hole. The GUARD goes out.*

RUBASHOV, *rubs his inflamed cheek, shakes his head, sighs, looks about, takes off his coat, slowly, painfully; throws it on the cot, murmurs to himself:* So, it's come. You're to die, Rubashov. Well, the old guard is gone! *He sits on the bed; rolls up his coat for a pillow, murmuring to himself.* For golden lads and girls all must as chimney sweepers come to dust. *He takes off his spectacles, places them on the floor, and lies back, staring grimly at the ceiling.* Yes. The old guard is gone. *He sighs again, repeats mechanically.* For golden lads and girls all must . . . *A ticking sound is heard. Three ticks, then a pause, then three more ticks. He sits up, listening* . . . as chimney sweepers . . . *The ticking becomes louder. He picks up his spectacles, rises, glances at the judas hole to make certain he is not being observed, places his ear to one wall, taps on it with his spectacles, listens, then tries another wall. Returning to the wall left, he listens, murmurs "Ah," taps three times. The answering taps become louder. He repeats the series, placing his ear to the wall; the taps now come in a different series, louder, rapid, more excited.* Easy! Slow. . . . Slow. *He taps slowly, deliberately. The answering taps slow down.* That's better. . . . *He counts the taps,* 5-3, W; 2-3, H; 3-5, O. "Who?" *The prisoner smiles and addresses himself softly to the wall.* Direct enough, aren't you, Comrade?

*The lights come up in the adjoining cell, the wall dissolves, the prisoner in 402 appears. He is verminous, caked with filth, his hair matted, his old Tsarist uniform in rags, but he has somehow preserved his monocle and the tatters of an old illusion. He strokes his moustache and swaggers about as if he were still a perfumed dandy.*

402, *as he taps on the wall, his lips unconsciously form the words and utter them. In their communications by tapping, all the prisoners unconsciously voice the messages as they tap them through:* Who are you? *Pause, as* RUBASHOV *shakes his head but doesn't answer. Taps again.* Is it day or night outside?

RUBASHOV, *glances again at the judas hole, taps:* Four A.M.

402, *taps:* What day?

RUBASHOV, *taps:* Tuesday.

402, *taps:* Month?

RUBASHOV, *taps:* March . . .

402, *taps:* Year?

RUBASHOV, *taps:* 1937.

402, *taps:* The weather?

RUBASHOV, *taps:* Snowing.

402, *to himself:* Snow. *Taps.* Who are you?

RUBASHOV, *to himself:* Well, why not? *He taps.* Nicolai Semonovitch Rubashov.

402, *straightens up with a cry:* Rubashov? *He bursts into wild, ugly laughter. He taps.* The wolves are devouring each other! *Crosses over to the opposite wall. Taps three times, and listens, his ear to the wall. The cell above lights up and the occupant rises painfully from his cot. He is a young man, thin, with a white ghostlike face, bruises and burns on it, and a split lip.*

*He crosses with effort to the wall, taps three times, then listens as 402 taps. New prisoner. Rubashov.*

302, *taps:* Nicolai Rubashov?

402, *laughing hoarsely as he taps:* N. S. Rubashov. Ex-Commissar of the People, ex-Member of the Central Committee, ex-General of the Red Army, Bearer of the Order of the Red Banner. Pass it along.

302, *crouches, stunned, cries out suddenly:* Oh! Father, Father, what have I done? . . . *He crosses to the opposite wall, taps three times. An answering tap is heard. The cell above lights up; 202, a peasant, with insane eyes, puts his head to the floor as 302 taps.*

302, *taps:* N. S. Rubashov arrested. Pass it along.

202: Rubashov? Well, well! *Crosses to other wall, taps.* N. S. Rubashov arrested. Pass it along.

*The tiers of cells darken and vanish, leaving only* RUBASHOV *visible, leaning against the wall, staring into space. The taps echo and reecho throughout the prison, to the whispering accompaniment:* "N. S. Rubashov arrested! N. S. Rubashov arrested!" *The whispers grow into the roar of a mighty throng calling out,* "Rubashov! Rubashov!" RUBASHOV's *voice is heard, young and triumphant, addressing the crowd.*

RUBASHOV'S VOICE: Comrades! *The tumult subsides.* Proletarians, soldiers, and sailors of the Revolution. The great, terrible, and joyful day has arrived! *The crowd roars.* RUBASHOV, *listening to the past, head bowed, paces his cell slowly.* Eight months ago the chariot of the blood-stained and mire-bespattered Romanov monarchy was tilted over at one blow. *The oceanic roar of the crowd.* The gray, stuttering Provisional Government of bourgeois democracy which followed was already dead and only waiting for the broom of History to sweep its putrid corpse into the sewer. In the name of the Revolutionary Committee, I now declare the Provisional Government overthrown. *The roar swells.* Power to the Soviets! Land to the peasants! Bread to the hungry! Peace to all the peoples!

*The victorious shouts of* "Rubashov! Rubashov!" *mount to a crescendo, fade away and die, leaving only the blanketed stillness of the cell and* RUBASHOV *listening to his memories. Three taps from 402's wall arouse him. He responds, ear to the wall. The wall dissolves, revealing 402.*

402, *taps, gloating:* Serves you right.

RUBASHOV, *to himself:* What is this? *Taps.* Who are you?

402, *taps:* None of your damned business. . . .

RUBASHOV, *taps:* As you like.

402, *taps:* Long live His Majesty, the Tsar!

RUBASHOV: So that's it. *Taps.* I thought you birds extinct.

402, *beats out the rhythm with his shoe:* Long live the Tsar!

RUBASHOV, *grins sardonically, taps:* Amen! Amen!

402, *taps:* Swine!

RUBASHOV, *amused, taps out:* Didn't quite understand.

402, *in a frenzy, hammers out:* Dirty swine . . .

RUBASHOV, *taps:* Not interested in your family tree.

402, *fury suddenly passes, taps out slowly:* Why have you been locked up?

RUBASHOV, *taps:* I don't know. *Pause.*

402, *taps:* Anything happened? Big? Assassination? War?

RUBASHOV, *taps:* No. Can you lend me tobacco?

402, *taps:* For you? I'd be castrated first.

RUBASHOV, *taps:* Good idea.

    *402 walks away, lies down on his cot. The lights fade out on him.*

RUBASHOV, *paces his cell, counting out the steps:* 1-2-3-4-5- and a half . . . *He wheels back.* 1-2-3-4 . . . *Strange ghostly voices are dimly heard. It starts.* So soon. *The vague outlines of ghostly faces hover above him. The waking, walking dreams. Other ghostly faces appear in space.* Yes, you sailors of Kronstadt—I shall pay. . . . And you nameless ones. *The face of a little hunchback appears, smoking a pipe and smiling.* And Comrade Luigi. *Some plates appear dancing in space—then a big moonface of a man, juggling them, grinning.* And Pablo. *The luminous face of a young woman appears in space. A striking face; large, soft brown eyes; dark hair; white skin.* And Luba. *The voices and faces fade away.* My debts will be paid—my debts will be paid.

    *The young woman materializes. The cell becomes the office of the Commissar of the Iron Works. Huge graphs hang on the walls. Through the window, a vista of factory chimneys and the skeletons of incompleted buildings may be seen. The young woman is bent over her notebook, taking down dictation.* RUBASHOV *walks up and down, dictating. In the pauses, she raises her head, and her soft, round eyes follow his wanderings through the room. There is wonder and worship in the way she looks at him. She wears a white peasant blouse, embroidered with little flowers at the high neck. Her body is generously formed and voluptuous.*

RUBASHOV, *dictates:* "To meet the Five-Year Plan we must step up our tempo. A twelve-hour day if necessary. Tempo! Tempo!" *The girl tosses her head as she writes, and her dangling earrings attract his attention. He frowns. Her head buried in her notebook, she does not observe this.* ". . . The Unions will dismiss workers who come late and deprive all laggards of their food cards . . ." *She quickly reaches down to scratch her ankle, and he notices she is wearing high-heeled slippers. He frowns again.* ". . . In the building of a new, hitherto undreamt-of Communist state, we must be guided by one rule, dash, the end justifies the means, period. Relentlessly, exclamation point."

*The girl bobs her head, the earrings sway. He suddenly growls:* Why do you wear those earrings? And those high heels? With a peasant blouse. Ridiculous! *The girl looks up.* What's you name?

LUBA: Loshenko.

RUBASHOV: Loshenko?

LUBA: Yes, Comrade Commissar. Luba Loshenko. *Her voice is low and hoarse, but gentle.*

RUBASHOV: And how long have you been working here?

LUBA: For you, Comrade Commissar?

RUBASHOV, *growls:* Yes, for me. Of course, for me.

LUBA: Three weeks.

RUBASHOV: Three? Really? Well, Comrade Loshenko, don't dress up like a ceremonial elephant in the office!

LUBA: Yes, Comrade Commissar, I'm sorry.

RUBASHOV: You weren't wearing those earrings yesterday?

LUBA: No, Comrade Commissar, I wasn't.

RUBASHOV: Then what are you getting dressed up for now? What's the occasion? This is an office. We've work to do. Ridiculous. . . . Where was I?

LUBA, *glances at her notebook:* "The end justifies the means, period. Relentlessly, exclamation point."

RUBASHOV: Mm! *He picks up some papers from the desk, glances at them.* "You liberals sitting on a cloud, dangling your feet in the air . . ." *He turns and looks at her; she is watching him but quickly turns back to her notebook.* You—you've really very pretty little ears. Why do you ruin them with those survivals of barbaric culture? *She plucks off the earrings.* That's better. And don't look so frightened. I'm not going to eat you. What do you people in the office think I am? An ogre? I don't eat little children.

LUBA, *looks at him:* I'm not frightened.

RUBASHOV: You're not?

LUBA: No.

RUBASHOV, *surprised:* Humph! Good! Good! Where was I?

LUBA, *scans her notebook:* "Sitting on a cloud, dangling your feet in the air."

RUBASHOV: Ah! *She looks up at him and smiles. In spite of himself, he returns her smile.* Yes . . . *Then soberly again.* "You liberals are wrong." *He begins to pace.* "And those who are wrong will pay! . . ." *The image of the girl fades; the office vanishes, and he is back in his cell.* Yes, Luba, I will pay. I will pay my debt to you, above all. . . . *Three taps are heard from 402's wall. He turns to the wall, fiercely.* But not you. I owe you nothing. How many of your people have I killed? No matter. You taught us to hate. *Three taps from 402.* You stood over us with the knout and the hangman. *Three taps from 402.* Your police made us fear this world, your priests the next, you poured melted lead down our throats, you massacred us in

Moscow, you slit the bellies of our partisans in Siberia and stuffed them with grain. No! *Crossing to the wall.* You? I owe no debt to you. *Three taps from 402.* RUBASHOV *places his ear to the wall, taps curtly.* What do you want?

402, *appears, tapping:* I'm sending tobacco.

RUBASHOV, *after a long pause, taps:* Thanks. *Sighs, murmurs to the wall.* Do I owe you a debt too? We at least acted in the name of humanity. Mm. But doesn't that double our debt? *He shakes his head, cynically.* What is this, Rubashov? A breath of religious madness? *A feverish chill shakes him. He puts on his coat.*

402, *rattles his door, peers through the judas hole, calls:* Guard! Guard! *The* GUARD *is heard shuffling across the corridor.*

GUARD, *through the bars of the judas hole:* What do you want?

402: Could you take this tobacco to cell 400?

GUARD: No.

402: I'll give you a hundred rubles.

GUARD: I'll give you my butt in your face.

402, *walks away:* For two rubles he'd cut his mother's throat.

GUARD, *returns to the judas hole, menacingly:* What did you say?

402, *cringes, whining:* Nothing! I said nothing. *The* GUARD *shuffles off.* 402 *crosses to wall, taps.* You're in for it.

RUBASHOV, *on sudden impulse goes to the iron door of his cell, bangs on it, shouting:* Guard! Guard! *The* GUARD *is heard approaching down the corridor.*

GUARD: Quiet! You're waking everyone. *His shadow appears in the judas hole.*

RUBASHOV, *peremptorily commands:* Tell the Commandant I must speak to him.

GUARD, *cackles:* Oh, sure.

RUBASHOV: At once!

GUARD: Who do you think you are?

RUBASHOV: Read your Party history.

GUARD: I know who you are.

RUBASHOV: Then don't ask idiotic questions.

GUARD: You're Number 400, in solitary, and you're probably going to be taken down in the cellar and shot. Now don't give me any more trouble or you'll get a butt in your face.

RUBASHOV: You try it and we'll see who'll be shot. *The* GUARD *hesitates.* RUBASHOV *again hammers on the door.*

GUARD: You're waking everyone. Stop that or I'll report you.

RUBASHOV: Do so! Report me! At once!

GUARD: I will. *He goes.*

RUBASHOV *continues to hammer on the cell door. The lights come up in the cell tier, bringing the other prisoners into vision. They have been listening to this exchange through the judas hole.* 302 *turns from the door and seats himself on his cot. Slowly, painfully, he begins to tap the signal to* 402. 402 *stands on his cot, responds, and listens.*

302, *taps:* Outside?

402, *taps:* It's morning, four A.M., Tuesday. March. Snowing.

302, *taps:* Send Rubashov my greetings.

402, *taps:* Who shall I say?

302, *taps:* Just say an old friend.

402, *crosses to Rubashov, summons him with a tap.* RUBASHOV *rises and listens at the wall as* 402 *taps:* 302 sends greetings.

RUBASHOV, *taps:* What's his name?

402, *taps:* Won't say. Just old friend. He was tortured last week.

RUBASHOV, *taps:* Why?

402, *taps:* Political divergencies.

RUBASHOV, *taps:* Your kind?

402, *taps:* No, your kind.

RUBASHOV, *taps:* How many prisoners here?

402, *taps:* Thousands. Come and go.

RUBASHOV, *taps:* Your kind?

402, *taps:* No. Yours. I'm extinct. Ha! Ha!

RUBASHOV, *taps:* Ha! Ha! *Footsteps approaching ring out in the corridor. He taps quickly.* Someone's coming.

402 *vanishes.* RUBASHOV *throws himself on the cot.*

*A huge young man in an officer's uniform enters. His shaven head, his deep-set, expressionless eyes, and his jutting, Slavic cheekbones give him the appearance of a death's-head. His stiff uniform creaks, as do his boots. The officer who arrested* RUBASHOV *and the* GUARD *are visible in the doorway. The young man enters the cell, which becomes smaller through his presence. His name is* GLETKIN.

GLETKIN, *fixes* RUBASHOV *with a cold stare:* Were you the one banging on the door? *He looks about.* This cell needs cleaning. *To* RUBASHOV. You know the regulations? *He glances behind the door, turns to the* GUARD. He has no mop. Get him a mop! *The* GUARD *hurries off.*

RUBASHOV: Are you the commandant here?

GLETKIN: No. Why were you banging on the door?

RUBASHOV: Why am I under arrest? Why have I been dragged out of a sickbed? Why have I been brought here?

GLETKIN: If you wish to argue with me you'll have to stand up.

RUBASHOV: If you're not the commandant, I haven't the slightest desire to argue with you . . . or even to speak to you for that matter.

GLETKIN: Then don't bang on the door again—or the usual disciplinary measures will have to be applied. *Turns to the* ARRESTING OFFICER. When was the prisoner brought in?

ARRESTING OFFICER: Ten minutes ago.

GLETKIN, *glances at his watch, sternly:* His arrest was ordered for three A.M. sharp. What happened?

ARRESTING OFFICER: The car broke down.

GLETKIN: That's inexcusable. It's the commandant's new car, and it was in perfect condition. This looks very suspicious. *He takes out a notebook and writes in it.* Send the driver up to my office at once!

RUBASHOV: It's not his fault. It wasn't sabotage.

GLETKIN, *writes, without glancing up:* How do you know it wasn't?

RUBASHOV: Make allowances.

GLETKIN: For what?

RUBASHOV: Our roads.

GLETKIN *puts away the notebook and measures* RUBASHOV *impersonally:* What's the matter with our roads?

RUBASHOV: They're primitive cow paths.

GLETKIN: Very critical, aren't we? I suppose the roads in the bourgeois countries are better?

RUBASHOV, *looks at* GLETKIN, *smiles cynically:* Young man, have you ever been outside of our country?

GLETKIN: No. I don't have to . . . to know. And I don't want to hear any fairy tales.

RUBASHOV: Fairy tales? *Sits up.* Have you read any of my books or articles?

GLETKIN: In the Komsomol Youth I read your political-education pamphlets. In their time I found them useful.

RUBASHOV: How flattering! And did you find any fairy tales in them?

GLETKIN: That was fifteen years ago. *Pause.* Don't think that gives you any privileges now! *The* GUARD *appears, flapping a dirty rag.* GLETKIN *takes it, throws it at* RUBASHOV's *feet.* When the morning bugle blows, you will clean up your cell. You know the rules. You've been in prison before?

RUBASHOV: Yes. Many of them. But this is my first experience under my own people. *He rubs his inflamed jaw.*

GLETKIN: Do you wish to go on sick call?

RUBASHOV: No, thanks. I know prison doctors.

GLETKIN: Then you're not really sick?

RUBASHOV: I have an abscess. It'll burst itself.

GLETKIN, *without irony:* Have you any more requests?

RUBASHOV: Tell your superior officer I want to talk to him and stop wasting my time!

GLETKIN: Your time has run out, Rubashov! *He starts to go, pulling the door behind him.*

RUBASHOV, *murmurs in French: Plus un singe monte . . .*

GLETKIN, *reenters quickly:* Speak in your own tongue! Are you so gone you can't even think any longer except in a filthy, foreign language?

RUBASHOV, *sharply, with military authority:* Young man, there's nothing wrong with the French language as such. Now, tell them I'm here and let's have a little Bolshevik discipline! GLETKIN *stiffens, studies* RUBASHOV *coldly, turns and goes, slamming the iron door. The jangle of the key in the lock; his footsteps as he marches off down the corridor. Suddenly* RUBASHOV *bounds to the door. He shouts through the judas hole.* And get me some cigarettes! Damn you! *Rubs his inflamed cheek, ruefully. To himself.* Now, why did you do that, Rubashov? What does this young man think of you? "Worn-out old intellectual! Self-appointed Messiah! Dares to question the party line! Ripe for liquidation . . ." There you go again, Rubashov—the old disease. *Paces.* 4 . . . 5. Revolutionaries shouldn't see through other people's eyes. Or should they? How can you change the world if you identify yourself with everybody? How else can you change it? *Paces.* 3 . . . 4. *He pauses, frowning, searching his memory.* What is it about this young man? Something? *Paces.* 3 . . . 4. Why do I recall a religious painting? A Pietà, a dead Christ in Mary's arms? Of course—Germany. The Museum, Leipzig, 1933.

*Slowly the prison becomes a museum in Germany. A large painting of the Pietà materializes. An S.S.* OFFICER *in black uniform and swastika armband is staring at the Pietà. His face, though different from* GLETKIN's *in features, has the same, cold, fanatical expression.* RUBASHOV, *catalogue in hand, walks slowly down, studying a row of invisible paintings front; then he crosses over, studies the Pietà. The S.S.* OFFICER *glances at him with hard, searching eyes, then goes.*

*A middle-aged man with a sensitive face, sunken cheeks, enters, looks alternately at the catalogue he is holding and the paintings in space. He halts next to* RUBASHOV, *squinting to make out the title.*

MAN, *softly, reading: Christ Crowned with Thorns.*

RUBASHOV, *turns, front, nods:* Titian.

MAN, *to* RUBASHOV: What page is it in your catalogue, please?

RUBASHOV, *without looking at him, hands over his catalogue.* MAN *glances at it, looks about hurriedly, returns it, whispers hoarsely.* Be very careful. They're everywhere.

RUBASHOV: I know. You're late, Comrade Richard.

RICHARD: I went a roundabout way.

RUBASHOV: Give me your report.

RICHARD: It's bad.

RUBASHOV: Give it to me.

RICHARD: Since the Reichstag fire, they've turned the tables on us. It's a massacre. All Germany is a shambles. Two weeks ago we had six hundred and twelve cells here—today there are fifty-two left. The Party is a thousand-headed mass of bleeding flesh. Two of my group jumped out of a window last night in order to avoid arrest! *His lips start to tremble; his entire body is suddenly convulsed.*

RUBASHOV, *sharply:* Control yourself! *Glances about.* You're one of the leaders here. If you go on this way, what can we expect of the other comrades?

RICHARD, *controls himself with an effort:* I'm sorry.

RUBASHOV: For a man who has written such heroic plays of the proletariat, this is surprising.

RICHARD: This is a bad moment for me. My wife, Comrade Truda, was arrested two days ago. The Storm Troopers took her and I haven't heard since.

RUBASHOV: Where were you at the time?

RICHARD: Across the street, on a roof. *His voice becomes shrill as he begins to lose control again. A stutter creeps into his speech.* I w-w-watched them take her away.

RUBASHOV, *glances around to see if they are observed, motions Richard to the bench under the Pietà:* Sit down. *They both sit on the bench.* We have a big job here. We have to pull the Party together. We have to stiffen its backbone. This is only a temporary phase.

RICHARD: We carry on, Comrade. We work day and night. We distribute literature in the factories and house to house.

RUBASHOV: I've seen some of these pamphlets. Who wrote them?

RICHARD: I did.

RUBASHOV: You did?

RICHARD: Yes. Why?

RUBASHOV: They're not quite satisfactory, Comrade Richard.

RICHARD: In what respect?

RUBASHOV: A bit off the line. We sense a certain sympathy with the Liberals and the Social Democrats.

RICHARD: The Storm Troopers are . . . *The stammer again creeps into his speech.* Sl . . . sl . . . slaughtering them, too, like animals in the street.

RUBASHOV: Let them! How does that affect us? In that respect the Nazis are clearing the way for us by wiping out this trash and saving us the trouble.

RICHARD: Trash?

RUBASHOV: The Liberals are our most treacherous enemies. Historically, they have always betrayed us.

RICHARD: But that's inhuman, man. You comrades back there act as if nothing had happened here. Try and understand! We're living in a j . . . j . . . jungle. All of us. We call ourselves "dead men on ho . . . holiday."

RUBASHOV: The party leadership here carries a great responsibility, and those who go soft now are betraying it. You're playing into the enemies' hands!

RICHARD: I . . . ?

RUBASHOV: Yes, Comrade Richard, you.

RICHARD: What is this? I supposed Truda betrayed the Party, too?

RUBASHOV: If you go on this way . . . *Suddenly, urgently.* Speak quietly, and don't turn your head to the door! *A tall young man in the uniform of a Storm Trooper has entered the room with a girl, and they stand nearby, studying their catalogues and the pictures. The S.S.* OFFICER *whispers to the girl. She titters.* RUBASHOV *rises. In a low calm voice.* Go on talking.

RICHARD, *rises, glances at his catalogue, talking rapidly:* Roger van der Weyden, the elder, 1400 to 1464. He's probably van Eyck's most famous pupil.

RUBASHOV: His figures are somewhat angular.

RICHARD: Yes, but look at the heads. There's real power there. And look at the depth of physiognomy. *Again the stammer.* Compare h . . . h . . . him with the other masters; you'll see his coloring is softer . . . and l . . . l . . . lighter. *His eyes stray to the S.S.* OFFICER *in panic and hatred.*

RUBASHOV: Did you stammer as a child? *Sharply.* Don't look over there!

RICHARD, *looks away quickly:* S . . . sometimes.

RUBASHOV: Breathe slowly and deeply several times. RICHARD *obeys. The* GIRL *with the* STORM TROOPER *giggles shrilly, and the pair move slowly toward the exit. In passing, they both turn their heads toward* RICHARD *and* RUBASHOV. *The* STORM TROOPER *says something to the girl. She replies in a low voice. They leave, the girl's giggling audible as their footsteps recede.*

RICHARD, *softly, to himself:* Truda used to laugh at my stutter. She had a funny little laugh.

RUBASHOV, *motioning* RICHARD *to reseat himself:* You must give me your promise to write only according to the lines laid down by the Comintern.

RICHARD, *sitting:* Understand one thing, Comrade: Some of my colleagues write easily. I don't. I write out of torment; I write what I believe and feel in here. I have no choice—I write what I must, because I must. Even if I'm wrong, I must write what I believe. That's how we arrive at the truth.

RUBASHOV: We have already arrived at the truth. Objective truth. And with us, Art is its weapon. I'm amazed at you, Comrade Richard. You're seeking the truth for the sake of your own ego! What kind of delusion is this? The individual is nothing! The Party is everything! And its policy as laid down by the Comintern must be like a block of polished granite. One conflicting idea is dangerous. Not one crack in its surface is to be tolerated. Nothing! Not a mustard seed must be allowed to sprout in it and split our solidarity! The "me," the "I," is a grammatical fiction. *He takes out his watch, glances at it.* My time is up. *He puts his watch back in his pocket, rises.* You know what's expected of you. Keep on the line. We will send you further instructions.

RICHARD, *rises:* I don't think I can do it.

RUBASHOV: Why not?

RICHARD: I don't believe in their policy.

RUBASHOV: Against our enemies, we're implacable!

RICHARD: That means . . . ?

RUBASHOV: You know what it means.

RICHARD: You'd t . . . turn me over to the Nazis?

RUBASHOV: Those who are not with us are against us.

RICHARD: Then what's the difference between us and them? Our people here are going over to them by the tens of thousands. It's an easy step. Too easy. *A pause. He speaks almost inaudibly.* Who can say what your Revolution once meant to me? The end of all injustice. Paradise! And my Truda now lies bleeding in some S.S. cellar. She may be dead even now. Yes. In my heart—I know she's dead.

RUBASHOV, *buttons his coat:* We'll have to break this off now. We'd better go separately. You leave first, I'll follow.

RICHARD: What are my instructions?

RUBASHOV: There are none. There's nothing more to be said.

RICHARD: And that's all?

RUBASHOV: Yes, that's all! *Walks off into the shadows.*

RICHARD, *groans:* Christ!

   RICHARD, *the Pietà, and the Museum vanish, leaving* RUBASHOV *alone, pacing his cell. A tap from 402 brings him across to 402's wall.* RUBASHOV *taps three times.*

402, *becomes visible, tapping:* I've a very important question.

RUBASHOV, *taps:* What?

402, *taps:* Promise answer?

RUBASHOV, *taps:* Your question?

402, *taps:* When did you last sleep with a woman?

RUBASHOV, *groans, after a long pause, laughs sardonically:* Now what would you like? *Taps.* Three weeks ago.

402, *taps:* Tell me about it.

RUBASHOV: Ach! *Turns away.*

402, *taps:* Tell me! Tell me! What were her breasts like?

RUBASHOV, *to the wall:* I suppose I have to humor you. *He taps.* Snowy,
fitting into champagne glasses. *Murmurs to the wall.* Is that your style?

402, *taps:* Go on. Details. Her thighs.

RUBASHOV, *taps:* Thighs like wild mares. *To the wall.* How's that?

402: Good fellow! *Taps.* Go on! More!

RUBASHOV, *taps:* That's all. You idiot—I'm teasing you.

402, *taps:* Go on, go on. Details, please.

   *Suddenly the joke goes stale.* RUBASHOV's *face clouds as a haunting
memory rises to torment him. Soft strains of distant music are heard. His
hand brushes his face as if to wipe away the memory.*

RUBASHOV, *taps:* No more.

402, *taps:* Go on, please. Please!

RUBASHOV, *to himself:* No more. No more. *He lies down on his cot, throws
his coat over him, brooding. The music rises.*

402, *taps:* Please! *On his knees, pleading.* Please! *Moans and taps.* Please!
*He buries his head in his cot, pleading inaudibly as the lights fade out
on him.*

   *The lights in* RUBASHOV's *cell dim. The music swells to the strains of a
piano recording of Beethoven's "Appassionata." As the lights come up, the
cell dissolves and becomes* LUBA LOSHENKO's *bedroom.* RUBASHOV's *cot becomes part of a large double bed. At the edge of the bed,* LUBA, *clad only in
her chemise, sits smoking, dreamily staring into space, listening to the music
that is coming from a small gramophone on the table nearby.*

LUBA: So tomorrow I'll have a new boss.

RUBASHOV: Yes.

LUBA: I'll hate him.

RUBASHOV: No. He'll be all right. *They listen in silence. He smiles, musing.*
This music is dangerous.

LUBA: You'll be gone long?

RUBASHOV: I don't know.

LUBA: I'll miss you terribly. *She hums the melody of the music.*

RUBASHOV, *taking out a cigarette:* Get me a match, will you, Luba?

LUBA, *smiles, rises, walks to the table, picks up some matches, crosses to
him, swaying to the music:* I love this. It always makes me feel like crying.
*She lights his cigarette.*

RUBASHOV, *smiling:* Do you enjoy that?

LUBA: Crying? *She blows out the match, laughs.* Sometimes.

RUBASHOV: Our racial weakness.

LUBA: What?

RUBASHOV: Tears and mysticism

LUBA: You mean the Slavic soul?

RUBASHOV, *smiling cynically:* The soul? Soul?

LUBA: I believe in it.

RUBASHOV: I know you do.

LUBA: Petty bourgeois?

RUBASHOV: Yes, Luba, you are. *He looks at her fondly, leans over, pulls her to him, kisses her throat. The music rises.* This music is dangerous. *They listen in silence awhile. She goes to the gramophone and winds it. She leans against the wall near* RUBASHOV.

LUBA: When I was a little girl in the Pioneer Youth I would start crying at the most unexpected moments.

RUBASHOV: You? In the Pioneer Youth? You, Luba?

LUBA: You're surprised? I wasn't in very long. I wasn't good material. *RUBASHOV smiles.* I would cry suddenly for no reason at all.

RUBASHOV: But there was a reason?

LUBA: I don't know. *She smokes for a moment.* Yes, I do. Our primer books made little Pavelik such a hero. All of us children wanted to turn our mothers and fathers over to the G.P.U. to be shot.

RUBASHOV: Was there anything to turn them in for?

LUBA, *laughs gently:* No. Nothing. But I would picture myself doing it anyway and becoming a great national hero like Pavelik. Then I would burst out crying. I loved my parents very much. Of course, no one knew why I was crying. So I was expelled, and my political career ended at the age of nine! *RUBASHOV smiles.* LUBA *hums the melody.* My father loved this. He and mother used to play it over and over and over.

RUBASHOV: Where are they now?

LUBA: They died in the famine after the Revolution. My father was a doctor.

RUBASHOV: Have you any family left?

LUBA: One brother. He's a doctor, too. He's married. My sister-in-law is very nice. She's a Polish woman . . . an artist. *LUBA picks up a small painting, crosses to* RUBASHOV, *kneels at his side.* She painted this picture. It's their baby. A little boy. Two years old. Isn't he fat?

RUBASHOV, *studies it:* Yes, he is fat. *He puts it aside, looks at* LUBA. Why don't you get married, Luba, and have some fat babies of your own? Isn't there a young man at the office . . . ?

LUBA: Yes.

RUBASHOV: I thought so. And he wants to marry you?

LUBA, *rests her cheek on his knee, lovingly caresses his hand:* Yes, he does.

RUBASHOV: Well . . . ?

LUBA: No!

RUBASHOV: Why not?

LUBA: I don't love him.

RUBASHOV: Mm, I see, I see. *A pause.*

LUBA, *suddenly:* You can do anything you wish with me.

RUBASHOV, *studies her:* Why did you say that? LUBA *shrugs her shoulders.* You don't reproach me?

LUBA: Oh, no, no, no! Why should I? *The music swells and fills the room.*

RUBASHOV: This music is dangerous. When you listen to this and you realize human beings can create such beauty, you want to pat them on the head. That's bad. They'll only bite your hand off.

LUBA, *takes his hand, and kisses it:* Like this?

RUBASHOV, *gently:* Luba, you know, with us, there can never be anything more.

LUBA: I don't expect anything more. Did I give you the impression I expected anything more?

RUBASHOV: No. You've been very kind, Luba, and sweet. *Pause.* I may be gone a long time. I may never see you again.

LUBA: Where are you going?

RUBASHOV, *hands her the painting:* Wherever the Party sends me.

LUBA, *rises:* I understand. I'm not asking anything. Only, wherever you go, I'll be thinking of you. I'll be with you in my mind always!

RUBASHOV, *snuffs out cigarette:* But this is exactly what I don't want.

LUBA, *turns toward him:* You don't?

RUBASHOV: No, Luba, no!

LUBA, *quietly:* Oh! *She crosses slowly to the gramophone.*

   *Suddenly, the phantasmagoria of* LUBA *and the bedroom vanishes as the lights are switched on in the cell. The jangle of the key in the lock. The door flies open. A young* GUARD *enters.*

GUARD: All right! Get up. Come with me.

RUBASHOV: Are you taking me to your commandant?

GUARD: Don't ask questions! Do as you're told.

RUBASHOV: Very well. *Rises.* All the posters show our young people smiling.

   *He puts on his overcoat.* Have you ever smiled?

GUARD, *humorlessly:* Yes.

RUBASHOV: Wonderful! When? On what occasion, short of an execution?

   *The* GUARD *grimly motions him out. They go. The light is switched off in his cell, as the lights come up on the prison tier.*

402, *crosses to 302's wall and taps:* They've taken him up.

302, *taps:* So soon?

402, *taps:* Pass it on.

302, *taps:* They've taken Rubashov up. Pass it on.

202, *taps:* I hope they give him a bad time.

302, *taps:* Oh, no! He was friend of the people.

202, *taps:* Yes. *His eyes bulge wildly as he addresses an imaginary group about him.* They're all friends of the people. Didn't they free us? Look at us. Free as birds! Everything's all right, Comrades. The land belongs to us! But the bread belongs to them. The rivers are ours! But the fish are theirs. The forests are ours, but not the wood! That's for them. Everything's for them. *He crosses, taps.* They've taken Rubashov up! Pass it on!

*The taps echo and reecho throughout the prison:* "Rubashov taken up," "Rubashov taken up." *The lights dim and the prisoners in the honeycomb of cells vanish behind the scrim, leaving only a huge pillar of granite and iron shrouded in shadows. The lights come up on an office in the prison. A barred window reveals dawn, and snow falling, outside. The bayonet of a guard cuts back and forth across the window like a metronome. On the wall, over the desk, is a portrait of The Leader seen vaguely in shadow. The rest of the wall is empty except for faded patches where other pictures have been hung and removed. Seated at the desk, smoking a long Kremlin cigarette, is a middle-aged man in officer's uniform. He is rough, heavy-set, jowly, graying at the temples, a face once handsome now dissipated and cynical. He is grimly examining some papers, carelessly dribbling cigarette ashes over his jacket. There is a knock at the door. The officer,* IVANOFF, *calls out,* "Come in." *The* GUARD *enters with* RUBASHOV.

IVANOFF, *gruffly, to the* GUARD: Shut the door. *Exit the* GUARD.

IVANOFF, *rises, shakes his head at* RUBASHOV, *laughs, then familiarly:* Kolya!

RUBASHOV: Well! . . .

IVANOFF: Surprised?

RUBASHOV: Nothing surprises me any more. IVANOFF *laughs, opens a drawer, takes out a box of cigarettes, limps across the room to him.* Are you the commandant here?

IVANOFF, *shaking his head:* I'm your investigator.

RUBASHOV: That makes it difficult.

IVANOFF: Not at all. Not if we're intelligent . . . which we are. *Offers him the box of cigarettes.* Cigarette? RUBASHOV *pauses.*

RUBASHOV: Have hostilities begun yet?

IVANOFF: Why?

RUBASHOV: You know the etiquette.

IVANOFF: Take one! *Forces the box into his hand.* Put them in your pocket, keep them.

RUBASHOV: All right. *He takes a cigarette, and puts the box in his pocket.* We'll call this an unofficial prelude.

IVANOFF: Why so aggressive?

RUBASHOV: Did I arrest you? Or did you people arrest me?

IVANOFF: You people? *Shakes his head, lights his own cigarette.* What's happened to you, Kolya? What a falling-off is here! *Sighs.* Ekh! Ekh!

RUBASHOV: Why have I been arrested?

IVANOFF, *gives* RUBASHOV *a match, genially:* Later. Sit down. Light your cigarette. Relax. *He limps to the door, closes the judas hole, and locks it.* RUBASHOV *sits down.* I saw you last three years ago.

RUBASHOV, *smoking his cigarette with relish:* Where?

IVANOFF: Moscow. *As he talks, he crosses up to the window and pulls the chain, letting down the iron shutters.* You were speaking. You'd just escaped from the German prison. They gave you a bad time, didn't they? They didn't dull your edge, though. *Crosses back to* RUBASHOV. Good speech, plenty of bite. I was proud of my old General.

RUBASHOV: Why didn't you come backstage?

IVANOFF: You were surrounded by all the big wigs.

RUBASHOV, *drily:* Mm, a fine assortment of opportunists, bureaucrats, and variegated pimps. IVANOFF *grins, shakes his head, hobbles to his desk.* RUBASHOV *points to his leg.* Your leg's very good. I hadn't even noticed.

IVANOFF, *nods, smiles, sits on the desk, tapping his leg:* Automatic joints, rustless chromium plating. I can swim, ride, drive a car, dance, make love. You see how right you were? And how stupid I was.

RUBASHOV: You were young and emotional, that's all. Tell me, Sascha, does the amputated foot still itch?

IVANOFF, *laughs:* The big toe. In rainy weather.

RUBASHOV, *smoking:* Curious.

IVANOFF, *lowers his lids, squints at* RUBASHOV, *blows a smoke ring:* Not at all. Doesn't your recent amputation itch?

RUBASHOV: Mine?

IVANOFF, *calmly, blowing smoke rings:* When did you cut yourself off from the Party? How long have you been a member of the organized opposition?

RUBASHOV, *throws his cigarette away, grinds it out under his foot:* The unofficial part is over.

IVANOFF, *rises, stands over him:* Don't be so aggressive, Nicolai!

RUBASHOV, *takes off his glasses, rubs his eyes:* I'm tired, and I'm sick, and I don't care to play any games with you. Why have I been arrested?

IVANOFF, *cynically, crossing back to his desk chair:* Supposing you tell me why.

RUBASHOV, *bounds to his feet, furious:* Stop this nonsense now! Who do you think you're dealing with? What are the charges against me?

IVANOFF, *shrugs his shoulders, leans back in his chair:* What difference does that make?

RUBASHOV: I demand that you either read the charges—or dismiss me at once!

IVANOFF, *blows a smoke ring:* Let's be sensible, shall we? Legal subtleties are all right for others, but for the likes of you and myself? *He taps his cigarette ash off into the tray.* Why put on an act? When did you ever trouble about formal charges? At Kronstadt? *He rises, confronts* RUBASHOV. After all—remember—I served under you. I know you.

RUBASHOV: No man fights a war without guilt. You don't win battles with rose water and silk gloves.

IVANOFF: Not our kind of battles, no!

RUBASHOV, *heatedly:* A bloodless revolution is a contradiction in terms. Illegality and violence are like dynamite in the hands of a true revolutionary—weapons of the class struggle.

IVANOFF: Agreed.

RUBASHOV: But you people have used the weapons of the Revolution to strangulate the Revolution! You've turned the Terror *against* the people. You've begun the bloodbath of the Thermidor. *He controls himself, speaks quietly.* And that's something quite different, my one-time friend and comrade. *Sits.*

IVANOFF: Damn it, Kolya, I'd hate to see you shot.

RUBASHOV, *polishing his glasses, smiles sarcastically:* Very touching of you. And exactly why do you people wish to shoot me?

IVANOFF, *flares up:* "You people!" Again. What the hell's happened to you? It used to be "we."

RUBASHOV, *on his feet again:* Yes, it used to be. But who is the "we" today? *He points to the picture on the wall.* The Boss? The Iron Man and his machine? Who is the "we"? Tell me.

IVANOFF: The people, the masses . . .

RUBASHOV: Leave the masses out. You don't understand them any more. Probably I don't either. Once we worked with them. We knew them. We made history with them. We were part of them. For one little minute we started them on what promised to be a new run of dignity for man. But that's gone! Dead! And buried. There they are. *He indicates the faded patches of wallpaper.* Faded patches on the wall. The old guard. Our old comrades. Where are they? Slaughtered! Your pockmarked leader has picked us off one by one till no one's left except a few broken-down men like myself, and a few careerist prostitutes like you!

IVANOFF: And when did you arrive at this morbid conclusion?

RUBASHOV: I didn't arrive at it. It was thrust on me.

IVANOFF: When? On what occasion would you say?

RUBASHOV: On the occasion when I came back from the Nazi slaughter-house, when I looked about for my old friends, when all I could find of them were those— *Again he waves his spectacles at the telltale patches.* —faded patches on every wall in every house in the land.

IVANOFF, *nods his head, murmurs reasonably:* Mm, hm! I see. That's logical. And that, of course, was when you . . . *The telephone rings.* IVANOFF *picks up the receiver, barks.* I'm busy. *Hangs up.* When you joined the organized opposition . . .

RUBASHOV, *slowly, deliberately:* You know as well as I do, I never joined the organized opposition.

IVANOFF: Kolya! Please! We both grew up in the tradition.

RUBASHOV, *sharply:* I never joined the opposition.

IVANOFF: Why not? You mean you sat by with your arms folded? You thought we were leading the Revolution to destruction and you did nothing? *Shakes his head.*

RUBASHOV: Perhaps I was too old and used up.

IVANOFF, *sits back again, clucks with good-natured disbelief:* Ekh, ekh, ekh!

RUBASHOV, *shrugging his shoulders:* Believe what you will.

IVANOFF: In any event, we have all the proofs.

RUBASHOV: Proofs of what? Sabotage?

IVANOFF: That, of course.

RUBASHOV: Of course.

IVANOFF: If that were all.

RUBASHOV: There's more?

IVANOFF, *nods:* And worse. *Rises.* Attempted murder.

RUBASHOV: Ah! And who am I supposed to have attempted to murder?

IVANOFF: Not personally. You instigated the act. Naturally.

RUBASHOV: Naturally.

IVANOFF: I told you we have proofs. *Picks up a sheaf of typewritten pages and waves them under his nose.*

RUBASHOV: For instance?

IVANOFF: Confessions.

RUBASHOV: Whose?

IVANOFF: For one, the man who was to do the killing.

RUBASHOV: Congratulations. And who was it I instigated to murder whom?

IVANOFF: Indiscreet question.

RUBASHOV: May I read the confession? RUBASHOV *reaches out for the papers.* IVANOFF *smiles, draws them out of his reach.* May I be confronted with the man? IVANOFF *smiles again, shakes his head.* Who the hell would I want to murder?

IVANOFF: You've been sitting there for ten minutes telling me. *He opens a drawer, drops in the sheaf of papers.* The man you tried to murder is the Leader. *He slams the drawer shut.* Our Leader.

RUBASHOV, *takes off his glasses, leans forward, speaks deliberately, between his teeth:* Do you really believe this nonsense? *He studies* IVANOFF. Or are you only pretending to be an idiot? *He suddenly laughs knowingly.* You don't believe it.

IVANOFF, *sits slowly, adjusting his prosthetic leg:* Put yourself in my place. Our positions could very easily be reversed. Ask yourself that question— and you have the answer. IVANOFF *rubs his thigh at the amputation line, stares moodily at the false leg.* I was always so proud of my body. Then to wake, to find a stump in a wire cage. I can smell that hospital room. I can see it as if it were happening now: you sitting there by my bed, soothing, reasoning, scolding, and I crying because they had just amputated my leg. *He turns to* RUBASHOV. Remember how I begged you to lend me your pistol? Remember how you argued with me for three hours, till you per- suaded me that suicide was petty bourgeois romanticism? *He rises, his voice suddenly harsh.* Today the positions are reversed. Now it's you who want to throw yourself into the abyss. Well, I'm not going to let you. Then we'll be quits.

RUBASHOV, *putting on his glasses, studies* IVANOFF *for a second, with an ironic smile:* You want to save me? You've a damned curious way of doing it. I am unimpressed by your bogus sentimentality. You've already tricked me into talking my head off my shoulders. Let it go at that!

IVANOFF, *beams:* I had to make you explode now, or you'd have exploded at the wrong time. Haven't you even noticed? *Gestures about the room.* No stenographer! *He crosses back to his desk, opens a drawer.* You're behav- ing like an infant. A romantic infant. Now you know what we're going to do? *Extracts a dossier from the drawer.*

RUBASHOV, *grimly:* No, what are we going to do?

IVANOFF: We are going to concoct a nice little confession.

RUBASHOV: Ah!

IVANOFF: For the public trial.

RUBASHOV, *nods his head in amused comprehension:* So that's it? There's to be a public trial? And I'm to make a nice little confession?

IVANOFF: Let me finish. . . .

RUBASHOV, *biting out each word:* That is to say, I'm to transform myself into a grinning chimpanzee in a zoo? I'm to beat my breast and spit at myself in a mirror, so the People can laugh and say, "The Old Guard— how ridiculous!" I'm to pick at my own excrement and put it in my own mouth, so the People can say, "The Old Guard—how disgusting!" No, Sascha, no! You've got the wrong man.

IVANOFF, *drawling with exaggerated patience:* Let me finish. *The patience vanishes. He shouts at* RUBASHOV. Which are we to save? Your dignity or your head? *He controls his impatience, begins to talk rapidly, thinking out the plan in his own mind, as he paces to and fro.* You make this confession now. You admit developing a deviation. You joined such-and-such an opposition bloc. You give us their names. (They've all been shot by now, anyway, so nothing's lost.) However, when you learned of their terroristic plans, you were shocked. You broke off with them. You see?

RUBASHOV: Yes, I see.

IVANOFF: Your case then goes to public trial. We refute the murder charge completely. Even so, you'll get twenty years. But in two, perhaps three years, a reprieve. In five years you'll be back in the ring again. And that is all that matters. *He stops and nods cheerfully at* RUBASHOV.

RUBASHOV: No, I'm sorry.

IVANOFF, *his smile fades, he lights a fresh cigarette, speaks slowly, drily:* Then your case will be taken out of my hands. You'll be tried in secret session administratively. You know what that means?

RUBASHOV: Yes. The rubber ball in my mouth, the bullet in the back of the neck.

IVANOFF, *shakes out the match, blows a perfect smoke ring, and smiles:* The methods follow logically. You just disappear into thin air. As far as your followers are concerned, no demonstrations. How can they? Perhaps you're off on a mission? Perhaps you've run away? Hidden somewhere? Suspicious, of course. But what does that matter? N. S. Rubashov has vanished. Pf! Quietly! Forever! That's your alternative. *The phone rings.* IVANOFF *picks up the receiver.* Look here, I'm . . . What? Oh! Yes? Yes. I see. I'll investigate at once. *He hangs up, turns to* RUBASHOV, *chuckles, and nods his head.* You fox! Oh, you old fox! *He picks up the phone, presses a button. An answering voice responds.* Gletkin? Ivanoff. Come to my office at once! The Rubashov arrest. You bungled it, that's what. Yes. At once! *He hangs up. Turns again to* RUBASHOV. Very adroit.

RUBASHOV: Really? What have I done now?

IVANOFF: You've no idea?

RUBASHOV: I have a small notion. Nuisance tactics! Of no real importance. You overestimate them.

 GLETKIN *enters, crosses above the desk, salutes stiffly.* IVANOFF *returns the salute.*

IVANOFF: I have just received a phone call from the prosecutor's office. Your men were instructed to arrest Citizen Rubashov as quietly as possible. What the hell went wrong?

GLETKIN: I'm interrogating the arresting officers now. The prisoner refused them entrance and barricaded his door against them.

IVANOFF: So they shot off the lock?

RUBASHOV, *with mock indignation:* Woke up the whole neighborhood.

GLETKIN, *not glancing at him:* There was no alternative.

RUBASHOV, *over his shoulder to* GLETKIN: There were five alternatives. You need some lessons in elementary tactics.

    *Stung,* GLETKIN *turns toward* RUBASHOV.

IVANOFF, *quickly, commanding:* Go on!

GLETKIN: Then he refused to accompany them on his feet. They were forced to pick him up and carry him out bodily, screaming like a woman.

RUBASHOV: Wrong! Roaring like a bear. A wounded bear. And they tore my pants.

    GLETKIN *stands there, straight as a ramrod, his eyes expressionless, in perfect control now.*

IVANOFF: Your instructions were to treat him with care. You will see that the prisoner gets cigarettes and medical attention.

RUBASHOV: Not unless you furnish an outside physician. I know these prison doctors.

GLETKIN: That is against regulations.

IVANOFF, *to* RUBASHOV: We'll see what can be done. *To* GLETKIN. Wait outside. *Exit* GLETKIN. You'll be given every consideration. Pencil and paper, if you wish . . .

RUBASHOV: Many thanks, but it won't work. I've had my bellyful of this farce. *He rises.* Kindly have me taken to my cell.

IVANOFF: As you like. *He picks up the phone, presses a button, and barks.* Guard! *He hangs up.* I didn't expect you to confess at once. Take your time. You have plenty of time. Think it over. When you are ready to confess, send me a note. *The men stare at each other.* IVANOFF *smiles.* You will. I'm sure you will.

RUBASHOV: Never, Sascha. Never. That's final!

    *The door is opened. The* GUARD *enters.*

IVANOFF: The next decade will decide the fate of the world in our era. Don't you want to be here to see it? RUBASHOV *glances at* IVANOFF, *then turns and goes off with the* GUARD.

    *As soon as* RUBASHOV *leaves,* IVANOFF *drops his monumental calm, rises and calls out irritably,* "Gletkin!" *As* GLETKIN *enters,* IVANOFF *speaks quickly and harshly, hobbling up and down nervously.*

IVANOFF: By now all Moscow knows. Make a full report. Send the arresting officers over to Headquarters. *Indicates the chair.* Sit down. GLETKIN *sits.* Now, look here! I want it clearly understood. This is no ordinary prisoner. We can't afford any more bungling. When you handle this man you dance on eggs! The political and historical importance of these trials is enormous. And N. S. Rubashov is the key figure. We must have his confession. Those are our orders. From the top.

GLETKIN: Then why not turn him over to me? I'll bring you his confession in three days.

IVANOFF: Thanks! And you'll carry N. S. Rubashov to the witness stand in pieces? Wonderful. No, your harsh methods won't work here. Not with this man. *Lights a fresh cigarette, calms down.* He'll confess. There's enough of the old Bolshevik left in him. He'll confess. You're to leave him in peace. I don't want him disturbed. He's to have paper, pencils, cigarettes, extra rations . . .

GLETKIN: Why?

IVANOFF: To accelerate the processes of thought. He has to work this out alone. *Taps his head.* In here.

GLETKIN: This approach, in my opinion, is all wrong.

IVANOFF, *looks at* GLETKIN *with veiled amusement:* You don't like him? You had a little trouble with him a few minutes ago, didn't you?

GLETKIN: That has nothing to do with it.

IVANOFF: Old Rubashov can still spit a sword! What'd he do? Cut you up the middle?

GLETKIN, *coldly:* His personality has nothing to do with it. I hope I'm a better Party member than that. I never allow likes or dislikes to interfere with my judgment.

IVANOFF: Very commendable.

GLETKIN: Only, since this confession is so important to the Party, I consider your method wrong. This won't get you results. I know how to handle these old-timers. They're all rotten at the core. They're all infected with the Western leprosy. If you want a confession, turn him over to me.

IVANOFF: You young people amuse me. You know everything, don't you? The Nazis captured this man, broke his leg, smashed his jaw, killed him, and brought him to life again—I don't know how many times—but they couldn't extract one admission out of him. And finally, he escaped. And you're going to break him for me in three days? *Musing.* No! If he confesses, it won't be out of cowardice. *To* GLETKIN. Your methods won't work with him. He's made out of a material, the more you hammer it, the tougher it gets.

GLETKIN: I don't agree. My experience with these old counter-revolutionaries proves otherwise. The human nervous system at best can only stand so much—and when they have these bourgeois flaws in them, a little pressure—in the right places—and they split like rotten logs.

IVANOFF, *laughs softly, shakes his head:* I'd hate to fall into your hands.

GLETKIN: It's my experience that every human nervous system has a break-

ing point under pain. It's only necessary to find the lever, the special
pain . . .

IVANOFF, *abruptly and harshly:* That'll do!

GLETKIN, *rises stiffly:* You asked me.

IVANOFF, *pause:* Comrade Gletkin, in the early days— *He goes to his desk,
opens a drawer, takes out a bottle and several glasses. He fills the glasses,
pushes one over to GLETKIN.* —before you were born, we started the Revolution with the illusion that some day we were going to abolish prisons
and substitute flower gardens. Ekh, ekh! Maybe, someday. *He tosses off
his drink.*

GLETKIN: Why are you all so cynical?

IVANOFF: Cynical? *Turns and surveys him.* Please explain that remark!

GLETKIN: I'd rather not, if you don't mind.

IVANOFF: I do mind. Explain it.

GLETKIN, *picks up the glass, drains it:* I notice you older men always talk as
if only the past were glorious . . . or some distant future. But we're already
far ahead of any other country, here and now! As for the past, we have to
crush it. The quicker, the better.

IVANOFF: I see. *He sits, shaking his head, amused.* In your eyes, then, *I* am
the cynic?

GLETKIN: Yes. I think so. *He crosses to the table, sets down the glass,
abruptly.*

IVANOFF: Well, that may be. As for Rubashov, my instructions remain. He's
to have time for reflection. He's to be left alone, and he will become his
own torturer.

GLETKIN: I don't agree.

IVANOFF: He'll confess. *He catches the expression in GLETKIN's face, then
sharply.* You're to leave him alone! That's an order.

GLETKIN: As you command. *Clicks his heels, jerks to attention, wheels
about, and marches out as if on parade. IVANOFF curls his lip in disgust,
pours himself a stiff drink, sighs heavily, and drinks . . . as the scene
fades out.*

   *The lights come up on all the cells. RUBASHOV is seated on his cot, smok-
ing, wrapped in thought. The other prisoners are passing communications
down the grapevine.*

202, *taps:* All the prisoners ask Rubashov not to confess. Die in silence.

302, *taps:* Prisoners ask Rubashov not to confess. Die in silence.

   *402 crosses to RUBASHOV's wall and signals. RUBASHOV raises his head,
pauses, slowly rises, glances at the judas hole, then crosses to the wall, responds to the signal.*

402, *taps:* Prisoners ask you not to give in. Don't let them make you go
on trial.

RUBASHOV, *pause, then taps:* How was 302 tortured?

402, *taps:* Steam.

RUBASHOV, *grimly, puffs at his lit cigarette till it glows, blows off the ashes, presses the live coal into the back of his hand, and holds it there without flinching, staring stoically at the blue wisps of smoke that curl up from his burning flesh. Finally, he grinds out the cigarette, tosses it away.*

402, *taps again:* You'll die in silence? You'll die in silence?

RUBASHOV, *taps wearily:* I will. Tell them. I will.

402, *taps:* My respects. You're a man! *He crosses, taps on 302's wall.* Rubashov will die in silence. Pass it on.

302, *taps:* Rubashov will die in silence. Pass it on.

*The news is tapped through the prison and a murmur like a wind rises and falls:* "Rubashov will die in silence . . . Rubashov will die in silence . . ." *The lights fade, and the prisoners in the tier vanish.*

RUBASHOV, *staring at the scorched hand, crosses to his cot, sits, nods his head, and murmurs:* As chimney sweepers come to dust . . . to dust . . . to dust . . . *The lights fade on him.*

*CURTAIN*

## ACT TWO

*Rubashov's cell, five weeks later.*

*At rise: Darkness. Bars of light from the judas hole illumine* Rubashov's *feverish face. His eyes are closed; he is dreaming evil dreams. He breathes heavily, moaning and tossing about fitfully on his cot. Ghostly images hover over and around him; ghostly voices whisper hollowly:* "Rubashov! Rubashov!" *Echoes of the past—* Richard's *voice calling:* "Christ crowned with thorns!," Luba's *voice, rich and low,* "You can do anything you want with me." *The nameless ones appear and disappear, whispering,* "Rubashov, Rubashov."

Rubashov, *dreaming, raises his head, his eyes shut, and cries out:* Death is no mystery to us. There's nothing exalted about it. It's the logical solution to political divergencies. *His head falls back again, turning from side to side, moaning.*

    *The lights come up in the corridor. A sound of heels on a stone floor.* Gletkin *enters from a door right, coming up from the execution cellar; he is followed by a young fellow officer. They move toward* Rubashov's *cell, talking inaudibly.* Ivanoff *enters through the gate, glimpses them, stops short, then calls out sharply:* "Gletkin!" Gletkin *halts, turns to face* Ivanoff.

Ivanoff, *hobbles down to* Gletkin, *scrutinizing him suspiciously:* What are you up to?

Gletkin, *very correct:* I don't understand you, Comrade.

Ivanoff: No, I'm sure you don't. Have you been at my prisoner?

Gletkin: Been at him?

Ivanoff, *irritably:* Laid your hands on him. You understand that, don't you?

Gletkin: I haven't seen Citizen Rubashov for five weeks. However, I am informed, in the line of duty, his fever is worse. I suggest it would be advisable I bring him to the prison doctor.

Ivanoff, *blows a smoke ring, then slowly, measuring his words:* Keep away from him. And keep that prison doctor away from him. *Sharply.* My orders still stand.

Gletkin: Very well, Comrade. They'll be obeyed.

    Ivanoff, *snorts, blows smoke into his face, then turns and limps off. They watch him go. The* Young Officer *turns to* Gletkin, *who has taken out his notebook and is writing in it.*

Young Officer: Comrade Ivanoff's nerves are wearing thin.

Gletkin: I'm afraid this prisoner is proving stubborn. I told them when they brought him in that I could break him.

YOUNG OFFICER: Easily.

GLETKIN: Comrade Ivanoff wants to use psychological methods only.

YOUNG OFFICER, *scornfully:* These old bookworms of the Revolution!

GLETKIN: Tonight I'm using psychological methods. *Closes his notebook, puts it away.* I'll break this prisoner.

YOUNG OFFICER: Against orders?

GLETKIN: No. I won't so much as go near his cell. But— *Glances at his watch.* —inside an hour he'll be ready to confess.

YOUNG OFFICER: How?

GLETKIN, *enigmatically:* It'll be very interesting.

> RUBASHOV *wakes, sits up with a sudden start, listening.*
> The lights in the tier of cells come up.
> *402 sits up abruptly, wakening suddenly, also listens, frozen. 302 and 202 also awaken suddenly and listen to the ominous stillness.*
> The lights fade on GLETKIN and the YOUNG OFFICER.
> *The prisoners rise, one by one, and begin to pace nervously to and fro like caged animals. Once in a while, one of them will pause, listen, and then continue to pace.* RUBASHOV *rises, wipes the perspiration from his face with the sleeve of his coat, listens, then crosses to 402's wall, taps, waits, and 402 responds.*

RUBASHOV, *taps:* Did I wake you?

402, *taps:* No.

RUBASHOV, *taps:* Something's happening. . . .

402, *taps:* You feel it too?

RUBASHOV, *taps:* What?

402, *taps:* Don't know. Something. How's your fever?

RUBASHOV, *taps:* Not good.

402, *taps:* Try to sleep. *Overhead, 302 taps signal.* Wait! *Crosses over to 302's segment of wall, and answers the signal.*

302, *taps:* Who is Bogrov?

402, *taps:* Don't know. *Returns, taps.* Who is Bogrov?

RUBASHOV, *taps:* Mischa Bogrov?

402, *taps:* No first name.

RUBASHOV, *taps:* I know a Mischa Bogrov. Why?

402, *taps:* Name tapped through.

RUBASHOV, *taps:* He arrested?

402, *taps:* Don't know. Name Bogrov. That is all.

RUBASHOV, *taps:* What connection?

402, *taps:* Don't know.

RUBASHOV, *to himself:* Curious.

> *The lights fade on the other prisoners as they start to pace nervously.*

RUBASHOV, *alone, thinking, smiles, murmurs:* Mischa. *He sits on his cot, shaking his head.* Mischa!

  *A chorus of men singing is faintly heard. It grows louder. The bronze glow of a flickering campfire. Russian soldiers and marines of the Revolution, in conglomerate uniforms, half-military, half-civilian, laden with assorted weapons, dangling stick grenades and daggers, are gathered around the fire, smoking, warming their hands, singing.* GENERAL RUBASHOV, *his face shining with reflected firelight, shakes his head and beats out the tune, as a big, snub-nosed, sandy-haired marine with thick shoulders and an enchanting smile sings out in a mellow, ringing voice.*

BOGROV: "In the dawn's light, faintly gleaming
            Stand the ancient Kremlin walls;
            And the land, no longer dreaming,
            Now awakes as morning calls.
            Though the winds are coldly blowing,
            Streets begin to hum with noise;
            And the sun with splendor glowing
            Greets the land with all its joys.
            We'll shout aloud for we are proud;
            Our power is invincible.
            We'll ne'er disband, we'll always stand
            Together for dear Moscow's land."

*The marine punctuates the finish by tossing his hat in the air. The others applaud and shout:* "Bravo Mischa! Bravo Mischa Bogrov!"

MISCHA, *laughs, crosses to* RUBASHOV, *unhooks from his belt a curved, elaborately chased, silver-handled dagger:* Kolya . . .

RUBASHOV: Yes, Mischa?

BOGROV, *presenting the dagger to him:* Here, I want you to have this. To remember me.

RUBASHOV, *laughs:* You may need it, yourself.

BOGROV, *shakes his head, grins. There is something of the good-natured, ingenuous child in this big man:* No. The Civil War is over. No more killing. Now we go home. We build a new life. *He extends the gift again.* Please, take it.

RUBASHOV, *accepts it:* All right, Mischa. Thank you. Now, I have something for you. Can you guess?

BOGROV, *thinks hard, frowning, then his eyes open wide:* Kolya, is it . . . Am I . . . They're . . . ?

RUBASHOV, *beaming, nods:* Tomorrow you'll be a member of the Party.

BOGROV, *overcome with joy:* Me? Me? Mischa Bogrov a member of the Party!

RUBASHOV: You've earned it. You fought well for the Revolution.

BOGROV: I'm ignorant, Kolya; I'm just a stupid peasant and I don't know enough yet—but I'd die for the Revolution.

RUBASHOV: We know that. Now you must learn the meaning of it. You must go to school. You must study, Mischa.

BOGROV: I will, I will. You'll see, you'll be very proud of me. Wherever I am, every year on this day, I'll send you a letter and I'll sign it "Your Comrade, Faithful to the Grave." *The soldiers call for more song,* "Come on, Mischa. More!" For you, I sing this just for you, Kolya.

BOGROV, *sings in a rich voice the chorus of "Red Moscow":*
"We'll shout aloud for we are proud,
Our power is invincible.
We'll ne'er disband, we'll always stand
Together for dear Moscow's land."

*Gradually* BOGROV *and the campfire and the men singing with him fade away, as do their voices, leaving* RUBASHOV *alone in his dank, silent, gray cell, nodding and humming the tune quietly to himself. Lights come up on 402, who is tapping on* RUBASHOV's *wall.* RUBASHOV *crosses to the wall, responds.*

402, *taps:* What day?

RUBASHOV, *taps:* Lost track.

402, *taps:* What you doing?

'BASHOV, *taps:* Dreaming.

\. L, *taps:* Sleeping?

RUBASHOV, *taps:* Waking.

402, *taps:* Bad. What dreams?

RUBASHOV, *taps:* My life.

402, *taps:* You won't confess?

RUBASHOV, *taps:* I told you no.

402, *taps:* Die in silence is best. *Pause.*

RUBASHOV, *to himself, sardonically:* Yes. Die in silence! Fade into darkness! Easily said. Die in silence! Vanish without a word! Easily said.

402, *taps:* Walking?

RUBASHOV, *taps:* Yes.

402, *taps:* Careful of blisters. Walking dreams bad for feet. I walked twelve hours in cell once. Wore out shoes. *He laughs hoarsely.* Didn't mind. *He licks his lips, rolls his eyes, and moans voluptuously.* Mm! I was dreaming women. Ah-h-h! Question: When is woman best? Answer: After hot bath, well soaped all over, slippery. Ha! Ha! *His laughter is tinctured with agony and madness.* Ha! Ha! *He stops, listens. The want of a response from* RUBASHOV *makes him suddenly angry.* What's matter? You didn't laugh. Joke!

RUBASHOV, *shrugs his shoulders, taps:* Ha ha!

402, *bursts into laughter again, taps:* Ha ha! Funny, ha!

RUBASHOV, *taps:* Funny.

402, *taps:* How many women you love? *Pause.* How many?

RUBASHOV, *taps:* None.

402, *taps:* Why not?

RUBASHOV, *taps:* My work. No time.

402, *taps:* You and Revolution. Some love affair! Don't you fellows have sex?

RUBASHOV, *taps:* Oh, yes.

402, *taps:* What you use it for? Write in snow? Ha! Ha! *He doubles up with laughter, plucking at the lean flesh on his arms and thighs.* Good joke?

RUBASHOV, *taps:* Not good.

402, *soured, taps:* No sense humor. No wonder. Your women are half men! Your women have moustaches. You killed the beauty of our women. Son of bitch, son of bitch, son of bitch!

RUBASHOV, *drily, taps:* Repeating yourself.

402, *taps:* Confess. Never in love? Once?

RUBASHOV, *taps:* No. Never. *He sighs heavily, frowns, thinking. 402 vanishes.*

   *A gray-haired man,* HRUTSCH, *materializes, sighing heavily and clutching his breast over the heart.*

HRUTSCH, *laughs timidly:* It's nothing. My heart skips about a bit.

   *The cell fades away.* HRUTSCH *is standing at the desk in the office of the Commissariat of the Iron Works. The vista outside the window reveals the now-completed factory buildings.* HRUTSCH *is obviously frightened and nervous.*

HRUTSCH, *squeezes his speech out in short spasmodic gasps:* Yes, the files are ready for you, and of course you'll want to see the charts. *He turns to the darkness.* LUBA LOSHENKO *materializes, standing there with the charts in her hand, staring at* RUBASHOV *with large, luminous eyes and parted lips. She hands the charts to* HRUTSCH, *but her eyes never leave* RUBASHOV. Ah, here we are. Now, anything you want explained, our secretary here knows them backwards. *He observes them staring at each other.* You remember Comrade Loshenko? *Hands the charts to* RU-BASHOV.

RUBASHOV, *leaning heavily on a cane, steps forward. He walks with a slight limp:* Yes. How have you been, Comrade Loshenko?

LUBA: Very well, thank you, Comrade Rubashov. Welcome back home.

HRUTSCH: Many changes since you've been gone. The factories are completed.

RUBASHOV, *depositing the charts on the desk:* You haven't filled your quota. Iron is off 23 percent, steel 38 percent.

HRUTSCH: Yes, yes, the sabotage is a problem. *He sighs, clutches his heart. He laughs apologetically, indicating his heart.* Every once in awhile it just starts hammering . . . I should complain—look at him. The stories you could tell, Comrade Rubashov? Those Nazis! What they did to you! And he escapes, comes home, and right to work. Wonderful spirit. Wonderful. What an example to us! *He laughs feebly, pants, holding his heart.* Of course, as for us filling the new quota, mechanically it can't be. It's physically . . .

RUBASHOV, *coldly, impersonal:* Those are the orders.

HRUTSCH, *again the fear rises, he essays a feeble smile:* Well, if those are the orders, it will just have to be done, won't it?

RUBASHOV: Yes. I'll send for you. *He dismisses him.* HRUTSCH *goes quickly.* RUBASHOV *turns. He looks at* LUBA *in silence, smiles.*

LUBA: I wondered if I'd ever see you again.

RUBASHOV: It was a question whether anyone would.

LUBA: I know. My prayers were answered. I prayed for you.

RUBASHOV: To which god?

LUBA: I did. I prayed.

RUBASHOV: The same little bourgeoise, Luba. Are you married yet?

LUBA: No.

RUBASHOV: Why not? LUBA *shrugs her shoulders.* Any babies?

LUBA: No. LUBA *laughs.* You've no idea of the excitement here when we read that you were alive and home. We saw a picture of you when you arrived at Moscow, and our Leader had his arm around you. I was so proud. *There is an embarrassed pause.*

RUBASHOV, *glances at the charts:* Hrutsch is in trouble.

LUBA: Poor man, it's not his fault.

RUBASHOV: Whose fault is it?

LUBA: No one's. The men are overworked, and . . . *She stops herself abruptly.*

RUBASHOV: Go on.

LUBA, *shakes her head:* That's all. Who am I to tell you?

RUBASHOV: Go on! Go on!

LUBA, *a sudden outpouring:* They're frightened. Last week more than forty workers were taken away by the G.P.U.

RUBASHOV: Well, we have to have discipline. Socialism isn't going to drop down on us from your nice, neat heaven.

LUBA: Yes, but the machines don't know that. The machines break down, too.

RUBASHOV: Why?

LUBA: The same reason. They're overworked.

RUBASHOV, *sighs:* Problems. *He puts the charts away, turns to her.* Tell me about yourself. Any lovers?

LUBA, *seriously:* No.

RUBASHOV, *teasing her:* No? Why not? Put on those old earrings and find yourself a lover.

LUBA: I thought you were dead, and I didn't want to go on living. I found that out. I wouldn't want to live in a world without knowing you were somewhere in it.

RUBASHOV: Come here. *LUBA goes to him. He puts his arms around her and kisses her.*

LUBA, *begins to tremble and cry:* I thought you were dead. I thought the Nazis had killed you.

RUBASHOV, *burying his face in her hair:* I'm hard to kill.

LUBA: But they hurt you so. Your poor legs—they broke them?

RUBASHOV: The pieces grow together.

LUBA: Was it awful?

RUBASHOV: I forget. *Holds her at arm's length, studies her face.* It's good to see you again, Luba.

LUBA: Do you mean that?

RUBASHOV, *impersonally:* Yes. *He turns from her, picks up the charts.* I have some dictation. Get your pad and pencil. And call in Hrutsch. I'm afraid we're going to have to get rid of that milksop. *Crossing away from her into the shadows.*

LUBA, *very quietly:* Yes, Comrade Commissar.

*The memory scene fades. RUBASHOV, alone, leaning against the stone wall, sighs heavily. Three taps are heard. He responds.*

402, *appears, taps:* Sad!

RUBASHOV, *taps:* What?

402, *taps:* You! Never in love. To die without ever being in love. Sad!

*A chill seizes RUBASHOV; he groans, puts his hand to his swollen cheek, and shivers.*

RUBASHOV, *taps:* Good night.

402, *taps:* What's wrong?

RUBASHOV, *taps:* My fever's back.

402, *taps:* Again? Maybe you should try the prison doctor?

RUBASHOV, *taps:* No, thanks.

402, *taps:* Don't blame you. A butcher!

*They both turn from the wall, pace a few steps, and simultaneously freeze, listening, listening as if the silence itself contained some unheard and unholy sound.*

RUBASHOV, *crosses to 402, taps:* What's that?

402, *taps:* You felt it again?

RUBASHOV, *taps:* In the air . . .

402, *taps:* Yes . . . *The lights fade on 402.*

RUBASHOV, *wipes his feverish brow with the back of his sleeve and slowly paces to and fro, to himself:* What if the Leader is right? In spite of everything. In spite of the dirt and blood and lies. Suppose the Leader is right? *A chill shakes him. He puts on his coat, continues to pace.* Suppose the true foundations of the future are being built here? History has always been an inhumane and unscrupulous builder, mixing its mortar of lies and blood and filth. *He shivers again, pulls his coat tighter.* Well, what of it, Rubashov? Be logical. Haven't you always lived under the compulsion of working things out to their final conclusions? *He accelerates his pacing, counting the steps.* 1 . . . 2 . . . 3 . . . 4 . . . 5 . . . and a half; 1 . . . 2 . . . 3 . . . 4 . . . 5 and a half. *He stops abruptly, as a thought strikes him.* Yes. Yes.

*A sound of distant laughter. Slowly, the figures of some dockworkers materialize, sitting at a small iron table in a pub on the waterfront on the Marseilles docks. They are eating bread and cheese and drinking wine, talking loudly and laughing good-naturedly. A big, stocky man wearing a sailor's sweater and stocking cap is seated next to a little hunchback who wears a sailor's cap and a seaman's pea jacket. Next to the little hunchback sits a third dockworker. The big man is juggling some apples, and the others are watching and roaring with laughter. On the wall over the table is a militant poster demanding sanctions against Mussolini for his rape of Ethiopia. Benito's caricature dominates the scene: the jutting jaw, the pop eyes, the little fez on the shaved dome.*

RUBASHOV, *accompanied by* ALBERT, *a sharp-featured, young French intellectual, with long expressive hands, which are forever gesturing, and a mincing, epicene manner, approaches the table. The little hunchback sees them and rises.*

ALBERT, *waving to him:* Comrade Luigi, head of the Dockworkers' Union. This is the comrade from Moscow.

LUIGI, *smiles and extends his hand:* We're honored. We're honored. *He shakes* RUBASHOV's *hand vigorously.* Please sit down. *He motions to the big dockworker.* Comrade Pablo, business manager of the union.

PABLO, *shakes hands:* How do you like the job we're doing here?

RUBASHOV: You've the strongest dockworkers' union in Europe.

PABLO: Nothing'll get by us. We'll strangle Il Duce.

LUIGI, *introduces the third dockworker:* Comrade André, our secretary.

ANDRÉ: Comrade. *They shake hands.* RUBASHOV *and* ALBERT *sit.*

PABLO: Those Italian ships out there will rot before we call off this strike.

LUIGI: Drink?

RUBASHOV: Coffee, black.

ALBERT: A double fine.

PABLO, *calls, off:* One coffee, black. One double fine.

VOICE, *off:* Coming.

PABLO, *pointing off, shouts a warning to* LUIGI: Luigi, look!—Here comes that cat again.

ANDRÉ: Meow! Meow!

LUIGI, *jumping to his feet in panic, growls at the unseen cat:* Get out! Fft—out! *He throws a spoon across the floor. The cat obviously flees.* ANDRÉ *and* PABLO *collapse in their chairs, holding their sides, filling the café with booming laughter.* LUIGI *looks at them, shakes his head, laughs sheepishly.*

PABLO, *to* RUBASHOV: Luigi don't like cats.

ANDRÉ: But they love him. They come to him like to a bowl of cream.

LUIGI: They got no reason to. *The three laugh.* LUIGI's *laughter becomes a racking cough. The* WAITER *enters and sets the drinks on the table. They are silent until he leaves.*

ANDRÉ: When Luigi escaped from Italy, he lived by killing cats.

PABLO: And selling their skins.

LUIGI: I had no papers. I couldn't get a job.

RUBASHOV: You're Italian?

LUIGI: I'm a man without a country. *He spits at Benito's caricature.* Three years ago I escaped. Benito was after me. I got here into France. No passport. The French police arrest me. Take me at night to the Belgian border. "We catch you here again, God help you!" In Belgium the Belgian police arrest me. . . . "No passport?" Take me to the French border. Kick me back here into France. Six times back and forth. Luigi, the human football. *He grimaces. His two comrades laugh appreciatively.* A man without a country. *They laugh louder and slap him on the back. He laughs.* Well, I can laugh now, too, thanks to Pablo. I meet him in jail. He gets me passport. Finds me this job with the union. I'm alive again, I belong.

PABLO, *leans across the table confidentially to* RUBASHOV: If you need any passports, I have a man will make you anything. A real artist.

RUBASHOV, *nods:* Thanks. I'll remember that.

ALBERT, *half rises, significantly:* The comrade from Moscow has a message for us.

LUIGI: For us? *They all lean forward, intent.*

RUBASHOV: In connection with this strike.

PABLO: Ah! The strike? Don't worry. Nothing'll get by us.

LUIGI: Sh, Pablo! *To* RUBASHOV. Your message?

RUBASHOV: As you know, our strength in the Soviet Union is the strength of the revolutionary movement all over the world.

PABLO, *hits the table with his fist:* You can count on us!

LUIGI: Sh, Pablo! *To RUBASHOV.* The strike?

RUBASHOV: The Italian shipyards are completing two destroyers and a cruiser for us.

ALBERT: For the Motherland of the Revolution!

RUBASHOV: The Italian Government has informed Moscow if we want these ships this strike must be called off at once.

PABLO: What?

ANDRÉ: You want us to call off this strike?

*The dockworkers look at each other, stunned, bewildered.*

LUIGI: But Moscow called on the world for sanctions!

ALBERT: The comrade from over there has explained this is in the interest of the defense of the Motherland of the Revolution.

PABLO, *angrily:* But the Fascists are taking on supplies to make war.

ANDRÉ: To kill Ethopian workers!

LUIGI: To make slaves of them.

ALBERT: Comrades, sentimentality gets us nowhere.

LUIGI, *gesticulates with his dirty handkerchief:* But this isn't right; we can't do this! It isn't fair, it isn't just, it isn't . . .

RUBASHOV, *quickly, sharply:* It isn't according to the rules laid down by the Marquis of Queensberry? No, it isn't. But revolutions aren't won by "fair play" morality. That's fine in the lulls of history, but in the crises, there is only one rule: The end justifies the means.

LUIGI: No, there are principles; the whole world looks to you back there for an example. . . . *He coughs violently into the handkerchief.*

ANDRÉ, *pointing at the scarlet stains on LUIGI's handkerchief:* You see? Blood. He spits blood. Benito gave him that. And took two brothers in exchange. If you knew . . .

LUIGI: That doesn't matter.

PABLO: This is just scabbing.

ANDRÉ: I vote to continue the strike.

PABLO: Strike.

LUIGI: Strike. The meeting is closed. *He stands up.*

RUBASHOV, *rises quickly, decisively:* No, it isn't! I'm in authority now. We have a job to be done here and it will be done.

ALBERT: In spite of agents provocateurs. *PABLO reaches over, grabs ALBERT by the lapels of his coat, and shakes him.*

LUIGI, *rises:* No, Pablo, stop that! Stop! *PABLO releases ALBERT. LUIGI addresses ALBERT.* Provocateurs? For who, in God's name?

ALBERT, *furious, his voice shrill:* For the Fascists.

PABLO: Because we won't load their ships? You hear, Comrades. That's a joke—a rotten joke, isn't it?

LUIGI, *softly:* No, it's not a joke, Pablo; it's rotten, but it's not a joke. *He looks up at the caricature of Mussolini.* The joke is Benito brought me into socialism, me and my two brothers. We lived in Forli, 1911. Italy was starting a war with Tripoli. There was a big anti-war meeting, banners, posters. Benito took the platform. Benito, the humble socialist, in a dirty black suit and a bow tie. *He imitates the crowd.* "Bravo, Benito!" *He mimics the gestures and facial expressions of Mussolini.* "Fellow workers, militarism is our enemy! We hate war!" *He becomes the crowd.* "Bravo, Benito!" *Again he is Mussolini.* "We don't want iron discipline, we don't want colonial adventures! We want bread and schools and freedom." "Bravo, Benito!" *He angrily admonishes the invisible crowd.* "Don't applaud me! Don't follow me. I hate fetishism. Follow my words!" *Softly, nodding to himself.* Benito. *He leans on the table, to* RUBASHOV. We followed his words; my two brothers and I. Ten years later he gives my brothers the castor-oil treatment. To some that sounds like a joke, too. You know what happens when a quart of castor oil is poured down your throat? It tears your intestines to pieces, like you put them in a butcher's grinder, to little pieces. Two brothers I had. Not like me. Well-formed, beautiful, like Michelangelo carved them out of Carrara marble—one a David and one a Moses. I, the ugly one, I escaped. *Softly, tenderly.* Two brothers I had . . . and now—*Fiercely.*—Mother of God, I'm a Fascist! *He coughs convulsively into his handkerchief.* Back where I started with Benito. *He spits at the caricature of Mussolini.*

PABLO, *fervently:* I swear to God it's all true.

ANDRÉ: Luigi's not a Fascist!

ALBERT, *rises, gesticulating with the long slender hands:* Now, Comrades, you're thinking mechanistically. Dialectically, the fact is that, whoever does not serve the long-distance aims of the Party is an enemy of the Party, and therefore, even though he may think himself subjectively an anti-Fascist, he is in fact objectively a Fascist . . .

PABLO, *ironically seizes some dishes, tosses them into the air, juggles them, catches them, then proffers them to* ALBERT *with an ironic bow:* Here! You do it better than I.

RUBASHOV, *rising:* The ships are to be unloaded tomorrow.

LUIGI: Over my dead body.

PABLO: And mine.

ANDRÉ: And mine.

RUBASHOV: You can tear up your cards! *Silence.* The meeting is adjourned.

*Indicating the phone.* Albert. ALBERT *nods, crosses to the phone, picks it up.*

LUIGI, *to the others:* Come. *The three men leave,* LUIGI *coughing as he does.*

ALBERT, *at phone:* André, Pablo, Luigi. Yes. Publish their pictures in tomorrow's press. Front page. Agents provocateurs. Any Party member who even talks to them will be dismissed at once.

RUBASHOV: Their passports!

ALBERT: Ah, of course. *On phone.* Also notify the French police their papers here are forged. Arrange for their immediate arrest and deportation. *He hangs up, grins smugly.* That'll do it! Now little Luigi is really a man without a country!

RUBASHOV, *stonily:* Yes. ALBERT *laughs.* RUBASHOV *turns a withering look of revulsion on him, and then, unable to endure it, shouts at him.* What the hell are you laughing at? What's so funny? ALBERT'S *laughter dies in his throat. He looks pained and puzzled. With an exclamation of disgust,* RUBASHOV *walks away.*

*The scene fades.* RUBASHOV *is back in his cell, pacing nervously.*

RUBASHOV: Yes. . . . We lived under the compulsion of working things out to their final conclusions. I thought and acted as I had to; I destroyed people I was fond of; I gave power to others I disliked. . . . Well—History put you in that position, Rubashov. What else could you do? . . . But I've exhausted the credit she gave me. Was I right? Was I wrong? I don't know. . . . The fact is, Rubashov, you no longer believe in your infallibility. That's why you're lost.

*A tapping.* RUBASHOV *crosses to the wall and replies. The lights come up on 402.*

402, *taps:* Knew something was happening.

RUBASHOV, *taps:* : Explain.

402, *taps:* Executions.

RUBASHOV, *to himself:* Executions? *Taps.* Who?

402, *taps:* Don't know.

RUBASHOV, *taps:* What time?

402, *taps:* Soon. Pass it on.

RUBASHOV, *goes to another wall of his cell, taps, receives an answering click, then he taps out the message:* Executions soon. Pass it on. *To himself, pacing.* Perhaps this time it is you, Rubashov. Well, so long as they do it quickly. *He stops, rubs his swollen cheek thoughtfully.* But is that right? You can still save yourself. One word—"Confess." *Fiercely.* What does it matter what you say or what you sign? Isn't the important thing to go on? Isn't that all that matters?—To go on? *An agonized look appears on his face, as an unbidden memory rises.*

*Faint strains of music.* LUBA's *voice humming the melody of the "Appas-sionata." The prison vanishes. We are in* LUBA's *room. It is a bright Sunday afternoon. The sun is pouring through the window, flooding the room with golden warmth.* LUBA, *kneeling, is snipping sprays of apple blossoms from a large bough spread out on a cloth laid on the floor. She is pruning the twigs preparatory to arranging them in a vase on the table. She hums hap-pily.* RUBASHOV *enters, stands, watching her. She turns.*

LUBA: Oh! I didn't hear you come in. *She rises, goes to him, holding out the flowers as an offering.*

RUBASHOV, *touches them:* Beautiful! Where did you get them?

LUBA: I took a long walk this morning in the country. They were lying on the ground. The branch had broken off an old apple tree. LUBA *notices that* RUBASHOV's *face is strained and lined with fatigue.* You look tired.

RUBASHOV: I am. I've been walking too.

LUBA: Not in the country?

RUBASHOV: No.

LUBA, *crosses to the table, arranges the flowers in the vase:* If you want to walk, you should go out to the country. *Disposing of the flowers, she opens a drawer, takes out a bar of chocolate, and hands it to him.* Yester-day was my lucky day.

RUBASHOV: Chocolate?

LUBA, *triumphantly:* Two bars. I ate one. They were the last in the store. I stood in line three hours. I had to battle for them, but I won.

RUBASHOV, *softly, under the strain of some deep emotion:* Thank you.

LUBA, *kneels, cutting more sprays off the branch, reminiscing:* We had some apple trees at home. On Sundays we'd help Father prune them. There was one huge old tree so gnarled and full of bumps. We had a special affection for that tree. Tch, the pains Father took to save it. We called it his "pa-tient." *Rises with the blooms.* One spring morning he took us out to look at the "patient." It was blossom time. The other apple trees didn't have many blossoms that year—but the "patient" . . . You've never seen so many blossoms on one tree. It took our breath away. The tree was all covered with blooms like snow. Then Father said, "I'm going to lose my patient."

RUBASHOV: Why'd he say that?

LUBA: An apple tree puts out its most beautiful bloom just before it dies.

RUBASHOV: I didn't know that.

LUBA: It's true. The next year the "patient" was gone.

RUBASHOV: Oh!

LUBA: When I'm working at the factory, everything seems matter-of-fact; but whenever I go out to the country, the world suddenly becomes full of mystery. LUBA *looks at* RUBASHOV. *He sits slowly, a strained expression on his face.* What is it? What's wrong?

RUBASHOV, *shakes his head:* Troubles.

LUBA: At the factory?

RUBASHOV, *tastes the chocolate:* There, too. All over. Upheavals. *He glances at the chocolate evasively.* This chocolate is made of soya beans. Tastes almost like real chocolate. *He sighs, pauses.* Luba . . .

LUBA: Yes?

RUBASHOV, *carefully places the chocolate on the table, speaks softly, deliberately:* Orders came in late yesterday, after you left. You'll have to report back to Moscow. LUBA's *hand, lifting a spray of blossoms to the vase, freezes in mid-air.* You're to leave tonight.

LUBA: Tonight?

RUBASHOV, *evading her glance:* Those are the orders. There's a train at ten o'clock.

LUBA, *trying desperately to control her mounting terror:* Why am I being sent back there?

RUBASHOV: They're investigating the files and production records.

LUBA: How long will I be gone?

RUBASHOV: I don't know that, Luba.

LUBA: Why didn't you tell me last night?

RUBASHOV: I wanted to find out what it is about.

LUBA: But I've so much work at the office to clean up. So many . . .

RUBASHOV, *rises:* It's hurried, I know. But that's the way the Bureau does things.

LUBA: What have I done wrong?

RUBASHOV: Nothing.

LUBA: Has my work been unsatisfactory?

RUBASHOV: It's been excellent.

LUBA, *the terror in her voice now:* Then why am I being sent back?

RUBASHOV, *patiently, soothingly:* I told you, they're examining the books.

LUBA, *dully wiping her wet hands on a cloth:* Someone else will take on my job here?

RUBASHOV: Only while you're gone.

LUBA, *turns to* RUBASHOV, *childishly:* I don't want to go.

RUBASHOV: You have to, Luba.

LUBA, *crossing to* RUBASHOV, *pleading:* Can't you help me?

RUBASHOV: You understand, I have enemies. It would look bad for you, if I interceded.

LUBA: For me?

RUBASHOV: For both of us. As if I wanted to conceal something.

LUBA, *her love and her fear for him taking precedent, she studies him:* You're not in any trouble?

RUBASHOV: No.

LUBA: You're sure?

RUBASHOV: Yes. *There is a long pause.*

LUBA, *very simply and directly:* They're not going to arrest me?

RUBASHOV: Of course not.

LUBA: I'm frightened. *She sits, looks about helplessly, a trapped animal.*

RUBASHOV, *goes to her, places his hands soothingly on her shoulders:* There's no need to be. If they should interrogate you, tell them the truth. You have nothing to fear. Just tell them the truth.

LUBA, *whispers:* I'm frightened. *Suddenly the waves of panic explode, and she cries out.* I'm not going to Moscow. I just won't go.

RUBASHOV, *quickly, trying to control the panic:* Then it would look as if you had done something wrong, wouldn't it?

LUBA, *turns to* RUBASHOV, *hysterically:* But I haven't, I haven't.

RUBASHOV: I know that, Luba.

LUBA, *her hysteria mounting, her body trembling, her voice becoming shrill:* Oh God! I want to run away. I want to hide! I want to run away.

RUBASHOV, *grips her arms tightly:* Nothing's going to happen to you. Understand? There are no charges against you. Nothing's going to happen. Nothing, nothing! *He holds her tight and kisses her. She clings to him with all her strength, wildly, passionately returning his embrace. Then she goes limp, withdraws, looks at him, smiles sadly, shakes her head.*

LUBA: I'm sorry. I'm stupid. *She turns to gather up the flowers from the floor.* I'll be all right. *Kneeling.* Ten o'clock?

RUBASHOV: Ten o'clock.

LUBA: The tickets? And my travel warrant? RUBASHOV *plucks them out of his pocket and hands them to her. She takes them quietly. She rises, and, tonelessly.* I'll have to pack now.

RUBASHOV: Yes. I'll go.

LUBA: Not yet.

RUBASHOV: It would be best . . . for both of us, at this time.

LUBA: Yes, I suppose so. *She looks at the bouquet of blossoms in her hands.* Wouldn't it be wonderful if we could just say "No" to them? If we could come and go as we wished, all of us?

RUBASHOV: But we can't, Luba. That would be anarchy. We haven't the right. *He crosses into the shadows.*

LUBA, *almost inaudibly:* No. Of course not. We haven't the right.

 LUBA, *flowers, room, and sunlight, all fade away, leaving* RUBASHOV *alone in his dank cell, talking to himself.*

RUBASHOV: And have I the right to say "No"? Even now? Have I the right to leave—to walk out, to die out of mere tiredness, personal disgust, and vanity? Have I this right?

*The lights come up in the other cells. The prisoners, ears to the wall, are listening for the news. 202 has just received a message. He crosses to 302's wall.*

202, *taps:* They're reading death sentence to him now. Pass it on. *He shuttles back to the other post to listen.*

302, *crosses, taps on 402's wall:* They're reading death sentence to him now. Pass it on. *Shuttles back to listen.*

402, *taps:* They're reading death sentence now. Pass it on.

RUBASHOV, *taps:* Who is he? *But 402 has crossed back to listen to the next messsage.* RUBASHOV *crosses to the rear wall, taps.* They're reading death sentence to him now. Pass it on. RUBASHOV *crosses back to 402's wall to listen.*

202, *crosses to wall, taps to 302:* They are bringing him, screaming and hitting out. Pass it on. *202 returns to his other post, listening.*

302, *crosses, taps to 402:* They are bringing him, screaming and hitting out. Pass it on. *302 returns to his other post.*

402, *taps to* RUBASHOV: They are bringing him, screaming and hitting out. Pass it on.

RUBASHOV, *taps, urgently:* Who is he? *But 402 has gone back to the opposite wall to listen for more news.* RUBASHOV *shuffles over to the rear wall and taps.* They are bringing him, screaming and hitting out. Pass it on. *Then he moves back to 402's wall and taps insistently.* Who is he? *402 crosses to* RUBASHOV's *wall, listening.* RUBASHOV, *very clearly.* What's his name?

402, *taps:* Mischa Bogrov.

RUBASHOV, *suddenly becomes faint, wipes the sweat from his forehead and for a moment braces himself against the wall, walks slowly to the rear wall and leans heavily against it as he taps through:* Mischa Bogrov, former sailor on Battleship Potemkin, Commander of the Baltic Fleet, bearer of Order of Red Banner, led to execution! Pass it on.

202, *taps:* Now! *He crosses to the door and starts drumming on the iron surface.*

302, *taps:* Now! *He crosses to the door and starts drumming on the iron surface.*

402, *taps:* Now! *He crosses to the door and starts drumming on the iron surface.*

RUBASHOV *taps:* Now! *Drags himself across the cell and starts drumming on the door's iron surface.*

*The prison becomes vibrant with the low beat of subdued drumming.*

*The men in the cells who form the acoustic chain stand behind their doors like a guard of honor in the dark, create a deceptive resemblance to the muffled solemn sound of the roll of drums, carried by the wind from the distance. At the far end of the corridor, the grinding of iron doors becomes louder. A bunch of keys jangle. The iron door is shut again. The drumming rises to a steady, muffled crescendo. Sliding and squealing sounds approach quickly, a moaning and whimpering like the whimpering of a child is heard. Shadowy figures enter the field of vision. Two dimly lit figures, both in uniform, drag between them a third, whom they hold under their arms. The middle figure hangs slack and yet with doll-like stiffness in their grasp, stretched out its full length, face turned to the ground, belly arched downwards, the legs trailing after, the shoes scraping on the toes. Whitish strands of hair hang over the face, the mouth is open. As they turn the corner of the corridor and open the trapdoor to the cellar, we see that this tortured, mangled face is* BOGROV'S. GLETKIN *now appears, whispers in his ear.* BOGROV *straightens up, looks about, flings off his captors for a moment, and moans out some vowels.*

BOGROV: Oo . . . a . . . ah; Oo . . . a . . . ah! *Then, with a mighty effort, he articulates the word and bellows out.* Rubashov! Rubashov!

RUBASHOV, *pounds on his door like a madman, screaming:* Mischa! Mischa!

*The other prisoners accelerate their drumming.* BOGROV *is dragged through the cellar door; it clangs shut, and we can hear his voice as he is being dragged down to the execution cellar, growing fainter and fainter, calling* "Rubashov! Rubashov!" *Gradually, the drumming dies down, the other prisoners vanish, a deep terrible silence settles on the prison.* RUBASHOV *stands in the middle of his cell, clutching his stomach to prevent himself from vomiting. He staggers to his cot, collapses on it, and is enveloped by complete darkness.*

*There is a long silence. From somewhere above a prisoner cries out,* "Arise, ye wretched of the earth!"

*The electric light in* RUBASHOV'S *cell is suddenly turned on.* IVANOFF *is standing next to his bed with a bottle of brandy and a glass.* RUBASHOV, *his eyes glazed, is staring, unseeing, into space.*

IVANOFF: You feel all right?

RUBASHOV: It's hot! Open the window! *He looks up at* IVANOFF. Who are you?

IVANOFF: Would you like some brandy? RUBASHOV'S *eyes follow him, dull, uncomprehending.* IVANOFF *pours a drink, extends it to* RUBASHOV. *Sits next to him.* Drink this. IVANOFF *holds the glass, feeding the drink to* RUBASHOV.

RUBASHOV, *finishes the drink, looks at him:* You been arrested too?

IVANOFF: No. I only came to visit you. *He places the bottle and the glass on the floor.* I think you're ill. Are you in pain?

RUBASHOV: No.

IVANOFF: Your cheek is swollen. I think you've a fever.

RUBASHOV: Give me a cigarette. IVANOFF *gives him a cigarette, lights it for him.* RUBASHOV *inhales the smoke deeply, hungrily. After a few moments of this, his eyes come into focus, his breathing becomes a little more regular, and he looks at* IVANOFF, *who is patiently blowing smoke rings.* What time is it?

IVANOFF: Two-thirty A.M.

RUBASHOV: How long have I been here?

IVANOFF: Five weeks tomorrow.

RUBASHOV, *examines* IVANOFF. *He is beginning to think quite clearly now:* What are you doing here?

IVANOFF: I want to talk to you. Some more brandy? *Picks up the bottle.*

RUBASHOV, *the iron creeping into his voice:* No, thank you.

IVANOFF: Lie down. Rest!

RUBASHOV, *sits up, spits out:* You pimp! Get out of here. You're a pimp like all the rest of them! You disgust me—you and your filthy tricks.

IVANOFF: Tricks? *Pours a drink.*

RUBASHOV, *raging:* You drag him by my cell—Bogrov—or what you've left of him, and when my bowels are split open, a savior appears with a bottle of brandy. You think I can be taken in by a cheap trick like that? You think you can wheedle a confession out of me with a bottle of brandy?

IVANOFF, *smiles and shows his gold teeth:* You really believe that I have such a primitive mind?

RUBASHOV: Take your whorish mind the hell out of here! It stinks! It's choking me.

IVANOFF, *drinks:* Very well. I'll go if you want me to.

RUBASHOV: You cannot begin to understand how you disgust me. All of you.

IVANOFF: But first, you listen to me for one second.

RUBASHOV, *shouts:* I don't want to hear any more . . .

IVANOFF, *outshouts him:* I'm afraid you'll have to! *Pauses, gently.* Now listen logically and calmly, if you can. First, to remove any doubts, Bogrov has already been shot!

*There is a long silence as* RUBASHOV *absorbs this news, then—*

RUBASHOV, *low, strangulated:* Good!

IVANOFF: He was also tortured for several days.

RUBASHOV: That was obvious.

IVANOFF: It was meant to be. But not by me. *Sits next to* RUBASHOV, *placing the bottle on the floor.* I'm going to put my life in your hands, Kolya.

RUBASHOV *looks at him.* If you mention what I tell you, to anyone, I am done for. This filthy trick, as you call it, was arranged by my young colleague, Gletkin, against my instructions. I would never make this mistake, not out of concern for you, but because it's bad psychology. You've recently been suffering humanitarian scruples? A scene with Bogrov could only intensify them. Obvious? Only a fool like Gletkin makes such mistakes. He's been urging me to use his methods on you too!

RUBASHOV: You can torture me; it will get you no results.

IVANOFF: Won't it? *He smiles cynically, reaches for the bottle.* You don't know Gletkin. *He fills the glass, studies it.* He's something new in the world—the Neanderthal Man! He came after the flood. He had no umbilical cord to the past. He was born without a navel. He doesn't approve of us old apes in general, and of *you* in particular. *He shakes his head at* RUBASHOV. It seems the other day you showed him your behind. He didn't like that. *Ominously.* He wants to lay his big hands on you.

RUBASHOV: I'm quite prepared to die.

IVANOFF: But I'm not prepared to let you die. Your martyrdom, Kolya, will consist of not being allowed to become a martyr. That's not why you're here. We need you, and we need you logical, because when you've thought the whole thing out clearly, then, but only then, will you make your confession. Am I right?

RUBASHOV: Go away, it's no use.

IVANOFF: Do you believe that I'm telling you the truth? *Pause.* Do you?

RUBASHOV: Yes . . . I suppose so.

IVANOFF: Then why do you want me to go? *He bends forward, pushing his face into* RUBASHOV'S, *mockingly.* Because you are afraid of me, because my way of reasoning is your way and you're afraid of the echoes in your own head.

RUBASHOV, *impatiently:* I've had enough of this reasoning. We've been running amok with it for thirty years. Enough.

IVANOFF: Get thee behind me, Satan. *Rises, goes to the door, peers out the judas hole, turns back.* In the old days temptation was carnal. It took the form of little naked women running around shaking their things in your face. Today it's cerebral. It takes the form of naked reason pushing facts in your face. Values change. *He drinks.*

RUBASHOV: Why was Bogrov tortured?

IVANOFF: He was stubborn like you.

RUBASHOV: Did you hear him whimpering?

IVANOFF: No. I didn't hear it. But I've heard and seen others. *He wheels on* RUBASHOV, *stabbing an accusing finger at him.* And so have you! And so have you, my General! *He hobbles to* RUBASHOV, *face thrust forward, accusingly.* What of it? A conscience is as unsuited to a revolutionary as a double chin. Since when did N. S. Rubashov develop this bourgeois conscience? Hm? When? *Pause.* Shall I tell you? The day, the hour, the minute? Nine months, two weeks ago—at 3:10 A.M.—when your little secretary, Luba Loshenko, was shot! *He sits next to* RUBASHOV. You were sleeping with her, weren't you? Now she's dead. So you're making the world a metaphysical brothel for your emotions. What have the shape of Luba Loshenko's breasts or Bogrov's whimperings to do with the new world we're creating?

RUBASHOV: Bogrov's dead, she's dead. You can afford a little pity.

IVANOFF: I have many vices—I drink, for a time, as you know, I took drugs; but so far I've avoided the vice of pity. One drop of that and a revolutionary's lost. *He fills his glass.* The great temptation! To renounce violence, to make peace with ourselves . . . hm? *He drinks.* I prefer my synthetic ecstasy in a glass. You get over it in the morning.

RUBASHOV, *after a long silence, shakes his head, murmurs sadly:* Our golden dream! *Then savagely.* What a stinking mess we've made of it.

IVANOFF, *setting down the glass, articulates carefully:* Have we? *He lights a fresh cigarette.* We've taken the land from the landlords. *He blows a smoke ring.* We've freed them from industrial exploitation. *He blows another.* For the first time in history a revolution is functional.

RUBASHOV: Functional? *He jumps to his feet, furious.* So functional in taking the land, in one year, we let five million farmers and their families die of starvation! Deliberately. So functional— *He begins to pace up and down.* —in freeing the people from industrial exploitation, we sent ten million of them to forced labor under worse conditions than galley slaves. *He plucks off his spectacles nervously and waves them at* IVANOFF. So functional, to settle a difference of opinion, the omnipotent Leader knows only one argument—Death!—whether it's a matter of submarines, manure, or the party line in Indochina. Death! *He replaces his spectacles and glares at* IVANOFF.

IVANOFF, *rises, belligerently:* That woman has really given you softening of the brain! What of the millions who die of starvation in China and India, of tuberculosis in rice fields, cotton plantations . . . ?

RUBASHOV: In negatives we agree. Where has it led us?

IVANOFF: Well, where?

RUBASHOV: Our standard of living is lower than the most backward country in Europe. Labor conditions are harder; discipline's more inhuman. Our country is run by the police. *Again he plucks off the glasses for emphasis.* We've torn the living skin off our people and left them standing with bare tissues, muscles and nerves quivering.

IVANOFF: Well, and what of it? *With warmth and conviction.* Don't you find that wonderful? Has anything more wonderful ever happened in history? We're tearing the old skin off mankind and giving it a new one! That's not an occupation for people with weak nerves, but there was a time it filled you with enthusiasm.

RUBASHOV: I know.

IVANOFF: Look at the pamphlets put out by the antivivisectionists. When you read how some poor cur who has just had his liver cut out, whines and licks his tormentor's hand, it breaks your heart. But if we listened to these sentimentalists, we'd have no cures for typhus, cholera, diphtheria . . .

RUBASHOV: I know, I know, I know. *He turns away, sits, moodily.*

IVANOFF, *following him, persistently:* Of course you do. Better than I. And you still insist on being a martyr? *He waits for an answer. Finally he throws up his hands and growls in disgust.* All right. Have it your way. *He picks up the bottle and glass.* If you must throw yourself into the dustbin of history, I can't stop you. Go. Let Gletkin have you. You're his. *He turns to the door, pauses, turns back. His voice becomes soft.* Only tell me, why? Why are you so in love with death? It stinks! Why do you want to die?

RUBASHOV, *hoarsely:* I don't want to die. No one does.

IVANOFF: You act as if you do.

RUBASHOV: It's a fake. *He clutches his throat.* From here up, I'm resigned. From here down, I'm frightened.

IVANOFF: Yet I offer you your life.

RUBASHOV: On what terms?

IVANOFF: The only terms that matter. To go on being useful. *He places the bottle on the floor and fumbles in his pocket.*

RUBASHOV: To act the fool in public trial? No, thanks. The terms are too high.

IVANOFF, *taking out an official communication, pushes it under* RUBASHOV's *nose:* Here's a confidential report I received today. RUBASHOV *takes it, glances at it.* Read between the lines.

RUBASHOV, *drily:* I need no instructions, thank you. *Studies the document.*

IVANOFF: What do you see?

RUBASHOV: War! It's coming.

IVANOFF: How soon?

RUBASHOV: Depends on how we play our cards. Perhaps years, perhaps months.

IVANOFF: The last war gave us Russia, Kolya; the next gives us the world. Or does it?

RUBASHOV: It could, if . . .

IVANOFF: If . . . ? Good! *He sits next to him.* There's a breach in the Party, in the whole country; the people are restless, dissatisfied; our economy is in pieces. The breach must be mended first; and you, and those who think like you, must mend it!

RUBASHOV: Hence the trials! *Hands him back the document, contemptuously.* They're better than the opera or the theatre.

IVANOFF: The goal, Kolya. It's coming. Nearer. Listen. You can hear it on the wind. And when that day comes . . .

RUBASHOV: The Gletkins take over.

IVANOFF: They're brutes. They don't count.

RUBASHOV, *plucking off his spectacles and glaring at* IVANOFF: Who made them brutes? We did! Their Byzantine leader worship is frightening. Their cultivated ignorance is disgusting.

IVANOFF: Would they have been any use to us any other way?

RUBASHOV: You'd trust our revolution to them?

IVANOFF: Why do you think I'm risking my neck to save you? It's your brain I want to save. When the day comes, your brain will be needed. We'll get rid of them. You'll be needed more than ever!

RUBASHOV, *studies him, replaces his spectacles, shakes his head:* If I thought that . . .

IVANOFF, *strongly:* Think it! Think it! *He watches* RUBASHOV *wrestle with the thought, then leans forward, and softly.* What other choice have you? To become a Christian martyr? For the Western democracies?

RUBASHOV, *rises, angrily:* What are you talking about, "the Western democracies"? What have I to do with those decadent humanists—those phantoms of religion and superstition?

IVANOFF, *pressing his point, sharpening his irony:* Do you want their liberal press, that hated your guts while you were alive, to sanctify you after your death?

RUBASHOV: The liberal press? Those puking jackals of holy property? What have I to do with them? I'd rather be two feet of manure in a Russian field. *He nervously polishes the glasses with his shirt.*

IVANOFF: Nevertheless, they'll put you in a stained-glass window. Saint Rubashov—the martyr for the Western world! Is that what you want?

RUBASHOV *looks at him, looks away, ponders, replaces the spectacles, sighs. For a long time he stands there, head bowed, wrapped in thought.* IVANOFF *watches him patiently.*

RUBASHOV, *finally, wearily:* I'll think it over.

IVANOFF, *triumphantly picks up his bottle, rises, and going to the judas hole, calls:* Guard! *He turns back to* RUBASHOV, *beaming.* You old warhorse.

You've had an attack of nerves. *The* GUARD *opens door.* But that's over now. Go to bed. Get some sleep. You'll need a clear head tomorrow when we make up your statement.

RUBASHOV, *frowning:* I said I'll think it over.

IVANOFF, *nods, laughs:* Good night, Kolya.

RUBASHOV: Good night, Sascha.

IVANOFF *goes.* RUBASHOV *stands, thinking, thinking. In the corridor,* IVANOFF *sees* GLETKIN, *leaning against the wall, watching* RUBASHOV'S *cell.*

IVANOFF, *crosses to* GLETKIN, *with supreme contempt:* What genius inspired you tonight? *Pause. He blows a smoke ring.* It's all right. He'll confess. But I had to sweat blood to repair the damage you did. You are all still suffering from personal feelings. In his place you'd be even more stubborn.

GLETKIN: I have some backbone, which he hasn't.

IVANOFF: But you're an idiot! For that answer alone, you ought to be shot before he is! *He blows a cloud of cigarette smoke directly into* GLETKIN'S *face, shows his gold teeth in a grin of utter disdain, and hobbles off down the corridor.*

GLETKIN *stands there as if he were made of stone, the face completely without expression, then he raises his hand and waves aside the fumes of smoke with a sudden, quick gesture.*

*DIM-OUT AND CURTAIN*

## ACT THREE

> RUBASHOV'S *cell; several days later.*
>
> *At rise:* RUBASHOV *seated on the cot, his shoes off, his coat thrown over his shoulders, a pad of blank paper on his knee, is writing intently, completely absorbed. He pauses, chews his pencil, studies the page, writes rapidly. Alongside him is a stack of completed pages. The tensions and the fever appear to have abated. As he writes, three taps are heard from 402's wall. He ignores them. Three more taps. Then three more. He glances up, annoyed, but continues to work. The taps now flow from 402's wall rapidly and insistently in a staccato stream. With an exclamation of annoyance,* RUBASHOV *tears off the page he has just completed, lays it carefully on the pile next to him, rises, and, crossing to the wall, taps. The lights come up on 402.*

402, *taps:* I tried to talk to you all day. Why didn't you answer?

RUBASHOV, *taps:* I've been busy.

402, *taps:* How?

RUBASHOV, *taps:* Writing.

402, *taps:* What?

RUBASHOV, *taps:* A new theory.

402, *taps:* What about?

RUBASHOV, *smiling ironically, taps:* The immaturity of the masses. The historical necessity for dictatorship.

402, *taps:* Repeat!

RUBASHOV, *taps:* Never mind.

402, *taps:* What's happened?

RUBASHOV, *taps:* I'm waiting for word. Upstairs.

402, *taps:* Why?

RUBASHOV, *taps:* I am confessing.

402, *pauses, stunned by this volte-face, then angrily, taps:* I'd rather hang.

RUBASHOV, *cynically, taps:* Each in his own way.

402, *taps slowly:* I thought you an exception. Have you no honor?

RUBASHOV, *taps:* Our ideas of honor differ.

402, *taps:* Honor is to live and die for your beliefs.

RUBASHOV, *taps:* I am living for mine.

402, *taps louder and more sharply:* Honor is decency.

RUBASHOV, *taps slowly, calmly:* What is decency?

402, *very excited, taps:* Something your kind will never understand.

RUBASHOV, *taps:* We have replaced decency by reason.

402, *taps:* What reason?

RUBASHOV, *taps:* Pure reason.

402, *taps:* You're pure son of bitch.

RUBASHOV, *amused, chuckles and taps:* Flattery does not impress me.

402, *taps:* I'll never talk to you again.

 *The scene is interrupted by a jangling sound. The door of* RUBASHOV'S *cell is thrown open. A* YOUNG OFFICER *enters.*

OFFICER: Put on your shoes!

RUBASHOV: Well! It's about time! *Crosses to the cot, sits, and proceeds to put on his shoes, leisurely.* I've been waiting on Commissar Ivanoff for several days.

OFFICER: Put on your shoes, and come with me.

RUBASHOV: You might have timed it a little more considerately. But I suppose you Neanderthal men only come out after midnight.

OFFICER: Don't talk so much. Just put on your shoes and hurry up.

RUBASHOV, *looks at the* OFFICER, *smiles, shakes his head as he ties the laces:* Brutes! *He rises, the* OFFICER *motions him out with a jerk of the head.* RUBASHOV *goes, remarking over his shoulder.* But then you wouldn't be any use to us if you weren't, would you? *Exit. The* OFFICER *frowns, follows him out. The lights in the cell dim out.*

402, *watching at the judas hole:* Son of a bitch! *He crosses up to 302's wall, taps.*

 *The lights come up in the tier above. 302 is pacing. He stops at the sound of tapping, crosses, and listens.*

402, *taps:* Rubashov is a filthy coward.

302, *taps:* You're wrong. He's brave. My father told me.

402, *taps:* Your father is mistaken . . .

302, *taps:* What's he done?

402, *taps:* He's saving his skin. He's confessing. They've taken him up now.

302, *taps:* Oh, my God! Pray for me.

402, *taps:* For you?

302, *taps:* Yes, for me. *He crosses, taps on 202's wall. The lights come up on 202, who responds and listens. 302 taps.* Rubashov confessing. Pass it on.

202, *groans, crosses to opposite wall, taps:* Rubashov confessing. Pass it on . . .

 *The tappings multiply and the murmur* "Rubashov confessing, Rubashov confessing" *echoes back and forth through the prison. The cells dim out slowly as the lights come up on* IVANOFF'S *office. Seated at the desk, his chair wheeled around, his back to us, is a man in uniform, apparently* IVANOFF. RUBASHOV *enters, accompanied by the* GUARD. *There is a faint ironic smile on* RUBASHOV'S *lips as he enters. The man seated at the desk swings his chair round to face* RUBASHOV. *It's not* IVANOFF, *it's* GLETKIN! *He looks at* RUBASHOV, *stony-faced. The smile on* RUBASHOV's *lips vanishes, he pauses in his stride, looks about quickly. Near* GLETKIN *a grim-lipped young woman, obviously a secretary, sits, sharpening her pencils.*

GLETKIN, *rises, waves the* GUARD *out:* Shut the door! *The* GUARD *goes, shutting the door behind him.* GLETKIN *turns to a heavy floor lamp nearby and switches it on. There is a humming sound, and a fierce, white light strikes* RUBASHOV *full in the eyes. He jerks his face away as if he'd been struck, then turns back to face* GLETKIN, *squinting and shielding his eyes with his hand.* GLETKIN *sits, picks up some official documents.* We will proceed with your examination. You wish to make a full confession?

RUBASHOV, *takes off his glasses and wipes his eyes:* Yes. To Commissar Ivanoff. Not to you.

GLETKIN: You will make your confession to me, here and now, or this investigation is closed, and you will be sentenced at once. Those are my orders from above. RUBASHOV *puts on his spectacles and tries to meet* GLETKIN's *gaze, but the harsh light blinds him. He removes his glasses again.* You have your choice. Which is it?

RUBASHOV, *avoiding the light:* I am ready to make a statement.

GLETKIN: Sit there.

RUBASHOV: On one condition. *He turns to* GLETKIN *firmly, even though he has to almost shut his eyes.* Turn off that dazzle-light! Save these devices for gangsters.

GLETKIN, *calmly:* You're in no position to make conditions. The fact is you are charged with being the worst kind of "gangster."

RUBASHOV, *controls his anger:* Exactly what are these charges? Please read them to me. Up till now this hasn't been done.

GLETKIN: Very well. Sit here! RUBASHOV *sits in the chair upon which the dazzle-light has been trained.* GLETKIN *reads the official statement in a rapid monotone.* "Enemy of the people, Nicolai Semonovitch Rubashov, you are charged with being a counterrevolutionary in the pay of hostile, foreign governments; of having, at the instigation of their agents, committed such acts of treason and wreckage as to cause vital shortages—undermining the military power of the U.S.S.R. You are also charged with having incited an accomplice to attempt the assassination of the Leader of the Party, i.e., you are charged with crimes covered by Articles 58-1A; 58-2; 58-7; 58-9; and 58-11 of the Criminal Code." *He drops the official papers and looks up.* You've heard the charges? You plead guilty?

RUBASHOV, *turns to face him, shielding his eyes with his hand:* I plead guilty to having fallen out of step with historical necessity. I plead guilty to bourgeois sentimentality. I plead guilty to having wanted an immediate alleviation of the Terror, and extension of freedom to the masses. *The secretary, who is writing this in shorthand, smiles contemptuously. RUBASHOV glances at her.* Don't be cynical, young woman *To GLETKIN.* I now realize fully that the regime is right and I am wrong. The times demand a tightening of the dictatorship; any sentimental aberrations at the present moment in history could become suicide. In this sense can you call me a counterrevolutionary, but in this sense only. With the insane charges made in the accusation I have nothing to do. I deny them categorically.

GLETKIN: Have you finished?

RUBASHOV: I deny that I, Rubashov, ever plotted against my country. I deny that I am in the pay of a foreign government. I deny any act of sabotage. I deny ever having taken the least part in any act of terror against the Leader of the Party. *To the stenographer, quietly.* Have you all that, young woman?

GLETKIN: Have you finished?

RUBASHOV: I have finished.

GLETKIN: Wipe your lips then. They're slimy with lies. Lies! Lies! Vomit! *He snatches a thick dossier off the desk, and cracks RUBASHOV across the face with it.* The statement you have just made is vomit. Enough nobility! Enough posturing! Enough strutting! What we demand of you is not high talk, but a full confession of your real crimes!

RUBASHOV, *his hand to his face, breathing hard, biting back the indignation, fighting for control:* I cannot confess to crimes I have not committed.

GLETKIN, *pressing a button on the desk:* Oh, no, that you cannot. *The GUARD enters, bringing in 302, whose eyes at once fix on GLETKIN, and who moves and talks like a sleepwalker. There is something in his manner of the helpless child, desperately eager to be "good" and to please. GLETKIN dismisses the GUARD with a nod, then points to a spot on the floor.* Step over here. *Immediately, 302 nods and shuffles over to stand correctly as designated. GLETKIN crosses above the desk. To RUBASHOV.* Do you know this person? *Pause. Harshly.* You will please pay attention! Do you know this person?

RUBASHOV: The light's in my eyes.

GLETKIN, *softly:* Stand up! *RUBASHOV hesitates. GLETKIN roars.* Stand up! *RUBASHOV rises.* Step over there! *He points to 302. RUBASHOV walks up closer.* Do you recognize him now?

RUBASHOV, *shielding his eyes from the blinding light, scrutinizes 302, then shakes his head:* No.

GLETKIN: You've never met him before?

RUBASHOV, *hesitates:* Mm . . . No.

GLETKIN: You hesitated. Why?

RUBASHOV, *studies 302's face:* I don't place him.

GLETKIN: Your memory was once proverbial in the Party. *A long pause.* You refuse to answer?

RUBASHOV: I do not refuse to answer. I simply do not place him.

GLETKIN: Good. Sit down. *RUBASHOV sits. GLETKIN turns to 302.* Help Citizen Rubashov's memory. Where did you last meet him?

302: Citizen Rubashov instigated me to murder the Leader of the Party by poison . . .

GLETKIN, *irritably:* I didn't ask you that. I asked you where you last met him.

RUBASHOV, *smiles grimly, and mutters:* Wrong lever.

GLETKIN, *turns on him, snaps:* What?

RUBASHOV: The automatic barrel organ played the wrong tune.

GLETKIN, *ominously:* I warn you. Remember where you are. We want none of your so-called wit. *Nods to 302.*

302: I met Citizen Rubashov in Brussels.

GLETKIN: Can you remember the date?

302: Distinctly. It was on the 17th anniversary of the Revolution. At his apartment!

RUBASHOV, *studying 302, suddenly puts his hand to his forehead:* Yes, of course. The date is correct. I didn't recognize Joseph Kieffer. *To GLETKIN.* Congratulations!

GLETKIN: You admit you knew him then? You met him on the day and occasion aforementioned?

RUBASHOV, *his eyes glued to the terrible spectacle of 302's mangled, ghostlike mask:* I've just told you that. If you'd informed me at once that he was the son of my unfortunate friend, Professor Kieffer, I'd have identified him sooner.

GLETKIN, *turns to 302:* How did this meeting come about?

302: After the reception at the Legation my father took me up to Citizen Rubashov's apartment.

GLETKIN, *nods:* Go on.

302: He and my father hadn't seen each other for years. They talked about the early days of the Revolution.

GLETKIN: They were drinking?

302: Yes. They drank and talked. *A faraway look and a gentle smile illumine his face at the memory.* In the last few years I've never seen my father in such a good mood.

GLETKIN, *quietly:* That was three months before the discovery of your father's counterrevolutionary crimes and his execution!

*302 darts a glance at him, licks his lips, and stands there dumb.*

*RUBASHOV turns to GLETKIN on a sudden impulse, but, blinded by the light, he shuts his eyes and turns slowly away, taking off his spectacles and wiping them on his sleeve. The secretary's pencil scratches on the paper and stops. After a long pause 302 regains himself.*

302: Yes.

GLETKIN: Proceed! Repeat their conversation. Only essentials.

302: He said . . .

GLETKIN: Rubashov?

302: Yes. Rubashov said, since the Boss sat on the Party with his broad posterior, the air underneath was no longer breathable. He said they must hold tight and wait the hour.

GLETKIN: What did he mean by that? "Wait the hour"?

302: The hour in which the Leader would be eliminated.

　　*RUBASHOV smiles.*

GLETKIN: These reminiscences seem to amuse you.

RUBASHOV: Two old friends get a little drunk, talk carelessly, and you make a conspiracy.

GLETKIN: So Rubashov spoke of the hour in which the Leader of the Party would be eliminated? How eliminated?

302: My father said someday the Party would force him to resign.

GLETKIN: And Rubashov?

302: Laughed. He said the Boss had made the Party bureaucracy his puppets. He said the Boss could only be removed by force.

RUBASHOV: By this I meant political action.

GLETKIN: As opposed to what?

RUBASHOV: Individual terrorism.

GLETKIN: In other words, you preferred civil war?

RUBASHOV: No, mass action.

GLETKIN: Which leads to civil war. Is that the distinction on which you place so much value?

RUBASHOV, *loses patience, shouting:* I cannot think straight with that damned light in my eyes.

GLETKIN, *outshouts him:* I can't change the lighting in this room to suit you. *To 302, quietly.* So Rubashov said they had to use violence? *302 nods.* And his wild talk, plus the alcohol he'd fed you, inflamed you?

302, *after a pause:* I didn't drink, but he—yes, he made a deep impression on me.

GLETKIN: And later that evening he outlined his plan for you to murder the Leader? *302 is silent. He blinks into the light. RUBASHOV raises his head. A pause, during which one hears only the lamp humming.* Would you like your memory refreshed?

302, *quivers as though struck by a whip:* It didn't happen that evening, but next morning.

RUBASHOV, *to* GLETKIN: I believe the defendant has the right to ask questions.

GLETKIN, *fiercely:* You have no rights here! *He leans forward to make some notations, and after a brief pause, without looking up.* Go ahead! Ask your questions.

RUBASHOV, *rises, steps toward 302, very gently:* Now, Joseph, if I remember correctly, your father received the Order of Lenin the day after the celebration of the 17th anniversary of the Revolution.

302, *whispers:* Yes.

RUBASHOV, *gently:* So that is correct. If I again remember rightly, Joseph, you were with him at the time he received it. *302 nods.* And as I recall it, the Order was presented at Moscow. Right, Joseph? *302 nods. RUBASHOV pauses, turns to GLETKIN.* Professor Kieffer took a midnight plane, and young Kieffer went with him. This alleged instigation to murder never took place, because at the alleged moment young Kieffer was hundreds of miles away, high in the clouds.

*The secretary's pencil comes to a sudden standstill. She turns to GLET-KIN. 302, his face twisting with bewilderment and fear, also looks to GLETKIN.*

GLETKIN, *calmly:* Have you any more questions?

RUBASHOV: That is all for the present. *Sits.*

GLETKIN: Now, Joseph—*Rises, assumes RUBASHOV's gentleness, even exaggerates it, crosses to 302.*—did you leave with your father? Or did you, in fact, join him later after your rendezvous with Rubashov?

302, *almost a sob of relief:* After! I joined my father later.

GLETKIN: In time to be with him for the presentation?

302: Yes. Yes.

GLETKIN, *nods, turns to RUBASHOV:* Have you any more questions?

RUBASHOV: No.

GLETKIN, *turns to 302:* You may go.

302: Thank you . . .

GLETKIN, *calls:* Guard!

*A uniformed GUARD enters and leads 302 out. At the door 302 turns his head once more to RUBASHOV. RUBASHOV meets 302's imploring glance for a second, then turns away. Exit 302.*

RUBASHOV, *angrily:* Poor devil! What have you done to him?

GLETKIN, *who has walked away, the full diameter of the room, turns, bellowing:* What can be done to you! *And, with incredible speed for such a huge man, he hurls himself across the room, grabs RUBASHOV by the throat, and pulls him to his feet.* We have many ways of making a man tell the truth.

RUBASHOV, *quickly:* Very well, what do you want me to sign? GLETKIN *re-*

*laxes his grip.* If you torture me, I will sign anything you place before me. I will say anything you wish me to say at once. But tomorrow I will recant. At the public trial I'll stand up in open court and I'll cry out for all the world to hear, "They are drowning the Revolution in blood. Tyranny is afoot. She strides over our dead bodies." You've become quite pale. It would end your career, wouldn't it? You hold me by the throat, young man, but I hold you by the throat too. Remember that!

GLETKIN, *slowly releasing* RUBASHOV: Why do you make this so personal?

RUBASHOV: Death, even in an impersonal cause, is a personal matter. Death and promotions. *Sits.*

GLETKIN: I am here only to serve the Party. I am nothing. *He sits at the desk, gathering up his papers.* The personal element in this case has been removed along with your friend Ivanoff.

RUBASHOV, *his face clouding, apprehensively:* Removed?

GLETKIN: There'll be no partial confessions; there'll be no bargains. We promise you nothing.

RUBASHOV: What's happened to Ivanoff?

GLETKIN: Enemy of the people Ivanoff was executed early this morning.

RUBASHOV, *after a long pause, nods to himself, murmurs:* I see. *Looks up at* GLETKIN. Why? Was it because of me?

GLETKIN: Perhaps.

RUBASHOV: Perhaps he thought I was innocent.

GLETKIN: Then he shouldn't have conducted your investigation.

RUBASHOV, *sighs heavily, murmurs:* Go, Sascha. Go, in peace!

GLETKIN: He was corrupt, like so many of your old guard, and his counter-revolutionary action in your examination . . .

RUBASHOV, *jumps to his feet, all his pent-up feelings exploding:* Counterrevolutionary? You ignorant young ass! What the hell do you know about the Revolution *or* the old guard? When you were peeing in your diapers, we were working and fighting and studying and writing one thing: Revolution! Revolution! Half our lives we lived like moles—underground; we rotted away in every prison in Europe; we knew poverty, we knew persecution, we knew starvation, but every living second we dreamed and built the Revolution with our blood and our bones! And now you have the gall to sit there and—*He waves his hand to the faded patches on the wall.*—spit at these, the heroes of your boyhood? Are you insane? Do you really believe that we have all suddenly become venal and corrupt?

GLETKIN, *leans forward, rising slowly, his face apoplectic:* Quiet! You washed-out, disgusting, rotten old man! You didn't make the Revolution—the Revolution made you. You adventurers rode along, scum on the flood of the people's uprising. But don't make any mistake! You never fooled our Leader! He used you, because he had to use whatever was at hand, but he knew you were defective. That's why our Leader has taken such pains with us. We have learned to recognize your defectiveness by the smell of you. You were needed for awhile, like the white-collared intelligentsia after the Revolution. But a new generation is at the helm now and your day is over. Understand! There'll be no bargains! You, we offer nothing! You are going to die! The only question is whether you'll die uselessly, or whether you will confess and perform a last service for the Party. But die you will, you understand?

RUBASHOV, *stares at him. Something dies; something of the will, and the battle, and the spirit go out of* RUBASHOV *forever. He suddenly becomes a very tired, sick old man. He nods, whispers hoarsely:* I understand.

GLETKIN, *harshly, triumphant:* Then let's have no more arrogance. *He pushes a button, picks up the phone.* Next witness! *The lights flicker, and as* RUBASHOV *slowly sits the scene vanishes.*

*The lights come up on the tier of cells. We see 402 and the wraithlike 302. They are eating their meager supper of black bread and cabbage soup.*

302, *taps to 402:* Is Rubashov back yet?

402, *taps:* No.

302, *taps:* How long?

402, *taps:* They've had him upstairs—it must be ten hours now.

302, *taps:* I wonder are they torturing him now.

402, *taps:* Why should they? He's confessed.

302, *taps:* They want more than that from him.

402, *taps:* What more is there?

302, *taps:* There's more. I hope he understood. I think he did. I looked into his eyes before I left. He seemed to understand. My father used to talk so well of him. *Suddenly overcome, to himself.* Oh, my father, my father!

402, *taps:* Eat your supper.

*The lights fade and the prisoners vanish. The lights come up again, revealing the office. A new* INTERROGATOR *and* SECRETARY *have replaced* GLETKIN *and the* YOUNG WOMAN. *As the scene appears, the* INTERROGATOR, *red-eyed, perspiration-soaked, purple-faced, is standing over* RUBASHOV, *hammering away at him. On the verge of fainting from fatigue, white-faced as the ghosts that haunt him,* RUBASHOV *exerts every ounce of willpower to resist the fanatical onslaught. The* SECRETARY *is also washed out with fatigue, his hair in disarray, his tie loosened.*

INTERROGATOR, *bellowing:* Is this true? Answer yes or no!

RUBASHOV: I can't . . .

INTERROGATOR: Yes or no!

RUBASHOV: Partially . . .

INTERROGATOR, *harshly:* Yes or no! Yes or no!

RUBASHOV, *wearily:* Yes. . . . Yes.

INTERROGATOR, *grunts:* Yes. Good. *Returns to the chair at the desk, seats himself.* And now we return to the Kieffer episode. *Picks up the documents.* You admit this conversation with Professor Kieffer? *Pause. He glances up;* RUBASHOV's *eyes have closed; his head, fallen, rests on his chest. The* INTERROGATOR *shouts.* You will pay attention!

RUBASHOV, *opens his eyes, raises his head:* What?

INTERROGATOR: Don't you feel well?

RUBASHOV: I'm all right.

INTERROGATOR, *with quiet threat:* Would you like me to call in the doctor?

RUBASHOV, *quickly, alert again:* No.

INTERROGATOR: Stand up! RUBASHOV *pulls himself to his feet.* Straight! Head up! Hands at your sides! At attention! RUBASHOV *obeys.* Perhaps that will keep you awake. You admit this conversation? *Pause.* Yes or no!

RUBASHOV: There were conversations.

INTERROGATOR: I didn't ask you about conversations, I ask you about this one.

RUBASHOV: In Hegel's philosophy, every yes has a no and every no has a yes.

INTERROGATOR: You're not here as a philosopher, you're here as a criminal. You'd better not talk about Hegel's philosophy. It'd be better first of all for Hegel. Do you admit this conversation? Yes or no.

RUBASHOV: Yes.

  *The door opens,* GLETKIN *and his* SECRETARY *enter briskly. They are fresh and rested. She has changed her dress.* GLETKIN *carries an armful of books, with slips inserted.*

INTERROGATOR: Yes. Good.

RUBASHOV: But I deny your conclusions.

GLETKIN, *interrupting:* That is to say you admit everything except the logical consequence of your admissions? *He nods to the seated* SECRETARY, *who folds his notebook and rises.* GLETKIN's SECRETARY *occupies the chair and proceeds to make notes.*

INTERROGATOR: Stop this crude lying!

RUBASHOV: I'm not lying, young man.

GLETKIN, *crosses to the desk:* You've been here for ten hours poisoning the air with your Jesuit tactics. What do you expect to gain by this?

RUBASHOV: Gain? Nothing.

GLETKIN, *touches the* INTERROGATOR, *who nods, rises:* Then admit your crimes and get it over with!

RUBASHOV: Admit to crimes I didn't commit? Even Danton in the French Revolution was allowed to defend himself.

INTERROGATOR, *now up out of the chair:* And what happened to the French Revolution?

GLETKIN, *sliding into the seat, leaning across the desk, without interrupting the interrogation. The effect is of a well-oiled machine:* Powdered pigtails declaiming about personal honor! All that mattered to Danton and Company was to go with a swan song. Is that what you want?

    The INTERROGATOR *and the male* SECRETARY *exit, stretching, yawning wearily.*

RUBASHOV: I certainly don't want to go howling like a wolf in the night.

GLETKIN: Whether it does good or harm to the Cause, that doesn't matter?

RUBASHOV: My whole life has but a single purpose: to serve the Cause.

GLETKIN: There's only one way you can serve it now. A full confession in open court. A voluntary confession of all these crimes.

RUBASHOV, *sways, leans on the desk to support himself:* I've pleaded guilty to a false and harmful policy. Isn't that enough?

GLETKIN: Our country today is the bastion of the new era. Everything depends on our keeping the bastion intact, keeping the country solidly united.

RUBASHOV: How does it unite the country? How does it serve the Party that her members have to grovel in the dust? The name N. S. Rubashov is a piece of Party history. By dragging me in the mud you besmirch the Revolution. I—

GLETKIN: I, I, me, me, I! *He picks up one of the books, opening it to a marked page.* Do you recognize this book?

RUBASHOV, *puts on his glasses. His hands are trembling. It takes him some time to focus his vision as he peers at the book:* Yes.

GLETKIN: Who wrote it?

RUBASHOV: I did.

GLETKIN, *reads from the page:* "With us the objective result is everything. With us objective good faith is of no interest. Those who prove wrong will pay!" You said that?

RUBASHOV, *his body sags again:* Yes.

GLETKIN: Well, you are wrong.

    *The ghostlike image of* RICHARD *appears, pointing a finger at* RUBASHOV.

RUBASHOV, *staring into space, nods:* Yes.

GLETKIN: And you will pay.

    *The phantom of* RICHARD *vanishes.*

RUBASHOV: I am paying.

GLETKIN: With your life!

RUBASHOV: My life has been the Party. My life would be worthless unless I could go on working for it. *His knees buckle, he sways, about to collapse.*

GLETKIN: Sit down! RUBASHOV *sinks to the chair.* There's only one way you can serve the Party now. As an example to the masses. *He opens another book, reading from it.* "For the masses, what is right must be gilded, what is wrong must be black as pitch." You wrote that?

RUBASHOV: Yes.

GLETKIN: Even if we let you go on living—as you say—what would you have to live for?

RUBASHOV, *to himself:* Nothing. A man without a country. *The ghostly image of* LUIGI *appears, smiling, gesticulating.* Like little Luigi.

GLETKIN: Who?

   LUIGI's *phantom vanishes.*

RUBASHOV, *shakes his head:* Never mind.

GLETKIN: You admit your guilt?

RUBASHOV: In thought.

GLETKIN: In thought? *Holds up a book.* And this?

RUBASHOV: Yes. Mine too.

GLETKIN, *reads:* "The consequences of our thinking will be felt unto the seventh generation. Hence a wrong thought from us is more criminal than a wrong deed from others." You wrote that?

RUBASHOV: Yes. I wrote it.

GLETKIN: Then, when you say you are not guilty, aren't you thinking mechanistically, Citizen Rubashov? ALBERT's *image appears. He is waving his hands with the ridiculously exaggerated gestures.* PABLO's *image appears, juggling plates.* RUBASHOV *laughs softly.*

GLETKIN: What are you laughing at?

   *The phantoms of* PABLO *and* ALBERT *vanish.*

RUBASHOV, *startled, looks up:* Was I laughing?

GLETKIN: Yes.

RUBASHOV, *passes his hand over his forehead:* I wasn't conscious of it.

GLETKIN: Do you usually do things you're not conscious of?

RUBASHOV: No. Not often.

GLETKIN: These acts of sabotage, for example.

RUBASHOV: I deny them.

GLETKIN: Perhaps you committed them unconsciously.

RUBASHOV: I didn't commit them at all.

GLETKIN: These factories had great losses.

RUBASHOV: Yes.

GLETKIN: Sabotage is a weapon of the class struggle.

RUBASHOV: Yes. But I didn't employ it.

GLETKIN: You've advocated its use again and again?

RUBASHOV: Yes. But I didn't employ it here.

GLETKIN: Didn't you? *Pause. He looks through the papers.* The case of the woman Luba Loshenko. She was your secretary? Correct?

RUBASHOV: Yes.

GLETKIN: And you were sleeping with her. RUBASHOV *straightens up.* Correct? *Silence.* Shall I give you the place, dates, conversations? *He waves the dossier.* They're all here.

RUBASHOV, *almost inaudible:* Yes, I was sleeping with her.

GLETKIN: Speak up!

RUBASHOV, *loudly:* Yes. I admit the relationship.

GLETKIN: You admit it?

RUBASHOV: I said yes.

GLETKIN: She was tried and shot for sabotage, correct?

RUBASHOV, *wildly:* She was innocent.

GLETKIN: Innocent? *He rises.*

RUBASHOV: Yes.

GLETKIN: She had no political motives? Is that what you mean?

RUBASHOV: Precisely.

GLETKIN: Precisely. She was an ordinary young woman, infatuated—blindly, stupidly, the slave and tool of one man who, however, did have considerable political motives—you!

RUBASHOV: What motives?

GLETKIN: You hated the Revolution, and you taught her to hate us.

RUBASHOV, *desperately:* That's not true. She was innocent.

GLETKIN: Why didn't you say so at the time?

RUBASHOV: You know as well as I there wasn't anything I could do to save her.

GLETKIN: So you did nothing?

RUBASHOV: Nothing.

GLETKIN: You were silent.

RUBASHOV: I was silent.

GLETKIN: To save your own neck!

RUBASHOV: To go on working.

GLETKIN: Without a neck one cannot work; hence, to save your own neck. And this silence of yours was finally responsible for her execution. Correct?

RUBASHOV: So I was informed.

GLETKIN: For your further information, I was one of her interrogators.

RUBASHOV, *raises his head:* You?

GLETKIN, *thumbs through the transcript:* I have here a transcript of her interrogation. I think it might interest you. Ninth day. Tenth day. Yes, here we
have it. This Loshenko woman was surprising. These thin delicate ones
sometimes really stand up. Listen! *He reads.* "Interrogator: 'Under whose
orders?' Loshensko: 'No one's' . . ."

  *LUBA's image appears in space, bowed, drenched with pain. She shakes
her head slowly, moving her lips silently at first, then her trembling voice
becomes barely audible, grows stronger, finally topping and supplanting
GLETKIN's voice. GLETKIN continues to read from the transcript.*

LUBA: No one's. I've told you a hundred times there were no orders.
GLETKIN: Stop lying.
LUBA: No matter what I say, you don't believe me. Oh, God! I'm so tired.
GLETKIN: I want the truth.
LUBA: I've told you the truth, over and over and over and over. I'm so tired,
  I can't . . .
GLETKIN: Who gave you these instructions?
LUBA: No one.
GLETKIN: You sabotaged without instructions?
LUBA: No, no, no. You're twisting my words.
GLETKIN: That's what you said.
LUBA: I didn't say that! I said I didn't do these things and no one asked me to.
GLETKIN: We've all the proofs.
LUBA: What are you trying to make me say?
GLETKIN: Stop shielding Rubashov!
LUBA: I'm not shielding anyone.
GLETKIN: You're shielding Rubashov.
LUBA: A man like that doesn't need shielding. A man like that . . .
GLETKIN: You were sleeping with him, weren't you?
LUBA: I loved him.
GLETKIN: You loved him?
LUBA: Yes.
GLETKIN: You'd do anything he asked you?
LUBA: He wouldn't ask me to commit crimes.
GLETKIN: Idiot! This man has used you.
LUBA: No!
GLETKIN: He's made a fool of you.
LUBA: No!
GLETKIN: And now when you need him, where is he? Where is he?
LUBA: Oh, God, God, make them leave me alone!
GLETKIN: God is dead, Luba Loshenko! God is dead.
LUBA: What do you want of me?

GLETKIN: Rubashov's making you responsible for his guilt.

LUBA: He's not.

GLETKIN: Use your head! He's refused to testify for you.

LUBA: I don't believe that.

GLETKIN: Here are the proofs! Look, look!

LUBA: I don't want to look.

GLETKIN: He was asked to testify and he's refused.

LUBA: I don't believe that. I don't believe you . . . I don't believe you. . . .

RUBASHOV, *staring into space, murmurs:* I had no choice, Luba. Don't you see? I had no choice. I couldn't have saved you. It was only a trap to destroy my usefulness. *The SECRETARY rises, leans forward to catch RUBASHOV's words and writes them down.* I tried! I went everywhere—to my friends in high places. They said no, nothing will help.

GLETKIN, *reads on:* Save yourself! This is your last chance, Luba Loshenko! You admit these acts of sabotage.

LUBA: I can't admit them because there weren't any. There was no sabotage. There were only tired men and sick men and frightened men.

GLETKIN, *slaps his hand as he reads:* You stupid bitch! *LUBA's IMAGE recoils as if she'd been struck.* All right! Then you'll be shot in the back of your neck!

LUBA: What are you doing to us? What are you doing to us? We're not stones, we're not machines! We're human beings. We feel, we think, we see, we dream, we're a part of God. Why have you done this to us? You say God is dead, but you've made your own god out of darkness, out of misery and lies and pain! Why? Why are you doing this to us?

RUBASHOV, *stands up unsteadily, staring into space, calls out:* This was not the way it was to be.

GLETKIN *glances quickly at* RUBASHOV *who is no longer aware of his surroundings, nods to the* SECRETARY. *She rises and leans closer to* RUBASHOV, *taking down his words.*

LUBA: You've made a prison . . . out of our wonderful country—a prison.

RUBASHOV: We wanted to build a new and better world.

LUBA: You've put chains on our people. Chains. In their hearts, inside their skulls. Why? Why?

RUBASHOV: I don't understand why, myself. Our principles were right.

LUBA: Our people are more miserable than before the Revolution.

RUBASHOV: We diagnosed the disease, but wherever we applied the healing knife . . .

LUBA: Our people are covered with sores.

RUBASHOV: Our will was pure. We should have been loved by the people . . .

LUBA: They hate you.

RUBASHOV: Why? Why are we so hated? We brought truth.

LUBA: In your mouths everything becomes a lie.

RUBASHOV: We brought living life . . .

LUBA: The trees in the forest wither.

RUBASHOV: I sang of hope.

LUBA: Your tongues stammer and bark.

RUBASHOV: Yes, yes, and every premise of unimpeachable truth has led me to this final weird and ghostly game. Why? Why?

LUBA: Kolya! Kolya, darling! Wherever you are . . . *She vanishes and only her voice is heard crying "Kolya! Kolya!"*

RUBASHOV: Luba! Luba! What have I done? What have I done? *He whispers.* Guilty, guilty, guilty! *Then, very simply.* I'm going to faint. *He slides gently and quietly out of the chair and falls to the floor.*

GLETKIN, *rings for his colleague, snaps his fingers at his* SECRETARY: The ammonia! *The* SECRETARY *rushes across to the table, opens a drawer, takes out a bottle of ammonia and hands it to him.* GLETKIN, *on one knee, slaps* RUBASHOV'S *face and administers the restorative. The door is thrown open and the other* INTERROGATOR *enters.*

GLETKIN, *nods, indicating* RUBASHOV'S *crumpled body:* We've got him. We've got the lever. *The sharp fumes of the ammonia begin to revive* RUBASHOV. Stand him up! *The other* INTERROGATOR *lifts* RUBASHOV *to his feet and holds him there, limp as a rag doll.* GLETKIN *waves the ammonia bottle under his nose until he responds, then, putting one huge hand gently on his shoulder, speaks softly, caressingly.* You haven't eaten your food today, Comrade Rubashov. Would you like some hot soup?

RUBASHOV, *murmurs:* Sleep. I must sleep.

GLETKIN: You understand, Comrade Rubashov, what the Party expects of you.

RUBASHOV: Yes.

GLETKIN: This is the last service you can perform for the Party.

RUBASHOV: I must sleep. Sleep.

GLETKIN: Very well. *To* GUARD. Take him back to his cell. *To* RUBASHOV, *gently.* I'll see that you are not disturbed.

RUBASHOV, *like a child, eagerly:* Thank you, Comrade Gletkin. *The* GUARD *takes* RUBASHOV *out.*

GLETKIN, *to the* INTERROGATOR: In exactly twenty minutes wake him up and bring him back here. I'll interrogate him till midnight, you take him till five A.M., and I'll take him again at five. *Blinks his eyes, avoids the dazzle-light.* This Loshenko thing—that's the lever. Work it around in his belly. Keep returning to it. It's simply a question of time now. *The* INTERROGATOR *nods, feels his aching back, and goes, yawning.* GLETKIN *snaps off the dazzle-light.*

SECRETARY: Congratulations, Comrade Gletkin.

GLETKIN, *sits down to his desk, stretches his legs, pleased:* It's just a matter of constitution.

*The scene fades out. The lights come up. The Supreme Court of the U.S.S.R. This scene is another memory in the mind of the brooding RUBA-SHOV after the event has occurred. The PRESIDENT, bathed in a hot white light, is seated at a long, covered table, three judges to his left, three to his right. The rest are shadowy figures.*

PRESIDENT: Comrade Judges, you have heard the evidence against Citizen Rubashov. Comrade Procurateur of the U.S.S.R. has summed up for the prosecution. Accused Rubashov step forward. *RUBASHOV appears in the white light before the judge's bench. The GUARD brings on a microphone and sets it in front of RUBASHOV.* Accused Rubashov may make his last plea.

RUBASHOV, *bending a little, speaking into the microphone, in a dead voice:* Citizen Judges. Covered with shame, trampled in the dust, about to die— let me serve my final purpose. Let my horrible story demonstrate how the slightest deflection from the Party line must inevitably drag one down into counter-revolutionary banditry. If I ask myself today: "For what am I dy- ing?" I am confronted by absolute nothingness. Therefore, on the thresh- old of my final hour, I bend my knees to my country and to my people. The political masquerade is over. We were dead long before the Public Prosecutor demanded our heads. With this my task is ended. I have paid my debts. To ask for mercy would be derision. You must hate me, and you must kill me! I have nothing more to say. *He stands with lowered head. The GUARD removes the microphone.*

PRESIDENT: I will announce the sentence of the Military Collegium of the Supreme Court. *He reads.* "The Sentence. The Military Collegium of the Supreme Court of the U.S.S.R. sentences N. S. Rubashov to the supreme penalty—to be shot, with the confiscation of all his personal property . . ."

*His voice trails off. The lights fade. The court vanishes. Only RUBASHOV remains, sitting in his cell, wrapped in meditation, his head between his hands, his brow furrowed, his face old and gray, as if all the blood had been drained out of him. An insistent tapping. 402 comes into view, tapping three times, waiting, and gently repeating the code.*

RUBASHOV, *coming out of his reverie, rises feebly, crosses unsteadily to the wall, taps:* Yes?

402, *taps:* I thought 302 behaved quite well. He went like a brave man.

RUBASHOV, *taps:* Yes.

402, *taps:* You still have about ten minutes. What are you doing?

RUBASHOV, *taps:* I'm thinking.

402, *taps:* Thinking's bad. You won't show the white feather! We know you're a man. A man. *Pause.* Do you still remember "Breasts fit champagne glasses"! Ha! Ha! What a man you are! RUBASHOV *listens for a sound from the corridor. 402 senses his thoughts.* Don't listen. I'll tell you in time when they are coming. *Pause.* What would you do if you were pardoned?

RUBASHOV, *thinks, taps:* I'd study astronomy.

402, *taps:* Ha! Ha! Me too, perhaps. But they say other stars are perhaps also inhabited. That would spoil it. *Pause.* May I give you some advice?

RUBASHOV *taps:* Yes.

402, *taps:* But don't take it wrong. Technical suggestion of an old soldier. Empty your bladder. Is always better in such case. The spirit is willing, but the flesh is weak. Ha! Ha!

RUBASHOV, *smiles, taps:* Thanks. *Pause.*

402, *taps:* Why astronomy?

RUBASHOV, *taps:* As a boy I loved to watch the stars. I wanted to solve the riddle of the universe.

402, *taps:* Why? Talk to me.

RUBASHOV, *to himself:* Recently I read they have discovered the Universe is finite. Forty years pass and I read that. If the Public Prosecutor has asked, "Defendant Rubashov, what about the Infinite?," I would not have been able to answer. Perhaps there is my real guilt.

402, *taps:* It's too late to worry about guilt.

RUBASHOV, *taps:* How can I die till I find out what I'm dying for? *Pause, taps.* Sorry! Tell me, what are your prospects?

402, *taps slowly:* Eighteen years more. Not quite. Only six thousand five hundred thirty days. *Pause.* Think of it. Another six thousand five hundred thirty days without a woman. I envy you, really. My brain is turning to water. I have returned to the habits of my childhood. I loathe myself!

RUBASHOV, *to the wall:* Oh, you poor, poor devil! *To the entire prison, to all Russia.* All of you! My hundred and eighty million fellow prisoners, what have I done to you? What have I created? If History is all calculation, Rubashov, give me the sum of a hundred and eighty million nightmares. Quickly calculate me the pressure of a hundred and eighty million cravings. Where in your mathematics, Rubashov, is the human soul? At the very beginning you forgot what you were searching for?

*Footsteps ring out in the corridor.*

402, *taps:* They're coming. *The footsteps grow louder.* What a shame. We were having such a pleasant talk.

RUBASHOV, *taps:* You've helped me a lot. Thanks.

402, *taps:* Farewell. I envy you, I envy you.

*The door of* RUBASHOV's *cell is thrown open with a clang.* GLETKIN *enters.*

GLETKIN: Enemy of the People Nicolai Semonovitch Rubashov, before you are executed, have you any last wish?

*A long pause.*

RUBASHOV: One. *He tries to catch* GLETKIN's *eyes.* If I could only make you understand where in the very beginning we failed.

GLETKIN: These are your last words. Don't waste them.

RUBASHOV, *passionately:* You don't build a Paradise out of concrete. My son . . .

GLETKIN, *quickly, distastefully:* I am not your son.

RUBASHOV, *after a long pause, sadly:* Yes, you are. That's the horror. *He shakes his head, bitterly.* The means have become the end; and darkness has come over the land.

GLETKIN: Have you any last wish?

RUBASHOV: To die.

GLETKIN *motions him to walk.* RUBASHOV *moves slowly out of the cell;* GLETKIN *takes out his pistol, cocks it, and follows. The* GUARD *opens the gate to the cellar, a shaft of light coming up catches them. 402 begins to drum on the door. From all over the prison comes the hollow muffled drumming, which mounts higher and higher as* RUBASHOV *and* GLETKIN *descend, and the iron gate clangs behind them. The drumming reaches a climax as the* CURTAIN *falls slowly.*

*Sidney Kingsley working in his study at his home in New Jersey, 1979. Reprinted by permission of the* North Jersey Herald & News, *Passaic, New Jersey.*